Contents

Chapter 6: Recent Developments

Series Introduction

The Sources of Christian Theology is a series of books to provide resources for the study of major Christian doctrines. The books are edited by expert scholars who provide an extended introductory discussion of the important dimensions of the doctrine. The main focus of each volume is on selections of source materials. These are drawn from major Christian theologians and documents that convey essential elements of theological formulations about each doctrine. The editor provides context and backgrounds in short introductory materials prior to the selections. A bibliography for further study is included.

There is no substitute in theological study for a return to the "sources." This series provides a wide array of source materials from the early church period to the present time. The selections represent the best Christian theological thinking and display the range of ways in which Christian persons have thought about the issues posed by the major aspects of Christian faith.

We hope that those interested in the study of Christian theology will find these volumes rich and valuable resources. They embody the efforts of Christian thinkers to move from "faith" to "understanding."

Donald K. McKim
Westminster John Knox Press

Acknowledgments

I would not have been able to put this reader together without help from a number of people. I am most grateful to Donald McKim for inviting me to work on this project. Sandy Lucas and Michele Blum at Westminster John Knox Press kept permissions organized and paid the bills; Julie Tonini supervised the process of producing the manuscript. My research assistants, Andrew Nelson and Justin Nickel, did extensive work in the library and on the computer, tracking down sources and preparing bibliographies. Karen Alexander at the Luther Seminary library went beyond the call of duty obtaining books and articles from libraries all over the country. Victoria Smith, our faculty secretary, not only proofread the manuscript but also did the difficult and time-consuming work of scanning most of the selections into electronic format. My colleague Alan Padgett discussed some of the text selections, as did Paul Sponheim, who also provided invaluable feedback on the introductions and readings for Kierkegaard and Whitehead. John McGuckin, a member of the editorial board, provided very incisive recommendations for the selection of texts. My father, Robert Malcolm, gave astute suggestions for the introductory essay. The influence of my teacher David Tracy is evident throughout the reader. And finally, I am especially grateful to my husband, David Watkins, for his constant encouragement and patience throughout the process of completing this project.

A Note on the Selection and Arrangement of Texts

Given the breadth and quantity of Christian literature on the doctrine of God, I have had to make some difficult choices. My primary goal in choosing material has been to identify thinkers who have had the most influence on later Christian theology and to select texts that most succinctly articulate why they have had such an impact. Most would agree that the following theologians have made significant contributions to the understanding and doctrine of God (at least within Western Christianity): Irenaeus, Tertullian, Origen, Athanasius, Gregory of Nazianzus, Gregory of Nyssa, Augustine, Dionysius the Areopagite, Anselm, Thomas Aquinas, Bonaventure, Martin Luther, John Calvin, Jonathan Edwards, Friedrich Schleiermacher, Karl Barth, Karl Rahner, and Paul Tillich. I have also included patristic and medieval figures currently being retrieved because of their contemporary relevance (Maximus Confessor, Nicholas of Cusa, Meister Eckhart, and Julian of Norwich) and modern philosophers who have influenced Christian theology (Descartes, Pascal, Kant, Hegel, Kierkegaard, and Whitehead). Among twentieth-century theologians, Wolfhart Pannenberg and Jürgen Moltmann have emerged as important Protestants; Hans Urs von Balthasar is a highly influential Roman Catholic; and Vladimir Lossky and Dumitru Stăniloae are noteworthy within the Orthodox tradition. Of course, a few others could have been added to the list of twentieth-century figures (e.g., Robert Jenson, Eberhard Jüngel, Thomas Torrance, David Tracy, and John Zizioulas). The last section on "recent developments" may be the most controversial; we do not know yet which of our contemporary theologians will have the most impact on later generations. My goal here has simply been to give readers a sense of the variety in contemporary Christian reflection on God—especially in view of Christianity's global character. Many other worthy texts could have been chosen in lieu of those selected.

I have arranged the selections historically rather than topically. The Christian doctrine of God covers a variety of themes: the Trinity, God's essence and nature, God's attributes, arguments for God's existence, God's relationship to the world, and so on. Since each thinker has a distinct approach to integrating these themes—emphasizing some and not others—I have organized the material around individual thinkers within a historical sequence in order to avoid artificially imposing categories that may not reflect their own sense of how the material fits together.

In my choice of excerpts, I have had to balance depth (providing as lengthy an excerpt as possible) and breadth (offering as much range as possible in my presentation of a thinker's work). In most cases, I have sought to use an excerpt from a theologian's most important theological treatise or *summa* (e.g., in selections for Origen, Augustine, Bonaventure, Aquinas, Calvin, and Barth). For those theologians who tended to write ad hoc pieces addressing specific issues (e.g., Athanasius, the Cappadocians, and Luther), I have had to include a number of shorter excerpts to give a sense of the range of their work. In a few instances, I have chosen a more accessible work rather than a more comprehensive one (e.g., Gregory of Nazianzus's shorter Trinitarian orations rather than the more famous *Five Theological Orations* or Schleiermacher's *On Religion* rather than *The Christian Faith*).

Each thinker's work is accompanied by a brief introduction to the main themes discussed in the excerpts. The introductory essay to the volume offers a historical overview introducing most of the authors in view of their major contributions to the history of Christian thought.

In my presentation of individual selections, I have revised the archaic language of older translations to make them more accessible to contemporary readers. I have retained most of the authors' footnotes in the originally published version of a text but have revised or excluded lengthy explanatory footnotes added by editors to pre-twentieth-century selections. I have also placed all additions of biblical references to pre-twentieth-century texts in brackets (rather than in footnotes) and have, for the sake of consistency in referencing conventions across the volume, revised both original and editorial footnotes where necessary. In these revisions, I followed standard academic format (i.e., *Chicago Manual of Style*) for citing monographs and articles and used abbreviations for frequently cited texts and Arabic numerals where possible in referencing premodern texts.

Introduction

After encountering the crucified Jesus raised from the dead, early Christians cried, "Abba! Father!" (Gal. 4:6; cf. Rom. 8). Through the Spirit within and among them, they boldly called out to the Father of Jesus, the God of Israel who is the great "I AM" (Exod. 3:14) and the one in whom all things "'live and move and have [their] being'" (Acts 17:28). In missionary witness and in clarifying their beliefs, those who followed them have sought to understand more fully the God addressed in this primitive prayer and what this God's purposes are for our world. This essay provides an overview of central themes and trajectories shaping the Christian understanding and doctrine of the God that has emerged over the centuries.

The Bible

The Old Testament tells the story of God's relationship to Israel, whose holiness is described as just and merciful, wise and loving (cf. Exod. 34:6). Active in the world, this God not only created the entire universe—imbuing all things with life—but chose a people among the nations and established a covenant with them. Having promised Abraham land and progeny, God rescued his descendants from slavery in Egypt at the exodus. Appearing to Moses in the burning bush, this God—called by various names, including the plural *Elohim*—revealed that the divine name is Yahweh, "I AM WHO I AM" (Exod. 3:14). God conversed with Moses and others, yet no one could see God's face and live. God's presence was palpable as the liberated Israelite slaves wandered through the desert. Bound by God's covenant made with Moses at Sinai, they were to keep God's commandments: to love the Lord their God with all their heart, soul, and might (Deut. 6:5) and to love their neighbors as themselves (Lev. 19:18). God was like a father to Israel and especially to David, the king chosen for Israel; as God's "sons," Israel's kings were to serve as God's representatives in the world (cf. 2 Sam. 7:14; Pss. 2:7; 89:26–27).

God's word also came on prophets who announced God's judgment on injustice and the worship of other gods. During and after Israel's exile in Babylon, they declared God's promise to create new life amidst her disaster. The God who had liberated the Israelites at the exodus was also the God who had subdued the primeval waters of chaos at creation; this God now had the power to redeem and rescue Israel. Not merely the God of a particular nation, Yahweh was now perceived as the Lord of the entire universe and history, who alone exists as the one, unique God; all other gods are illusory (Isa. 40–55). Promising a new messianic age, God would create a new heaven and a new earth (Isa. 65:17–25). At this time, the Spirit, who infuses life in all creatures and had raised up prophets and leaders in the past, would come as God's palpable presence among all people—regardless of status, gender, or ethnicity (Joel 2:28–32)—writing God's law on their hearts (Jer. 31:33).

What the New Testament says about the message of Jesus Christ is warranted by God's promises to Israel. A wandering prophet and teacher, Jesus proclaimed and embodied God's reign of justice and mercy. Everything he did—forgiving sins, healing the sick, exorcising demons, and calling disciples to follow him—was rooted in his intimacy with his "Abba" and in the Spirit's inspiration. Although his life ended in crucifixion, his disciples soon declared that he was raised from the dead and was, in fact, the anticipated messiah of David's line. Drawing on Old Testament themes, they declared that he is God's "beloved Son" (Mark 1:11; 10:45)—both as the "Son of Man," an apocalyptic figure who represents the God's judgment over all in the messianic kingdom (cf. Dan. 7:13), and as the "Suffering Servant," a figure whose debasement brings atonement and healing for others (cf. Isa. 52:13–53:12).

If Jesus proclaimed the reign of God during his lifetime, then his followers proclaimed a message about him. The apostle Paul declared that Jesus is the Messiah (in Greek: the "Christ")—the "Son" God has sent to redeem the world from law, sin, and death. In Christ there is a new creation (2 Cor. 5:17; cf. Isa. 65). God's promise to Abraham—now linked with the promise of the Spirit—is offered to all people through Christ's death and resurrection (Gal. 3:13–14). Now all can, through faith and baptism in Christ, be adopted as God's children in whose hearts "God has sent the Spirit of his Son . . . crying 'Abba! Father!'" (Gal. 4:6). The Spirit who raised Jesus from the dead had now descended among his followers at Pentecost in a fashion similar to Moses' experience at Sinai (Acts 2)—sending them in missionary proclamation throughout the world to tell the story about Jesus not only among Jews (interpreting it in relation to Israel's history with God, e.g., in Acts 2) but also among Gentiles (interpreting it in relation to Hellenistic ideas about God, e.g., in Acts 17).

As Paul makes clear, what the Spirit reveals is the crucified Christ, the wisdom and power of God (1 Cor. 1:18–25; cf. Phil. 2:5–11). Raised from the dead, Jesus is now recognized as the one "from whom are all things and for whom we exist" (1 Cor. 8:6; Col. 1:15) and thus related to the personified figure of Wisdom in the Old Testament—identified not only with God's Word in the Law and the Prophets but also as God's agent in creation and even redemption (Prov. 8:27–30). Echoing how Wisdom was with God before the world's creation, the Gospel of John presents the most highly developed account of how Jesus is the Word who "was with

God, and . . . was God" (John 1:1). By faith in the "Word made flesh," we too enter the intimacy he has with his Father, and through their intimacy we are united with one another (John 17). Central, then, to the Christian understanding of God is that "God is love": God has sent God's only Son to be the world's Savior, and through this love, we are to love one another (1 John 4:7, 19).

Although an explicitly Trinitarian theology would not emerge until later, the New Testament affirms both that God is one (e.g., Gal. 3:20) and that something new happens in Jesus through the power of the Spirit. Depicting the individual identities of Father, Son, and Spirit and their relationship with one another, it also contains binitarian references—to "God and Christ" (e.g., Rom. 1:7) and less frequently to "Christ and the Spirit" (e.g., 1 Cor. 6:11)—and of its few Trinitarian references, the most important deals with our baptism into the "the Father, . . . the Son, and . . . the Holy Spirit" (Matt. 28:19).

Patristic Theology

In its missionary expansion, the church interpreted its new experience of God in light of Scripture and the worldview of the ancient Greco-Roman world. Early apologists like Justin Martyr (d. ca. 165) argued that Christians worshiped the one true God and that Jesus not only fulfills Old Testament expectation but is also the incarnate Logos who embodies the true wisdom of Greek philosophers.

This Christian identification of Jesus with the Logos resonated with the work of the Jewish philosopher Philo of Alexandria (20 B.C.E.–50 C.E.). Influenced by Middle Platonism (a fusion of Stoic and Aristotelian elements into Platonism), Philo had not only related biblical depictions of God's Word (*memra*) and personified Wisdom to Greek conceptions of the *logos* (the reason and intelligence linking the cosmic order with truth in human beings), but he had also distinguished God's *ousia* (essential nature) from God's powers (*dynameis*) and their works or effects (*energeia*) apprehensible to us through God's Word (*logos*). Similarly, Christians depicted how the one transcendent God is immanently present in the world through Jesus and the Spirit. Drawing on biblical imagery, they spoke of Jesus as a "second God" alongside the Father—God's "Word," "Wisdom," and "Offspring" (John 1:1–4; Col. 1:15; cf. Prov. 8). Initially binitarian and Trinitarian, their depictions of God from the third century onwards would become explicitly Trinitarian, analogous to the way Neoplatonist Plotinus (ca. 205–70) depicted a Trinity with three hypostases (*hypostaseis*)—One, Mind, and Soul—that enacted Being, Life, and Wisdom.

In general, however, the apologists and other pre-Nicene theologians were less interested in clarifying how there could be plurality within the inner being of God than in describing how God's being and purposes were manifest in creation and salvation through the Son and the Spirit. Drawing on Ephesians 3:9—"the plan [*oikonomia*] of the mystery hidden for ages in God who created all things"—they used the term *oikonomia* (management, organization, and dispensation) to speak about the way God's gracious dispensation in creation and salvation culminates in the incarnation of Jesus Christ.

This "economic" Trinitarianism would be further clarified through theological debate. In *Against the Heresies,* Irenaeus of Lyons (ca. 135–300) rejected "Gnostic" heresies that supplanted the "evil" God of the Old Testament with the gracious and loving God of the New Testament. Christians, he argued, worshiped the one true God who created all things. The Son and the Spirit are the "two hands" God uses within creation. As the Logos both eternally with God and expressed in the incarnation—generated from God before (and not in the act of) the creation—Jesus Christ "recapitulates" or "sums up" all of nature and history within his divine and human person, bringing it to completion within God's life (Eph. 1:10).

Some, however, were suspicious of Logos theology, fearing it introduced a plurality into the Godhead. Called the "monarchians"—because they sought to preserve God's unity (i.e., God's *monarchia* or sole rule over all things)—they would be identified by future historians with two positions. The first, "dynamic monarchianism," describes how Jesus is adopted into deity by the indwelling Spirit (identified with Paul of Samosata). The second, "modalist monarchianism," refuses distinctions within God: the titles Father, Son, and Spirit merely refer to different aspects of God's work (identified with Sabellius, who spoke of God's three modes of being, and Praxeas, who held that the Father entered the virgin's womb and suffered and died on Calvary).

In *Against Praxeas,* Tertullian countered the monarchians, arguing that the "monarchy" of God must not be separated from the "economy." Within the monarchy, he argued, Father, Son, and Spirit share the same divine "substance" (*substantia*) even though they are distinct "persons" (*persona*) in terms of their "sequence, manifestation, and aspect" within the economy. (In his usage, *persona* refers not to the modern sense of a psychological subject but rather to the "presentation of a face.") Using visual metaphors to describe the Trinity (e.g., root-tree-fruit, fountain-river-stream, and sun-ray-point), Tertullian also drew an analogy between the way our words express inner thoughts and the way the Son is God's Word and Wisdom—distinct yet never separate from him. Moreover, anticipating later arguments, he drew on a Stoic understanding of "relative disposition" to describe how the titles "Father" and "Son" refer to a relationship and not to intrinsic qualities.

If Tertullian provided new terms, then Origen (ca. 185–ca. 254) laid the conceptual groundwork for later Nicene debates. In *On First Principles,* he maintained that as a "simple intellectual nature" characterized by unity and oneness, God is incomprehensible and immeasurable; we only know God through the "divine sense" of a pure heart. Nonetheless, God exists in three coeternal and divine hypostases: Father, Son, and Spirit. Important for later arguments, he averred that the Son is eternally generated from the Father and thus uncreated: "There never was a time when he was not." As God's Wisdom, Christ is the express image of the Father present alongside him before the creation, who emerges from the Father analogous to the way an act of the will proceeds from the mind (Col. 1:15; cf. Prov. 8; Wis. 7). Likewise, the Spirit is divine and coeternal with the Father and the Son. Not merely a force or energy, the Spirit is a distinct hypostasis who sanctifies believers and endows them with charismatic gifts. Although Origen stressed the divinity and coeternity of all three persons, he nonetheless distinguished their roles and activities in ways that implied hierarchy; thus, he would be used by various sides in later debates.

In the fourth century, a conflict between two close readers of Origen—Arius of Alexandria and his bishop, Alexander—initiated a series of controversies. Arius contended that Christ must be inferior to the Father and thus not divine in the same sense (drawing, e.g., on John 14:28—"The Father is greater than I"—and Proverbs 8:22—where Wisdom states, "The LORD created me"). In turn, Alexander maintained that the Son of God was eternally generated: "uncreated" but "begotten." Alexander's position triumphed at the Council of Nicaea in 325, where the word *homoousios* (one substance) was adopted to affirm the Son's shared deity with the Father.

The consensus reached at this council was short-lived. In ensuing debates, Athanasius of Alexandria (ca. 296–373) emerged as defender of the pro-Nicene cause. In *Orations against the Arians*, he answered what he described as the "Arian" question of whether there is only one "unoriginate" or two with this response: both are "unoriginate" (*agenetos*, uncreated or unborn and thus eternal), but the Father is "ungenerated" (*agennetos*), and the Son is "generated" (*gennetos*). Thus, the titles "Father" and the "Son" depict a "relation." Radically different from the biological relationship between human "fathers" and "sons," this divine relationship is defined by an "eternal generation" whereby the Son expresses the Father analogous to the way humans express their words and wisdom (recall Tertullian's and Origen's use of a similar argument); thus, we speak of the "Son" as the Father's "Word and Wisdom." In this way, the Father and Son are truly *homoousios* in the eternally generative character of God's existence. At stake in this argument was the claim, also made in *On the Incarnation*, that Christ must be fully divine in order to redeem us from sin and the devil and lead us, through his incarnate humanity, into the divinization (*theosis*) that characterizes union with God. In addition, in *Letters to Serapion concerning the Holy Spirit*, Athanasius reproached those who accepted the *homoousion* of the Son but still believed the Spirit was a creature. The Spirit must be divine, he argued, if the Spirit sanctifies or "deifies" believers, something creatures cannot do. Although he died in 373, his arguments influenced the Council of Constantinople in 381 (the outcome of which is popularly known as the Nicene Creed), which affirmed the deity of the Son and the Holy Spirit.

The Cappadocians—Basil of Caesarea, his friend Gregory of Nazianzus, and his younger brother Gregory of Nyssa—would articulate the classical defense of pro-Nicene Trinitarian theology. They were especially critical of two points they identified with a subordinationist position linked with the schools of Aetius and his disciple Eunomius: (1) that we can know God's essence rationally; and (2) that God's essence is defined by being "Father" of all (that is, unbegotten or ungenerated). By contrast, the Cappadocians maintained that God's infinite nature is incomprehensible and ineffable; we only know God through purity of heart and contemplation. God's Trinitarian name does not tell us *what* God is (i.e., God's "essence") but *that* and *how* God is (i.e., that God exists and relates to us in the economy of salvation). Baptized into this name, we are not only redeemed by Christ but united with him by the sanctifying work of the Spirit—and through Jesus, the Word and Wisdom of God, we are united with the Father. Thus, "theology" (*theologia*) contemplates the incomprehensible God whose "economy" (*oikonomia*) of salvation is named in our baptism.

This economy reveals distinctions among the Trinitarian persons even though all three share the same divine nature. In contrast to the Eunomian claim that "Fatherhood" defines God's essence, the names Father, Son, and Spirit refer to their "relations" (*skésis*) to one another. As source, origin, and cause, the Father bestows his deity on the Son and the Spirit: generating the former and "breathing" the latter or causing it to proceed (cf. John 15:26). In turn, what distinguishes the Son and the Spirit from each other (and from the Father) are their unique modes of being generated (begetting versus procession). With their source in the Father, these relations express the dynamic way the three persons participate in one another in a dynamic movement toward unity; God's generative nature eternally produces the Trinity as the perfection of divine existence. Although the term *perichoresis* (in Latin, *circumincessio*) does not occur before Maximus in seventh century—and was later related to Trinitarian doctrine by John of Damascus (ca. 676–749)—it expresses well the Cappadocian understanding of how the three persons interpenetrate one another in mutual "relations."

As the Cappadocians would become the main theological source for Eastern Christianity, so Augustine would emerge as a crucial influence in the West. A convert from Manichaeism to Neoplatonism, and then to

Christianity, his theology emphasized the illumination that comes from turning away from the world of sense experience to our most primal acts of knowing and loving, which lead us not only to perceive truth and goodness (even in the face of skepticism), but ultimately to contemplate God—the eternal and immutable source of all truth and goodness. Though influenced by Neoplatonism, Augustine rejected its assumption that the soul could ascend to God on its own power. Because our fall into sin has disordered our will and what it loves—and thus clouded our vision—we need Christ, the redeemer who heals and restores us.

The Trinity presents Augustine's most elaborate account of how we contemplate the triune God by reflecting on the image of God within our mind (Latin: *mens*, understood broadly as our capacity to think, to feel, to desire, and to will). Interpreting biblical texts discussed by earlier "economic" Trinitarian theologians (from Justin to Tertullian), he argues that the two divine "missions" into the world—the sending of the Son and the sending of the Spirit into the world (cf. Gal. 4:4–6)—in fact, reveal their eternal "processions" from the Father (since we are adopted into "sonship" through Christ's redemptive work and sanctified by the Spirit). He then interprets the Nicene understanding of the Trinity (in particular, that of Gregory of Nazianzus) as emphasizing the coequality of the three persons, their sharing in the same divine essence, and their co-inhering in a mutuality of love and communion. He also argues that as an expression of their mutual love, the Spirit proceeds from both the Father *and* the Son (*filioque*)—a claim that would cause a schism between the East and the West centuries later. In addition, he develops the theme of "appropriation": the application of certain attributes belonging to the entire Godhead to one of the Trinitarian persons (e.g., although the divine attributes "wisdom" and "love" belong to the entire Trinity, we preeminently apply the former to the Son and the latter to the Spirit).

Turning to a more inward approach (*modo interiore*), Augustine asks, as an act of "faith seeking understanding," how—since we are created in God's image—our human activities of knowing and loving enable us to contemplate the Trinity. In addition to reflecting on the activity of love (which leads us to a Trinity of lover, beloved, and the love binding them together), he leads us through a series of mental exercises, drawing an analogy (following earlier Trinitarians) between the way our mind produces thoughts and the way the Logos, as God's Word and Wisdom, proceeds from the Father. Among these exercises, the most significant involve the connection he makes between Trinitarian processions and our activities of remembering, understanding, and willing. Although he warns of the inadequacies of these analogies—since the Trinity is incomprehensible—he nonetheless urges us to contemplate the God who is "nearer to me than I am to myself" (*interior intimo meo*; cf. Ps. 139), which leads us not only to our personal history but to the history of God's self-revelation within us. The fall and sin may have effaced God's image within us—turning all our acts of knowing and loving into misdirected activities—but we can be healed through the incarnation of Christ and his redemptive death on the cross. Instead of a further descent into false and disordered loves, our "minds" can thus be reoriented by participating in Christ, the Wisdom of God, who leads us in an ascent toward true integration: the restoration and renewal of God's image within us.

Yet another important figure, Dionysius the Areopagite (early sixth century), would be significant for both Eastern and the Western theology. An unknown Syrian bishop or priest, he used a pseudonym (from Paul's convert of the same name, Acts 17:34) and thus is often referred to as "Pseudo-Dionysius." His *Divine Names* portrays how the Deity, though incomprehensible and beyond all human discourse and knowledge, nonetheless lovingly reveals itself, drawing us through the Spirit into as much contemplation, participation, and resemblance of God *(theoria, koinonia, homoiosis)* as we can attain. Influenced by Neoplatonism, he depicts God as not only the "One," a *monad* or *henad*, utter simplicity and indivisible unity, but also as the "Good," the source and cause of all life, overflowing with divine abundance and generosity. Moreover, as the Trinity, God's transcendent fecundity is manifest as three persons—Father, Son, and Spirit—a triadic unity possessing the same divinity and the same goodness. Because the Trinity loves humanity, one of its persons, the Son in Jesus, shares fully in our humanity—the simple becoming complex—in order to raise us back to God. Through the "veils" of sacred revelation, which culminate in the incarnation, the transcendent is clothed in "being," with shape and form. Thus, God's single all-creative providence uses a range of names, which Dionysius organizes around a Neoplatonic pattern of God's procession into the world and our return back to God. As source of all, God is "good" (God's preeminent name) and enters the world as "being," "life," and "wisdom" (to the latter, he adds "mind," "Word," "truth," and "faith"). Our return back to God is enabled not only by God's "power" (under which he discusses "righteousness," "salvation," and "redemption") but also by God's infinite and eternal presence in the world and by God's "holiness," culminating in the God who is "perfect" and "one."

Dionysius's *Mystical Theology* describes the soul's ascent to union with God by transcending all sense, discourse, and knowledge in a threefold process: purification (through moral virtue); contemplation and illumination; and perfection into union in the "darkness of unknowing." It also introduces the influential distinction between "cataphatic theology" (making affirmative statements about God drawing on analogies and symbols) and "apophatic theology" (negating and denying all assertions about the incomprehensible God). Only by transcending *both*—in a double negation—do we enter fully into union with God in a "darkness of unknowing."

Medieval Theology

Centuries later, the monk Anselm of Canterbury (1033–1109) would follow Augustine and Dionysius in conceiving of theology as a contemplative exercise. Nonetheless, he would also anticipate later scholastics by providing "necessary reasons" for Christian beliefs—for both believers and nonbelievers. Among his arguments for God's existence, his so-called ontological proof (found in the *Proslogion*) would especially be influential. Often ignored in later discussions, however, is that Anselm not only embeds it within a prayer but also presents it for the purpose of providing a way of integrating the full range of God's attributes, which he contemplates in the rest of the treatise.

The proof itself takes its point of departure in the believer's idea of God as "that than which no greater can be conceived" followed by the observation that even a "fool" who says there is no God can conceive this idea of God in his mind. If this idea is, in fact, about that which no greater can be conceived, then it cannot exist solely in the mind, since existing in reality is greater than existing merely as a concept (a classical philosophical and theological assumption). Thus, one must admit God also exists in reality. This proof would receive varied responses in the history of thought. Anselm's contemporary, the monk Guanilon (and later Thomas Aquinas and Immanuel Kant) would reject it, saying, in a nutshell, that merely thinking about something does not entail that it exists. Many others (including Bonaventure, G. W. F. Hegel, Karl Barth, Paul Tillich, and Charles Hartshorne) would, albeit in different ways, draw on its significance for clarifying what the idea of God entails.

A couple of centuries later, a Franciscan friar named Bonaventure (1221–74) also integrated contemplation with rigorous reflection by pursuing a unified Christian wisdom centered on three elements: (1) emanation, the procession of creatures from the Creator; (2) exemplarism, the existence of "exemplary" ideas in God's eternal Word and Wisdom, which give us traces of the Trinity throughout creation; and (3) consummation, the fulfillment of creation's destiny in its return to God. Although presented explicitly elsewhere, these themes inform his most influential work, *The Journey of the Mind into God*, which describes how the mind (understood broadly in the Augustinian sense as encompassing all we think, feel, desire, and will) moves from the external world of sensation into its own interiority and transformation through grace, and then finally upward into the contemplation of God. With the crucified Christ as our road and door on this journey, our ascent to God—following Augustine—entails a transformation not only of our sense and intellectual capacities but also of our affections. Yet Bonaventure placed a greater emphasis than Augustine did on knowing God through our senses and the created world (following Aristotle and Francis of Assisi). In addition (following Dionysius), he portrayed the God we contemplate both as "being" (and thus as simple, perfect, and one) and as the "good" (and thus as a Trinity of three persons). At the end of the journey, we enter into the fiery darkness of affective union with God through the crucified Christ.

At this time, much of Aristotle's work was translated into Latin (either directly from the Greek or from earlier Arabic translations). This had an enormous impact on philosophical reflection on revealed traditions—not only among Christians but also among Jews (e.g., Maimonedes) and Muslims (e.g., Avicenna and Averroes). Moreover, universities were founded in the thirteenth century along with preaching orders (like those of the Franciscans and Dominicans), which in contrast to older monastic orders sought to be actively engaged in the world. In addition to Bonaventure, yet another theologian, a Dominican named Thomas Aquinas (1225–74), would also be deeply engaged in this new intellectual milieu. Unlike Bonaventure, however, Thomas countered an Augustinian reliance on an immediate intuition of God's illumination. Instead, he argued that theology (as "sacred doctrine") must be conceived of as a "science" (*scientia*) that makes clear what revelation sets forth by way of reasoning discursively from data given to our senses. Although theology is ultimately rooted in divinely revealed "wisdom" (*sapientia*)—since it has as its subject matter the God who transcends everything we perceive—it is still possible to reflect discursively on God's *effects* on us through the created world and the revelation of grace.

By conceiving of theology as a science, Thomas countered the Platonic assumption that things are real only to the extent that they reflect the "essence" of eternal forms. Things are real, he argued, to the extent that they "exist." Presupposing Aristotle's theory that all corporeal reality consists of matter and form—and that *matter* is related to *form* as *potency* (or potential) is related to *act* (or actualization)—Thomas broadened this theory by applying it to *esse*: what it means "to exist" or "to be." A finite being's degree of existence (or perfection) is measured by the degree to which it realizes its essence (or potency). Moreover, if God's revealed name is "I AM WHO I AM" (Exod. 3:14), then God is the one being whose *essence* is *existence*—in contrast to created beings whose existence (or actualization) as individuals differs from their essence (or potency). God is God's own existence. Indeed, God is existence itself (*ipsum esse*), the one from whom all things derive their existence (*esse*). God is the one self-subsistent being (*esse subsistens*) who bestows existence on all that is.

Thus, the proposition "God exists" is self-evident: its subject ("God") contains the predicate ("exists"). Yet since God wholly transcends human knowledge, we need arguments for God's existence—not to "prove" that God exists (an article of faith) but to provide a means for making God's revelation intelligible to us. Hence Thomas presents "five ways" for understanding what we mean when we use the word *God*. Referencing Paul's observation that creation displays God's invisible eternal power and divine nature (cf. Rom. 1:20), Thomas rejected Anselm's ontological proof, which relies on intuiting an a priori concept. Instead he presented a posteriori arguments based on what we perceive. Organized around Aristotle's four-fold understanding of causality,[1] the first three (later called "cosmological arguments") observe how things work in the world: what moves must ulti-mately be moved by an "unmoved mover" (cf. Aristotle); efficient causes must have an ultimate cause (cf. efficient causality); and contingent things must ultimately depend on something necessary (cf. material causal-ity). The fourth presupposes degrees of perfection that imply something more perfect (later described as a kind of "moral" argument; cf. formal causality). The fifth argues that the order or design in the world implies an intelligent source (later described as a "teleological" argument; cf. final causality).

But Thomas is clear that we can only know *that* God is, not *what* God is. We can only truly know and love God because of God's own Trinitarian knowing and loving communicated to us through Christ and the Spirit. Nonetheless, our created intelligence does tell us something about what God's nature is *not*. Unlike creatures, whose "existence" differs from their "essence," God is *simple*: God is the one being whose essence is God's exis-tence. And because God is the most actual of all beings—embracing within the divine existence the complete fulfillment of all that exists—God is also *perfect*. These two attributes entail all the others (e.g., goodness, infinity, omnipresence, immutability, eternity, unity), and together they provide a grammar for thinking and speaking about God. Influenced by Dionysius, Thomas concurred that our knowledge and discourse about God must go beyond both affirmations and denials. Nonetheless, he argued that we can think and speak about God by way of "analogy"—beyond both "equivo-cation" (i.e., negation) and "univocal predication" (i.e., affirmation)—because our entire existence already participates in the perfection of God's pure act of existing.

Although Thomas separated his treatment of *De Deo Uno* (the one God) from that of *De Deo Trino* (the triune God), his discussion of God's "inter-nal" activity at the end of *De Deo Uno* as knowing and willing (enacted as love, justice, and mercy) anticipates *De Deo Trino*, which elaborates on the divine processions and missions, and the mutual perichoresis of the three persons (following Augustine). In turn, his discussion of God's "external activity" in the same section anticipates his treatment of God's creative activity in the world (at the end of the first part of *Summa*); of human exis-tence, sin, and grace (in the second part); and of our return back to God through Christ, the Wisdom of God (in the third part).

---

1. Aristotle described four types of causes: a thing's *material cause* is the stuff it consists of (e.g., a statue is made from bronze or marble); its *formal cause* gives shape to its matter; its *efficient cause* is the reason it changes or rests; and its *final cause* gives it aim or purpose.

Thomas's synthesis would not last. The Franciscan thinker Duns Scotus (d. 1308) argued that existence cannot be differentiated from essence: only individual things exist. Thus, "infinity" is what distinguishes God from creatures, not "being," which is merely a neutral, univocal concept applying to both God and creatures. Eliminating the distinction between essence and existence did away with Thomas's basis for analogical predication and led to an emphasis on God's will—free from all constraints—and the radical contingency of the created world. Another Franciscan, William Ockham (ca. 1285–1349), intensified these emphases by arguing that God can do anything God chooses. Human acts are good and moral simply because God commands them to be so and not because they conform to eternal law or divine ideas. His well-known principle of parsimony— "Ockham's razor"—stipulated that we must explain things with as few assumptions as possible. It did away with the assumption—presupposed from the patristic period on to Thomas—that we participate in eternal ideas in the divine mind: rather, we exist only as individual beings. Critical of earlier arguments for God's existence because they assumed too much, he allowed only for those based on efficient causality, but even here—in order to avoid difficulties with infinite regress—he focused primarily on God's *conserving* activity, which, he maintained, was the most easy to demonstrate. Moreover, he argued we have no basis, using reason, for arriving at God's attributes (e.g., unity, omnipotence, or freedom). For these, we must rely solely on faith. These shifts in thought led to an increased differentiation between reason and revelation—relegating all knowledge transcending experience to the realm of revelation and faith, and opening the way for a secular science based solely on empirical observation.

Yet others would seek to retrieve Christian Neoplatonist mystical themes. A Dominican preacher and philosopher, Meister Eckhart (ca. 1260–1327) identified the *intellectus* (intellect) as the place where we meet God in a space he described as "nothing." While Thomas argued that God's primary name was "Being" (as pure act) and used "analogy" to think and talk about God, Eckhart maintained that God's primary name is the "One" and that we encounter God in a paradoxical space characterized both by identity (between God and creatures) and dialectical difference (the transcendence not only of all thought and speech but even of our very own selves—out of "something" into "nothing"). Since God is "neither this nor that"—empty, free, utterly one, and simple—we are united with God only when we sink down into the pure, unmixed "One" distinct from all duality. True to Christian Neoplatonism, Eckhart also depicted the one God as the Trinitarian God in whom the Father eternally gives birth to the coequal Son through the Spirit. Adopted into Christ's "sonship," we too experience this birth in our souls—a birth ultimately leading to a "breakthrough" into the hidden God, the innermost divine ground that, in a paradoxical identity, is also dialectally related to the Trinity.

Also drawing on Christian Neoplatonism, Nicholas of Cusa (1401–64) maintained that human beings are wise when they understand the limits of their knowledge—what he called "learned ignorance." Finite reason can only approximate but never fully possess absolute truth, which is infinite. Nonetheless, God contains the "coincidence of opposites" between the infinite and the finite. As "absolute maxim," God's fullness (as infinite being) encompasses the "minimum" (finite being)—"enfolding" (*complicatio*) all reality within God's being and "unfolding" (*explicatio*) it within the world. The ultimate union of divine and human, Christ is the apex of the union between infinite and finite.

Mention must also be made of the distinctive theology and spirituality centered on the cross that emerged amidst the political and intellectual upheaval of the late medieval and early modern periods—e.g., in Johannes Tauler (1300–61), Henry Suso (ca. 1295–1366), Julian of Norwich (1343–ca. 1416), Catherine of Siena (1347–80), Teresa of Avila (1515–82), and John of the Cross (1542–91). Among these, Julian of Norwich is notable because she drew on latent biblical, patristic, and medieval themes to describe how the Trinitarian persons reform, restore, and bring us into union with them with a fatherly and motherly care. Centered on our solidarity with Christ in sin, grace, and redemption, her deeply Pauline theology has the distinctive twist of describing this solidarity as a union with Christ, our mother.

Reformation Theology

The later medieval emphasis on divine freedom and the contingency of finite created beings led to an understanding of grace, which (based on the biblical idea of covenant) affirmed that God has bound himself to reward with grace through the sacraments those who try their best to do what is in them. For the Augustinian monk Martin Luther (1483–1546), this led to anxiety and a "disturbed conscience," even though his life was "beyond reproach." His great breakthrough came while meditating on Paul's Epistle to the Romans when he understood that God's "righteousness" has to do not with God's judging us for failing to enact the righteousness of which we are capable but with God's power to justify sinners. From this point on, the idea of "justification by faith," which affirmed salvation as a free gift of God's grace, would be the rallying cry for the Protestant Reformation.

Though influenced by Augustine, Luther reversed the directions of his theology. Instead of our ascending to God in knowing and loving contemplation, God comes to us in the preached Word and in the bread and wine, declaring the forgiveness of sins "for you." We cannot bear God's "naked," terrifying majesty on our own. Our wisdom and morality only lead us to God's law (which, though good in itself, is impotent to save sinners). Thus, God "clothes" himself with external means—disguises, veils, and masks—that the Holy Spirit uses to bring Christ's redeeming flesh to us. Reading the apostle Paul in light of the psalms—especially the lament psalms—Luther reworked Dionysius's cataphatic and apophatic theology in terms of the way God's Word addresses us as law and gospel. As the crucified Christ who brings us into conformity with his death and resurrection, the Word both kills the old sinful self within the devil's grip (as law) and makes us alive in Christ (as the gospel). Thus, God's righteousness has to do with God's power to create out of nothing. In turn, Luther observed, if our faith and trust make the gods we rely and depend on, then justification by faith has to do with trusting in the God who has the power to create "something" out of "nothing"—sin, death, and hell—and not in impotent idols (even those we create through our own supposed wisdom and goodness).

Whereas Luther observed that whatever we place our trust in is our God, John Calvin (1509–64)—the other great Reformer of the sixteenth century—made a corollary observation: knowledge of God and knowledge of self are intrinsically related. But Calvin's focus was not on how God's judgment and mercy meet us in the flesh of the crucified Christ but on how God's creative majesty and grandeur confront our human misery—with its ignorance, depravity, and corruption—and thus lead us to Christ, the redeemer. Like Augustine, he averred that when we examine ourselves, we find that we live and move and have our being in God, the creator of all things (Acts 17:28). Recognizing God's majesty leads us to acknowledge our misery and our need for Christ. Yet in spite of sin, we have a *sensus divinitas* (sense of the divine) implanted in our nature. Even the way our mind is a "factory of idols"—continually fabricating false gods—is an indication of this sense of God's presence manifest throughout creation, the "beautiful theatre" of God's glory.

For Calvin, this general knowledge of God is further clarified by knowing Christ, the redeemer, who leads us to the true knowledge of God: "Reverence joined with the love of God that the knowledge of his benefits induces."[2] Such reverence and love enable us to trust God's providence in all that happens to us and to our world—in spite of the evil that befalls us. Calvin even addressed the topic of predestination (whether and whom God chooses for salvation and for damnation, a source of controversy for later Calvinists) from the standpoint of trusting and being comforted by God's providence for us and others, in spite of our inability fully to comprehend God's purposes.

After the Reformation, doctrinal distinctions among various Christian groups became more clearly defined. Following the Council of Trent (1545–63), the Counter-Reformation spawned a period of Catholic revival marked by intellectual rigor and spiritual zeal—as exemplified by the

---

2. John Calvin, *Institutes of the Christian Religion*, vol. 1, ed. John T. McNeill, trans. Ford Lewis Battles, Library of Christian Classics (Philadelphia: Westminster Press, 1960), 41.

founding of the Jesuit order. The period of Protestant scholasticism also emerged at this time, consolidating and systematizing the major ideas of the Reformation. The great scholastics of this period reintroduced Aristotelian logic and sought to define, on rational grounds, the doctrinal authority of Scripture. Natural theology became a distinct subdiscipline that provided rational proofs for God's existence and miracles. Faith and mystical union (*unio mystica*) were distinguished more explicitly: the former as intellectual assent to doctrine and the latter as an experiential state reached through sanctifying grace.

As theology became more rational, spontaneous spiritual movements erupted—from early German Pietism to the Great Awakenings in Britain and North America—which laid greater stress on the living experience of faith and its implications for morality. While Protestant scholasticism resonated with the rationalism of the Enlightenment, pietistic revivals resonated with its emphasis on individual experience. Indeed, many believers and Enlightenment thinkers felt they were participating in the age of the Spirit (beyond the ages of the Father and the Son) described by the medieval Franciscan Joachim de Fiore (ca. 1135–1202), when every individual would be taught directly by the Spirit, even slaves and women.

Modernity

The Enlightenment's emphasis on personal autonomy and the power of science to understand the universe and improve the human lot led many to question classical theological assumptions. The philosopher David Hume (1711–76), for example, questioned the empirical basis for the argument from design as a proof for God's existence. Yet others sought to interpret classical Christian claims in light of the changing intellectual milieu. In many ways a thoroughly modern theologian, Jonathan Edwards (1703–58) was both an important preacher in the first Great Awakening in North America and an intellectual who took Enlightenment themes seriously (especially John Locke's emphasis on experience and Isaac Newton's understanding of nature). He was also, however, deeply influenced by Calvin and classical Christian understandings of beauty and harmony. Integrating these various influences, his theology depicted how God's infinite fullness overflows into all creation, profoundly shaping all our dispositions, activities, and relations.

In France, René Descartes (1596–1650) rooted his landmark attempt to establish an indubitable foundation for knowledge in the face of skepticism—*cogito ergo sum* ("I am thinking, therefore I exist")—in an argument drawing on Augustine that grounds our finite existence in God's infinite being. A century later, Blaise Pascal (1623–62) would follow another strain in Augustine (through the Jansenists). His famous "wager" gambles on the "reasons of the heart" that call one to live a life shaped by belief in an infinite and good God.

In Germany, Immanuel Kant (1724–1804) sought to mediate a compromise between empiricists like Hume and rationalists like Descartes by developing a metaphysics based on the way the mind both limits and is the source of what we perceive in the world. He was especially critical of three types of proofs for God's existence found in the theology textbooks of his day: the ontological (based on the idea of God); the cosmological (based on observations of things in the world); and the teleological (based on an apparent design in the world). Like Thomas, he argued that the first was illegitimate because it moves from a concept to what exists. The other two were illegitimate because they presuppose causality, which for Kant is something the human mind imposes on experience and is therefore only applicable to the world of "appearance" presenting itself to our experience and not to the real world of "things in themselves." In this way, Kant rejected the whole enterprise of modern natural theology and (in an echo of classical apophatic theology) reinstated a sharp contrast between what humans can know and the reality of God.

But if Kant denied knowledge of God in the realm of "speculative reason" (thinking about what transcends the limits of sense experience), then he made "room for faith" within the realm of "practical reason" (thinking about morality). For Kant, the *summum bonum* (complete good) is one where virtue and happiness are commensurate. Yet we must act virtuously despite the consequences. This leads to the antinomy of the moral life: reason demands that morality be rewarded with happiness, yet life provides no guarantee we can simultaneously attain both. To deal with this antinomy, Kant postulated the existence of God as the one who guarantees the realization of the complete good: the agreement of moral goodness and happiness.

Friedrich Schleiermacher (1768–1834), a Reformed theologian influenced by Moravian Pietism, accepted Kant's rejection of speculation. Later credited with founding liberal Protestant theology, he argued that theology must be rooted in our immediate experience of self-consciousness: it must explicate what Christians actually experience of Christ as redeemer. Further, our experience of redemption fleshes out more fully the "original revelation of God" all people experience as an "absolute dependence" on a "whence"—the unconditioned reality affecting everything while not being reciprocally related to it. For Schleiermacher, this intuitive certainty of a "whence," which gives us a "sense and a taste for the Infinite," replaces all so-called rational proofs for God's existence.

Schleiermacher's contemporary Georg W. F. Hegel (1770–1831) took a different approach. Countering Kant's dismissal of speculation, he sought to embody how the "Absolute Spirit"—the "thing-in-itself"—unfolds both conceptually and historically according to certain laws. Reformulating Anselm's ontological proof, he argued that the task of speculative philosophy is to demonstrate how the concept and reality of God are, in fact, related in the very way thought moves through history. There is, he argued, a dialectical movement to the way the Absolute Spirit moves through a dialectic of self-consciousness from (1) immediacy or identity ("being in itself") to (2) differentiation or cleavage ("being for another") and then (3) a return to itself ("reconciliation"). Encompassing all of history, this dialectic enacts the idea of God in Trinitarian form: God realizes God's existence in a historical figure, Jesus of Nazareth. Here Hegel's Lutheranism becomes especially explicit: the infinite takes on the finite in all its distinctness, including its estrangement and separation from God. In Jesus' death—as depicted in the Lutheran hymn "God himself lies dead"—God not only takes into God's own being the radical separation between God and humanity but also achieves their reconciliation through this act of "absolute love." Culminating in the resurrection, this reconciliation is verified by the immediate witness of the Spirit to human spirits, which explicates and interprets it so we can intuit its truth within our own self-consciousness.

Hegel would have a profound, if implicit, influence on modern theology, especially twentieth-century Trinitarian theology. He would also have famous critics, particularly among those who rejected his theological assumptions. One of his students, Ludwig Feuerbach (1804–72), would radically reverse his conceptual framework: instead of participating in the Absolute Spirit, Feuerbach argued that God is merely a projection—and thus an invention—of our highest ideals. In turn, Karl Marx (1818–83) would appropriate Hegel's ideas in terms of a historical materialism that had class conflict at the heart of its dialectic—with religion merely serving as an "opiate" the powerful use to subjugate the masses. Analogous interpretations of religion as a function of something else would be reiterated by a range of thinkers—from Sigmund Freud (1856–1939), who depicted religion as a function of subconscious drives, to Friedrich Nietzsche (1844–1900), who portrayed it as (in contrast to Marx) something the weak employ to conceal their own "will to power."

The Danish Lutheran Søren Kierkegaard (1813–55) was Hegel's most influential Christian critic. For Kierkegaard, the absolute conceptual synthesis Hegel sought was impossible: concepts cannot be merged with single individuals existing in time. Instead, Kierkegaard (reminiscent of Pascal) argued for a faith resting transparently in the God who embraces all of life, even its particulars. We can only be certain of truth by taking a leap; only through faith do we find a "repetition" of the "paradox" that God has appeared in the cross of Christ for our salvation.

Hegel was not the only one who sought to rethink metaphysics in dynamic terms. In the early part of the twentieth century, Alfred North Whitehead (1861–1947) endeavored to develop a "process philosophy" in line with Heraclitus's ancient claim that all reality is in flux. Rejecting the modern reduction of causality to efficient causation, Whitehead constructed a theory of "relations" that conceived of the "now" as emerging out of both the past and the future. Consisting of interdependent organisms continually in a process of creative and responsive development, reality is best conceived of not as "being" but as "becoming." Deeply involved in these processes, God provides finite creatures with creative possibilities through a dipolar nature: God's primordial nature is changeless and necessary, but God's consequent nature undergoes change and is affected by actual events in the cosmos. Revising traditional ideas of divine immutability and impassibility, Whitehead—along with Charles Hartshorne (1897–2000)—has been influential on process theologians, who argue that his philosophical idea of God is more compatible with the biblical God (who responds and is affected by human agency and events in history) than the one earlier Christians had developed (drawing on Platonic and Aristotelian assumptions about God).

Twentieth-Century Theology

Some of the most influential Western theologians of the twentieth century, however, retrieved the great patristic and medieval syntheses, but they did so in a post-Kantian fashion: they located our relation to God not in a Neoplatonic conception of God's procession and return in the cosmos but in a modern depiction of (in Martin Buber's words) an "I-thou" encounter: God's personal address to us through Jesus Christ. Moreover, writing after Luther and Hegel, they placed greater emphasis than their premodern counterparts did on God's fully entering human history through Christ's incarnation and death (cf. Phil. 2:5–11).

Drawing on Luther and Calvin, the Protestant Karl Barth (1886–1968) stressed the primacy of God's Word. Rejecting what he perceived to be the anthropocentrism of liberal theology, Barth argued that dogmatics must begin not with human experience but with God's own act of self-revelation—as Father, Son, and Holy Spirit. In an appropriation of Anselm's ontological argument, he argued for the priority of God's address to us in judgment and grace. In this address, we encounter the full contemporaneity (cf. Kierkegaard) of God's being God as "act, event, and life," where the unique and singular one reveals himself as the God who "loves in freedom." Although Barth was as vehement in his critique of the Roman Catholic "analogy of being" as he was of a liberal Protestant anthropocentrism, he did have a place for an "analogy of faith." Following Luther, he reworked the classical ways of negation and analogy in terms of the Word's functions as law and gospel. As law, God's judgment negates our sin and idolatry, but in the proclamation of the gospel, God's eternal grace and mercy enable us to know God through God's Word—through an "analogy of faith"—even though all human knowing falls short of what is given. In this, Barth (like Luther) defined God's incomprehensibility in terms of the hiddenness of divine freedom—a hiddenness paradoxically expressed in God's self-revelation. In a similar vein, although he refused to use the classical idea of divine simplicity as an all-controlling principle, he emphasized how God's single act of love and freedom in revelation "unites the multiplicity, individuality, and diversity of the divine perfections" in the inviolable unity of God's being.

Barth sought to correct liberal Protestant anthropocentrism by retrieving the Reformers' emphasis on proclaiming God's Word. By contrast, Karl Rahner (1904–84)—a Jesuit steeped in the Ignatian practice of discerning God in all things—sought to correct a different kind of problem, the "extrinsicism" of neoscholastic readings of Thomism, by enacting a mystagogy that leads us to God's self-communication through Jesus and the Spirit in our inmost selves. In this, Rahner (like Barth) sought to retrieve the Trinity as the matrix for theological reflection. His famous expression—"the immanent Trinity [God in God's self] is the economic Trinity [God in God's self-revelation], and vice versa"—had a profound influence on the twentieth-century revival of Trinitarian theology. Instead of proving God's existence, Rahner sought to make his readers aware of how God is the "term," the source and goal, of human transcendence. Like Augustine, he presupposed that God, although incomprehensible, is present in our everyday acts of knowing things and acting freely—even when we are unaware of God's presence. Moreover, not merely an eternally unreached or "asymptotic" term of human transcendence, God has self-communicated God's very own self to us: as the Logos or Son, Jesus Christ is God's irreversible offer of God's own self to human beings as our true fulfillment; through the Spirit, we experience Christ's presence within us not only as forgiving love but also as the divinization of our inmost selves.

Like Rahner and his patristic and medieval predecessors, Paul Tillich (1886–1965) maintained God can never be depicted as a *being* alongside (or even on top of) other finite beings. Like Barth, he affirmed the Reformers' biblical understanding of the "living God": God has not only created finite beings with an autonomy of their own but has also entered, as the Logos and the "new being" in Christ, the very nonbeing of our finitude—with its tragic evil and intentional sin—in order to reunite us with the infinite God through the Spirit. Beyond and prior to everything else, God's infinity encompasses all finite reality—including the element of nonbeing in finitude. Thus, the living Trinitarian God is the "power of being" overcoming all nonbeing. As ultimate and transcendent, God judges every one of our idolatrous or "demonic" obsessions; as palpably immanent, God resists any "profaning" tendency to negate God's presence within us and the world around us. Following Luther's observation that our gods are what we trust or have faith in, Tillich stressed that only this "holy God" must be our "ultimate concern."

The next generation of Protestant theologians placed an even greater emphasis on God's presence in history. Relating biblical eschatology to a post-Ockhamist understanding of the world, Wolfhart Pannenberg (1928–) rejected analogical discourse about God and the notions of divine transcendence it implied. Instead, he depicted divine transcendence as the in-breaking of the future infinitely eluding our grasp. This notion of transcendence, he argued, is more faithful to the primitive biblical message that the history of Jesus, crucified and raised from the dead, is God's own self-demonstration of who God is. The truth of this claim, however, is hidden (cf. Luther); it will only be definitely revealed at the end of history. Nonetheless, we can still seek to understand the reality it reveals and anticipates: the immanent Trinity disclosed in the economy of salvation, which points to the way God's very essence and existence (and the various attributes of God revealed in Scripture) are unified in the unfolding of divine love, a loved grounded in the true Infinite—the Trinitarian God manifest as Father, Son, and Spirit.

Jürgen Moltmann (1926–) also centered his theology in the reality of God's eschatological future breaking into our lives. Nonetheless, following Luther, he emphasized how this future only becomes a reality in our lives through the cross. Rejecting the classical axiom that the divine nature is incapable of suffering, Moltmann maintained that in the event of the cross the Son truly suffers death—and even godforsakenness (Mark 15:34)— and the Father truly suffers an infinite grief of love over his Son's death. In this way, the community of divine life takes within itself the infinite curse of sin, guilt, and death. But as God's indestructible life, the Spirit raises Jesus from the dead, thus opening up a new future, creating life anew for all.

Within Roman Catholicism, Hans Urs von Balthasar (1905–88) also presented a Trinitarian theology centered on the cross. Influenced by the Gospel of John, the early church fathers, and Barth, he sought to "walk on a knife edge" between the negative theology of the early church—which excluded any "tragic mythology" within God's life—and the biblical revelation of the economy of salvation—which proclaimed "something happens in God" through Jesus' life, death, and resurrection. Walking this knife edge, von Balthasar maintained that the infinite distance between the Father and Son—which reaches its apex in Jesus' cry of forsakenness on the cross—is sustained by their even more profound unity in the Spirit. In this distance and unity, our creaturely freedom and its sinful perversion are always only enacted within the Son's self-giving, which for von Balthasar is the only true condition for any possible and real world.

If twentieth-century Western theologians sought to retrieve the biblical emphasis on God's personal address to us within history, then their Eastern Orthodox counterparts sought to retrieve the mystical theology of the early church. Vladimir Lossky (1903–58) argued that we can only fully understand dogmatic theology by entering into the mystical union it enacts. Drawing on the Orthodox distinction between God's unspeakable "essence" and God's self-revealing "energies," he depicted how apophatic theology (following Dionysius and the Cappadocians) leads not to sheer emptiness or negation, but rather to participation in the fullness of Trinitarian life: the deification leading ultimately to union with God. In a similar vein, Dumitru Stăniloae (1903–93) also drew on the distinction between God's "essence" (which cannot even be experienced) and "energies" (which can be experienced but not defined). Interpreting this distinction in light of Maximus Confessor's distinction between Logos and the *logoi* and modern accounts of personhood and intersubjectivity, he integrated an experiential account of apophatic theology with a profound understanding of how the Holy Trinity—as "divine intersubjectivity""—ensures not only our existence as human persons but also the world's existence as a sacrament of God's personal presence.

In the past few decades, there have been a great variety of proposals for thinking and speaking about the God of Christian faith. Some have sought to address what has been called the "crisis of cognitive claims" brought about by the Enlightenment. Christian philosophers, for example, have argued for the reasonableness of Christian beliefs even if they cannot be inferred from other modern assumptions about reality. By contrast, revisionist theologians have sought to reconstruct traditional images and ideas of God in light of modern understandings of evolutionary and historical processes. Even some evangelical theologians have sought to revise assumptions in "classical theism" with an "open theism" that emphasizes God's responsive relationship to the world. Yet others have argued that what needs to be addressed is not a cognitive crisis but a "crisis of power." Liberation theologians in a variety of contexts have sought to name God's liberating activity in the midst of poverty, injustice, and suffering; and feminist, mujerista, and womanist theologians have sought to name God's emancipating presence in the experience of women.

Overall, the global character of Christianity has increasingly been emphasized. While Western Christians have sought to understand the God of Christian faith by appropriating Neoplatonic and German idealist categories, African Christians have sought to do so by engaging traditional African religious and metaphysical ideas, and Asian Christians, by appropriating themes from Buddhism and Hinduism.

Finally, the "postmodern" horizon (identified with thinkers like Heidegger, Nietzsche, and Wittgenstein) has opened up ways of thinking and speaking about God that are both fresh and yet ancient. Like their secular counterparts, many postmodern Christian thinkers reject the "modern" idea of a "God" defined as the metaphysical foundation that grounds the existence of all beings (identified, e.g., with Descartes). However, for them, this rejection leads not to atheism or nihilism but to an embrace of classical biblical and theological ways of thinking and speaking after the pattern of God's own way of revealing God's identity through Jesus in the power of the Spirit. Not only has there has been renewed interest in patristic and medieval ways of naming God and of contemplating God in the Eucharist and in prayer, but, in line with the Reformers, the inner logic of biblical categories for thinking and speaking about the Trinitarian God has increasingly been brought to the fore, with an emphasis placed on their practical import for everyday life.

We have barely scratched the surface of the history of Christian thought and only hinted at the fullness, depth, and breadth of its subject matter. Since the God of Jesus Christ is also the great "I AM" in whom all things have their source and goal, Christian reflection on God must encompass all of reality—if it is to be true to its theme. Yet as all the great theologians have acknowledged, human minds are not only finite and frail but also prone to sin. We put our trust in the wrong things, and our misdirected passions cloud our vision. Even our best ideas about the God we proclaim and believe in can lead us away from loving God with all we have and from loving others as we ought to love ourselves. Thus many of the selections that follow will remind us that God cannot be encompassed in human ideas or words but only addressed. Most importantly, they will affirm that—in spite of ourselves—the just and merciful God has, indeed, addressed us through Jesus in the Spirit, offering to all not only forgiveness but also the power to become children of God, and thus coheirs of all that Jesus had when he boldly cried out, "Abba! Father!"

Abbreviations

The following abbreviations are used for texts frequently cited.

ANF   *The Ante-Nicene Fathers: Translations of the Writings of the Fathers down to A.D. 325.* 9 vols. Ed. Alexander Roberts, James Donaldson, et al. Edinburgh, 1885–1897.

BC   *Book of Concord: The Confessions of the Evangelical Lutheran Church.* Ed. Robert Kolb, Timothy Wengert, James Schaffer. Minneapolis, 2000.

LCC   *The Library of Christian Classics.* 26 vols. Ed. John Baillie, John T. McNeill, and Henry P. Van Dusen. Philadelphia, 1953–1966.

LW   *Luther's Works.* American ed. 55 vols. Ed. Jaroslav Pelikan. Philadelphia/St. Louis, 1955–1986.

NPNF *A Select Library of the Nicene and Post-Nicene Fathers of the Christian Church.* First Series. 14 vols. Ed. Philip Schaff. Edinburgh, 1866–1889. Second Series. 14 vols. Ed. Philip Schaff and Henry Wace. Edinburgh, 1890–1900.

PG   *Patrologiae Cursus Completus, Series Graeca.* 161 vols. Ed. J.-P. Migne. Paris, 1857–1866.

TDNT *Theological Dictionary of the New Testament.* Ed. Gerhard Kittel and Gerhard Friedrich. 10 vols. Grand Rapids: Wm. B. Eerdmans Publishing Co., 1964–1976.

TDOT *Theological Dictionary of the Old Testament.* Ed. G. Johannes Botterweck and Helmer Ringgren. 6 vols. Grand Rapids: Wm. B. Eerdmans Publishing Co., 1974–1990.

CHAPTER 1

God in the Early Church

Exodus 3:13–15 and Significant New Testament Passages

The texts below include some of the biblical texts that were most influential on later Christian reflections on God; many others, of course, could have been chosen. Exodus 3 presents the divine name as "I AM WHO I AM," a passage that would be highly influential on all later Christian theological and philosophical reflection on God. Romans 8 and John 17 provide the lengthiest descriptions in the New Testament of how members of what later theology would call the Trinity—the Father, the Son, and the Spirit—interact with one another and with our lives. The prayers in Ephesians 1 and 3 provide shorter descriptions of the Trinity's involvement in our lives and in the world. The passage from Romans 1 would be an important source for understanding how we know God through the created world, as would Acts 17, which refers to our attempts to search and grope for the God "in [whom] we live and move and have our being."

Exodus 3:13–15

Here God says to Moses, "I AM WHO I AM" or "I will be whatever I will be" (echoing Exod. 33:19: "I will be gracious to whom I will be gracious"). The name is a pun on the divine Yahweh and connotes God's "being there" for Moses and the Israelites.

From the *New Revised Standard Version Bible*
(San Francisco: HarperCollins Publishers, 1989).

[13]But Moses said to God, "If I come to the Israelites and say to them, 'The God of your ancestors has sent me to you,' and they ask me, 'What is his name?' what shall I say to them?" [14]God said to Moses, "I AM WHO I AM." He said further, "Thus you shall say to the Israelites, 'I AM has sent me to you.'" [15]God also said to Moses, "Thus you shall say to the Israelites, 'The LORD, the God of your ancestors, the God of Abraham, the God of Isaac, and the God of Jacob, has sent me to you':

> This is my name for ever,
> and this my title for all generations."

Romans 8:14–30

This passage contains fecund insights into the way the Father, the Son, and the Spirit interact with one another as they sustain and respond to us as we cry out to God. Adopted as God's children (through faith and baptism into Christ's death and resurrection), we have now received the same Spirit of God who enabled Jesus to cry, "Abba! Father!" As we "groan" with the rest of creation in our sufferings in the present time, this Spirit not only bears witness with our spirit that we are children of God but also intercedes for us to God (the Father), who, in turn, "knows what is the mind of the Spirit."

From the *New Revised Standard Version Bible*
(San Francisco: HarperCollins Publishers, 1989).

[14]For all who are led by the Spirit of God are children of God. [15]For you did not receive a spirit of slavery to fall back into fear, but you have received a spirit of adoption. When we cry, "Abba! Father!" [16]it is that very Spirit bearing witness with our spirit that we are children of God, [17]and if children, then heirs, heirs of God and joint heirs with Christ—if, in fact, we suffer with him so that we may also be glorified with him.

[18]I consider that the sufferings of this present time are not worth comparing with the glory about to be revealed to us. [19]For the creation waits with eager longing for the revealing of the children of God; [20]for the creation was subjected to futility, not of its own will but by the will of the one who subjected it, in hope [21]that the creation itself will be set free from its bondage to decay and will obtain the freedom of the glory of the children of God. [22]We know that the whole creation has been groaning in labor pains until now; [23]and not only the creation, but we ourselves, who have the first fruits of the Spirit, groan inwardly while we wait for adoption, the redemption of our bodies. [24]For in hope we were saved. Now hope that is seen is not hope. For who hopes for what is seen? [25]But if we hope for what we do not see, we wait for it with patience.

[26]Likewise the Spirit helps us in our weakness; for we do not know how to pray as we ought, but that very Spirit intercedes with sighs too deep for words. [27]And God, who searches the heart, knows what is the mind of the Spirit, because the Spirit intercedes for the saints according to the will of God.

[28]We know that all things work together for good for those who love God, who are called according to his purpose. [29]For those whom he foreknew he also predestined to be conformed to the image of his Son, in order that he might be the firstborn within a large family. [30]And those whom he predestined he also called; and those whom he called he also justified; and those whom he justified he also glorified.

John 17:17–26

Following Jesus' promise in John 14–16 to send the Spirit or Advocate (*Paraclete*) after he "leaves" the disciples and "returns" to the Father, this chapter depicts Jesus' final prayer to the Father before his crucifixion. In the prayer, we overhear Jesus describing his mission and relationship to the Father from "before the world existed" (cf. John 1:1–4). We then overhear his prayers for our protection and unity: "that they may be one, as we are one." In the same way that the Father is in Jesus and Jesus is in the Father, so Jesus prays that we will be in them (the Father and Jesus) so that we may be "one" as they are "one."

From the *New Revised Standard Version Bible*
(San Francisco: HarperCollins Publishers, 1989).

[1]After Jesus had spoken these words, he looked up to heaven and said, "Father, the hour has come; glorify your Son so that the Son may glorify you, [2]since you have given him authority over all people, to give eternal life to all whom you have given him. [3]And this is eternal life, that they may know you, the only true God, and Jesus Christ whom you have sent. [4]I glorified you on earth by finishing the work that you gave me to do. [5]So now, Father, glorify me in your own presence with the glory that I had in your presence before the world existed.

[6]"I have made your name known to those whom you gave me from the world. They were yours, and you gave them to me, and they have kept your word. [7]Now they know that everything you have given me is from you; [8]for the words that you gave to me I have given to them, and they have received them and know in truth that I came from you; and they have believed that you sent me. [9]I am asking on their behalf; I am not asking on behalf of the world, but on behalf of those whom you gave me, because they are yours. [10]All mine are yours, and yours are mine; and I have been glorified in them. [11]And now I am no longer in the world, but they are in the world, and I am coming to you. Holy Father, protect them in your name that you have given me, so that they may be one, as we are one. [12]While I was with them, I protected them in your name that you have given me. I guarded them, and not one of them was lost except the one destined to be lost, so that the scripture might be fulfilled. [13]But now I am coming to you, and I speak these things in the world so that they may have my joy made complete in themselves. [14]I have given them your word, and the world has hated them because they do not belong to the world, just as I do not belong to the world. [15]I am not asking you to take them out of the world, but I ask you to protect them from the evil one. [16]They do not belong to the world, just as I do not belong to the world. [17]Sanctify them in the truth; your word

is truth. [18]As you have sent me into the world, so I have sent them into the world. [19]And for their sakes I sanctify myself, so that they also may be sanctified in truth.

[20]"I ask not only on behalf of these, but also on behalf of those who will believe in me through their word, [21]that they may all be one. As you, Father, are in me and I am in you, may they also be in us, so that the world may believe that you have sent me. [22]The glory that you have given me I have given them, so that they may be one, as we are one, [23]I in them and you in me, that they may become completely one, so that the world may know that you have sent me and have loved them even as you have loved me. [24]Father, I desire that those also, whom you have given me, may be with me where I am, to see my glory, which you have given me because you loved me before the foundation of the world.

[25]"Righteous Father, the world does not know you, but I know you; and these know that you have sent me. [26]I made your name known to them, and I will make it known, so that the love with which you have loved me may be in them, and I in them."

Ephesians 1:3–14

This passage was especially influential on Irenaeus's understanding of God's "economy" [*oikonomia*] or purposive activity, for the salvation of the world—God's plan "for the fullness of time, to gather up all things" in Christ.

From the *New Revised Standard Version Bible*
(San Francisco: HarperCollins Publishers, 1989).

[3]Blessed be the God and Father of our Lord Jesus Christ, who has blessed us in Christ with every spiritual blessing in the heavenly places, [4]just as he chose us in Christ before the foundation of the world to be holy and blameless before him in love. [5]He destined us for adoption as his children through Jesus Christ, according to the good pleasure of his will, [6]to the praise of his glorious grace that he freely bestowed on us in the Beloved. [7]In him we have redemption through his blood, the forgiveness of our trespasses, according to the riches of his grace [8]that he lavished on us. With all wisdom and insight [9]he has made known to us the mystery of his will, according to his good pleasure that he set forth in Christ, [10]as a plan [*oikonomian*] for the fullness of time, to gather up all things in him, things in heaven and things on earth. [11]In Christ we have also obtained an inheritance, having been destined according to the purpose of him who accomplishes all things according to his counsel and will, [12]so that we, who were the first to set our hope on Christ, might live for the praise of his glory. [13]In

him you also, when you had heard the word of truth, the gospel of your salvation, and had believed in him, were marked with the seal of the promised Holy Spirit; [14]this is the pledge of our inheritance toward redemption as God's own people, to the praise of his glory.

Ephesians 3:14–19

This prayer to the Father describes how we are "strengthened in [our] inner being with power through his Spirit" so that Christ may "dwell" in our hearts through faith and we may "know the love of Christ that surpasses knowledge" and be "filled with all the fullness of God."

From the *New Revised Standard Version Bible*
(San Francisco: HarperCollins Publishers, 1989).

[14]For this reason I bow my knees before the Father, [15]from whom every family in heaven and on earth takes its name. [16]I pray that, according to the riches of his glory, he may grant that you may be strengthened in your inner being with power through his Spirit, [17]and that Christ may dwell in your hearts through faith, as you are being rooted and grounded in love. [18]I pray that you may have the power to comprehend, with all the saints, what is the breadth and length and height and depth, [19]and to know the love of Christ that surpasses knowledge, so that you may be filled with all the fullness of God.

Romans 1:16–25

In this passage, the apostle Paul depicts the power of the gospel of Jesus Christ against the backdrop of humanity's guilt, given the fact that although "invisible," God's "eternal power and divine nature" can be understood and seen throughout the created world.

From the *New Revised Standard Version Bible*
(San Francisco: HarperCollins Publishers, 1989).

[16]For I am not ashamed of the gospel; it is the power of God for salvation to everyone who has faith, to the Jew first and also to the Greek. [17]For in it the righteousness of God is revealed through faith for faith; as it is written, "The one who is righteous will live by faith."

[18]For the wrath of God is revealed from heaven against all ungodliness and wickedness of those who by their wickedness suppress the truth. [19]For what can be known about God is plain to them, because God has shown

it to them. [20]Ever since the creation of the world his eternal power and divine nature, invisible though they are, have been understood and seen through the things he has made. So they are without excuse; [21]for though they knew God, they did not honor him as God or give thanks to him, but they became futile in their thinking, and their senseless minds were darkened. [22]Claiming to be wise, they became fools; [23]and they exchanged the glory of the immortal God for images resembling a mortal human being or birds or four-footed animals or reptiles.

[24]Therefore God gave them up in the lusts of their hearts to impurity, to the degrading of their bodies among themselves, [25]because they exchanged the truth about God for a lie and worshiped and served the creature rather than the Creator, who is blessed forever! Amen.

Acts 17:16–31

This passage presents Paul's speech at the Areopagus, where he seeks to counter the idolatry he finds in Athens with a warning of divine judgment. Unlike many other speeches in Acts, which address Jews and draw on the Hebrew Scriptures, this speech addresses a Gentile audience; Epicureans and Stoics were among Paul's interlocutors. Starting with a reference to an "unknown god," Paul goes on to say that God is not made by humans but is the very source of life we "search for" and "perhaps grope for" and "find." This God is the one in whom "we live and move and have our being" (perhaps a quote from the sixth-century B.C.E. philosopher-poet Epimenides), who now calls for repentance.

From the *New Revised Standard Version Bible*
(San Francisco: HarperCollins Publishers, 1989).

[16]While Paul was waiting for them in Athens, he was deeply distressed to see that the city was full of idols. [17]So he argued in the synagogue with the Jews and the devout persons, and also in the marketplace every day with those who happened to be there. [18]Also some Epicurean and Stoic philosophers debated with him. Some said, "What does this babbler want to say?" Others said, "He seems to be a proclaimer of foreign divinities." (This was because he was telling the good news about Jesus and the resurrection.) [19]So they took him and brought him to the Areopagus and asked him, "May we know what this new teaching is that you are presenting? [20]It sounds rather strange to us, so we would like to know what it means." [21]Now all the Athenians and the foreigners living there would spend their time in nothing but telling or hearing something new.

[22]Then Paul stood in front of the Areopagus and said, "Athenians, I see how extremely religious you are in every way. [23]For as I went through the

city and looked carefully at the objects of your worship, I found among them an altar with the inscription, 'To an unknown god.' What therefore you worship as unknown, this I proclaim to you. [24]The God who made the world and everything in it, he who is Lord of heaven and earth, does not live in shrines made by human hands, [25]nor is he served by human hands, as though he needed anything, since he himself gives to all mortals life and breath and all things. [26]From one ancestor he made all nations to inhabit the whole earth, and he allotted the times of their existence and the boundaries of the places where they would live, [27]so that they would search for God and perhaps grope for him and find him—though indeed he is not far from each one of us. [28]For 'In him we live and move and have our being'; as even some of your own poets have said,

'For we too are his offspring.'

[29]Since we are God's offspring, we ought not to think that the deity is like gold, or silver, or stone, an image formed by the art and imagination of mortals. [30]While God has overlooked the times of human ignorance, now he commands all people everywhere to repent, [31]because he has fixed a day on which he will have the world judged in righteousness by a man whom he has appointed, and of this he has given assurance to all by raising him from the dead."

SELECTION **2**

Irenaeus of Lyons

**Against the Heresies,
Book 4, Chapter 20:1–8**

As bishop of Lyons, Irenaeus (ca. 135–200) was an early church father whose writings were formative for early Christian theology. His most influential work, the five-volume *Against the Heresies*, refuted what he described as a "Gnostic" distinction between the "Father" of Christ and the "wicked god" of the Old Testament who created the material cosmos. Instead, he affirmed the one God in whom all things exist. As creator of heaven and earth, God is not only just and powerful but also good, wise, and merciful. Although humans cannot comprehend who God is, they can know, love, and have fellowship with God because of the divine love manifest in his Word, Jesus Christ.

Boundless and incomprehensible, God uses "two hands" to enact God's work in creation: the Son and the Spirit (which Irenaeus also identified as Word and Wisdom). Coeternal with God, and thus present with God when God created the world, these "two hands" are the means by which God creates and arranges all things and brings them to fulfillment. God has a singular purpose for the world manifest in the divine "economy" of salvation: God's plan for the redemption of the world (also described as God's "dispensations" within history) centered on the Word's becoming fully human.

In Old Testament prophecies, the Spirit of God announced the Word's advent in the flesh, anticipating God's activities among the people of Israel as a "type" of what would be enacted through Christ in the church. What these prophecies anticipated was Christ's work of "recapitulation" that "sums up" and "gathers together" the entire cosmos into his divine and human person, bringing it to completion (Eph. 1:10). As Second Adam, Christ not only liberates us from sin and death, but he also fulfills and perfects the humanity created in Adam and Eve, granting it immortality, incorruptibility, and the power to "see" God's face. In Jesus Christ, God becomes human so that human beings might receive deification (*theosis*) and thus participate in divine life.

From *The Apostolic Fathers, Justin Martyr, Irenaeus*, ANF 1:487–93.

Chapter 20
That one God formed all things in the world, by means of the Word and the Holy Spirit: and that although God is invisible and incomprehensible to us in this life, nevertheless God is not unknown; inasmuch as God's works do declare Who God Is, and God's Word has shown that in many modes God may be seen and known.

1. With regard to God's greatness, therefore, it is impossible to know God—for it is impossible for the Father to be measured. But with regard to God's love (for this is what leads us to God by God's Word), when we obey God, we do always learn that there is so great a God, and that it is God who by Himself has established, and selected, and adorned, and contains all things. And among all things, both ourselves and this our world, we also were made, along with those things that are contained by God. And this is the One of whom the Scripture says, "And God formed man, taking clay of the earth, and breathed into his face the breath of life" [Gen. 2:7]. Thus, it was not angels who made us, nor who formed us, neither had angels power to make an image of God, nor anyone else, except the Word of the Lord, nor any Power remotely distant from the Father of all things. For God did not stand in need of these [beings], in order to accomplish what God had Himself determined with Himself beforehand should be done—as if God did not possess God's own hands. For with God were always present the Word and Wisdom, the Son and the Spirit, by whom and in whom, freely and spontaneously, God made all things, to whom also God speaks, saying, "Let Us make humankind after Our image and likeness" [Gen. 1:26]— God taking from Himself the substance of the creatures [formed], and the pattern of things made, and the type of all the adornments in the world.

2. Truly, then, the Scripture has declared—which says "First[1] of all believe that there is one God, who has established all things and completed them, having caused that from what had no being all things should come into existence"—that God contains all things and is contained by no one. Rightly also Malachi has said among the prophets: "Is it not one God who has established us? Have we not all one Father?" [Mal. 2:10]. In accordance with this, too, does the apostle say, "There is one God, the Father, who is above all, and in us all" [Eph. 4:6]. Likewise does the Lord also say: "All things are delivered to Me by My Father" [Matt. 11:27], manifestly by the One who made all things, for God did not deliver to Him the things of another, but God's own. But in *all things* [it is implied that] nothing has been kept back [from God], and for this reason the same person is the Judge of the living and the dead; "having the key of David: He shall open, and no one shall shut: He shall shut, and no one shall open" [Rev. 3:7]. For no one was able, either in heaven or in earth, or under the earth, to open the book of the Father, or to behold Him, with the exception of the Lamb who was slain and who redeemed us with His own blood, receiving power over all things from the same God who made all things by the Word, and adorned them by God's Wisdom, when "the Word was made flesh": that even as the Word of God had sovereignty in the heavens, so also might He have sovereignty in earth, inasmuch as [He was] a righteous man "who did no sin, neither was there found guile in His mouth" [1 Pet. 2:23]; and that He might have the pre-eminence over those things that are under the earth, He Himself being made "the first-begotten of the dead" [Col. 1:18]; and that all things, as I have already said, might behold their King; and that the paternal light might meet with and rest upon the flesh of our Lord, and come to us from His resplendent flesh; and that thus humans might attain to immortality, having been invested with the Father's light.

3. I have also largely demonstrated, that the Word, namely the Son, was always with the Father; and that Wisdom also, which is the Spirit, was present with Him, anterior to all creation, declaring by Solomon: "God by Wisdom founded the earth, and by understanding has God established the heaven. By [Wisdom's] knowledge the depths burst forth, and the clouds dropped down the dew" [Prov. 3:19, 20]. And again: "The Lord created me the beginning of His ways in His work: He set me up from everlasting, in the beginning, before He made the earth, before He established the depths, and before the fountains of waters gushed forth; before the mountains were made strong, and before all the hills, He brought me forth" [Prov. 8:22–25].[2] And again: "When He prepared the heaven, I was with Him, and when He established the fountains of the deep; when He made the

---

1. This quotation is taken from the *Shepherd of Hermas*, book 2, sim. 1.

2. This is one of the favorite Messianic quotations from the Fathers, and is considered as the basis of the first chapter of St. John's Gospel.

foundations of the earth strong, I was with Him preparing [them]. I was [the One] in whom He rejoiced, and throughout all time I was daily glad before His face, when He rejoiced at the completion of the world, and was delighted in the [human race]" [Prov. 8:27-31].

4. There is therefore one God, who by the Word and Wisdom created and arranged all things. This is the Creator (Demiurge) who has granted this world to the human race, and who, with regard to God's greatness, is indeed unknown to all who have been made by God (for no one has searched out God's height, either among the ancients who have gone to their rest, or any of those who are now alive). But with regard to God's love, God is always known through Him by whose means He ordained all things. Now this is God's Word, our Lord Jesus Christ, who in the last times was made a human among humans so that He might join the end to the beginning, that is, humans to God. Therefore the prophets, receiving the prophetic gift from the same Word, announced His advent according to the flesh by which the blending and communion of God and humans took place according to the Father's good pleasure—the Word of God foretelling from the beginning that God would be seen by humans and hold converse with them upon earth; that God would confer with them and would be present with God's own creation, saving it, and becoming capable of being perceived by it, and freeing us from the hands of all that hate us, that is, from every spirit of wickedness, causing us to serve God in holiness and righteousness all our days [Luke 1:71, 75] in order that humans, having embraced the Spirit of God, might pass into the glory of the Father.

5. The prophets set forth these things in a prophetical manner. But they did not, as some allege, [proclaim] that the One who was seen by the prophets was a different God, the Father of all being invisible. Yet this is what those [heretics] declare, who are altogether ignorant of the nature of prophecy. For prophecy is a prediction of future things, that is, a setting forth beforehand of those things that shall be afterwards. The prophets, then, indicated beforehand that God would be seen by humans; as the Lord also says, "Blessed are the pure in heart, for they shall see God" [Matt. 5:8]. But in respect to God's greatness, and God's wonderful glory, "no one shall see God and live" [Exod. 33:20], for the Father is incomprehensible. But in regard to God's love and kindness, and as to God's infinite power, even this God grants to those who love God, that is, to see God, which the prophets did also predict. "For those things that are impossible with humans, are possible with God" [Luke 18:27]. For humans do not see God by their own powers; but when God pleases God is seen by humans, by whom God wills, and when God wills, and as God wills. For God is powerful in all things, having been seen at that time indeed, prophetically through the Spirit, and seen, too, adoptively through the Son; and God shall also be seen paternally in the kingdom of heaven, the Spirit truly

preparing humans in the Son[3] of God, and the Son leading them to the Father, while the Father, too, confers on them incorruption for eternal life, which comes to everyone from the fact of their seeing God. For as those who see the light are within the light, and partake of its brilliancy; even so, those who see God are in God, and receive of God's splendor. But God's splendor vivifies them; those, therefore, who see God, do receive life. And for this reason, God, although beyond comprehension, and boundless and invisible, rendered Himself visible, and comprehensible, and within the capacity of those who believe, that God might vivify those who receive and behold God through faith.[4] For as God's greatness is beyond comprehension, so also God's goodness is beyond expression; and thus by having been seen, God bestows life upon those who see God. It is not possible to live apart from life, and the means of life is found in fellowship with God; but fellowship with God is to know God, and to enjoy God's goodness.

6. Humans therefore shall see God so that they might live—being made immortal by that sight and even attaining to God. This, as I have already said, was declared figuratively by the prophets: that God should be seen by humans who bear God's Spirit and do always wait patiently for God's coming. As also Moses says in Deuteronomy, "Today we have seen that God may speak to someone and the person may still live" [Deut. 5:24]. For certain people used to see the prophetic Spirit and the Spirit's active influences poured forth for all kinds of gifts. Others, again, [beheld] the advent of the Lord, and the dispensation that obtained from the beginning, by which He accomplished the will of the Father with regard to things both celestial and terrestrial; and others [beheld] paternal glories adapted to the times, and to those who saw and who heard them then, and to all who were subsequently to hear them. Thus, therefore, God was revealed; for God the Father is shown forth through all these activities, the Spirit indeed working, and the Son ministering, while the Father was approving, and humanity's salvation being accomplished. As God also declares through Hosea the prophet: "I," God says, "have multiplied visions, and have used similitudes by the ministry of the prophets" [Hos. 12:10]. But the apostle explained this very passage, when he said, "Now there are diversities of gifts, but the same Spirit; and there are diversities of ministries, but the same Lord; and there are diversities of activities, but it is the same God that works all in all. But the manifestation of the Spirit is given to everyone for the common good" [1 Cor. 12:4–7]. But as the One who works all things in all is God, [as to the points] of what nature and how great God is, God is invisible and indescribable to all things that have been made by God, but God is by no means unknown. For all things learn

3. Some read "in filium" instead of "in filio" as above.

4. A part of the original Greek text is preserved here, and has been followed, as it makes the better sense.

through God's Word that there is one God the Father, who contains all things and who grants existence to all, as is written in the Gospel: "No one has seen God at any time, except the only-begotten Son, who is in the bosom of the Father, Who has made him known" [John 1:18].

7. Therefore the Son of the Father has made God known from the beginning, inasmuch as He was with the Father from the beginning, who did also show to the human race prophetic visions, and diversities of gifts, and His own ministries, and the glory of the Father, in regular order and connection, at the fitting time for the benefit of humankind. For where there is a regular succession, there is also fixedness; and where fixedness, there suitability to the period; and where suitability, there also utility. And for this reason did the Word become the dispenser of the paternal grace for the benefit of humans, for whom He made such great dispensations, revealing God indeed to humans and presenting humans to God: on the one hand, preserving the invisibility of the Father (lest humans should at any time become despisers of God, and that they should always possess something towards which they might advance) but, on the other hand, revealing God to humans through many dispensations (lest humans, falling away from God altogether, should cease to exist). For the glory of God is a living human being; and the life of human beings consists in beholding God. For if the manifestation of God, which is made by means of the creation, gives life to all those living in the earth, how much more does that revelation of the Father, which comes through the Word, give life to those who see God!

8. Inasmuch, then, as the Spirit of God pointed out things to come through the prophets—forming and adapting us beforehand for the purpose of our being made subject to God, though it was still a future thing that humans (through the good pleasure of the Holy Spirit) should see God—it necessarily behooved those through whose instrumentality future things were announced to see God (whom they intimated as to be seen by humans) in order that God and the Son of God, and the Son and the Father, should not only be prophetically announced but that God should also be seen by all God's members who are sanctified and instructed in the things of God: that humans might be disciplined beforehand and previously exercised for a reception into the glory that will afterwards be revealed in those who love God. For the prophets used to prophesy not only in word alone, but also in visions, and in their mode of life, and in the actions they performed according to the suggestions of the Spirit. After this invisible manner, therefore, did they see God, as also Isaiah says, "I have seen with my eyes the King, the Lord of hosts" [Isa. 6:5], pointing out that humans should behold God with their eyes, and hear God's voice. In this manner, therefore, did they also see the Son of God as a man conversant with humans, while they prophesied what was to happen, saying that He who was not come as yet was present proclaiming also the impassible as subject

to suffering, and declaring that He who was then in heaven had descended into the dust of death [Ps. 22:15]. Moreover, [with regard to] the other arrangements concerning the summing up that He should make, some of these they beheld through visions, others they proclaimed by word, while others they indicated typically by means of [outward] action, seeing visibly those things that were to be seen; heralding by word of mouth those which should be heard; and performing by actual activity what should take place by action; but [at the same time] announcing all prophetically. Thus also Moses declared that God was indeed a consuming fire [Deut. 4:24] to the people who transgressed the law, and threatened that God would bring on them a day of fire; but to those who had the fear of God he said, "The Lord God is merciful and gracious, and long-suffering, and of great compassion, and true, and keeps justice and mercy for thousands, forgiving unrighteousness, and transgressions, and sins" [Exod. 34:6, 7].

SELECTION **3**

Tertullian

**Against Praxeas,
Chapters 1–2, 7–9**

In *Against Praxeas*, Tertullian of North Africa (ca. 160–225) refuted the "monarchian" position of a certain Praxeas (meaning "busybody" and thus probably not a real name). Tertullian criticized two positions identified with Praxeas: first, that the Father had become incarnate and was crucified (what would later be called *Patripassionism*), and second, that the Spirit had no place within the Godhead. Moreover, Tertullian was angry about the way monarchians had maligned the followers of Montanism (a movement centered on the experience of the Spirit).

Since the monarchians sought to preserve the unity of God, Tertullian argued that God's "monarchy" (God's sole rule) cannot be separated from the "economy of salvation" (the divine plan of salvation). If the monarchy of God requires the identity of Father, Son, and Spirit, then the economy of salvation requires that they be distinguished. Thus, although the three are one in "quality, substance, and power," they are distinct in "sequence, aspect, and manifestation" (chap. 2). Tertullian used the term "substance" (*substantia*) to refer to the "stuff" that unifies and joins the inner life of God, and "person" (*persona*) to refer to the distinct individuals existing within that inner life.

Comparing the relationship between the Father and Son to the relationship between thought and speech—drawing on a Stoic distinction between an inner and uttered *logos* used by earlier Christian apologists—Tertullian described how the Son emanates from the Father as God's Word and Wisdom (and thus is distinct but not separate from him) (chaps. 5–6). He also used visual metaphors to describe the Trinity: root-tree-fruit, fountain-river-stream, and sun-ray-point (chap. 8). Moreover, he appropriated the Stoic category of "relative disposition" to describe how the Trinity is a matter of substantial relations: the words "Father" and "Son" do not point to intrinsic qualities but to the character of their relationship (e.g., a father is a father because he has a son) (chap. 10).

From *Latin Christianity: Its Founder, Tertullian*, ANF 3:597–628.

Chapter 1

Satan's Wiles Against the Truth; How They Take the Form of the Praxean Heresy; Account of the Publication of This Heresy

In various ways has the devil rivaled and resisted the truth. Sometimes his aim has been to destroy the truth by defending it. He maintains that there is one only Lord, the Almighty Creator of the world, in order that out of this *doctrine of the* unity he may fabricate a heresy. He says that the Father Himself came down into the Virgin, was Himself born of her, Himself suffered, indeed was Himself Jesus Christ.

Here the *old* serpent has fallen out with himself, since, when he tempted Christ after John's baptism, he approached Him as "the Son of God;" surely intimating that God had a Son, even on the testimony of the very Scriptures, out of which he was at the moment forging his temptation: "If you are the Son of God, command that these stones be made bread" [Matt. 4:3]. Again: "If you are the Son of God, cast yourself down from here [Matt 4:6] for it is written, He shall give His angels charge over you"—referring no doubt, to the Father—"and in their hands they shall bear you up, that you not hurt your foot against a stone" [Ps. 91:11]. Or perhaps, after all, he was only reproaching the Gospels with a lie, saying in fact: "Away with Matthew; away with Luke! *Why heed their words*? In spite of them, *I declare* that it was God Himself that I approached; it was the Almighty Himself that I tempted face to face; and it was for no other purpose than to tempt Him that I approached Him. If, on the contrary, it had been *only* the Son of God, most likely I should never have condescended to deal with Him."

However, he is himself a liar from the beginning [John 8:44], and whomever he instigates in his own way; as, for instance, Praxeas. For *he* was the first to import into Rome from Asia this kind of heretical corruption, a man in other respects of restless disposition, and above all inflated with the pride of confessorship[5] simply and solely because he had to bear for a short time the annoyance of a prison; on which occasion, even "if

---

5. Ed. note: "Confessorship" means the act or state of suffering persecution for religious faith.

he had given his body to be burned, it would have profited him nothing," not having the love of God [1 Cor. 13:3], whose very gifts he has resisted and destroyed. For after the Bishop of Rome had acknowledged the prophetic gifts of Montanus, Prisca, and Maximilla, and, in consequence of the acknowledgment, had bestowed his peace[6] on the churches of Asia and Phrygia, *he*, by importunately urging false accusations against the prophets themselves and their churches, and insisting on the authority of the bishop's predecessors in the see, compelled him to recall the peacemaking letter that he had issued, as well as to desist from his purpose of acknowledging the *said* gifts. By this Praxeas did a twofold service for the devil at Rome: he drove away prophecy and he brought in heresy; he put to flight the Paraclete and he crucified the Father. . . .

Chapter 2
The Catholic Doctrine of the Trinity and Unity,
Sometimes Called the Divine Economy, or Dispensation
of the Personal Relations of the Godhead

In the course of time, then, the Father indeed was born, and the Father suffered, God Himself, the Lord Almighty, whom in their preaching they declare to be Jesus Christ. We, however, as we indeed always have done (and more especially since we have been better instructed by the Paraclete, who leads humans indeed into all truth), believe that there is one only God, but under the following dispensation, or *oikonomia*, as it is called, that this one only God has also a Son, God's Word, who proceeded from Himself, by whom all things were made, and without whom nothing was made. *We believe* Him to have been sent by the Father into the Virgin, and to have been born of her—being both Man and God, the Son of Man and the Son of God, and to have been called by the name of Jesus Christ. *We believe* Him to have suffered, died, and been buried, according to the Scriptures, and, after He had been raised again by the Father and taken back to heaven, to be sitting at the right hand of the Father, *and* that He will come to judge the quick and the dead; who sent also from heaven from the Father, according to His own promise, the Holy Spirit, the Paraclete [the "Comforter"], the sanctifier of the faith of those who believe in the Father, and in the Son, and in the Holy Spirit.

That this rule of faith has come down to us from the beginning of the gospel, even before any of the older heretics, much more before Praxeas, *a pretender* of yesterday, will be apparent both from the lateness of date that marks all heresies and also from the absolutely novel character of our new-fangled Praxeas. In this principle also we must find a presumption of equal force against all heresies whatsoever—that whatever is first is true, whereas whatever is later in date is spurious.

---

6. Had admitted them to communion.

But keeping this prescriptive rule inviolate, still some opportunity must be given for reviewing the statements of heretics, with a view to the instruction and protection of different persons—were it only that it may not seem that each perversion *of the truth* is condemned without examination and simply prejudged—especially in the case of this heresy, which supposes itself to possess the pure truth in thinking that one cannot believe in One Only God in any other way than by saying that the Father, the Son, and the Holy Spirit are the very selfsame Person.

As if in this way also one were not All (in that All are of One by unity of substance) while the mystery of the dispensation [*oikonomia*] is still guarded, which distributes the Unity into a Trinity, placing in their order the three *Persons* (the Father, the Son, and the Holy Spirit)—three, however, not in condition but in degree, not in substance, but in form, not in power but in aspect, yet of one substance and of one condition and of one power inasmuch as God is one God from whom these degrees and forms and aspects are reckoned under the name of the Father, and of the Son, and of the Holy Spirit. How they are susceptible of number without division, will be shown as our treatise proceeds.

Chapter 7
The Son by Being Designated Word and Wisdom (According to the Imperfection of Human Thought and Language) Liable to Be Deemed a Mere Attribute; He is Shown to Be a Personal Being

Then, therefore, does the Word also Himself assume His own form and glorious garb, *His own* sound and vocal utterance, when God says, "Let there be light" [Gen. 1:3]. This is the perfect nativity of the Word, when He proceeds forth from God—*formed* by Him first to devise and think out *all things* under the name of Wisdom—"The Lord created *or formed* me as the beginning of His ways" [Prov. 8:22]; then afterward *begotten*, to carry all into effect—"When He prepared the heaven, I was present with Him" [Prov. 8:27].

Thus does He make Him equal to Him: for by proceeding from Himself He became His first-begotten Son, because begotten before all things [Col. 1:15]; and His only-begotten also, because alone begotten of God, in a way peculiar to Himself, from the womb of His own heart—even as the Father Himself testifies: "My heart," says He, "has emitted my most excellent Word" [Ps. 45:1]. *The Father* took pleasure evermore in Him, who equally rejoiced with a reciprocal gladness in the Father's presence: "Thou art my Son, today have I begotten Thee" [Ps. 2:7]; even before the morning star did I beget Thee.

The Son likewise acknowledges the Father, speaking in His own person, under the name of Wisdom: "The Lord formed Me as the beginning of His ways, with a view to His own works; before all the hills did He beget Me" [Prov. 8:22, 25]. For if indeed Wisdom in this passage seems to say that She was created by the Lord with a view to His works, and to accomplish His ways, yet proof is given in another Scripture that "all things were made by the Word, and without Him was there nothing made" [John 1:3], as again in another place (it is said), "By His word were the heavens established, and all the powers thereof by His Spirit" [Ps. 33:6]—that is to say, by the Spirit (or Divine Nature) which was in the Word.

Thus is it evident that it is one and the same power which is in one place described under the name of Wisdom and in another passage under the appellation of the Word, which was initiated for the works of God [Prov. 8:22] which "strengthened the heavens" [v. 8]; "by which all things were made" [John 1:3], "and without which nothing was made" [John 1:3]. Nor need we dwell any longer on this point, as if it were not the very Word Himself, who is spoken of under the name both of Wisdom and of Reason, and of the entire Divine Soul and Spirit. He became also the Son of God, and was begotten when He proceeded forth from Him.

Do you then (you ask) grant that the Word is a certain substance, constructed by the Spirit and the communication of Wisdom? Certainly I do. But you will not allow Him to be really a substantive being, by having a substance of His own; in such a way that He may be regarded as an objective thing and a person, and so be able (as being constituted second to God *the Father*) to make two, the Father and the Son, God and the Word. For you will say, what is a word but a voice and sound of the mouth, and (as the grammarians teach) air when struck against, intelligible to the ear, but for the rest a sort of void, empty, and incorporeal thing.

I, on the contrary, contend that nothing empty and void could have come forth from God, seeing that it is not put forth from that which is empty and void; nor could that possibly be devoid of substance which has proceeded from so great a substance, and has produced such mighty substances: for all things which were made through Him, He Himself (personally) made. How could it be, that He Himself is nothing, without whom nothing was made? How could He who is empty have made things which are solid, and He who is void have made things which are full, and He who is incorporeal have made things which have body? For although a thing may sometimes be made different from him by whom it is made, yet nothing can be made by that which is a void and empty thing.

Is that Word of God, then, a void and empty thing, which is called the Son, who Himself is designated God? "The Word was with God, and the Word was God" [John 1:1]. It is written, "Thou shalt not take God's name in vain" [Exod. 20:7]. This for certain is He "who, being in the form of God, thought it not robbery to be equal with God" [Phil. 2:6]. In what form of God? Of course he means in some form, not in none. For who will deny that God is a body, although "God is a Spirit" [John 4:24]? For Spirit has a bodily substance of its own kind, in its own form. Now, even if invisible things, whatsoever they be, have both their substance and their form in God whereby they are visible to God alone, how much more shall that which has been sent forth from God's substance not be without substance! Whatever, therefore, was the substance of the Word that I designate a Person, I claim for it the name of *Son*; and while I recognize the Son, I assert His distinction as second to the Father.

Chapter 8
Though the Son or Word of God Emanates from the Father,
He is Not Separable from the Father; Nor Is the Holy Spirit
Separable from Either; Illustrations from Nature

. . . With us, however, the Son alone knows the Father [Matt.11:27] and has Himself unfolded "the Father's bosom" [John 1:18]. He has also heard and seen all things with the Father; and what He has been commanded by the Father, that also does He speak [John 8:26]. And it is not His own will, but the Father's, which He has accomplished [John 6:38] which He had known most intimately, even from the beginning. "For who knows the things that are in God, but the Spirit that is in God?" [1 Cor. 2:11]. But the Word was formed by the Spirit, and (if I may so express myself) the Spirit is the body of the Word.

The Word, therefore, is both always in the Father, as He says, "I am in the Father" [John 14:11] and is always with God, according to what is written, "And the Word was with God" [John 1:1]; and never separate from the Father, or other than the Father, since "I and the Father are one" [John 10:30]. This will be the prolation,[7] taught by the truth,[8] the guardian of the Unity, wherein we declare that the Son is a prolation from the Father, without being separated from Him. For God sent forth the Word, as the Paraclete also declares, just as the root puts forth the tree, and the fountain the river, and the sun the ray. For these are *probalaí* (*or emanations*) of the substances from which they proceed.

I should not hesitate, indeed, to call the tree the son or offspring of the root, and the river of the fountain, and the ray of the sun; because every original source is a parent, and everything which issues from the origin is an offspring. Much more is (this true of) the Word of God, who has actually received as His own peculiar designation the name of *Son*. But still the tree is not severed from the root, nor the river from the fountain, nor the ray from the sun; nor, indeed, is the Word separated from God. Following, therefore, the form of these analogies, I confess that I call God and God's Word—the Father and His Son—*two*. For the root and the tree are distinctly two things, but correlatively joined; the fountain and the river are also two forms, but indivisible; so likewise the sun and the ray are

---

7. Ed. note: "Prolation" (*probolē*) refers to the production or bringing forth of the Logos or divine word.

8. Literally, the *probolē* "of the truth."

two forms, but coherent ones. Everything that proceeds from something else must be second to that from which it proceeds, without being on that account separated. Where, however, there is a second, there must be two; and where there is a third, there must be three.

Now the Spirit indeed is third from God and the Son; just as the fruit of the tree is third from the root, or as the stream out of the river is third from the fountain, or as the apex of the ray is third from the sun. Nothing, however, is alien from that original source whence it derives its own properties. In like manner the Trinity, flowing down from the Father through intertwined and connected steps, does not at all disturb the *Monarchy*,[9] whilst it at the same time guards the state of the *Economy*.[10]

Chapter 9
The Catholic Rule of Faith Expounded, Especially in the Unconfused Distinction of the Several Persons of the Blessed Trinity

Bear always in mind that this is the rule of faith which I profess; by it I testify that the Father, and the Son, and the Spirit are inseparable from each other, and so will you know in what sense this is said. Now, observe, my assertion is that the Father is one, and the Son one, and the Spirit one, and that They are distinct from Each Other. This statement is taken in a wrong sense by every uneducated as well as every perversely disposed person, as if it predicated a diversity, in such a sense as to imply a separation among the Father, and the Son, and the Spirit.

I am, moreover, obliged to say this, when (extolling the *Monarchy* at the expense of the *Economy*) they contend for the identity of the Father and Son and Spirit—that it is not by way of diversity that the Son differs from the Father but by distribution. It is not by division that He is different but by distinction because the Father is not the same as the Son, since they differ one from the other in the mode of their being. For the Father is the entire substance, but the Son is a derivation and portion of the whole, as He Himself acknowledges: "My Father is greater than I" [John 14:28]. In the Psalm His inferiority is described as being "a little lower than the angels" [Ps. 8:5]. Thus the Father is distinct from the Son, being greater than the Son, inasmuch as He who begets is one, and He who is begotten is another; He, too, who sends is one, and He who is sent is another; and He, again, who makes is one, and He through whom the thing is made is another.

Happily the Lord Himself employs this expression of the person of the Paraclete, so as to signify not a division or severance, but a disposition (of mutual relations in the Godhead); for He says, "I will pray the Father, and He shall send you another Comforter . . . even the Spirit of truth" [John 14:16], thus making the Paraclete distinct from Himself, even as we say

---

9. Or oneness of the divine empire.
10. Or dispensation of the divine tripersonality. See above chap. 2.

that the Son is also distinct from the Father; so that He showed a third degree in the Paraclete, as we believe the second degree is in the Son, by reason of the order observed in the *Economy*.

Besides, does not the very fact that they have the distinct names of *Father* and *Son* amount to a declaration that they are distinct in personality? For, of course, all things will be what their names represent them to be—and what they are and ever will be that will they be called. And the distinction indicated by the names does not at all admit of any confusion because there is none in the things that they designate. "Yes is yes, and no is no; for what is more than these, comes of evil" [Matt. 5:37].

SELECTION **4**

Origen of Alexandria

On First Principles, Book 1, Chapters 1–3

A major theologian in the period before the Council of Nicaea, Origen of Alexandria (ca. 185–ca. 254) influenced various sides in later Trinitarian debates. His best-known work, *On First Principles*, presents some of his contributions to later Trinitarian theology, which center on the teaching that the one God exists in three coeternal hypostases—as Father, Son, and Holy Spirit.

Drawing on Scripture and Greek philosophy, Origen avers that God is Spirit (i.e., without a body), incomprehensible and immeasurable (1.1.5), and a "simple intellectual nature" characterized by "unity" and "oneness" (1.1.6). As the source and goal of all existence, God alone is true and substantial being; all other beings only exist "accidentally" by participating in God. Because God so surpasses creatures, we can only know God through the "divine sense" that characterizes the "pure in heart" (1.1.9)

Only the Father is unborn or unbegotten; Christ and the Spirit derive their divinity from God the Father, the primal source from which the Son is "born" and the Holy Spirit "proceeds" (1.2.13). Nonetheless, Christ is the Father's only-begotten Son, the express "image" of the Father, who is given birth by the Father in the internal way an act of the will internally proceeds from the mind (1.2.6). Generated before any beginning that can be comprehended or expressed (1.2.2), the Son is eternal (1.2.4): "There never was a time when he was not" (1.2.9). The Father has always generated the Son, who as Wisdom not only makes human beings wise and capable of receiving virtue and intelligence but also contains within herself the beginnings, forms, and species of all creation (1.2.2; Col. 1:15; cf. Prov. 8:22ff.; Wis. 7:25ff.).

The Holy Spirit is also divine, hypostatically distinct, and coeternal with the Father and Son (1.3.4). Not merely a force or energy, the Spirit is an active and personal substance who sanctifies believers and endows them with spiritual gifts in the same way the Spirit inspired the prophets in the Old Testament (1.3.4).

Although Origen stressed that there is nothing greater or lesser in the Trinity (1.3.7), he also distinguished roles and activities within the Trinity: the Father is superior to all because he holds all things together; the Son is lesser because he derives his deity from the Father by contemplating the Father (a process that is, in turn, mirrored in the way all rational or spiritual creatures contemplate the Word and Wisdom who mediates the Father to them); and the Spirit is still less, and dwells only in the saints (1.3.5–8). Yet Origen also stressed that all three hypostases share in the "same stuff" or substance of God. Not only do all three transcend time and all eternity (4.28), but the Son and the Spirit are united with the Father, bringing to completion the one divine will of redeeming the world.

From *Fathers of the Third Century*, ANF 4:242–257.

Chapter 1
On God

1. I know that some will attempt to say that even according to the declarations of our own Scriptures God is a body because in the writings of Moses they find it said, that "our God is a consuming fire" [Deut. 4:24] and in the Gospel according to John that "God is a Spirit and they who worship God must worship God in spirit and in truth" [John 4:24]. Fire and spirit, according to them, are to be regarded as nothing else than a body.

Now, I should like to ask these persons what they have to say about that passage where it is declared that God is light. As John writes in his Epistle, "God is light and in God there is no darkness at all" [1 John 1:5]. Truly God is the light that illuminates the whole understanding of those who are capable of receiving truth, as is said in the thirty-sixth Psalm, "In Your light we shall see light" [Ps. 36:9]. For what other light of God can be named "in which any one sees light" save an influence of God by which a person, being enlightened, either thoroughly sees the truth of all things or comes to know God Himself who is called the truth? Such is the meaning of the expression, "In Your light we shall see light;" i.e., in Your Word and Wisdom which is Your Son, in Himself we shall see You the Father. Because God is called light, shall God be supposed to have any resemblance to the light of the sun? Or how should there be the slightest ground for imagining that from that corporeal light any one could derive the cause of knowledge and come to the understanding of the truth?

2. If, then, they acquiesce in our assertion that reason itself has demonstrated regarding the nature of light, and acknowledge that God cannot be understood to be a body in the sense that light is, similar reasoning

will hold true of the expression "a consuming fire." For what will God consume in respect of God being fire? Shall God be thought to consume material substance, as wood, or hay, or stubble? And what in this view can be
called worthy of the glory of God if God be a fire consuming materials of
that kind?

But let us reflect that God does indeed consume and utterly destroy—
that God consumes evil thoughts, wicked actions, and sinful desires when
they find their way into the minds of believers; and that inhabiting along
with God's Son those souls that are rendered capable of receiving God's
Word and Wisdom, according to His own declaration, "I and the Father
shall come, and We shall make our abode with him?" [John 14:23]. He
makes them, after all their vices and passions have been consumed, a holy
temple, worthy of Himself.

Those, moreover, who, on account of the expression "God is a Spirit,"
think that God is a body, are to be answered, I think, in the following
manner. It is the custom of sacred Scripture, when it wishes to designate
anything opposed to this gross and solid body, to call it spirit, as in the
expression, "The letter kills, but the spirit gives life" [2 Cor. 3:6] where
there can be no doubt that by "letter" are meant bodily things and by
"spirit" intellectual things that we also term "spiritual." The apostle, moreover, says, "Even to this day, when Moses is read, the veil is on their heart.
Nevertheless, when it shall turn to the Lord, the veil shall be taken away,
and where the Spirit of the Lord is, there is liberty" [2 Cor. 3:15–17].

For so long as anyone is not converted to a spiritual understanding, a
veil is placed over his heart, with which veil (i.e., a gross understanding)
Scripture itself is said or thought to be covered. And this is the meaning of
the statement that a veil was placed over the countenance of Moses when
he spoke to the people, i.e., when the law was publicly read aloud. But if we
turn to the Lord, where also is the word of God, and where the Holy Spirit
reveals spiritual knowledge, then the veil is taken away and with unveiled
face we shall behold the glory of the Lord in the holy Scriptures.

3. And since many saints participate in the Holy Spirit He cannot therefore be understood to be a body, which being divided into corporeal parts
is partaken of by each one of the saints, but He is manifestly a sanctifying
power in which all are said to have a share who have deserved to be sanctified by the Spirit's grace.

And in order that what we say may be more easily understood, let us
take an illustration from things that are dissimilar. There are many persons
who take a part in the science [*disciplina*] or art of medicine. Are we therefore to suppose that those who do so take to themselves the particles of
some body called medicine, which is placed before them, and in this way
participate in the same? Or must we not rather understand that all who
with quick and trained minds come to understand the art and discipline

itself may be said to be partakers of the art of healing? But these are not to be deemed altogether parallel instances in a comparison of medicine to the Holy Spirit, as they have been adduced only to establish that that is not necessarily to be considered a body, a share in which is possessed by many individuals. For the Holy Spirit differs widely from the method or science of medicine, in respect that the Holy Spirit is an intellectual existence [*substantia*] and subsists and exists in a peculiar manner, whereas medicine is not at all of that nature.

4. But we must pass on to the language of the Gospel itself, in which it is declared that "God is a Spirit" and where we have to show how that is to be understood agreeably to what we have stated. For let us inquire on what occasion these words were spoken by the Savior before whom He uttered them, and what was the subject of investigation. We find, without any doubt, that He spoke these words to the Samaritan woman, saying to her, who thought, agreeably to the Samaritan view, that God ought to be worshipped on Mount Gerizim—that "God is a Spirit." For the Samaritan woman, believing Him to be a Jew, was inquiring of Him whether God ought to be worshipped in Jerusalem or on this mountain; and her words were, "All our fathers worshipped on this mountain, and you say that in Jerusalem is the place where we ought to worship" [John 4:20]. To this opinion of the Samaritan woman, therefore, who imagined that God was less rightly or duly worshipped, according to the privileges of the different localities—either by the Jews in Jerusalem or by the Samaritans on Mount Gerizim—the Savior answered that he who would follow the Lord must lay aside all preference for particular places, and thus expressed Himself: "The hour is coming when neither in Jerusalem nor on this mountain shall the true worshippers worship the Father. God is a Spirit, and those who worship God must worship God in spirit and in truth" [John 4:23, 24]. And observe how logically He has joined together the spirit and the truth: He called God a Spirit, that He might distinguish God from bodies; and He named God the truth, to distinguish God from a shadow or an image. For they who worshipped in Jerusalem worshipped God neither in truth nor in spirit, being in subjection to the shadow or image of heavenly things; and such also was the case with those who worshipped on Mount Gerizim.

5. Having refuted, then, as well as we could, every notion that might suggest that we were to think of God as in any degree corporeal, we go on to say that, according to strict truth, God is incomprehensible and incapable of being measured. For whatever might be the knowledge that we are able to obtain of God, either by perception or reflection, we must of necessity believe that God is by many degrees far better than what we perceive God to be. For, as if we were to see any one unable to bear a spark of light, or the flame of a very small lamp, and were desirous to acquaint such a one, whose vision could not admit a greater degree of light than

what we have stated with the brightness and splendor of the sun, would it not be necessary to tell him that the splendor of the sun was unspeakably and incalculably better and more glorious than all this light that he saw? So our understanding, when shut in by the fetters of flesh and blood and rendered, on account of its participation in such material substances duller and more obtuse, although, in comparison with our bodily nature, it is esteemed to be far superior, yet, in its efforts to examine and behold incorporeal things, scarcely holds the place of a spark or lamp. But among all intelligent, that is, incorporeal beings what is so superior to all others— so unspeakably and incalculably superior—as God, whose nature cannot be grasped or seen by the power of any human understanding, even the purest and brightest?

6. But it will not appear absurd if we employ another similitude to make the matter clearer. Our eyes frequently cannot look upon the nature of the light itself—that is, upon the substance of the sun. But when we behold its splendor or its rays pouring in, perhaps, through windows or some small openings to admit the light, we can reflect how great is the supply and source of the light of the body. So, in like manner, the works of Divine Providence and the plan of this whole world are a sort of rays, as it were, of the nature of God in comparison with God's real substance and being. As, therefore, our understanding is unable of itself to behold God Himself as God is, it knows the Father of the world from the beauty of God's works and the comeliness of God's creatures. God, therefore, is not to be thought of as being either a body or as existing in a body, but as an uncompounded intellectual nature [*simplex intellectualis natura*] admitting within Himself no addition of any kind; so that God cannot be believed to have within him a greater and a lesser, but is such that God is in all parts *Monas*, and, so to speak, *Henas*, and is the mind and source from which all intellectual nature or mind takes its beginning. But mind, for its movements or activities, needs no physical space, nor sensible magnitude, nor bodily shape, nor color, nor any other of those adjuncts that are the properties of body or matter. Wherefore that simple and wholly intellectual nature [*natura illa simplex et tota mens*] can admit of no delay or hesitation in its movements or activities, lest the simplicity of the divine nature should appear to be circumscribed or in some degree hampered by such adjuncts, and lest that which is the beginning of all things should be found composite and differing, and that which ought to be free from all bodily intermixture, in virtue of being the one sole species of deity, so to speak, should prove, instead of being one, to consist of many things. . . .

9. Here, if any one lay before us the passage where it is said, "Blessed are the pure in heart, for they shall see God" [Matt. 5:8] from that very passage, in my opinion, will our position derive additional strength. For what else is seeing God in heart, but, according to our exposition as above,

understanding and knowing God with the mind? For the names of the organs of sense are frequently applied to the soul so that it may be said to see with the eyes of the heart (i.e., to perform an intellectual act by means of the power of intelligence). So also it is said to hear with the ears when it perceives the deeper meaning of a statement. So also we say that it makes use of teeth, when it chews and eats the bread of life that comes down from heaven. In like manner, also, it is said to employ the services of other members, which are transferred from their bodily appellations and applied to the powers of the soul, according to the words of Solomon, "You will find a divine sense" [cf. Prov. 2:5]. For he knew that there were within us two kinds of senses: the one mortal, corruptible, human; the other immortal and intellectual, which he now termed divine. By this divine sense, therefore, not of the eyes, but of a pure heart, which is the mind, God may be seen by those who are worthy. For you will certainly find in all the Scriptures, both old and new, the term "heart" repeatedly used instead of "mind" (i.e., intellectual power). In this manner, therefore, although far below the dignity of the subject, have we spoken of the nature of God, as those who understand it under the limitation of the human understanding. In the next place, let us see what is meant by the name of Christ.

Chapter 2
On Christ

1. In the first place, we must note that the nature of the deity that is in Christ with respect to His being the only-begotten Son of God is one thing, and that human nature which He assumed in these last times for the purposes of the dispensation (of grace) is another. Thus we have first to ascertain what the only-begotten Son of God is, seeing He is called by many different names, according to the circumstances and views of individuals. For He is termed Wisdom, according to the expression of Solomon: "The Lord created me—the beginning of His ways, and among His works, before He made any other thing; He founded me before the ages. In the beginning, before He formed the earth, before He brought forth the fountains of waters, before the mountains were made strong, before all the hills, He brought me forth" [Prov. 8:22–25].[11] He is also styled First-born, as the apostle has declared: "who is the first-born of every creature" [Col. 1:15]. The first-born, however, is not by nature a different person from Wisdom, but one and the same. Finally, the Apostle Paul says that "Christ (is) the power of God and the wisdom of God" [1 Cor. 1:24].

2. Let no one, however, imagine that we mean anything impersonal [*aliquid insubstantivum*] when we call Him the Wisdom of God; or suppose, for example, that we understand Him to be not a living being

---

11. The reading in the text differs considerably from that of the Vulgate.

endowed with wisdom but something that makes humans wise, giving itself to, and implanting itself in, the minds of those who are made capable of receiving His virtues and intelligence.

If, then, it is once rightly understood that the only-begotten Son of God is God's wisdom hypostatically [*substantialiter*] existing, I know not whether our curiosity ought to advance beyond this or entertain any suspicion that that *hupóstasis* or *substantia* contains anything of a bodily nature since everything that is corporeal is distinguished either by form, or color, or magnitude. And who in his sound senses ever sought for form, or color, or size, in wisdom, in respect of its being wisdom?

And who that is capable of entertaining reverential thoughts or feelings regarding God, can suppose or believe that God the Father ever existed, even for a moment of time without having generated this Wisdom? For in that case he must say either that God was unable to generate Wisdom before God produced Her—so that God afterwards called into being Her who formerly did not exist—or that God possessed the power indeed but (what cannot be said of God without impiety) was unwilling to use it. Both of these suppositions, it is patent to all, are alike absurd and impious. For they amount to this: either that God advanced from a condition of inability to one of ability or that, although possessed of the power, God concealed it and delayed the generation of Wisdom. Thus we have always held that God is the Father of God's only-begotten Son, who was born indeed of God and derives from God what He is but without any beginning—not only such as may be measured by any divisions of time but even that which the mind alone can contemplate within itself or behold, so to speak, with the naked powers of the understanding.

And therefore we must believe that Wisdom was generated before any beginning that can be either comprehended or expressed. And since all the creative power of the coming creation [*omnis virtus ac deformatio futurae creaturae*] was included in this very existence of Wisdom (whether of those things that have an original existence or of those that have a derived existence, having been formed beforehand and arranged by the power of foreknowledge), on account of these very creatures that had been described, as it were, and prefigured in Wisdom Herself, does Wisdom say, in the words of Solomon, that She was created the beginning of the ways of God, inasmuch as She contained within Herself either the beginnings, or forms, or species of all creation.

3. Now, in the same way in which we have understood that Wisdom was the beginning of the ways of God and is said to be created, forming beforehand and containing within Herself the species and beginnings of all creatures, so must we understand Her to be the Word of God, because of Her disclosing to all other beings (i.e., to universal creation) the nature of the mysteries and secrets that are contained within the Divine Wisdom. And on this account, She is called the Word, because She is, as it were, the

interpreter of the secrets of the mind. And therefore that language found in the *Acts of Paul*,[12] where it is said "here is the Word a living being" appears to me to be rightly used. John, however, with more sublimity and propriety, says in the beginning of his Gospel, when defining God by a special definition to be the Word, "And God was the Word, and this was in the beginning with God" (John 1:1).

Let him, then, who assigns a beginning to the Word or Wisdom of God, take care that he be not guilty of impiety against the unbegotten Father Himself, seeing he denies that He had always been a Father, and had generated the Word, and had possessed wisdom in all preceding periods, whether they be called times or ages, or anything else that can be so entitled.

4. This Son, accordingly, is also the Truth and Life of all things that exist. And with reason. For how could those things that were created live, unless they derived their being from Life? Or how could those things that are, truly exist unless they came down from the Truth? Or how could rational beings exist unless the Word or Reason had previously existed? Or how could they be wise unless there were Wisdom? But since it was to come to pass that some also should fall away from life and bring death upon themselves by their declension—for death is nothing else than a departure from life—and as it was not to follow that those beings that had once been created by God for the enjoyment of life should utterly perish, it was necessary that, before death, there should be in existence such a power as would destroy the coming death and that there should be a resurrection, the type of which was in our Lord and Savior, and that this resurrection should have its ground in the Wisdom and Word and Life of God.

And then, in the next place, since some of those who were created were not to be always willing to remain unchangeable and unalterable in the calm and moderate enjoyment of the blessings which they possessed, but, in consequence of the good that was in them being theirs not by nature or essence, but by accident, were to be perverted and changed, and to fall away from their position, therefore was the Word and Wisdom of God made the Way.

And it was so termed because it leads to the Father those who walk along it. Whatever, therefore, we have predicated of the Wisdom of God, will be appropriately applied and understood of the Son of God, in virtue of His being the Life, and the Word, and the Truth and the Resurrection. For all these titles are derived from His power and activities and in none of them is there the slightest ground for understanding anything of a corporeal nature which might seem to denote either size, or form, or color.

---

12. This work is mentioned by Eusebius, *Hist. Eccles.*, iii. c. 3 and 25, as among the spurious writings current in the Church. The *Acts of Paul and Thecla* was a different work from the *Acts of Paul*. The words quoted, "Hic est verbum animal vivens," seem to be a corruption from Heb. 4:12. . . .

For those children of humans that appear among us, or those descendants of other living beings, correspond to the seed of those by whom they were begotten, or derive from those mothers, in whose wombs they are formed and nourished, whatever it is that they bring into this life and carry with them when they are born. But it is monstrous and unlawful to compare God the Father, in the generation of His only-begotten Son and in the substance [*subsistentia*][13] of the same, to any person or other living thing engaged in such an act. For we must of necessity hold that there is something exceptional and worthy of God that does not admit of any comparison at all—not merely in things but that cannot even be conceived by thought or discovered by perception so that a human mind should be able to apprehend how the unbegotten God is made the Father of the only-begotten Son—because His generation is as eternal and everlasting as the brilliancy which is produced from the sun. For it is not by receiving the breath of life that He is made a Son, by *any outward act*, but by His own nature.

5. Let us now ascertain how those statements that we have advanced are supported by the authority of Holy Scripture. The Apostle Paul says, that the only-begotten Son is the "image of the invisible God," and "the firstborn of every creature" [Col. 1:15]. And when writing to the Hebrews, he says of Him that He is "the brightness of God's glory, and the express image of God's person" [Heb. 1:3]. Now, we find in the treatise called the Wisdom of Solomon the following description of the Wisdom of God: "For She is the breath of the power of God, and the purest efflux of the glory of the Almighty. Nothing that is polluted can therefore come upon Her. For She is the splendor of the eternal light, and the stainless mirror of God's working, and the image of God's goodness" [Wis. 7:25, 26]. Now we say, as before, that Wisdom has Her existence nowhere else save in Him who is the beginning of all things—from whom also is derived everything that is wise, because He Himself is the only one who is by nature a Son, and is therefore termed the Only-begotten.

6. Let us now see how we are to understand the expression "invisible image," that we may in this way perceive how God is rightly called the Father of His Son; and let us, in the first place, draw our conclusions from what are customarily called images among humans. That is sometimes called an image which is painted or sculptured on some material substance, such as wood or stone; and sometimes a child is called the image of his parent, when the features of the child in no respect belie their resemblance to the father. I think, therefore, that that person who was formed after the image and likeness of God may be fittingly compared to the first illustration. Respecting him, however, we shall see more precisely, God willing, when we come to expound the passage in Genesis.

13. Some would read here, "substantia."

But the image of the Son of God, of whom we are now speaking, may be compared to the second of the above examples, even in respect of this, that He is the invisible image of the invisible God, in the same manner as we say, according to the sacred history, that the image of Adam is his son Seth. The words are, "And Adam begat Seth in his own likeness, and after his own image" [Gen. 5:3]. Now this image contains the unity of nature and substance belonging to Father and Son. For if the Son do, in like manner, all those things that the Father does, then, in virtue of the Son doing all things like the Father, is the image of the Father formed in the Son, who is born of Him, like an act of His will proceeding from the mind. And I am therefore of opinion that the will of the Father ought alone to be sufficient for the existence of that which He wishes to exist. For in the exercise of His will He employs no other way than that which is made known by the counsel of His will. And thus also the existence [*subsistentia*] of the Son is generated by Him. For this point must above all others be maintained by those who allow nothing to be unbegotten (i.e., unborn) save God the Father only.

We must be careful not to fall into the absurdities of those who picture to themselves certain emanations, so as to divide the divine nature into parts, and who divide God the Father as far as they can, since even to entertain the remotest suspicion of such a thing regarding an incorporeal being is not only the height of impiety, but a mark of the greatest folly—it being most remote from any intelligent conception that there should be any physical division of any incorporeal nature. Rather, therefore, as an act of the will proceeds from the understanding, and neither cuts off any part nor is separated or divided from it, so after some such fashion is the Father to be supposed as having begotten the Son, His own image—namely, so that, as He is Himself invisible by nature, He also begat an image that was invisible.

For the Son is the Word, and therefore we are not to understand that anything in Him is cognizable by the senses. He is Wisdom, and in Wisdom there can be no suspicion of anything corporeal. He is the true Light, which enlightens everyone who comes into this world, but He has nothing in common with the light of this sun. Our Savior, therefore, is the Image of the invisible God, inasmuch as compared with the Father Himself He is the Truth: and as compared with us, to whom He reveals the Father, He is the image by which we come to the knowledge of the Father, whom no one knows save the Son, and he to whom the Son is pleased to reveal Him. And the method of revealing Him is through the understanding. For He by whom the Son Himself is understood, understands, as a consequence, the Father also, according to His own words: "He that has seen Me, has seen the Father also" [John 14:9]. . . .

Chapter 3
On the Holy Spirit

4. . . . For as it is said of the Son, that "no one knows the Father but the Son, and he to whom the Son will reveal Him" [Luke 10:22], the same also is said by the apostle of the Holy Spirit, when he declares, "God has revealed them to us by the Holy Spirit; for the Spirit searches all things, even the deep things of God" [1 Cor. 2:10]; and again in the Gospel, when the Savior, speaking of the divine and profounder parts of His teaching, which His disciples were not yet able to receive, thus addresses them: "I have yet many things to say unto you, but you cannot bear them now; but when the Holy Spirit, the Comforter, comes, He will teach you all things, and will bring all things to your remembrance, whatsoever I have said unto you" [cf. John 16:12, 13]. We must understand, therefore, that as the Son, who alone knows the Father, reveals Him to whom He will, so the Holy Spirit, who alone searches the deep things of God, reveals God to whom He will: "For the Spirit blows where He wills" [John 3:8].

We are not, however, to suppose that the Spirit derives His knowledge through revelation from the Son. For if the Holy Spirit knows the Father through the Son's revelation, He passes from a state of ignorance into one of knowledge; but it is alike impious and foolish to confess the Holy Spirit, and yet to ascribe to Him ignorance. For even though something else existed before the Holy Spirit, it was not by progressive advancement that He came to be the Holy Spirit; as if anyone should venture to say, that at the time when He was not yet the Holy Spirit He was ignorant of the Father, but that after He had received knowledge He was made the Holy Spirit. If this were the case, the Holy Spirit would never be reckoned in the Unity of the Trinity (i.e., along with the unchangeable Father and His Son), unless He had always been the Holy Spirit. When we use, indeed, such terms as "always" or "was," or any other designation of time, they are not to be taken absolutely, but with due allowance; for while the significations of these words relate to time, and those subjects of which we speak are spoken of by a stretch of language as existing in time, they nevertheless surpass in their real nature all conception of the finite understanding.

5. Nevertheless it seems proper to inquire what is the reason why he who is regenerated by God to salvation has to do with Father and Son and Holy Spirit, and does not obtain salvation unless with the cooperation of the entire Trinity; and why it is impossible to become partaker of the Father or the Son without the Holy Spirit. And in discussing these subjects, it will undoubtedly be necessary to describe the special working of the Holy Spirit, and of the Father and the Son.

I am of opinion, then, that the working of the Father and of the Son takes place as well in saints as in sinners, in rational beings and in dumb animals—no, even in those things that are without life, and in all things universally that exist—but that the activity of the Holy Spirit does not take place at all in those things that are without life, or in those which, although living, are yet dumb—no, is not found even in those who are endowed indeed with reason, but are engaged in evil courses and not at all converted to a better life. In those persons alone do I think that the activity of the Holy Spirit takes place—who are already turning to a better life and walking along the way which leads to Jesus Christ, i.e., who are engaged in the performance of good actions, and who abide in God.

6. That the working of the Father and the Son is active, both in saints and in sinners, is manifest from this: that all who are rational beings are partakers of the Word, (i.e., of Reason) and by this means bear certain seeds implanted within them of Wisdom and Justice—that is Christ.

Now, all things, whatever they are, participate in God who truly exists and who said by Moses, "I AM WHO I AM," [Exod. 3:14]. Such participation in God the Father is shared both by just persons and sinners, by rational and irrational beings, and by all things universally that exist.

The Apostle Paul also shows truly that all have a share in Christ, when he says, "Say not in your heart, Who shall ascend into heaven (i.e., to bring Christ down from above)? Or who shall descend into the deep (i.e., to bring up Christ again from the dead)? But what does Scripture say? 'The word is near you, even in your mouth, and in your heart'" [Rom. 10:6–8]. By this he means that Christ is in the heart of all, in respect of His being the Word or Reason, by participating in which they are rational beings. That declaration also in the Gospel, "If I had not come and spoken to them, they had not had sin but now they have no excuse for their sin" [John 15:22] renders it manifest and patent to all who have a rational knowledge of how long a time humans are without sin, and from what period they are liable to it, how, by participating in the Word or Reason, humans are said to have sinned—that from the time they are made capable of understanding and knowledge, when the reason implanted within has suggested to them the difference between good and evil, and after they have already begun to know what evil is, they are made liable to sin, if they commit it. And this is the meaning of the expression, that "humans have no excuse for their sin"—that from the time the Divine Word or Reason has begun to show them internally the difference between good and evil, they ought to avoid and guard against that which is wicked: "For to him who knows to do good, and does it not, to him it is sin" [Jas. 4:17].

Moreover, that all humans are not without communion with God, is taught in the Gospel thus, by the Savior's words: "The kingdom of God comes not with observation; neither shall they say, Lo here! Or, lo there! But the kingdom of God is within you" [Luke 17:20, 21]. But here we must see whether this does not bear the same meaning with the expression in Genesis: "And He breathed into his face the breath of life, and man became a living soul" [Gen. 2:7]. For if this be understood as applying generally to all humans, then all humans have a share in God.

7. But if this is to be understood as spoken of the Spirit of God, since Adam also is found to have prophesied of some things, it may be taken not as of general application, but as confined to those who are saints. Finally, also, at the time of the flood, when all flesh had corrupted their way before God, it is recorded that God spoke thus, as of undeserving humans and sinners: "My Spirit shall not abide with those humans forever, because they are flesh" [Gen. 6:3]. By this, it is clearly shown that the Spirit of God is taken away from all who are unworthy. In the Psalms also it is written: "You take away their spirit, and they will die, and return to their earth. You send forth Your Spirit, and they shall be created, and You will renew the face of the earth" [Ps. 104:29, 30], which is manifestly intended of the Holy Spirit, who, after sinners and unworthy persons have been taken away and destroyed, creates for Himself a new people, and renews the face of the earth when, laying aside through the grace of the Spirit the old person with his deeds, they begin to walk in newness of life.

And therefore the expression is competently applied to the Holy Spirit because He will take up His dwelling, not in all people, nor in those who are flesh, but in those whose land has been renewed. Lastly, for this reason was the grace and revelation of the Holy Spirit bestowed by the imposition of the apostles' hands after baptism. Our Savior also, after the resurrection, when old things had already passed away, and all things had become new, Himself a new person, and the first-born from the dead, His apostles also being renewed by faith in His resurrection, says, "Receive the Holy Spirit" [John 20:22]. This is doubtless what the Lord the Savior meant to convey in the Gospel, when He said that new wine cannot be put into old bottles, but commanded that the bottles should be made new, i.e., that humans should walk in newness of life, that they might receive the new wine, i.e., the newness of grace of the Holy Spirit.

In this manner, then, is the working of the power of God the Father and of the Son extended without distinction to every creature; but a share in the Holy Spirit we find possessed only by the saints. And therefore it is said, "No one can say that Jesus is Lord, but by the Holy Spirit" [1 Cor. 12:3]. And on one occasion, scarcely even the apostles themselves are deemed worthy to hear the words, "You shall receive the power of the Holy Spirit coming upon you" [Acts 1:8].

For this reason, also, I think it follows that he who has committed a sin against the Son of man is deserving of forgiveness; because if he who is a participator of the Word or Reason of God cease to live agreeably to reason, he seems to have fallen into a state of ignorance or folly, and therefore to deserve forgiveness; whereas he who has been deemed worthy to have a portion of the Holy Spirit, and who has relapsed, is, by this very act and work, said to be guilty of blasphemy against the Holy Spirit.

Let no one indeed suppose that we, from having said that the Holy Spirit is conferred upon the saints alone, but that the benefits or activities of the Father and of the Son extend to good and bad, to just and unjust, by so doing give a preference to the Holy Spirit over the Father and the Son, or assert that His dignity is greater, which certainly would be a very illogical conclusion. For it is the peculiarity of Holy Spirit's grace and activities that we have been describing. Moreover, nothing in the Trinity can be called greater or less, since the Fountain of Divinity alone contains all things by God's Word and Reason and by the Spirit of God's mouth sanctifies all things that are worthy of sanctification, as it is written in the Psalm: "By the word of the Lord were the heavens strengthened, and all their power by the Spirit of His mouth" [Ps. 33:6].

There is also a special working of God the Father, besides that by which He bestowed upon all things the gift of natural life. There is also a special ministry of the Lord Jesus Christ to those upon whom He confers by nature the gift of Reason, by means of which they are enabled to be rightly what they are. There is also another grace of the Holy Spirit, which is bestowed upon the deserving, through the ministry of Christ and the working of the Father, in proportion to the merits of those who are rendered capable of receiving it. This is most clearly pointed out by the Apostle Paul, when demonstrating that the power of the Trinity is one and the same, in the words, "There are diversities of gifts, but the same Spirit; there are diversities of ministries, but the same Lord; and there are diversities of activities, but it is the same God who works all in all. But the manifestation of the Spirit is given to everyone for the common good" [1 Cor. 12:4–7]. From this it most clearly follows that there is no difference in the Trinity, but that which is called the gift of the Spirit is made known through the Son and activated by God the Father. "All these are activated by one and the same Spirit, who allots to each one individually just as the Spirit chooses" [1 Cor. 12:11].

8. Having made these declarations regarding the Unity of the Father, and of the Son, and of the Holy Spirit, let us return to the order in which we began the discussion. God the Father bestows upon all existence; and participation in Christ, in respect of His being the Word of reason, renders them rational beings. From this it follows that they are deserving either of praise or blame, because capable of virtue and vice. On this account, therefore, is the grace of the Holy Spirit present, that those beings who are not holy in their essence may be rendered holy by participating in it.

Seeing then that first they derive their existence from God the Father; second, their rational nature from the Word; and third, their holiness from the Holy Spirit—those who have been previously sanctified by the Holy Spirit are again made capable of receiving Christ, in respect that He is the righteousness of God; and those who have earned advancement to this grade by the sanctification of the Holy Spirit will nevertheless obtain the gift of wisdom according to the power and working of the Spirit of God. And this I consider is Paul's meaning when he says that to "some is given the word of wisdom, to others the word of knowledge, according to the same Spirit" [1 Cor. 12:8]. And while pointing out the individual distinction of gifts, he refers the whole of them to the source of all things in the words, "There are diversities of activities, but one God who works all in all" [1 Cor. 12:6].

Thus also the working of the Father, which confers existence upon all things, is found to be more glorious and magnificent, while each one, by participation in Christ—as being wisdom and knowledge and sanctification—makes progress and advances to higher degrees of perfection; and seeing it is by partaking of the Holy Spirit that any one is made purer and holier, he obtains, when he is made worthy, the grace of wisdom and knowledge, in order that—after all stains of pollution and ignorance are cleansed and taken away—he may make so great an advance in holiness and purity that the nature he received from God may become such as is worthy of the One who gave it to be pure and perfect, so that the being which exists may be as worthy as the One who called it into existence.

For, in this way, he who is such as his Creator wished him to be will receive from God power always to exist and to abide forever. That this may be the case and that those whom God has created may be unceasingly and inseparably present with God, Who IS, it is the business of Wisdom to instruct and train them, and to bring them to perfection by confirmation of the Holy Spirit and unceasing sanctification, by which alone are they capable of receiving God.

In this way, then, by the renewal of the ceaseless working of Father, Son, and Holy Spirit in us, in its various stages of progress, shall we be able at some future time perhaps, although with difficulty, to behold the holy and the blessed life, in which (as it is only after many struggles that we are able to reach it) we ought so to continue, that no satiety of that blessedness should ever seize us, but the more we perceive its blessedness, the more should be increased and intensified within us the longing for the same, while we ever more eagerly and freely receive and hold fast the Father, and the Son, and the Holy Spirit.

But if satiety should ever take hold of any one of those who stand on the highest and perfect summit of attainment, I do not think that such a one would suddenly be deposed from his position and fall away, but that he must decline gradually and little by little, so that it may sometimes happen that if a brief lapsus take place, and the individual quickly repent and return to himself, he may not utterly fall away, but may retrace his steps, and return to his former place, and again make good what had been lost by his negligence.

Athanasius of Alexandria

Orations against the Arians and Letters to Serapion on the Holy Spirit

As bishop of Alexandria, Athanasius (ca. 296–373) promulgated the Creed of Nicaea (325), playing an important role in defining the Nicene confession that the Logos, the Son of God, is eternally divine and consubstantial (of "one substance," *homoousios)* with the Father.

In the excerpt below from *Orations against the Arians,* Athanasius argues that the Triad (the Trinity) is everlasting because the Word was with God from eternity: "There never was a time when the Word was not." In contrast to created beings, who do not have the same essence as their creator, the Son is the Father's own "Offspring, Word, and Wisdom" and "Image." Like the Father (and unlike creatures), the Son is eternal, sharing in all the Father's divine attributes—what is "proper" to the Father as his own. The titles "Father" and "Son" refer to their relationship; unlike human relations between fathers and sons (where sons, in turn, become fathers of their own sons), the divine Father and Son are eternally Father and Son.

Athanasius based his argument for the Son's consubstantiality with the Father on a soteriological claim: the Son is divine because he saves and deifies humans; God became human so that we might be deified. As he argued in *On the Incarnation,* "only a God can save." In a similar vein, he argued that the Spirit who sanctifies us must be divine and not a creature. In *Letters to Serapion on the Holy Spirit* (375), which was addressed to the Tropici (who considered the Holy Spirit to be merely a creature), he maintained that the Spirit belongs to Christ in the same way that the Son belongs to the Father: as the Son is the Father's Word and Wisdom, so the Spirit is the Son's "energy" *(energeia),* present in and completing the Son's work.

Orations against the Arians, Discourse 1.6

From *Athanasius: Select Works and Letters, NPNF* 2:4, 316–20.

Discourse 1
Chapter 6

17. . . . If God be Maker and Creator and create God's works through the Son, and we cannot regard things that come to be except as being through the Word, is it not blasphemous—God being Maker—to say that God's

Framing Word and God's Wisdom once was not? It is the same as saying, that God is not Maker, if God had not God's proper Framing Word which is from God, but that that by which God frames, accrues to God from without, and is alien from God, and unlike in essence.

Next, let them tell us this, or rather learn from it how irreligious they are in saying, "Once He was not" and "He was not before His genera-tion"—for if the Word is not with the Father from everlasting, the Triad is not everlasting but a Monad was first and afterwards by addition it became a Triad. And so as time went on, it seems what we know concerning God grew and took shape.

And further, if the Son is not the proper offspring of the Father's essence, but of nothing has come to be, then of nothing the Triad con-sists. And once there was not a Triad, but a Monad, and a Triad once with deficiency and then complete—deficient before the Son was originated, complete when He had come to be—and henceforth a thing originated is reckoned with the Creator and what once was not has divine worship and glory with the One who was ever. No, what is more serious still, the Triad is discovered to be unlike Itself, consisting of strange and alien natures an essences. And this, in other words, is saying, that the Triad has an origi-nated consistence.

What sort of a religion then is this, which is not even like itself, but is in the process of completion as time goes on, and is now not thus, and then again thus? For probably it will receive some new attainment, and so on without limit, since at first and at the start it took its consistence by way of attainments. And so undoubtedly it may decrease on the contrary, for what is added plainly admits of being subtracted.

18. But this is not so: perish the thought! The Triad is not originated, but there is an eternal and one Godhead in a Triad; and there is one Glory of the Holy Triad. You presume to divide it into different natures: the Father being eternal yet you say of the Word that is seated by Him, "Once He was not"; and, whereas the Son is seated by the Father, yet you think to place Him far from Him. The Triad is Creator and Framer, and you fear not to degrade It to things which are from nothing. You scruple not to equal servile beings to the nobility of the Triad and to rank the King, the Lord of Sabaoth with subjects. Cease this confusion of things not associated, or rather of things which are not with the One who is. Such statements do not glorify and honor the Lord, but the reverse: for he who dishonors the Son, dishonors also the Father. For if the doctrine of God is now perfect in a Triad and this is the true and only Religion—and this is the good and the truth—it must have been always so, unless the good and the truth be something that came after and the doctrine of God is completed by addi-tions. I say, it must have been eternally so. But if not eternally, not so at present either, but at present so, as you suppose it was from the begin-ning—I mean, not a Triad now.

But such heretics no Christian would bear: it belongs to Greeks to introduce an originated Triad and to level It with things originate. For these do admit of deficiencies and additions, but the faith of Christians acknowledges the blessed Triad as unalterable and perfect and ever what It was—neither adding to It what is more nor imputing to It any loss (for both ideas are irreligious). Therefore it dissociates It from all things generated; it guards as indivisible and worships the unity of the Godhead Itself; and it shuns the Arian blasphemies, confessing and acknowledging that the Son was ever. For He is eternal, as is the Father, of whom He is the Eternal Word—to which subject let us now return again.

19. If God is, and is called, the Fountain of wisdom and life—as He says by Jeremiah, "They have forsaken Me the Fountain of living waters" [Jer. 2:13]; and again, "A glorious high throne from the beginning, is the place of our sanctuary; O Lord, the Hope of Israel, all that forsake You shall be ashamed, and they that depart from Me shall be written in the earth, because they have forsaken the Lord, the Fountain of living waters" [Jer. 17:12, 13]; and in the book of Baruch it is written, "Thou hast forsaken the Fountain of wisdom" [Bar. 3:12]—this implies that life and wisdom are not foreign to the Essence of the Fountain, but are proper to It, nor were at any time without existence, but were always.

Now the Son is all this, who says, "I am the Life" [John 14:6], and, "I Wisdom dwell with prudence" [Prov. 8:12]. Is it not then irreligious to say, "Once the Son was not?" for it is all one with saying, "Once the Fountain was dry, destitute of Life and Wisdom." But a fountain it would then cease to be; for what begets not from itself, is not a fountain. What a load of extravagance! For God promises that those who do God's will shall be as a fountain that the water fails not, saying by Isaiah the prophet, "And the Lord shall satisfy your soul in drought and make your bones fat; and you shall be like a watered garden, and like a spring of water whose waters fail not" [Isa. 58:11].

And yet these, whereas God is called and is a Fountain of wisdom, dare to insult God as barren and void of God's proper Wisdom. But their doctrine is false—truth witnessing that God is the eternal Fountain of God's proper Wisdom and if the Fountain be eternal, the Wisdom also must be eternal. For in It were all things made, as David says in the Psalm, "In Wisdom, You have made them all" [Ps. 104:24]; and Solomon says, "The Lord by Wisdom has formed the earth, by understanding has He established the heavens" [Prov. 3:19]. And this Wisdom is the Word and by Him, as John says, "all things were made," and "without Him was made not one thing" [John 1:3]. And this Word is Christ; for "there is One God, the Father, from whom are all things, and we for Him; and One Lord Jesus Christ, through whom are all things, and we through Him" [1 Cor. 8:6].

And if all things are through Him, He Himself is not to be reckoned with that "all." For he who dares to call Him, through whom are things, one of that "all," surely will have like speculations concerning God from whom are all. But if he shrinks from this as unseemly and excludes God from that all, it is but consistent that he should also exclude from that all the Only-Begotten Son, as being proper to the Father's essence. And, if He be not one of the all, it is sin to say concerning Him, "He was not," and "He was not before His generation." Such words may be used of creatures; but as to the Son, He is such as the Father is, of whose essence He is proper Offspring, Word, and Wisdom. For this is proper to the Son, as regards the Father, and this shows that the Father is proper to the Son; that we may neither say that God was ever without Word [*álogon*] nor that the Son was non-existent. For wherefore a Son, if not from Him? Or wherefore Word and Wisdom, if not ever proper to Him?

20. When then was God without that which is proper to Him? Or how can one consider that which is proper as foreign and alien in essence? For other things, according to the nature of things originate, are without likeness in essence with the Maker; but are external to the Maker made by the Word at His grace and will and thus admit of ceasing to be, if it so pleases the One who made them; for such is the nature of things originate. But as to what is proper to the Father's essence (for this we have already found to be the Son), what daring is it in irreligion to say that "This comes from nothing," and that "It was not before generation," but was adventitious and can at some time cease to be again? Let a person only dwell upon this thought, and he will discern how the perfection and the plenitude of the Father's essence is impaired by this heresy.

However, he will see its unseemliness still more clearly, if he considers that the Son is the Image and Radiance of the Father, and Expression, and Truth. For if, when Light exists, there is with it its Image (viz. Radiance); and a Subsistence existing, there is of it the entire Expression; and a Father existing, there be His Truth (viz. the Son). Let them consider what depths of irreligion they fall into—those who make time the measure of the Image and Form of the Godhead. For if the Son was not before His generation, Truth was not always in God, which it is a sin to say. For since the Father was, there was ever in Him the Truth, which is the Son, who says, "I am the Truth" [John 14:6]. And the Subsistence existing, of course, there was without delay its Expression and Image. For God's Image is not delineated from without, but God Himself has begotten it in which seeing Himself, God has delight, as the Son Himself says, "I was His delight" [Prov. 8:30]. When then did the Father not see Himself in His own Image? Or when had He not delight that one should dare to say, "The Image is out of nothing," and "The Father had not delight before the Image was originated?" and how should the Maker and Creator see Himself in a created and originated essence? For such as is the Father, such must be the Image.

21. We proceed then to consider the attributes of the Father and we shall come to know whether this Image is really His. The Father is eternal,

immortal, powerful, light, King, Sovereign, God, Lord, Creator, and Maker. These attributes must be in the Image, to make it true that he "that hath seen" the Son "has seen the Father" [John 14:9]. If the Son be not all this but, as the Arians consider, originate and not eternal, this is not a true Image of the Father unless indeed they give up shame and go on to say that the title of Image given to the Son is not a token of a similar essence [*homoías ousías*] but His name only. But this, on the other hand, O you enemies of Christ, is not an Image, nor is it an Expression. For what is the likeness of what is out of nothing to Him who brought what was nothing into being? Or how can that which is not, be like Him that is, being short of Him in once not being and in its having its place among things originate?

However, such the Arians wishing Him to be devised for themselves arguments such as this—"If the Son is the Father's offspring and Image, and is like in all things to the Father, then it necessarily holds that as He is begotten, so He begets, and He too becomes father of a son. And again, he who is begotten from Him, begets in his turn, and so on without limit; for this is to make the Begotten like Him that begat Him."

Authors of blasphemy, verily, are these foes of God! Who, sooner than confess that the Son is the Father's Image, conceive material and earthly ideas concerning the Father Himself, ascribing to Him splitting and effluences and influences. If then God be as a human, let God become also a parent as a human, so that God's Son should be father of another, and so in succession one from another, until the series they imagine grows into a multitude of gods. But if God is not a human, as God is not, we must not impute to God the attributes of humans. For animals and humans, after a Creator has created them, are begotten by succession; and the son, having been begotten of a father who was a son, becomes accordingly in his turn a father to a son, in inheriting from his father that by which he himself has come to be. Hence in such instances there is not, properly speaking, either father or son, nor do the father and the son stay in their respective characters, for the son himself becomes a father, being son of his father, but father of his son.

But it is not so in the Godhead. For God is not like a human being. For the Father is not from a father; therefore He does not beget one who shall become a father. Nor is the Son from effluence of the Father, nor is He begotten from a father that was begotten; therefore neither is He begotten so as to beget. Thus it belongs to the Godhead alone that the Father is properly father, and the Son properly son, and in Them and Them only, does it hold that the Father is ever Father and the Son ever Son.

22. Therefore he who asks why the Son is not to beget a son, must inquire why the Father had not a father. But both suppositions are unseemly and full of impiety. For as the Father is ever Father and never could become Son, so the Son is ever Son and never could become Father. For in this rather is He shown to be the Father's Expression and Image, remaining

what He is and not changing, but thus receiving from the Father to be one and the same. If then the Father change, let the Image change; for so is the Image and Radiance in its relation towards the One who begat It. But if the Father is unalterable, and what He is that He continues, necessarily does the Image also continue what He is and will not alter. Now He is Son from the Father; therefore He will not become other than is proper to the Father's essence. Idly then have the foolish ones devised this objection also, wishing to separate the Image from the Father, that they might level the Son with things originated.

Letters to Serapion on the Holy Spirit, 1:24–25

From *Athanasius*, ed. Anatolios Khaled (London: Routledge, 2004), 223–25.

24. Moreover, all things are said to be participants of God through the Spirit. For it says, "Do you not know that you are the temple of God and that the Spirit of God dwells in you? If anyone destroys the temple of God, God will destroy that one. For the temple of God, which you are, is holy" (1 Cor. 3:16, 17). But if the Holy Spirit were a creature, there would not be for us any participation of God in the Spirit. Indeed, if we were merely united to a creature, we would still be foreigners to the divine nature, having no participation in it.[14] But now that we are called participants of Christ and participants of God, it is thereby shown that the unction and seal which is in us is not of a created nature but of the nature of the Son, who unites us to the Father through the Spirit that is in him. This is what John teaches, when he writes, as has been cited above, "This is how we know that we remain in God and he in us, in that he has given us his Spirit" (1 John 4:13). But if we become sharers in the divine nature through participation in the Spirit, one would have to be crazy to say that the Spirit is of a created nature and not of the nature of God, for that is how those in whom the Spirit is become divinized. But if the Spirit divinizes, it is not to be doubted that it is of the nature of God himself.[15]

And for a still clearer negation of this heresy, the psalmist sings in the one-hundred-and-third [*sic*] psalm, as we have previously quoted: "You will take away their spirit and they will perish and return to their dust. You will send forth your spirit and they will be created, and you will renew the face of the earth" (Ps. 104:29–30). And Paul writes to Titus: "Through the bath of regeneration and the renewal of the Holy Spirit, which he poured out richly upon us through Jesus Christ" (Titus 3:5–6). But if the Father

14. A creature cannot join other creatures to God and grant other creatures participation in divine life. This argument had been used by Athanasius in defense of the divinity of the Son; cf. for example, *Orations against the Arians* 2:41, 2:69, 2:70. This reasoning is taken up by Gregory of Nazianzus, *Oration* 31:4.

15. Cf. Basil, *On the Holy Spirit* 36.

creates and renews all things through the Son and in the Holy Spirit, what likeness or kinship can there be between creatures and the Creator? Or how can it at all be the case that the one in whom everything is created is a creature?

Such foul talk would consistently lead to blasphemy against the Son, so that those who say that the Spirit is a creature should say also that the Son, through whom all things were created, is a creature as well. For the Spirit is said to be and is the Image of the Son; for "those whom he foreknew he also predestined to be conformed to the Image of his Son" (Rom. 8:29). Therefore, if it is confessed even by them that the Son is not a creature, then neither could his Image be a creature. For as the Image is, so must be that of which it is an Image. Therefore, the Son is quite fittingly and properly confessed not to be a creature, since he is the Image (*eikon*) of the Father. Yet, the one who counts the Spirit among creatures will surely end up counting the Son also among creatures and uttering impropriety against the Father through this improper speech about his Image.

25. Thus, the Spirit is other than the creatures, and is shown rather to belong (*idion*) to the Son and to be not foreign to God. But then there is that foolish question they ask: "If the Spirit is from God, why is it not also called Son?" This question has already been shown to be rash and reckless in what we have said above, and we will equally show it to be so now. Even though it is not called "Son" in the Scriptures but "Spirit of God," nevertheless it is said to be in God himself and from God himself, as the apostle has written (cf. 1 Cor. 2:11–12). If the Son belongs (*idios*) to the being of the Father because he is from the Father, then necessarily the Spirit also, who is said to be from God, belongs (*idion*) to the being of the Son. Of course, the Lord is Son; but then the Spirit is called the Spirit of sonship (Rom. 8:15).[16] And, again, while the Son is Wisdom (1 Cor. 1:24) and Truth (cf. John 14:6), it is written that the Spirit is Spirit of Wisdom (cf. Isa. 11:2) and Truth (cf. John 14:17; 15:26). Yet again, while the Son is Power of God (1 Cor. 1:24) and Lord of glory (1 Cor. 2:8), the Spirit is said to be Spirit of Power and Spirit of glory. And that is how Scripture speaks of each of them, respectively. So Paul writes to the Corinthians: "If they had known, they would not have crucified the Lord of glory" (1 Cor. 2:8); and in another place, "For you did not receive a spirit of slavery to fall back into fear, but you received a spirit of sonship"[17] (Rom. 8:15), and furthermore, "God sent the Spirit of his Son into our hearts, crying 'Abba, Father'" (Gal. 4:6). Peter [589B] wrote: "If you are insulted for the name of Christ,

16. Having elaborated on the names and designations of the Spirit's work in the Scriptures, Athanasius now focuses on the scriptural patterns of correlating the Spirit and the Son.

17. In the Pauline text cited by Athanasius, the adoption granted by the Spirit is identified with "glorification," which is presumably what Athanasius had in mind when referring to this passage for evidence that the Spirit is "Spirit of glory." Cf. Rom. 8:16: "The Spirit itself bears witness with our spirit that we are children of God, and if children, then heirs, heirs of God and joint heirs with Christ, if only we suffer with him so that we may also be glorified with him."

blessed are you, for the Spirit of glory and of God rests upon you" (1 Pet. 4:14). As for the Lord, he said that the Spirit is Spirit of Truth and Comforter (John 14:16), which shows that the Trinity is complete in the Spirit. Therefore, it is in the Spirit that the Word glorifies creation and presents it to the Father by divinizing it and granting it adoption. But the one who binds creation to the Word could not be among the creatures and the one who bestows sonship upon creation could not be foreign to the Son. Otherwise, it would be necessary to look for another spirit to unite this one to the Word.[18] But that is senseless. Therefore, the Spirit is not among the things that have come into being but belongs (*idion*) to the divinity of the Father, and is the one in whom the Word divinizes the things that have come into being. But the one in whom creation is divinized cannot be extrinsic to the divinity of the Father.

SELECTION **6**

Gregory of Nazianzus

Orations 20, 23, and 25

One of the Cappadocian Fathers—along with the brothers Basil the Great and Gregory of Nyssa—Gregory of Nazianzus (ca. 329–90) is widely recognized as the chief architect of classical Trinitarian theology. His most well-known Trinitarian writings are his *Five Theological Orations* (Ors. 27–31), which counter objections from Eunomians (who denied the Son's consubstantiality with the Father) and Pneumatochians (who denied the deity of the Spirit). Although less well-known, the excerpts below present a succinct and more positive statement of his Trinitarian doctrine.

In Oration 20 (which deals with the responsibility of theologians and bishops), Gregory opposes Sabellians, who negate distinctions within the Trinity, and Arians, who negate the unity and equality of the three persons. Instead, he argues that we worship Father, Son, and Spirit "by distinguishing their individual characteristics while maintaining their divine unity." Nonetheless, because God and creatures are incomparable, he guards against "meaningless speculation" about the Son's generation and the Spirit's procession. Rather, we are to "be content with what abides within [us]": we can only know God by way of "purification" and "the illumination of the Holy Trinity."

In Oration 23 (which seeks to reconcile competing theological factions),

---

18. The same argument is used by Athanasius in reference to the Son's joining the world to the Father; cf. *Orations against the Arians* 2:26, *On the Council of Nicaea* 8.

Gregory describes the Trinity as a "monad" whose "superabundance" transcends a "dyad" or "synthesis of duality"—going beyond form and matter—thereby becoming a "triad" so that the Godhead might neither be "constricted" (and thus without generosity) nor "diffused" (and thus without order). Beyond the grasp of "our minds and our human condition," the true meaning of the Trinity lies in "our confession of faith" and "our rebirth, our Godhead, our deification, our hope"—and not in rhetorical controversies.

In Oration 25 (written in praise of Maximus, a Cynic convert to Christianity who later betrayed Gregory), Gregory describes the unique characteristics of Father, Son, and Holy Spirit and their interrelations as well as their equality and unity. Sharing the same uncreated divinity, the special characteristic of the Father is "his ingeneratedness"; of the Son, "his generation"; and the Spirit, "its procession." We cannot comprehend what takes place within the Godhead; nonetheless, "unity is worshiped in Trinity and Trinity in unity, both its union and its distinction miraculous."

From *The Fathers of the Church, St. Gregory of Nazianzus, Select Orations,* trans. Martha Vinson, Orations 20:5–12, 23:6–12, 25:15–19 (Washington, D.C.: Catholic University Press of America, 2003), 110–16, 135–40, 170–74.

Oration 20.5–12

5. Now that we have cleansed our theologian with our sermon,[19] come, let us talk a little about God too, drawing our inspiration from the Father himself and the Son and the Holy Spirit who form the topic of our sermon. I pray that I may be like Solomon and avoid eccentricity in what I think and say about God. For when he says, *For I am the most simple of all men, and there is not in me the wisdom of men* [Prov. 30:2 LXX], he presumably does not mean that he is guilty of a lack of discernment. How could he? Did he not, after all, ask God for this understanding above everything else [1 Kgs. 3:9–14] and obtain wisdom and insight and *largeness of mind* in richer and greater abundance than the grains of sand [1 Kgs. 4:29; LXX 2:35a and 5:9]? How does one so wise and blessed with such a gift call himself the most simple of all men? Clearly, because his understanding is not his own but the fullness of God's understanding working in him. This is also why, when Paul said, *it is no longer I who live, but Christ who lives in me* [Gal. 2:20], he of course was not speaking of himself as dead, but meant rather that he had attained a life beyond the ordinary by partaking of the true life, the one bounded by no death. Hence we worship the Father and the Son and the Holy Spirit, distinguishing their individual characteristics while maintaining their divine unity; and we neither confound the three into one, thus avoiding the plague of Sabellius, nor adopt the insanity of Arius and divide them into three entities that are unnaturally estranged from one another. Why must we violently swing in the opposite direction,

19. There is a play on words between theologian (*theológos*) and sermon (*logos*).

attempting to correct one distortion with another, much as one might try to straighten a plant that leans completely to one side, when we can, by moving directly to the center, stay within piety's pale?

6. Now when I speak of the center I am talking about truth, the only object worthy of our consideration as we reject both the evil of contraction and the greater absurdity of division. We ought not, on the assumption that Father, Son, and Holy Spirit are the same, adopt language that from a fear of polytheism contracts its reference to a single individually existing entity, keeping the names but stripping them of any distinction; we may just as well call all three one as say that each by definition is nothing, for they would hardly be what they are if they were interchangeable with one another. Nor, on the other hand, ought we divide them into three substances that are either foreign, dissimilar, and unrelated (which is to follow what is well called the insanity of Arius), or lack order and authority and are, so to speak, rival gods. In the first instance we are locked into the narrow position of the Jews, who restrict deity only to the ungenerated; in the second, we plunge into the equal but opposite evil of positing three individual sources and three gods, something even more absurd than the first case. We must neither be so partial to the Father that we actually strip him of his fatherhood, for whose father would he in fact be if his son were different in nature and estranged from him along with the rest of creation? Nor, by the same token, should we be so partial to Christ that we fail to preserve this very distinction, his Sonhood, for whose son would he in fact be if there were no causal relationship between his Father and himself? Nor again should we diminish the Father's status as source, proper to him as Father and generator, since he would be the source of small and worthless things were he not the cause of deity contemplated in Son and Spirit. It is our duty then both to maintain the oneness of God and to confess three individual entities, or Persons, each with his distinctive property.

7. The oneness of God would, in my view, be maintained if both Son and Spirit are causally related to him alone without being merged or fused into him and if they all share one and the same divine movement and purpose, if I may so phrase it, and are identical in essence. And the three individually existing entities will be maintained if we do not think of them as fusing or dissolving or mingling, lest those with an excessive devotion to unity end up destroying the whole. And the individual properties will be maintained if, in the case of the Father, we think and speak of him as being both source and without source (I use the term in the sense of causal agent, fount, and eternal light); and, in the case of the Son, we do not think of him as without source but the source of all things. But when I speak of "source," do not think of time or imagine something midway between Creator and created, or by a false interposition split the nature of beings that are coeternal and conjoined. For if time were older than the Son, it would clearly be the first product of the Father's causal activity, and how

can one who is in time be the creator of all time? And in what sense is he in fact the *Lord of all* [Rom. 10:12] if he is preceded by and subject to the lordship of time? The Father, then, is without source: his existence is derived neither from outside nor from within himself. In turn, the Son is not without source if you understand "Father" to mean causal agent, since the Father is the source of the Son as causal agent, but if you take source in the temporal sense, he too is without source because the Lord of all time does not owe his source to time.

8. If, however, you are going to claim that the Son is subject to time for the reason that bodies are too, you will in fact be attributing corporeality to the incorporeal, and if you insist that the Son too made the transition from nonexistence to existence on the grounds that whatever is generated in our world does not exist at one point but comes into being after a time, you are comparing the incomparable, God and man, corporeal and incorporeal; hence because our bodies both suffer and perish so will he too. Your claim, then, is that, because bodies are generated in this way, so too is God; while I say that because bodies are so generated, God is not. Things that have a different kind of existence also have a different mode of generation, unless he is a slave to material influences in all other respects too, as for example pain and suffering and hunger and thirst and all the other afflictions either corporeal or corporeal and incorporeal together. But these are the things your mind does not accept; we are in fact speaking about God. So stop supposing that his generation too is anything other than of a divine sort.

9. But, someone retorts, if he is generated, what form did this generation take? Answer me, unerring dialectician that you are. If he has been created, how has he been created? And go ahead and ask me this: how was he generated? Does generation involve passion? Then so does creation. Are not mental conception and thought and the analysis of a single idea into its discrete parts a kind of passion? Is there time involved in generation? The created world also exists in time. Does space apply to this world? It does in the other too. Can generation miscarry? So too can creation. These are the arguments I have heard you make: the hand often fails to execute what the mind calls up. But, you argue, he brought everything into existence by his word and will, for *he spoke, and they were made; he commanded, and they were created* [Ps. 148:5 LXX]. When you say that everything was created by God's word, you are not positing creation in human terms. None of us makes things happen by word. Nothing would be more sublime or effortless than ourselves if statement sufficed to bring about fact; hence, although God creates what he creates by word, his creation is not of human sort. Either show me a human being who also brings something about by word, or else admit that God does not create in a human way. All you need do is picture to yourself a city and lo! have it come into being; will yourself a son, and lo! have a boy appear; wish for anything

else that can possibly happen and have your will become accomplished fact. But as surely as none of these things comes to pass as a result of our willing it so, while with God the act of will and its fulfillment are identical, man creates in one way and God, the Creator of all, in another. So if God does not create like a human being, how does it follow that he must beget like one? Once upon a time you did not exist; then you did, and now you beget. Accordingly, you bring into existence someone who did not previously exist or, in a deeper sense, perhaps it is not you at all who are doing the bringing, since Levi also, Scripture says, *was still in the loins of his ancestor* [Heb. 7:10] before he was born. And let no one sneer at my words. I am not suggesting that the Son derives his being from the Father in that he first existed in the Father and later made his way into being, nor that he was first unformed and was then formed, as is the case with human generation.

10. These are the views of malcontents, the views of those who are quick to jump on every word. They are not our thoughts or beliefs. We think that the ungenerated existence of the Father—he has always existed, for the mind's reach does not extend to a time when he did not—is coextensive with the generated existence of the Son. Hence the existence of the Father is concurrent with the generation of his only-begotten Son, who takes his being both from the Father and not after him, except in the sense that the Father is the source, that is, causal agent. I am repeating myself because your crassly materialistic cast of mind frightens me. And if you are going to refrain from inquiring impertinently into the Son's—what should I call it? generation? person? or anything better one can think of (the notion and its expression confound my powers of speech)—do not be too inquisitive about the procession of the Spirit, either. I am satisfied with the declaration that he is Son and that he is from the Father, and that the one is Father and the other Son; and I refuse to engage in meaningless speculation beyond this point. I have no wish to be like the man who loses his voice from overuse or his eyesight from staring directly into the sun: the more fully and sharply one wants to see, the more he damages his eyes and is blinded altogether, for his vision is overwhelmed by the magnitude of the sight if he insists on taking in the whole instead of only that portion that is without risk . . . .

12. So if you have been listening to me at all, wary theologian that I am, you have understood something; now ask to understand what remains. Be content with what abides within you; let the rest abide in the treasuries of heaven. Ascend by an upright life; through purification obtain the pure. Do you wish to be a theologian one day, worthy of divinity? Seek to keep the commandments; walk in his statutes [cf. 1 Kgs. 6:12]. Conduct is the stepping-stone to contemplation. Devote your body to the service of your soul. Is there any man who can equal Paul's lofty status? Yet, for all that, he says that he sees *in a mirror dimly*, but that there is a time when he will see

face to face. Are you better at discourse than another? You are most assuredly inferior to God. More sagacious perhaps than another? Your grasp of the truth is as deficient as your existence in comparison to God's. We have the promise that one day we shall know to the degree that we are known [1 Cor. 13:12]. If while on this earth I may not possess to perfection knowledge of all that exists, what remains to me? What may I hope for? The kingdom of heaven, you will surely say. And I believe this to be nothing other than the attainment of that which is most pure and perfect; and the most perfect of the things that are is the knowledge of God. So one part let us secure and let us reach another while we are on the face of the earth; and the remainder let us reserve for the other life that we may receive, as the fruit of our labor, this, the illumination of the Holy Trinity in the fullness of its being and character and magnitude (if to speak so violates no law of God), in Christ himself, our Lord, to whom be the power and the glory forever and ever. Amen.

Oration 23.6–12

6. What, then, is your wish? Are you convinced? There is no need for any further effort on my part? You do not require a second discourse on the Deity and so spare my infirmity, thanks to which I can hardly address you even now? Or should the same message reverberate over and over again, as for the hard of hearing, so that the constant din may penetrate your ears and we be heard? Your silence seems to be an invitation to speak. As the saying goes, Silence is assent. So listen to us both: we speak with one heart and one mouth. I am sorry that I cannot climb a high mountain, find a voice equal to the strength of my feeling and declaim before the world and all the wrongheaded people in it as though before a grand theater: *O ye sons of men, how long will ye be slow of heart? Wherefore do ye love vanity, and seek falsehood* [Ps. 4:2 LXX]? You posit not a single nor an uncompounded nature of divinity but either three that are alienated and disjoined from one another and, not surprisingly, in conflict by virtue of their being proportionately superior or inferior; or you posit a single nature, but one that is constricted and mean, and which is not in a position to be the source of anything significant precisely because it cannot or will not, and this for two reasons, either envy or fear: envy, because it wishes to avoid the introduction of something that is of equal importance; fear, lest it take on a hostile and belligerent element. In fact, God is the object of proportionately more honor than his creatures are to the degree that it is more in keeping with the greater majesty of the first cause to be the source of divinity rather than of creatures and to reach the creatures through the medium of divinity rather than the reverse, that is, for divinity to acquire substantive existence for their sakes, as our very subtle and high-flown thinkers imagine.

7. For if, while admitting the dignity of the Son and the Holy Spirit, we

implied that they are either without source or from a different source, we should in fact face the terrible risk of dishonoring God or of setting up a rival deity. But if, no matter how highly you exalt the Son or the Spirit, you do not proceed to place them above the Father, or alienate them from him as their cause, but attribute their noble generation and marvelous procession to him, I shall simply ask you, my friend, you who are so fond of the expressions "unbegotten" and "without source," who dishonors God more, the one who regards him as the source of the kinds of beings you yourself introduce, or the one who regards him as the source not of such, but of those which are like him in nature and equal to him in honor, the kind that our doctrine professes? Your own son is to you a great, indeed, a very great, cause for honor, and all the more so if he takes after his father in all respects, and bears the true stamp of his sire, and you would prefer to be the parent of a single child rather than the master of countless slaves. Similarly, is there any greater cause for honor in God's case than being the Father of his Son? This adds to his glory, not detracts from it, as does the fact that the Holy Spirit also proceeds from him. Or are you unaware that in regarding God as the source of "creatures," by which I mean the Son and the Holy Spirit, you not only fail to honor the source but you also dishonor whatever issues from it? You dishonor the source by referring it to beings that are inconsequential and unworthy of divinity; you dishonor the issue, by making them inconsequential, and not merely creatures, but of all creatures the least honored. If in fact it was for the sake of these creatures that the Son and the Spirit came into existence at some point in time, like a craftsman's tools that do not exist before the craftsman has made them, their only reason for being would be that God chose to use them to create something, on the grounds that his will was not enough; for everything that exists for the sake of something else is held in less esteem than the thing for which it was produced.

8. I, on the other hand, by positing a source of divinity that is independent of time, inseparable, and infinite, honor both the source as well as its issue: the source, because of the nature of the things of which it is the source; the issue, because of their own nature as well as of the nature of the source from which they are derived, because they are disparate neither in time, nor in nature, nor in holiness. They are one in their separation and separate in their conjunction, even if this is a paradoxical statement; revered no less for their mutual relationship than when they are thought of and taken individually; a perfect Trinity of three perfect entities; a monad taking its impetus from its superabundance, a dyad transcended (that is, it goes beyond the form and matter of which bodies consist), a triad defined by its perfection since it is the first to transcend the synthesis of duality in order that the Godhead might not be constricted or diffused without limit, for constriction bespeaks an absence of generosity; diffusion, an absence of order. The one is thoroughly Judaic; the other, Greek and polytheistic.

9. I also take into consideration the possibility, one that perhaps does not reflect ignorance and naivete on my part so much as careful thought, that you do not assume any risk at all when you posit the Son as begotten. For, you may be sure, the ingenerate does not experience generation in the way that bodies and material substances do since he is not a body. This even the popular conceptions about God concede. So why do we feel fear *where there is no fear* [Ps. 13:5; 14:5 LXX] and why do we engage in vain impiety, as Scripture says? I, on the other hand, believe I do run the risk of compromising the Deity if I admit the creature, for what is created is not God, and what shares the yoke of servitude cannot be defined as master, even if it represents the very best that the world of servitude and creation has to offer and is the only thing in this vile station to display the quality of loving-kindness.[20] For whoever withholds the honor due bestows not honor through what he gives but rather dishonor through what he takes away, even though his act gives the semblance of honor.

10. And if you start to speculate on passions in connection with generation, I too shall do so in the matter of creation; I am, of course, aware that no created thing is created without passion. But if he was not begotten and if you were not created, admit the rest of your argument since your use of the term "creature" presumes the like for all practical purposes. There is nothing that you hesitate to venture or attempt, perverse judge and critic of the Deity that you are. The only way that you could gain any credibility at all is by relegating God to a position far removed from any real power, just as on earth those of a tyrannical or avaricious bent do to those weaker than they. As for myself, I shall say only one thing, succinctly and in a few words. The Trinity, my brothers, is truly a trinity. Trinity does not mean an itemized collection of disparate elements; if it did, what would prevent us from calling it a decad, or a centad,[21] or a myriad, if the number of components so justified? The arithmetical possibilities are many; indeed, more than these examples. Rather, Trinity is a comprehensive relationship between equals who are held in equal honor; the term unites in one word members that are one by nature and does not allow things that are indivisible to suffer fragmentation when their number is divided.

11. Our minds and our human condition are such that a knowledge of the relationship and disposition of these members with regard to one another is reserved for the Holy Trinity itself alone and those purified souls to whom the Trinity may make revelation either now or in the future. We, on the other hand, may know that the nature of divinity is one and the same, characterized by lack of source, generation, and procession (these

---

20. The divinity of Christ was compromised by the Arian view that he was a created being, albeit the first of creatures. The reference to Christ's mercy despite his sufferings on earth is a patristic commonplace.

21. Gregory's term, *centad*, that is, a hundred, has been retained for the sake of euphony.

correspond to mind, word, and spirit in humans, at least insofar as one can compare things spiritual with things perceptible and things that are very great with those that are small, for no comparison ever represents the true picture exactly); a nature that is in internal agreement with itself, is ever the same, ever perfect, without quality or quantity, independent of time, uncreated, incomprehensible, never self-deficient, nor ever so to be, lives and life, lights and light, goods and good, glories and glory, true and the truth, and *Spirit of truth* [John 16:13], holies and holiness itself; each one God, if contemplated separately, because the mind can divide the indivisible; the three God, if contemplated collectively, because their activity and nature are the same; which neither rejected anything in the past as superfluous to itself nor asserted superiority over any other thing for there has been none; nor shall leave anything to survive it or will assert superiority over anything in the future, for there will be none such; nor admits to its presence anything of equal honor since no created or servile thing, nothing which participates or is circumscribed can attain to its nature, which is both uncreated and sovereign, participated in and infinite. For some things are remote from it in every respect; others come close to it with varying success and will continue to do so, and this not by nature, but as a result of participation, and precisely when, by serving the Trinity properly, they rise above servitude, unless in fact freedom and dominion consist of this very thing, attaining a proper knowledge of sovereignty and refusing to confound things that are distinct because of a poverty of intellect. If to serve is so great an office, how great must be the sovereignty of those whom one serves? And if knowledge is blessedness, how great must be that which is known?

12. This is the meaning of our great mystery, this, our faith and rebirth in the Father, Son, and Holy Spirit, and in our common name, our rejection of godlessness and our confession of the Godhead. This is the meaning of our common name. And so, to dishonor or separate any one of the three is to dishonor our confession of faith, that is, our rebirth, our Godhead, our deification, our hope. You see how gracious the Holy Spirit is to us when we confess him as God and how he punishes us when we deny him. I will not speak of the fear and the wrath that threatens, not those who do him honor, but those who dishonor him. This brief discussion has been offered in the interests of doctrine, not of controversy; as a fisherman would, not some precious Aristotelian; with spiritual, not mischievous intent; in a manner suited to the Church, not the market place; as a benefit to others, not as a rhetorical show. Our object is to inform those of you who agree only on the desirability of making pompous and defamatory speeches against us that we are united in our views and are of one inspiration and breathe one spirit; and to keep you from pecking like starvelings at our tiny scraps, call them faults or follies, and broadcasting

them indiscriminately. It is the nadir of depravity to base one's security not on one's own sources of strength but on the weaknesses of others.

Oration 25.15–19

15. Define too for us our orthodox faith by teaching us to recognize one God, unbegotten, the Father, and one begotten Lord, his Son, referred to as God when he is mentioned separately, but Lord when he is named in conjunction with the Father, the one term on account of his nature, the other on account of his monarchy; and one Holy Spirit proceeding, or, if you will, going forth from the Father, God to those with the capacity to apprehend things that are interrelated, but in fact resisted by the impious though so recognized by their betters and actually so predicated by the more spiritual. Neither should we place the Father beneath first principle, so as to avoid positing a first of the first, thus necessarily destroying primary existence; nor say that the Son or the Holy Spirit is without beginning. Thus we shall avoid depriving the Father of his special characteristic. Paradoxically, they are not without beginning, and, in a sense, they are: they are not in terms of causation, since they are indeed from God although they are not subsequent to him, just as light is not subsequent to the sun, but they are without beginning in terms of time since they are not subject to it. Otherwise, that which is transitory would be antecedent to things that abide, and that which has no independent existence to things that do.

16. Neither should we posit three first principles if we want to avoid the polytheism of the Greeks, nor a single one, Judaic in its narrowness as well as grudging and ineffectual, whether by positing a self-absorbing deity (the preferred view of those who have the Son issue from the Father only to be absorbed into him again) or by disallowing their natures and stripping them of Godhead, as our current experts like to do, as though the Godhead feared some rival opposition from them or could produce nothing higher than creatures. Likewise, we should not claim that the Son is unbegotten, for the Father is one; nor the Holy Spirit is Son, for the Only-Begotten Son is one. In this way, the divinity of each will be defined in terms of the property that is unique to each, in the case of the Son, his Sonship, in the case of the Holy Spirit, its procession and not sonship. We should believe that the Father is truly a father, far more truly father, in fact, than we humans are, in that he is uniquely, that is, distinctively so, unlike corporal beings; and that he is one alone, that is, without mate, and Father of one alone, his Only-Begotten; and that he is a Father only, not formerly a son; and that he is wholly Father, and father of one wholly his son, as cannot be affirmed of human beings; and that he has been Father from the beginning and did not become Father in the course of things. We should believe that the Son is truly a Son in that he is the only Son of one only Father and only in one way and only a Son. He is not also Father

but is wholly Son, and Son of one who is wholly Father, and has been Son from the beginning, since there was never a time when he began to be a Son, for his divinity is not due to a change of purpose nor his deification to progress in time; otherwise, there would be a time when the one was not a Father and the other not a Son. We should also believe that the Holy Spirit is truly holy in that there is no other like it in quality or manner and in that its holiness is not conferred but is holiness in the absolute, and in that it is not more or less nor did it begin or will it end in time. For what the Father and Son and Holy Spirit have in common is their divinity and the fact that they were not created, while for the Son and the Holy Spirit it is the fact that they are from the Father. In turn, the special characteristic of the Father is his ingeneratedness, of the Son his generation, and of the Holy Spirit its procession. But if you seek after the means, what will you leave to them—in the words of Scripture, they alone know and are known by one another [Matt. 11:27]—or also for those of us who will one day receive illumination from on high?

17. First get to be one of the things that we have talked about, or someone of like sort, and then you will come to know in the same measure as they are known by one another [1 Cor. 13:12]. But for now, we ask you to teach us to see just this much, that unity is worshipped in Trinity and Trinity in unity, both its union and its distinction miraculous. Do not worry about the passions when you confess generation: the divine is impassible even if it has generated. This I can assure you: its generation takes place in a divine, not a human, fashion since its existence is not human either. Do worry about time and creation: He is not God if he was created; otherwise, you mount a useless defense of God and do away with him altogether by making what belongs to the same Godhead—and in fact frees you from servitude if you sincerely profess his lordship—a servant like yourself. Do not worry about the procession: the all-abounding Deity is under no compulsion either to bring forth, or not to bring forth, in a similar way. Do worry about estrangement and the ominous fate that lies in store not for those who acknowledge the divinity of the Spirit, but for those who impiously discount it.

18. Neither show a perverse reverence for divine monarchy by contracting or truncating deity, nor feel embarrassed when you are accused of worshipping three gods. Someone else is equally liable to a charge of worshipping two. For you will either manage to rebut the charge in common with him or you will be in common difficulty; or else his deity will founder along with his arguments while yours will remain intact. Even if your powers of reasoning are not up to the task, it is still better to falter with rational arguments directed by the Spirit than to adopt easy but impious solutions out of indolence. Be contemptuous of objections and counter-arguments, and the newfangled piety and piddling wisdom; more contemptuous than of spiders' webs, which can snare a fly but are easily

snagged by a wasp, not to mention a finger or anything with some mass behind it. Be our instructor in our learning to fear one thing alone: seeing our faith dissolve in sophistics. It is not terrible to be bested in argument, since skillful argumentation is not a universal attainment. What is terrible is experiencing the loss of one's God, because hope is universal to all. These matters you will, of course, pursue on your own more intently as well as more thoroughly. Your wounds are my assurance, and your body, which has labored in the defense of piety. And we shall join you ourselves to the extent of our ability.

19. And when you embark on your noble journey, remember, if you will, the Trinity that dwells in tents—if God can at all be said to dwell in things made by human hands—and this small harvest, one not from seeds of piety that are small, to be sure, but one still thin and immature and being gathered a little at a time. For we are become *as* those gathering *straw in harvest* (if the prophet's words are here apropos) and *grape gleanings in the vintage, when there is no cluster* [Mic. 7:1 LXX]. Do you see how small our gathering is? For this very reason help make our threshing floor richer and our wine-vat more full [Joel 2:24]. Speak of our calling as well as of our remarkable visit here, undertaken not for common enjoyment but as a way of participating in suffering, so that by sharing affliction we may also share the glory. You have in this people a prayerful ally and comrade in your travels, the flock that is small in number but not in piety, whose smallness I respect more than others' size. These are the words of the Holy Spirit; with it you will go through fire (Ps. 65:12; 66:12 LXX) and lull to sleep the wild beasts and turn princes to moderation. With this intent set out; with this intent be on your way and come back to us again, richly enriched, laureate a second time, to sing with us the hymn of victory now and in the future in Christ Jesus our Lord, to whom be the glory forever. Amen.

SELECTION **7**

Gregory of Nyssa

Refutation of Eunomius' Confession, The Great Catechism, and The Life of Moses

Along with his older brother, Basil of Caesarea, and his friend, Gregory of Nazianzus, Gregory of Nyssa (ca. 331–395) played a significant role in the events leading to the Council of Constantinople in 381. The excerpts below exemplify some of his contributions to Trinitarian doctrine and mystical theology.

In his *Refutation of Eunomius' Confession*, Gregory argues against the Eunomian assertion that God's essence is defined by being "Father," ungenerated (*agennēssia*). Instead, Gregory maintains that God's uncreated essence is incomprehensible and ineffable. Nonetheless, we have been baptized into the "unnameable name" of "Father, Son, and Spirit" (Matt. 28:19), and this name tells us that by becoming incarnate in Jesus Christ, God has given us what we need to receive new birth and be transformed into the image of the Son. In this name, "Father" refers not to God's "essence" (*ousia*) but to his "relation" (*skesis*) to the Son. If the Father exists in eternity as Father—and if the name Father implies the Son—then the Son also exists in eternity. Thus, all that we attribute to God as Father belongs to the Son and by implication to the Spirit as well. Relations among the three divine "persons" (*prosopon*) define their distinct "subsistences" (*hypostases*); they are unified by sharing in the same uncreated nature. In this way, God is "divided without separation and united without confusion."

In the *Great Catechism* used in baptismal instruction, Gregory presents a range of arguments for Christian belief in God. To atheists, he appeals to the order of the universe. To polytheists, he argues that the very idea of God requires the unity of God and not a plurality of gods. To Jews (who deny the Logos), he uses the analogy of the way words express yet are different from ideas in our minds to describe how the Logos of God is the living Word of God who, as life-creating power, is distinct from and yet of the same divine nature as the Father. Likewise, he uses an analogy from human breathing to depict the Holy Spirit as the divine energy that is distinct yet inseparable from God in whom it exists and the Word of God it accompanies.

The *Life of Moses* uses Moses' journey to Mount Sinai as a paradigm for the Christian's journey through temptations to an endless growth (*epektasis*) into God's infinite goodness. In contrast to Origen (who had argued that God is limited, since to be limited is to be clearly defined and knowable), Gregory argues that God is infinite, without boundaries or limits. Incomprehensible, the infinite God is encountered only in a "luminous darkness," beyond all sense knowledge and intellectual concepts. Such encounter is possible because of the incarnation, which enables us to be transformed into the likeness of God in an endless growth in moral perfection by an ever-greater participation in God's goodness.

Refutation of Eunomius' Confession, Book 2.1–3

From *Gregory of Nyssa: Dogmatic Treatises, Etc., NPNF* 2.5.101–5.[22]

Book 2

1. The Incarnation of God the Word and the Faith Delivered by the Lord to His Disciples

The Christian Faith, which in accordance with the command of our Lord has been preached to all nations by his disciples, is neither of human beings nor by human beings, but by our Lord Jesus Christ himself, Who is the Word, the Life, the Light, the Truth, and God, and Wisdom, and all else that He is by nature. For this cause above all was made in the likeness of human beings and shared our nature, becoming like us in all things yet without sin. He was like us in all things in that He took upon Himself humanity in its entirety, with soul and body, so that our salvation was accomplished by means of both. He, I say, appeared on earth and "conversed with humans" [Bar. 3:37]: that humans might no longer have opinions according to their own notions about the Self-existent, formulating into a doctrine the hints that come to them from vague conjectures, but that we might be convinced that God has truly been manifested in the flesh, and believe that to be the only true "mystery of godliness" [1 Tim. 3:16], which was delivered to us by the very Word and God who by himself spoke to his apostles, and that we might receive the teaching concerning the transcendent nature of the Deity that is given to us, as it were, "through a glass darkly" [1 Cor. 13:12] from the older Scriptures—from the Law, and the Prophets, and the Sapiential Books—as an evidence of the truth fully revealed to us, reverently accepting the meaning of the things which have been spoken, so as to accord in the Faith set forth by the Lord of the whole Scriptures. This Faith we guard as we received it: word for word, in purity, without falsification, judging even a slight divergence from the words delivered to us an extreme blasphemy and impiety. We believe, then, even as the Lord set forth the Faith to his disciples, when he said, "Go, teach all nations, baptizing them in the name of the Father, and of the Son, and of the Holy Spirit" [Matt. 28:19]. This is the word of the mystery whereby through new birth from above our nature is transformed from the corruptible to the incorruptible, being renewed from "the old self," "according to the image of its Creator" [cf. Col. 3:9, 10], at the beginning the likeness to the Godhead.

In the Faith then that was delivered by God to the Apostles we admit neither subtraction, nor alteration, nor addition, knowing assuredly that he who presumes to pervert the Divine utterance by dishonest quibbling, the same "is of his father the devil," who leaves the words of truth and

---

22. Note that *Against Eunomius* 2 in *NPNF* 5:191ff. is actually *Refutation of Eunomius' Confession*; the true *Against Eunomius* 2 is found in *NPNF* 5:250ff.

"speaks of his own," becoming the father of a lie [cf. John 8:44]. For whatsoever is said otherwise than in exact accord with the truth is assuredly false and not true.

2. The Eternal Father, the Son, and the Holy Spirit

Since then this doctrine is put forth by the Truth itself, it follows that anything that the inventors of pestilent heresies devise besides to subvert this Divine utterance—as, for example, calling the Father "Maker" and "Creator" of the Son instead of "Father"; and the Son a "result," a "creature," a "product," instead of "Son"; and the Holy Spirit the "creature of a creature" and the "product of a product," instead of his proper title the "Spirit"; and whatever those who fight against God are pleased to say of him. All such fancies we term a denial and violation of the Godhead revealed to us in this doctrine. For once for all we have learned from the Lord, through whom comes the transformation of our nature from mortality to immortality, from him, I say, we have learned to what we ought to look with the eyes of our understanding—that is, the Father, the Son, and the Holy Spirit. We say that it is a terrible and soul-destroying thing to misinterpret these Divine utterances and to devise in their stead assertions to subvert them—assertions pretending to correct God the Word, who appointed that we should maintain these statements as part of our faith. For each of these titles understood in its natural sense becomes for Christians a rule of truth and a law of piety. For while there are many other names by which Deity is indicated in the Historical Books, in the Prophets and in the Law, our Master Christ passes by all these and commits to us these titles as better able to bring us to the faith about the Self-Existent, declaring that it suffices us to cling to the title, "Father, Son, and Holy Spirit," in order to attain to the apprehension of him who is absolutely Existent, who is one and yet not one. In regard to essence God is one, thus the Lord ordained that we should look to one Name. But in regard to the attributes indicative of the Persons, our belief in God is distinguished into belief in the Father, the Son, and the Holy Spirit. God is divided without separation, and united without confusion.

For when we hear the title "Father" we apprehend the meaning to be this: that the name is not understood with reference to itself alone, but also by its special signification indicates the relation to the Son. For the term "Father" would have no meaning apart by itself, if "Son" were not connoted by the utterance of the word "Father." When, then, we learnt the name "Father" we were taught at the same time, by the selfsame title, faith also in the Son. Now since Deity by its very nature is permanently and immutably the same in all that pertains to its essence, nor did it at any time fail to be anything that it now is, nor will it at any future time be anything that it now is not, and since he who is the very Father was named Father by the

Word, and since in the Father the Son is implied—since these things are so, we of necessity believe that he who admits no change or alteration in his nature was always entirely what he is now, or, if there is anything which he was not, *that* he assuredly is not now. Since then he is named Father by the very Word, he assuredly always was Father, and is and will be even as he was. For surely it is not lawful in speaking of the Divine and unimpaired Essence to deny that what is excellent always belonged to it. For if he was not always what he now is, he certainly changed either from the better to the worse or from the worse to the better, and of these assertions the impiety is equal either way, whichever statement is made concerning the Divine nature. But in fact the Deity is incapable of change and alteration. So, then, everything that is excellent and good is always contemplated in the fountain of excellency. But "the Only-begotten God, Who is in the bosom of the Father" [John 1:18] is excellent, and beyond all excellency—mark you, He says, "Who *is* in the bosom of the Father," not "Who came to be" there.

Well then, it has been demonstrated by these proofs that the Son is from all eternity to be contemplated in the Father, in whom he is, being Life and Light and Truth, and every noble name and conception—to say that the Father ever existed by himself apart from these attributes is a piece of the utmost impiety and infatuation. For if the Son, as the Scripture says, is the Power of God, and Wisdom, and Truth, and Light, and Sanctification, and Peace, and Life, and the like, then before the Son existed, according to the view of the heretics, these things also had no existence at all. And if these things had no existence they must certainly conceive the bosom of the Father to have been devoid of such excellences.

To the end, then, that the Father might not be conceived as destitute of the excellences that are his own, and that the doctrine might not run wild into this extravagance, the right faith concerning the Son is necessarily included in our Lord's utterance with the contemplation of the eternity of the Father. And for this reason he passes over all those names which are employed to indicate the surpassing excellence of the Divine nature, and delivers to us as part of our profession of faith the title of "Father" as better suited to indicate the truth, being a title which, as has been said, by its relative sense connotes with itself the Son, while the Son, who is in the Father, always is what he essentially is, as has been said already, because the Deity by its very nature does not admit of augmentation. For it does not perceive any other good outside of itself, by participation in which it could acquire any accession, but is always immutable, neither casting away what it has, nor acquiring what it has not: for none of its properties are such as to be cast away.

And if there is anything whatsoever blessed, unsullied, true and good, associated with him and in him, we see of necessity that the good and Holy Spirit must belong to him, not by way of accretion. That Spirit is indisputably a princely Spirit, a quickening Spirit, the controlling and sanctifying force of all creation, the Spirit that "works all in all" as he wills [cf. 1 Cor. 8:6]. Thus we conceive no gap between the anointed Christ and his anointing, between the King and his sovereignty, between Wisdom and the Spirit of Wisdom, between Truth and the Spirit of Truth, between Power and the Spirit of Power, but as there is contemplated from all eternity in the Father the Son, who is Wisdom and Truth, and Counsel, and Might, and Knowledge, and Understanding, so there is also contemplated in him the Holy Spirit, who is the Spirit of Wisdom, and of Truth, and of Counsel, and of Understanding, and all else that the Son is and is called.

For this reason we say that to the holy disciples the mystery of godliness was committed in a form expressing at once union and distinction—that we should believe on the Name of the Father, and of the Son, and of the Holy Spirit. For the differentiation of the subsistences [*hupostaséōn*] makes the distinction of Persons [*prosōpōn*] clear and free from confusion, while the one Name standing in the forefront of the declaration of the Faith clearly expounds to us the unity of essence of the Persons [*prosōpōn*] whom the Faith declares—I mean, of the Father, and of the Son, and of the Holy Spirit. For by these appellations we are taught not a difference of nature, but only the special attributes that mark the subsistences [*hupostaséōn*], so that we know that neither is the Father the Son, nor the Son the Father, nor the Holy Spirit either the Father or the Son, and recognize each by the distinctive mark of his Personal Subsistence [*hupostaséōn*], in illimitable perfection, at once contemplated by himself and not divided from that with which he is connected.

3. The Unnameable Name of the Holy Trinity and the Mutual Relation of the Persons, and the Unknowable Character of the Divine Essence

What then does that unnameable name mean concerning which the Lord said, "Baptizing them into the name," and did not add the actual significant term which "the name" indicates? We have concerning it this notion: that all things that exist in the creation are defined by means of their several names. Thus whenever a person speaks of "heaven" he directs the notion of the hearer to the created object indicated by this name, and whenever one mentions "human being" or some animal, at once by the mention of the name impresses upon the hearer the form of the creature, and in the same way all other things, by means of the names imposed upon them, are depicted in the heart of him who by hearing receives the appellation imposed upon the thing.

The uncreated Nature alone, which we acknowledge in the Father, and in the Son, and in the Holy Spirit, surpasses all significance of names. For this cause the Word, when He spoke of "the name" in delivering the Faith, did not add what it is—for how could a name be found for that which is above every name?—but gave authority that whatever name our intelligence by pious effort be enabled to discover to indicate the transcendent Nature, that name should be applied alike to Father, Son, and Holy Spirit, whether it be "the Good" or "the Incorruptible," whatever name each may think proper to be used to indicate the undefiled Nature of Godhead.

And by this deliverance the Word seems to me to lay down for us this law—that we are to be persuaded that the Divine Essence is ineffable and incomprehensible: for it is plain that the title of Father does not present to us the Essence, but only indicates the relation to the Son. It follows, then, that if it were possible for human nature to be taught the essence of God, the one "who will have all people to be saved and to come to the knowledge of the truth" [1 Tim. 2:4] would not have suppressed the knowledge upon this matter. But as it is, by saying nothing concerning the Divine Essence, he showed that the knowledge thereof is beyond our power, while when we have learnt that of which we are capable, we stand in no need of the knowledge beyond our capacity, as we have in the profession of faith in the doctrine delivered to us what suffices for our salvation. For to learn that he is the absolutely existent, together with whom by the relative force of the term there is also declared the majesty of the Son, is the fullest teaching of godliness—the Son, as has been said, implying in close union with Himself the Spirit of Life and Truth, inasmuch as he is himself Life and Truth.

These distinctions being thus established, while we anathematize all heretical fancies in the sphere of divine doctrines, we believe, even as we were taught by the voice of the Lord, in the Name of the Father and of the Son and of the Holy Spirit, acknowledging together with this faith also the dispensation that has been set on foot on behalf of human beings by the Lord of the creation. For he "being in the form of God thought it not robbery to be equal with God, but made himself of no reputation, and took upon him the form of a servant" [Phil. 2:6], and being incarnate in the Holy Virgin redeemed us from death "in which we were held," "sold under sin" [cf. Rom. 7:7 and 14] giving as the ransom for the deliverance of our souls his precious blood which he poured out by his Cross, and having through himself made clear for us the path of the resurrection from the dead, shall come in his own time in the glory of the Father to judge every soul in righteousness, when "all that are in the graves shall hear His voice, and shall come forth, they that have done good unto the resurrection of life, and they that have done evil unto the resurrection of damnation [John 5:28–29]." But that the pernicious heresy that is now being sown broadcast by Eunomius may not, by falling upon the mind of some of the simpler sort and being left without investigation, do harm to guileless faith, we are constrained to set forth the profession which they circulate and to strive to expose the mischief of their teaching.

The Great Catechism, Prologue, Chapters 1–3

From *Gregory of Nyssa: Dogmatic Treatises, Etc., NPNF* 2:5:131–137.

Prologue

The presiding ministers of the "mystery of godliness" [1 Tim. 3:16] have need of a system in their instructions, in order that the Church may be replenished by the addition of those who were being saved [Acts 2:47] through the teaching of the word of Faith brought home to the hearing of unbelievers. Not that the same method of instruction will be suitable in the case of all who approach the word. The catechism must be adapted to the diversities of their religious worship—with an eye, indeed, to the one aim and end of the system, but not using the same method of preparation in each individual case. The Judaizer has been preoccupied with one set of notions, one conversant with Hellenism, with others; while the Eunomian, and the Manichean, with the followers of Marcion, Valentinus, and Basilides, and the rest on the list of those who have wandered into heresy, each of them being prepossessed with their peculiar notions, require a special controversy with their several opinions.

The method of recovery must be adapted to the form of the disease. You will not by the same means cure the polytheism of the Greek, and the unbelief of the Jew as to the Only-begotten God. Nor as regards those who have wandered into heresy will you, by the same arguments in each case, upset their misleading romances as to the tenets of the Faith. No one could set Sabellius right by the same instruction as would benefit the Eunomian. The controversy with the Manichean is profitless against the Jew. It is necessary, therefore, as I have said, to regard the opinions that the persons have taken up and to frame your argument in accordance with the error into which each has fallen, by advancing in each discussion certain principles and reasonable propositions, that thus, through what is agreed upon on both sides, the truth may conclusively be brought to light.

When, then, a discussion is held with one of those who favor Greek ideas, it would be well to make the ascertaining of this the commencement of the reasoning, i.e. whether he presupposes the existence of a God, or concurs with the atheistic view. Should he say there is no God, then, from the consideration of the skillful and wise economy of the universe he will be brought to acknowledge that there is a certain overmastering power manifested through these channels.

If, on the other hand, he should have no doubt as to the existence of Deity, but should be inclined to entertain the presumption of a plurality of Gods, then we will adopt against him some such train of reasoning as this: "Does he think Deity is perfect or defective?" and if, as is likely, he bears testimony to the perfection in the Divine nature, then we will demand of him to grant a perfection throughout in everything that is observable in that divinity, in order that Deity may not be regarded as a mixture of opposites, defect and perfection. But whether as respects power, or the conception of goodness, or wisdom and imperishability and eternal existence, or any other notion besides suitable to the nature of Deity, that is found to lie close to the subject of our contemplation, in all he will agree that perfection is the idea to be entertained of the Divine nature, as being a just inference from these premises.

If this, then, be granted us, it would not be difficult to bring round these scattered notions of a plurality of Gods to the acknowledgment of a unity of Deity. For if he admits that perfection is in every respect to be ascribed to the subject before us, though there is a plurality of these perfect things which are marked with the same character, he must be required by a logical necessity, either to point out the particularity in each of these things which present no distinctive variation, but are found always with the same marks, or, if (he cannot do that, and) the mind can grasp nothing in them in the way of particular, to give up the idea of any distinction. For if neither as regards "more and less" a person can detect a difference (in as much as the idea of perfection does not admit of it), nor as regards "worse" and "better" (for he cannot entertain a notion of Deity at all where the term "worse" is not got rid of), nor as regards "ancient" and "modern" (for what exists not for ever is foreign to the notion of Deity), but on the contrary the idea of Godhead is one and the same, no peculiarity being on any ground of reason to be discovered in any one point, it is an absolute necessity that the mistaken fancy of a plurality of Gods would be forced to the acknowledgment of a unity of Deity. For if goodness, and justice, and wisdom, and power may be equally predicated of it, then also imperishability and eternal existence, and every orthodox idea would be in the same way admitted. As then all distinctive difference in any aspect whatever has been gradually removed, it necessarily follows that together with it a plurality of Gods has been removed from his belief, the general identity bringing round conviction to the Unity.

Chapter 1

But since our system of religion is accustomed to observe a distinction of persons in the unity of the Nature—to prevent our argument in our contention with Greeks sinking to the level of Judaism—there is need again of a distinct technical statement in order to correct all error on this point. For not even by those who are external to our doctrine is the Deity held to be without Logos [cf. John 1:1]. Now this admission of theirs will quite enable our argument to be unfolded. For he who admits that God is not without Logos, will agree that a being who is not without Logos (or word) certainly possesses Logos. Now it is to be observed that the utterance of man is expressed by the same term. If, then, he should say that he understands what the Logos of God is according to the analogy of things with us, he will thus be led on to a loftier idea, it being an absolute necessity for him to believe that the utterance, just as everything else, corresponds with the nature. Though, that is, there is a certain sort of force, and life, and wisdom, observed in the human subject, yet no one from the similarity of the terms would suppose that the life, or power, or wisdom, were in the case of God of such a sort as that, but the significations of all such terms are lowered to accord with the standard of our nature. For since our nature is liable to corruption and weak, therefore is our life short, our strength unsubstantial, our word unstable. But in that transcendent nature, through the greatness of the subject contemplated, everything that is said about it is elevated with it. Therefore though mention be made of God's Word it will not be thought of as having its realization in the utterance of what is spoken, and as then vanishing away, like our speech, into the nonexistent. On the contrary, as our nature, liable as it is to come to an end, is endued with speech which likewise comes to an end, so that, imperishable and ever-existing nature has eternal, and substantial speech.

If, then, logic requires him to admit this eternal subsistence of God's Word, it is altogether necessary to admit also that the subsistence of that word consists in a living state—for it is an impiety to suppose that the Word has a soulless subsistence after the manner of stones. But if it subsists, being as it is something with intellect and without body, then certainly it lives, whereas if it be divorced from life, then as certainly it does not subsist; but this idea that the Word of God does not subsist, has been shown to be blasphemy. By consequence, therefore, it has also been shown that the Word is to be considered as in a living condition. And since the nature of the Logos is reasonably believed to be simple, and exhibits in itself no duplicity or combination, no one would contemplate the existence of the living Logos as dependent on a mere participation of life, for such a supposition, which is to say that one thing is within another, would not exclude the idea of compositeness; but, since the simplicity has been admitted, we are compelled to think that the Logos has an independent life, and not a mere participation of life. If, then, the Logos, as being life, lives, it certainly has the faculty of will, for no one of living creatures is without such a faculty.

Moreover that such a will has also capacity to act must be the conclusion of a devout mind. For if you admit not this potency, you prove the reverse to exist. But no; impotence is quite removed from our conception of Deity. Nothing of incongruity is to be observed in connection with the Divine nature, but it is absolutely necessary to admit that the power of that word is as great as the purpose, lest mixture, or concurrence, of contradictions be found in an existence that is incomposite, as would be the case if, in the same purpose, we were to detect both impotence and power, if, that is, there were power to do one thing, but no power to do something else.

Also we must suppose that this will in its power to do all things will have no tendency to anything that is evil (for impulse towards evil is foreign to the Divine nature), but that whatever is good, this it also wishes, and, wishing, is able to perform, and, being able, will not fail to perform; but that it will bring all its proposals for good to effectual accomplishment. Now the world *is* good, and all its contents are seen to be wisely and skillfully ordered. All of them, therefore, are the works of the Word, of one who, while he lives and subsists, in that he is God's Word, has a will too, in that he lives; of one too who has power to effect what he wills, and who wills what is absolutely good and wise and all else that connotes superiority. Whereas, then, the world is admitted to be something good, and from what has been said the world has been shown to be the work of the Word, who both wills and is able to effect the good, this Word is other than he of whom he is the Word.

For this, too, to a certain extent is a term of "relation," inasmuch as the Father of the Word must be thought of with the Word, for it would not be word were it not a word of some one. If, then, the mind of the hearers, from the relative meaning of the term, makes a distinction between the Word and him from whom he proceeds, we should find that the Gospel mystery, in its contention with the Greek conceptions, would not be in danger of coinciding with those who prefer the beliefs of the Jews. But it will equally escape the absurdity of either party, by acknowledging both that the living Word of God is an effective and creative being, which is what the Jew refuses to receive, and also that the Word itself, and he from whom he is, do not differ in their nature. As in our own case we say that the word is from the mind and no more entirely the same as the mind, than altogether other than it (for, by its being from it, it is something else, and not it. Still by its bringing the mind in evidence it can no longer be considered as something other than it; and so it is in its essence one with mind, while as a subject it is different). In like manner, too, the Word of God by its self-subsistence is distinct from the One from whom it has its subsistence; and yet by exhibiting in itself those qualities that are recognized in God it is the same in nature with the One who is recognizable by the same distinctive marks. For whether one adopts goodness, or power, or wisdom, or eternal existence, or the incapability of vice, death, and decay, or an entire perfection, or anything whatever of the kind, to mark one's conception of the Father, by means of the same marks he will find the Word that subsists from him.

Chapter 2

As, then, by the higher mystical ascent [*anagōgikōs*] from matters that concern ourselves to that transcendent nature we gain a knowledge of the Word, by the same method we shall be led on to a conception of the Spirit, by observing in our own nature certain shadows and resemblances of his ineffable power.

Now in us the spirit (or breath) is the drawing of air, a matter other than ourselves, inhaled and breathed out for the necessary sustainment of the body. This, on the occasion of uttering the word, becomes an utterance that expresses in itself the meaning of the word. And in the case of the Divine nature it has been deemed a point of our religion that there is a Spirit of God, just as it has been allowed that there is a Word of God, because of the inconsistency of the Word of God being deficient as compared with our word, if, while this word of ours is contemplated in connection with spirit, that other Word were to be believed to be quite unconnected with spirit. Not indeed that it is a thought proper to entertain of Deity— that like our breath something foreign from without flows into God and in God becomes the Spirit. But when we think of God's Word we do not deem the Word to be something unsubstantial, nor the result of instruction, nor an utterance of the voice, nor what after being uttered passes away, nor what is subject to any other condition such as those which are observed in our word, but to be essentially self-subsisting, with a faculty of will ever-working, all-powerful.

Thus, our doctrine about God's Spirit: we regard it as that which goes with the Word and manifests its energy, and not as a mere effluence of the breath; for by such a conception the grandeur of the Divine power would be reduced and humiliated, that is, if the Spirit that is in it were supposed to resemble ours. But we conceive of it as an essential power, regarded as self-centered in its own proper person, yet equally incapable of being separated from God in whom it is, or from the Word of God whom it accompanies, as from melting into nothingness; but as being, after the likeness of God's Word, existing as a person, able to will, self-moved, efficient, ever choosing the good, and for its every purpose having its power concurrent with its will.

Chapter 3

And so one who thoroughly studies the depths of the mystery, receives secretly in his spirit, indeed, a moderate amount of apprehension of the doctrine of God's nature, yet he is unable to explain clearly in words the ineffable depth of this mystery. As, for instance, how the same thing is capable of being numbered and yet rejects numeration, how it is observed with distinctions yet is apprehended as a monad, how it is separate as to personality yet is not divided as to subject matter. For, in personality, the Spirit is one thing and the Word another, and yet again that from which the Word and Spirit is, another. But when you have gained the conception of what the distinction is in these, the oneness, again, of the nature admits not division, so that the supremacy of the one First Cause is not split and cut up into differing Godships, neither does the statement harmonize with the Jewish dogma, but the truth passes in the mean between these two conceptions, destroying each heresy, and yet accepting what is useful to it from each. The Jewish dogma is destroyed by the acceptance of the Word, and by the belief in the Spirit; while the polytheistic error of the Greek school is made to vanish by the unity of the Nature abrogating this imagination of plurality. While yet again, of the Jewish conception, let the unity of the Nature stand; and of the Hellenistic, only the distinction as to persons; the remedy against a profane view being thus applied, as required, on either side. For it is as if the number of the triad were a remedy in the case of those who are in error as to the One, and the assertion of the unity for those whose beliefs are dispersed among a number of divinities.

The Life of Moses, Book 1.5–10, Book 2.162–69

From *Gregory of Nyssa: The Life of Moses*, trans. Abraham J. Malherbe and Everett Ferguson (New York: Paulist Press, 1978), 30–31, 94–97.

Book 1
The Life of Moses or Concerning Perfection in Virtue

Prologue 5. The perfection of everything which can be measured by the senses is marked off by certain definite boundaries. Quantity, for example, admits of both continuity and limitation, for every quantitative measure is circumscribed by certain limits proper to itself.[23] The person who looks at a cubit or at the number ten knows that its perfection consists in the fact that it has both a beginning and an end. But in the case of virtue we have learned from the Apostle that its one limit of perfection is the fact that it has no limit. For that divine Apostle, great and lofty in understanding, ever running the course of virtue, never ceased *straining toward those things that are still to come* [Phil. 3:13].[24] Coming to a stop in the race was not safe for him. Why? Because no Good has a limit in its own nature but is limited by the presence of its opposite, as life is limited by death and light by darkness. And every good thing generally ends with all those things which are perceived to be contrary to the good.

6. Just as the end of life is the beginning of death, so also stopping in the race of virtue marks the beginning of the race of evil. Thus our statement that grasping perfection with reference to virtue is impossible was not false, for it has been pointed out that what is marked off by boundaries is not virtue.

I said that it is also impossible for those who pursue the life of virtue to attain perfection. The meaning of this statement will be explained.

7. The Divine One is himself the Good (in the primary and proper sense of the word),[25] whose very nature is goodness. Since, then, it has not

23. See Aristotle, *Categories* 4b 20ff.
24. Phil 3:13 is the theme of the whole treatise: that perfection is a continual progress.
25. Cf. Aristotle, *Nicomachean Ethics* 1157a30.

been demonstrated that there is any limit to virtue except evil, and since the Divine does not admit of an opposite, we hold the divine nature to be unlimited and infinite. Certainly whoever pursues true virtue participates in nothing other than God, because he is himself absolute virtue. Since, then, those who know what is good by nature desire participation in it, and since this good has no limit, the participant's desire itself necessarily has no stopping place but stretches out with the limitless.

8. It is therefore undoubtedly impossible to attain perfection, since, as I have said, perfection is not marked off by limits: The one limit of virtue is the absence of a limit. How then would one arrive at the sought-for boundary when one can find no boundary?[26]

9. Although on the whole my argument has shown that what is sought for is unattainable, one should not disregard the commandment of the Lord which says, *Therefore be perfect, just as your heavenly father is perfect* [Matt. 5:48]. For in the case of those things which are good by nature, even if reasonable people were not able to attain everything, by attaining even a part they could yet gain a great deal.

10. We should show great diligence not to fall away from the perfection that is attainable but to acquire as much as is possible: To that extent let us make progress within the realm of what we seek. For the perfection of human nature consists perhaps in its very growth in goodness.

Book 2
Contemplation on the Life of Moses

The Darkness 162. What does it mean that Moses entered the darkness and then saw God in it? [Exod. 20:21] What is now recounted seems somehow to be contradictory to the first theophany, for then the Divine was beheld in light but now he is seen in darkness. Let us not think that this is at variance with the sequence of things we have contemplated spiritually. Scripture teaches by this that religious knowledge comes at first to those who receive it as light. Therefore what is perceived to be contrary to religion is darkness, and the escape from darkness comes about when one participates in light. But as the mind progresses and, through an ever greater and more perfect diligence, comes to apprehend reality, as it approaches more nearly to contemplation, it sees more clearly what of the divine nature is uncontemplated.

163. For leaving behind everything that is observed, not only what sense comprehends but also what the intelligence thinks it sees, it keeps on penetrating deeper until by the intelligence's yearning for understanding it gains access to the invisible and the incomprehensible, and there it sees God. This is the true knowledge of what is sought; this is the seeing that

---

26. The basis of the perpetual progress in virtue is divine infinity.

consists in not seeing, because that which is sought transcends all knowledge, being separated on all sides by incomprehensibility as by a kind of darkness. Wherefore John the sublime, who penetrated into the luminous darkness, says, *No one has ever seen God* [John 1:18], thus asserting that knowledge of the divine essence is unattainable not only by men but also by every intelligent creature.

164. When, therefore, Moses grew in knowledge, he declared that he had seen God in the darkness, that is, that he had then come to know that what is divine is beyond all knowledge and comprehension, for the text says, Moses *approached the dark cloud where God was* [Exod. 20:21]. What God? He who *made darkness his hiding place* [Ps. 18:11], David says, who also was initiated into the mysteries in the same inner sanctuary.

165. When Moses arrived there, he was taught by word what he had formerly learned from darkness, so that, I think, the doctrine on this matter might be made firmer for us for being testified to by the divine voice. The divine word at the beginning forbids that the Divine be likened to any of the things known by men [Exod. 20:2], since every concept which comes from some comprehensible image by an approximate understanding and by guessing at the divine nature constitutes an idol of God and does not proclaim God.

166. Religious virtue is divided into two parts, into that which pertains to the Divine and that which pertains to right conduct (for purity of life is a part of religion). Moses learns at first the things which must be known about God (namely, that none of those things known by human comprehension is to be ascribed to him). Then he is taught the other side of virtue, learning by what pursuits the virtuous life is perfected.

167. After this he comes to the tabernacle not made with hands. Who will follow someone who makes his way through such places and elevates his mind to such heights, who, as though he were passing from one peak to another, comes ever higher than he was through his ascent to the heights? First, he leaves behind the base of the mountain and is separated from all those too weak for the ascent. Then as he rises higher in his ascent he hears the sounds of the trumpets. Thereupon, he slips into the inner sanctuary of divine knowledge. And he does not remain there, but he passes on to the tabernacle not made with hands [Heb. 9:11]. For truly this is the limit that someone reaches who is elevated through such ascents.

168. For it seems to me that in another sense the heavenly trumpet becomes a teacher to the one ascending as he makes his way to what is not made with hands. For the wonderful harmony of the heavens proclaims the wisdom which shines forth in the creation and sets forth the great glory of God through the things which are seen, in keeping with the statement, the heavens declare the glory of God [Ps. 19:1]. It becomes the loud sounding trumpet of clear and melodious teaching, as one of the Prophets says, "The heavens trumpeted from above" [Sir. 46:17].

169. When he who has been purified and is sharp of hearing in his heart hears this sound (I am speaking of the knowledge of the divine power which comes from the contemplation of reality), he is led by it to the place where his intelligence lets him slip in where God is. This is called darkness by the Scripture [Exod. 20:21; 24:15, 18], which signifies, as I said, the unknown and unseen. When he arrives there, he sees that tabernacle not made with hands, which he shows to those below by means of a material likeness [Exod. 25–27].

SELECTION **8**

Augustine

The Trinity, Book 15.1–14

A North African bishop, Augustine of Hippo (354–430) has had a profound influence on Western Christianity. The excerpt below is from the first section of the last book of *The Trinity,* his most comprehensive work. Throughout the work, Augustine's goal is to lead his readers to contemplate the image of God within our minds (*mens*; understood broadly as our capacity to think, to feel, to desire, and to will). Contemplating this image, we are led to the reality of God, who created us in the divine image (no. 1). Faith leads us to such contemplation so that we can understand more deeply what it means to know God (nos. 2, 3).

Augustine then gives a brief overview of the previous fourteen books (nos. 4, 5). Books 1–4 argue for the unity and equality of the Trinitarian persons in an extensive biblical exegesis dealing with the way the *temporal missions* of the Son and the Spirit (in the economy of redemption and sanctification) reveal the mystery of *eternal processions* within God (see Gal. 4:4–6). Books 5–7 interpret and further develop Cappadocian arguments against Arianism and Eunomianism, stressing the equality and mutual relations of the Trinitarian persons. Book 8 shifts to a "more inward way," which moves from reflecting on one's own self-awareness to reflecting on God's presence within that self-awareness. Through this contemplative exercise, Augustine leads us to the image of the Trinity within the very way the mind—in reflecting on itself—knows itself and loves itself (Book 9). Likewise, we can discern an image of the Trinity in the way the inner self remembers, understands, and wills (or loves) itself (Book 10)—and even in the way we see things both outside of us and within our imaginations (Book 11). Knowledge, of course, is different from wisdom, which is what ultimately mirrors the divine image within us. Moreover, because of humanity's fall into sin, only Christ, the incarnate wisdom of God, can truly restore this divine image within us (Books 13, 14). By faith in Christ's redeeming work—the mission of the Son—our inner self's remembering, understanding, and willing itself is transformed into true wisdom: remembering, understanding, and loving the triune God within us (Book 14).

Augustine then moves to a more "direct" search for God's very being, which can be discerned in what we inherently value (e.g., life, feeling, intelligence, immortality, potency, righteousness, the beautiful, the good, and so on) (no. 6). From here, Augustine discerns a range of divine attributes that he then condenses to three terms—*eternal, wise,* and *blessed* (nos. 7, 8)— which, in turn, are all implied in the single term *wisdom* (no. 9). Although the Trinity (as lover, the beloved, and love) may be too brilliant for us to grasp, we can perceive through our own knowing and loving that God's gift of wisdom to us is indeed the Trinity who—in knowing and loving itself— gives us the power to know and love ourselves (no. 10).

Yet this analogy is insufficient. The "trinity of wisdom" is *in* us as something we possess; the divine Trinity, by contrast, constitutes the very divine nature or essence (no. 11). Further, our remembering, understanding, and willing are discrete activities; they are not interchangeable. In God, memory, understanding, and will are mutually related and interchangeable; they belong to all three persons (no. 12). And, since we live in time, we cannot comprehend how God's eternal wisdom embraces both the past and the future (no. 13). Thus, we only see through the veil of a "mirror"—an "image"—that needs to be transformed by grace before it can see God face to face (2 Cor. 3:18) (nos. 14–16).

From *Augustine: Later Works,* trans. John Burnaby, *LCC* 8:128–142.

1. Our design of preparing the reader, by the study of the things that are made, for the knowledge of their maker, has brought us to the image of God which man presents, in virtue of that which sets him above all other animals: namely, reason or intelligence, with any other characteristic of the reasonable or intellectual soul that is properly to be assigned to what we call *mens* or *animus* (mind). The word *animus* is used by some Latin writers as a technical term to distinguish the higher element in man, which is lacking in the beast, from the *anima* or soul which is present in beast as well as man. If we look for a being above this, and look for an existing reality, it must be God, the being not created but Creator. And whether this being is a Trinity is a question not only to be decided for faith by the authority of Holy Scripture; but one to which we ought, if we can, to give some rational answer, satisfactory to the understanding. My reason for saying "if we can," will emerge in the course of our actual discussion of the question.

2. The God whom we seek will, I doubt not, give us the help we need, that our labor be not fruitless. Then shall we understand what is written in the Psalm: "Let the heart of them rejoice that seek the Lord: seek the

Lord and be strengthened; seek his face always" [Ps. 105:3–4]. One might suppose that what is always sought is never found; and that the heart of them that seek must rather grieve than rejoice, if they cannot find what they seek.

It is not said, "Let the heart of them that find rejoice," but "of them that seek the Lord." Yet that the Lord God can be found through seeking, we are assured by the word of the prophet Isaiah: "Seek the Lord, and call upon him that ye may find him presently; and when he draweth near to you, let the ungodly leave his ways and the wicked man his thoughts" [Isa. 55:6f.]. If then, he can be found when he is sought, why are we bidden "seek his face always"? Perhaps because even when he is found he must be sought. Enquiry concerning the incomprehensible is justified, and the enquirer has found something, if he has succeeded in finding how far what he sought passes comprehension. Comprehending the incomprehensibility of what he seeks, yet he will go on seeking, because he cannot slacken his pursuit so long as progress is made in the actual enquiry into things incomprehensible: so long as he is continually bettered by the search after so great a good—both sought that it may be found, and found that it may be sought: still sought that the finding may be sweeter, still found that the seeking may be more eager. So we may interpret the words put into Wisdom's mouth in the book of Ecclesiasticus: "They that eat me shall still hunger, and they that drink me shall still thirst" [24:21]. They eat and drink, because they find: because they hunger and thirst, they still seek. Faith seeks, understanding finds: wherefore the prophet says: "Unless ye believe, ye shall not understand" [Isa. 7:9]. And again understanding yet seeks him whom it finds: for "God hath looked upon the sons of men," we sing in the Psalm, "to see if there be one that is understanding, or a seeker after God" [Ps. 14:2]. Man is called to be understanding, to the end that he may seek after God.

3. Thus, the care with which we have dwelt on that which God has made will have been justified by its purpose, that thereby we might come to know the maker. "For the invisible things of him from the creation of the world, being understood through the things which are made, are clearly seen" [Rom. 1:20]. Hence the reproof in the Book of Wisdom, of those who "could not out of the good things that are seen know him that is; neither by considering the works did they acknowledge the artificer, but deemed either fire or wind or the swift air or the circling of the stars or the violence of waters or the luminaries of heaven to be the gods which govern the world: with whose beauty if they were so delighted as to account them gods, let them know how much better the ruler of them is. For the first author of beauty hath created them. Or if they marveled at their strength and working, let them understand from these things how much mightier is he that ordered them; for by the greatness of the beauty and the creation, the creator of them might recognizably have been discerned" [Wis.

13:1ff.]. I quote these verses from the Book of Wisdom, that in my search for pointers to that supreme Trinity which we seek when we seek for God, I may not seem to any of the faithful to have wasted my labor in beginning with the creature, and so moving by stages through a number of special trinities up to the mind of man.

4. The necessities of discourse and argument have obliged us to deal in the course of fourteen Books with many matters which we can hardly embrace in a single view, so as to apply them without hesitation to the point we desire to grasp. I shall therefore do my best, God helping, to summarize without discussion the results of our discussions in each Book, and so to make accessible at a glance, not the grounds of our conclusions but the conclusions themselves. In this way our later results will not be so far separated from the earlier that examination of the later will drive the earlier from our minds; or if it does, we shall be able readily to look back and recollect what was forgotten.

5. Book 1 showed the testimony of Holy Scripture to the unity and equality of the supreme Trinity.

Books 2, 3, and 4 dealt with the same theme; but the detailed enquiry into the missions of the Son and of the Holy Spirit occupies the three Books. It was shown that the Person sent is not less than the Sender because of that relationship: the Trinity, which is equal throughout, working inseparably without any difference in the changelessness, invisibility and omnipresence of its being.

Book 5 met the argument that the substance of the Father and of the Son is not the same, on the ground that nothing can be predicated of God which does not denote substance, and that therefore begetting and being begotten, or the begotten and the unbegotten, being different predicates must denote different substances. It was shown that not all that is predicated of God denotes substance, as do the predicates "good" and "great" and any others denoting what he is in himself; but that there are also predicates of relation, denoting not what he is in himself but what he is in relation to something which is not himself; as he is called Father in relation to the Son, or Lord in relation to the creature that is subject to him. If he is given a relative predicate such as implies temporal process, as for example "Lord, thou hast become our refuge" [Ps. 90:1], that does not denote a happening to him involving change: he himself in his nature or essence remains altogether changeless.

Book 6 discussed the meaning of the apostolic titles of Christ, "the power of God and the wisdom of God," postponing for further consideration the question whether he of whom Christ is begotten is not wisdom himself but only the Father of his own wisdom, or whether wisdom has begotten wisdom. But however that should be answered, this Book also served to make clear the equality of the Trinity, and that God is not treble—God three times over, but Trinity: Father and Son do not make up a double as against the singleness of the Holy Spirit, and the Three are not anything "more" than any one of them. The Book ended with a discussion of the meaning of Bishop Hilary's phrase: "Eternity in the Father, form in the image, use in the gift."[27]

Book 7 dealt with the question adjourned, to the effect that God as begetter of the Son is not only Father of his own power and wisdom, but also power and wisdom in himself; the same holding of the Holy Spirit. Yet there are not three powers or wisdoms but one power and one wisdom, as there is one God and one essence. Then it was asked in what sense we speak of one essence and three Persons, or in the Greek manner of one essence and three substances. The terms were found to meet the need of a form of speech that would provide a single answer to the question "What are the three, whom we truly confess as three?"—namely, Father, Son, and Holy Spirit.

Book 8 applied the method of reasoning to make it clear to the understanding that in true substance not only is the Father no "greater" than the Son, but neither are both together a "greater" thing than the Holy Spirit alone; nor are any two in the Trinity a "greater" thing than one, nor all three together "greater" than each severally. Then I endeavored to make intelligible, so far as that may be, the incorporeal and changeless nature of God: using the notions of the Truth which is understood and seen, the supreme Good from which all good proceeds, the righteousness for which a righteous soul is loved by one not yet righteous, and finally the charity which in Holy Scripture is called God, and in which an actual Trinity begins to show itself to the understanding, in the form of lover, the beloved, and love.

Book 9 carried the argument to that image of God which is presented by man in his mental nature. There we find a kind of trinity, in the mind, the knowledge whereby it knows itself, and the love whereby it loves itself and its knowledge; and these three are shown to be equal to one another and of one essence.

Book 10 gave a more thorough and precise investigation to the same subject, which led to the discovery in the mind of a trinity more manifest, in the form of memory, understanding and will. But it was also found that the mind can never have been without the memory, understanding, and love of itself, although it does not always think of itself; and when it does, the same act of thought does not cause it to distinguish itself from what is corporeal. We therefore postponed our consideration of the Trinity of which this is an image, in order to discover a trinity in the actual process of bodily perception, and thereby to offer the reader a less obscure field in which to exercise his power of penetration.

Book 11 accordingly took the visual sense as an example, findings in

---

27. Hilary, *On the Trinity*, 2.34.

which could be recognized as valid for the other four senses. Thus was disclosed a trinity of the outward man, first in external vision, composed of the physical object seen, the form impressed from it upon the view of the beholder, and the act of voluntary attention which links the two. But the members of this triad are plainly neither equal to one another nor of one substance; and we proceeded to the discovery of another trinity in the mind itself, imported from the field of outward sense, in which the same three appeared as consubstantial: the imaging of the object as retained in the memory, the actualizing of the form derived from it when the thinker's view is directed thither, and the act of voluntary attention which unites them. Even this trinity was recognized as belonging to the outward man, inasmuch as it results from the perception of external objects.

Book 12 laid down the distinction between wisdom and knowledge, and looked first in the inferior realm of knowledge in the strict sense of the word, for a special kind of trinity. This belongs indeed to the inward man, but cannot yet be regarded as the image of God, or so entitled.

Book 13 developed this enquiry by way of an exposition of Christian faith.

Book 14 proceeded to a discourse on man's true wisdom—the wisdom, distinct from knowledge, conferred by God's gift through a partaking in God himself; and this led to the emergence of a trinity in the image of God constituted by man in his mental nature, which is in the knowledge of God after the image of him who created man in his image [Col. 3:10; Gen. 1:27], and in that renewal acquires the wisdom in which there is a contemplation of things eternal.

6. And now the time has come for us to direct our search for the Trinity, which is God, upon that eternal world, bodiless and changeless, in whose perfect contemplation we have the promise of a blessed life—the life that must needs be eternal. The being of God is not only asserted by the authority of divine Scripture. The universe of nature which environs us and to which we ourselves belong, proclaims its dependence on a supremely good establisher. He has given us a mind and a natural reason, whereby we discern the relative values of things: preferring the living to what is without life, the sentient to what is without feeling, the understanding to what is without intelligence; immortal to mortal, potent to impotent, righteous to unrighteous, beautiful to ugly, good to evil, incorruptible to corruptible, immutable to mutable, invisible to visible, incorporeal to corporeal, blessed to miserable. And inasmuch as we do not hesitate to set a higher value on the Creator than on things created, we are obliged to allow that he must have life at its highest, and awareness and understanding of all things; that he cannot suffer death, corruption, or change; that he is no body, but a Spirit most potent, righteous, beautiful, good, and blessed.

7. But all these attributes, and any others that human modes of expression may worthily assign to God, belong both to the whole Trinity which

is the one God and to the several Persons in that same Trinity. Neither of the one God, the Trinity itself, nor of Father or Son or Holy Spirit, may any man presume to speak as without life, sentience or understanding; or to suggest that any of them, in that being in respect of which they are accounted equal to one another, is either mortal or corruptible or changeable or corporeal; or to deny to any of them the fullest power, righteousness, beauty, goodness, and blessedness. If then these and all similar terms are to be predicated both of the Trinity itself and of the several Persons therein, where or how can they display the nature of Trinity?

Let us begin by reducing their indefinite number to something smaller. What we call "life" in God is his very essence and nature: the life by which God lives is what he is to himself. But that life is not the life of a tree, without understanding or sentience; nor the life of a beast, which possesses sentience in its five divisions, but no understanding. The life that is God has consciousness and understanding of all things; and its consciousness is mental not corporeal, since God is spirit [John 4:24]. It is not through a body that God is conscious, like the embodied animal; for he is not composed of soul and body. His uncompounded nature is conscious as it understands, and understands as it is conscious: his understanding is the same as his consciousness. Nor is the life of God such as ever to cease or ever to begin, for it is immortal. Rightly is it said of him that he "alone hath immortality" [1 Tim. 6:16]; for true immortality belongs only to him in whose nature there is no possibility of change. And the changelessness of God is the effect of his true eternity, without beginning, without end; from which follows his incorruptibility. So it is one and the same thing to call God eternal or immortal or incorruptible or changeless, and it is the same thing to call him living and understanding, which implies wisdom. He has not acquired a wisdom to make him wise, but is himself wisdom. And this is his life, and at the same time the strength or power, and the beauty, for which he is called potent and beautiful. Nothing could have more power and beauty than the wisdom which "reacheth mightily from one end to the other, and sweetly ordereth all things" [Wis. 8:1]. Again, goodness and righteousness cannot lie apart from one another in God's nature, as they do in his works: there are not two different qualities of God, one goodness, and another righteousness. His righteousness is his goodness, and his goodness is his blessedness. As for the term incorporeal, it is used of God simply in the sense that for our faith or understanding he is spirit and not body.

8. If then we call God eternal, immortal, incorruptible, changeless, living, wise, potent, beautiful, righteous, good, blessed, spirit—the last of these terms may be thought to denote substance only, and all the rest qualities of that substance. But this distinction does not exist in the ineffable and uncompounded nature of God. Terms which appear to denote quality must here be taken as denoting substance or essence. We may never say

that God is spirit in substance, and good in quality: he is both in substance. The same applies to all the terms we have applied to him: as we have argued at length in previous Books.[28]

The first four of these terms as above enumerated in order were eternal, immortal, incorruptible, changeless. Since these four denote one thing, as I have explained, let us select some one of them in order to concentrate our thought: say the one that comes first, "eternal." Let us do the same with the second four, living, wise, potent, beautiful. Here, we note that life of a sort belongs to the beast who is without wisdom; that wisdom and power may in a man be so contrasted with one another that Scripture can say: "Better is the wise than the strong" [Wis. 6:12 LXX]; and that we normally use the word beautiful of corporeal things. Our best choice among these four will therefore be "wise": although in God there is no inequality between the four, since the four words stand for one thing. In the case of the last group of four terms, it is true that righteousness in God is identical with goodness and blessedness, and "spirit" is identical with all three. But in men there can be an unblessed spirit, there can be one righteous and good who is not yet blessed; whereas none can be blessed who is not a spirit both righteous and good. Let us then choose the term which even in men must carry the three others with it, namely "blessed."

9. Can we then say that these three terms, "eternal," "wise," "blessed," constitute the Trinity which we call God? We have reduced our terms from twelve to three; but possibly we might make a further reduction of these three to some one of them. If wisdom and power, or life and wisdom, may be one and the same thing in the nature of God, why should not this hold of eternity and wisdom, or of blessedness and wisdom? Then, just as in our reduction of the larger to the smaller number it made no difference whether we used the twelve terms or the three, so it will make no difference whether we use the three, or the single one to which we have suggested that the two others might similarly be reduced. And then we shall hardly find a line of argument, a force or power of understanding, a vigor of reasoning or a penetration of thought, sufficient to show without regard to all the rest how the Trinity may be found in the application to God of this single term—wisdom. God does not learn wisdom from any other source as we do from him: he is his own wisdom, since, in him for whom to be is to be wise, his wisdom and his essence are not distinguishable things. It is true that in Holy Scripture Christ is called the power of God and the wisdom of God [1 Cor. 1:24]. But we discussed in our seventh Book the interpretation of this text so as to avoid implying that the Son makes the Father wise; and our conclusion was that the Son is Wisdom from Wisdom, as he is Light from Light, God from God. And we were forced to extend the same argument to the Holy Spirit, admitting that he

---

28. The reference is especially to Book 5 and 6.

also is himself wisdom—all together constituting one wisdom, as they do one God and one essence. Of this wisdom, then, which is God, how shall we understand that it is Trinity? I do not say, How shall we believe? For of that there should be no question among the faithful. But if there is any way by which understanding may give us a vision of what we believe, what can that way be?

10. We may recall that it was in the eighth Book that the manifestation of the Trinity to our understanding began. There we essayed to lift up, so far as might be, the effort of our mind to the understanding of that most excellent and changeless being which is other than our mind. In contemplation we were aware of it as not far from us and yet above us—not spatially but by its own most reverend and wonderful excellence, so that we found it present in us in virtue of its own pervading light. But so far we had no glimpse of the Trinity, because we could not in that dazzling brightness direct our mind's eye steadily to look for it (Book 8.3). All that we could with some clearness distinguish was that it was no measurable mass in which the quantity of two or three must be believed greater than that of the two. Only when we came to consider charity, which in Holy Scripture is called God, the light began to break upon a Trinity, consisting in lover, the beloved, and love. But from that ineffable light our gaze flinched away: we had to confess that our mind in its weakness was not yet strong enough to be conformed to it. And therefore, in order to recruit our laboring efforts, we paused in the pursuit of our undertaking and turned back to the more familiar consideration of that same mind of ours, in which man has been made after the image of God; and from the ninth to the fourteenth Book we occupied ourselves with our own creaturely nature, in order that we might be able to apprehend and perceive the invisible things of God through the things that are made [Rom. 1:20].

And now the time has come, when after this exercise of our understanding in a lower sphere for so long as need required (and maybe for longer), we would lift ourselves up to perceive the supreme Trinity which is God. Yet our strength fails us. Many trinities we can see most surely. There are those which are produced by the action of corporeal objects on the outward senses, and those which occur when the sense perception becomes matter of thought. There are trinities when things arising in the mind apart from the bodily senses are distinguished by clear reasoning and comprehended in knowledge, such as our faith, and those virtues which are ways of living. There are trinities when the mind itself, by which we know all that we truthfully claim to know, is known to itself or thinks of itself, or when it perceives an eternal and unchanging object other than itself. In all these processes we see trinities with assurance, since they occur or exist in us as we remember, regard, and will. But can we perceive therein by an act of understanding a Speaker and his Word, the Father and the Son, and proceeding thence the Charity common to both which is the

Holy Spirit? It may be urged that while trinities belonging to the sphere of sense or mind are for us objects of sight rather than belief, the fact that God is Trinity must be believed rather than seen. If that be so, it must follow, either that the invisible things of him are nowhere apprehended and perceived by us through the things that are made; or, that in none of them which we perceive can we perceive the Trinity—that there is something in that sphere which we may perceive, but something also which we are obliged to believe though unperceived. Yet the eighth Book showed that we do perceive a changeless good, other than ourselves; and the same was indicated in the fourteenth Book when we spoke of the wisdom which comes to man from God. Why then can we not recognize there the Trinity? It is impossible to maintain that this wisdom which is called God neither understands nor loves itself; and it is patent that where there is no knowledge there cannot possibly be wisdom. That the wisdom which is God knows or loves other things but neither knows nor loves itself, cannot be asserted or believed without foolishness and impiety; and if so, here surely is Trinity: wisdom, its knowledge of itself, and its love of itself. That was how we discovered a trinity in man: the mind, the knowledge whereby it knows itself; and the love whereby it loves itself.

11. But these three are in man, without by themselves constituting man; for if we follow the definition of the ancients, man is a rational and mortal animal. The three things named are then man's highest part, but not by themselves man. Moreover, the one person which is the individual man possesses those three in his mind. Even if we adopt a different definition of man, to the effect that he is a rational substance composed of soul and body, it remains indubitable that man possesses a soul which is not body and a body which is not soul. And then our triad is not equivalent to man but belongs to man or is in man. If we set aside the body and think of the soul alone, we find that the mind is a part of it, as it might be its head or eye or face—though we may not think of the soul's parts as bodies. Thus it is not the soul but the highest thing in it which we call the mind. But we cannot say that the Trinity is in God in this manner—a part of God but not itself God. The individual man, who is called the image of God not in respect of all that belongs to his nature but in respect of his mind alone, is a personal unity, having the image of the Trinity in his mind. But the Trinity of whom he is image is as a whole nothing but God, is as a whole nothing but Trinity. Nothing belongs to God's nature that does not belong to this Trinity. The three Persons are of one essence, not like the individual man one person.

12. In another respect also there is a wide difference to be noted. In man, whether we speak of mind, its knowledge and its love, or of memory, understanding, and will, nothing in the mind is remembered but through memory, or understood but through understanding, or loved but through will. In the divine Trinity, reverence forbids us to say that the Father

understands neither himself nor his Son nor the Holy Spirit, save through the Son, nor loves save through the Holy Spirit; or that through himself he does no more than remember either himself or the Son or the Holy Spirit. Or similarly, that the Son remembers himself and the Father only through the Father, and loves only through the Holy Spirit; while through himself he can only understand both Father and himself and Holy Spirit. Or in the same way that it is through the Father that the Holy Spirit remembers Father, Son, and himself, through the Son that he understands Father, Son, and himself, while through himself he can only love himself, the Father and the Son. This would amount to saying that the Father is memory of himself, Son, and Holy Spirit, the Son is understanding of himself, Father, and Holy Spirit, the Holy Spirit is charity to himself, Father and Son. But to hold or express such opinions concerning the divine Trinity would be extreme presumption. If only the Son understands for himself and Father and Holy Spirit, we are back in the irrational notion that the Father is wise not of himself but by the Son: that wisdom has not begotten wisdom, but the Father is called wise in virtue of the wisdom he has begotten. For where understanding is lacking, there can be no wisdom: if the Father understands not for himself but the Son for the Father, clearly the Son makes the Father wise. And if for God to be is to be wise, and his essence is his wisdom, it will not be the Son who has his essence from the Father (as he truly does), but the Father who has his essence from the Son—which is entirely irrational and false. We may be satisfied with our discussion, refutation and rejection of this irrationality in the seventh Book. God the Father is wise by that same wisdom which is his own being; and the Son is the wisdom of the Father, as being derived from the wisdom which is identical with the Father of whom he is begotten. And accordingly the Father is understanding by the same understanding which is his own being; for wisdom implies understanding; and the Son is the understanding of the Father, as begotten of the understanding which is the Father's being. The same may properly be said of memory. He who remembers nothing, or does not remember himself; cannot be wise. Since therefore the Father is wisdom, and the Son is wisdom, the Son will remember himself no less than the Father remembers himself; and just as the Father remembers himself and the Son with a memory that is his own and not the Son's, the Son will remember himself and the Father with a memory that is not the Father's but his own. Finally, we cannot predicate wisdom where there is no love; from which it follows that the Father is his own love, no less than his own understanding and his own memory. We seem forced to the conclusion that our triad of memory, understanding and love or will, in that supreme and changeless essence that is God, are not to be identified with Father, Son and Holy Spirit, but with the Father by himself. And because the Son is wisdom begotten of wisdom, it is equally true that he understands for himself and not the Father or the Holy Spirit for him, and that neither does the Father remember nor the Holy Spirit love for him, but he does both for himself; for he is his own memory, his own understanding, his own love, though that property comes to him from the Father of whom he is begotten. Again, since the Holy Spirit is wisdom proceeding from wisdom, it is not true that the memory which belongs to him is the Father, the understanding the Son, and the love himself; for he would not be wisdom if another remembered for him, and another understood for him, while for himself he did no more than love. All three belong to him, and in such a manner that he is all three; but this property comes to him from that Source from which he proceeds.

13. No man can comprehend the wisdom by which God knows all things, a wisdom wherein that which we call past does not pass, and that which we call future is not awaited as though not yet available, but both past and future are all together present with what is present: a wisdom wherein there is no thinking on particular things severally, or movement of thought from one thing to another, but the whole universe is presented simultaneously in one single view. No man, I say, can comprehend such a wisdom, which is both foresight and knowledge; inasmuch as even our own wisdom passes our comprehension. We can perceive, in various ways, what is present to our senses or our understanding: what is absent but was once present, we know by memory if we have not forgotten it. We conjecture, not the past from the future, but the future from the past, though we cannot have certain knowledge of it. To some of our thoughts we look forward with a degree of clearness and assurance as about to occur in the immediate future; but when we do so with the maximum of security, we do it by an act of memory, which is evidently concerned not with what is going to happen but with what is past. This is open to experience in the case of speeches or songs which we render from memory in a certain order: did we not foresee in thought what comes next, we could not speak it. But what enables us to foresee is not pre-vision but memory. Until the whole speech or song is ended, there is nothing in its recitation that was not foreseen and looked forward to. Yet in the process our singing and speaking is not ascribed to pre-vision but to memory; and we remark, in those who display exceptional powers of such extended recitation, a strength not of foresight but of memory. We know, without any doubt, that such processes are carried on in our mind, or by our mind; but the more closely we try to observe the manner of the process, the more surely does description fail us and effort exhaust itself in the attempt to reach lucidity of understanding, if not of language. Can we expect then that our feeble minds will be able to comprehend the identity of God's providence with his memory and understanding—the providence of God who does not regard each thing severally in discursive thought, but embraces all that he knows in one eternal, changeless and ineffable vision? In the strait of such perplexity we may well cry out to the living God: "From myself thy

knowledge has become wonderful: its strength is shown, and I shall not be able to reach it" [Ps. 139:6]. For from myself I understand how marvelous and incomprehensible is thy knowledge whereby thou halt made me; and yet in my meditation the fire is kindled, so that I seek thy face evermore [Ps. 39:3; 105:4].

14. I know that wisdom is an incorporeal substance, a light in which are seen things not seen by the eye of flesh. And yet a man of such spiritual greatness as Paul says that "we see now through a mirror, in an enigma; but then face to face" [1 Cor. 13:12]. If we ask of what manner or of what nature is this mirror, we think immediately of the fact that in a mirror what is seen is no more than an image. What we have tried to do is to gain through this image which is ourselves some vision, as through a mirror, of him who made us. We find the same sense in other words of the apostle's: "We with unveiled face beholding in a mirror the glory of the Lord, are transformed into the same image from glory unto glory, as by the Spirit of the Lord" [2 Cor. 3:18]. (The word *speculantes* means "seeing in a mirror," not "observing from a watch-tower": as is clear in the original Greek, in which the *speculum* that reflects an image is described by a quite different-sounding word from the *specula* or height from the top of which we look out at distant objects, and it is plain enough that *speculantes*, in the phrase *gloriam Domini speculantes*, is derived from *speculum* and not *specula*). The words "transformed into the same image" refer to the image of God—the "same," that is, that very image which we behold in the mirror. For this same image is also the glory of God, as Paul says elsewhere: "the man ought not to veil his head, since he is the image of God and glory of God" [1 Cor. 11:7] a text which we discussed in the twelfth Book. "We are transformed"—that is, we are changed from one form into another, from a form of obscurity into a form of clear light. Even in obscurity, the form is God's image; and if his image, then assuredly, his glory, wherein we were created as men, excelling all other animals. For of human nature itself it is said that "a man ought not to veil his head, since he is the image and glory of God." And it is this nature, the most excellent of things created, which when justified by its Creator from its ungodliness is brought over from a form that is deformed into a form of perfect beauty. For even in its very ungodliness, the more severe our condemnation of its fault, the more unhesitating must be our appreciation of its natural dignity. Hence the addition of the words, "from glory to glory": from the glory of creation into the glory of justification. Another interpretation of these words is indeed possible: they may mean, from the glory of faith into the glory of sight: from that glory in which we are the sons of God into that glory in which we shall be like him, for we shall see him as he is. Finally, the words "as from the Spirit of the Lord" indicate that the blessing of a transformation so devoutly prayed for is granted to us by the grace of God.

SELECTION 9

Dionysius the Areopagite

Divine Names and Mystical Theology

A Syrian monk from the early part of the sixth century, Dionysius the Areopagite (also "Denys" or "Pseudo-Dionysius") is known by a pseudonym presumably taken from Acts 17:34. Drawing on Origen, the Cappadocian Fathers, and the Neoplatonists Plotinus and Proclus, he developed a Christian Neoplatonism that was to influence theology in the East (e.g., Maximus Confessor and Gregory Palamas) and in the West (e.g., John Scotus Eriugena, Thomas Aquinas, and Bonaventure). He was also an important inspiration for later mystics (e.g., the anonymous author of the *Cloud of Unknowing*, Meister Eckhart, Johannes Tauler, and later Spanish mystics).

In four surviving treatises—*Divine Names, Mystical Theology, Celestial Hierarchy*, and *Ecclesiastical Hierarchy*—Dionysius presents a comprehensive theology that depicts how the multiplicity within creation comes from and returns to God. The incarnation of the Word, or Son of God, in Jesus is at the center of this emanation and return: in Christ, the One enters the world of multiplicity; Christ expresses the ineffable in the universe.

The *Divine Names* treats the multiplicity of God's names (or attributes) that speak of God's emanation and return in all things. Throughout, Dionysius presupposes contemplative prayer: the disciplined leaving behind of all speech and knowledge in order to attain a union with God that "exceeds our abilities and any exercise of discursive or intuitive reason." He distinguishes *kataphatic* or affirmative theology (which attributes names to God drawing on Scripture and philosophical texts) from *apophatic* or negative theology (which explores the limits and speech-transcending character of language about God). We must simultaneously affirm and deny everything we say about the God who, as source and goal of all reality, is incomprehensible.

The *Mystical Theology* uses Moses' ascent to Mount Sinai to describe how the soul ascends to deification. In a threefold process of purification, illumination, and perfection into union, the soul finally transcends all sense experience, thought, and speech in an encounter with divine silence, darkness, and unknowing. In this encounter, we not only negate all our positive assertions about God but also our negation of those assertions as we enter into union with the God who transcends all our experiences, thoughts, and words.

Divine Names, Chapter 1

From *On the Divine Names and On the Mystical Theology*,
trans. C. E. Rolt (London: SPCK, 1920), 51–81, 191–201.

Chapter 1

Dionysius the Elder, to His fellow-Elder Timothy;
The Purpose of the Discourse,
and the Tradition concerning the Diving Names

1. Now, Blessed Timothy, having finished the *Outlines of Divinity*, I will proceed, so far as in me lies, to an Exposition of the Divine Names. Here also let us set before our minds the scriptural rule that in speaking about God we should declare the Truth—not with enticing words of human wisdom but in demonstration of the power that the Spirit [1 Cor. 2:4] stirred up in the Sacred Writers. In this way, in a manner surpassing speech and knowledge, we embrace those truths that in like manner surpass them in a Union that exceeds our faculty and exercise of discursive and of intuitive reason. We must not then dare to speak, or indeed to form any conception, of the hidden super-Godhead except those things that are revealed to us from the Holy Scriptures. For a super-essential understanding of It is proper to Unknowing, which lies in the Super-Essence surpassing Discourse, Intuition and Being.

Acknowledging this truth, let us lift our eyes toward the steep height so far as the effluent light of the Divine Scriptures grants its aid. As we strive to ascend to those Supernal Rays, let us gird ourselves for the task with holiness and the reverent fear of God. For, if we may safely trust the wise and infallible Scriptures, Divine things are revealed to each created spirit in proportion to its powers. In this measure perception is granted through the workings of the Divine goodness that in just care for our preservation divinely tempers to finite measure the infinitude of things that pass human understanding. For even as things that are intellectually discerned cannot be comprehended or perceived by means of those things that belong to the senses—nor simple and imageless things by means of types and images, nor the formless and intangible essence of disembodied things by means of those that have bodily form—by the same law of truth the boundless Super-Essence surpasses Essences, the Super-Intellectual Unity surpasses Intelligences, the One that is beyond thought surpasses the apprehension of thought, and the Good that is beyond utterance surpasses the reach of words.

Yes, it is a Unity that is the unifying Source of all unity and a Super-Essential Essence—a Mind beyond the reach of mind [*nous anoētos*] and a Word beyond utterance, eluding Discourse, Intuition, Name, and every kind of being. It is the Universal Cause of existence while Itself existing not, for It is beyond all Being and such that It alone can give with proper understanding a revelation of Itself.

2. Now concerning this hidden Super-Essential Godhead we must not dare, as I have said, to speak or even to form any conception Thereof except those things that are divinely revealed to us from the Holy Scriptures. For as It has lovingly taught us in the Scriptures concerning Itself [Ps. 145:3; Matt. 11:27; Rom. 11:33; 1 Cor. 2:11; Eph. 3:8], the understanding and contemplation of Its actual nature is not accessible to any being; for such knowledge is superessentially exalted above them all. And you will find that many of the Sacred Writers have declared that It is not only invisible and incomprehensible but also unsearchable and past finding out, since there is no trace of any that have penetrated the hidden depths of Its infinitude.

Not that the Good is wholly incommunicable to anything. No, rather, while dwelling alone by Itself, and having there firmly fixed Its super-essential Ray, It lovingly reveals Itself by illuminations corresponding to each separate creature's powers, and thus draws upwards holy minds into such contemplation, participation and resemblance [*theōria, koinonía, homoiōsis*; cf. 1 John 3:2] of Itself as they can attain—even those that holily and duly strive after and do not seek with impotent presumption the Mystery beyond that heavenly revelation that is so granted as to fit their powers, nor yet through their lower propensity slip down the steep descent but with unwavering constancy press onwards toward the ray that casts its light upon them and, through the love responsive to these gracious illuminations, speed their temperate and holy flight on the wings of a godly reverence.

3. In obedience to these divine biddings that guide all the holy dispositions of the heavenly hosts, we worship with reverent silence the unutterable Truths and, with the unfathomable [cf. 1 Cor. 2:10, 11] and holy veneration of our mind, approach that Mystery of Godhead that exceeds all Mind and Being, and we press upwards to those beams that in the Holy Scripture shine upon us. From them we gain the light that leads us to the Divine praises, being supernaturally enlightened by them and conformed to that sacred hymnody, even so as to behold the Divine enlightenments that through them are given in such wise as fits our powers, and so as to praise the bounteous Origin of all holy illumination in accordance with that Doctrine, as concerning Itself, whereby It has instructed us in the Holy Scriptures. Thus do we learn that It is the Cause and Origin and Being and Life of all creation [Gen. 1].

It is to those that fall away from It a Voice that recalls them and a Power by which they rise. To those that have stumbled into a corruption of the Divine image within them, It is a Power of Renewal and Reform. It is a sacred Grounding to those that feel the shock of unholy assault and a Security to those that stand; an upward Guidance to those that are being drawn to It and a Principle of Illumination to those that are being enlightened; a Principle of Perfection to those that are being perfected [cf. 1 Cor.

2:6; Phil. 3:15] and of Simplicity to those that are being brought to simplicity [cf. Matt. 6:22] and of Unity to those that are being brought to unity.

Yes, in a super-essential manner, above the category of origin, It is the Origin of all origin, and the good and bounteous Communication (so far as such may be) of hidden mysteries. In a word, It is the life of all things that live and the Being of all that are, the Origin and Cause of all life and being through Its bounty that both brings them into existence and maintains them.

4. These mysteries we learn from the Divine Scriptures and you will find that in almost all the utterances of the Sacred Writers the Divine Names refer in a Symbolical Revelation to Its beneficent Emanations. Thus, in almost all consideration of Divine things we see the Supreme Godhead celebrated with holy praises as One and an Unity, through the simplicity and unity of Its supernatural indivisibility, from whence (as from a unifying power) we attain to unity and through the supernal conjunction of our diverse and separate qualities are knit together each into a Godlike Oneness and all together into a mutual Godly union.

And It is called the Trinity because Its supernatural fecundity is revealed in a Threefold Personality, wherefrom all Fatherhood in heaven and on earth exists and draws Its name. And It is called the Universal Cause since all things came into being through Its bounty, whence all being springs. And It is called Wise and Fair because all things that keep their own nature uncorrupted are full of all Divine harmony and holy Beauty.

And especially It is called Benevolent because, in one of Its Persons, It verily and wholly shared in our human lot, calling to Itself and uplifting the low estate of humans, wherefrom in an ineffable manner the simple Being of Jesus assumed a compound state [*ho haplous Iēsous sunetéthē*][29] and the Eternal has taken a temporal existence, and He who supernaturally transcends all the order of all the natural world was born in our Human Nature without any change or confusion of His ultimate properties.

And in all the other Divine enlightenments that the secret Tradition of our inspired teachers have by mystic Interpretation accordant with the Scriptures bestowed upon us, we also have been initiated—apprehending these things in the present life (according to our powers) through the sacred veils of that loving kindness that in the Scriptures and the Hierarchical Traditions wraps spiritual truths in terms drawn from the world of sense and super-essential truths in terms drawn from Being, clothing with shapes and forms things that are shapeless and formless, and by a variety of separable symbols, fashioning manifold attributes of the imageless and supernatural Simplicity.

But hereafter, when we are corruptible and immortal and attain the blessed lot of being like Christ, then (as the Scripture says) we shall be

---

29. Cf. *Mystical Theology* 3, "Super Essential Jesus."

forever with the Lord [1 Thess. 4:16], fulfilled with the visible Theophany that shall shine about us in holy contemplations with radiant beams of glory (even as it once shone around the Disciples at the Divine Transfiguration). So shall we, with our mind made passionless and spiritual, participate in a spiritual illumination from Him and in a union transcending our mental faculties. And there, amidst the blinding blissful impulsions of His dazzling rays, we shall, in a diviner manner than at present, be like heavenly Intelligences [i.e., the angels]. For, as the infallible Scripture says, we shall be equal to the angels and shall be the Sons of God, being Sons of the Resurrection [Luke 20:36].

But at present we employ (so far as in us lies) appropriate symbols for things Divine and then from these we press on upwards according to our powers to behold in simple unity the Truth perceived by spiritual contemplations. Leaving behind us all human notions of godlike things, we still the activities of our minds and reach (so far as this may be) into the Super-Essential Ray,[30] wherein all kinds of knowledge so have their pre-existent limits (in a transcendently inexpressible manner) that we cannot conceive nor utter It, nor in any wise contemplate the same, seeing that It surpasses all things and wholly exceeds our knowledge and super-essentially contains beforehand (all conjoined within Itself) the bounds of all natural sciences and forces (while yet Its force is not circumscribed by any) and so possesses, beyond the celestial Intelligences, Its firmly fixed abode. For if all the branches of knowledge belong to things that have being, and if their limits have reference to the existing world, then that which is beyond all Being must also be transcendent above all knowledge.

5. But if It is greater than all Reason and all knowledge—and has Its firm abode altogether beyond Mind and Being and circumscribes, compacts, embraces and anticipates all things while Itself is altogether beyond the grasp of them all and cannot be reached by any perception, imagination, conjecture, name, discourse, apprehension, or understanding—how then is our Discourse concerning the Divine Names to be accomplished, since we see that the Super-Essential Godhead is unutterable and nameless?

Now, as we said when setting forth our *Outlines of Divinity*, the One, the Unknowable, the Super-Essential, the Absolute Good (I mean the Threefold Unity of Persons possessing the same Deity and Goodness) is impossible to describe or to conceive in Its ultimate Nature. No, even the angelical communions of the heavenly Powers Therewith that we describe as either Impulsions or from the Unknowable and blinding Goodness are themselves beyond utterance and knowledge, and belong to none but those angels who, in a manner beyond angelic knowledge, have been counted worthy thereof. And godlike Minds—angelically entering (according to

---

30. Meditation leads on to contemplation; and the higher kind of contemplation is performed by the *via negativa*.

their powers) such states of union and being deified and united through the ceasing of their natural activities to the Light That surpasses Deity— can find no more fitting method to celebrate its praises than to deny It every manner of Attribute.[31] For by a true and supernatural illumination from their blessed union Therewith, they learn that It is the Cause of all things and yet Itself is nothing, because It super-essentially transcends them all. Thus, as for the Super-Essence of the Supreme Godhead (if we would define the Transcendence of its Transcendent Goodness) it is not lawful to any lover of that Truth that is above all truth to celebrate It as Reason or Power or Mind or Life or Being, but rather as most utterly surpassing all condition, movement, life, imagination, conjecture, name, discourse, thought, conception, being, rest, dwelling, union, limit, infinity, everything that exists.

And yet since as the Subsistence of goodness It, by the very fact of Its existence, is the Cause of all things, in celebrating the bountiful Providence of the Supreme Godhead we must draw upon the whole creation. For It is both the central Force of all things and also their final Purpose and *is* Itself before them all, and they all subsist in It, and through the fact of Its existence the world is brought into being and maintained. It is that which all things desire—those that have intuitive or discursive Reason seeking It through knowledge, the next rank of beings through perception, and the rest through vital movement or the property of mere existence belonging to their state. Conscious of this, the Sacred Writers celebrate It by every Name while yet they call It Nameless.[32]

6. For instance, they call It Nameless when they say that the Supreme Godhead Itself, in one of the mystical visions whereby It was symbolically manifested, rebuked him who said: "What is your name?" [Judg. 13:18] and, as though bidding him not seek by any means of any Name to acquire a knowledge of God, made the answer: "Why do you ask in this way about My name knowing it is secret?" Now is not the secret Name precisely that which is above all names [Phil. 2:9; Eph. 1:21] and nameless and is fixed beyond every name that is named, not only in this world but also in that which is to come? On the other hand, they attribute many names to It when, for instance, they speak of It as declaring: "I am that I am" [Exod. 3:14], or "I am the Life" [John 14:6], or "the Light" [John 8:12], or "God" [Gen. 28:13], or "the Truth" [John 14:6] and when the Inspired Writers themselves celebrate the Universal Cause with many titles drawn from the whole created universe, such as "Good" [Matt. 19:17], and "Fair" [Ps. 27:4], and "Wise" [Rom. 16:27], as "Beloved" [Isa. 5:1], as "God of Gods" and "Lord of Lords" [Ps. 136:2, 3] and "Holy of Holies" [Isa. 6:3], as "Eternal" [Deut. 33:27], as "Existent" [Exod. 3:14] and as "Creator of Ages" [Gen.

---

31. This shows that the *via negativa* is based on experience and not on mere speculation.
32. This shows that there is a positive element in Dionysius's *via negativa*.

1:1–8], as "Giver of Life" [Gen. 1:20; 2:7; Job 10:12; John 10:10] as "Wisdom" [Prov. 8], as "Mind" [1 Cor. 2:16], as "Word" [John 1:1], as "Knower" [Ps. 44:21], as "possessing beforehand all the treasures of knowledge" [Col. 2:3], as "Power" [Rev. 19:1], as "Ruler" [Rev. 1:5], as "King of kings" [Rev. 17:14], as "Ancient of Days" [Dan. 7]; and as "Him that is the same and whose years shall not fail" [Ps. 102:25], as "Salvation" [Exod. 15:2], as "Righteousness" [Jer. 23:6], as "Sanctification" [1 Cor. 1:30], as "Redemption" [1 Cor. 1:30], as "Surpassing all things in greatness" [Isa. 40:15], and yet as being in "the still small breeze" [1 Kgs. 19:12].

Moreover, they say that He dwells within our minds, and in our souls [John 14:17] and bodies [1 Cor. 6:19] and in heaven and in earth [Isa. 66:1] and that, while remaining Himself, He is at one and the same time within the world around it and above it (yes, above the sky and above existence). And they call Him a Sun [Ps. 84:11], a Star [Rev. 22:16] and a Fire [Deut. 4:24] and Water [Ps. 84:6], a Wind or Spirit [John 4:24; Acts 2:2], a Dew [Hos. 14:5], a Cloud [Exod. 13:21], an Archetypal Stone [Ps. 118:22], and a Rock [Ps. 31:2, 3] and All Creation [1 Cor. 15:28] Who yet (they declare) is no created thing.

Thus, then, the Universal and Transcendent Cause must both be nameless and also possess the names of all things in order that It may truly be an universal Dominion, the Center of creation on which all things depend, as on their Cause and Origin and Goal. And that, according to the Scriptures, It may be all in all, and may be truly called the Creator of the world, originating and perfecting and maintaining all things; their Defense and Dwelling, and the Attractive Force that draws them: and all this in one single, ceaseless, and transcendent act [God is above Time]. For the Nameless Goodness is not only the cause of cohesion or life or perfection in such a way as to derive Its Name from this or that providential activity alone; no, rather It contains all things beforehand within Itself, after a simple and uncircumscribed manner through the perfect excellence of Its one and all-creative Providence, and thus we draw from the whole creation Its appropriate praises and Its Names.

8. Moreover, the sacred writers proclaim not only such titles as these (titles drawn from universal [e.g. "I am that I am," "Good," "Fair"] or from particular [e.g. Sun," "Star," "Rock," etc.] providences or providential activities) but sometimes they have gained their images from certain heavenly visions[33] (which in the holy precincts or elsewhere have illuminated the Initiates or the Prophets) and ascribing to the super-luminous nameless Goodness titles drawn from all manner of acts and functions, have clothed It in human (fiery or amber) shapes [Ezek. 1:26, 27] or forms, and have spoken of Its Eyes [Ps. 10:5], and Ears [James 5:4] and Hair [Dan. 7:9] and

---

33. Thus the complete classification is: (1) analogies drawn from the material world, (a) universal, (b) particular; (2) psychic visions.

Face [Ps. 33:17] and Hands [Job 10:8] and Wings and Feathers [Ps. 91:4] and Arms [Deut. 33:27] and Back Parts [Exod. 33:23] and Feet [Exod. 24:10]; and fashioned such mystical conceptions as its Crown [Rev. 14:14], and Throne [Ezek. 1:26, 27] and Cup [Ps. 75:8] and Mixing Bowl [Prov. 9:5], etc., concerning those things we will attempt to speak when we treat of Symbolical Divinity.

At present, collecting from the Scriptures what concerns the matter in hand, and employing as our canon the rule we have described, and guiding our search thereby, let us proceed to an exposition of God's Intelligible Names; and as the Hierarchical Law directs us in all study of Divinity, let us approach these godlike contemplations (for such indeed they are [i. e. actually godlike because human beings are deified by them]) with our hearts predisposed to the vision of God, and let us bring holy ears to the exposition of God's holy Names, implanting holy Truths in holy instruments according to the Divine command, and withholding these things from the mockery and laughter of the uninitiated,[34] or, rather, seeking to redeem those wicked people (if any such there be) from their enmity towards God.

You, therefore, O good Timothy, must guard these truths according to the holy Ordinance, nor must you utter or divulge the heavenly mysteries to the uninitiated. And for myself I pray God grant me worthily to declare the beneficent and manifold Names of the Unutterable and Nameless Godhead, and that He do not take away the word of Truth out of my mouth.

Mystical Theology, Chapters 1–5

From Dionysius the Areopagite, *On the Divine Names and On the Mystical Theology*, trans. C. E. Rolt (London: SPCK, 1920), 191–201.

Chapter 1
What Is the Divine Darkness?
Trinity that exceeds all Being, Deity, and Goodness![35] You that instruct Christians in Your heavenly wisdom! Guide us to that topmost height of mystic lore[36] that exceeds light and more than exceeds knowledge, where the simple, absolute, and unchangeable mysteries of heavenly Truth lie hidden in the dazzling obscurity of the secret Silence, outshining all brilliance with the intensity of their darkness, and surcharging our blinded intellects with the utterly impalpable and invisible fairness of glories that exceed all beauty! Such be my prayer; and you, dear Timothy, I counsel that, in the earnest exercise of mystic contemplation, you leave the senses

---

34. See *Mystical Theology* 1.2; and cf. Matt. 7:6.
35. Lit. "Super-Essential, Supra-Divine, Super-Excellent."
36. Lit. "Oracles" i.e., to the most exalted and mystical teaching of Holy Scripture.

and the activities of the intellect and all things that the senses or the intellect can perceive, and all things in this world of nothingness or in that world of being, and that, your understanding being laid to rest,[37] you strain (so far as you may) towards a union with Him whom neither being nor understanding can contain. For, by the unceasing and absolute renunciation of yourself and all things, you shall in pureness cast all things aside, and be released from all, and so shall be led upwards to the Ray of that divine Darkness that exceeds all existence.[38]

These things you must not disclose to any of the uninitiated, by whom I mean those who cling to the objects of human thought and imagine there is no super-essential reality beyond, and fancy that they know by human understanding the One Who has made Darkness His secret place. And, if the Divine Initiation is beyond such people as these, what can be said of others yet more incapable thereof, who describe the Transcendent Cause of all things by qualities drawn from the lowest order of being while they deny that it is in any way superior to the various ungodly delusions that they fondly invent in ignorance of this truth? That while it possesses all the positive attributes of the universe (being the universal Cause), yet in a stricter sense It does not possess them since It transcends them all, wherefore there is no contradiction between affirming and denying that It has them inasmuch as It precedes and surpasses all deprivation, being beyond all positive and negative distinctions?

Such at least is the teaching of the blessed Bartholomew.[39] For he says that the subject-matter of the Divine Science is vast and yet minute, and that the Gospel combines in itself both width and restriction. I thinks he has shown by these his words how marvelously he has understood that the Good Cause of all things is eloquent yet speaks few words, or rather none—possessing neither speech nor understanding because It exceeds all things in a super-essential manner, and is revealed in Its naked truth to those alone who pass right through the opposition of fair and foul, and pass beyond the topmost altitudes of holy ascent and leave behind them all divine enlightenment and voices and heavenly utterances and plunge into the Darkness where truly dwells, as says the Scripture, that One Who is beyond all things.

For not without reason[40] is the blessed Moses bidden first to undergo purification himself and then to separate himself from those who have not undergone it, and after all purification hears the many-voiced trumpets and sees many lights flash forth with pure and diverse-streaming rays,

37. Gk. *agnōstōs* refers to a transcendent or spiritual Unknowing (as distinguished from mere ignorance).
38. "The Super-Essential Ray of Divine Darkness."
39. No writings of St. Bartholomew are extant. Possibly Dionysius is inventing, though not necessarily.
40. In the following passage we get the three stages tabulated by later mystical theology: (1) purgation, (2) illumination, and (3) union.

and then stands separate from the multitudes and with the chosen priests presses forward to the topmost pinnacle of the Divine Ascent. Nevertheless he meets not with God Himself, yet he beholds—not God indeed (for God is invisible)—but the place wherein God dwells.

And this I take to signify that the divinest and the highest of the things perceived by the eyes of the body or the mind are but the symbolic language of things subordinate to the One Who transcends them all. Through these things God's incomprehensible presence is shown walking upon those heights of God's holy places that are perceived by the mind. And then It breaks forth, even from the things that are beheld and from those that behold them, and plunges the true initiate unto the Darkness of Unknowing wherein he renounces all the apprehensions of his understanding and is wrapped in that which is wholly intangible and invisible, belonging wholly to the One Who is beyond all things and to none else (whether himself or another), and being through the passive stillness of all his reasoning powers united by his highest faculty to the One Who is wholly Unknowable, of whom thus by a rejection of all knowledge he possesses a knowledge that exceeds his understanding.

Chapter 2
How It Is Necessary to Be United With and Render Praise to Him Who Is the Cause of All and Above All

To this Darkness that is beyond Light we pray that we may come, and may attain vision through the loss of sight and knowledge, and that in ceasing thus to see or to know we may learn to know that which is beyond all perception and understanding (for this emptying of our faculties is true sight and knowledge), and that we may offer the One Who transcends all things the praises of a transcendent hymnody, which we shall do by denying or removing all things that are, like people who, carving a statue out of marble, remove all the impediments that hinder the clear perceptive of the latent image and by this mere removal display the hidden statue itself in its hidden beauty. Now we must wholly distinguish this negative method from that of positive statements. For when we were making positive statements we began with the most universal statements and then through intermediate terms we came at last to particular titles.[41] But now ascending upwards from particular to universal conceptions we strip off all qualities

---

41. In the *Divine Names* Dionysius begins with the notion of Goodness (which he holds to be possessed by all things) and proceeds to Existence (which is not possessed by things that are either destroyed or yet unmade) and then to Wisdom (which is not possessed either by unconscious or irrational forms of Life), and then to qualities (such as Righteousness, Salvation, Omnipotence) or combinations of opposite qualities (such as Greatness and Smallness) that are not, in the full sense, applicable to any creature as such. Thus by adding quality to quality ("Existence" to "Goodness," "Life" to "Existence," "Wisdom" to "Life," "Salvation," etc., to "Wisdom") he reaches the conception of God. But he constantly reminds us in the *Divine Names* that these qualities apply adequately only to the manifested Godhead that, in Its ultimate Nature, transcends them.

in order that we may attain a naked knowledge of that Unknowing that in all existent things is wrapped by all objects of knowledge and that we may begin to see that super-essential Darkness that is hidden by all the light that is in existent things.

Chapter 3

What Are the Affirmative Expressions Respecting God, and What Are the Negative

Now I have in my *Outlines of Divinity* set forth those conceptions that are most proper to the affirmative method, and have shown in what sense God's holy nature is called single and in what sense triple; what is the nature of the Fatherhood and Sonship that we attribute unto It; what is meant by the articles of faith concerning the Spirit; how from the immaterial and indivisible Good the interior rays of Its goodness have their being and remain immovably in that state of rest that both within their Origin and within themselves is co-eternal with the act by which they spring from It; in what manner Jesus being above all essence[42] has stooped to an essential state in which all the truths of human nature meet; and all the other revelations of Scripture that my *Outlines of Divinity* treat.

And in the book of the *Divine Names* I have considered the meaning concerning God of the titles Good, Existent, Life, Wisdom, Power, and of the other titles that the understanding frames. And in my *Symbolic Divinity* I have considered what are the metaphorical titles drawn from the world of sense and applied to the nature of God; what are the mental or material images we form of God or the functions and instruments of activity we attribute to God; what are the places where God dwells and the robes God is adorned with; what is meant by God's anger, grief, and indignation, or the divine inebriation and wrath; what is meant by God's oath and God's malediction, by God's slumber and awaking, and all the other inspired imagery of allegoric symbolism.

And I doubt not that you have also observed how far more copious are the last terms than the first for the doctrines of God's Nature and the exposition of God's Names could not but be briefer than the *Symbolic Divinity*.[43] For the more that we soar upwards the more our language becomes restricted to the compass of purely intellectual conceptions, even as in the present instance plunging into the Darkness that is above the intellect we shall find ourselves reduced not merely to brevity of speech but even to absolute dumbness both of speech and thought. Now in the former treatises the course of the argument, as it came down from the highest to the

---

42. This is a case of *communicatio idiomatum* (cf. the title "Mother of God" applied to the Blessed Virgin Mary). The Godhead of our Lord is Super-Essential, not His Manhood.

43. The *Symbolical Divinity* was an attempt to spiritualize "popular" theology; the *Divine Names* sought to spiritualize philosophical theology; the present treatise is a direct essay on Spiritual Theology.

lowest categories, embraced an ever-widening number of conceptions that increased at each stage of the descent, but in the present treatise it mounts upwards from below towards the category of transcendence, and in proportion to its ascent it contracts its terminology, and when the whole ascent is passed it will be totally dumb, being at last wholly united with the One Whom words cannot describe.

But why is it, you will ask, that after beginning from the highest category when one method was affirmative, we begin from the lowest category where it is negative?[44] Because, when affirming the existence of that which transcends all affirmation, we were obliged to start from that which is most akin to It, and then to make the affirmation on which the rest depended. But when pursuing the negative method, to reach that which is beyond all negation, we must start by applying our negations to those qualities that differ most from the ultimate goal. Surely it is truer to affirm that God is life and goodness than that God is air or stone, and truer to deny that drunkenness or fury can be attributed to God than to deny that we may apply to God the categories of human thought.

Chapter 4
That God Who Is the Pre-eminent Cause of Everything Sensibly Perceived Is Not Himself Any One of the Things Sensibly Perceived

We therefore maintain that the universal Cause transcending all things is neither impersonal nor lifeless, nor irrational nor without understanding: in short, that It is not a material body and therefore does not possess outward shape or intelligible form, or quality, or quantity, or solid weight; nor has It any local existence that can be perceived by sight or touch; nor has It the power of perceiving or being perceived; nor does It suffer any vexation or disorder through the disturbance of earthly passions, or any feebleness through the tyranny of material chances, or any want of light; nor any change, or decay, or division, or deprivation, or ebb and flow, or anything else that the senses can perceive. None of these things can be either identified with it or attributed unto It.

Chapter 5
That God Who is the Pre-eminent Cause of Everything Intelligibly Perceived Is Not Himself Any One of the Things Intelligibly Perceived

Once more, ascending yet higher we maintain[45] that It is not soul, or mind, or endowed with the faculty of imagination, conjecture, reason, or understanding; nor is It any act of reason or understanding; nor can It be described by the reason or perceived by the understanding, since It is not

44. In the *Divine Names* the order of procedure was: Goodness, Existence, Life, etc. Now it passes from sense-perception to thought.

45. It is not (1) a Thinking Subject; nor (2) an Act or Faculty of Thought; nor (3) an Object of Thought.

number, or order, or greatness, or littleness, or equality, or inequality, and since It is not immovable nor in motion, or at rest, and has no power, and is not power or light, and does not live, and is not life; nor is It personal essence, or eternity, or time; nor can It be grasped by the understanding since It is not knowledge or truth; nor is It kingship or wisdom; nor is It one, nor is It unity, nor is It Godhead or Goodness; nor is It a Spirit, as we understand the term, since It is not Sonship or Fatherhood; nor is It any other thing such as we or any other being can have knowledge of; nor does It belong to the category of non-existence or to that of existence; nor do existent beings know It as it actually is, nor does It know them as they actually are; nor can the reason attain to It to name It or to know It; nor is it darkness, nor is It light, or error, or truth; nor can any affirmation or negation apply to it. For while applying affirmations or negations to those orders of being that come next to It, we apply not unto It either affirmation or negation, inasmuch as It transcends all affirmation by being the perfect and unique Cause of all things, and transcends all negation by the pre-eminence of Its simple and absolute nature—free from every limitation and beyond them all.[46]

SELECTION **10**

Maximus Confessor

**Chapters on Knowledge,
"Second Century," 1–11**

One of the most important Byzantine theologians, Maximus Confessor (ca. 580–662) integrated the Trinitarian and christological emphases of Origen and the Cappadocians with a profound ascetical theology of prayer (drawn primarily from Dionysius the Areopagite). His various writings depict how the divine Logos, who is reflected in the various *logoi* of creatures, brings all creatures into communion with the will of God. Although created to align our wills with our Creator, we have separated ourselves from God by misusing God's creation for the sake of our passions. But through the incarnation, Jesus Christ, the Logos of God, has become our future destiny, taking within himself the oppositions that break the unity of the created universe. Assuming our humanity, Christ is the means for our divinization, which begins in the baptismal rebirth that renews our "mode of existence" (*tropos*) without changing the "essential principle" (*logos*) for which we were created.

46. It is (1) richer than all concrete forms of positive existence; (2) more simple than the barest abstraction.

Maximus is best known for his contribution to the Monothelite controversy. Countering those who contended that Christ had only one will and activity (*energeia*), Maximus argued (following the Council of Chalcedon, which affirmed that Christ was one person with two natures) that "will" and "activity" pertained to a nature rather than to a person. Thus Christ (although one person) had two wills: a divine will and a human will. In line with the patristic principle that whatever was not assumed in the incarnation was not healed in the redemption, he argued that Christ's not having a human will would have meant that our human sinful will would have not have been saved.

For Maximus, this argument was grounded not merely in speculative reason but also in a spirituality deeply rooted in Trinitarian and christological assumptions that, in turn, were central to his reinterpretation of Dionysius the Areopagite's apophatic theology. Following the Cappadocians who (in their critique of Eunomius) emphasized that the divine nature transcends all human reason, Maximus appropriated Dionysius's "apophaticism" (from *apophasis*, the Greek work for "negation") in a way that stressed the way it leads to our union with God through the Word incarnate, Jesus Christ—a union that ultimately transcends all human concepts and words.

The following selection, from his *Chapters on Knowledge*, discusses how the Trinity is the one God, "identically monad and triad," and how we might rally from the "division caused by disobedience" so that we can, through the "grain of mustard . . . sown by faith in the Spirit in the hearts of those who receive him" reach the very of Word of God himself in a way that "transcends knowledge."

From *Maximus Confessor: Selected Writings*, trans. with notes by George Berthold; intro. by Jaroslav Pelikan (New York: Paulist Press, 1985), 147–50.

1. There is one God because one Godhead, one, without beginning, simple and supersubstantial, without parts and undivided, identically monad and triad; entirely monad and entirely triad; wholly monad as to substance, and wholly triad as to hypostases. For the Father, Son, and Holy Spirit are the Godhead, and the Godhead is in Father and Son and Holy Spirit. The whole is in the whole Father and the whole Father is in the whole of it; the whole is in the Son and the whole Son is in the whole of it. And the whole is in the Holy Spirit and the whole Holy Spirit is in the whole of it. The whole is the Father and in the whole Father; and the whole Father is the whole of it. And the whole is the whole Son and the whole is in the whole Son and the whole Son is the whole of it, and the Son is in the whole of it. And the whole is the Holy Spirit and in the Holy Spirit and the Holy Spirit is the whole of it and the whole Holy Spirit is in the whole of it. For neither is the Godhead partly in the Father nor is the Father partly God; nor is the Godhead partly in the Son nor the Son partly God; nor is the Godhead

partly in the Holy Spirit nor the Holy Spirit partly God. For neither is the Godhead divisible nor are Father, Son, and Holy Spirit imperfectly God. Rather the whole and complete Godhead is entirely in the entire Father and wholly complete it is entirely in the entire Son; and wholly complete it is entirely in the entire Holy Spirit. For the whole Father is entirely in the whole Son and Holy Spirit, and the whole Son is entirely in the whole Father and Holy Spirit; and the whole Holy Spirit is entirely in the whole Father and Son. This is why there is only one God, Father, Son, and Holy Spirit. For there is one and the same essence, power, and act of the Father and Son and Holy Spirit, and no one of them can exist or be conceived without the others.[47]

2. Every concept involves those who think and what is thought, subject and object. But God is neither of those who think nor of what is thought for he is beyond them. Otherwise he would be limited if as a thinker he stood in need of the relationship to what was thought or as an object of thought he would naturally lapse to the level of the subject thinking through a relationship. Thus there remains only the rejoinder that God can neither conceive nor be conceived but is beyond conception and being conceived. To conceive and to be conceived pertain by nature to those things which are secondary to him.[48]

3. Every concept has its motion about substance, as a quality clearly has its place in a substance. For it is not possible that what is completely free and simple and existing by itself could admit something which is not free and simple. But God is altogether simple in both ways and is a substance which is not present in a subject and a conception which has nothing of the subject in him, is not of those things which conceive or are conceived because he is obviously above essence and thought.

4. Just as straight lines which proceed from the center are seen as entirely undivided in that position, so the one who has been made worthy to be in God will recognize in himself with a certain simple and undivided knowledge all the preexisting principles of things.[49]

5. Formed by its objects, the one concept gives rise to many concepts when each of the objects takes formal shape.[50] But when it has gone beyond a multitude of sense experiences and thoughts which have formed

47. This trinitarian chapter, the longest of the entire treatise, parallels the theological prologue of the first century (1–10) and like it is meant to serve as a theological framework and foundation for the ascetical and mystical chapters to follow. In accordance with contemporary Byzantine standards it is arranged not only in proper theological but also rhetorical structure.

48. Evagrius approaches this subject in *Kephalia Gnostica* 4:77 but without the intellectual precision of Maximus, who insists on the unknowableness of God. Cf. Dionysius, *Mystical Theology* 1:1, and so on.

49. The image of unity at a circle's center . . . stems from Proclus through Dionysius. Cf. Hans Urs von Balthasar, *Kosmische Liturgie: Das Weltbild Maximus des Bekenners* (Einsiedeln: Johannes-Verlag, 1961), 593–594.

50. I.e., one object of thought can be viewed under many aspects and formalities, and thus the thought multiplies.

it, it becomes completely without form. It is then that the Word which is above thought aptly holds it fast and makes it his own, causing it to cease from those forms produced from thoughts of another sort; thus the one who experiences this "rests from his works just as God did from his" [Heb. 4:10].

6. The one who achieves a perfection attainable to men here below bears as fruit for God love, joy, peace, endurance for the future, incorruption and eternity, and things similar to these. And perhaps the first things belong to the one who is perfect in the active life while the second belong to the one who through genuine knowledge has gone beyond created things.[51]

7. Just as sin is the fruit of disobedience so is virtue the fruit of obedience. And just as a transgression of the commandments is a concomitant of disobedience and a separation[52] from the one who enjoined them, so does the keeping of the commandments and union with the one who gave them follow obedience. Therefore the one who has observed a commandment out of obedience has both fulfilled righteousness and also has preserved unbroken the union of love with the giver of the commandments. But the one who out of disobedience transgresses a commandment has both committed sin and separated himself as well from loving union with the giver of the commandments.

8. The one who rallies from the division caused by disobedience first separates himself from the passions, then from passionate thoughts, then from nature and the things of nature, then from concepts and knowledge derived from them, and finally getting away from the abundant variety of the reasons concerning Providence he reaches in a way which transcends knowledge the very Word of God himself. In him the mind considers its own stability and "rejoices with unutterable joy" [1 Pet. 1:8], as a peace comes from God which surpasses all understanding [cf. Phil. 4:7] and which continually keeps secure the one who is worthy of it.

9. The fear of hell trains beginners to flee from evil, the desire for the reward of good things gives to the advanced the eagerness for the practice of virtues. But the mystery of love removes the mind from all created things, causing it to be blind to all that is less than God. Only those who have become blind to all that is less than God does the Lord instruct by showing them more divine things.[53]

10. The word of God is like a grain of mustard seed; before its cultivation it appears to be very small, but when it has been properly cultivated

---

51. Two Pauline lists (cf. Gal 5:22 and Rom 2:7), which Maximus assigns to praxis and gnosis.

52. *Diairesis*. For Maximus this term has the negative connotation of disruption of the harmony of nature brought on by sin. See the Cappadocian references in von Balthasar, *Kosmische Liturgie*, 516.

53. This mystical blindness, which Hans Urs von Balthasar calls a negative description of love, can be found in Evagrius, *Praktikos* 62. The fear/desire contrast is another instance of Maximus' use of these important categories (*Phobos/Pothos*).

it shows itself to be so evidently big that the noble reasons of creatures of sense and mind come as birds to rest in it [cf. Matt. 13:31–32]. For the reasons of all things are set in it as finite beings, but it is limited by none of these beings. Thus the Lord said that the one who has faith as a mustard seed could move a mountain by his word, which means to chase away the might of the devil from us and to change over from his sway [cf. Matt. 17:20].

11. The grain of mustard seed is the Lord, who is sown by faith in the Spirit in the hearts of those who receive him. The one who carefully cultivates it through the virtues moves the mountain of earthly purpose by driving away from himself with authority the tenacious habit of wickedness. Then the reasons and forms of the commandments, which are the divine powers, will come as birds from heaven to rest in him.

CHAPTER 2

God in the Medieval Period

Anselm of Canterbury

Proslogion, **Preface,**
Chapters 1–5, 18–19, 22–26

A Benedictine monk and archbishop of Canterbury, Anselm (1033–1109) bridged the contemplative theology of the patristic period with the scholastic theology of the medieval period. Influenced primarily by Augustine but also by Boethius, Pseudo-Dionysius, John Scotus Erigena, and his own reading of Plato, he assumed the following: Truth is eternal; there are degrees of reality (with God as the supremely real being); and truth in all things is ultimately one truth. Given these premises, he presupposed not only that theology entails "faith seeking understanding" but also that it could provide "necessary reasons" (*ratio necessaria*) for Christian beliefs—for both believers and nonbelievers.

One of his most well-known works is the *Proslogion*, originally titled *Fides quaerens intellectum (Faith Seeking Understanding)*. Written after the *Monologion*, a meditation on why the various divine attributes are necessary, the *Proslogion* seeks to make a more elegant argument. It seeks to demonstrate not only that God exists and that all beings depend on God for their existence but also that all the divine attributes cohere within a single proof. Beginning with a prayer that calls on God to renew and restore the image of God created within him, Anselm declares that he does not seek to understand in order to believe but rather to "believe in order to understand." His famous proof begins in chapter 2 with the observation that even a "fool" (who says there is no God) can imagine "something than which nothing greater can be thought." Although it is one thing to exist in thought and another to exist in reality, something "than which nothing greater can be thought" cannot exist only in thought because if it exists only in thought then it cannot be "that than which nothing greater can be thought." (Note the assumption here that what exists in reality must be greater than that which exists only in thought). Therefore, a being than which nothing greater can be conceived must exist not only in thought but also in reality, and this being must be God. The proof is then restated in negative form in chapter 3.

With this proof as an organizing principle, the rest of the treatise contemplates the various attributes that manifest God, the highest of all beings, who alone exists through itself and in whom all other beings exist (chaps. 5–23). It concludes with a meditation that praises God, the supreme good, for enabling us to participate in the goods these divine attributes manifest (chaps. 24–26).

From *St. Anselm,* trans. Sidney Norton Deane
(Chicago: Open Court, 1903), 1–35.

Preface

After I had published, at the solicitous entreaties of certain brethren, a brief work [the *Monologium*] as an example of meditation on the grounds of faith in the person of one who investigates in a course of silent reasoning with himself matters of which he is ignorant—considering that this book was knit together by the linking of many arguments—I began to ask myself whether there might be found a single argument that would require no other for its proof than itself alone and alone would suffice to demonstrate that God truly exists and that there is a supreme good requiring nothing else, which all other things require for their existence and well-being, and whatever we believe regarding the divine Being.

Although I often and earnestly directed my thought to this end—and at some times that which I sought seemed to be just within my reach while again it wholly evaded my mental vision—at last in despair I was about to cease, as if from the search for a thing which could not be found. But when I wished to exclude this thought altogether—lest, by busying my mind to no purpose, it should keep me from other thoughts in which I might be successful—then more and more, though I was unwilling and shunned it, it began to force itself upon me, with a kind of importunity. So, one day, when I was exceedingly wearied with resisting its importunity, in the very conflict of my thoughts, the proof of which I had despaired offered itself so that I eagerly embraced the thoughts which I was strenuously repelling.

Thinking, therefore, that what I rejoiced to have found would if put in writing be welcome to some readers, of this very matter, and of some others, I have written the following treatise in the person of one who strives to lift his mind to the contemplation of God and seeks to understand what he believes. In my judgment, neither this work nor the other that I mentioned above deserved to be called a book or to bear the name of an author. And yet I thought they ought not to be sent forth without some title by which they might, in some sort, invite one into whose hands they fell to their perusal. I accordingly gave each a title, that the first might be known as, *An Example of Meditation on the Grounds of Faith*, and its sequel as, *Faith Seeking Understanding*. But, after, both had been copied by many under these titles, many urged me, and especially Hugo, the reverend Archbishop of Lyons, who discharges the apostolic office in Gaul, who instructed me to this effect on his apostolic authority—to prefix my name to these writings. And that this might be done more fitly, I named the first, *Monologion*, that is, A Soliloquy; but the second, *Proslogion*, that is, A Discourse.

Chapter 1

Exhortation to Contemplate God

Up now, slight man! Flee, for a little while, your occupations; hide yourself for a time, from your disturbing thoughts. Cast aside, now, your burdensome cares, and put away your toilsome business. Yield room for some little time to God and rest for a little time in him. Enter the inner chamber of your mind. Shut out all thoughts save that of God, and such as can aid you in seeking him. Close your door and seek him. Speak now, my whole heart! Speak now to God, saying, I seek your face; your face, Lord, will I seek [Ps. 27:8]. And come you now, O Lord my God, teach my heart where and how it may seek you, where and how it may find you.

Lord, if you are not here, where shall I seek you, being absent? But if you are everywhere, why do I not see you present? Truly you dwell in unapproachable light. But where is unapproachable light, or how shall I come to it? Or who shall lead me to that light and into it, that I may see you in it? Again, by what marks, under what form, shall I seek you? I have never seen you, O Lord, my God. I do not know your form. What, O most high Lord, shall this man do, an exile far from you? What shall your servant do, anxious in his love of you, and cast out afar from your face? He wants to see you and your face is too far from him. He longs to come to you and your dwelling-place is inaccessible. He is eager to find you and knows not your place. He desires to seek you and does not know your face. Lord, you are my God, and you are my Lord, and never have I seen you. It is you that have made me, and have made me anew, and have bestowed on me all the blessing I enjoy. And not yet do I know you. Finally, I was created to see you and not yet have I done that for which I was made.

O wretched lot of man, when he has lost that for which he was made! O hard and terrible fate! Alas, what has he lost, and what has he found? What has departed and what remains? He has lost the blessedness for which he was made and has found the misery for which he was not made. That has departed without which nothing is happy and that remains which, in itself, is only miserable. Man once did eat the bread of angels, for which he hungers now. He eats now the bread of sorrows, of which he knew not then. Alas! For the mourning of all humankind, for the universal lamentation of the sons [and daughters] of Hades! He choked with satiety, we sigh with hunger. He abounded, we beg. He possessed in happiness, and miserably forsook his possession; we suffer want in unhappiness, and feel a miserable longing, and alas! We remain empty.

Why did he not keep for us, when he could so easily, that whose lack we should feel so heavily? Why did he shut us away from the light and cover us over with darkness? With what purpose did he rob us of life and inflict death upon us? Wretches that we are, whence have we been driven out? Whither are we driven on? Whence hurled? Whither consigned to ruin?

From a native country into exile, from the vision of God into our present blindness, from the joy of immortality into the bitterness and horror of death. Miserable exchange of how great a good, for how great an evil! Heavy loss, heavy grief, heavy all our fate!

But alas! Wretched that I am, one of the sons of Eve, far removed from God! What have I undertaken? What have I accomplished? Whither was I striving? How far have I come? To what did I aspire? Amid what thoughts am I sighing? I sought blessings, and lo! Confusion. I strove toward God, and I stumbled on myself. I sought calm in privacy and I found tribulation and grief in my inmost thoughts. I wished to smile in the joy of my mind and I am compelled to frown by the sorrow of my heart. Gladness was hoped for, and lo! A source of frequent sighs!

And you too, O Lord, how long? How long, O Lord, do you forget us? How long do you turn your face from us? When will you look upon us and hear us? When will you enlighten our eyes and show us your face? When will you restore yourself to us? Look upon us, Lord. Hear us, enlighten us, reveal yourself to us. Restore yourself to us—that it may be well with us—yourself, without whom it is so ill with us. Pity our toiling and striving toward you since we can do nothing without you. You do invite us; do help us. I beseech you, O Lord, that I may not lose hope in sighs but may breathe anew in hope. Lord, my heart is made bitter by its desolation. Sweeten it, I beseech you, with your consolation. Lord, in hunger I began to seek you. I beseech you that I may not cease to hunger for you. In hunger I have come to you; let me not go unfed. I have come in poverty to the Rich, in misery to the Compassionate; let me not return empty and despised. And if before I eat I sigh, grant—even after sighs—that which I may eat. Lord, I am bowed down and can only look downward; raise me up that I may look upward. My iniquities have gone over my head. They overwhelm me. And, like a heavy load, they weigh me down. Free me from them. Unburden me, that the pit of iniquities may not close over me.

Be it mine to look up to your light—even from afar, even from the depths. Teach me to seek you and reveal yourself to me when I seek you, for I cannot seek you except you teach me, nor find you except you reveal yourself. Let me seek you in longing. Let me long for you in seeking. Let me find you in love and love you in finding. Lord, I acknowledge and I thank you that you have created me in this your image in order that I may be mindful of you, may conceive of you, and love you. But that image has been so consumed and wasted away by vices and obscured by the smoke of wrong-doing that it cannot achieve that for which it was made except you renew it and create it anew. I do not endeavor, O Lord, to penetrate your sublimity, for in no wise do I compare my understanding with that. But I long to understand in some degree your truth, which my heart believes and loves. For I do not seek to understand that I may believe, but I believe in order to understand. For this also I believe—that unless I believed, I should not understand.

Chapter 2
Truly There Is a God, although the Fool Has Said in His Heart, "There is no God"

And so, Lord, you who give understanding to faith, give me so far as you know it to be profitable to understand that you are as we believe—and that you are that which we believe. And indeed, we believe that you are a being than which nothing greater can be conceived. Or is there no such nature since the fool has said in his heart, there is no God? [Ps. 14:1]. But, at any rate, this very fool, when he hears of this being of which I speak—a being than which nothing greater can be conceived—understands what he hears and what he understands is in his understanding, although he does not understand it to exist.

For, it is one thing for an object to be in the understanding and another to understand that the object exists. When a painter first conceives of what he will afterwards perform, he has it in his understanding, but he does not yet understand it to be because he has not yet performed it. But after he has made the painting, he both has it in his understanding and he understands that it exists because he has made it.

Hence, even the fool is convinced that something exists in the understanding, at least, than which nothing greater can be conceived. For, when he hears of this, he understands it. And whatever is understood exists in the understanding. And assuredly that than which nothing greater can be conceived cannot exist in the understanding alone. For suppose it exists in the understanding alone: then it can be conceived to exist in reality, which is greater.

Therefore, if that than which nothing greater can be conceived exists in the understanding alone, the very being than which nothing greater can be conceived is one than which a greater can be conceived. But obviously this is impossible. Hence, there is no doubt that there exists a being than which nothing greater can be conceived and it exists both in the understanding and in reality.

Chapter 3
God Cannot Be Conceived Not to Exist

And it assuredly exists so truly, that it cannot be conceived not to exist. For, it is possible to conceive of a being which cannot be conceived not to exist, and this is greater than one which can be conceived not to exist. Hence, if that than which nothing greater can be conceived can be conceived not to exist, it is not that than which nothing greater can be conceived. But this is an irreconcilable contradiction. There is then so truly a being than which nothing greater can be conceived to exist that it cannot even be conceived not to exist. And you are this being, O Lord, our God.

So truly, therefore, do you exist, O Lord, my God, that you cannot be conceived not to exist, and rightly. For if a mind could conceive of a being better than you, the creature would rise above the Creator, and this is most absurd. And, indeed, whatever else there is, except you alone, can be conceived not to exist. To you alone, therefore, it belongs to exist more truly than all other beings, and hence in a higher degree than all others. For, whatever else exists does not exist so truly, and hence in a less degree it belongs to it to exist. Why, then, has the fool said in his heart, there is no God [Ps. 14:1] since it is so evident to a rational mind that you do exist in the highest degree of all? Why except that he is dull and a fool?

Chapter 4
How the Fool Has Said in His Heart What Cannot Be Conceived

But how has the fool said in his heart what he could not conceive? Or how is it that he could not conceive what he said in his heart? Since it is the same to say in the heart and to conceive.

But, if really, no, since really he both conceived because he said in his heart and did not say in his heart because he could not conceive. There is more than one way in which a thing is said in the heart or conceived. For, in one sense, an object is conceived when the word signifying it is conceived; and in another when the very entity that the object is, is understood.

In the former sense, then, God can be conceived not to exist, but in the latter not at all. For no one who understands what fire and water are can conceive fire to be water, in accordance with the nature of the facts themselves, although this is possible according to the words. So, then, no one who understands what God is can conceive that God does not exist—although he says these words in his heart, either without any or with some foreign, signification. For God is that than which a greater cannot be conceived. And he, who thoroughly understands this, assuredly understands that this being so truly exists, that not even in concept can it be non-existent. Therefore, he who understands that God so exists cannot conceive that he does not exist.

I thank you, gracious Lord, I thank you because what I formerly believed by your bounty, I now so understand by your illumination—that if I were unwilling to believe that you do exist, I should not be able not to understand this to be true.

Chapter 5
Only God Is Self-existent Being, Who Creates from Nothing

What are you, then, Lord God, than whom nothing greater can be conceived? But what are you, except that which, as the highest of all beings, alone exists through itself and creates all other things from nothing? For, whatever is not this is less than a thing which can be conceived of. But this cannot be conceived of you. What good, therefore, does the supreme Good lack, through which every good is? Therefore, you are just, truthful, blessed, and whatever it is better to be than not to be. For it is better to be just than not just; better to be blessed than not blessed.

Chapter 18
God Is Life, Wisdom, Eternity, and Every True Good

And lo, again confusion. Lo, again grief and mourning meet him who seeks for joy and gladness. My soul now hoped for satisfaction, and lo, again it is overwhelmed with need. I desired now to feast, and lo, I hunger more. I tried to rise to the light of God, and I have fallen back into my darkness. No, not only have I fallen into it, but I feel that I am enveloped in it. I fell before my mother conceived me. Truly, in darkness I was conceived, and in the cover of darkness I was born. Truly, in him we all fell, in whom we all sinned. In him we all lost, who kept easily, and wickedly lost to himself and to us that which when we wish to seek it, we do not know; when we seek it, we do not find; when we find, it is not that which we seek.

Do help me for your goodness' sake! Lord, I sought your face; your face, Lord, will I seek; hide not your face far from me [Ps. 27:8]. Free me from myself toward you. Cleanse, heal, sharpen, enlighten the eye of my mind, that it may behold you. Let my soul recover its strength, and with all its understanding let it strive toward you, O Lord. What are you, Lord, what are you? What shall my heart conceive you to be?

Assuredly you are life, you are wisdom, you are truth, you are goodness, you are blessedness, you are eternity, and you are every true good. Many are these attributes. My restricted understanding cannot see so many at one view, that it may be gladdened by all at once. How, then, O Lord, are you all these things? Are they parts of you, or is each one of these rather the whole, which you are? For whatever is composed of parts is not altogether one, but is in some sort plural, and different from itself, and either in fact or in concept is capable of dissolution.

But these things are alien to you than whom nothing better can be conceived of. Hence, there are no parts in you, Lord, nor are you more than one. But you are so truly a unitary being, and so identical with yourself, that in no respect are you unlike yourself; rather you are unity itself, indivisible by any conception. Therefore, life and wisdom and the rest are not parts of you, but all are one; and each of these is the whole, which you are, and which all the rest are.

In this way, then, it appears that you have no parts, and that your eternity, which you are, is nowhere and never a part of you or of your eternity. But everywhere you are as a whole and your eternity exists as a whole forever.

Chapter 19

God Does Not Exist in Place or Time, but All Things Exist in God

But if through your eternity you have been and are and will be—and to have been is not to be destined to be and to be is not to have been or to be destined to be—how does your eternity exist as a whole forever? Or is it true that nothing of your eternity passes away, so that it is not now; and that nothing of it is destined to be, as if it were not yet?

You were not, then, yesterday, nor will you be tomorrow but yesterday and today and tomorrow you are. Or, rather, neither yesterday nor today nor tomorrow you are but simply you are, outside all time. For yesterday and today and tomorrow have no existence, except in time. But you, although nothing exists without you, nevertheless do not exist in space or time, but all things exist in you. For nothing contains you, but you contain all things.

Chapter 22

God Alone Is What God Is and Who God Is;
All Things Need God for Their Being and Their Well-being

Therefore, you alone, O Lord, are what you are; and you are he who you are. For, what is one thing in the whole and another in the parts, and in which there is any mutable element, is not altogether what it is. And what begins from non-existence and can be conceived not to exist, and unless it subsists through something else, returns to non-existence. And what has a past existence, which is no longer, or a future existence, which is not yet—this does not properly and absolutely exist.

But you are what you are, because, whatever you are at any time, or in any way, you are as a whole and forever. And you are he who you are, properly and simply. For you have neither a past existence nor a future, but only a present existence; nor can you be conceived as at any time non-existent. But you are life, and light, and wisdom, and blessedness, and many goods of this nature. And yet you are only one supreme good. You are all-sufficient to yourself, and need none. And you are he whom all things need for their existence and wellbeing.

Chapter 23

This Good Is Equally Father, and Son, and Holy Spirit

This good that you are God the Father; this is your Word, that is, your Son. For nothing, other than what you are, or greater or less than you, can be in the Word by which you express yourself. For your Word is true, as you are truthful. And, hence, it is truth itself, just as you are. No other truth than you; and you are of so simple a nature, that of you nothing can be born other than what you are. This very good is the one love common to you and to your Son, that is, the Holy Spirit proceeding from both. For this love is not unequal to you or to your Son; seeing that you do love yourself and him, and he, you and himself, to the whole extent of your being and his. Nor is there anything else proceeding from you and from him, which is not unequal to you and to him. Nor can anything proceed from the supreme simplicity, other than what this, from which it proceeds, is.

But what each is, separately, this is all the Trinity at once, Father, Son, and Holy Spirit; seeing that each separately is none other than the supremely simple unity, and the supremely unitary simplicity which can neither be multiplied nor varied. Moreover, there is a single necessary Being. Now, this is that single, necessary Being, in which is every good; no, which is every good, and a single entire good, and the only good.

Chapter 24
If Created Life is Good, How Good Is the Creative Life!
And now, my soul, arouse and lift up all your understanding, and conceive, so far as you can, of what character and how great is that good! For, if individual goods are delectable, conceive in earnestness how delectable is that good that contains the pleasantness of all goods; and not such as we have experienced in created objects, but as different as the Creator from the creature. For, if the created life is good, how good is the creative life! If the salvation given is delightful, how delightful is the salvation that has given all salvation! If wisdom in the knowledge of the created world is lovely, how lovely is the wisdom that has created all things from nothing! Finally, if there are many great delights in delectable things, what and how great is the delight in him who has made these delectable things!

Chapter 25
What Goods Belong to Those Who Enjoy This Good!
Who shall enjoy this good? And what shall belong to him, and what shall not belong to him? At any rate, whatever he shall wish shall be his, and whatever he shall not wish shall not be his. For, these goods of body and soul will be such as eye has not seen nor ear heard, neither has the heart conceived [Isa. 64:4; 1 Cor. 2:9].

Why, then, do you wander abroad, slight man, in your search for the goods of your soul and your body? Love the one good in which are all goods, and it suffices. Desire the simple good which is every good, and it is enough. For, what do you love, my flesh? What do you desire, my soul? There, there is whatever you love, whatever you desire.

If beauty delights you, there shall the righteous shine forth as the sun [Matt. 13:43]. If swiftness or endurance, or freedom of body, which nothing can withstand, delight you, they shall be as angels of God—because it is sown a natural body, it is raised a spiritual body [1 Cor. 15:44]—in power certainly, though not in nature. If it is a long and sound life that pleases you, there a healthful eternity is, and an eternal health. For the righteous shall live forever [Wis. 5:15], and the salvation of the righteous is of the Lord [Ps. 37:39]. If it is satisfaction of hunger, they shall be satisfied when the glory of the Lord has appeared [Ps. 17:15]. If it is quenching of thirst, they shall be abundantly satisfied with the fatness of your house [Ps. 36:8]. If it is melody, there the choirs of angels sing forever, before God. If it is any not impure, but pure, pleasure, you shall make them drink of the river of your pleasures, O God [Ps. 36:8].

If it is wisdom that delights you, the very wisdom of God will reveal itself to them. If friendship, they shall love God more than themselves, and one another as themselves. And God shall love them more than they themselves—for they love God, and themselves, and one another, through God, and God, himself and them, through himself. If concord, they shall all have a single will.

If power, they shall have all power to fulfill their will, as God to fulfill his. For, as God will have power to do what he wills, through himself, so they will have power, through him, to do what they will. For, as they will not will nothing else than he, he shall will whatever they will; and what he shall will cannot fail to be. If honor and riches, God shall make his good and faithful servants rulers over many things [Luke 12:42]. No, they shall be called sons of God, and gods— and where his Son shall be, there they shall be also, heirs indeed of God, and joint-heirs with Christ [Rom. 8:17].

If true security delights you, undoubtedly they shall be as sure that those goods, or rather that good, will never and in no wise fail them; as they shall be sure that they will not lose it of their own accord; and that God, who loves them, will not take it away from those who love him against their will; and that nothing more powerful than God will separate him from them against his will and theirs.

But what, or how great, is the joy, where such and so great is the good! Heart of humans, needy heart, heart acquainted with sorrows, no, over-whelmed with sorrows, how greatly would you rejoice, if you did abound in all these things! Ask your inmost mind whether it could contain its joy over so great a blessedness of its own.

Yet assuredly, if any other whom you did love altogether as yourself possessed the same blessedness, your joy would be doubled, because you would rejoice not less for him than for yourself. But, if two, or three, or many more, had the same joy, you would rejoice as much for each one as for yourself, if you did love each as yourself. Hence, in that perfect love of innumerable blessed angels and sainted men, where none shall love another less than himself, every one shall rejoice for each of the others as for himself.

If, then, the heart of a human will scarce contain its joy over its own so great good, how shall it contain so many and so great joys? And doubtless, seeing that everyone loves another so far as he rejoices in the other's good, and as, in that perfect felicity, each one should love God beyond compare, more than himself and all the others with him; so he will rejoice beyond reckoning in the felicity of God, more than in his own and that of all the others with him.

But if they shall so love God with all their heart, and all their mind, and all their soul, that still all the heart, and all the mind, and all the soul shall not suffice for the worthiness of this love; doubtless they will so rejoice with all their heart, and all their mind, and all their soul, that all the heart, and all the mind, and all the soul shall not suffice for the fullness of their joy.

Chapter 26
The Joy the Lord Promises

My God and my Lord, my hope and the joy of my heart, speak unto my soul and tell me whether this is the joy of which you tell us through your Son: "Ask and you shall receive, that your joy may be full" [John 16:24]. For I have found a joy that is full, and more than full. For when heart and mind and soul and the entire person are full of that joy, joy beyond measure will still remain. Hence, not all of that joy shall enter into those who rejoice but they who rejoice shall wholly enter into that joy.

Show me, O Lord, show your servant in his heart whether this is the joy into which your servants shall enter, who shall enter into the joy of their Lord. But that joy, surely, with which your chosen ones shall rejoice, eye has not seen nor ear heard, neither has it entered into the heart of a human [Isa. 64:4; 1 Cor. 2:9]. Not yet, then, have I told or conceived, O Lord, how greatly those blessed ones of yours shall rejoice. Doubtless they shall rejoice according as they shall love; and they shall love according as they shall know. How far they will know you, Lord, then! And how much they will love you! Truly, eye has not seen, nor ear heard, neither has it entered into the heart of a human in this life, how far they shall know you, and how much they shall love you in that life.

I pray, O God, to know you, to love you that I may rejoice in you. And if I cannot attain to full joy in this life may I at least advance from day to day, until that joy shall come to the full. Let the knowledge of you advance in me here, and there be made full. Let the love of you increase, and there let it be full, that here my joy may be great in hope, and there full in truth. Lord, through your Son you do command, no, you do counsel us to ask; and you do promise that we shall receive, that our joy may be full. I ask, O Lord, as you do counsel through our wonderful Counselor. I will receive what you promise by virtue of your truth, that my joy may be full. Faithful God, I ask. I will receive, that my joy may be full. Meanwhile, let my mind meditate upon it. Let my tongue speak of it. Let my heart love it. Let my mouth talk of it. Let my soul hunger for it. Let my flesh thirst for it. Let my whole being desire it, until I enter into your joy, O Lord, who are the Three and the One God, blessed for ever and ever. Amen.

SELECTION **2**

Bonaventure

The Journey of the Mind into God, Chapters 5–7

A leader in the Franciscan order, Bonaventure (1221–1274) was one of the most influential theologians of the medieval period. On St. Francis's feast day in October 1259, Bonaventure visited Mt. Alverna, where Francis had received the stigmata, the wounds of Christ. There he received a vision of the crucified Christ as a six-winged seraph, which served as inspiration for his most influential work, *The Journey of the Mind into God*.[1] In seven chapters, the book traces a journey through the crucified Christ as road and door and up the six wings of the seraph in three stages: from the exterior world to the interior mind to an encounter with God. The first two chapters are the two lower wings, where we contemplate God (following Francis) in the beauty and goodness of the natural world. The next two chapters are the middle wings, where we contemplate God (following Augustine) in our own selves as those created in God's image—first in our natural capacities (memory, understanding, and will) and then in those capacities reformed by grace (in faith, hope, and love).

The selection below is from the last three chapters. The fifth and sixth chapters are the highest wings—where (following Dionysius) we contemplate God as "being" and the "good." In discussing God as "being," Bonaventure distinguishes divine being from both nonbeing and particular beings. With five attributes (primary, eternal, simple, perfect, and one), God as being is contemplated as a coincidence of opposites "whose center is everywhere and circumference nowhere" and "who is within all things, not as included, outside of all things, not as excluded, above all things, not as lifted up, below all things, not as prostrated."

Bonaventure uses a syllogism in discussing God as "good": if the good is self-diffusive (Dionysius) and the highest is that which nothing better can be thought (Anselm), then the highest good must be the most self-diffusive. Moreover, the highest self-diffusive goodness must be the Trinity, since it must transcend time and creation. In making this argument, Bonaventure presupposes emanation—not in the Neoplatonic sense of descending opposites but in the consubstantial sense of the Christian Trinity. Drawing on the Greek Fathers, he understands the Father to be the source of divine fecundity out of which he generates the Son (his Word and Image) and the Spirit (the Gift who imparts all other gifts). With six characteristics (communicable,

---

1. The Latin title is *Itinerarium Mentis in Deum*. "Mind" (*mentis*) includes both the intellect and the affections; it refers to all that the human being has as created in God's image.

consubstantial, configurable, coequal, coeternal, and cointimate), the Trinity is contemplated as a coincidence of opposites whose differentiation in three Persons nonetheless constitutes a unity.

In the final chapter—the last stage of the journey—we move from contemplating God as Being and Trinity to contemplating Christ, the God-Man, in whom opposites coincide even more deeply. Gazing into Christ as the mercy seat, we transcend not only the sensible world but our very selves through an "excess of contemplation." Leaving our intellect behind and having our affections completely transferred and transformed into God, we enter—through the Crucified—the fire that totally inflames and transfers us into God.

From the *Opera Omnia S. Bonaventurae*, vol. 5
(Quaracchi: Collegii S. Bonaventurae, 1890), 295–316.[2]

Chapter 5
Contemplating the Divine Unity through Its Primary Name, Which Is "Being"
1. God is contemplated
not only outside of us and within us, but also above us:
outside through vestige, within through image
and above through the light, which has been marked upon our mind
    [Ps. 4:7],
which is the light of Eternal Truth,
since "our very mind is formed immediately by Truth Itself."[3]
Those who have been exercised in the first way
have entered already into the entrance-hall before the Tabernacle;
those in the second have entered into the Holies;
moreover, those in the third enter with the high priest into the Holy of
    Holies
where above the Ark are the Cherubim of glory overshadowing the
    Mercy Seat [cf. Exod. 25:10–22; 26:33; Heb. 9:2–5].
By these two Cherubim we understand two ways or steps
of contemplating the invisible and eternal things of God:
one hovering around the things essential to God
and the other around the things proper to the persons.
2. The first way fixes its gaze first and principally on "being" itself
    (*ipsum esse*),
saying, that *He who is* [Exod. 3:14] is the first Name of God.
The second way fixes its gaze upon the good itself,
saying, that this is the first Name of God.

2. The arrangement of some parts of this translation in poetry form follows *Bonaventure*, trans. and ed. Ewert Cousins (New York: Paulist Press, 1978).

3. Augustine, *Eighty-Three Different Questions* 8:3, q. 51, no. 2, 4.

The first looks chiefly at the Old Testament,
which preaches most of all the unity of the Divine Essence;
hence Moses said: *I am who am* [Exod. 3:14].
The second looks at the New Testament, which determines the plurality
    of persons,
by baptizing *in the Name of*
the Father and of the Son and of the Holy Spirit [Matt. 28:19].
For that reason Christ Our Teacher,
    wishing to raise to evangelical perfection the youth who observed
    the Law
attributed the name of goodness to God principally and precisely,
saying *No one, is good except God alone* [Mark 10:18; Luke 18:19].
Therefore the Damascene following Moses says,
that *He who is* is the first Name of God.[4]
Dionysius following Christ says,
that "the Good" is the first Name of God.[5]

3. Let the mind, desiring to contemplate the invisible things of God in regard to his unity of essence, first fix its gaze upon "being" itself (*ipsum esse*). Let it see that "being" itself is so certain in itself that it cannot be thought not to be. For pure "being" itself does not occur except in full flight from "non-being" (*non-esse*), just as nothing is also in full flight from "being." Therefore, as it has entirely nothing from "being," or from its conditions, so conversely "being" itself has nothing from "non-being"— neither in act nor in power, nor according to the truth of a thing, nor according to our estimation. Moreover since "non-being" is a privation of the act of being (*privatio essendi*), it does not fall in the intellect except through "being." Moreover "being" does not fall through something else, because everything that is understood either is understood as a non-being (*non ens*), or as a being in potency (*ens in potentia*), or as a being in act. If therefore "non-being" can only be understood through a being and a being in potency only through a being in act—and if "being" names the pure act itself of a being—then "being" is what first falls in the intellect and "being" is pure act. But this is not particular "being," which is constrained "being" (*esse arctatum*) since it is mixed with potency; nor is it analogous "being" because it has the least actuality (*minime de actu*) for the reason that it scarcely is (*minime est*). It follows, therefore, that that "being" is the Divine "Being".

4. Strange, then, is the blindness of the intellect, which does not consider that which it sees first and without which it can become acquainted with nothing. The eye intent upon various differences of colors does not see the light through which it sees other things—and if it does see it, it

---

4. John of Damascus, *The Orthodox Faith* 1, 9.
5. Dionysius, *Divine Names* 3, 1; 4, 1.

does not advert to it. Likewise, the eye of our mind, intent upon particular and universal beings, does not advert to being itself, which is outside every genus, even though it first occurs to the mind and through it to other beings. Hence it most truly appears that "as the eye of the bat holds itself towards the light, so the eye of our mind holds itself towards the most manifest things of nature."[6] Accustomed to the shadows of beings and to the phantasms of senses, when it looks upon the light itself of Most High "Being," it seems to itself to see nothing—not understanding that that darkness is the Most High Illumination of our mind (Ps. 138:11)—just as when the eye sees pure light, it seems to itself to see nothing.

5. Therefore see that most pure "Being," if you can, and it occurs to you that It cannot be thought of as received from another. From this, It must necessarily be thought of as first in every way (*omnimode*), because It can be neither from nothing nor from something. For what is It per se, if "Being" itself is not through itself nor from itself? It occurs also to you as lacking entirely in "non-being" and through this as never beginning, never stopping, but eternal. It occurs to you also as having nothing in itself, except that which is "being" itself, and through this as composed with nothing, but most simple. It occurs to you as having nothing of possibility, because every possibility has in some way something from "non-being" and through this as most actual. It occurs as having no defect and through this as most perfect. It occurs lastly as having no diversity, and through this as most highly one. Therefore, "being," which is pure "being" and simply "being" and absolute "being," is the primary, the eternal, the most simple, the most actual, the most perfect and the most highly one "being."

6. These things are so certain that the opposite cannot be thought by understanding "being" itself, and one necessarily infers the other. Because It is simply "being," for that reason It is simply first. Because It is simply first, for that reason It has not been made from another, nor by itself could It, therefore It is eternal. Likewise, because it is first and eternal, for that reason it is not from others, therefore it is most simple. Likewise, because It is first, eternal, most simple, for that reason there is nothing in It of possibility mixed with act, for that reason it is most actual. Likewise, because It is first, eternal, most simple, most actual, therefore It is most perfect—to such nothing is lacking, nor can there be any addition to it. Because It is first, eternal, most simple, most actual, most perfect, for that reason most highly one. For what is through an omnimodal (*omnimodam*) superabundance is said in respect to all things. "What is said through superabundance can be said of only one thing."[7] Hence, if "God" names the primary, eternal, most simple, most actual, most perfect "being," it is impossible

---

6. Aristotle, *Metaphysics* I minor (II), t. 1, c. 1 (993b 9–11).
7. Aristotle, *Topics* 5, c. 5 (134b 23–24).

that God is thought not to be, nor to be other than the only one. *Listen therefore, O Israel, God your God is one God* [Deut. 6:4]. If you see this in the pure simplicity of your mind, you will in somehow be filled with the brightening of eternal light.

7. But you have that from which you will be lifted into wonder.

For "Being" itself is first and last,
is eternal and most present,
is most simple and greatest,
is most actual and most immutable,
is most perfect and immense,
is most highly one and nevertheless omnimodal (*omnimodum*).
If you wonder at these things with a pure mind,
you shall be filled with a greater light,
while you see further, that It is for that reason last,
because it is first.
For because It is first,
It works all things on account of Its very self;
and for that reason it is necessary,
that It be the last end, the beginning and the consummation,
the Alpha and Omega [Rev. 1:8, 21:6; 22:13].
For that reason it is the most present, because it is eternal.
For because it is eternal,
It does not flow from another
nor fails by itself
nor passes from one state into another:
therefore it has neither a past nor a future, but only a present "being."
For that reason It is the greatest, because It is the most simple.
For because It is the most simple in essence,
for that reason It is the greatest in virtue, because virtue,
as much as it is more united, so much is it more infinite.
For that reason It is the most immutable,
because It is the most actual.
For because It is the most actual, for that reason it is the Pure Act;
and because It is such it acquires nothing new, looses nothing had,
and through this cannot be changed.
For that reason It is immense, because It is most perfect.
For because It is most perfect,
one can think of nothing beyond it better, more noble, or more worthy,
and through this nothing greater; and everything that is such is
  immense.
For that reason It is omnimodal, because It is most highly one.
For what is most highly one, is the universal principle of every multitude;
and through this It is the universal efficient, exemplary,
and final cause of all things,

as "the cause of existing, the reason of understanding and the order of
living."
Therefore It is omnimodal not as the Essence of all things,
but as the most superexcellent
and most universal and most sufficient Cause of all other essences;
whose virtue, because it is most highly united in an Essence,
is for that reason most-highly most infinite and most manifold in
efficacy.
8. Returning again to this, let us say that
therefore the most pure and absolute "being,"
which is simply "being," is primary and last,
is for that reason the Origin and consummating End of all things.
Because It is eternal and most present,
It for that reason comprises and enters all durations,
as if existing at the same time as their center and circumference.
Because It is most simple and the greatest,
for that reason wholly within all and wholly outside,
and through this "it is an intelligible sphere,
whose center is everywhere and circumference nowhere."[8]
Because It is most actual and most immutable,
for that reason "remaining stable, it grants motion to all things."[9]
Because it is most perfect and immense,
for that reason it is within all things,
not as included, outside of all things,
not as excluded, above all things,
not as lifted up, below all things, not as prostrated.
On the other hand, because It is most highly one and in every measure,
for that reason It is all in all,
although all things be many and It itself is not but one;
and this, because through the most simple unity,
the most serene truth,
and the most sincere goodness
there is in Him every virtuosity,
every exemplarity and every communicability;
and through this, *from Him and through Him and in Him are all things*
[1 Cor. 15:28];
and this, because He is the omnipotent, omniscient and in every measure Good,
which to see perfectly is to be blessed,
as was said by Moses:
I will you show you all good [Exod. 33:19].

---

8. Alan of Lille, *Regulae Theologicae* reg. 7.
9. Boethius, *The Consolations of Philosophy* 3, metr. 9.

Chapter 6

Contemplating the Most Blessed Trinity in Its Name,
Which Is "The Good"

1. After considering the essential conditions of God,
the eye of the intelligence must be lifted up to survey the Most Blessed
  Trinity,
so as to set up the one Cherub alongside the other.
Moreover just as "being" itself is the radical principle
and name of the vision of essential conditions,
through which all others become known;
so the Good itself is the principle foundation for contemplating the
  emanations.

2. Therefore see and attend to this,
that "the best" is what is simply speaking
"that than which nothing better can be thought."
And so is this of which we speak,
because It cannot be rightly thought not to be,
because "to be" is entirely better than "not to be."[10]
Thus it is, that It cannot rightly be thought,
if it is not thought of as Triune and One.
For "the good is said to be diffusive of itself";[11]
therefore the Most High Good is most highly diffusive of Itself.
But a most high diffusion cannot be, unless it be
actual and intrinsic,
substantial and hypostatic,
natural and voluntary,
liberal and necessary,
unfailing and perfect.
Therefore unless there be eternally in the Most High Good
an actual and consubstantial production,
and a hypostasis equally noble,
as is one producing through the way of generation and spiration
so that there be an eternal production of an eternally co-principiant
  principle,
so that there would be a beloved and a co-beloved, a begotten and a
  spirated,
that is, the Father and the Son and the Holy Spirit—
it would never be the Most High Good,
because it would not diffuse itself most highly.
For diffusion in time into creatures

---

10. Cf. Anselm, *Proslogion*, c. 2–5, 15.
11. Cf. Dionysius, *Celestial Hierarchy* 4.1; *Divine Names* 4.1, 20.

is not but as a center or point
in respect to the immensity of the eternal Goodness.
Hence any diffusion can also be thought greater than that,
namely that, in which diffusing itself it
communicates to the other its whole substance and nature.
Therefore it would not be the Most High Good,
if it were able in reality,
or in understanding to be lacking.
Therefore, if you can, with the eye of your mind survey the purity of
goodness,
which is the pure act of the Principle loving in a charitable way
with a love, free and due and commingled from both,
which is the fullest diffusion by means of a nature and will,
which is a diffusion by means of the Word, in which all things are said,
and by means of the Gift, in whom all other gifts are given;
then you can see, through the most high communicability of the Good,
that the Trinity, of the Father and of the Son and of the Holy Spirit, is
necessary,
among Whom it is necessary on account of Most High Goodness
that there be a most high communicability,
and from the most high communicability a most high consubstantiality,
and from the most high consubstantiality a most high configurability,
and from these a most high co-equality,
and through this a most high co-eternity,
and from all that has been said a most high co-intimacy,
by which One is in the Other necessarily
through a most high interpenetration (*circumincessio*)
and One works with an Other
through the omnimodal indivision of the Substance and Virtue and
Activity
of the Most Blessed Trinity Itself.
3. But when you contemplate these,
see, that you do not consider yourself able to comprehend the
incomprehensible.
For in these six conditions you still have to consider
what leads the eye of our mind fervently into a trance of wonder.
For there is a most high communicability with the property of the
Persons,
a most high consubstantiality with the plurality of the hypostases,
a most high configurability with distinct personality,
a most high co-equality with order,
a most high co-eternity with emanation,
a most high co-intimacy with a sending-forth.

Who at the sight of such great wonders
does not rise up together with them in wonder?
But all these we most certainly understand to be (*esse*) in the Most
    Blessed Trinity,
if we raise our eyes to Its most superexcellent Goodness.
For if there is a most high communication and true diffusion,
there is a true origin and a true distinction;
and because the whole is communicated, not the part,
for that reason That which is given, is what is possessed, and it is the
    whole.
Therefore the One emanating and the One producing
are both distinguished in properties, and are essentially One.
Therefore because They are distinguished in properties,
for that reason They have
personal properties and a plurality of hypostases
and an emanation of origin
and order not of posteriority, but of origin,
and a sending-forth,
not of a change of place but by the gratuity of inspiration,
on account of the authority of the One producing,
which the One sending has in respect to the One being sent.
Moreover, because They are substantially One,
for that reason it is proper that there be a Unity
in essence and form, dignity and eternity, and existence and
    unlimitedness.
Therefore while you consider these conditions singly in themselves,
you have that from which to contemplate the Truth;
while comparing these one to another,
you have that from which to be suspended into the highest wonder.
For that reason, as your mind ascends through wonder into wondrous
    contemplation, these conditions must be considered together.
4. For the Cherubim, who looked at each other also signify this.
Nor was it free from mystery
when they looked backwards at each other
with faces turned toward the Mercy Seat [Exod. 25:30]
to verify what the Lord says in (the Gospel of) John:
This is eternal life, to know you the only true God,
and Jesus Christ, whom you have sent [John 17:3].
For we should wonder
not only at the essential and personal properties of God in themselves,
but also in a comparison with the super-wonderful union of God
    and man
in the unity of the Person of Christ.

5. For if you are a Cherub contemplating the essential properties of God,
and you wonder, because at the same time the Divine "Being" is
First and Last,
Eternal and Most Present,
Most Simple and Greatest or Uncircumscribed,
wholly everywhere and never comprehended,
Most Actual and never moved,
Most Perfect and having nothing superfluous nor diminished,
and nevertheless Immense and Infinite without bounds,
Most Highly One and nevertheless Omnimodal,
as having all things in himself,
as All Virtue, All Truth, All Good—
look back towards the Mercy Seat and wonder,
that in himself the First Principle has been joined with the last,
God with the man formed on the sixth day [Gen. 1:26],
the Eternal One has been joined with temporal man,
in the fullness of times born from the Virgin,
the most Simple with the most highly composite,
the most Actual with one who has most highly suffered and died,
the most Perfect and Immense with the little measure,
the most Highly One and Omnimodal
with the composite individual and distinct from all others,
that is, with the human Christ Jesus.
6. Moreover if you are the other Cherub
by contemplating the things proper to the Persons,
and you wonder, that
communicability is joined with property,
consubstantiality with plurality,
configurability with personality,
co-equality with order,
co-eternality with production,
co-intimacy with sending-forth,
because the Son has been sent from the Father,
and the Holy Spirit from Them both,
who nevertheless is with Them and never recedes from Them—
look back upon the mercy seat and wonder,
because in Christ a personal union exists
with a trinity of substances and a duality of natures;
an omnimodal consensus exists with a plurality of wills,
a co-predication of God and man exists with a plurality of properties,
a co-adoration exists with a plurality of nobilities,
a co-exaltation above all things exists with a plurality of dignities,
a co-domination exists a plurality of powers.

7. Moreover, in this consideration is
the perfection of the mind's illumination,
when, as on the sixth day, one sees
that humans have been made to the image of God [Gen. 1:26].
For if the image is an expressed likeness,
when our mind contemplates in Christ the Son of God,
who is the invisible Image of God by nature,
our humanity so wonderfully exalted, so ineffably united,
by seeing together in one thing
the First and last,
the Most High and most deep,
the Circumference and center,
the Alpha and the Omega [Rev. 1:8; 21:6; 22:13],
the caused and the Cause,
the Creator and the creature,
that is, *the book written inside and out* [Rev. 5:1; Ezek. 2:9]—
it has already arrived at a certain perfect reality,
so that it may with God arrive at the perfection of his illuminations
on the sixth step as if on the sixth day,
and so that nothing more ample may now remain
except the day of rest,
in which through an excess of the mind
the mind's discernment rests from every work
that it would accomplish [Gen. 2:2].

Chapter 7
On the Mental and Mystical Excess, in Which, Rest Is Given
to the Intellect by an Affection Passing-over Wholly into
God through Excess

1. Having passed through these six considerations—
as if they were the six steps of the throne of the true Solomon,
by which one arrives at peace,
where the true Peacemaker rests in a peaceful state of mind
as if in the interior Jerusalem;
as if they were like the six wings of the Cherub,
by which the mind of the true contemplative
can be driven above by a full brightening of supernal wisdom;
as if they were also the first six days,
in which the mind has to be exercised,
to arrive at last to the Sabbath of quiet—
after which our mind has beheld God
outside of itself through vestiges and in vestiges,
within itself through image and in image,

and above itself through a similitude of the divine light glittering
  above us
and in that Light itself,
according to what is possible according to our state as wayfarers
and the exercise of our mind;
when one arrives on the sixth step as far as this,
that in the First and Most High Principle
and the mediator of God and human beings, Jesus Christ [1 Tim. 2:5],
one gazes upon those things
the like of which can in no way be discovered among creatures,
and which exceed every insight of the human intellect:
it follows, that this mind by gazing transcends and passes-over
not only this sensible world, but also its very self.
In this passing over
Christ is *the Way and the Gate* [cf. John 14:6; 10:7],
Christ is the ladder and the vehicle
like the Mercy Seat placed above the ark of God
and the *mystery hidden from eternity* [Eph. 3:9].
2. Whoever looks at the Mercy Seat with a full conversion of face,
seeing him suspended upon the Cross—
with faith, hope and charity,
devotion, wonder, exultation,
appreciation, praise, and jubilation—
makes the Passover, that is the passing over [Exod. 12:11], together with
  Christ:
passing over the Red Sea through the rod of the Cross,
entering the desert from Egypt, where he tastes the hidden manna
  [Rev. 2:17],
and resting together with Christ in the tomb, as if dead to the outer
  world,
but sensing, nevertheless,
as much as is possible in this transient state,
what was said to the thief handing on a cross with Christ:
Today you shall be with me in paradise [Luke 23:43].
3. This was also shown to blessed Francis,
when in an excess of contemplation on the exalted mountain,
where these things were written,
there appeared the six-winged Seraph fastened upon a cross in that very
  place,
as I and many others have heard
from his companion, who was with him at that time.[12]

---

12. Cf. Bonaventure's *Life of St. Francis* 8:3, 305–6.

There he passed-over into God through an excess of contemplation
and has become an example of perfect contemplation;
as previously he had been a man of action, like another Jacob and Israel
[Gen. 35:10],
so that through him, more by example than by word,
God may invite all truly spiritual persons
to a passing-over of this kind and an excess of the mind.
4. If this passing-over is to be perfect,
it is fitting that all intellectual activities be left behind
and our whole apex of affection be transferred and transformed into
God.
This, however, is mystical and most secret,
because *no one knows it, except the one who receives it* [Rev. 2:17],
nor does one receive it, unless one desires it,
nor does one desire it, unless one is be inflamed in the marrow of one's
bones
by the fire of the Holy Spirit, whom Christ sent upon earth [Luke 12:49].
Thus, the Apostle says that
this mystical wisdom has been revealed through the Holy Spirit [1 Cor.
2:10ff.].
5. Since, therefore, there can be nothing by nature,
only a limited amount by industry,
only a little by inquiring,
but much by unction;
little must be given to the tongue,
and most to internal joy;
little must be given to word and to writing,
and the whole to the Gift of God, that is to the Holy Spirit;
little or nothing must be given to the creature,
and the whole to the creative Essence,
to the Father and to the Son, and to the Holy Spirit,
by saying with Dionysius
to God the Trinity:
"O Trinity, super-essential and super-God, and super-eminent,
the overseer of divine wisdom among Christians,
direct us into
the super-unknown and super-shining and most sublime summit of
mystical speech.
There the new and absolute and unspeakable mysteries of theology are,
according to the super-shining darkness of an instructing silence,
secretly hidden in the one most obscure,
and yet Most Manifest, Super-resplendent, and That in which everything glitters,

and Super-fulfilling invisible intellects with the splendors of invisible
    super-goods."[13]
This he says to God.
But to the friend, to whom these things were written:
"Moreover you, O friend, concerning mystical visions,
having been strengthened on the journey,
desert both your senses and your intellectual activities,
both sensible things and invisible things,
and all non-being and being,
and unknowingly re-establish yourself,
insofar as is possible,
according to Unity with Him,
who is above every essence and knowledge.
For indeed deserting all things and absolved from all,
you shall ascend by yourself,
by the immeasurable and absolute excess of pure mind,
to the super-essential Ray of divine shadows."[14]
6. Moreover if you inquire into,
how these things occur,
ask grace, not doctrine,
desire, not understanding,
the groan of praying, not the study of reading,
the spouse, not the teacher,
God, not human beings,
darkness, not clarity,
not light, but the Fire totally inflaming,
transferring one into God
both by its excessive unctions and by its most ardent affections.
This fire indeed is God, and *God's furnace is in Jerusalem* [Isa. 31:9],
and Christ ignites this in the fervor of his most ardent Passion,
which he alone truly perceived, who said:
My soul has chosen hanging, and my bones death [Job 7:15].
Whoever who loves this death can see God, because it is indubitably
    true:
No one will see me and live [Exod. 33:20].
Let us then die and step into the darkness.
Let us impose silence upon our cares, our desires, and our imaginings.
With Christ Crucified,
let us pass over *from this world to the Father* [John 13:1]
so that when the Father is shown to us, we may say with Philip:
It suffices for us [John 14:8].

13. Dionysius, *Mystical Theology* 1:1.
14. Ibid.

Let us hear with Paul:
My grace is sufficient for you [2 Cor. 12:9].
Let us exult with David saying:
My flesh and my heart failed, God of my heart and my portion: God forever.
Blessed be the Lord forever, and every people shall say:
Let it be; let it be. Amen [Ps. 73:26; 106:48].
Here ends the journey of the mind into God.

SELECTION **3**

Thomas Aquinas

Summa Theologica,
1.1–4, 12–13

A Dominican, Thomas Aquinas (1225–1274) is widely recognized as the most influential theologian and philosopher in the Roman Catholic Church. The excerpts below are from the prologue of the *Summa Theologica* and its first two sections on the nature of God, which deal with whether God exists and the manner of God's existence.

Peter Lombard's *Sentences*—the theological textbook of Thomas's day—sought to interpret the "things" (*res*) and "signs" (*signa*) of divine revelation by way of inward illumination (following Augustine). By contrast, Thomas sought to develop a definite knowledge of God as a "science," which (following Aristotle) could be demonstrated by way of what reason abstracts from data provided by the senses (q.1, art.7). As a science, "sacred doctrine" does not seek to prove the articles of Christian faith—it presupposes them—rather, it simply seeks to clarify what faith sets forth in terms we can understand. Since reason can only give us direct knowledge of what we apprehend with our senses, it cannot provide us with direct knowledge of God's nature, which transcends us. However, since grace never destroys but instead perfects nature, reason can make use of God's effects on creatures (either in nature or through grace) in order to say something demonstrable about God.

Thus, Thomas begins his famous "five ways" for proving God's existence (q.2, art.3) with the divine revelation "I AM WHO I AM" (Exod. 3:14). These proofs do not rationally justify belief in God—they presuppose biblical revelation and faith—rather, they provide a means for thinking and speaking about God in terms we can understand. The statement "God exists" is self-evident in itself (because, as he will demonstrate, God's essence implies his existence), yet it is not self-evident to us (since we have no access to God's nature). Rejecting Anselm's argument that simply having the word *God* in our minds means that God actually exists, Thomas argues that we need discursive arguments based on what our senses perceive. We cannot demonstrate God's existence with a priori arguments— since God transcends us— but we can do so by way of a posteriori arguments based on God's effects in creation (cf. Rom. 1:20). Derived from the many names attributed to God based on these effects, the meaning of the word *God* serves as the "middle term" in these a posteriori arguments—enabling us to move from God's effects in creation to the recognition that God, in fact, exists.

Each of the five ways infers God as the cause of an observable effect: (1) what moves is moved by something that moves it; (2) every efficient cause has a prior cause; (3) what is contingent depends on what is necessary; (4) degrees of perfection imply something more perfect; and (5) the order and design in the world implies an intelligent source. The first three infer from a series of causes a first and uncaused cause (presupposing that an infinite regress in a series of causes is impossible). The fourth presupposes that there must a cause for our notions of what is good and true, and the fifth, that the evidence of design in the world implies an originating intelligence. Together, these proofs integrate Aristotle's four causes around a Neoplatonic pattern of all things coming from and returning to God. They begin with God as the *unmoved mover*, the source of all movement in the world, and end with God as the intelligent being who guides all things, as their *final cause*, toward their true end or purpose. Between these, God is the *efficient cause* of all things other than God, the necessary *material cause* of contingent beings, and the *formal cause* enabling us to perceive the best, the truest, and the most real in our sensible experience.

Although we can demonstrate *that* God exists, we cannot know *what* God is. Thus, Thomas warns that we can only treat God's nature by discussing what God is *not*. His intent, however, is not merely negative: he seeks to depict how we can think and speak about the God who far exceeds anything we might say about God. Indeed, the first two divine attributes—simplicity and perfection—entail that we speak about God in this way. As Thomas explains in his discussion of God's *simplicity* (q.3), all particular beings are composed of form (their essence or nature) and matter (which individuates them); thus the "actuality" of their "existence" (as form and matter) differs from the "potentiality" inherent in their "essence." By contrast, God is not only God's own essence or nature, but God is God's own existence as well. Unlike particular beings, which are composites of form and matter, essence and existence, God is simple: God's essence is God's existence. God is God's own being—the pure act of existing ("I AM WHO I AM," Exod. 3:14).

Moreover, God's simplicity implies God's *perfection* (q.4). If God is God's own essence and existence, then God is the most actual and the most perfect of all—embracing within God's being without limitation the perfection of all things, which preexist in God but in a more perfect way. In other words, God is the "very existence of all subsisting things," which entails not only *goodness in general* (q.5) but the fact that God is good (q.6). In an analogous fashion, all the other divine attributes that explicitly distinguish God's nature from that of other beings are entailed in God's simplicity and perfection: *infinity* (q.7) and *omnipresence* (q.8); *immutability* (q.9) and *eternity* (q.10); and *unity* or oneness (q.11).

How we think and speak about God must be consistent with God's nature and attributes. Following Dionysius, Thomas contends that we know God in three ways: (1) the *way of causality* enables us to understand that God exists through God's effects in creation; (2) *the way of negation* acknowledges that we cannot know God's nature; and (3) *the way of eminence* provides the means for thinking about the God who superexceeds all creature beings (q.12). Unlike Dionysius, however, who advocated a mystical transcendence of all our theological affirmations and negations, Thomas argues for the possibility of analogical discourse about God (q.13) based on the third "way of eminence." Although we move from effect to cause epistemologically in these three ways, in reality the cause precedes all effects, which preexist within God but in a more perfect and eminent way. Thus, although our theological affirmations and negations always belong to our "mode of signification," there is some sort of analogy between what we think and say, on the one hand, and who God is, on the other, since what is signified by our names for God (goodness, life, etc.) belongs most properly to God. Thus Thomas rejects both univocal predication about God (which is impossible because of the radical difference between God and creatures) and equivocal predication about God (which is problematic because our knowledge of God, based on God's effects in creation, is not strictly arbitrary). Instead, he argues for the possibility of analogical discourse about God since all that we think or say already participates in God, the pure act of being in which all exist (cf. q.4, a.3).

From *Summa Theologica, First Part*, trans. Fathers of the English Dominican Province (New York: Benziger, 1947).

Question 1: The Nature and Extent of Sacred Doctrine
Article 7: Whether God Is the Object of This Science?

Objections: 1: It seems that God is not the object of this science.[15] For in every science, the nature of its object is presupposed. But this science cannot presuppose the essence of God, for Damascene says: "It is impossible to define the essence of God."[16] Therefore God is not the object of this science.

---

15. Ed. note: In developing his arguments, Thomas follows the scholastic method of dealing with "questions" (major topics) and "articles" (issues within a topic). In each article, he proceeds by listing various authorities who have "objections" to what he will argue followed by a position "on the contrary," and then giving his "answer" and "replies" to the various objections.

16. *On the Orthodox Faith* 1.4.

2: Further, whatever conclusions are reached in any science must be comprehended under the object of the science. But in Holy Writ we reach conclusions not only concerning God, but concerning many other things, such as creatures and human morality. Therefore God is not the object of this science.

On the Contrary: The object of the science is that of which it principally treats. But in this science, the treatment is mainly about God; for it is called theology, as treating of God. Therefore God is the object of this science.

Answer: God is the object of this science. The relation between a science and its object is the same as that between a habit or faculty and its object. Now properly speaking, the object of a faculty or habit is the thing under the aspect of which all things are referred to that faculty or habit, as man and stone are referred to the faculty of sight in that they are colored. Hence colored things are the proper objects of sight. But in sacred science, all things are treated of under the aspect of God: either because they are God Himself or because they refer to God as their beginning and end. Hence it follows that God is in very truth the object of this science. This is clear also from the principles of this science, namely, the articles of faith, for faith is about God. The object of the principles and of the whole science must be the same, since the whole science is contained virtually in its principles. Some, however, looking to what is treated of in this science, and not to the aspect under which it is treated, have asserted the object of this science to be something other than God—that is, either things and signs; or the works of salvation; or the whole Christ, as the head and members. Of all these things, in truth, we treat in this science, but so far as they have reference to God.

Replies to Objections: 1: Although we cannot know in what consists the essence of God, nevertheless in this science we make use of God's effects, either of nature or of grace, in place of a definition, in regard to whatever is treated of in this science concerning God; even as in some philosophical sciences we demonstrate something about a cause from its effect, by taking the effect in place of a definition of the cause.
2: Whatever other conclusions are reached in this sacred science are comprehended under God, not as parts or species or accidents but as in some way related to God.

Treatise on the One God
Because the chief aim of sacred doctrine is to teach the knowledge of God, not only as God is in himself, but also as God is the beginning of things and their last end, and especially of rational creatures, as is clear

from what has been already said,[17] therefore, in our endeavor to expound this science, we shall treat: (1) Of God; (2) Of the rational creature's journey towards God; (3) Of Christ, who as man, is our way to God.[18]

In treating of God there will be a threefold division: (1) the nature of God; (2) the distinctions of persons in God; (3) the procession of creatures from God.[19]

Concerning the nature of God, we must consider: (1) whether God exists; (2) the manner of God's existence, or, rather, what is not the manner of God's existence; (3) God's activity—that is, God's knowledge, will, and power.[20]

Question 2: Whether God exists

Concerning whether God exists, there are three points of inquiry:
  (1) Whether the proposition "God exists" is self-evident?
  (2) Whether it is demonstrable?
  (3) Whether God exists?

Article 1: Whether the Existence of God Is Self-evident?

Objections: 1: It seems that the existence of God is self-evident. Now those things are said to be self-evident to us the knowledge of which is naturally implanted in us, as we can see in regard to first principles. But as Damascene says, "the knowledge of God is naturally implanted in all."[21] Therefore the existence of God is self-evident.

2: Further, those things are said to be self-evident which are known as soon as the terms are known, which the Philosopher says is true of the first principles of demonstration.[22] Thus, when the nature of a whole and of a

---

17. Cf. Ia.1, 7.

18. Ed. note: Organized around the Neoplatonic pattern of emanation and return (*exitus-reditus*)—where all things come from and return to God—the *Summa Theologica* consists of three parts. Part 1 (*Prima Pars*) discusses the nature of God and God's works in creation. Part 2 (*Secunda Pars*) discusses human beings as the image of God and the movement of the human person toward God. Part 3 (*Tertia Pars*) discusses Christ, who unites God and humanity and is our way back to God.

19. Ed. note: In the *Prima Pars* Aquinas examines (1) the unity of divine nature (*De Deo Uno*) (qq.2–26) and (2) the trinity of persons (*De Deo Trino*) (qq.27–43) followed by the (3) creation of all things in the movement of God outward toward the creature and then the ultimate return of creatures to God (qq.44–119).

20. Ed. note: Thomas's discussion of the divine nature moves from treating whether God exists (q.2) and how God exists (qq.3–13) to discussing God's activity, which includes both God's internal activities of knowing and willing and God's external activity of creating the world *ad extra* ("towards the outside," or what is other than God) through divine power (qq.14–26). By placing his discussion of God's activity between his discussion of God's unity (*De Deo Uno*) and the Trinity (*De Deo Trino*), Thomas provides a means for linking the two. The procession of Trinitarian persons within God is understood (following Augustine) through God's internal activities of knowing and willing (qq.27–43) and God's procession to creatures in creating what is other than God is understood through God's activity *ad extra* in creative power (qq.44–119).

21. *On the Orthodox Faith* 1.1.

22. Aristotle, *Posterior Analytics* 1.2.

part is known, it is at once recognized that every whole is greater than its part. But as soon as the signification of the word "God" is understood, it is at once seen that God exists. For by this word is signified that thing than which nothing greater can be conceived.[23] But that which exists actually and mentally is greater than that which exists only mentally. Therefore, since as soon as the word "God" is understood it exists mentally, it also follows that it exists actually.[24] Therefore the proposition "God exists" is self-evident.

3: Further, the existence of truth is self-evident. For whoever denies the existence of truth grants that truth does not exist: and, if truth does not exist, then the proposition "Truth does not exist" is true: and if there is anything true, there must be truth. But God is truth itself: "I am the way, the truth, and the life" [John 14:6]. Therefore "God exists" is self-evident.

On the Contrary: No one can mentally admit the opposite of what is self-evident; as the Philosopher states concerning the first principles of demonstration.[25] But the opposite of the proposition "God is" can be mentally admitted: "The fool said in his heart, There is no God" [Ps. 53:1]. Therefore, that God exists is not self-evident.

Answer: A thing can be self-evident in either of two ways: on the one hand, self-evident in itself, though not to us; on the other, self-evident in itself, and to us. A proposition is self-evident because the predicate is included in the essence of the subject, as "The human is an animal," for animal is contained in the essence of human. If, therefore the essence of the predicate and subject be known to all, the proposition will be self-evident to all; as is clear with regard to the first principles of demonstration, the terms of which are common things that no one is ignorant of, such as being and non-being, whole and part, and such like. If, however, there are some to whom the essence of the predicate and subject is unknown, the proposition will be self-evident in itself, but not to those who do not know the meaning of the predicate and subject of the proposition. Therefore, it happens, as Boethius says "that there are some mental concepts self-evident only to the learned, as that incorporeal substances are not in space."[26] Therefore I say that this proposition, "God exists," of itself is self-evident, for the predicate is the same as the subject, because God is God's own existence as will be hereafter shown.[27] Now because we do not know the essence of God, the proposition is not self-evident to us; but needs to

23. See Anselm, *Proslogion.*
24. Ibid.
25. Aristotle, *Metaphysics* 4.3. *Posterior Analytics* 1.10.
26. Boethius, *De Hebdomadibus.* Boethius (d. 524–5); his works were one of the main channels through which Greek speculation passed to the early Latin middle ages.
27. Cf. Ia.3.4.

be demonstrated by things that are more known to us, though less known in their nature—namely, by effects.

Replies to Objections: 1: To know that God exists in a general and confused way is implanted in us by nature, inasmuch as God is man's beatitude. For human beings naturally desire happiness, and what is naturally desired by human beings must be naturally known to them. This, however, is not to know absolutely that God exists; just as to know that someone is approaching is not the same as to know that Peter is approaching, even though it is Peter who is approaching; for many there are who imagine that humanity's perfect good, which is happiness, consists in riches, and others in pleasures, and others in something else.

2: Perhaps not everyone who hears this word "God" understands it to signify something than which nothing greater can be thought, seeing that some have believed God to be a body. Yet, granted that everyone understands that by this word "God" is signified something than which nothing greater can be thought, nevertheless, it does not therefore follow that he understands that what the word signifies exists actually, but only that it exists mentally. Nor can it be argued that it actually exists, unless it be admitted that there actually exists something than which nothing greater can be thought; and this precisely is not admitted by those who hold that God does not exist.

3: The existence of truth in general is self-evident but the existence of a Primal Truth is not self-evident to us.

Article 2: Whether It Can Be Demonstrated That God Exists?

Objections: 1: It seems that the existence of God cannot be demonstrated. For it is an article of faith that God exists. But what is of faith cannot be demonstrated, because a demonstration produces scientific knowledge; whereas faith is of the unseen [Heb. 11:1]. Therefore it cannot be demonstrated that God exists.

2: Further, the essence is the middle term of demonstration. But we cannot know in what God's essence consists, but solely in what it does not consist; as Damascene says.[28] Therefore we cannot demonstrate that God exists.

3: Further, if the existence of God were demonstrated, this could only be from God's effects. But God's effects are not proportionate to God, since God is infinite and God's effects are finite; and between the finite and infinite there is no proportion. Therefore, since a cause cannot be demonstrated by an effect not proportionate to it, it seems that the existence of God cannot be demonstrated.

---

28. John of Damascus, *On the Orthodox Faith* 1.4.

On the Contrary: The Apostle says: "The invisible things of him are clearly seen, being understood by the things that are made" [Rom. 1:20]. But this would not be unless the existence of God could be demonstrated through the things that are made; for the first thing we must know of anything is whether it exists.

Answer: Demonstration can be made in two ways: One is through the cause, and is called "a priori," and this is to argue from what is prior absolutely. The other is through the effect, and is called a demonstration "a posteriori"; this is to argue from what is prior relatively only to us. When an effect is better known to us than its cause, from the effect we proceed to the knowledge of the cause. And from every effect the existence of its proper cause can be demonstrated, so long as its effects are better known to us; because since every effect depends upon its cause, if the effect exists, the cause must pre-exist. Hence the existence of God, in so far as it is not self-evident to us, can be demonstrated from those of God's effects that are known to us.

Replies to Objections: 1: The existence of God and other like truths about God that can be known by natural reason are not articles of faith, but are preambles to the articles; for faith presupposes natural knowledge, even as grace presupposes nature, and perfection supposes something that can be perfected. Nevertheless, there is nothing to prevent a person, who cannot grasp a proof, accepting, as a matter of faith, something that in itself is capable of being scientifically known and demonstrated.

2: When the existence of a cause is demonstrated from an effect, this effect takes the place of the definition of the cause in proof of the cause's existence. This is especially the case in regard to God, because, in order to prove the existence of anything, it is necessary to accept as a middle term the meaning of the word, and not its essence, for the question of its essence follows on the question of its existence. Now the names given to God are derived from God's effects;[29] consequently, in demonstrating the existence of God from God's effects, we may take for the middle term the meaning of the word "God."

3: From effects not proportionate to the cause no perfect knowledge of that cause can be obtained. Yet from every effect the existence of the cause can be clearly demonstrated, and so we can demonstrate the existence of God from God's effects; though from them we cannot perfectly know God as God is in God's essence.

Article 3: Whether God exists?

Objections: 1: It seems that God does not exist; because if one of two contraries be infinite, the other would be altogether destroyed. But

29. Cf. Ia.13.1ff.

the word "God" means that God is infinite goodness. If, therefore, God existed, there would be no evil discoverable; but there is evil in the world. Therefore God does not exist.

2: Further, it is superfluous to suppose that what can be accounted for by a few principles has been produced by many. But it seems that everything we see in the world can be accounted for by other principles, supposing God did not exist. For all natural things can be reduced to one principle which is nature; and all voluntary things can be reduced to one principle which is human reason, or will. Therefore there is no need to suppose God's existence.

On the Contrary: It is said in the person of God: "I am who am" [Exod. 3:14].

Answer: The existence of God can be proved in five ways.

The first and more manifest way is the argument from motion. It is certain, and evident to our senses, that in the world some things are in motion. Now whatever is in motion is put in motion by another, for nothing can be in motion except it is in potentiality to that towards which it is in motion; whereas a thing moves inasmuch as it is in act. For motion is nothing else than the reduction of something from potentiality to actuality. But nothing can be reduced from potentiality to actuality, except by something in a state of actuality. Thus that which is actually hot, as fire, makes wood, which is potentially hot, to be actually hot, and thereby moves and changes it. Now it is not possible that the same thing should be at once in actuality and potentiality in the same respect, but only in different respects. For what is actually hot cannot simultaneously be potentially hot; but it is simultaneously potentially cold. It is therefore impossible that in the same respect and in the same way a thing should be both mover and moved, i.e. that it should move itself. Therefore, whatever is in motion must be put in motion by another. If that by which it is put in motion be itself put in motion, then this also must needs be put in motion by another, and that by another again. But this cannot go on to infinity, because then there would be no first mover, and, consequently, no other mover; seeing that subsequent movers move only inasmuch as they are put in motion by the first mover; as the staff moves only because it is put in motion by the hand. Therefore it is necessary to arrive at a first mover, put in motion by no other; and this everyone understands to be God.

The second way is from the nature of the efficient cause. In the world of sense we find there is an order of efficient causes. There is no case known (neither is it, indeed, possible) in which a thing is found to be the efficient cause of itself; for so it would be prior to itself, which is impossible. Now in efficient causes it is not possible to go on to infinity, because in all efficient causes following in order, the first is the cause of the intermediate cause, and the intermediate is the cause of the ultimate cause, whether the intermediate cause be several, or only one. Now to take away the cause is to take away the effect. Therefore, if there be no first cause among efficient causes, there will be no ultimate, nor any intermediate cause. But if in efficient causes it is possible to go on to infinity, there will be no first efficient cause, neither will there be an ultimate effect, nor any intermediate efficient causes; all of which is plainly false. Therefore it is necessary to admit a first efficient cause, to which everyone gives the name of God.

The third way is taken from possibility and necessity, and runs thus. We find in nature things that are possible to be and not to be, since they are found to be generated, and to corrupt, and consequently, they are possible to be and not to be. But it is impossible for these always to exist, for that which is possible not to be at some time is not. Therefore, if everything is possible not to be, then at one time there could have been nothing in existence. Now if this were true, even now there would be nothing in existence, because that which does not exist only begins to exist by something already existing. Therefore, if at one time nothing was in existence, it would have been impossible for anything to have begun to exist; and thus even now nothing would be in existence—which is absurd. Therefore, not all beings are merely possible, but there must exist something the existence of which is necessary. But every necessary thing either has its necessity caused by another, or not. Now it is impossible to go on to infinity in necessary things which have their necessity caused by another, as has been already proved in regard to efficient causes. Therefore we cannot but postulate the existence of some being having of itself its own necessity, and not receiving it from another, but rather causing in others their necessity. This all human beings speak of as God.

The fourth way is taken from the gradation to be found in things. Among beings there are some more and some less good, true, noble and the like. But "more" and "less" are predicated of different things, according as they resemble in their different ways something which is the maximum, as a thing is said to be hotter according as it more nearly resembles that which is hottest; so that there is something which is truest, something best, something noblest and, consequently, something which is uttermost being; for those things that are greatest in truth are greatest in being, as it is written in *Metaphysics* 2, "Now the maximum in any genus is the cause of all in that genus; as fire, which is the maximum heat, is the cause of all hot things." Therefore there must also be something which is to all beings the cause of their being, goodness, and every other perfection; and this we call God.

The fifth way is taken from the governance of the world. We see that things which lack intelligence, such as natural bodies, act for an end, and this is evident from their acting always, or nearly always, in the same way, so as to obtain the best result. Hence it is plain that not fortuitously, but designedly, do they achieve their end. Now whatever lacks intelligence cannot move towards an end, unless it be directed by some being endowed with knowledge and intelligence; as the arrow is shot to its mark by the archer. Therefore some intelligent being exists by whom all natural things are directed to their end; and this being we call God.

Replies to Objections: 1: As Augustine says: "Since God is the highest good, God would not allow any evil to exist in God's works, unless God's omnipotence and goodness were such as to bring good even out of evil."[30] This is part of the infinite goodness of God, that God should allow evil to exist, and out of it produce good.

2: Since nature works for a determinate end under the direction of a higher agent, whatever is done by nature must be traced back to God, as to its first cause. So also whatever is done voluntarily must also be traced back to some higher cause other than human reason or will, since these can change or fail; for all things that are changeable and capable of defect must be traced back to an immovable and self-necessary first principle, as was shown in the body of the Article.

Question 3: God's Simplicity

Having recognized that a certain thing exists, there remains the further question of the way it exists in order to understand what it is that exists.[31] Now, because we cannot know what God is, but rather what God is not, we have no means for considering how God is, but rather how God is not.

Therefore, we must consider: (1) how God is not; (2) how God is known by us; (3) how God is named.[32]

Now it can be shown how God is not, by denying him whatever is opposed to the idea of God, such as composition, motion, and the like. Therefore (1) we must discuss God's simplicity, whereby we deny composition in God; and because whatever is simple in material things is imperfect and a part of something else, we shall discuss (2) God's perfection; (3) God's infinity; (4) God's immutability; (5) God's unity.[33]

---

30. Augustine, *Enchiridion* 11.

31. Ed. note: The excerpts from questions 3–13 that follow will contain only selected articles and only Thomas's "answer" to each question.

32. Ed. note: Thomas begins with God's reality (how God is himself) (qq.3–11) and then discusses how we know God (q.12) and how we name God (q.13). Cf. q.13 and Aristotle's triadic understanding of the relationship among word, concept, and thing in *On Interpretation*, chap. 1.

33. Ed. note: Thomas's discussion of the names of God follows and yet revises Dionysius's discussion in the *Divine Names* in that for Thomas, "being" rather than the "good" is the primary name for God. Although Thomas only lists five primary attributes here, he actually discusses eight attributes. After discussing God's simplicity (q.3), he treats God's perfection (q.4), which entails not only the goodness of being in general (q.5) but also God's goodness (q.6). God's simplicity, in turn, implies God's infinity (q.7), with its corresponding affirmation of God's omnipresence (q.8), God's immutability (q.9), with its corresponding affirmation of God's eternity (q.10), and finally God's unity or oneness (q.11).

Concerning God's simplicity, there are eight points of inquiry:

(1) Whether God is a body?

(2) Whether God is composed of matter and form?

(3) Whether God is to be identified with God's own essence of nature, with that which makes God what God is?

(4) Whether God is composed of essence and existence?

(5) Whether God is composed of genus and difference?

(6) Whether God is composed of subject and accident?

(7) Whether God is in any way composite, or wholly simple?

(8) Whether God enters into composition with other things?

Article 3: Whether God Is the Same as God's Essence or Nature?

Answer: God is the same as God's essence or nature. To understand this, it must be noted that in things composed of matter and form, the nature or essence must differ from the "*suppositum*," because the essence or nature connotes only what is included in the definition of the species; as, humanity connotes all that is included in the definition of being human, for it is by this that a human being is human, and it is this that humanity signifies, that, namely, whereby a human being is human. Now individual matter, with all the individualizing accidents, is not included in the definition of the species. For this particular flesh, these bones, this blackness or whiteness, etc., are not included in the definition of a human. Therefore this flesh, these bones, and the accidental qualities distinguishing this particular matter, are not included in humanity; and yet they are included in the thing that is human. Hence the thing that is a human has something more in it than has humanity. Consequently humanity and a human are not wholly identical; but humanity is taken to mean the formal part of a human, because the principles whereby a thing is defined are regarded as the formal constituent in regard to the individualizing matter. On the other hand, in things not composed of matter and form, in which individualization is not due to individual matter—that is to say, to "this" matter—the very forms being individualized of themselves—it is necessary the forms themselves should be subsisting "*supposita*." Therefore "*suppositum*" and nature in them are identified. Since God then is not composed of matter and form,[34] God must be God's own Godhead, God's own life, and whatever else is thus predicated of God.

Article 4: Whether Essence and existence are the same in God?

Answer: God is not only God's own essence, as shown in the preceding article, but also God's own existence.[35] This may be shown in several

34. Cf. Ia.3.2.
35. Cf. Ia.3.3.

ways. First, whatever a thing has besides its essence must be caused either by the constituent principles of that essence (like a property that necessarily accompanies the species—as the faculty of laughing is proper to a human—and is caused by the constituent principles of the species), or by some exterior agent—as heat is caused in water by fire. Therefore, if the existence of a thing differs from its essence, this existence must be caused either by some exterior agent or by its essential principles. Now it is impossible for a thing's existence to be caused by its essential constituent principles, for nothing can be the sufficient cause of its own existence, if its existence is caused. Therefore that thing, whose existence differs from its essence, must have its existence caused by another. But this cannot be true of God; because we call God the first efficient cause.[36] Therefore it is impossible that in God God's existence should differ from God's essence.

Secondly, existence is that which makes every form or nature actual; for goodness and humanity are spoken of as actual, only because they are spoken of as existing. Therefore existence must be compared to essence, if the latter is a distinct reality, as actuality to potentiality. Therefore, since in God there is no potentiality, as shown above,[37] it follows that in God essence does not differ from existence. Therefore God's essence is God's existence.

Thirdly, because, just as that which has fire, but is not itself fire, is on fire by participation; so that which has existence but is not existence, is a being by participation. But God is God's own essence, as shown above;[38] if, therefore, God is not God's own existence God will be not essential, but participated being. God will not therefore be the first being—which is absurd. Therefore God is God's own existence, and not merely God's own essence.

Question 4: The Perfection of God
Article 1: Whether God Is Perfect?

Answer: As the Philosopher relates,[39] some ancient philosophers, namely, the Pythagoreans and Leucippus, did not predicate "best" and "most perfect" of the first principle. The reason was that the ancient philosophers considered only a material principle; and a material principle is most imperfect. For since matter as such is merely potential, the first material principle must be simply potential, and thus most imperfect. Now God is the first principle, not material, but in the order of efficient cause, which must be most perfect. For just as matter, as such, is merely potential, an agent, as such, is in the state of actuality. Hence, the first active

36. Cf. Ia.2.3.
37. Cf. Ia.3.1.
38. Cf. Ia.2.3.
39. *Metaphysics* 12.

principle must needs be most actual, and therefore most perfect; for a thing is perfect in proportion to its state of actuality, because we call that perfect which lacks nothing of the mode of its perfection.

Article 2: Whether the Perfections of All Things Are in God?

Answer: All created perfections are in God. Hence God is spoken of as universally perfect, because God lacks not (says the Commentator)[40] any excellence which may be found in any genus. This may be seen from two considerations. First, because whatever perfection exists in an effect must be found in the effective cause: either in the same formality, if it is a univocal agent—as when a human reproduces a human; or in a more eminent degree, if it is an equivocal agent—thus in the sun is the likeness of whatever is generated by the sun's power. Now it is plain that the effect pre-exists virtually in the efficient cause: and although to pre-exist in the potentiality of a material cause is to pre-exist in a more imperfect way, since matter as such is imperfect, and an agent as such is perfect; still to pre-exist virtually in the efficient cause is to pre-exist not in a more imperfect, but in a more perfect way. Since therefore God is the first effective cause of things, the perfections of all things must pre-exist in God in a more eminent way. Dionysius implies the same line of argument by saying of God: "It is not that God is this and not that, but that God is all, as the cause of all."[41] Secondly, from what has been already proved, God is existence itself, of itself subsistent.[42] Consequently, God must contain within Himself the whole perfection of being. For it is clear that if some hot thing has not the whole perfection of heat, this is because heat is not participated in its full perfection; but if this heat were self-subsisting, nothing of the virtue of heat would be wanting to it. Since therefore God is subsisting being itself, nothing of the perfection of being can be wanting to him. Now all created perfections are included in the perfection of being; for things are perfect, precisely so far as they have being after some fashion. It follows therefore that the perfection of no one thing is wanting to God. This line of argument, too, is implied by Dionysius, when he says that, "God exists not in any single mode, but embraces all being within Himself, absolutely, without limitation, uniformly;" and afterwards he adds that, "God is the very existence to subsisting things."[43]

Article 3: Whether Any Creature Can Be Like God?

Answer: Since likeness is based upon agreement or communication in form, it varies according to the many modes of communication in form.

40. *Metaphysics* 5.
41. *Divine Names* 5.
42. Cf. Ia.3.4.
43. *Divine Names* 5.

Some things are said to be like, which communicate in the same form according to the same formality, and according to the same mode; and these are said to be not merely like, but equal in their likeness; as two things equally white are said to be alike in whiteness; and this is the most perfect likeness. In another way, we speak of things as alike which communicate in form according to the same formality, though not according to the same measure, but according to more or less, as something less white is said to be like another thing more white; and this is imperfect likeness. In a third way some things are said to be alike which communicate in the same form, but not according to the same formality; as we see in non-univocal agents. For since every agent reproduces itself so far as it is an agent, and everything acts according to the manner of its form, the effect must in some way resemble the form of the agent. If therefore the agent is contained in the same species as its effect, there will be a likeness in form between that which makes and that which is made, according to the same formality of the species; as humanity reproduces humanity. If, however, the agent and its effect are not contained in the same species, there will be a likeness, but not according to the formality of the same species; as things generated by the sun's heat may be in some sort spoken of as like the sun, not as though they received the form of the sun in its specific likeness, but in its generic likeness. Therefore if there is an agent not contained in any "genus," its effect will still more distantly reproduce the form of the agent, not, that is, so as to participate in the likeness of the agent's form according to the same specific or generic formality, but only according to some sort of analogy; as existence is common to all. In this way all created things, so far as they are beings, are like God as the first and universal principle of all being.

Question 12: How God Is Known by Us
Since we have considered God as he is in himself, we now go on to consider in what manner he is in the knowledge of creatures; concerning which there are thirteen points of inquiry:

(1) Whether any created intellect can see the essence of God?

(2) Whether the essence of God is seen by the intellect through any created image?

(3) Whether the essence of God can be seen by the corporeal eye?

(4) Whether any created intellectual substance is sufficient by its own natural powers to see the essence of God?

(5) Whether the created intellect needs any created light in order to see the essence of God?

(6) Whether of those who see God, one sees God more perfectly than another?

(7) Whether any created intellect can comprehend the essence of God?

(8) Whether the created intellect seeing the essence of God, knows all things in it?

(9) Whether what is there known is known by any similitudes?

(10) Whether the created intellect knows at once what it sees in God?

(11) Whether in the state of this life any man can see the essence of God?

(12) Whether by natural reason we can know God in this life?

(13) Whether there is in this life any knowledge of God through grace above the knowledge of natural reason?

Article 12: Whether God Can Be Known in This Life by Natural Reason?

Answer: Our natural knowledge begins from sense. Hence our natural knowledge can go as far as it can be led by sensible things. But our mind cannot be led by sense so far as to see the essence of God; because the sensible effects of God do not equal the power of God as their cause. Hence from the knowledge of sensible things the whole power of God cannot be known; nor therefore can God's essence be seen. But because they are God's effects and depend on their cause, we can be led from them so far as to know of God "whether God exists," and to know of God what must necessarily belong to God, as the first cause of all things, exceeding all things caused by God.

Hence we know that God's relationship with creatures so far as to be the cause of them all; also that creatures differ from God, inasmuch as God is not in any way part of what is caused by God; and that creatures are not removed from God by reason of any defect on God's part, but because God super-exceeds them all.

Article 13: Whether by Grace a Higher Knowledge of God Can Be Obtained Than by Natural Reason?

Answer: We have a more perfect knowledge of God by grace than by natural reason. This is proved in this way. The knowledge which we have by natural reason contains two things: images derived from the sensible objects; and the natural intelligible light, enabling us to abstract from them intelligible conceptions.

Now in both of these, human knowledge is assisted by the revelation of grace. For the intellect's natural light is strengthened by the infusion of gratuitous light; and sometimes also the images in the human imagination are divinely formed, so as to express divine things better than those do which we receive from sensible objects, as appears in prophetic visions; while sometimes sensible things, or even voices, are divinely formed to express some divine meaning; as in the Baptism, the Holy Ghost was seen in the shape of a dove, and the voice of the Father was heard, "This is My beloved Son" [Matt 3:17].

Question 13: The Names of God

After the consideration of those things which belong to the divine knowledge, we now proceed to the consideration of the divine names. For everything is named by us according to our knowledge of it.

Under this head, there are twelve points for inquiry:

(1) Whether God can be named by us?

(2) Whether any names applied to God are predicated of him substantially?

(3) Whether any names applied to God are said of God literally, or are all to be taken metaphorically?

(4) Whether any names applied to God are synonymous?

(5) Whether some names are applied to God and to creatures univocally or equivocally?

(6) Whether, supposing they are applied analogically, they are applied first to God or to creatures?

(7) Whether any names are applicable to God from time?

(8) Whether this name "God" is a name of nature, or of the operation?

(9) Whether this name "God" is a communicable name?

(10) Whether it is taken univocally or equivocally as signifying God, by nature, by participation, and by opinion?

(11) Whether this name, "Who is," is the supremely appropriate name of God?

(12) Whether affirmative propositions can be formed about God?

Article 1: Whether a Name Can Be Given to God?

Answer: Since according to the Philosopher,[44] words are signs of ideas, and ideas the similitude of things, it is evident that words relate to the meaning of things signified through the medium of the intellectual conception. It follows therefore that we can give a name to anything in as far as we can understand it. Now it was shown above,[45] that in this life we cannot see the essence of God; but we know God from creatures as their principle, and also by way of excellence and remotion. In this way therefore he can be named by us from creatures, yet not so that the name which signifies him expresses the divine essence in itself. Thus the name "man" expresses the essence of man in himself, since it signifies the definition of man by manifesting his essence; for the idea expressed by the name is the definition.

44. *On Interpretation* 1.
45. Cf. Ia.12.11, 12.

Article 2: Whether Any Name Can Be Applied to God Substantially?

Answer: Negative names applied to God, or signifying God's relation to creatures manifestly do not at all signify God's substance, but rather express the distance of the creature from God, or God's relation to something else, or rather, the relation of creatures to himself.

But as regards absolute and affirmative names of God, as "good," "wise," and the like, various and many opinions have been given. For some have said that all such names, although they are applied to God affirmatively, nevertheless have been brought into use more to express some emotion from God, rather than to express anything that exists positively in God. Hence they assert that when we say that God lives, we mean that God is not like an inanimate thing; and the same in like manner applies to other names; and this was taught by Rabbi Moses.[46] Others say that these names applied to God signify God's relationship towards creatures: thus in the words, "God is good," we mean, God is the cause of goodness in things; and the same rule applies to other names.

Both of these opinions, however, seem to be untrue for three reasons. First because in neither of them can a reason be assigned why some names more than others are applied to God. For God is assuredly the cause of bodies in the same way as God is the cause of good things; therefore if the words "God is good," signified no more than, "God is the cause of good things," it might in like manner be said that God is a body, inasmuch as God is the cause of bodies. So also to say that God is a body implies that God is not a mere potentiality, as is primary matter. Secondly, because it would follow that all names applied to God would be said of God by way of being taken in a secondary sense, as healthy is secondarily said of medicine, forasmuch as it signifies only the cause of the health in the animal which primarily is called healthy. Thirdly, because this is against the intention of those who speak of God. For in saying that God lives, they assuredly mean more than to say the God is the cause of our life, or that God differs from inanimate bodies.

Therefore we must hold a different doctrine—viz. that these names signify the divine substance, and are predicated substantially of God, although they fall short of a full representation of him. This is proved in this way. For these names express God, so far as our intellects know him. Now since our intellect knows God from creatures, it knows God as far as creatures represent him. Now it is shown above that God prepossesses in himself all the perfections of creatures, being himself simply and universally perfect.[47] Hence every creature represents God, and is like God so far as it possesses some perfection; yet it represents God not as something

46. Ed. note: Maimonedes.
47. Cf. Ia.4.2.

of the same species or genus, but as the excelling principle of whose form the effects fall short, although they derive some kind of likeness thereto, even as the forms of inferior bodies represent the power of the sun. This was explained above, in treating of the divine perfection.[48] Therefore the aforesaid names signify the divine substance, but in an imperfect manner, even as creatures represent it imperfectly. So when we say, "God is good," the meaning is not, "God is the cause of goodness," or "God is not evil"; but the meaning is, "Whatever good we attribute to creatures, pre-exists in God," and in a more excellent and higher way. Hence it does not follow that God is good, because he causes goodness; but rather,

On the Contrary: God causes goodness in things because God is good; according to what Augustine says, "Because God is good, we are."[49]

Article 3: Whether Any Name Can Be Applied to God in Its Literal Sense?

Answer: According to the preceding article, our knowledge of God is derived from the perfections that flow from God to creatures—perfections that are in God in a more eminent way than in creatures. Now our intellect apprehends them as they are in creatures, and as it apprehends them it signifies them by names. Therefore as to the names applied to God—viz. the perfections which they signify, such as goodness, life and the like, and their mode of signification. As regards what is signified by these names, they belong properly to God, and more properly than they belong to creatures, and are applied primarily to him. But as regards their mode of signification, they do not properly and strictly apply to God; for their mode of signification applies to creatures.

Article 5: Whether What Is Said of God and of Creatures Is Univocally Predicated of Them?

Answer: Univocal predication is impossible between God and creatures. The reason of this is that every effect that is not an adequate result of the power of the efficient cause receives the similitude of the agent not in its full degree, but in a measure that falls short, so that what is divided and multiplied in the effects resides in the agent simply, and in the same manner; as for example the sun by exercise of its one power produces manifold and various forms in all inferior things. In the same way, as said in the preceding article, all perfections existing in creatures divided and multiplied, pre-exist in God unitedly. Thus when any term expressing perfection is applied to a creature, it signifies that perfection distinct in idea from other

48. Cf. Ia.4.3.
49. *On Christian Doctrine* 1.32.

perfections; as, for instance, by the term "wise" applied to man, we signify some perfection distinct from a man's essence, and distinct from his power and existence, and from all similar things; whereas when we apply to it God, we do not mean to signify anything distinct from God's essence, or power, or existence. Thus also this term "wise" applied to man in some degree circumscribes and comprehends the thing signified; whereas this is not the case when it is applied to God; but it leaves the thing signified as incomprehended, and as exceeding the signification of the name. Hence it is evident that this term "wise" is not applied in the same way to God and to man. The same rule applies to other terms. Hence no name is predicated univocally of God and of creatures.

Neither, on the other hand, are names applied to God and creatures in a purely equivocal sense, as some have said. Because if that were so, it follows that from creatures nothing could be known or demonstrated about God at all; for the reasoning would always be exposed to the fallacy of equivocation. Such a view is against the philosophers, who proved many things about God, and also against what the Apostle says: "The invisible things of God are clearly seen being understood by the things that are made" [Rom. 1:20]. Therefore it must be said that these names are said of God and creatures in an analogous sense, i.e. according to proportion.

Now names are thus used in two ways: either according as many things are proportionate to one, thus for example "healthy" predicated of medicine and urine in relation and in proportion to health of a body, of which the former is the sign and the latter the cause: or according as one thing is proportionate to another, thus "healthy" is said of medicine and animal, since medicine is the cause of health in the animal body. And in this way some things are said of God and creatures analogically, and not in a purely equivocal nor in a purely univocal sense. For we can name God only from creatures.[50] Thus whatever is said of God and creatures, is said according to the relation of a creature to God as its principle and cause, wherein all perfections of things pre-exist excellently. Now this mode of community of idea is a mean between pure equivocation and simple univocation. For in analogies the idea is not, as it is in univocals, one and the same, yet it is not totally diverse as in equivocals; but a term which is thus used in a multiple sense signifies various proportions to some one thing; thus "healthy" applied to urine signifies the sign of animal health, and applied to medicine signifies the cause of the same health.

Article 11: Whether This Name, HE WHO IS, Is the Most Proper Name of God?

Answer: This name HE WHO IS is most properly applied to God, for three reasons:

50. Cf. Ia.13.1.

First, because of its signification. For it does not signify form, but simply existence itself. Hence since the existence of God is God's essence itself, which can be said of no other,[51] it is clear that among other names this one specially denominates God, for everything is denominated by its form.

Secondly, on account of its universality. For all other names are either less universal, or, if convertible with it, add something above it at least in idea; hence in a certain way they inform and determine it. Now our intellect cannot know the essence of God itself in this life, as it is in itself, but whatever mode it applies in determining what it understands about God, it falls short of the mode of what God is in himself. Therefore the less determinate the names are, and the more universal and absolute they are, the more properly they are applied to God. Hence Damascene says that, "HE WHO IS, is the principal of all names applied to God; for comprehending all in itself, it contains existence itself as an infinite and indeterminate sea of substance."[52] Now by any other name some mode of substance is determined, whereas this name HE WHO IS, determines no mode of being, but is indeterminate to all; and therefore it denominates the "infinite ocean of substance."

Thirdly, from its consignification, for it signifies present existence; and this above all properly applies to God, whose existence knows not past or future, as Augustine says.[53]

SELECTION **4**

Meister Eckhart

Sermon 6: Justi vivent in aeternum (Wis. 5:16)[54]

A Dominican monk and preacher, Meister Eckhart (1260–1327) developed a distinctive Christian Neoplatonist understanding of our union with God. At the heart of his theology is a dynamic Neoplatonic depiction of how all things "flow out" (*exitus, uzvliezen*) from and "flow back" or return (*reditus, durchbrechen*) to God, their source and goal. The first movement of "flowing out" has two stages: (1) the inner *bullitio* (literally "boiling over") of Trinitarian persons from the innermost, hidden divine ground (*Grund*) and (2) the outward *ebullitio*

---

51. Cf. Ia.3.4.
52. *On the Orthodox Faith* 1.
53. *On the Trinity* 5.
54. "Justice Lives Eternally." For an important study of this sermon, see K. Kertz, "Meister Eckhart's Teaching on the Birth of the Divine Word in the Soul," *Traditio* 15 (1959): 336–39, 359–62.

(or creation) of all things patterned after it. Likewise, the second movement of "flowing back" has two stages: (1) the birth of God in the soul and (2) the "breaking through" or penetration of the soul into the ineffable divine ground. Eckhart used paradoxical language to describe our emanation from and return back to God—language that dialectically stresses both God's distinction from creatures (as the "one" God beyond all distinctions) and God's identity with creatures (who though nothing in themselves, nonetheless have their being in God's existence).

In the following sermon, Eckhart describes God's birth within the soul. He begins by discussing the "just man" (which refers to who we are in God's being and not to a concrete, existing individual). In God, the just man is perfectly detached, seeking no reward—not even holiness. United with God, the just man participates in God's justice since he derives his very existence from God: "God's existence must be my existence and God's is-ness is my is-ness." He then describes not only how the Father eternally gives birth to the coequal Son but also how this eternal birth also takes place in our lives (since we have been baptized into union with the Son). Going further, Eckhart says, "He gives birth, me, his Son, and the same Son," and going further still, he describes how the just man participates in the inner Trinitarian *bullitio*: "[The Father] gives birth to me as himself and himself as me and to me as his being and nature. In the innermost source, there I spring out in the Holy Spirit." Moreover, if the soul participates in the inner Trinitarian *bullitio*, then it must also participate in God's work in creation (or *ebullitio*). In other sermons, Eckhart goes on to depict yet another stage, beyond the soul's birth through the Son's birth: the summons to penetrate—or to "break through"—even further into the hidden God, who in a dialectical relation to the Trinity, lies beyond it as the innermost divine ground.

From *Meister Eckhart: The Essential Sermons, Commentaries, Treatises, and Defense*, trans. Edmund Colledge and Bernard McGinn (New York: Paulist Press, 1981), 185–89.

"The just will live forever, and their reward is with God." See exactly what this means; though it may sound simple and commonplace, it is really noteworthy and excellent.

"The just will live." Which are the just? Somewhere it is written: "That man is just who gives everyone what belongs to him";[55] those who give God what is his, and the saints and the angels what is theirs, and their fellow man what is his.

Honor belongs to God [cf. 1 Tim. 1:17]. Who are those who honor God? Those who have wholly gone out of themselves, and who do not seek for what is theirs in anything, whatever it may be, great or little, who are not

---

55. Justinian, *Institutes* I, 1.

looking beneath themselves or above themselves or beside themselves or at themselves, who are not desiring possessions or honors or ease or pleasure or profit or inwardness or holiness or reward or the kingdom of heaven, and who have gone out from all this, from everything that is theirs, these people pay honor to God,[56] and they honor God properly, and they give him what is his.

People ought to give joy to the angels and the saints. What, does this amaze you? Can a man in this life give joy to those who are in everlasting life? Yes, indeed, he can! Every saint has such great delight and such unspeakable joy from every good work; from a good will or an aspiration they have such great joy that no tongue can tell, no heart can think how great is the joy they have from this. Why is that? Because their love for God is so immeasurably great, and they have so true a love for him, that his honor is dearer to them than their blessedness. And not only the saints or the angels, for God himself takes such delight in this, just as if it were his blessedness; and his being depends upon it, and his contentment and his well-being. Yes, mark this well: If we do not want to serve God for any other reason than the great joy they have in this who are in everlasting life, and that God himself has, we could do it gladly and with all our might.

And one ought also to give help and support to those who are in purgatory, and improvement and edification[57] to those who are still living.

Such a man is just in one way, and so in another sense are all those who accept all things alike from God, whatever it may be, great or small, joy or sorrow, all of it alike, less or more, one like the other. If you account anything more than something else, you do wrong. You ought to go wholly out from your, own will.

Recently I had this thought: If God did not wish as I do, then I would still wish as he does. There are some people who want to have their own will in everything; that is bad, and there is much harm in it. Those are a little better who do want what God wants, and want nothing contrary to his will; if they were sick, what they would wish would be for God's will to be for them to be well. So these people want God to want according to their will, not for themselves to want according to his will. One has to endure this, but still it is wrong. The just have no will at all; what God wills is all the same to them, however great distress that may be.

For just men, the pursuit of justice is so imperative that if God were not just, they would not give a fig for God; and they stand fast by justice, and

---

56. "Who are not desiring possessions . . . these people pay honor to God": this is the material for art. 8 of "In agro dominico," which is condemned as heretical.

57. "Improvement and edification" is supplied, where the German manuscripts have a lacuna, from J. Quint's citation of a parallel passage in *Commentary on Wisdom*, n. 59 in *Meister Eckhart: Die Deutschen und Lateinischen Werke* (Stuttgart and Berlin: W. Kohlhammer, 1936–), 386.

they have gone out of themselves so completely that they have no regard for the pains of hell or the joys of heaven or for any other thing. Yes, if all the pains that those have who are in hell, men or devils, or all the pains that have ever been or ever will be suffered on earth were to be joined on to justice, they would not give a straw for that, so fast do they stand by God and by justice. Nothing is more painful or hard for a just man than what is contrary to justice.[58] In what way? If one thing gives them joy and another sorrow, they are not just; but if on one occasion they are joyful, then they are always joyful; and if on one occasion they are more joyful and on others less, then they are wrong. Whoever loves justice stands so fast by it that whatever he loves, that is his being; nothing can deflect him from this, nor does he esteem anything differently. Saint Augustine says: "When the soul loves, it is more properly itself than when it gives life."[59] This sounds simple and commonplace, and yet few understand what it means, and still it is true. Anyone who has discernment in justice and in just men, he understands everything I am saying.

"The just will live." Among all things there is nothing so dear or so desirable as life. However wretched or hard his life may be, a man still wants to live. It is written somewhere that the closer anything is to death, the more it suffers. Yet however wretched life may be, still it wants to live. Why do you eat? Why do you sleep? So that you live. Why do you want riches or honors? That you know very well; but—why do you live? So as to live; and still you do not know why you live. Life is in itself so desirable that we desire it for its own sake. Those in hell are in everlasting torment, but they would not want to lose their lives, not the devils or the souls of men, for their life is so precious that it flows without any medium from God into the soul. And because it flows from God without medium they want to live. What is life? God's being is my life. If my life is God's being, then God's existence must be my existence and God's is-ness is my is-ness,[60] neither less nor more.

They live eternally "with God,"[61] directly close to God, not beneath or above. They perform all their works with God, and God with them. Saint John says: "The Word was with God" [John 1:1]. It was wholly equal, and it was close beside, not beneath there or above there, but just equal. When

---

58. On the basis of one manuscript, Quint here supplies a phrase that could be translated something like: "that he is not indifferent to all things."

59. This is actually from Bernard of Clairvaux, *Of Precept and Dispensation*, 20.60; the Latin is making a play on *amat, animat.*

60. *Isticheit,* a term coined perhaps by Eckhart. This sentence appears in the Cologne proceedings in G. Théry, "Edition critique des pièces relatives au process d'Eckhart," *Arches d'historie littéraire et doctrinal du moyen âge* 1 (1926), p. 240, where *isticheit* is rendered as *quidditas* ("what-it-is"), but it is not certain that this is what Eckhart had in mind, for his response here is totally in terms of *esse* or "existence."

61. *Bî gote;* Eckhart makes much play with *bî's* two senses, "close beside" and "at the home of."

God made man, he made woman from man's side, so that she might be equal to him. He did not make her out of man's head or his feet, so that she would be neither woman nor man for him, but so that she might be equal. So should the just soul be equal with God and close beside God, equal beside him, not beneath or above.

Who are they who are thus equal? Those who are equal to nothing, they alone are equal to God. The divine being is equal to nothing, and in it there is neither image nor form. To the souls who are equal, the Father gives equally, and he withholds nothing at all from them. Whatever the Father can achieve, that he gives equally to this soul, yes, if it no longer equals itself more than anything else, and it should not be closer to itself than to anything else. It should desire or heed its own honor, its profit and whatever may be its own, no more than what is a stranger's. Whatever belongs to anyone should not be distant or strange to the soul, whether this be evil or good. All the love of this world is founded on self-love. If you had forsaken that, you would have forsaken the whole world.

The Father gives birth to his Son in eternity, equal to himself. "The Word was with God, and God was the Word" [John 1:1]; it was the same in the same nature. Yet I say more: He has given birth to him in my soul. Not only is the soul with him, and he equal with it, but he is in it, and the Father gives his Son birth in the soul in the same way as he gives him birth in eternity, and not otherwise. He must do it whether he likes it or not. The Father gives birth to his Son without ceasing; and I say more: He gives me birth, me, his Son and the same Son. I say more: He gives birth not only to me, his Son, but he gives birth to me as himself and himself as me and to me as his being and nature. In the innermost source, there I spring out in the Holy Spirit, where there is one life and one being and one work. Everything God performs is one; therefore he gives me, his Son, birth without any distinction.[62] My fleshly father is not actually my father except in one little portion of his nature, and I am separated from him; he may be dead and I alive. Therefore the heavenly Father is truly my Father, for I am his Son and have everything that I have from him, and I am the same Son and not a different one. Because the Father performs one work, therefore his work is me, his Only-Begotten Son without any difference.

"We shall be completely transformed and changed into God" [2 Cor. 3:18]. See a comparison. In the same way, when in the sacrament bread is changed into the Body of our Lord, however many pieces of bread there were, they still become one Body. Just so, if all the pieces of bread were changed into my finger, there would still not be more than one finger. But if my finger were changed into the bread, there would be as many of one as of the other. What is changed into something else becomes one with it.

---

62. Art. 22 from "In agro dominico," deplored as suspect of heresy, is extracted from this.

I am so changed into him that he produces his being in me as one, not just similar.[63] By the living God, this is true! There is no distinction.[64]

The Father gives his Son birth without ceasing. Once the Son has been born he receives nothing from the Father because he has it all, but what he receives from the Father is his being born. In this we ought not to ask for something from God as if he were a stranger. Our Lord said to his disciples: "I have not called you servants, but friends" [John 15:14]. Whoever asks for something from someone else is a servant, and he who grants it is a master. Recently I considered whether there was anything I would take or ask from God. I shall take careful thought about this, because if I were accepting anything from God, I should be subject to him as a servant, and he in giving would be as a master. We shall not be so in life everlasting.[65]

Once I said here, and what I said is true: If a man obtains or accepts something from outside himself, he is in this wrong. One should not accept or esteem God as being outside oneself, but as one's own and as what is within one; nor should one serve or labor for any recompense, not for God or for his honor or for anything that is outside oneself, but only for that which one's own being and one's own life is within one. Some simple people think that they will see God as if he were standing there and they here. It is not so. God and I, we are one. I accept God into me in knowing; I go into God in loving. There are some who say that blessedness consists not in knowing but in willing. They are wrong; for if it consisted only in the will, it would not be one. Working and becoming are one. If a carpenter does not work, nothing becomes of the house. If the axe is not doing anything, nothing is becoming anything. In this working God and I are one; he is working and I am becoming. The fire changes anything into itself that is put into it and this takes on fire's own nature. The wood does not change the fire into itself, but the fire changes the wood into itself. So are we changed into God, that we shall know him as he is [1 John 3:2]. Saint Paul says: "So shall we come to know him, I knowing him just as he knows me" [1 Cor. 13:12], neither less nor more, perfectly equal. "The just will live forever, and their reward is with God," perfectly equal.

That we may love justice, for its own sake and for God, without asking return, may God help us to this. Amen.

---

63. This is Quint's interpretation of a difficult and doubtful phrase—MHG: *ein unglich*; Latin: *unum, non simile.*

64. "We shall be completely transformed . . . . There is no distinction": this is the material for art. 10 from "In agro dominico," beginning, "We are wholly transformed and changed into God," as if the notion were Eckhart's and not Paul's, and omitting the conceit about Eckhart's little finger. The article was condemned as heretical.

65. "Recently I thought . . . life everlasting": this is the material for art. 9 from "In agro dominico," very accurately translated and condemned as heretical.

SELECTION **5**

Julian of Norwich

Revelations of Divine Love,
Chapters 58–63

A well-known English mystic, Julian
of Norwich (1342–1416) lived as an anchorite in a cell attached to St.
Julian's Church, Norwich. After a series of visions of Christ's sufferings
while being healed of a serious illness, she wrote *Revelations of Divine Love*
(also titled *Showings*) in two accounts: a shorter one (written earlier) and a
longer one (written twenty or thirty years later). In these accounts, Julian
emphasized God's love, developing a Pauline theology of sin, grace, and
redemption centered on our solidarity with Christ, our mother. Her unique
contribution lies not in her reference to God as mother (early church and
medieval writers had already done this) but in her portrayal of Trinitarian interrelationships and activities in terms of God's fatherly and motherly
care for us.

As our "almighty Father" and our "all-wise Mother" with all "the love
and goodness of the Holy Spirit," the Trinity relates to us in three ways: in
nature (giving us our "being"); in *mercy* ("increasing" our participation in
Christ's passion, death, and resurrection, which "reforms" and "restores"
us); and in *grace* ("fulfilling" us beyond all we could desire as we yield to
the Holy Spirit's "rewarding" and "giving"). In these three ways, the Trinity participates in our lives in a "doubling" that gives us not only our (1)
"substance" (our "being") in each of the three persons as one God but also
(2) our "sensual nature" (our created nature as finite beings) in our mother
Christ Jesus, who is one with the Father and the Holy Spirit.

As loving mother, Christ Jesus does for us all the "sweet offices of
motherhood." He gives his life for us in his incarnation, death, and resurrection—opposing sin, taking us out of hell and our wretched condition,
suffering for us, nourishing and feeding us with the blessed sacraments,
and bringing us ultimately into the blissful unity of eternal life with God.
Moreover, as loving mother, Christ Jesus attunes herself to her children's
needs—allowing them to fall, be chastised, and healed in the course of time
by being united with her. In all this activity, nature and grace work together;
both are of God.

Our response is simply to be like children. Neither despairing nor trusting solely in ourselves, we are simply called to trust in Christ our loving
mother as she reassures us, "All will be well": all the blessed children who
come from Christ by nature will be brought again into him by grace.

From Julian of Norwich, *Revelations of Divine Love*, trans. Grace Warrack
(London: Musuen & Co. Ltd., 1901), 140–57.

Chapter 58

"All our life is in three: 'Nature, Mercy, Grace.' The high Might of the Trinity is our Father, the deep Wisdom of the Trinity is our Mother, and the great Love of the Trinity is our Lord."

God, the blessed Trinity, who is everlasting Being—just as God is endless from without beginning, just so it was in God's endless purpose to make humankind, whose fair Kind first was prepared to God's own Son, the Second Person. And when God would, by full accord of all the Trinity, God made us all at once; and in our making God knit us and oned us to himself: by which oneing we are kept as clear and as noble as we were made.[66] By the virtue of the same precious oneing, we love our Maker and seek God, praise God and thank God, and endlessly enjoy God. And this is the work that is wrought continually in every soul that shall be saved: which is the Godly Will aforesaid.[67] And thus in our making, God, Almighty, is our Nature's Father; and God, All-Wisdom, is our Nature's Mother; with the Love and the Goodness of the Holy Spirit: which is all one God, one Lord. And in the knitting and the oneing God is our Very, True Spouse, and we God's loved Wife, God's Fair Maiden—a Wife with whom God is never displeased. For God says: I love you and you love me, and our love shall never be disparted in two.

I beheld the working of all the blessed Trinity. In this beholding I saw and understood these three properties: the property of the Fatherhood, the property of the Motherhood, and the property of the Lordhood, in one God. In our Father Almighty we have our keeping and our bliss in regard to our natural Substance, which is to us by our making, without beginning. And in the Second Person in skill and wisdom we have our keeping in regard to our Sense-soul: our restoring and our saving; for he is our Mother, Brother, and Savior.[68] And in our good Lord, the Holy Spirit,

---

66. Ed. note: Julian uses "one" as a verb to mean "join."

67. Ed. note: Julian's use of the "godly will of the soul" (never separated from God by sin; cf. 1 John 3:9) and of "God our Mother" suggest familiarity with the writings of William of St. Thierry, a theologian and mystic, and abbot of the Benedictine monastery of Saint-Thierry (ca. 1075–1148). See *Julian of Norwich: Showings*, trans. with an intro. by Edmund Colledge and James Walsh (New York: Paulist Press, 1978), 20.

68. Ed. note: Cf. Anselm's prayer to St. Paul, "But you, too, good Jesus, are not you also a mother? Is not he a mother who like a hen gathers his chicks beneath his wing? Truly Lord, you are a mother too. . . ." See also Augustine's comment on Psalm 101:7: "I am made like a pelican in the desert," where he writes that "Christ exercises fatherly authority and maternal love," making the same comparison as Anselm "just as Paul is also father and mother . . . through his gospel preaching" [Cf. 1 Thess. 2:11; 1 Cor. 4:14; 2 Cor. 6:13; Gal. 4:1]. See also the depiction of Christ as mother in Mechtild of Hackborn, Bridget of Sweden, and Catherine of Siena. These references are discussed in *Julian of Norwich: Showings*, 87, 90–91.

we have our rewarding and our meed-giving for our living and our travail, and endless overpassing of all that we desire in his marvelous courtesy of his high plenteous grace.[69] For all our life is in *three*: in the first we have our Being, in the second we have our Increasing, and in the third we have our Fulfilling: the first is Nature, the second is Mercy, and the third is Grace.

For the first, I understood that the high Might of the Trinity is our Father, and the deep Wisdom of the Trinity is our Mother, and the great Love of the Trinity is our Lord: and all this have we in Nature and in the making of our Substance.

And furthermore I saw that the Second Person, which is our Mother in regard to the Substance, that same dearworthy Person is become our Mother in regard to the Sense-soul. For we are double by God's making: that is to say, Substantial and Sensual. Our Substance is the higher part, which we have in our Father, God Almighty; and the Second Person of the Trinity is our Mother in Nature, in making of our Substance: in whom we are grounded and rooted. And he is our Mother in Mercy, in taking of our Sense-part. And thus our Mother is to us in diverse manners working: in whom our parts are kept undisparted. For in our Mother Christ we profit and increase, and in Mercy he reforms us and restores, and, by the virtue of his Passion and his Death and Uprising, ones us to our Substance. Thus works our Mother in Mercy to all his children that are to him yielding and obedient.

And Grace works with Mercy, and especially in two properties, as it was shown. This working belongs to the Third Person, the Holy Spirit, who works *rewarding* and *giving*. Rewarding is a large giving-of-truth that the Lord does to him that has travailed; and giving is a courteous working which he does freely of Grace, fulfilling and overpassing all that is deserved of creatures.

Thus in our Father, God Almighty, we have our being; and in our Mother of Mercy we have our reforming and restoring: in whom our Parts are oned and all made perfect Man; and by reward-yielding and giving in Grace of the Holy Spirit, we are fulfilled.

And our Substance is in our Father, God Almighty, and our Substance is in our Mother, God, All-wisdom; and our Substance is in our Lord the Holy Spirit, God All-goodness. For our Substance is whole in each Person of the Trinity, which is one God. And our Sense-soul is only in the Second Person Christ Jesus, in whom is the Father and the Holy Spirit. In him and by him we are mightily taken out of hell, and out of the wretchedness in Earth worshipfully brought up into heaven and blissfully oned to our Substance—increased in riches and in nobleness by all the virtues of Christ, and by the grace and working of the Holy Spirit.

---

69. Ed. note: "Meed-giving" means "reward-giving." "Meed" refers to a fitting reward or recompense.

Chapter 59

"Jesus Christ that does Good against evil is our Very Mother: we have our Being of him where the Ground of Motherhood begins—with all the sweet Keeping by Love, that endlessly follows."

And all this bliss we have by Mercy and Grace. This manner of bliss we might never have had nor known but if that property of Goodness which is God had been contraried: whereby we have this bliss. For wickedness has been suffered to rise contrary to Goodness, and the Goodness of Mercy and Grace contraried against the wickedness and turned all to goodness and to worship, to all these that shall be saved. For it is the property in God that does good against evil. Thus Jesus Christ that does good against evil is our Very Mother: we have our Being of him—where the Ground of Motherhood begins—with all the sweet Keeping of Love that endlessly follows. As truly as God is our Father, so truly God is our Mother; and this God showed in all, and especially in these sweet words where God says: *It is I.* That is to say, *I it am, the Might and the Goodness of the Fatherhood; I it am, the Wisdom of the Motherhood; I it am, the Light and the Grace that is all blessed Love: I it am, the Trinity, I it am, the Unity: I am the sovereign Goodness of all manner of things. I am that makes you love: I am that makes you long: I it am, the endless fulfilling of all true desires* [cf. Exod. 3:14].

For there the soul is highest, noblest, and worthiest, where it is lowest, meekest, and mildest: and out of this *Substantial Ground* we have all our virtues in our Sense-part by gift of Nature, by helping and speeding of Mercy and Grace: without which we may not profit. Our high Father, God Almighty, which is Being, he knew and loved us from before all time: of which knowing, in his marvelous deep charity and the foreseeing counsel of all the blessed Trinity, he willed that the Second Person should become our Mother [cf. Col. 2:9–19]. Our Father wills, our Mother works, our good Lord the Holy Spirit confirms. Therefore it belongs to us to love our God in whom we have our being—reverently thanking and praising the Father for our making, mightily praying to our Mother for mercy and pity, and to our Lord the Holy Spirit for help and grace.

For in these three is all our life: Nature, Mercy, Grace. In these we have meekness and mildness, patience and pity, and hating of sin and of wickedness—for it belongs properly to virtue to hate sin and wickedness. And thus is Jesus our Very Mother in Nature by virtue of our first making; and Jesus is our Very Mother in Grace, by taking our nature made. All the fair working, and all the sweet natural office of dearworthy Motherhood is appropriated to the Second Person: for in him we have this Godly Will whole and safe without end, both in Nature and in Grace, of his own proper Goodness.

I understood three manners of beholding of Motherhood in God: the first is grounded in our Nature's *making*; the second is *taking* of our nature—and there begins the Motherhood of Grace; the third is Motherhood of *working*—and therein is an overflowing by the same Grace, of length and breadth and height and of deepness without end.[70] And all is one Love.

Chapter 60

"The Kind, loving Mother"

But now I need to say a little more of this overflowing, as I understand in the meaning of our Lord: how that we be brought again by the Motherhood of Mercy and Grace into our Nature's place, where that we were made by the Motherhood of Nature-Love whose Kindly-love never leaves us.

Our Mother by Nature, our Mother in Grace—because he would all wholly become our Mother in all things, he took the Ground of his Works full low and full mildly in the Maiden's womb. (And this he showed in the First Showing where he brought that meek Maid before the eye of my understanding in the simple stature as she was when she conceived.)[71] That is to say, our high God is sovereign Wisdom of all. In this low place he arrayed and adorned him full ready in our poor flesh, himself to do the service and the office of Motherhood in all things.

The Mother's service is nearest, readiest, and surest: nearest, for it is most of nature; readiest, for it is most of love; and surest for it is most of truth. This office none might, nor could, nor ever should do to the full, but he alone. We know that all our mothers' bearing is bearing of us to pain and to dying: and what is this but that our Very Mother, Jesus, he—All-Love—bears us to joy and to endless living?—blessed may he be! Thus he sustains us within himself in love; and travailed, until the full time that he would suffer the sharpest throes and the most grievous pains that ever were or ever shall be; and died at the last. And when he had finished, and so borne us to bliss, yet might not all this make full content to his marvelous love; and that he shows in these high overpassing words of love: *If I might suffer more, I would suffer more.* He might no more die, but he would not stint of working: wherefore then it behooves him to feed us; for the dearworthy love of Motherhood has made him debtor to us.

The mother may give her child suck of her milk, but our precious Mother, Jesus, he may feed us with himself, and does it, full courteously and full tenderly, with the Blessed Sacrament that is precious food of my life; and with all the sweet Sacraments he sustains us full mercifully and graciously. And so he meant in this blessed word where he said: *It is I that Holy Church preaches to you and teaches you.* That is to say: *All the health and life of Sacraments, all the virtue and grace of my Word, all the Goodness that is ordained in Holy Church for you, it is I.*

---

70. Ed. note: I am using "overflowing" instead of "forthspreading," the word Julian uses to translate *circumincessio* (the mutual interpenetration of the Trinitarian persons), which describes the expansion of God's love in Christ (Eph. 3:18–19).

71. Ed. note: Here Julian recalls an earlier revelation about Mary.

The Mother may lay the child tenderly to her breast, but our tender Mother Jesus may homely lead us into his blessed breast, by his sweet open side, and show therein part of the Godhead and the joys of heaven, with spiritual sureness of endless bliss. And that he shows in the Tenth Showing, giving the same understanding in this sweet word where he says: *Lo! how I loved you;* looking to the Wound in his side, rejoicing. This fair lovely word *Mother*, it is so sweet and so close in Nature of itself that it may not verily be said of none but of *him*; and to her that is very Mother of him and of all. To the property of Motherhood belongs natural love, wisdom, and knowing; and it is good: for though it be so that our bodily bringing forth be but little, low, and simple in regard of our spiritual bringing forth, yet it is he that does it in the creatures by whom that it is done. The Kind loving Mother that perceives and knows the need of her child, she keeps it full tenderly, as the nature and condition of Motherhood will. And as it waxes in age, she changes her working, but not her love. And when it is waxen of more age, she suffers that it be beaten in breaking down of vices, to make the child receive virtues and graces. This working, with all that be fair and good, our Lord does it in them by whom it is done: thus he is our Mother in Nature by the working of Grace in the lower part for love of the higher part. And he wills that we know this: for he will have all our love fastened to him.

And in this I saw that all our duty that we owe, by God's bidding, to Fatherhood and Motherhood, for reason of God's Fatherhood and Motherhood is fulfilled in true loving of God; which blessed love Christ works in us. And this was shown in all the Revelations and especially in the high plenteous words where he says: *It is I that you love.*

Chapter 61
"By the assay of this falling we shall have a high marvelous knowing of Love in God, without end. For strong and marvelous is that love which may not, nor will not, be broken for trespass."

And in our spiritual bringing forth he uses more tenderness of keeping, without any likeness: by as much as our soul is of more price in his sight. He kindles our understanding, he directs our ways, he eases our conscience, he comforts our soul, he lightens our heart, and gives us, in part, knowing and believing in his blissful Godhead, with gracious mind in his sweet Manhood and his blessed Passion, with reverent marveling in his high, overpassing Goodness; and makes us to love all that he loves, for his love, and to be well-pleased with him and all his works. And when we fall, hastily he raises us by his lovely calling and gracious touching. And when we be thus strengthened by his sweet working, then we with all our will choose him, by his sweet grace, to be his servants and his lovers lastingly without end.

And after this he suffers some of us to fall more hard and more grievously than ever we did afore, as we think. And then suppose we (who be
not all wise) that all were naught that we have begun. But this is not so.
For it needs us to fall, and it needs us to see it. For if we never fell, we
should not know how feeble and how wretched we are of our self, and also
we should not fully know that marvelous love of our Maker. For we shall
truly see in heaven, without end, that we have grievously sinned in this
life, and notwithstanding this, we shall see that we were never hurt in his
love, we were never the less of price in his sight. And by the assay of this
falling we shall have a high, marvelous knowing of love in God, without
end. For strong and marvelous is that love which may not, nor will not, be
broken for trespass. And this is one understanding of our profit. Another
is the lowness and meekness that we shall get by the sight of our falling:
for thereby we shall highly be raised in heaven; to which raising we could
never have come without that meekness. And therefore it needs us to see
it; and if we see it not, though we fell it should not profit us. And commonly, first we fall and later we see it: and both of the Mercy of God.

The mother may suffer the child to fall sometimes, and to be hurt in
diverse manners for its own profit, but she may never suffer that any manner of peril come to the child, for love. And though our earthly mother
may suffer her child to perish, our heavenly Mother, Jesus, may not suffer
us that are his children to perish: for he is All-mighty, All-wisdom, and
All-love; and so is none but he,—blessed may he be!

But oftentimes when our falling and our wretchedness is showed us,
we are so sore adread, and so greatly ashamed of our self, that scarcely we
find where we may hold us. But then wills not our courteous Mother that
we flee away, for him were nothing loathed. But he wills then that we use
the condition of a child: for when it is hurt, or adread, it runs hastily to the
mother for help, with all its might. So wills he that we do, as a meek child
saying thus: *My kind Mother, my Gracious Mother, my dearworthy Mother,
have mercy on me: I have made myself foul and unlike to You, and I nor may
nor can amend it but with your help and grace.* And if we do not feel eased
once, we can be sure that he uses the condition of a wise mother. For if he
see that it be more profit to us to mourn and to weep, he suffers it, with
ruth and pity, unto the best time, for love. And he wills then that we use the
property of a child, that evermore of nature trusts to the love of the mother
in weal and in woe.

And he wills that we take us mightily to the Faith of Holy Church and
find there our dearworthy Mother, in solace of true Understanding, with
all the blessed Common. For one single person may oftentimes be broken, as it seems to himself, but the whole Body of Holy Church was never
broken, nor never shall be, without end. And therefore a sure thing it is, a
good and a gracious, to will meekly and mightily to be fastened and oned
to our Mother, Holy Church. that is, Christ Jesus. For the food of mercy

that is his dearworthy blood and precious water is plenteous to make us fair and clean; the blessed wounds of our Savior be open and enjoy to heal us; the sweet, gracious hands of our Mother be ready and diligently about us. For he in all this working uses the office of a kind nurse that has naught else to do but to give heed about the salvation of her child. It is his office to save us: it is his worship to do it and it is his will that we know it: for he wills that we love him sweetly and trust in him meekly and mightily. And this showed he in these gracious words: *I keep you full surely*.

Chapter 62
"God is Very Father and Very Mother of Nature: and all natures that God has made to flow out of God to work God's will shall be restored and brought again into God by the salvation of Humankind through the working of Grace."

For in that time God showed our frailty and our fallings, our afflictions and our nothings, our despites and our outcastings, and all our woe so far forth as I thought it might befall in this life. And soon afterwards God showed God's blessed Might, God's blessed Wisdom, God's blessed Love: that God keeps us in this time as tenderly and as sweetly to God's worship, and as surely to our salvation, as God does when we are in most solace and comfort. And there he raises us spiritually and highly in heaven, and turns it all to God's worship and to our joy, without end. For God's love suffers us never to lose time.

And all this is of the Nature-Goodness of God, by the working of Grace. God is kind in God's being: that is to say, that Goodness that is Nature, it is God. God is the ground, God is the substance, God is the same thing that is Nature-hood. And God is very Father and very Mother of Nature: and all natures that God has made to flow out of him to work God's will shall be restored and brought again into God by the salvation of humanity through the working of Grace.

For of all natures that God has set in diverse creatures by part, in humans is all the whole; in fullness and in virtue, in fairness and in goodness, in royalty and nobleness, in all manner of majesty, of preciousness and worship. Here may we see that we are all beholden to God for nature, and we are all beholden to God for grace. Here may we see us needs not greatly to seek far out to know sundry natures, but to Holy Church, to our Mother's breast: that is to say, to our own soul where our Lord dwells; and there shall we find all now in faith and in understanding. And afterward verily in himself clearly, in bliss.

But let no man nor woman take this singularly to himself or herself: for it is not so, it is general: for it is of our precious Christ, and to him was this fair nature made ready for the worship and nobility of humanity's making, and for the joy and the bliss of humanity's salvation even as he saw, perceived, and knew from without beginning.

Chapter 63
"'As verily as sin is unclean, so verily is it unkind'—a disease or
monstrous thing against nature. 'He shall heal us full fair.'"

Here may we see that we have verily of Nature to hate sin, and we have
verily of Grace to hate sin. For Nature is all good and fair in itself, and
Grace was sent out to save Nature and destroy sin, and bring again fair
nature to the blessed point from whence it came: that is God; with more
nobleness and worship by the virtuous working of Grace. For it shall be
seen before God by all God's Holy in joy without end that Nature has been
assayed in the fire of tribulation and therein has been found no flaw, no
fault. Thus are Nature and Grace of one accord: for Grace is God, as Nature
is God: God is two in manner of working and one in love; and neither of
these works without other: they be not disparted.

And when we by Mercy of God and with God's help accord us to Nature
and Grace, we shall see verily that sin is in sooth viler and more painful
than hell, without likeness: for it is contrary to our fair nature. For as verily as sin is unclean, so verily is it unnatural, thus an horrible thing to see
for the loved soul that would be all fair and shining in the sight of God,
as Nature and Grace teaches. Yet be we not adread of this, save inasmuch
as dread may speed us: but meekly make we our moan to our dearworthy
Mother, and he shall besprinkle us in his precious blood and make our
soul full soft and full mild, and heal us full fair by process of time, right
as it is most worship to him and joy to us without end. And of this sweet
fair working he shall never cease nor stint till all his dearworthy children
be born and brought forth. (And that he showed where he showed me
understanding of the spiritual Thirst, that is the love-longing that shall last
till Doomsday.)

Thus in our Very Mother, Jesus, our life is grounded in the foreseeing
Wisdom of himself from without beginning, with the high Might of the
Father, the high sovereign Goodness of the Holy Spirit. And in the taking of our nature he quickened us; in his blessed dying upon the Cross he
bare us to endless life; and from that time, and now, and evermore unto
Doomsday, he feeds us and furthers us: even as that high sovereign Kindness of Motherhood, and as Kindly need of Childhood asks.

Fair and sweet is our heavenly Mother in the sight of our souls; precious and lovely are the Gracious Children in the sight of our heavenly
Mother, with mildness and meekness, and all the fair virtues that belong
to children in Nature. For of nature the Child despairs not of the Mother's
love, of nature the Child presumes not of itself, of nature the Child loves
the Mother and each one of the other children. These are the fair virtues,
with all other that be like, wherewith our heavenly Mother is served and
pleased.

And I understood none higher stature in this life than Childhood, in
feebleness and failing of might and of wit, unto the time that our Gracious

Mother has brought us up to our Father's Bliss. And then shall it verily be known to us his meaning in those sweet words where he says: *All shall be well: and you shall see, yourself, that all manner of things shall be well*. And then shall the Bliss of our Mother, in Christ, be new to begin in the Joys of our God: which new beginning shall last without end, new beginning. Thus I understood that all his blessed children which be come out of him by Nature shall be brought again into him by Grace.

SELECTION **6**

Nicholas of Cusa

Vision of God, Chapter 10

As one of the most influential German thinkers of the fifteenth century, Nicholas of Cusa (1401–1464) developed a distinctive Christian Neoplatonist view of reality. Among his many works, he is best known for *On Learned Ignorance*. Using the central concept of the "maximum," it contrasts God as absolute maximum and the universe as "contracted" or restricted maximum, and concludes with Christ as the maximum uniting both the absolute and contracted. Because "there is no proportion between the infinite and finite," human concepts (which measure the limited world of the more or less) cannot comprehend God (who is unlimited and transcendent). God lies beyond the world governed by the principle of noncontradiction. Nonetheless, within God's infinite oneness, God "enfolds" all reality, and all reality "unfolds" from God. Thus, in God, there is a "coincidence of opposites" where both differentiation and limitation meet in undifferentiated unity. Although God is incomprehensible, we can approach God through exercises of the mind and heart that indirectly enable us to understand something of God's "incomprehensibility"—thus the title: "On Learned Ignorance."

The *Vision of God* draws on these insights in a prayer that enacts a series of meditative exercises. Written in response to a request from the Benedictines of Tegernsee, the prayer was accompanied by an "all-seeing" icon (probably an image of the suffering Jesus looking at the viewer) that symbolized two aspects of the "vision of God": God's seeing us and our seeing God. Gazing at the icon enacts a dialectic of presence and absence—of seeing and not seeing. On the one hand, our seeing God (or God seen) is identical with God's seeing us. On the other, there is distance: Jesus' eyes in the painting are an icon; they are not his real eyes. We cannot see God's face, yet precisely by our gazing at the icon, God sees us even as we see God.

Cusanus uses another metaphor in this prayer: the wall of paradise, which symbolizes the "coincidence of opposites." Outside the wall, human reason can understand the difference between things *enfolded* (or identical) with God and the same things *unfolded* in the universe. The wall depicts where we are with Christ, at the door of the wall. Here enfolding and unfolding coincide in the coincidence of opposites. God exists, infinite and unknowable, inside the wall in eternity, where enfolding and unfolding fall away.

In the selection below, Cusanus describes how the door in the wall—of the coincidence of opposites—lies precisely where God's seeing and speaking coincide with our being seen and spoken into existence. We receive our being from God by seeing God as God sees us; our being is equally God's seeing and God's being seen by us. In this, God speaks and conceives all things at once (simultaneously), even though all things come into existence successively. Thus, our "now" and "then" *coincide* in the "wall" surrounding where God dwells in absolute eternity—beyond our now and then—as the one who exists and speaks.

From *Selected Spiritual Writings*, trans. H. Lawrence Bond
(New York: Paulist Press, 1997), 252–54.

Chapter 10
How God Is Seen Beyond the Coincidence of Contradictories, and How Seeing is Being

I stand before this image of your face, my God, which I observe with the eyes of sense, and I attempt with inward eyes to behold the truth that is designated in the picture. The thought occurs to me, O Lord, that your gaze speaks, for your speaking is not other than your seeing, because they are not in reality different in you, who are absolute simplicity itself. Therefore, I experience clearly that you see all things and each thing together. For when I preach, I speak at one and the same time both to the church congregated and to each individual present in the church. I preach only one word, and with this one word, I speak to each person individually. What is for me the church is for you, O Lord, the entire world and every single creature which exists or can exist. Thus, you speak to individuals, and you see those to which you speak.

O Lord, you are the supreme comfort of those who hope in you. You inspire me to praise you from myself. For, as you willed, you have given me one face, and those to whom I preach see it individually and at the same time. Each one sees my individual face, and each hears in whole this simple sermon of mine. However, I cannot at the same moment hear separately all who speak, but only one at a time, nor can I at the same moment see them separately, but only one by one. But if such great power existed in me that being heard would coincide with hearing and being seen with seeing and also speaking with hearing, as in you, O Lord, who are the highest power, then I would hear and see all and each one at the same time. Just as I would speak to individuals simultaneously, so also in the very same moment in which I were speaking I would see and hear the responses of all and each.[72]

Consequently, when I am at the door of the coincidence of opposites, guarded by the angel stationed at the entrance of paradise [cf. Gen. 3:24], I begin to see you, O Lord. For you are there where speaking, seeing, hearing, tasting, touching, reasoning, knowing, and understanding are the same and where seeing coincides with being seen, hearing with being heard, tasting with being tasted, touching with being touched, speaking with hearing, and creating with speaking. If I were to see just as I am visible, I would not be a creature, and if you, O God, did not see just as you are visible, you would not be God, the Almighty. You are visible by all creatures and you see all. In that you see all you are seen by all. For otherwise creatures cannot exist since they exist by your vision. If they did not see you who see, they would not receive being from you. The being of a creature is equally your seeing and your being seen.[73]

By your word, you speak to all that are and call into existence all that are not [Rom. 4:17]. You call them to hear you, and when they hear you, then they are. When, therefore, you speak, you speak to all and all to which you speak hear you. You speak to the earth, and you call it into human nature. The earth hears you, and its hearing this is its becoming human being. You speak to nothing as if it were something, and you call nothing into something, and nothing hears you since what was nothing becomes something [Gen. 1:3ff; Ps. 49 (50):1; John 1:1–3].

O infinite Power, your conceiving is your speaking. You conceive sky, and it exists as you conceive it. You conceive earth, and it exists as you conceive it. While conceiving, you see and you speak and you work and you do all else that one is able to name.

You inspire wonder, my God. You speak once; you conceive once. How is it, therefore, that all things do not exist simultaneously, but many come into being successively? How do so many diverse things exist out of a single concept? You enlighten me, stationed at the threshold of the door, for your concept is simplest eternity itself. Nothing, however, can be made subsequent to simplest eternity. Infinite duration, which is eternity itself, embraces all succession. Everything, therefore, that appears to us in succession in no way exists subsequent to your concept, which is eternity. For your unique concept, which is also your Word, enfolds all things and each single thing. Your eternal Word cannot be manifold, diverse, variable, or subject to change, because it is simple eternity. Thus, O Lord, I see that nothing exists subsequent to your concept, but all things exist because you

---

72. On the analogy of the preacher, see Augustine, *Epistolae* 137.2.7.
73. On the soul's relationship to God's seeing and being seen, cf. Meister Eckhart, *Predigten* 10, 173, and *Predigten* 12, 201.

conceive them. Moreover, you conceive in eternity. But in eternity succession is, without succession, eternity itself, your Word itself, O Lord my God. You have not conceived before it existed anything that appears to us in time. For in eternity, in which you conceive, all temporal succession coincides in the same now of eternity. Therefore, nothing is past or future where future and past coincide with the present.

But that things in this world exist according to earlier and later stems from the fact that you did not conceive such things earlier so that they would exist. Had you conceived them earlier, they would have existed earlier. But one is not almighty in whose thought earlier and later occur, so that one first conceives one thing and afterward another. Thus, since you are God the Almighty, you are in Paradise inside its wall. The wall, moreover, is that coincidence where later coincides with earlier, where the end coincides with the beginning, and where the alpha and the omega are the same [Rev. 1:8; 2:8; 21:6; 22:13; cf. Isa. 41:4; 44:6; 48:12].

Therefore, things exist always because you tell them to exist, and they do not exist earlier because you do not earlier speak. When I read that Adam existed so many years ago and that one such as he was born today, it seems impossible that Adam existed then because you then willed it and likewise that someone else was born today because now you have willed it, and that nevertheless you did not earlier will Adam to exist than you willed the one born today to exist. But that which seems impossible is necessity itself. For now and then exist after your word. And, therefore, to one approaching you, now and then meet in coincidence within the wall that surrounds the place where you dwell. For now and then coincide in the circle of the wall of paradise. But it is beyond now and then that you, my God, who are absolute eternity, exist and speak.

CHAPTER 3

God in the Reformation

Martin Luther

**"Luther's Experience of
the 'Righteousness of God,'"
The Heidelberg Disputation,
The Large Catechism,
"The Right Hand of God,"
and "God Is a Supernatural,
Inscrutable Being"**

An Augustinian monk, Martin Luther (1483–1546) initiated the Protestant Reformation. Outraged by clergy corruption and anxious about God's judgment, he came upon the idea of justification by faith: the doctrine that salvation is a free gift of God's grace. Initially thinking that the "righteousness of God" had to do with God's judgment and punishment, he discovered while meditating that Scripture uses it to speak about God's mercy that justifies us by faith (Rom. 1:17): God's righteousness has to do with God's making us become what God is. Further, something comparable happens with all of God's other attributes—strength, wisdom, salvation, glory, and so on: they describe "what God does in us" when God shares himself and allows us to participate in his being.

All people may have a general (*generalis*) knowledge of God as creator and righteous judge (cf. Rom. 1:20), but such knowledge lacks certainty about the true and proper (*propria*) knowledge of God—that God saves us as sinners. General or natural knowledge of God merely shows us the law (God's "left hand" or God's backside; cf. Exod. 33:18–20). Only by clinging to the gospel's evangelical proclamation (God's "right hand") are we able to look straight into God's face. Reason may lead to monotheism—*that* God is—but it cannot lead to the Trinity—*who* God is and what takes place "inside" God, where God opens his heart to us in mercy in the Son's incarnation.

Revealed in the crucified Christ, God is only known in the cross and in suffering (1 Cor. 1:25). The *Heidelberg Disputation* describes how "theologians of glory" use human wisdom and morality to seek God's invisible nature and majestic attributes (Rom. 1:20). But without the cross, we misuse the best in the worst way—calling evil good and good evil. We need the cross, which "calls a thing what it actually is." Not speculative, the knowledge of God has to do with our entire existence. God meets us in death—Christ's death—which we experience as our own when we die together with him. Here in contrast to human love, which seeks what it desires, God's love "creates what is pleasing to him."

Thus, justification has to do with God's power to create "something" even out of its opposite—the "nothing" of sin and death. In turn, faith is fundamentally about the first commandment. If whatever we rely and depend on with our whole being becomes our god—and faith and trust can make either God or an idol—then we must rely on the God who, as the creed affirms, has the power to provide, nourish, and preserve us with every good gift, even in danger or calamity.

Indeed, as Luther notes in his teaching on the Lord's Supper, when Scripture speaks about God (e.g., God's arm, hand, nature, face, Spirit, wisdom, etc.), it deals with one thing: God's power, which is simple and not divided. Thus, the "right hand of God" is not a specific place but the almighty power of God, paradoxically nowhere and yet everywhere. Not determined or measured, God's power is uncircumscribed and immeasurable, beyond and above all that is or may be, yet also present in all places, preserving every single creature in its innermost and outermost being, even the tiniest leaf.

Moreover, faith asserts something more: God is not only present in Christ as God is present in all others, but God dwells in him bodily in such a way that Christ is God himself, whose righteousness alone can make us righteous.

"Luther's Experience of the 'Righteousness of God'"

From *LW*, vol. 34, *Career of the Reformer* 4, 336–38.

Meanwhile, I had already during that year returned to interpret the Psalter anew. I had confidence in the fact that I was more skillful, after I had lectured in the university on St. Paul's epistles to the Romans, to the Galatians, and the one to the Hebrews. I had indeed been captivated with an extraordinary ardor for understanding Paul in the Epistle to the Romans. But up till then it was not the cold blood about the heart,[1] but a single word in Chapter 1 [v. 17], "In it the righteousness of God is revealed," that had stood in my way. For I hated that word "righteousness of God," which, according to the use and custom of all the teachers, I had been taught to understand philosophically regarding the formal or active righteousness, as they called it, with which God is righteous and punishes the unrighteous sinner.

Though I lived as a monk without reproach, I felt that I was a sinner before God with an extremely disturbed conscience. I could not believe that he was placated by my satisfaction. I did not love, yes, I hated the righteous God who punishes sinners, and secretly, if not blasphemously, certainly murmuring greatly, I was angry with God, and said, "As if, indeed, it is not enough, that miserable sinners, eternally lost through original sin,

1. Cf. Virgil *Georgics* 2, 484.

are crushed by every kind of calamity by the law of the decalogue, without having God add pain to pain by the gospel and also by the gospel threatening us with his righteousness and wrath!" Thus I raged with a fierce and troubled conscience. Nevertheless, I beat importunately upon Paul at that place, most ardently desiring to know what St. Paul wanted.

At last, by the mercy of God, meditating day and night, I gave heed to the context of the words, namely, "In it the righteousness of God is revealed, as it is written, 'He who through faith is righteous shall live.'" There I began to understand that the righteousness of God is that by which the righteous lives by a gift of God, namely by faith. And this is the meaning: the righteousness of God is revealed by the gospel, namely, the passive righteousness with which merciful God justifies us by faith, as it is written, "He who through faith is righteous shall live." Here I felt that I was altogether born again and had entered paradise itself through open gates. There a totally other face of the entire Scripture showed itself to me. Thereupon I ran through the Scriptures from memory. I also found in other terms an analogy, as, the work of God, that is, what God does in us, the power of God, with which he makes us strong, the wisdom of God, with which he makes us wise, the strength of God, the salvation of God, the glory of God.

And I extolled my sweetest word with a love as great as the hatred with which I had before hated the word "righteousness of God." Thus that place in Paul was for me truly the gate to paradise. Later I read Augustine's *The Spirit and the Letter*, where contrary to hope I found that he, too, interpreted God's righteousness in a similar way, as the righteousness with which God clothes us when he justifies us.[2] Although this was heretofore said imperfectly and he did not explain all things concerning imputation clearly, it nevertheless was pleasing that God's righteousness with which we are justified was taught. Armed more fully with these thoughts, I began a second time to interpret the Psalter. And the work would have grown into a large commentary, if I had not again been compelled to leave the work begun, because Emperor Charles V in the following year convened the diet at Worms.[3]

The Heidelberg Disputation

From *LW*, vol. 31, *Career of the Reformer* 1, 39–41.

Distrusting completely our own wisdom, according to that counsel of the Holy Spirit, "Do not rely on your own insight" [Prov. 3:5], we humbly present to the judgment of all those who wish to be here these theological paradoxes, so that it may become clear whether they have been deduced

2. Augustine *The Spirit and the Letter*, lib. i, ix, x, 15–16.
3. Luther received the summons to Worms at the end of March, 1521, and had to interrupt his exegesis at Psalm 21.

well or poorly from St. Paul, the especially chosen vessel and instrument of Christ, and also from St. Augustine, his most trustworthy interpreter.

1. The law of God, the most salutary doctrine of life, cannot advance man on his way to righteousness, but rather hinders him.

2. Much less can human works, which are done over and over again with the aid of natural precepts, so to speak, lead to that end.

3. Although the works of man always seem attractive and good, they are nevertheless likely to be mortal sins.

4. Although the works of God always seem unattractive and appear evil, they are nevertheless really eternal merits.

5. The works of men are thus not mortal sins (we speak of works which are apparently good), as though they were crimes.

6. The works of God (we speak of those which he does through man) are thus not merits, as though they were sinless.

7. The works of the righteous would be mortal sins if they would not be feared as mortal sins by the righteous themselves out of pious fear of God.

8. By so much more are the works of man mortal sins when they are done without fear and in unadulterated, evil self-security.

9. To say that works without Christ are dead, but not mortal, appears to constitute a perilous surrender of the fear of God.

10. Indeed, it is very difficult to see how a work can be dead and at the same time not a harmful and mortal sin.

11. Arrogance cannot be avoided or true hope be present unless the judgment of condemnation is feared in every work.

12. In the sight of God sins are then truly venial when they are feared by men to be mortal.

13. Free will, after the fall, exists in name only, and as long as it does what it is able to do, it commits a mortal sin.

14. Free will, after the fall, has power to do good only in a passive capacity, but it can always do evil in an active capacity.

15. Nor could free will endure in a state of innocence, much less do good, in an active capacity, but only in its passive capacity.

16. The person who believes that he can obtain grace by doing what is in him adds sin to sin so that he becomes doubly guilty.

17. Nor does speaking in this manner give cause for despair, but for arousing the desire to humble oneself and seek the grace of Christ.

18. It is certain that man must utterly despair of his own ability before he is prepared to receive the grace of Christ.

19. That person does not deserve to be called a theologian who looks upon the invisible things of God as though they were clearly perceptible in those things which have actually happened [Rom. 1:20].

20. He deserves to be called a theologian, however, who comprehends the visible and manifest things of God seen through suffering and the cross.

21. A theologian of glory calls evil good and good evil. A theologian of the cross calls the thing what it actually is.

22. That wisdom which sees the invisible things of God in works as perceived by man is completely puffed up, blinded, and hardened.

23. The law brings the wrath of God, kills, reviles, accuses, judges, and condemns everything that is not in Christ [Rom. 4:15].

24. Yet that wisdom is not of itself evil, nor is the law to be evaded; but without the theology of the cross man misuses the best in the worst manner.

25. He is not righteous who does much, but he who, without work, believes much in Christ.

26. The law says, "do this," and it is never done. Grace says, "believe in this," and everything is already done.

27. Actually one should call the work of Christ an acting work and our work an accomplished work, and thus an accomplished work pleasing to God by the grace of the acting work.

28. The love of God does not find, but creates, that which is pleasing to it. The love of man comes into being through that which is pleasing to it.

The Large Catechism

From *The Book of Concord: The Confessions of the Evangelical Lutheran Church,* ed. R. Kolb, T. J. Wengert, and C. P. Arand (Minneapolis: Fortress Press, 2000), 386–90, 432–33.

The First Commandment
"You are to have no other gods."

That is, you are to regard me alone as your God. What does this mean, and how is it to be understood? What does "to have a god" mean, or what is God?

Answer: A "god" is the term for that to which we are to look for all good and in which we are to find refuge in all need. Therefore, to have a god is nothing else than to trust and believe in that one with your whole heart. As I have often said, it is the trust and faith of the heart alone that make both God and an idol. If your faith and trust are right, then your God is the true one. Conversely, where your trust is false and wrong, there you do not have the true God. For these two belong together, faith and God. Anything on which your heart relies and depends, I say, that is really your God.

The intention of this commandment, therefore, is to require true faith and confidence of the heart, which fly straight to the one true God and cling to him alone. What this means is: "See to it that you let me alone be your God, and never search for another." In other words: "Whatever good thing you lack, look to me for it and seek it from me, and whenever you suffer misfortune and distress, crawl to me and cling to me. I, I myself, will give you what you need and help you out of every danger. Only do not let your heart cling to or rest in anyone else."

So that it may be understood and remembered, I must explain this a little more plainly by citing some everyday examples of the opposite. There are some who think that they have God and everything they need when they have money and property; they trust in them and boast in them so stubbornly and securely that they care for no one else. They, too, have a god—mammon [Matt. 6:24] by name, that is, money and property—on which they set their whole heart. This is the most common idol on earth. Those who have money and property feel secure, happy, and fearless, as if they were sitting in the midst of paradise. On the other hand, those who have nothing doubt and despair as if they knew of no god at all. We will find very few who are cheerful, who do not fret and complain, if they do not have mammon. This desire for wealth clings and sticks to our nature all the way to the grave.

So, too, those who boast of great learning, wisdom, power, prestige, family, and honor and who trust in them have a god also, but not the one, true God. Notice again, how presumptuous, secure, and proud people are when they have such possessions, and how despondent they are when they lack them or when they are taken away. Therefore, I repeat, the correct interpretation of this commandment is that to have a god is to have something in which the heart trusts completely. . . .

Thus you can easily understand what and how much this commandment requires, namely, that one's whole heart and confidence be placed in God alone, and in no one else. To have a God, as you can well imagine, does not mean to grasp him with your fingers, or to put him into a purse, or to shut him up in a box. Rather, you lay hold of God when your heart grasps him and clings to him. To cling to him with your heart is nothing else than to entrust yourself to him completely. He wishes to turn us away from everything else apart from him, and to draw us to himself, because he is the one, eternal good. It is as if he said: "What you formerly sought from the saints, or what you hoped to receive from mammon or from anything else, turn to me for all of this; look on me as the one who will help you and lavish all good things upon you richly."

Look, here you have the true honor and worship that please God, which God also commands under penalty of eternal wrath, namely, that the heart should know no other consolation or confidence than in him, nor let itself be torn from him, but for his sake should risk everything and disregard everything else on earth. On the other hand, you will easily see and judge how the world practices nothing but false worship and idolatry. There has never been a nation so wicked that it did not establish and maintain some sort of worship. All people have set up their own god, to whom they looked for blessings, help, and comfort. . . .

This much, however, should be said to the common people, so that they may mark well and remember the sense of this commandment: We are to trust in God alone, to look to him alone, and to expect him to give us only good things; for it is he who gives us body, life, food, drink, nourishment, health, protection, peace, and all necessary temporal and eternal blessings. In addition, God protects us from misfortune and rescues and delivers us when any evil befalls us. It is God alone (as I have repeated often enough) from whom we receive everything good and by whom we are delivered from all evil. This, I think, is why we Germans from ancient times have called God by a name more elegant and worthy than found in any other language, a name derived from the word "good,"[4] because he is an eternal fountain who overflows with pure goodness and from whom pours forth all that is truly good.

Although much that is good comes to us from human beings, nevertheless, anything received according to his command and ordinance in fact comes from God. Our parents and authorities—as well as everyone who is a neighbor—have received the command to do us all kinds of good. So we receive our blessings not from them, but from God through them. Creatures are only the hands, channels, and means through which God bestows all blessings. For example, he gives to the mother breasts and milk for her infant or gives grain and all sorts of fruits from the earth for sustenance— things that no creature could produce by itself. No one, therefore, should presume to take or give anything unless God has commanded it. This forces us to recognize God's gifts and give him thanks, as this commandment requires. Therefore, we should not spurn even this way of receiving such things through God's creatures, nor are we through arrogance to seek other methods and ways than those God has commanded. For that would not be receiving them from God, but seeking them from ourselves.

Let each and everyone, then, see to it that you esteem this commandment above all things and not make light of it. Search and examine your own heart thoroughly, and you will discover whether or not it clings to God alone. If you have the sort of heart that expects from him nothing good but good, especially in distress and need, and renounces and forsakes all that is not God, then you have the one, true God. On the contrary, if your heart clings to something else and expects to receive from it more good and help than from God and does not run to God but flees from him when things go wrong, then you have another god, an idol.

Consequently, in order to show that God will not have this commandment taken lightly but will strictly watch over it, he has attached to it, first, a terrible threat, and, then, a beautiful comforting promise. Both of these should be thoroughly emphasized and impressed upon the young people so that they may take them to heart and remember them.

---

4. German: *gut*. This derivation is etymologically incorrect. The words for "God" (*Gott*) and "good" (*gut*) are not related in either Gothic or in Middle High German.

The First Article (of the Apostles' Creed)
  "I believe in God, the Father almighty,
  CREATOR *of heaven and earth . . ."*

This is the shortest possible way of describing and illustrating the nature, will, acts, and work of God the Father. Because the Ten Commandments have explained that we are to have no more than one God, so it may now be asked: "What kind of person is God? What does he do? How can we praise or portray or describe him in such a way so we may know him?" This is taught here and in the following articles. Thus the Creed is nothing else than a response and confession of Christians based on the First Commandment. If you were to ask a young child, "My dear, what kind of God do you have? What do you know about him?" he or she could say: "First, my God is the Father, who made heaven and earth. Aside from this one alone I regard nothing as God, for there is no one else who could create heaven and earth."

For the highly educated and those somewhat more well informed, however, all three articles can be treated more fully and divided into as many parts as there are words. But for the young pupils it is now enough to indicate the most necessary points, namely, as we have said, that this article deals with creation. We should emphasize the words "creator of heaven and earth." What is meant by these words or what do you mean when you say, "I believe in God, the Father almighty, creator," etc.? Answer: I hold and believe that I am God's creature, that is, that he has given me and constantly sustains my body, soul, and life, my members great and small, all my senses, my reason and understanding, and the like; my food and drink, clothing, nourishment, spouse and children, servants, house and farm, etc. Besides, he makes all creation help provide the benefits and necessities of life—sun, moon, and stars in the heavens; day and night; air, fire, water, the earth and all that it yields and brings forth; birds, fish, animals, grain, and all sorts of produce. Moreover, he gives all physical and temporal blessings—good government, peace, security. Thus we learn from this article that none of us has life—or anything else that has been mentioned here or can be mentioned—from ourselves, nor can we by ourselves preserve any of them, however small and unimportant. All this is comprehended in the word "Creator."

Moreover, we also confess that God the Father has given us not only all that we have and what we see before our eyes, but also that he daily guards and defends us against every evil and misfortune, warding off all sorts of danger and disaster. All this he does out of pure love and goodness, without our merit, as a kind father who cares for us so that no evil may befall us. But further discussion of this subject belongs in the other two parts of this article, where it says, "Father almighty."

Hence, because everything we possess, and everything in heaven and on earth besides, is daily given, sustained, and protected by God, it inevitably follows that we are in duty bound to love, praise, and thank him without ceasing, and, in short, to devote all these things to his service, as he has required and enjoined in the Ten Commandments.

Here much could be said if we were to describe how few people believe this article. We all pass over it; we hear it and recite it, but we neither see nor think about what the words command us to do. For if we believed it with our whole heart, we would also act accordingly, and not swagger about and boast and brag as if we had life, riches, power, honor, and such things of ourselves, as if we ourselves were to be feared and served. This is the way the wretched, perverse world acts, drowned in its blindness, misusing all the blessings and gifts of God solely for its own pride, greed, pleasure, and enjoyment, and never once turning to God to thank him or acknowledge him as Lord or Creator.

Therefore, if we believe it, this article should humble and terrify all of us. For we sin daily with eyes, ears, hands, body and soul, money and property, and with all that we have, especially those who even fight against the Word of God. Yet Christians have this advantage, that they acknowledge that they owe it to God to serve and obey him for all these things.

For this reason we ought daily to practice this article, impress it upon our minds, and remember it in everything we see and in every blessing that comes our way. Whenever we escape distress or danger, we should recognize how God gives and does all of this so that we may sense and see in them his fatherly heart and his boundless love toward us. Thus our hearts will be warmed and kindled with gratitude to God and a desire to use all these blessings to his glory and praise.

Such, very briefly, is the meaning of this article. It is all that ordinary people need to learn at first, both about what we have and receive from God and about what we owe him in return. This is knowledge of great significance, but an even greater treasure. For here we see how the Father has given to us himself with all creation and has abundantly provided for us in this life, apart from the fact that he has also showered us with inexpressible eternal blessings through his Son and the Holy Spirit, as we shall hear.

"The Right Hand of God"

From "That These Words of Christ, 'This is my Body,' etc., Still Stand Firm against the Fanatics," *LW*, vol. 37, *Word and Sacrament 3*, 57–60.

The Scriptures teach us, however, that the right hand of God is not a specific place in which a body must or may be, such as on a golden throne, but is the almighty power of God, which at one and the same time can be nowhere and yet must be everywhere. It cannot be at any one place, I say. For if it were at some specific place, it would have to be there in a circumscribed and determinate manner, as everything which is at one place must be at that place determinately and measurably, so that it cannot meanwhile be at any other place. But the power of God cannot be so determined and measured, for it is uncircumscribed and immeasurable, beyond and above all that is or may be.

On the other hand, it must be essentially present[5] at all places, even in the tiniest tree leaf. The reason is this: It is God who creates, effects, and preserves all things through his almighty power and right hand, as our Creed confesses. For he dispatches no officials or angels when he creates or preserves something, but all this is the work of his divine power itself. If he is to create or preserve it, however, he must be present and must make and preserve his creation both in its innermost and outermost aspects.

Therefore, indeed, he himself must be present in every single creature in its innermost and outermost being, on all sides, through and through, below and above, before and behind, so that nothing can be more truly present and within all creatures than God himself with his power. For it is he who makes the skin and it is he who makes the bones; it is he who makes the hair on the skin, and it is he who makes the marrow in the bones; it is he who makes every bit of the hair, it is he who makes every bit of the marrow. Indeed, he must make everything, both the parts and the whole. Surely, then, his hand which makes all this must be present; that cannot be lacking.

At this point the passage of Isaiah 66 [v. 2] derived from Genesis 1, undeniably applies: "Has not my hand made all these things?" Psalm 139 [vv. 7–10]: "Whither shall I go from thy Spirit? Or whither shall I flee from thy presence? If I ascend to heaven, thou art there! If I make my bed in hell, thou art there! If I take the wings of the morning dawn (and these are certainly great wings, as great as half the world) and dwell in the uttermost parts of the sea, even there thy hand shall hold me."

Why should I say a great deal? The Scriptures ascribe all miracles and works of God to his right hand, e.g. Acts 4 [5:31], Christ is exalted by the right hand of God; Psalm 118 [vv. 15f.], "The right hand of God does wonders, the right hand of the Lord exalts me." In Acts 17 [vv. 27 f.] Paul says, "God is not far from each one of us, for in him we live and move and have our being." And Romans 11 [v. 36], "From him and through him and to him are all things." And Jeremiah 23[vv. 23 f.], "Am I not[6] a God at hand, and not a God afar off? Do I not fill heaven and earth?" Isaiah 66 [v. 1], "Heaven is my throne and the earth is my footstool." He does not say, "A part of heaven is my throne, a part or spot of the earth is my footstool," but, "Whatever and wherever heaven is, there is my throne, whether heaven is beneath, above, or beside the earth. And whatever and wherever earth is,

---

5. *Wesentlich* and *gegenwertig*. *Wesentlich*, "essentially" or "substantially," means for Luther "in essence" in the ancient philosophical sense, cf. *Against Latomus*, *LW* 32, 202; it does not have the modern connotation of "for all practical purposes."

6. Jeremiah's text does not contain the negative here.

whether at the bottom of the sea, in the grave of the dead, or at the middle of the earth, there is my footstool." Come and tell me now, where are his head, arm, breast, body, if with his feet he fills the earth and with his legs he fills heaven? He reaches out ever so far over and beyond the world, above heaven and earth.

What can Isaiah intend with this saying but, as St. Hilary[7] also says on this subject, that God in his essence is present everywhere, in and through the whole creation in all its parts and in all places, and so the world is full of God and he fills it all, yet he is not limited or circumscribed by it, but is at the same time beyond and above the whole creation? All this is an infinitely incomprehensible thing, yet these are articles of our faith, clearly and powerfully attested in the Scriptures. In comparison with this it is a trivial matter that Christ's body and blood are at the same time in heaven and in the Supper. And if the fanatics began to approach this point with their reason and their eyes, they would quickly fall headlong and say that it is nothing and (as it is the great virtue of the ungodly to say), "There is no God," Psalm 14 [v. 1].

For how can reason tolerate it that the Divine Majesty is so small as to be present in essence in a kernel, on a kernel, above a kernel, throughout a kernel, inside and outside—and, even though it is one single Majesty, can nevertheless be completely and entirely present in every individual thing, countless in number though they be? For he certainly makes every single kernel in particular, in all its parts, on the inside and throughout, so his power must be present there throughout, in and on the kernel. But now, his power is one and simple and is not divided, as if he made the husk of the kernel with his fingers and the pith of the kernel with his feet. Thus the entire divine power must be present throughout, in and on the kernel. For he alone makes it all. On the other hand, the same Majesty is so great that neither this world nor even a thousand worlds could embrace it and say, "See, there it is!"

Here, now, let the fanatics answer me. Body, of course, has still another relation with other bodies; they may fit together, as for example bread is a body, wine is a body, Christ's flesh is a body. Here one body may be in another, as I can be in the open air, and in a garment or a house, as money can be in a purse, or wine in a cask or tankard. But here, where we are dealing not with body but spirit—indeed, who knows what this is[8] that we call God? He is above body, above spirit, above everything man can say or hear or think: how at one and the same time can such a being be completely and entirely present in every single body, every creature and object everywhere, and on the other hand, must and can be nowhere, beyond and above all creatures and objects, as our Creed and the Scriptures confess

---

7. Hilary of Poitiers, *On the Trinity*, 1.6.
8. I.e. something beyond our comprehension.

both truths about God? Here reason must conclude without further ado: Oh, surely this is utter nonsense and can be nothing but nonsense. Now if he has found the way whereby his own divine nature can be wholly and entirely in all creatures and in every single individual being, more deeply, more inwardly, more present than the creature is to itself, and yet on the other hand may and can be circumscribed nowhere and in no being, so that he actually embraces all things and is in all, but no one being circumscribes him and is in him—should not this same God also know some way whereby his body could be wholly and completely present in many places at the same time, and yet none of these places could be where he is? Ah, we miserable children of men, who judge God and his doings according to our own imagination, and think of him as a cobbler or a day laborer!

Yes, they say, of course we believe that God's power is everywhere. But it is not necessary on that account for his divine nature or his right hand to be everywhere. Answer: I believe also, of course, that at the bottom of your hearts you believe nothing either about God or about God's power. I am certain, moreover, that you will, of course, leap over all these irrefutable Scripture passages which I am adducing and expounding here, and that you will curl your lips and say, "Humph! He speaks of kernels and tree leaves, but he produces no Scripture." For this is what you are accustomed to do. And then you jabber something about your forbearance or babble about irrelevant matters, and that must serve as Scripture. We know, however, that God's power, arm, hand, nature, face, Spirit, wisdom, etc., are all one thing; for apart from the creation there is nothing but the one simple Deity himself. And thus, if before the creation of the universe there doubtless existed the power and hand of God, God's nature itself, then it did not become something else after the creation of the universe. Indeed, he makes and does nothing except through his Word, Genesis 1, John 1 [cf. Gen. 1:3, 6, 9, etc.; John 1:3, 10], i.e. his power. And his power is not an ax, hatchet, saw, or file with which he works, but is himself. Then if his power and Spirit are present everywhere and in all things to the innermost and outermost degree, through and through, as it must be if he is to make and preserve all things everywhere, then his divine right hand, nature, and majesty must also be everywhere. He must surely be present if he makes and preserves them.

"God is a Supernatural, Inscrutable Being"

From "Confession Concerning Christ's Supper, 1528,"
in *LW*, vol. 37, *Word and Sacrament 3*, 228–30.

. . . We say that God is no such extended, long, broad, thick, high, deep being. He is a supernatural, inscrutable being who exists at the same time in every little seed, whole and entire, and yet also in all and above all and outside all created things. There is no need to enclose him here, as this spirit dreams, for a body is much, much too wide for the Godhead; it could contain many thousand Godheads. On the other hand, it is also far, far too narrow to contain one Godhead. Nothing is so small but God is still smaller, nothing so large but God is still larger, nothing is so short but God is still shorter, nothing so long but God is still longer, nothing is so broad but God is still broader, nothing so narrow but God is still narrower, and so on. He is an inexpressible being, above and beyond all that can be described or imagined. . . .

If we wish to be Christians and think and speak rightly about Christ, we must regard his divinity as extending beyond and above all creatures. Secondly, we must assert that though his humanity is a created thing, yet since it is the only creature so united with God as to constitute it one person with the divinity, it must be higher than all other creatures and above and beyond them, under God alone. Well, this is our faith. Here we come with a Christ beyond all creatures, both according to his humanity and his divinity; with his humanity we enter a different land from that in which it moved here on earth, viz. beyond and above all creatures and purely in the Godhead. Now let faith be the judge and arbiter here. Beyond the creatures there is only God; accordingly, since this humanity also is beyond the creatures, it must be wherever God is, without fail. In essence, however, it cannot be God, but because it reaches up above all creation to the essential God and is united with him and is wherever God is, it must be at least in person God and thus exist everywhere that God is.

Of course, our reason takes a foolish attitude, since it is accustomed to understanding the word "in" only in a physical, circumscribed sense like straw in a sack and bread in a basket. Consequently, when it hears that God is in this or that object, it always thinks of the straw-sack and the breadbasket. But faith understands that in these matters "in" is equivalent to "above," "beyond," "beneath," "through and through," and "everywhere." . . .

SELECTION **2**

John Calvin

Institutes of the Christian Religion, Book 1, Chapters 1–3, 14.20–22

A French pastor and theologian, John Calvin (1509–1564) was, after Luther, the second most important figure in the Protestant Reformation. His most important work is the two-volume

Institutes of the Christian Religion, which in four books contains (1) the knowledge of God the creator; (2) the knowledge of the redeemer in Christ; (3) the way we receive Christ's grace (through the Spirit); and (4) the external means of grace in the church.

In the first book on God as creator, Calvin observes that true wisdom consists of "the knowledge of God and of ourselves." We cannot look at ourselves without recognizing that we live and move and have our being in God (Acts 17:28). Even our human misery—with its ignorance, depravity, and corruption—causes us to seek God. In turn, contemplating God, we scrutinize ourselves, measuring our lives by the standard of God's majesty. Not mere speculation, the knowledge of God involves piety (*pietas*): the "reverence joined with the love of God that the knowledge of his benefits induces." It entails both an understanding of God's majesty as the creator (discussed in the first book) and an understanding of God as redeemer, which we see in the face of Christ who saves us and reconciles us to God (discussed in the second book).

God has implanted the first kind of knowledge—the knowledge of God as creator—in human minds, giving all people by natural instinct an awareness of divinity, a "seed of religion." Even the impulse to idolatry (the worship of creatures instead of the creator) is proof of this. God's creative activity is manifest throughout creation, the "beautiful theatre" of God's glory, and especially in human beings who are the most excellent example of God's works. All of creation mirrors God's attributes—wisdom, power, justice, and goodness. We have true faith in God as creator when we recognize two things: (1) that God's powers are evident in the creation of the universe—in the way God arranges and fits all things together in a wonderful order—and (2) that God has, with fatherly care, destined all things for our good and salvation so that as we feel his power and grace within us and receive his benefits, we are inspired to trust and love God.

God's creative activity cannot be separated from God's providence. Divine power continues to shine throughout creation as much as it did in its inception. Not only does God govern and preserve the world in a general way, but God sustains and nourishes all things in very particular ways, even the specific circumstances of our lives. All things are governed by God's secret plan; nothing happens that is not knowingly or willingly decreed by God. Throughout his discussion of God's providence, Calvin's intent is to offer comfort for those who are anxious and fearful in a seemingly capricious world. Whether one experiences prosperity or adversity, the world remains the "theatre of God's glory," the locus of God's ongoing providential care.

"The Knowledge⁹ of God the Creator"

From *Calvin: Institutes of the Christian Religion*, vol. 1, ed. John T. McNeill and trans. Ford Lewis Battles (Philadelphia: Westminster Press, 1960), 35–44, 179–82, 197–98, 200–201.

Chapter 1

How the Knowledge of God and That of Ourselves Are Connected and How They Are Interrelated

1. Without Knowledge of Self There Is No Knowledge of God Nearly all the wisdom we possess, that is to say, true and sound wisdom, consists of two parts: the knowledge of God and of ourselves.[10] But, while joined by many bonds, which one precedes and brings forth the other is not easy to discern. In the first place, no one can look upon himself without immediately turning his thoughts to the contemplation of God, in whom he "lives and moves" [Acts 17:28]. For, quite clearly, the mighty gifts with

---

9. The word "knowledge" in the title, chosen rather than "being" or "existence" of God, emphasizes the centrality of revelation in both the structure and content of Calvin's theology. Similarly, the term "Creator," subsuming the doctrines of the Trinity, Creation, and Providence, stresses God's revealing work or acts rather than God in himself. The latter is more prominent in Scholastic doctrines of God, both medieval and later "Calvinist." Despite the titles of Books 1 and 2. Calvin's epistemology is not fully developed in the *Institutes* until Book 3, "The Way in Which We Receive the Grace of Christ." Cf. especially the meaning of knowledge in faith, 3.2, passim.

The Latin for "knowledge" is here *cognitio*, while in the title of chap. 1 following it is *notitia*. The words are used interchangeably by Calvin, and both are by him here translated into French (1541) as *cognoissance*. Knowledge, whatever word is employed, is for Calvin never "mere" or "simple" or purely objective knowledge. Cf. 3.2.4, which is his most definitive brief statement on the meaning of knowledge in a religious context. Probably "existentialist" apprehension is the nearest equivalent in contemporary parlance. Among other closely related words used by Calvin are *agnitio*, recognition or acknowledgement; *intelligentia*, primarily meaning perception; and *scientia*, primarily meaning expert knowledge.

10. This statement, thrice revised, stands at the beginning of every edition of the *Institutes*. The French version of 1560 expresses even more strongly the association of the two aspects of sound knowledge: "In knowing God, each of us also knows himself." These decisive words set the limits of Calvin's theology and condition every subsequent statement. They are echoed in the introductory words of Book 3 and at such important junctures in 1.15.1 and 2.8.1.... Calvin's basic concept here is discoverable in Clement of Alexandria's *Instructor* 3 ("If one knows himself, he will know God"), and finds frequent expression in Augustine. In his *Soliloquies* 1.2.7, Augustine has this dialogue: "I desire to know God and the soul." "Nothing more?" "Nothing whatever"; and in 2.1.1 occurs the prayer, "Let me know myself, let me know thee." Cf. Aquinas: "Sacred doctrine is not concerned with God and the creatures equally. It is concerned with God fundamentally, and with the creatures in so far as they relate to God as their beginning or end." *Summa Theologica* 1.1.3. Calvin makes explicit the same order of importance between knowledge of God and of the creatures in the "Argument" preceding his Commentary on Genesis.... It is worth noting that Descartes, in an important letter to Father Martin Mersene, April 15, 1630, parallels Calvin's language here. Having referred to "human reason," Descartes continues: "I hold that all those to whom God has given the use of this reason are bound to employ it in the effort to know him and to know themselves" (*Oeuvres de Descartes*, 1.144). In his *Discourse on Method* (1637), he aims, unlike Calvin, to "demonstrate the existence of God and the soul," and he is concerned with the same issue in his *Meditations in Prime Philosophy* (1641); see especially Meditation 3, 5, and 6. George Berkeley, in his *Treatise on the Principles of Human Knowledge* (1710), holds that existence can be predicated of God and the soul only.

which we are endowed are hardly from ourselves; indeed, our very being is nothing but subsistence in the one God. Then, by these benefits shed like dew from heaven upon us, we are led as by rivulets to the spring itself. Indeed, our very poverty better discloses the infinitude of benefits reposing in God. The miserable ruin, into which the rebellion of the first man cast us, especially compels us to look upward. Thus, not only will we, in fasting and hungering, seek thence what we lack; but, in being aroused by fear, we shall learn humility.[11] For, as a veritable world of miseries is to be found in mankind, and we are thereby despoiled of divine raiment, our shameful nakedness exposes a teeming horde of infamies. Each of us must, then, be so stung by the consciousness of his own unhappiness as to attain at least some knowledge of God. Thus, from the feeling of our own ignorance, vanity, poverty, infirmity, and—what is more—depravity and corruption, we recognize that the true light of wisdom, sound virtue, full abundance of every good, and purity of righteousness rest in the Lord alone. To this extent we are prompted by our own ills to contemplate the good things of God; and we cannot seriously aspire to him before we begin to become displeased with ourselves. For what man in all the world would not gladly remain as he is—what man does not remain as he is—so long as he does not know himself, that is, while content with his own gifts, and either ignorant or unmindful of his own misery? Accordingly, the knowledge of ourselves not only arouses us to seek God, but also, as it were, leads us by the hand to find him.

2. *Without Knowledge of God There Is No Knowledge of Self* Again, it is certain that man never achieves a clear knowledge of himself [12] unless he has first looked upon God's face, and then descends from contemplating him to scrutinize himself. For we always seem to ourselves righteous and upright and wise and holy—this pride is innate in all of us—unless by clear proofs we stand convinced of our own unrighteousness, foulness, folly, and impurity. Moreover, we are not thus convinced if we look merely to ourselves and not also to the Lord, who is the sole standard by which this judgment must be measured. For, because all of us are inclined by nature to hypocrisy, a kind of empty image of righteousness in place of righteousness itself abundantly satisfies us. And because nothing appears within or around us that has not been contaminated by great immorality, what is a little less vile pleases us as a thing most pure—so long as we confine our minds within the limits of human corruption. Just so, an eye to which

---

11. The close relation of humility and self-knowledge constitutes an often repeated theme for Calvin. Cf. 2.2.10–11; 2.16.1; 3.2.23; 3.12.5.6; 4.16.40 (end). Without humility, self-knowledge serves pride and is the root of all error in philosophy: 1.5.4; 2.1.1–3.

12. "*Sui notitiam.*" Our knowledge of ourselves may be construed to conclude both all mankind and all creation (of which man is a microcosm, 1.5.3). Hence 1.14 and 15 may be subsumed here along 2.1–5.

nothing is shown but black objects judges something dirty white or even rather darkly mottled to be whiteness itself. Indeed, we can discern still more clearly from the bodily senses how much we are deluded in estimating the powers of the soul. For if in broad daylight we either look down upon the ground or survey whatever meets our view round about, we seem to ourselves endowed with the strongest and keenest sight; yet when we look up to the sun and gaze straight at it, that power of sight which was particularly strong on earth is at once blunted and confused by a great brilliance, and thus we are compelled to admit that our keenness in looking upon things earthly is sheer dullness when it comes to the sun. So it happens in estimating our spiritual goods. As long as we do not look beyond the earth, being quite content with our own righteousness, wisdom, and virtue, we flatter ourselves most sweetly, and fancy ourselves all but demigods. Suppose we but once begin to raise our thoughts to God, and to ponder his nature, and how completely perfect are his righteousness, wisdom, and power—the straightedge to which we must be shaped. Then, what masquerading earlier as righteousness was pleasing in us will soon grow filthy in its consummate wickedness. What wonderfully impressed us under the name of wisdom will stink in its very foolishness. What wore the face of power will prove itself the most miserable weakness. That is, what in us seems perfection itself corresponds ill to the purity of God.

Chapter 2
What It Is to Know God, and to What Purpose the Knowledge of God Tends

1. Piety Is Requisite for the Knowledge of God Now, the knowledge of God, as I understand it, is that by which we not only conceive that there is a God but also grasp what befits us and is proper to his glory, in fine, what is to our advantage to know of him. Indeed, we shall not say that, properly speaking, God is known where there is no religion or piety.[13] Here I do not yet touch upon the sort of knowledge with which men, in themselves lost and accursed, apprehend God the Redeemer in Christ the Mediator; but I speak only of the primal and simple knowledge to which the very order of nature would have led us if Adam had remained upright.[14] In this ruin of mankind no one now experiences God either as Father or as Author of salvation, or favorable in any way, until Christ the Mediator comes forward

---

13. It is a favorite emphasis in Calvin that *pietas*, piety, in which reverence and love of God are joined, is prerequisite to any true knowledge of God. Cf. 1.4.4.

14. "*Si integer stetisset Adam.*" The controlling thought of 1.2–5, which is the *locus classicus* for a discussion of "natural theology" in Calvin, is contained in this phrase. The revelation of God in creation, for Calvin, would have been the basis of a sound natural theology only "*if* Adam had remained upright." Because of sin no sound theology of this type is possible. Scripture is the only medium of knowing the Creator, and of apprehending his revelation in creation (1.6ff.).

to reconcile him to us. Nevertheless, it is one thing to feel that God as our Maker supports us by his power, governs us by his providence, nourishes us by his goodness, and attends us with all sorts of blessings—and another thing to embrace the grace of reconciliation offered to us in Christ. First, as much in the fashioning of the universe as in the general teaching of Scripture the Lord shows himself to be simply the Creator. Then in the face of Christ [cf. 2 Cor. 4:6] he shows himself the Redeemer. Of the resulting twofold knowledge of God[15] we shall now discuss the first aspect; the second will be dealt with in its proper place.[16]

Moreover, although our mind cannot apprehend God without rendering some honor to him, it will not suffice simply to hold that there is One whom all ought to honor and adore, unless we are also persuaded that he is the fountain of every good, and that we must seek nothing elsewhere than in him. This I take to mean that not only does he sustain this universe (as he once founded it) by his boundless might, regulate it by his wisdom, preserve it by his goodness, and especially rule mankind by his righteousness and judgment, bear with it in his mercy, watch over it by his protection; but also that no drop will be found either of wisdom and light, or of righteousness or power or rectitude, or of genuine truth, which does not flow from him, and of which he is not the cause. Thus we may learn to await and seek all these things from him, and thankfully to ascribe them, once received, to him. For this sense of the powers of God[17] is for us a fit teacher of piety, from which religion is born. I call "piety" that reverence joined with love of God which the knowledge of his benefits induces. For until men recognize that they owe everything to God, that they are nourished by his fatherly care, that he is the Author of their every good, that they should seek nothing beyond him—they will never yield him willing service. Nay, unless they establish their complete happiness in him, they will never give themselves truly and sincerely to him.

2. Knowledge of God Involves Trust and Reverence What is God? Men who pose this question are merely toying with idle speculations. It is more important for us to know of what sort he is and what is consistent with his nature. What good is it to profess with Epicurus some sort of God nature who has cast aside the care of the world only to amuse himself in

---

15. "*Duplex . . . cognitio.*" The distinction, "twofold" knowledge, added to the *Institutes* in 1559, is basic to the structure of the completed work. Calvin calls attention to this repeatedly in a striking series of methodological statements, all added in 1559 to clarify the course of the argument. Cf. 1.6.1, 2; 10.1; 8.9, 11, 23, 24; 14.20, 21, and 2.6.1. Hence, nothing in Book 1 belongs to the knowledge of the Redeemer, although everything after chap. 5 is based in the *special* revelation of Scripture.

16. What is called "first" makes up the entire remainder of Book 1. "The second" broadly corresponds to the whole material of Books 2–4.

17. "*Virtutum Dei sensus.*"

idleness?[18] What help is it, in short, to know a God with whom we have nothing to do? Rather, our knowledge should serve first to teach us fear and reverence; secondly, with it as our guide and teacher, we should learn to seek every good from him, and, having received it, to credit it to his account. For how can the thought of God penetrate your mind without your realizing immediately that, since you are his handiwork, you have been made over and bound to his command by right of creation, that you owe your life to him?—that whatever you undertake, whatever you do, ought to be ascribed to him? If this be so, it now assuredly follows that your life is wickedly corrupt unless it be disposed to his service, seeing that his will ought for us to be the law by which we live. Again, you cannot behold him clearly unless you acknowledge him to be the fountainhead and source of every good. From this too would arise the desire to cleave to him and trust in him, but for the fact that man's depravity seduces his mind from rightly seeking him.

For, to begin with, the pious mind does not dream up for itself any god it pleases, but contemplates the one and only true God. And it does not attach to him whatever it pleases, but is content to hold him to be as he manifests himself; furthermore, the mind always exercises the utmost diligence and care not to wander astray, or rashly and boldly to go beyond his will. It thus recognizes God because it knows that he governs all things; and trusts that he is its guide and protector, therefore giving itself over completely to trust in him. Because it understands him to be the Author of every good, if anything oppresses, if anything is lacking, immediately it betakes itself to his protection, waiting for help from him. Because it is persuaded that he is good and merciful, it reposes in him with perfect trust, and doubts not that in his loving-kindness a remedy will be provided for all its ills. Because it acknowledges him as Lord and Father, the pious mind also deems it meet and right to observe his authority in all things—reverence his majesty, take care to advance his glory, and obey his commandments. Because it sees him to be a righteous judge, armed with severity to punish wickedness, it ever holds his judgment seat before its gaze, and through fear of him restrains itself from provoking his anger. And yet it is not so terrified by the awareness of his judgment as to wish to withdraw, even if some way of escape were open. But it embraces him no less as punisher of the wicked than as benefactor of the pious. For the pious mind realizes that the punishment of the impious and wicked and the reward of life eternal for the righteous equally pertain to God's glory. Besides, this mind restrains itself from sinning, not out of dread of punishment alone; but, because it loves and reveres God as Father, it worships and adores him as Lord. Even if there were no hell, it would still shudder at offending him alone.

18. Epicurus (342–270 B.C), whose extensive writings are extant in fragments only, seems to have been known to Calvin chiefly through Cicero's *De finibus* and *De natura deorum*.

Here indeed is pure and real religion: faith so joined with an earnest fear of God that this fear also embraces willing reverence, and carries with it such legitimate worship as is prescribed in the law. And we ought to note this fact even more diligently: all men have a vague general veneration for God, but very few really reverence him; and wherever there is great ostentation in ceremonies, sincerity of heart is rare indeed.

Chapter 3
The Knowledge of God Has Been Naturally Implanted in Human Minds

1. The Character of This Natural Endowment There is within the human mind, and indeed by natural instinct, an awareness of divinity.[19] This we take to be beyond controversy. To prevent anyone from taking refuge in the pretense of ignorance, God himself has implanted in all men a certain understanding of his divine majesty. Ever renewing its memory, he repeatedly sheds fresh drops.[20] Since, therefore, men one and all perceive that there is a God and that he is their Maker, they are condemned by their own testimony because they have failed to honor him and to consecrate their lives to his will. If ignorance of God is to be looked for anywhere, surely one is most likely to find an example of it among the more backward folk and those more remote from civilization. Yet there is, as the eminent pagan says, no nation so barbarous, no people so savage, that they have not a deep-seated conviction that there is a God.[21] And they who in other aspects of life seem least to differ from brutes still continue to retain some seed of religion. So deeply does the common conception occupy the minds of all, so tenaciously does it inhere in the hearts of all! Therefore, since from the beginning of the world there has been no region, no city, in short, no household, that could do without religion, there lies in this a tacit confession of a sense of deity inscribed in the hearts of all.

Indeed, even idolatry is ample proof of this conception. We know how man does not willingly humble himself so as to place other creatures over himself. Since, then, he prefers to worship wood and stone rather than to be thought of as having no God, clearly this is a most vivid impression of a

---

19. *"Divinitatis sensum."* This term and "seed of religion," used immediately below (cf. I.4.1), refer generally to a numinous awareness of God, and are closely related to conscience, which is a moral response to God. Cf. 1.1.3 and Comm. John 1:5, 9. On verse 5, Calvin writes: "There are two principles parts of the light which still remains in corrupt nature: first, the seed of religion is planted in all men; next, the distinction between good and evil is engraved on their consciences."

20. Cf. Cicero, *Tusculan Disputations* 2.10.

21. The pagan (*ethnicus*) is Cicero. Calvin's view that all men have a natural sense or intimation of deity is in accord with the presupposition of all the characters of Cicero's dialogue *On the Nature of the Gods.*

divine being. So impossible is it to blot this from man's mind that natural disposition would be more easily altered, as altered indeed it is when man voluntarily sinks from his natural haughtiness to the very depths in order to honor God!

Chapter 14
Even in the Creation of the Universe and of All Things,
Scripture by Unmistakable Marks Distinguishes
the True from False Gods (The Spiritual Lessons of Creation, 20-22)

20. Greatness and Abundance of Creation Meanwhile let us not be ashamed to take pious delight in the works of God open and manifest in this most beautiful theater.[22] For, as I have elsewhere said,[23] although it is not the chief evidence for faith, yet it is the first evidence in the order of nature, to be mindful that wherever we cast our eyes, all things they meet are works of God, and at the same time to ponder with pious meditation to what end God created them. Therefore, that we may apprehend with true faith what it profits us to know of God, it is important for us to grasp first the history of the creation of the universe, as it has been set forth briefly by Moses [Gen. 1-2], and then has been more fully illustrated by saintly men, especially by Basil and Ambrose.[24] From this history we shall learn that God by the power of his Word and Spirit created heaven and earth out of nothing; that thereupon he brought forth living beings and inanimate things of every kind, that in a wonderful series he distinguished an innumerable variety of things, that he endowed each kind with its own nature, assigned functions, appointed places and stations; and that, although all were subject to corruption, he nevertheless provided for the preservation of each species until the Last Day. We shall likewise learn that he nourishes some in secret ways, and, as it were, from time to time instills new vigor into them; on others he has conferred the power of propagating, lest by their death the entire species perish; that he has so wonderfully adorned heaven and earth with as unlimited abundance, variety, and beauty of all things as could possibly be, quite like a spacious and splendid house, provided and filled with the most exquisite and at the same time most abundant furnishings. Finally, we shall learn that in forming man and in adorning

22. Cf. 1.5.8, note 27; 1.6.2; 2.6.1; 3.9.2.
23. 1.5.15.
24. Basil, *Hexaemeron* (homilies on the six days of Creation); Ambrose, *Hexameron*. The prevailing Christian view of creation is that God created the world out of nothing *(ex nihilo)*. Cf. 1.15.5. In antiquity the possibility of this was denied by the Epicureans: "*Nil posse creari de nilo*," wrote Lucretius *(De rerum natura i.* 155). Augustine (apart from the doctrine of the origin of individual souls, on which his position is indeterminate) asserts *creatio ex nihilo,* e.g., in *Faith and the Creed* 2. 2. It is thus stated in the Westminster Confession 4.1: "It pleased God . . . to create, or make of nothing, the world, and all things therein."

him with such goodly beauty, and with such great and numerous gifts, he put him forth as the most excellent example of his works. But since it is not my purpose to recount the creation of the universe, let it be enough for me to have touched upon these few matters again in passing. For it is better, as I have already warned my readers, to seek a fuller understanding of this passage from Moses and from those others who have faithfully and diligently recorded the narrative of Creation [Gen. 1–2].

21. How Should We View God's Works? Nothing is to be gained by further discussing what direction the contemplation of God's works should take and to what goal such contemplation ought to be applied, inasmuch as the greater part of this topic has been disposed of in another place,[25] and it is possible to accomplish in a few words whatever concerns our present purpose. Indeed, if we chose to explain in a fitting manner how God's inestimable wisdom, power, justice, and goodness shine forth in the fashioning of the universe no splendor, no ornament of speech, would be equal to an act of such great magnitude. There is no doubt that the Lord would have us uninterruptedly occupied in this holy meditation; that, while we contemplate in all creatures, as in mirrors, those immense riches of his wisdom, justice, goodness, and power, we should not merely run over them cursorily, and, so to speak, with a fleeting glance; but we should ponder them at length, turn them over in our minds seriously and faithfully, and recollect them repeatedly. But because our purpose here is to teach, it is proper for us to omit those matters which require long harangue. Therefore, to be brief, let all readers know that they have with true faith apprehended what it is for God to be Creator of heaven and earth, if they first of all follow the universal rule, not to pass over in ungrateful thoughtlessness or forgetfulness those conspicuous powers which God shows forth in his creatures, apply it to themselves that their very hearts are touched. The first part of the rule exemplified when we reflect upon the greatness of the Artificer who stationed, arranged, and fitted together the starry host of heaven in such wonderful order that nothing more beautiful in appearance can be imagined; who so set and fixed some in their stations that they cannot move; who granted to others a freer course, but so as not to wander outside their appointed course; who so adjusted the motion of all that days and nights, months, years, and seasons of the year are measured off; who so proportioned the inequality of days, which we daily observe, that no confusion occurs. It is so too when we observe his power in sustaining so great a mass, in governing the swiftly revolving heavenly system,[26] and the like. For these few examples make sufficiently clear what it is to recognize God's powers, in the creation of the universe. Otherwise, as I have said, if I decide to set forth the whole matter in my discourse, there will be no end.

25. 1.5.1–4.
26. "*Caelestis machinae.*" Cf. 1.10.1, note 2.

For there are as many miracles of divine power, as many tokens of goodness, and as many proofs of wisdom, as there are kinds of things in the universe, indeed, as there are things either great or small.

22. *The Contemplation of God's Goodness in His Creation Will Lead Us to Thankfulness and Trust* There remains the second part of the rule, more closely related to faith. It is to recognize that God has destined all things for our good and salvation but at the same time to feel his power and grace in ourselves and in the great benefits he has conferred upon us, and so bestir ourselves to trust, invoke, praise, and love him.[27] Indeed, as I pointed out a little before,[28] God himself has shown by the order of Creation that he created all things for man's sake. For it is not without significance that he divided the making of the universe into six days [Gen. 1:31], even though it would have been no more difficult for him to have completed in one moment the whole work together in all its details than to arrive at its completion gradually by a progression of this sort. But he willed to commend his providence and fatherly solicitude toward us in that, before he fashioned man, he prepared everything he foresaw would be useful and salutary for him. How great ingratitude would it be now to doubt whether this most gracious Father has us in his care, who we see was concerned for us even before we were born! How impious would it be to tremble for fear that his kindness might at any time fail us in our need, when we see that it was shown, with the greatest abundance of every good thing, when we were yet unborn! Besides, from Moses we hear that, through His liberality, all things on earth are subject to us [Gen. 1:28; 9:2]. It is certain that He did not do this to mock us with the empty title to a gift. Therefore nothing that is needful for our welfare will ever be lacking to us.

To conclude once for all, whenever we call God the Creator of heaven and earth, let us at the same time bear in mind that the dispensation of all those things which he has made is in his own hand and power and that we are indeed his children, whom he has received into his faithful protection to nourish and educate. We are therefore to await the fullness of all good things from him alone and to trust completely that he will never leave us destitute of what we need for salvation, and to hang our hopes on none but him! We are therefore, also, to petition him for whatever we desire; and we are to recognize as a blessing from him, and thankfully to acknowledge, every benefit that falls to our share. So, invited by the great sweetness of his beneficence and goodness, let us study to love and serve him with all our heart.

---

27. The belief that the material universe was made for the sake of man was espoused by the Stoics in opposition to the Epicureans.

28. 1.15.2.

CHAPTER 4

God in Modernity

Jonathan Edwards

The End for Which God Created the World and "Discourse on the Trinity"

Widely recognized to be America's most important and original theologian, Jonathan Edwards (1703–1758) was also a philosopher and a great preacher who played a crucial role in America's Great Awakening.

Influenced by both Calvin and the philosophical and scientific emphases of the Enlightenment, Edwards developed a theology centered on the glory of God experienced as an active and harmonious communication or emanation of the fullness of God's perfect Being. Against Arminians, he defended a Calvinist understanding of human depravity and God's sovereign grace in redemption. Yet he also engaged Enlightenment perspectives, in particular John Locke's emphasis on experience and Isaac Newton's characterization of nature as a network of relational laws and active forces. Nonetheless, Edwards negated materialism and argued that the laws of nature are intimately linked with the harmony and beauty of God's own being, which continually overflows into all of creation. Describing the essence of God and the nature of reality in general in terms of dispositions, activities, and relations, Edwards maintained that God's primary disposition is love. As God exercises this disposition, God diffuses God's infinite fullness and thereby increases God's own being, which is both fully actualized and perfect yet is also infinitely disposed to self-communication and emanation. God's being is pure actuality (*actus purus*) rooted in God's disposition to communicate *ad extra* (outside God's self). Like Calvin, Edwards believed that every moment is rooted in God's creative and redemptive activity.

In the last chapter of *The End for Which God Created the World*, Edwards argues that the end of creation is the "glory of God." Scripture's various names for God and for the many attributes of God (power, infinity, eternity, immutability, etc.) all express one thing: God's *internal glory*, which is also God's *external glory*. If God's internal glory is God's understanding and will—which Edwards further defines as God's infinite knowledge, on the one hand, and God's holiness or virtue and happiness or joy, on the other—then this internal glory is also God's external glory. All things are an "emanation and remanation," a proceeding from and returning to God. As those created in God's image, thus also having understanding and will, human beings are completed or fulfilled by knowing, loving, and delighting in God, which, in turn, is a participation in—and a repetition of— God's own internal glory.

The greater the union between God and creatures, the more both are fulfilled. Like Gregory of Nyssa, Edwards speaks of a continual increase of this union—an eternal motion and progression with God at its center.

As the next selection from "Discourse on the Trinity" makes clear, God's activities *ad extra* are the external extensions of God's triune life *ad intra* (within God's self) whereby God knows and loves God's self. The Father is the deity subsisting in the primary, unoriginate, and most absolute manner. The Son, who is begotten, is the reflexive act of God's knowing God's self. And since the Father loves what he knows, the Spirit is the deity repeated and self-communicated affectionally—the divine essence flowing out and breathed forth in love and joy. God's actuality, then, is the Father's eternal and infinitely full actuality and its complete repetition in the Son and the Holy Spirit.

The End for Which God Created the World, Section 7

From *Works of Jonathan Edwards*, vol. 8, *Ethical Writings*, ed. Paul Ramsey (New Haven, CT: Yale University Press, 1989), 526–36.

Section 7
Showing That the Ultimate End of the Creation of the World Is but One, and What That One End Is

From what has been observed in the last section, it appears that however the last end of the creation is spoken of in Scripture under various denominations; yet if the whole of what is said relating to this affair be duly weighed, and one part compared with another, we shall have reason to think that the design of the Spirit of God does not seem to be to represent God's ultimate end as manifold, but as one. For though it be signified by various names, yet they appear not to be names of different things, but various names involving each other in their meaning; either different names of the same thing, or names of several parts of one whole, or of the same whole viewed in various lights, or in its different respects and relations. For it appears that all that is ever spoken of in the Scripture as an ultimate end of God's works is included in that one phrase, "the glory of God"; which is the name by which the last end of God's works is most commonly called in Scripture: and seems to be the name which most aptly signifies the thing.

The thing signified by that name, "the glory of God," when spoken of as the supreme and ultimate end of the work of creation, and of all God's works, is the emanation and true external expression of God's internal glory and fullness; meaning by his fullness, what has already been explained. Or in other words, God's internal glory extant, in a true and just exhibition, or external existence of it. It is confessed that there is a degree of obscurity in these definitions: but perhaps an obscurity which is unavoidable, through the imperfection of language, and words being less fitted to express things of so sublime a nature. And therefore the thing may possibly be better understood, by using many words and a variety of expressions, by a particular consideration of it, as it were by parts, than by any short definition.

There is included in this the exercise of God's perfections to produce a proper effect, in opposition to their lying eternally dormant and ineffectual: as his power being eternally without any act or fruit of that power; his wisdom eternally ineffectual in any wise production, or prudent disposal of anything, etc. The manifestation of his internal glory to created understandings. The communication of the infinite fullness of God to the creature. The creature's high esteem of God, love to God, and complacence and joy in God; and the proper exercises and expressions of these.

These at first view may appear to be entirely distinct things: but if we more closely consider the matter, they will all appear to be one thing, in a variety of views and relations. They are all but the emanation of God's glory; or the excellent brightness and fullness of the divinity diffused, overflowing, and as it were enlarged; or in one word, existing *ad extra*. God's exercising his perfection to produce a proper effect is not distinct from the emanation or communication of his fullness: for this is the effect, viz. his fullness communicated, and the producing this effect is the communication of his fullness; and there is nothing in this effectual exerting of God's perfection, but the emanation of God's internal glory.

The emanation or communication is of the internal glory or fullness of God, as it is. Now God's internal glory, as it is in God, is either in his understanding or will. The glory or fullness of his understanding is his knowledge. The internal glory and fullness of God, which we must conceive of as having its special seat in his will, is his holiness and happiness. The whole of God's internal good or glory, is in these three things, viz. his infinite knowledge; his infinite virtue or holiness, and his infinite joy and happiness. Indeed there are a great many attributes in God, according to our way of conceiving or talking of them: but all may be reduced to these; or to the degree, circumstances and relations of these. We have no conception of God's power, different from the degree of these things, with a certain relation of them to effects. God's infinity is not so properly a distinct kind of good in God, but only expresses the degree of the good there is in him. So God's eternity is not a distinct good; but is the duration of good. His immutability is still the same good, with a negation of change. So that, as I said, the fullness of the Godhead is the fullness of his understanding, consisting in his knowledge, and the fullness of his will, consisting in his virtue and happiness. And therefore the external glory of God consists in the communication of these.

The communication of his knowledge is chiefly in giving the knowledge of himself: for this is the knowledge in which the fullness of God's understanding chiefly consists. And thus we see how the manifestation of God's glory to created understandings, and their seeing and knowing it, is not distinct from an emanation or communication of God's fullness, but clearly implied in it.

Again, the communication of God's virtue or holiness is principally in communicating the love of himself (which appears by what has before been observed). And thus we see how, not only the creature's seeing and knowing God's excellence, but also supremely esteeming and loving him, belongs to the communication of God's fullness. And the communication of God's joy and happiness consists chiefly in communicating to the creature that happiness and joy, which consists in rejoicing in God and in his glorious excellency; for in such joy God's own happiness does principally consist. And in these things, viz. in knowing God's excellency, loving God for it, and rejoicing in it; and in the exercise and expression of these, consists God's honor and praise: so that these are clearly implied in that glory of God, which consists in the emanation of his internal glory.

And though we suppose all these things, which seem to be so various, are signified by that "glory" which the Scripture speaks of as the last end of all God's works, yet it is manifest there is no greater, and no other variety in it, than in the internal and essential glory of God itself. God's internal glory is partly in his understanding, and partly in his will. And this internal glory, as seated in the will of God, implies both his holiness and his happiness: both are evidently God's glory, according to the use of the phrase. So that as God's external glory is only the emanation of his internal glory, this variety necessarily follows.

And again, it hence appears that here is no other variety or distinction, but what necessarily arises from the distinct faculties of the creature, to which the communication is made, as created in the image of God; even as having these two faculties of understanding and will. God communicates himself to the understanding of the creature, in giving him the knowledge of his glory; and to the will of the creature, in giving him holiness, consisting primarily in the love of God: and in giving the creature happiness, chiefly consisting in joy in God. These are the sum of that emanation of divine fullness called in Scripture, "the glory of God." The first part of this glory is called "truth," the latter, "grace."

John 1:14, "We beheld his glory, the glory of the only begotten of the Father, full of *grace* and *truth*."

Thus we see that the great and last end of God's works which is so variously expressed in Scripture, is indeed but *one*; and this *one* end is most properly and comprehensively called, "the glory of God"; by which name it is most commonly called in Scripture. And is fitly compared to an effulgence or emanation of light from a luminary, by which this glory of God is abundantly represented in Scripture. Light is the external expression, exhibition and manifestation of the excellency of the luminary, of the sun for instance: it is the abundant, extensive emanation and communication of the fullness of the sun to innumerable beings that partake of it. 'Tis by this that the sun itself is seen, and his glory beheld, and all other things are discovered: 'tis by a participation of this communication from the sun that surrounding objects receive all their luster, beauty and brightness. 'Tis by this that all nature is quickened and receives life, comfort and joy. Light is abundantly used in Scripture to represent and signify these three things, knowledge, holiness and happiness.

What has been said may be sufficient to show how those things, which are spoken of in Scripture as ultimate ends of God's works, though they may seem at first view to be distinct, all are plainly to be reduced to this one thing, viz. God's internal glory or fullness extant externally, or existing in its emanation. And though God in seeking this end, seeks the creature's good; yet therein appears his supreme regard to himself.

The emanation or communication of the divine fullness, consisting in the knowledge of God, love to God, and joy in God, has relation indeed both to God and the creature: but it has relation to God as its fountain, as it is an emanation from God; and as the communication itself, or thing communicated, is something divine, something of God, something of his internal fullness; as the water in the stream is something of the fountain; and as the beams are of the sun. And again, they have relation to God as they have respect to him as their object: for the knowledge communicated is the knowledge of God; and so God is the object of the knowledge: and the love communicated, is the love of God; so God is the object of that love: and the happiness communicated, is joy in God; and so he is the object of the joy communicated. In the creature's knowing, esteeming, loving, rejoicing in, and praising God, the glory of God is both exhibited and acknowledged; his fullness is received and returned. Here is both an *emanation* and *remanation*. The refulgence shines upon and into the creature, and is reflected back to the luminary. The beams of glory come from God, and are something of God, and are refunded back again to their original. So that the whole is *of* God, and *in* God, and *to* God; and God is the beginning, middle and end in this affair.

And though it be true that God has respect to the creature in these things; yet his respect to himself, and to the creature in this matter, are not properly to be looked upon as a double and divided respect of God's heart. . . .

When God was about to create the world, he had respect to that emanation of his glory, which is actually the consequence of the creation, just as it is with regard to all that belongs to it, both with regard to its relation to himself, and the creature. He had regard to it as an emanation from himself, and a communication of himself, and as the thing communicated, in its nature returned to himself, as its final term. And he had regard to it also as the emanation was to the creature, and as the thing communicated was in the creature, as its subject. And God had regard to it in this manner, as he had a supreme regard to himself, and value for his own infinite internal glory. It was this value for himself that caused him to value and seek that his internal glory should flow forth from himself. It was from his value for his glorious perfections of wisdom and righteousness, etc., that he valued the proper exercise and effect of these perfections, in wise and righteous acts and effects. It was from his infinite value for his internal glory and fullness, that he valued the thing itself, which is communicated, which is something of the same, extant in the creature. Thus, because he infinitely values his own glory, consisting in the knowledge of himself, love to himself, and complacence and joy in himself; he therefore valued the image, communication or participation of these, in the creature. And 'tis because he values himself, that he delights in the knowledge and love and joy of the creature; as being himself the object of this knowledge, love and complacence. For it is the necessary consequence of the true esteem and love of any person or being (suppose a son or friend) that we should approve and value others' esteem of the same object, and disapprove and dislike the contrary. For the same reason it is the consequence of a being's esteem and love of himself that he should approve of others' esteem and love of himself.

Thus 'tis easy to conceive how God should seek the good of the creature, consisting in the creature's knowledge and holiness, and even his happiness, from a supreme regard to himself; as his happiness arises from that which is an image and participation of God's own beauty; and consists in the creature's exercising a supreme regard to God and complacence in him; in beholding God's glory, in esteeming and loving it, and rejoicing in it, and in his exercising and testifying love and supreme respect to God: which is the same thing with the creature's exalting God as his chief good, and making him his supreme end.

And though the emanation of God's fullness which God intended in the creation, and which actually is the consequence of it, is to the creature as its object, and the creature is the subject of the fullness communicated, and is the creature's good; and was also regarded as such, when God sought it as the end of his works: yet it doesn't necessarily follow, that even in so doing, he did not make himself his end. It comes to the same thing. God's respect to the creature's good, and his respect to himself, is not a divided respect; but both are united in one, as the happiness of the creature aimed at is happiness in union with himself. The creature is no further happy with this happiness which God makes his ultimate end than he becomes one with God. The more happiness the greater union: when the happiness is perfect, the union is perfect. And as the happiness will be increasing to eternity, the union will become more and more strict and perfect; nearer and more like to that between God the Father and the Son; who are so united, that their interest is perfectly one. If the happiness of the creature be considered as it will be, in the whole of the creature's eternal duration, with all the infinity of its progress, and infinite increase of nearness and union to God; in this view, the creature must be looked upon as united to God in an infinite strictness.

If God has respect to something in the creature, which he views as of everlasting duration, and as rising higher and higher through that infinite duration, and that not with constantly diminishing (but perhaps an increasing) celerity: then he has respect to it as, in the whole, of infinite height; though there never will be any particular time when it can be said already to have come to such an height.

Let the most perfect union with God be represented by something at an infinite height above us; and the eternally increasing union of the saints with God, by something that is ascending constantly towards that infinite height, moving upwards with a given velocity; and that is to continue thus to move to all eternity. God who views the whole of this eternally increasing height views it as an infinite height. And if he has respect to it, and makes it his end, as in the whole of it, he has respect to it as an infinite height, though the time will never come when it can be said it has already arrived at this infinite height.

God aims at that which the motion or progression which he causes aims at, or tends to. If there be many things supposed to be so made and appointed, that by a constant and eternal motion, they all tend to a certain center; then it appears that he who made them and is the cause of their motion, aimed at that center, that term of their motion to which they eternally tend, and are eternally, as it were, striving after. And if God be this center, then God aimed at himself. And herein it appears that as he is the first author of their being and motion, so he is the last end, the final term, to which is their ultimate tendency and aim.

We may judge of the end that the Creator aimed at, in the being, nature and tendency he gives the creature, by the mark or term which they constantly aim at in their tendency and eternal progress; though the time will never come when it can be said it is attained to, in the most absolutely perfect manner.

But if strictness of union to God be viewed as thus infinitely exalted; then the creature must be regarded as infinitely, nearly and closely united to God. And viewed thus, their interest must be viewed as one with God's interest; and so is not regarded properly with a disjunct and separate, but an undivided respect. . . .

If by reason of the strictness of the union of a man and his family, their interest may be looked upon as one, how much more one is the interest of Christ and his church (whose first union in heaven is unspeakably more perfect and exalted, than that of an earthly father and his family), if they be considered with regard to their eternal and increasing union! Doubtless it may justly be esteemed as so much one that it may be supposed to be aimed at and sought, not with a distinct and separate, but an undivided respect.

'Tis certain that what God aimed at in the creation of the world was the good that would be the consequence of the creation, in the whole continuance of the thing created. . . .

"Discourse on the Trinity"

From *Works of Jonathan Edwards*, vol. 21, *Writings on Trinity, Grace, and Faith,* ed. Sang Hyun Lee (New Haven, CT: Yale University Press, 2003), 113–14, 131–32.

When we speak of God's happiness, the account that we are wont to give of it is that God is infinitely happy in the enjoyment of himself, in perfectly beholding and infinitely loving, and rejoicing in, his own essence and perfections. And accordingly it must be supposed that God perpetually and eternally has a most perfect idea of himself, as it were an exact image and representation of himself ever before him and in actual view. And from hence arises a most pure and perfect energy in the Godhead, which is the divine love, complacence and joy.

Though we cannot conceive of the manner of the divine understanding, yet if it be understanding or anything that can be anyway signified by that word of ours, it is by idea. Though the divine nature be vastly different from that of created spirits, yet our souls are made in the image of God: we have understanding and will, idea and love, as God hath, and the difference is only in the perfection of degree and manner. The perfection of the manner will indeed infer this, that there is no distinction to be made in God between power or habit and act; and with respect to God's understanding, that there are no such distinctions to be admitted as in ours between perception or idea, and reasoning and judgment—excepting what the will has to do in judgment—but that the whole of the divine understanding or wisdom consists in the mere perception or unvaried presence of his infinitely perfect idea. And with respect to the other faculty, as it is in God, there are no distinctions to be admitted of faculty, habit and act, between will, inclination and love: but that it is all one simple act. But the divine perfection will not infer that his understanding is not by idea, and that there is not indeed such a thing as inclination and love in God.

That in John, "God is love" [1 John 4:8, 16], shows that there are more persons than one in the Deity: for it shows love to be essential and necessary to the Deity, so that his nature consists in it; and this supposes that there is an eternal and necessary object, because all love respects another, that is, the beloved. By love here the Apostle certainly means something beside that which is commonly called self-love, that is very improperly called love, and is a thing of an exceeding diverse nature from that affection or virtue of love the Apostle is speaking of.

The sum of the divine understanding and wisdom consists in his having a perfect idea of himself, he being indeed the all-comprehending Being, he that is and there is none else. So the sum of his inclination, love and joy is his love to and delight in himself. God's love to himself, and complacency and delight in himself, they are not to be distinguished, they are the very same thing in God; which will easily be allowed. Love in man being scarcely distinguishable from the complacence he has in any idea, if there be any difference it is merely modal, and circumstantial.

The knowledge or view which God has of himself must necessarily be conceived to be something distinct from his mere direct existence. There must be something that answers to our reflection. The reflection, as we reflect on our own minds, carries something of imperfection in it. However, if God beholds himself so as thence to have delight and joy in himself, he must become his own object: there must be a duplicity. There is God and the idea of God, if it be proper to call a conception of that that is purely spiritual an idea. . . .

And this I suppose to be that blessed Trinity that we read of in the holy Scriptures. The Father is the Deity subsisting in the prime, unoriginated and most absolute manner, or the Deity in its direct existence. The Son is the Deity generated by God's understanding, or having an idea of himself, and subsisting in that idea. The Holy Ghost is the Deity subsisting in act or the divine essence flowing out and breathed forth, in God's infinite love to and delight in himself. And I believe the whole divine essence does truly and distinctly subsist both in the divine idea and divine love, and that therefore each of them are properly distinct persons.

And it confirms me in it, that this is the true Trinity, because reason is sufficient to tell us that there must be these distinctions in the Deity, viz. of God (absolutely considered), and the idea of God, and love and delight; and there are no other real distinctions in God that can be thought (of). There are but these three distinct real things in God; whatsoever else can be mentioned in God are nothing but mere modes or relations of existence. There are his attributes of infinity, eternity and immutability: they are mere modes of existence. There is God's understanding, his wisdom and omniscience, that we have shown to be the same with his idea. There is God's will: but that is not really distinguished from his love, but is the same, but only with a different relation. As the sum of God's understanding consists in his having an idea of himself, so the sum of his will or inclination consists in his loving himself, as we have already observed. There is God's power or ability to bring things to pass. But this is not really distinct from his understanding and will; it is the same, but only with the relation they have to those effects that are or are to be produced. There is God's holiness, but this is the same— as we have shown in what we have said of the nature of excellency— with his love to himself. There is God's justice, which is not really distinct from his holiness. There are the attributes of goodness, mercy and grace, but these are but the overflowings of God's infinite love. The sum of all God's love is his love to himself. These three— God, and the idea of God, and the inclination, affection or love of God— must be conceived as really distinct. But as for all those other things—of extent, duration, being with or without change, ability to do—they are not distinct real things, even in created spirits, but only mere modes and relations. So that our natural reason is sufficient to tell us that there are these three in God, and we can think of no more.

It is a maxim amongst divines that everything that is in God is God, which must be understood of real attributes and not of mere modalities. If a man should tell me that the immutability of God is God, or that the omnipresence of God and authority of God (is God), I should not be able to think of any rational meaning of what he said. It hardly sounds to me proper to say that God's being without change is God, or that God's being everywhere is God, or that God's having a right of government over creatures is God. But if it be meant that the real attributes of God, viz. his understanding and love, are God, then what we have said may in some measure explain how it is so: for Deity subsists in them distinctly, so they are distinct divine persons. We find no other attributes of which it is said that they are God in Scripture, or that God is they, but *Logos* and *Agape*, the reason and the love of God [John 1:1; 1 John 4:8, 16]. Indeed, it is said that God is light [1 John 1:5]. But what can we understand by divine light different from the divine reason or understanding? The same Apostle tells us that Christ is the true light [John 1:9], and the apostle Paul tells us that he is the effulgence of the Father's glory [Heb. 1:3].

This is the light that the Holy Ghost in the prophet Daniel says dwells with God. Daniel 2:22, "And the light dwelleth with him." The same with that Word or reason that the apostle John says [John 1] was with God, and was God; that he there says is the "true Light," and speaks much of under that character [vv. 4–5, 7–9]. This is that Wisdom that says in Proverbs 8:30 that he was by God "as one brought up with him." This is that light with respect to which especially, God the Father may be called the Father of Lights. . . .

René Descartes

***Meditations*, 3.1–4, 13–16, 22–39**

A French philosopher, René Descartes (1596–1650) is credited with originating modern philosophy. He is best known for attempting to establish an indubitable foundation for knowledge in the face of radical skepticism (see his *Discourse on Method* and *Principles of Philosophy*). Declaring, "I think, therefore I am" (*cogito ergo sum*), he was most certain of his own awareness of being a "thinking thing." Even doubting his existence proved that he existed since someone or something must be doing the doubting.

Influenced by Augustine, the third of his *Meditations on First Philosophy* seeks to prove God's existence with two different exercises that reflect on the ideas he perceives most vividly and distinctly in his immediate consciousness. (A third proof is found in the fifth meditation.) The first exercise is rooted in a distinction between the "formal" reality of an idea (by which he means its "actual" existence) and its "objective" reality (that is, the degree of perfection it represents). It also presupposes a ranking of things based on their degree of independent existence: 1) the infinite substance (i.e., God, dependent on nothing else); 2) finite substances (e.g., humans); and 3) modes or accidents (attributes of a substance). Descartes observes that a cause of something must have as much reality as its effect. Not only does something not come from nothing, but what is more perfect cannot arise from what is less perfect. From this, he infers that there must be as much formal (i.e., actual) reality in the cause of an idea as there is in the objective content represented by the idea. This inference enables him to deduce the actual existence of a cause based on the content of an idea (the cause's effect) in his mind. Thus, the idea of God demands God for its cause: only a perfect and infinite reality could cause the idea in his mind of a perfect and infinite being.

The second exercise begins with the question "Could I exist if there were no God?" Descartes considers possible sources of his existence—himself, his parents, his always having existed, or some cause less perfect than God—and observes the following: 1) If he created himself, he would have made himself perfect (which he is not); 2) he could not have always existed since every moment of his existence is sustained by the power that initially created it; 3) if he came solely from his parents, asking where they came from leads to infinite regress; and 4) a perfect idea cannot come from an imperfect cause. Moreover, because the idea of God is neither a sense perception nor a product of his imagination (since he cannot add to or subtract from it), it must be innate, as his idea of himself is innate. God created him in God's image, and because of this likeness, he is able to perceive both himself and the idea of God. He could not be what he is—an imperfect, finite being—and still have the idea of a perfect, infinite God if God in reality did not exist.

He concludes the entire meditation by observing that the exercise of contemplating God's majesty is the greatest source of happiness in this life—just as it will be, far more perfectly, in another life.

From *The Method, Meditations and Philosophy of Descartes,*trans. John Veitch (Washington, DC: M. Walter Dunne, 1901), my italics.

Meditation 3
"On God: That God Exists"

1. I will now close my eyes. I will stop my ears. I will turn my senses away from their objects. I will even remove from my consciousness all the images of bodily things or at least, because this can hardly be accomplished, I will consider them empty and false. Conversing only with myself, closely examining my nature, I will attempt to attain a more intimate and familiar knowledge of myself. I am a thinking (conscious) thing, that is, a being who doubts, affirms, denies, knows a few objects, and is ignorant of many—(who loves, hates), wills, refuses, who imagines likewise, and perceives. As I remarked before, although what I perceive or imagine is perhaps nothing at all apart from me (and in themselves), I am nonetheless assured that my perceptions and imaginations, insofar as they are modes of consciousness, exist in me.

2. In the little I have said I think I have summed up all that I really know, or at least all that up to this point I was aware I knew. Now, as I attempt to extend my knowledge more widely, I will use introspection, and consider with care whether I can still discover in myself anything more that I have not yet observed. I am certain that I am a thinking thing, but what is required to make me certain of a truth? In this first item of knowledge, there is nothing that assures me of its truth except the clear and distinct perception of what I affirm. This would not be sufficient to assure me that what I say is true, if it could ever happen that anything I thus clearly and distinctly perceived should prove false. Accordingly, it seems to me that I may now take as a general rule that all that is very clearly and distinctly apprehended (conceived) is true.

3. Nonetheless there are many things I received and affirmed as wholly certain and evident, which I doubted later. What were these things? They were the earth, the sky, the stars, and all the other objects that I perceived by the senses. But what did I clearly (and distinctly) perceive in them? Nothing more than the ideas and the thoughts of those objects present

in my mind. And even now I do not deny I have these ideas in my mind. But there was yet another thing that I affirmed, and which, because I was accustomed to believe it, I thought I clearly perceived, although, in truth, I did not perceive it at all: the existence of objects external to me, from which those ideas came, and to which they had a perfect resemblance. In fact, I was mistaken, or if I judged correctly, this could not be traced to the force of my perception.

4. But when I considered something like arithmetic and geometry, which was very simple and easy—as, for example, that two and three added together make five, and things of this sort— did I not perceive them with sufficient clearness to warrant my affirming their truth? Indeed, if I afterward judged that we ought to doubt these things, it was for no other reason than because it occurred to me that a God might perhaps have given me such a nature as that I should be deceived, even with regard to those things that appeared most evidently true. But whenever the belief in the supreme power of a God presents itself to my mind, I must admit that it would be easy for him, if he wishes it, to make me err, even in matters where I think I possess the greatest evidence. On the other hand, whenever I direct my attention to things that I think I apprehend with great clearness, I am so persuaded of their truth that I exclaim: "Deceive me! No one has yet to convince me that I am nothing, as long as I am conscious that I am; or at any future point to convince me that I have never been, it being now true that I am; or make two and three more or less than five, in supposing that and other similar absurdities, I discover an obvious contradiction." In truth, I have no basis for believing that God is deceitful and as, indeed, I have not even considered the reasons for establishing that God exists, the basis for my doubt is very slight and theoretical. But, in order to remove this doubt entirely, I must ask whether there is a God, as soon as I can, and if I find that there is a God, I must also examine whether he is a deceiver. Without knowledge of these two truths, I do not see that I can ever be certain of anything. . . .

13. But there is still another way of asking whether, of the objects whose ideas are in my mind, there are any which exist out of me. If ideas are taken as modes of consciousness, I do not see any difference or inequality among them. All seem to proceed from myself. But considering them as images presenting different things, it is evident that there is a great diversity among them. For, without doubt, those that represent substances are something more and contain in themselves, so to speak, more objective reality (that is, participate by representation in greater degrees of being or perfection), than those that represent only modes or accidents. Moreover, the idea by which I conceive a God—(supreme), eternal, infinite, (immutable), all-knowing, all-powerful, and the creator of all things that are out of himself—certainly has in it more objective reality than ideas that represent finite substances.

14. Now, it is evident by the natural light[1] that there must at least be as much reality in an efficient and total cause as in its effect: for from where does an effect receive its reality if not from its cause? And how could the cause communicate this reality to it unless it possessed it in itself? Thus it follows not only that *what is* cannot be produced by *what is not*, but likewise that the *more perfect*—in other words, what contains within itself more reality—cannot be the effect of the *less perfect*. And this is not only true of those effects, whose reality is *actual or formal*, but also of ideas, whose reality is only considered as *objective*. Thus, for example, a stone that is not yet in existence cannot begin to exist unless it is produced by something that possesses in itself, formally or eminently, all that enters into its composition (in other words, by something that contains in itself the same properties that are in the stone, or others superior to them); and heat can only be produced in a subject that did not have it by a cause that is of an order (degree or kind) at least as perfect as heat; and so of the others. Further, even the idea of heat, or of a stone, cannot exist in me unless it was put there by a cause that contains, at least, as much reality as I conceive exists in heat or in a stone because although that cause may not transmit into my idea anything of its actual or formal reality, we ought not because of this imagine that it is less real. Rather we ought to consider that (since every idea is a work of the mind) its nature is such that it demands no other formal reality than what it borrows from our consciousness, of which it is but a mode (that is, a manner or way of thinking). But in order for an idea to contain *objective reality*, it must derive it from a cause that has at least as much *formal reality* as the idea contains of objective reality; for, if we suppose that there is in an idea anything that was not in its cause, it must, of course, derive this from nothing. But, however imperfect the mode of existence may be by which a thing is *objectively* (or by representation) understood by its idea, we certainly cannot, for all that, claim that this mode of existence is nothing, nor, consequently, that the idea owes its origin to nothing.

15. Nor must we imagine that, since the reality considered in these ideas is only objective, the same reality need not be formally (actually) in the causes of these ideas, but only objectively: for, just as the mode of existing objectively belongs to ideas by their distinctive nature, so likewise the mode of existing formally pertains to the causes of these ideas (at least to the first and principal) by their distinctive nature. And although an idea may give rise to another idea, this regress cannot, nevertheless, be infinite. We must in the end reach a first idea, the cause of which is, as it were, the archetype in which all the reality (or perfection) that is found objectively (or by representation) in these ideas is contained formally (and in act). I

---

1. Ed. note: Descartes uses "natural light" to mean human reason.

am thus clearly taught by the natural light that ideas exist in me as pictures or images, which may, in truth, readily fall short of the perfection of the objects from which they are taken, but can never contain anything greater or more perfect.

16. As I examine these matters with time and care, my confidence in their truth becomes more vivid and distinct. What should I conclude from all this? It is this: if the objective reality (or perfection) of any one of my ideas is such that it clearly convinces me that this same reality exists in me neither formally nor eminently, and if, as follows, I myself cannot be the cause of it, it is a necessary consequence that I am not alone in the world, but that there is some other being besides myself who exists as the cause of that idea; while, on the contrary, if no such idea is found in my mind, I shall have no sufficient ground of assurance of the existence of any other being besides myself, for, after a most careful search, I have, up to this moment, been unable to discover any other ground . . . .

22. There only remains, therefore, the idea of God, in which I must consider whether there is anything that cannot be supposed to originate with myself. By the name God, I understand a substance infinite, (eternal, immutable), independent, all-knowing, all-powerful, and by which I myself, and every other thing that exists, if they do exist, were created. But these properties are so great and excellent, that the more attentively I consider them the less I feel persuaded that the idea I have of them owes its origin to myself alone. Thus it is absolutely necessary to conclude, from all I have said, that God exists.

23. For although the idea of substance is in my mind, because I myself am a substance, I would not, however, have the idea of an infinite substance, as I am a finite being, unless it were given me by some substance that is, in reality, infinite.

24. And I must not imagine that I do not apprehend the infinite by a true idea, but only by negating the finite, in the same way that I comprehend repose and darkness by negating motion and light. On the contrary, I clearly perceive that there is more reality in the infinite substance than in the finite, and therefore that in some way I possess the perception (notion) of the infinite before that of the finite, that is, the perception of God before that of myself, for how could I know that I doubt, desire, or that I lack something and am not entirely perfect, if I possessed no idea of a being more perfect than myself, by comparison of which I knew my nature's deficiencies?

25. And it cannot be said that this idea of God is perhaps materially false, and consequently that it may have arisen from nothing. . . . On the contrary, as this idea is very clear and distinct, and contains in itself more objective reality than any other, there can be no one of itself more true, or less open to the suspicion of falsity. The idea, I say, of a being supremely perfect, and infinite, is in the greatest degree true; for although, perhaps,

we may imagine that such a being does not exist, we cannot, nevertheless, suppose that his idea represents nothing real, as I have already said of the idea of cold. It is likewise clear and distinct in the greatest degree, since whatever the mind clearly and distinctly conceives as real or true, and as implying any perfection, is contained completely in this idea. And this is true, even though I do not comprehend the infinite, and although there may be in God an infinity of things that I cannot comprehend or even encompass by thought in any way. For the nature of the infinite is such that it cannot be comprehended by the finite. It is enough that I rightly understand this, and judge that all that I clearly perceive—and in which I know there is some perfection and perhaps also an infinity of properties of which I am ignorant—is formally or eminently in God, in order that the idea I have of him may become the most true, clear, and distinct of all the ideas in my mind.

26. But perhaps I am something more than I suppose myself to be, and it may be that all those perfections that I attribute to God in some way exist potentially in me, although they do not yet show themselves, and are not yet enacted. Indeed, I am already conscious that my knowledge can be increased (and perfected) by degrees. I see nothing to prevent it from gradually increasing to infinity, nor any reason why, after such increase and perfection, I should not be able to acquire all the other perfections of the divine nature; nor why my capacity to acquire those perfections, if it really does now exist in me, should not be sufficient to produce the ideas of them.

27. Yet, in examining the matter more closely, I discover that this cannot be. In the first place, even if it were true that my knowledge acquired daily new degrees of perfection—and although there were potentially in my nature much that was not as yet actually in it—still all these excellences could not even make the slightest approach to the idea I have of God, in whom there is no perfection that is merely potentially (but all actually) are existent. For the very fact that my knowledge can be augmented by degrees is but a sign of its imperfection. Further, even if my knowledge continually increases, this does not induce me to think that it will ever be actually infinite, since it can never reach that point beyond which it shall be incapable of further increase. But I conceive God as actually infinite, so that nothing can be added to his perfection. And I readily perceive that the objective being of an idea cannot be produced by a being that is merely potentially existent, which, properly speaking, is nothing, but only by a being existing formally or actually.

28. And, truly, I see nothing in all that I have said that would not be easy for anyone who carefully considers it to discern by the natural light. But when I allow my attention to relax to some degree, the vision of my mind becomes obscured and blinded by the images of sensible objects. I do not readily remember the reason why the idea of a being more perfect

than myself, must of necessity have proceeded from a being in reality more perfect. Because of this, I desire to ask further whether I, who possess this idea of God, could exist if there were no God.

29. From whom, then, would I derive my existence? Perhaps from myself, or from my parents, or from some other causes less perfect than God; for anything more perfect, or even equal to God, cannot be thought or imagined.

30. But if I (were independent of every other existence, and) were myself the creator of my being, I would doubt nothing; I would desire nothing and want no further perfection. I would have given to myself every perfection I have an idea of, and would thus be God. And it must not be imagined that what is now lacking in me is perhaps more difficult to acquire than what I already possess. On the contrary, it is quite evident that it was a matter of much greater difficulty that I, a thinking being, should arise from nothing, than it would be for me to acquire the knowledge of many things of which I am ignorant, and which are merely the accidents of a thinking substance. And certainly, if I possessed in myself the greater perfection I have spoken about (in other words, if I were the creator of my own existence), I would not at least have denied to myself things that may be more easily obtained (as that infinite variety of knowledge of which I am at present destitute). I could not, indeed, have denied to myself any property that I perceive is contained in the idea of God, because none of these would be more difficult for me to make or acquire. And if there were any that were more difficult to acquire, they would certainly appear so to me (supposing that I myself were the source of the other things I possess), because I would discover in them a limit to my power.

31. And though I were to suppose that I always was as I now am, I would not, on this basis, escape the import of this reasoning, since it would not follow, even on this supposition, that no creator of my existence needed to be sought after. For all the moments of my life can be divided into an infinity of parts, each of which is in no way dependent on any other. Because I was in existence a short time ago, it does not follow that I must now exist, unless in this moment some cause create me anew—that is, conserve me. In truth, it is perfectly clear and evident to all who will attentively consider the nature of duration that the conservation of a substance, in each moment of its duration, requires the same power and act that would be necessary to create it when it was not yet in existence. Thus, it is evidently a dictate of the natural light that conservation and creation differ merely in respect of our mode of thinking (and not in reality).

32. All that is here required, therefore, is that I ask myself to discover whether I possess any power by means of which I can bring it about that I, who now am, should exist the next moment. For since I am merely a thinking thing (or least, this is the part of myself that I am now inquiring about), if such a power resided in me, I would, without doubt, be aware of

it. But I am aware of no such power, and thereby I evidently know that I am dependent upon some being different from myself.

33. But perhaps the being upon whom I am dependent is not God and I have been produced either by my parents, or by some causes less perfect than God. This cannot be. As I said before, it is perfectly evident that there must at least be as much reality in the cause as in its effect. Accordingly, since I am a thinking thing and possess in myself an idea of God, whatever in the end is the cause of my existence must of necessity also be a thinking being that possesses in itself the idea and all the perfections I attribute to God. Then it may again be asked: Does this cause owe its origin and existence to itself, or to some other cause? If it were self-existent, it follows, from what I have already laid down, that this cause is God. For, since it possesses the perfection of self-existence, it must likewise, without doubt, have the power of actually possessing every perfection of which it has the idea—in other words, all the perfections I conceive to belong to God. But if it owes its existence to another cause than itself, we demand again, for a similar reason, whether this second cause exists of itself or through some other, until, from stage to stage, we at length arrive at an ultimate cause, which will be God.

34. And it is quite evident that in this matter there can be no infinite regress of causes, since the question raised deals not so much with the cause that produced me initially as with what conserves me at this very moment.

35. Nor can it be supposed that several causes worked together in my production and that from one I received the idea of one of the perfections I attribute to God, and from another yet another perfection, and thus that all those perfections are indeed found somewhere in the universe, but do not all exist together in a single being who is God. On the contrary, the unity, the simplicity, or inseparability of all the properties of God is one of the chief perfections I conceive him to possess. The idea of the unity of all of God's perfections could certainly not be put into my mind by any cause from which I did not also receive the ideas of all the other perfections. No power could enable me to embrace them in an inseparable unity without at the same time giving me the knowledge of what they were and of their existence in a particular mode.

36. Finally, with regard to my parents (from whom it appears I came), even if all that I believed with regard to them were be true, it does not follow that I am conserved by them, or even that I was produced by them, in so far as I am a thinking being. All that, at the most, they contributed to my origin was giving certain dispositions (or modifications) to the matter in which I have so far judged that I or my mind, which is all that I consider myself to be, is enclosed. Thus, there can here be no difficulty with respect to them, and it is absolutely necessary to conclude from this alone—that I

am and possess the idea of a being absolutely perfect, that is, of God—that God's existence is most clearly demonstrated.

37. There remains only the question: the way I received this idea from God. For I have not drawn it from the senses, nor is it even presented to me unexpectedly, as is usual with the ideas of sensible objects when these are presented, or appear to be presented, to the external organs of the senses. It is not even a pure invention or fiction of my mind, for it is not in my power to take from or add to it. Consequently all that remains is the alternative: that it is innate, in the same way that the idea I have of myself is innate.

38. In truth, it is not to be wondered at that God, at my creation, implanted this idea in me, that it might serve, as it were, as the mark of the workman impressed on his work. It is also not necessary that the mark should be something different from the work itself. Considering only that God is my creator, it is highly probable that he in some way fashioned me after his own image and likeness and that I perceive this likeness, in which is contained the idea of God, by the same faculty by which I apprehend myself. In other words, when I make myself the object of my reflection, I not only find that I am an incomplete, imperfect, and dependent being, and one who unceasingly aspires after something better and greater than he is but, at the same time, I am assured likewise that the one upon whom I depend possesses in himself all the goods I aspire after (and the ideas of which I find in my mind)—not merely indefinitely and potentially, but infinitely and actually—and that he is God. The entire force of the argument I have used to establish the existence of God consists in this: that I perceive I could not possibly be what I am, with the nature that I have, and yet have in my mind the idea of a God, if God did not in reality exist—this God, whose idea is in my mind—that is, a being who possesses all the lofty perfections my mind has some slight conception of, without, however, being able fully to comprehend them, and who is wholly superior to all defect (and has nothing that marks imperfection). From this, it is sufficiently evident that God cannot be a deceiver, since it is a dictate of the natural light that all fraud and deception spring from some defect.

39. But before I examine this with more attention and proceed to consider other truths that may evolve from it, I think it proper to remain here for some time contemplating God himself—pondering at leisure his wonderful attributes—beholding, admiring, and adoring the beauty of this light so unspeakably great, as far, at least, as the strength of my mind, dazzled by the sight, will permit. For just as we learn by faith that the supreme happiness of another life consists in contemplating the Divine majesty alone, so even now we learn from experience that a similar meditation, though incomparably less perfect, is the source of the greatest satisfaction we can have in this life.

SELECTION **3**

Blaise Pascal

**"The Wager," Sections
3.227–33, 4.277–82**

A French philosopher, Blaise Pascal (1623–1662) advocated experiencing God through the heart rather than through reason. His most influential book, posthumously titled *Pensées* (*Thoughts*), was put together from scraps of notes he had written for a book he had originally titled *Defense of the Christian Religion*. In these reflections, he presents a number of paradoxes (infinity and nothing, faith and reason, death and life, meaning and vanity, etc.) in a series of exercises that lead to confusion and thus an experience of reason's limits.

His famous "wager" begins with the despairing observation that God is incomprehensible: the infinite God has no affinity with us. We cannot prove God's existence. Christians can only profess their faith as "foolishness" to the world (1 Cor. 1:21). Belief in God is a gamble. If you win, you gain everything—an eternity of life and happiness. If you lose, you lose nothing. The choices are all or nothing. There is an infinite distance between the certainty of your finite reason and the uncertainty of infinite gain, which is as likely to happen as the loss of nothingness.

Even if you cannot believe, Pascal goes on, at least experience your inability to believe. Stop trying to develop "proofs" for God's existence and focus instead on taming your passions. What harm will come from your being faithful, humble, grateful, generous, sincere, and truthful? In the end, you will recognize that you wagered for something certain and infinite, for which you have given nothing. And finally, whatever is persuasive in all this only comes from prayer to the infinite one, who gives you all that he has so that you can give him all that you have for your own good.

The next short selection contains his famous line "The heart has its reasons, which reason does not know." Only the heart experiences God, not reason. Faith is a gift of God felt by the heart, not by reason. Even reason's first principles (e.g., space, time, motion, number) are intuitions of the heart, although aside from these, nature gives us very little by way of intuition; the rest must be acquired by reasoning. Those who experience God through intuition are fortunate; the rest can only be given reasons as they wait for God to give them the spiritual insight, without which faith is only human and useless for salvation.

From *The Thoughts of Pascal*, trans. W. F. Trotter (from the edition
prepared by Léon Brunschvieg) (London: Gollancz, 1904).

Section 3

Of the Necessity of the Wager

227. Order by dialogues—"What ought I to do? I see only darkness everywhere. Shall I believe I am nothing? Shall I believe I am God?"

All things change and succeed each other. . . .

228. Objection of atheists: "But we have no light."

229. This is what I see and what troubles me. I look on all sides, and I see only darkness everywhere. Nature presents to me nothing that is not a matter of doubt and concern. If I saw nothing there that revealed a God, I would come to a negative conclusion; if I saw everywhere the signs of a Creator, I would remain peacefully in faith. But, seeing too much to deny and too little to be sure, I am in a state to be pitied; thus, I have a hundred times wished that if a God maintains Nature, she should testify to him unequivocally, and that, if the signs she gives are deceptive, she should suppress them altogether; that she should say everything or nothing, that I might see which cause I ought to follow. But in my present state, ignorant of what I am or of what I ought to do, I know neither my condition nor my duty. My heart inclines wholly to know where the true good is, in order to follow it; nothing would be too dear to me for eternity.

I envy those I see living in the faith with such carelessness and who make such a bad use of a gift that, it seems to me, I would make such a different use.

230. It is incomprehensible that God should exist, and it is incomprehensible that he should not exist; that the soul should be joined to the body, and that we should have no soul; that the world should be created, and that it should not be created, etc.; that original sin should be, and that it should not be.

231. Do you believe it to be impossible that God is infinite, without parts? Yes. I wish, therefore, to show you an infinite and indivisible thing. It is a point moving everywhere with an infinite velocity; for it is one in all places and is all totality in every place.

Let this effect of nature, which previously seemed to you impossible, make you know that there may be others of which you are still ignorant. Do not draw from your experiment the conclusion that there remains nothing for you to know, but rather that there remains an infinity for you to know.

232. Infinite movement, the point that fills everything, the moment of rest; infinite without quantity, indivisible and infinite.

233. Infinite—nothing. Our soul is cast into a body where it finds

number, dimension. Thus, it reasons, and calls this nature necessity, and can believe nothing else.

Unity joined to infinity adds nothing to it, no more than one foot to an infinite measure. The finite is annihilated in the presence of the infinite, and becomes pure nothing. So our spirit before God, so our justice before divine justice. There is not so great a disproportion between our justice and God's as between unity and infinity.

God's justice must be as vast as his compassion. Now God's justice to the outcast is less vast and ought less to offend our feelings than God's mercy towards the elect.

We know that there is an infinite without knowing its nature, just as we know it to be false that numbers are finite. Thus, it is true that there is an infinite number, but we do not know what it is. It is false that it is even, and it is false that it is odd, because adding a unit does not change its nature. Yet it is a number, and every number is odd or even (this is certainly true of every finite number). So we may well know that there is a God without knowing what he is. Is there not one substantial truth, seeing there are so many things that are not the truth itself?

We know then the existence and nature of the finite, because we also are finite and have extension. We know the existence of the infinite and are ignorant of its nature, because it has extension like us, but not limits like us. But we know neither the existence nor the nature of God, because he has neither extension nor limits.

But by faith we know his existence; in glory we shall know his nature. Now, I have already shown that we may well know the existence of a thing, without knowing its nature.

Let us now speak according to natural lights.

If there is a God, he is infinitely incomprehensible, since, having neither parts nor limits, he has no affinity to us. We are then incapable of knowing either what he is or if he is. This being so, who will dare to decide on the question? Not we, who have no affinity to him.

Who then will blame Christians for not being able to give a reason for their belief, since they profess a religion for which they cannot give a reason? They declare, in expounding it to the world, that it is foolishness (*stultitiam*) [1 Cor. 1:21]; and then you complain that they do not prove it! If they proved it, they would not keep their word; it is in lacking proofs that they are not lacking in sense. "Yes, but although this excuses those who offer it as such and takes away from them the blame of putting it forward without reason, it does not excuse those who receive it." Let us then examine this point, and say, "God is, or he is not." But to which side shall we be inclined? Reason can decide nothing here. Infinite chaos separates us. A game is being played at the extremity of this infinite distance where heads or tails will turn up. What will you wager? According to reason, you can do neither the one thing nor the other; according to reason, you can defend neither of the propositions.

Do not, then, reprove for error those who have made a choice, because you know nothing about it. "No, but I blame them for having made, not this choice, but a choice. For again, both the one who chooses heads and the one who chooses tails are equally at fault. They are both in the wrong. The true course is not to wager at all."

Yes, but you must wager. It is not optional. You are embarked. What, then, will you choose? Let us see. Since you must choose, let us see what interests you least. You have two things to lose: the true and the good. And two things to stake: your reason and your will, your knowledge and your happiness. And your nature has two things to shun: error and misery. Your reason is no more shocked in choosing one rather than the other, since you must of necessity choose. This is one point settled. But your happiness? Let us weigh the gain and the loss in wagering that God is. Let us estimate these two chances. If you gain, you gain all; if you lose, you lose nothing. Wager, then, without hesitation that he is. "That is very fine. Yes, I must wager; but I may perhaps wager too much." Let us see. Since there is an equal risk of gain and of loss, if you had only to gain two lives, instead of one, you might still wager. But if there were three lives to gain, you would have to play (since you are under the necessity of playing), and you would be imprudent, when you are forced to play, not to chance your life to gain three at a game where there is an equal risk of loss and gain. But there is an eternity of life and happiness. And this being so, if there were an infinity of chances of which one only would be for you, you would still be right in wagering one to win two, and you would act stupidly, being obliged to play, by refusing to stake one life against three at a game in which out of an infinity of chances there is one for you, if there were an infinity of an infinitely happy life to gain. But there is here an infinity of an infinitely happy life to gain, a chance of gain against a finite number of chances of loss, and what you stake is finite. It is all divided. Wherever there is infinity, and where there are not infinite chances of losing against winning, there is no time to hesitate: you must give all. And thus, when forced to play, you must renounce reason to preserve your life, rather than risk it for infinite gain, as likely to happen as the loss of nothingness.

For it is no use to say it is uncertain if we will win, and it is certain that we risk, and that the infinite distance between the certainty of what is staked and the uncertainty of what will be gained, equals the finite good that is certainly staked against the uncertain infinite. It is not so, as every player stakes a certainty to gain an uncertainty, and yet he stakes a finite certainty to gain a finite uncertainty, without transgressing against reason. There is not an infinite distance between the certainty staked and the uncertainty of the gain; that is untrue. In truth, there is an infinity between the certainty of gain and the certainty of loss. But the uncertainty of the gain is proportioned to the certainty of the stake according to the proportion of the chances of gain and loss. Hence it comes that, if there are as many risks on one side as on the other, the course is to play even; and then the certainty of the stake is equal to the uncertainty of the gain, so far is it from fact that there is an infinite distance between them. And so our proposition is of infinite force, when there is the finite to stake in a game where there are equal risks of gain and of loss, and the infinite to gain. This is demonstrable; and if humans are capable of any truths, this is one.

"I confess it, I admit it. But, still, is there no means of seeing the faces of the cards?" Yes, Scripture and the rest, etc. "Yes, but I have my hands tied and my mouth closed; I am forced to wager, and am not free. I am not released, and am so made that I cannot believe. What, then, would you have me do?"

True. But at least learn your inability to believe, since reason brings you to this, and yet you cannot believe. Make an effort, then, to convince yourself, not by multiplying your proofs for God's existence, but by taming your passions. You would like to attain faith and do not know the way; you would like to cure yourself of unbelief and ask the remedy for it. Learn from those who were once bound like you, and who now wager all their possessions. These are people who know the way that you would follow, and who are cured of the affliction of which you would be cured. Follow the way by which they began—by acting as if they believed, taking the holy water, having masses said, etc. That will make you believe naturally, and mute your intensity. "But this is what I am afraid of." And why? What have you to lose?

But to show you that this leads you there—that it is lessen the passions, which are your great stumbling-blocks . . .

The End of This Discourse

Now, what harm will come to you from choosing this course? You will be faithful, humble, grateful, generous, a sincere friend, truthful. Certainly you will not have those toxic pleasures, glory and luxury; but will you not have others? I will tell you that you will gain even in this life, and that, at each step you take on this road, you will see so great certainty of gain, so much nothingness in what you risk, that you will at last recognize that you have wagered for something certain and infinite—for which you have given nothing.

"Ah! This discourse transports me, charms me," etc.

If this discourse pleases you and seems impressive, know that it is made by a person who has knelt, both before and after it, in prayer to that Being, infinite and without parts, before whom he lays all he has, for you also to lay before him all you have for your own good and for his glory, so that strength may be given to lowliness.

Section 4

Of the Means of Belief

277. The heart has its reasons that reason does not know. We feel it in a thousand things. I say that the heart naturally loves the Universal Being, and also itself naturally, according as it gives itself to them; and it hardens itself against one or the other at its will. You have rejected the one and kept the other. Is it by reason that you love yourself?

278. It is the heart that experiences God, and not the reason. This, then, is faith: God felt by the heart, not by the reason.

279. Faith is a gift of God; do not believe that we said it was a gift of reasoning. Other religions do not say this of their faith. They only gave reasoning in order to arrive at it, and yet it does not bring them to it.

280. The knowledge of God is very far from the love of him.

281. Heart, instinct, principles.

282. We know truth, not only by reason, but also through the heart, and it is in this latter way that we know first principles; and reason, which has no part in it, tries in vain to impugn them. The skeptics, who have only this for their object, labor to no purpose. We know that we do not dream, and, however impossible it is for us to prove it by reason, this inability demonstrates only the weakness of our reason, but not, as they affirm, the uncertainty of all our knowledge. For the knowledge of first principles—as space, time, motion, number—is as sure as any of those that we get from reasoning. And reason must trust these intuitions of the heart, and must base them on every argument. (We have intuitive knowledge of the tri-dimensional nature of space and of the infinity of number, and reason then shows that there are no two square numbers one of which is double of the other. Principles are intuited, propositions are inferred, all with certainty, though in different ways.) And it is as useless and absurd for reason to demand from the heart proofs of her first principles before admitting them, as it would be for the heart to demand from reason an intuition of all demonstrated propositions before accepting them.

This inability ought, then, to serve only to humble reason, which would judge all, but not to impugn our certainty, as if only reason were capable of instructing us. Would to God, on the contrary, that we had never need of it, and that we knew everything by instinct and intuition! But nature has refused us this boon. On the contrary, she has given us but very little knowledge of this kind; all the rest can be acquired only by reasoning.

Therefore, those to whom God has imparted religion by intuition are very fortunate and justly convinced. But to those who do not have it, we can give it only by reasoning, waiting for God to give them spiritual insight, without which faith is only human and useless for salvation.

Immanuel Kant

"The Existence of God as a Postulate of Pure Practical Reason"

The German philosopher Immanuel Kant (1724–1804) sought to integrate modern rationalism and empiricism in a "critical philosophy" centered on the autonomy of human understanding: not only does it provide general laws that enable us to structure our experience, but it also gives us the moral law, which grounds our belief in God, freedom, and immortality.

In the *Critique of Pure Reason*, Kant criticized traditional forms of metaphysics for pretending to know what lies beyond experiential evidence. Nonetheless, he established another kind of metaphysics based on the structure, range, use, and validity of concepts (e.g., "cause" or "duty") that—although not derived from experience—are essential for making sense of our experience. By demonstrating that a priori principles structure experience, Kant claimed to have accomplished a "Copernican revolution" in philosophy.

In his critique of traditional metaphysics, Kant rejected traditional proofs for God's existence: the *ontological argument*, which moves from an idea of God to the existence of God; the *cosmological argument*, which moves from the contingent world to God as its noncontingent source; and the *teleological argument*, which moves from the apparent order of the world to a divine designer. The first proof fails because simply having an idea of something does not prove that it exists. The other two proofs fail because you cannot apply causality, which the mind imposes on our experiences in the world, to prove a reality like God, who transcends the limits of the world.

Nonetheless, in his *Critique of Practical Reason,* Kant replaced these proofs with a *moral argument* for God. Assuming that the complete or highest good (*summum bonum*) takes place when virtue receives its due reward of happiness, he observed that there is no basis within morality for a necessary connection between virtue and proportionate happiness. To be moral we must be virtuous regardless of the consequences. Yet we have no guarantee of happiness because we cannot control whether what happens to us will conform to our desires; we can only do our duty. This is the antinomy at the heart of the moral life. The only solution is to postulate a holy and wise God as the condition for harmony between virtue and happiness. However, this moral necessity is subjective (a want) and not objective (a duty); it is a hypothesis and thus is called faith.

The *summum bonum* is the "end of creation" depicted in the Christian concept of the kingdom of God. This "end" is not the happiness of rational beings but the condition of being worthy of happiness. We can say that the "end of creation" is the "glory of God" since nothing glorifies God more than respect for God's commandments—our holy duty—with the proportionate happiness added to it. The latter makes God worthy of love, the former an object of adoration. In turn, human beings are also "ends" in themselves because they are subject to the moral law, which is holy in itself, even as this law is grounded in the autonomy of their will.

In a footnote on God's attributes, Kant observes that three attributes—holiness, blessedness, and wisdom—belong exclusively to God, for they depict God as the "holy lawgiver" (as creator), the "good governor" (as preserver), and the "just judge."

From Kant's Critique of Practical Reason and Other Works on the Theory of Ethics, trans. Thomas Kingsmill Abbott (London: Longmans, Green, & Co., 1909), 220–29.

In the foregoing analysis the moral law led to a practical problem which is prescribed by pure reason alone, without the aid of any sensible motives, namely, that of the necessary completeness of the first and principle element of the *summum bonum,* viz., morality; and, as this can be perfectly solved only in eternity, to the postulate of immortality. The same law must also lead us to affirm the possibility of the second element of the *summum bonum,* viz., happiness proportioned to that morality, and this on grounds as disinterested as before, and solely from impartial reason; that is, it must lead to the supposition of the existence of a cause adequate to this effect; in other words, it must postulate the existence of God, as the necessary condition of the possibility of the *summum bonum* (an object of the will which is necessarily connected with the moral legislation of pure reason). We proceed to exhibit this connection in a convincing manner.

Happiness is the condition of a rational being in the world with whom everything goes according to his wish and will; it rests, therefore, on the harmony of physical nature with his whole end and likewise with the essential determining principle of his will. Now the moral law as a law of freedom commands by determining principles, which ought to be quite independent of nature and of its harmony with our faculty of desire (as springs). But the acting rational being in the world is not the cause of the world and of nature itself. There is not the least ground, therefore, in the moral law for a necessary connection between morality and proportionate happiness in a being that belongs to the world as part of it, and therefore dependent on it, and which for that reason cannot by his will be a cause of this nature, nor by his own power make it thoroughly harmonize, as far as his happiness is concerned, with his practical principles. Nevertheless, in the practical problem of pure reason, i.e., the necessary pursuit of the *summum bonum,* such a connection is postulated as necessary: we ought to endeavor to promote the *summum bonum*, which, therefore, must be possible. Accordingly, the existence of a cause of all nature, distinct from nature itself and containing the principle of this connection, namely, of the exact harmony of happiness with morality, is also postulated. Now this supreme cause must contain the principle of the harmony of nature, not merely with a law of the will of rational beings, but with the conception of this law, in so far as they make it the supreme determining principle of the will, and consequently not merely with the form of morals, but with their morality as their motive, that is, with their moral character. Therefore, the *summum bonum* is possible in the world only on the supposition of a Supreme Being having a causality corresponding to moral character. Now a being that is capable of acting on the conception of laws is an intelligence (a rational being), and the causality of such a being according to this conception of laws is his will; therefore the supreme cause of nature, which must be presupposed as a condition of the *summum bonum* is a being which is the cause of nature by intelligence and will, consequently its author, that is God. It follows that the postulate of the possibility of the highest derived good (the best world) is likewise the postulate of the reality of a highest original good, that is to say, of the existence of God. Now it was seen to be a duty for us to promote the *summum bonum*; consequently it is not merely allowable, but it is a necessity connected with duty as a requisite, that we should presuppose the possibility of this *summum bonum*; and as this is possible only on condition of the existence of God, it inseparably connects the supposition of this with duty; that is, it is morally necessary to assume the existence of God.

It must be remarked here that this moral necessity is subjective, that is, it is a want, and not objective, that is, itself a duty, for there cannot be a duty to suppose the existence of anything (since this concerns only the theoretical employment of reason). Moreover, it is not meant by this that it is necessary to suppose the existence of God as a basis of all obligation in general (for this rests, as has been sufficiently proved, simply on the autonomy of reason itself). What belongs to duty here is only the endeavor to realize and promote the *summum bonum* in the world, the possibility of which can therefore be postulated; and as our reason finds it not conceivable except on the supposition of a supreme intelligence, the admission of this existence is therefore connected with the consciousness of our duty, although the admission itself belongs to the domain of speculative reason. Considered in respect of this alone, as a principle of explanation, it may be called a hypothesis, but in reference to the intelligibility of an object given us by the moral law (the *summum bonum*), and consequently of a requirement for practical purposes, it may be called faith, that is to say a pure rational faith, since pure reason (both in its theoretical and practical use) is the sole source from which it springs.

From this deduction it is now intelligible why the Greek schools could never attain the solution of their problem of the practical possibility of the *summum bonum*, because they made the rule of the use which the will of man makes of his freedom the sole and sufficient ground of this possibility, thinking that they had no need for that purpose of the existence of God. No doubt they were so far right that they established the principle of morals of itself independently of this postulate, from the relation of reason only to the will, and consequently made it the supreme practical condition of the *summum bonum*; but it was not therefore the whole condition of its possibility. The Epicureans had indeed assumed as the supreme principle of morality a wholly false one, namely that of happiness, and had substituted for a law a maxim of arbitrary choice according to every man's inclination; they proceeded, however, consistently enough in this, that they degraded their *summum bonum* likewise, just in proportion to the meanness of their fundamental principle, and looked for no greater happiness than can be attained by human prudence (including temperance and moderation of the inclinations), and this as we know would be scanty enough and would be very different according to circumstances; not to mention the exceptions that their maxims must perpetually admit and which make them incapable of being laws. The Stoics, on the contrary, had chosen their supreme practical principle quite rightly, making virtue the condition of the *summum bonum*; but when they represented the degree of virtue required by its pure law as fully attainable in this life, they not only strained the moral powers of the man whom they called the wise beyond all the limits of his nature, and assumed a thing that contradicts all our knowledge of men, but also and principally they would not allow the second element of the *summum bonum*, namely, happiness, to be properly a special object of human desire, but made their wise man, like a divinity in his consciousness of the excellence of his person, wholly independent of nature (as regards his own contentment); they exposed him indeed to the evils of life, but made him not subject to them (at the same time representing him also as free from moral evil). They thus, in fact, left out the second element of the *summum bonum*, namely, personal happiness, placing it solely in action and satisfaction with one's own personal worth, thus including it in the consciousness of being morally minded, in which they might have been sufficiently refuted by the voice of their own nature.

The doctrine of Christianity,[2] even if we do not yet consider it as a

---

2. It is commonly held that the Christian precept of morality has no advantage in respect of purity over the moral conceptions of the Stoics; the distinction between them is, however, very obvious. The Stoic system made the consciousness of strength of mind the pivot on which all moral dispositions should turn; and although its disciples spoke of duties and even defined them very well, yet they placed the spring and proper determining principle of the will in an elevation of the mind above the lower springs of the senses, which owe their power only to weakness of mind. With them therefore, virtue was a sort of heroism in the wise man who, raising himself above the animal nature of man, is sufficient for himself, and, while he prescribes duties to others, is himself raised above them, and is not subject to any temptation to transgress the moral law. All this, however, they could not have done

religious doctrine, gives, touching this point, a conception of the *summum bonum* (the kingdom of God), which alone satisfies the strictest demand of practical reason. The moral law is holy (unyielding) and demands holiness of morals, although all the moral perfection to which man can attain is still only virtue, that is, a rightful disposition arising from respect for the law, implying consciousness of a constant propensity to transgression, or at least a want of purity, that is, a mixture of many spurious (not moral) motives of obedience to the law, consequently a self-esteem combined with humility. In respect, then, of the holiness which the Christian law requires, this leaves the creature nothing but a progress in infinitum, but for that very reason it justifies him in hoping for an endless duration of his existence. The worth of a character perfectly accordant with the moral law is infinite, since the only restriction on all possible happiness in the judgement of a wise and all powerful distributor of it is the absence of conformity of rational beings to their duty. But the moral law of itself does not promise any happiness, for according to our conceptions of an order of nature in general, this is not necessarily connected with obedience to the law. Now Christian morality supplies this defect (of the second indispensable element of the *summum bonum*) by representing the world in which rational beings devote themselves with all their soul to the moral law, as a kingdom of God, in which nature and morality are brought into a harmony foreign to each of itself, by a holy Author who makes the derived *summum bonum* possible. Holiness of life is prescribed to them as a rule even in this life, while the welfare proportioned to it, namely, bliss, is represented as attainable only in an eternity; because the former must always be the pattern of their conduct in every state, and progress towards it is already possible and necessary in this life; while the latter, under the name of happiness, cannot be attained at all in this world (so far as our own power is concerned), and therefore is made simply an object of hope. Nevertheless, the Christian principle of morality itself is not theological (so as

---

if they had conceived this law in all its purity and strictness, as the precept of the Gospel does. When I give the name moral idea to a perfection to which nothing adequate can be given in experience, it does not follow that the moral ideas are things transcendent, that is something of which we could not even determine the concept adequately, or of which it is uncertain whether there is any object corresponding to it at all, as is the case with the ideas of speculative reason. On the contrary, being types of practical perfection, they serve as the indispensable rule of conduct and likewise as the standard of comparison. Now if I consider Christian morals on their philosophical side, then compared with the ideas of the Greek schools, they would appear as follows: the ideas of the Cynics, the Epicureans, the Stoics, and the Christians are simplicity of nature, prudence, wisdom, and holiness. In respect of the way of attaining them, the Greek schools were distinguished from one another: the Cynics only required common sense, the others the path of science, but both found the mere use of natural powers sufficient for the purpose. Christian morality, because its precept is framed (as a moral precept must be) so pure and unyielding, takes from humanity all confidence of being fully adequate to it, at least in this life, but again sets it up by enabling us to hope that if we act as well as it is in our power to do, then what is not in our power will come in to our aid from another source, whether we know how this may be or not. Aristotle and Plato differed only as to the origin of our moral conceptions.

to be heteronomy), but is autonomy of pure practical reason, since it does not make the knowledge of God and God's will the foundation of these laws, but only of the attainment of the *summum bonum*, on condition of following these laws, and it does not even place the proper spring of this obedience in the desired results, but solely in the conception of duty, as that of which the faithful observance alone constitutes the worthiness to obtain those happy consequences.

In this manner, the moral laws lead through the conception of the *summum bonum* as the object and final end of pure practical reason to religion, that is, to the recognition of all duties as divine commands, not as sanctions, that is to say, arbitrary ordinances of a foreign and contingent in themselves, but as essential laws of every free will in itself, which, nevertheless, must be regarded as commands of the Supreme Being, because it is only from a morally perfect (holy and good) and at the same time all-powerful will, and consequently only through harmony with this will, that we can hope to attain the *summum bonum* which the moral law makes it our duty to take as the object of our endeavors. Here again, then, all remains disinterested and founded merely on duty; neither fear nor hope being made the fundamental springs, which if taken as principles would destroy the whole moral worth of actions. The moral law commands me to make the highest possible good in a world the ultimate object of all my conduct. But I cannot hope to effect this otherwise than by the harmony of my will with that of a holy and good Author of the world; and although the conception of the *summum bonum* as a whole, in which the greatest happiness is conceived as combined in the most exact proportion with the highest degree of moral perfection (possible in creatures), includes my own happiness, yet it is not this that is the determining principle of the will which is enjoined to promote the *summum bonum*, but the moral law, which, on the contrary, limits by strict conditions my unbounded desire of happiness.

Hence also morality is not properly the doctrine how we should make ourselves happy, but how we should become worthy of happiness. It is only when religion is added that there also comes in the hope of participating some day in happiness in proportion as we have endeavored to be not unworthy of it. A man is worthy to possess a thing or a state when his possession of it is in harmony with the *summum bonum*. We can now easily see that all worthiness depends on moral conduct, since in the conception of the *summum bonum* this constitutes the condition of the rest (which belongs to one's state), namely, the participation of happiness. Now it follows from this that morality should never be treated as a doctrine of happiness, that is, an instruction how to become happy; for it has to do simply with the rational condition (*conditio sine qua non*) of happiness, not with the means of attaining it. But when morality has been completely expounded (which merely imposes duties instead of providing rules for selfish desires), then first, after the moral desire to promote the *summum bonum* (to bring the kingdom of God to us) has been awakened, a desire founded on a law, and which could not previously arise in any selfish mind, and when for the behoof of this desire the step to religion has been taken, then this ethical doctrine may be also called a doctrine of happiness because the hope of happiness first begins with religion only.

We can also see from this that, when we ask what is God's ultimate end in creating the world, we must not name the happiness of the rational beings in it, but the *summum bonum*, which adds a further condition to that wish of such beings, namely, the condition of being worthy of happiness, that is, the morality of these same rational beings, a condition which alone contains the rule by which only they can hope to share in the former at the hand of a wise Author. For as wisdom, theoretically considered, signifies the knowledge of the *summum bonum* and, practically, the accordance of the will with the *summum bonum*, we cannot attribute to a supreme independent wisdom an end based merely on goodness. For we cannot conceive the action of this goodness (in respect of the happiness of rational beings) as suitable to the highest original good, except under the restrictive conditions of harmony with the holiness of his will.[3] Therefore, those who placed the end of creation in the glory of God (provided that this is not conceived anthropomorphically as a desire to be praised) have perhaps hit upon the best expression. For nothing glorifies God more than that which is the most estimable thing in the world, respect for God's command, the observance of the holy duty that God's law imposes on us, when there is added thereto God's glorious plan of crowning such a beautiful order of things with corresponding happiness. If the latter (to speak humanly) makes God worthy of love, by the former God is an object of adoration. Even human beings can never acquire respect by benevolence alone, though they may gain love, so that the greatest beneficence only procures them honor when it is regulated by worthiness.

It follows that, in the order of ends, human beings (and with them every rational being) are ends in themselves, that is, that they can never be used merely as a means by any (not even by God) without being at the same time an end also themselves, that therefore humanity in our person must be holy to ourselves. This follows now of itself because they are the

---

3. In order to make the characteristics of these conceptions clear, I add the remark that while we ascribe to God various attributes, the quality of which we also find applicable to creatures—only that in God they are raised to the highest degree (e.g., power, knowledge, presence, goodness, etc.) under the designations of omnipotence, omniscience, omnipresence, etc.—there are three that are ascribed to God exclusively, and yet without the addition of greatness, and which are all moral. God is the only holy, the only blessed, the only wise, because these conceptions already imply the absence of limitation. In the order of these attributes God is also the holy lawgiver (and creator), the good governor (and preserver) and the just judge—three attributes that include everything by which God is the object of religion, and in conformity with which the metaphysical perfections are added of themselves in the reason.

subject of the moral law, in other words, of that which is holy in itself, and on account of which and in agreement with which alone can anything be termed holy. For this moral law is founded on the autonomy of their will, as a free will which by its universal laws must necessarily be able to agree with that to which it is to submit itself.

SELECTION **5**

Friedrich Schleiermacher

"God and Immortality"

A Reformed theologian influenced by Moravian Pietism, Friedrich Schleiermacher (1768–1834) is often described as the "father of modern liberal theology." His most important work, *The Christian Faith*, provides a systematic interpretation of Christian dogmatics for believers in light of a modern scientific view of the world. For Schleiermacher, all talk about God has to be rooted in our immediate experience of self-consciousness. When we reflect on this experience, we find that we are in a reciprocal relationship with the rest of nature and with other selves. But within this experience, we find that we are also aware of being "absolutely dependent" on a "whence"—an unconditioned reality that affects everything yet is not reciprocally related to it in the same way that the rest of life is. Neither merely a "knowing" (as in doctrinal orthodoxy) nor merely a "doing" (as in pietism or a religion reduced to ethics), nor even simply an emotion, this "feeling" of absolute dependence is a universal part of life— although it varies in strength since we only experience it along with the rest of our sensible experience, which does not uniformly encourage the emergence of a "higher" consciousness within us. All that we have to say about God comes from this original revelation of God; our intuitive certainty of it replaces all so-called "proofs" for God's existence. The root of all "piety," this original revelation is found in all true religions, but it is most completely experienced through Christ's redemptive work, which overcomes all obstructions to our experience of it.

Schleiermacher wrote *On Religion: Speeches to Its Cultured Despisers* earlier in his life as an apology for Christian faith to skeptics, many of whom were his friends. Here, he describes the feeling of absolute dependence as "true religion"—a "sense and taste for the Infinite." Schleiermacher contrasts this understanding of God with two other more limited views. Against pantheism, which equates God consciousness with world consciousness, it presupposes divine causality as the world's eternal ground. Against the traditional notion of a personal God who intervenes in the world supernaturally, it describes God as a "living God" whose "omniscient" spirit always works within and through natural processes (and not through "supernatural" incursions). From within our experience of absolute dependence, we can understand that immortality is not about an "endless temporal existence" but about being one with the Infinite in the midst of finitude, something we can experience even now in this life whenever we surrender our lives to God—losing our lives for Christ's sake so that we can gain eternal life.

From *On Religion: Speeches to Its Cultured Despisers*, trans. John Oman
(London: K. Paul, Trench, Trubner & Co., Ltd., 1893), 92–101.[4]

I have tried, as best I could, therefore, to show you what religion really is. Have you found anything there unworthy of you or of the highest human culture? Do you long all the more for that universal union with the world that is only possible through feeling, the more you are separated and isolated by definite culture and individuality? Have you not often felt this holy longing, as something unknown? I urge you to become conscious of the call of your deepest nature and follow it. Banish the false shame of a century that should not determine you but should be made and determined by you. Return to what lies so near to you—yes, even to you—the violent separation from which cannot fail to destroy the most beautiful part of your nature.

It appears to me, however, that many among you do not believe that I can here mean to end my present business. How can I have spoken thoroughly of the nature of religion, seeing I have not treated at all of immortality, and of God only a little in passing? Is it not incumbent upon me, most of all, to speak of these two things and to present to you how unhappy you would be without belief in them? For are not these two things, for most pious people, the very poles and first articles of religion?

But I do not agree with you. First of all, I do not believe I have said nothing about immortality and so little about God. Both, I believe, are in all and in everything that I have discussed as an element of religion. Had I not presupposed God and immortality I could not have said what I have said, for, only what is divine and immortal has room in which to speak of religion.

In the second place, I do not consider the conceptions and doctrines of God and of immortality, as they are usually understood, to be the principal things in religion. Only what is in feeling and in immediate consciousness can belong to religion. God and immortality, however, as they are found in such doctrines, are ideas. How many among you—possibly most of you—are firmly convinced of one or other or both of those doctrines, without

---

4. *On Religion: Speeches to Its Cultured Despisers* was initially published in 1799, but Schleiermacher revised it twice (in 1806 and 1821). Included in this excerpt are the explanatory notes he added to the 1821 revision.

being on that account pious or having religion? As ideas, they have no greater value in religion than ideas generally.

But lest you think I am afraid to give a straightforward word on this matter, because it would be dangerous to speak until some definition of God and existence that has stood its trial, has been brought to light, and has been accepted in the German Empire as good and valid—or lest you should, on the other hand, perhaps, believe that I am playing a pious fraud and wish on you in order to be all things to all people, with seeming indifference to make light of what must be of far greater importance to me than I will confess—lest you should think these things, I will gladly be questioned and attempt to make clear to you that, on the basis of my deepest conviction, it really is as I have just maintained.

Remember in the first place that any feeling is not an emotion of piety because in it a single object as such affects as, but only insofar as in it and along with it, it affects us as revelation of God. It is, therefore, not an individual or finite thing, but God, in whom alone the particular thing is one and all, that enters our life. Nor do we stand over against the world and in it at the same time by any one faculty, but by our whole being. The divine in us, therefore, is immediately affected and called forth by the feeling.[5] Seeing then that I have presented nothing but just this immediate and original existence of God in us through feeling, how can anyone say that I have depicted a religion without God? Is God not the highest and the only unity? Is it not God alone before whom and in whom all particular things disappear? And if you see the world as a whole, a universe, can you do it otherwise than in God? If not, how could you distinguish the highest existence—the original and eternal Being—from a temporal and derived individual? We do not claim to have God in our feeling outside of the emotions produced in us by the world. Thus, I have not said more of God.

If you will not admit that this is what it means to have God, and to be conscious of him, I can neither teach nor direct you further. How much you may know I do not judge, for it does not at present concern me, but in respect of feeling and sentiment, you would to me be godless. Science,

5. By what is said in my "Glaubenslehre" [*The Christian Faith*] § 3–5, I trust that what is here said—and especially the statement that all pious emotions exhibit through feeling the immediate presence of God in us—may be set in a clearer light. It is hardly necessary to remind you that the existence of God generally can only be active, and as there can be no passive existence of God, the divine activity upon any object is the divine existence in respect of that object. It may, however, require to be explained why I represent the unity of our being in contrast to the multiplicity of function, as the divine in us. And you may ask why I say of this unity that it appears in the emotions of piety, seeing it can be shown from other manifestations also that self-consciousness is but a single function. In respect of the former the divine in us must be that in which the capacity to be conscious of God has its seat. Even were the criticisms just, it might still be the divine that is awakened in us in the pious emotions, and that is here the main point. For the rest, the unity of our being cannot, certainly, appear by itself, for it is absolutely inward. Most immediately it appears in the self-consciousness, in so far as single references are in the background. On the other hand, when references to single things are most prominent, the self-consciousness then most appears as a single function.

it is true, is extolled as giving an immediate knowledge about God as the source of all other knowledge. But we are not speaking of science now, but of religion. This way of knowing about God that most praise—and that I will also extol—is neither the idea of God as the undivided unity and source of all, which you place at the head of all knowledge, nor is it the feeling of God in the heart, of which we ourselves boast. It lags far behind the demands of science, and is for piety something quite subordinate. It is an idea made up of characteristics, from what are called attributes of God. These attributes correspond to the different ways the unity of the individual and the whole expresses itself in feeling. Thus I can only say of this idea what I have said of ideas generally with reference to religion: that there can be much piety without it and that it is only formed when piety is made an object of contemplation.

Yet this idea of God, as it is usually conceived, is different from the other ideas I discussed before. Although it seeks to be the highest and to stand above all, God, being thought of as like us—as a thinking and a willing Person—is drawn down into the domain of opposition. It therefore appears natural that the more like humans God is conceived, the more easily another mode of presentation is set over against it. Thus, we have an idea of the highest being, not as personally thinking and willing but as exalted above all personality, as the universal, productive, connecting necessity of all thought and existence.

Nothing seems less appropriate to me than for the supporters of the former view to charge with godlessness those who, in dread of this anthropomorphism, take refuge in the other, or for the supporters of the latter view to make the humanness of the idea of God a ground for charging the supporters of the former with idolatry, or for declaring their piety void.

It matters not what conceptions a person adheres to, he can still be pious. His piety, the divine in his feeling, may be better than his concepts, and his desire to put the essence of his piety into concepts only makes him misunderstand himself. Consider how narrow the presentation of God is the one conception, and how dead and rigid in the other. Neither corresponds to its object, and thus cannot be a proof of piety, except insofar as it rests on something in the mind, of which it falls far short. Rightly understood, both present, at least, one element of feeling, but, without feeling, neither is of any value. Many believe in and accept a God presented in conception, and yet are nothing less than pious,[6] and in no case is this

---

6. This exposition also, it is hoped, will be made clearer and at the same time be completed by what is said in the "Glaubenslehre," especially in § 8, note 2. As everyone can compare them, it is not necessary for me to enter on a defense of myself against the supposition—I would not willingly call it accusation—which those whom I greatly honor, and some of whom have already gone hence, have drawn from this Speech. For myself I am supposed to prefer the impersonal form of thinking of the highest being, and this has been called now my atheism and again my Spinozism. I, however, thought that it is truly Christian to seek for piety everywhere, and to acknowledge it under every form. I find,

conception the germ from which their piety could ever spring, for it has no life in itself. Neither conception is any sign of a perfect or of an imperfect religion, but perfection and imperfection depend upon the degree of cultivation of the religious sense. As I know of nothing more that could bring us to an understanding on this subject of concept, let us now go on to consider the development of the religious sense.

As long as a person's whole relation to the world has not arrived at clearness, this feeling is but a vague instinct; the world can only appear to him as a confused unity. Nothing of its complexity is definitely distinguishable. It is chaos to him, uniform in its confusion, without division, order, or law. Apart from what most immediately concerns his survival, he distinguishes nothing as individual except by arbitrarily cutting it off in time and space. Here you will find but few traces of any conceptions, and you will scarcely discern to which side they incline. You will not set much value on the difference, whether a blind fate—only to be indicated by magic rites—exhibits the character of the whole, or a being, alive indeed, but without definite characteristics—an idol, a fetish, one, or, if many, only distinguishable by the arbitrarily appointed limits of their sphere.

As we advance, the feeling becomes more conscious. Circumstances display themselves in their complexity and definiteness. The multiplicity of the heterogeneous elements and powers, by whose constant and

---

at least, that Christ enjoined this upon his disciples, and that Paul obeyed not only among the Jews and the Proselytes, but among the Heathen at Athens. When I had said in all simplicity that it is still not indifferent whether one does not acquire or quite rejects a definite form of representing the highest being, and thereby obstructs generally the growth of his piety, I did not think it necessary to protest further against all consequences. I did not remember how often a person going straightforward seems to be going to the left to a person going to the right. But none who reflect on the little that is said about pantheism will suspect me of any materialistic pantheism. And if any one look at it rightly, he will find that, on the one side, everyone must recognize it as an almost absolute necessity for the highest stage of piety to acquire the conception of a personal God, and on the other he will recognize the essential imperfection in the conception of a personality of the highest being, nay, how hazardous it is, if it is not most carefully kept pure. The conception is necessary whenever one would interpret to himself or to others immediate religious emotions, or whenever the heart has immediate intercourse with the highest being. Yet the profoundest of the church fathers have ever sought to purify the idea. Were the definite expressions they have used to clear away what is human and limited in the form of personality put together, it would be as easy to say that they denied personality to God as that they ascribed it to him. As it is so difficult to think of a personality as truly infinite and incapable of suffering, a great distinction should be drawn between a personal God and a living God. The latter idea alone distinguishes from materialistic pantheism and atheistic blind necessity. Within that limit any further wavering in respect of personality must be left to the representative imagination and the dialectic conscience, and where the pious sense exists, they will guard each other. Does the former fashion a too human personality, the latter restrains by exhibiting the doubtful consequences; does the latter limit the representation too much by negative formulas, the former knows how to suit it to its need. I was especially concerned to show that, if one form of the conception does not in itself exclude all piety, the other as little necessarily includes it. How many people are there in whose lives piety has little weight and influence, for whom this conception of personality is indispensable as a general supplement to their chain of causality which on both sides is broken off; and how many, on the other band, show the deepest piety who, in what they say of the highest being, have never rightly developed the idea of personality!

determined strife, phenomena are determined, becomes more prominent in man's consciousness of the world. To the same degree, the result of contemplating this feeling changes. The opposite forms of the idea stand more distinctly apart. Blind fate changes into a higher necessity, in which, though unattainable and unsearchable, reason and connection rest. Similarly, the idea of a personal God becomes higher, but at the same time divides and multiplies; each power and element becomes animate, and gods arise in endless number. They are now distinguishable by means of the different objects of their activity, and different inclinations and dispositions. You must acknowledge that a stronger, more beautiful life of the universe in feeling is here exhibited. It is most beautiful when this new won complexity and this innate highest unity are most intimately bound together in feeling, as for example, among the Greeks, whom you so justly revere. Both forms then unite in reflection, one being of more value for thought, the other for art—one showing more of the complexity, the other of the unity. But this stage, even without such a union is more perfect than the former, especially if the idea of the highest being is placed rather in the eternal unattainable necessity, than in single gods.

Let us now mount higher where opposing elements are again united—where existence, by exhibiting itself as totality, as unity in variety, as system, first deserves its name. Is not the person who perceives existence both as one and as all—who stands over against the whole, and yet is one with it in feeling—to be accounted happier in his religion, let his feeling mirror itself in idea as it may? There as elsewhere then, the way in which the Deity is present to humans in feeling is decisive of the worth of their religion, not the manner, always inadequate, in which it is copied in idea. Suppose there is someone who arrived at this stage but rejected the idea of a personal God. I will not decide on the justice of the names you are accustomed to apply to him, whether pantheist or Spinozist. This rejection of the idea of a personal Deity does not decide against the presence of the Deity in his feeling. The ground of such a rejection might be a humble consciousness of the limits of personal existence, and particularly of personality joined to consciousness. He might stand as high above a worshipper of the twelve gods whom you would rightly name after Lucretius, as a pious person at that stage would be above an idolater.

But we have here the old confusion, the unmistakable sign of defective culture. Those who are at the same stage, only not at the same point, are most strongly repudiated. The proper standard of religiousness, which announces the stage to which a person has attained, is his sense for the Deity. But to which idea he will attach himself depends purely on what he requires it for, and whether his imagination chiefly inclines towards existence and nature or consciousness and thought.

You will not, I trust, consider it blasphemy or incongruity that such a matter should depend on how we direct our imagination. By imagination

I do not mean anything subordinate or confused, but the highest and most original faculty in man. All else in the human mind is simply reflection upon it, and is therefore dependent on it. Imagination in this sense is the free generation of thoughts, whereby you come to a conception of the world; such a conception you cannot receive from without, nor compound from inferences. From this conception you are then impressed with the feeling of omnipotence. The subsequent translation into thought depends on whether one is willing, being conscious of his own weakness, to be lost in the mysterious obscurity, or whether, first of all, seeking definiteness of thought, he cannot think of anything except under the one form given to us, that of consciousness or self-consciousness. Recoil from the obscurity of indefinite thought is one tendency of the imagination; recoil from the appearance of contradiction in transferring the forms of the finite to the Infinite is the other.

Now can we not combine the same inwardness of religion with both? Would not a closer consideration show that the two ways of conceiving are not very wide apart? But the pantheistic idea is not to be thought of as death, and no effort is to be spared to surpass in thought the limits of the personal idea.

So much I have thought it necessary to say, not so much in explanation of my own position, as to prevent you from thinking that all who will not accept the personality of the highest being as it is usually set forth are despisers of religion. And I am quite convinced that what has been said will not make the idea of the personality of God more uncertain for anyone who truly has it; nor will anyone more easily rid himself of the almost absolute necessity to acquire it by knowing from where this necessity comes. Among truly religious men there have never been zealots, enthusiasts, or fanatics for this idea. Even when timidity and hesitation about it is called atheism, truly pious persons will leave it alone with great tranquility. Not to have the Deity immediately present in one's feeling has always seemed to them more irreligious. They would most unwillingly believe that anyone could in point of fact be quite without religion. They believe that only those who are quite without feeling, and whose nature has become brutish, can have no consciousness of the God that is in us and in the world, and of the divine life and operation whereby all things consist. But whoever insists—it matters not how many excellent people he excludes—that the highest piety consists in confessing that the highest being thinks as a person and wills outside the world, cannot be too familiar with the domain of piety. No, the profoundest words of the most zealous defenders of his own faith must still be strange to him.

The number who would have something from this God, that is alien to piety, is only too great. He is to give an outward guarantee of their blessedness and to spur them on to morality. They want to have it before their eyes. They would not have God working on humans by freedom, but in the only way in which one free being can work on another: by necessity, by making himself known either by pain or by pleasure. But this cannot spur us on to morality. Every external stimulus is alien to morality, whether it be hope or fear. To follow it where it concerns morality is un-free, and thus immoral. But the highest being, particularly when he is thought of as free, cannot wish to make freedom itself not free, and morality not moral.[7]

This now brings me to the second point, to immortality. I cannot conceal that in the usual way of dealing with this matter there is still more that seems to me inconsistent with the nature of piety. I believe I have just shown you in what way each one bears in himself an unchangeable and eternal nature. If our feeling nowhere attaches itself to the individual, but if its content is our relation to God wherein all that is individual and fleeting disappears, there can be nothing fleeting in it, but all must be eternal. In religious life, then, we may well say we have already offered up and disposed of all that is mortal, and that we actually are enjoying immortality. But the immortality that most people imagine and their longing for it, seem to me irreligious—indeed, quite opposed to the spirit of piety. Their wish to be immortal is grounded in a dislike of the very aim of religion. Recall how religion earnestly strives to expand the sharply defined outlines of personality. They are gradually lost in the infinite so that we, becoming conscious of the universe, might as much as possible be one with it. But people struggle against this aim. They are anxious about their personality, and do not wish to overstep its accustomed limits or to be anything other than a manifestation of it. And they are very far from wishing to embrace the one opportunity death gives them of transcending it. On the contrary, they are concerned with how they are to carry it with them beyond this life, and their utmost endeavor is for longer sight and better limbs. But God speaks to them as it stands written: "Whoever loses his life for my sake, will keep it, and whoever keeps it, will lose it" [Mark 8:35]. The life they would keep is one that cannot be kept. If they are concerned with the eternity of their individual identity, why are they not as anxious about what it has been as about what it is to be? Why be concerned about what is

---

7. This passage is different from the former edition. Partly the statement that morality generally cannot be manipulated, though right in the connection, seemed to require closer definition if there was not to be misunderstanding; partly the whole view seemed to me only rightly completed by the addition that freedom and morality would be endangered by the prospect of divine recompense. In the strife on this point, especially as it is carried on between the Kantians and the Eudaemonists, the great difference between presenting divine recompense as an inducement and using it theoretically to explain the order of the world has very often been overlooked. The former is an immoral and therefore specially an unchristian procedure, and is never employed by true heralds of Christianity and has no place in the Scriptures; the other is natural and necessary, for it alone shows how the divine law extends over the whole nature of humanity, and so far from causing a rift in human nature, it most fully guards its unity. But this explanation will be very different in proportion as love of truth and desire of knowledge are free from all foreign ingredients. It is hardly to be denied that the demands of self-love will most claim arbitrariness for the divine recompense, and as arbitrariness can only have its seat in personality, it will be accompanied by the narrowest conceptions of the divine personality.

ahead of them when they cannot go backwards? They desire an immortality that is no immortality. They are not even capable of comprehending it, for who can bear the effort of conceiving an endless temporal existence? Thus, they lose the immortality always available them and, in addition, their mortal life is distressed and tortured by useless thoughts. Would they but attempt to surrender their lives to God in love! Would they but strive to annihilate their personality and to live in the One and in the All! Whoever has learned to be more than himself knows that he loses little when he loses himself. Only the person who, in denying himself, sinks himself into as much of the entire universe as he can attain, and in whose soul a greater and holier longing has arisen, has a right to the hopes that death gives. With him alone is it really possible to hold further conversation about the endlessness to which, through death, we infallibly soar.[8]

This, then, is my understanding of these matters. The usual conception of God as a single being outside of the world and behind the world is neither the beginning nor the end of religion. It is only one manner of expressing God, seldom entirely pure and always inadequate. Such an idea may emerge from mixed motives, from the need for such a being to console and help, and such a God may be believed in without piety, at least in my sense, and I think in the true and right sense. If, however, this idea is formed, not arbitrarily, but somehow by the necessity of a person's way of thinking—if he needs it for the security of his piety—then the imperfections of his idea will neither burden him nor pollute his piety. Yet the true nature of religion is neither this idea nor any other, but an immediate

---

8. This passage has met very much the same fate as the passage which treated of the personality of God. It was also directed against narrow and impure conceptions and it has raised the same misunderstandings. I am supposed to disparage the hope of immortality in the usual sense of the word, representing it as a weakness and contending against it. But this was not the place to declare myself in respect of the truth of the matter, or to offer the view of it which I, as a Christian, hold. This will be found in the second part of my "Glaubenslehre," and both passages should supplement each other. There I had only to answer the question whether this hope was so essential to a pious direction of the mind that the two stood or fell together. What could I do but answer in the negative, seeing it is now usually accepted that the people of the old Covenant did not, in earlier times, have this hope, and seeing also that it is easy to show that, in the state of pious emotion, the soul is rather absorbed in the present moment than directed towards the future? Only it appears hard that this Speech should deduce not doubtfully the hope so widely diffused among the noblest people of a restoration of the individual life not again to be interrupted, from the lowest stage of self-love, seeing it might as well have been ascribed to the interest of love in the beloved objects. All the forms under which the hope of immortality can present itself as the highest self-consciousness of the spirit being before me, just in contrast to the opponents of the faith it seemed to me natural and necessary to utter the warning that any particular way of conceiving immortality and especially that which has unmistakable traces of a lower interest hidden behind it, is not to be confused with the reality. I thus sought to prepare for grasping the question, not as it is entirely limited to personality or to a self-consciousness chained to single affinities, but as it is natural in one in whom personal interest is purified by subordination to a self-consciousness that is ennobled by the consciousness of the human race and of human nature. On the other side, in order to avoid endless and wide-spreading explanations, it was necessary to make the opponents of religion observe that there could be no religious discussion of this matter except among those who have already cultivated in themselves the higher life, given by true piety,

consciousness of the Deity as we find him in ourselves and in the world. Likewise, the goal and the character of the religious life is not the immortality desired and believed in by many, or what their craving to be too wise about it would suggest, pretended to be believed in by many. It is not the immortality that is outside of time, behind it, or after it, but still is in time. It is the immortality that we can now have in this temporal life: it is the problem in the solution with which we are forever to be engaged. To be one with the infinite in the midst of finitude, and in every moment to be eternal, is the immortality of religion.

SELECTION **6**

G. W. F. Hegel

**"The Development
of the Idea of God"**

A German philosopher, Georg Wilhelm Friedrich Hegel (1770–1831) was a major figure in the period of "German idealism" following Kant. Reformulating Anselm's proof for God's existence, Hegel argued that the task of speculative philosophy is not only to demonstrate the unity between concept and reality in this proof, but also to account for the difference between them by showing that the concept or logical idea of God simply *is* the movement by which it determines itself to be. Hegel's science of logic demonstrates this dialectical movement. As

---

which is worthy to conquer death. If I am somewhat severe on the self-deception of a mean way of thinking and feeling, which is proud that it can comprehend immortality and that it is guided by the accompanying hope and fear, I can only say in self-defense that there is nothing of mere rhetoric in it, but that it has always been with me a very strong feeling. I desire no more than that each person, if he would test his piety, should see, not merely, as Plato says, that souls appear before the judges of the Underworld stripped of all alien ornament conferred by the external relations of life, but, laying aside these claims to endless existence and considering himself just as he is, that he then decide whether these claims are anything more than the titles of lands, never possessed and never to be possessed, wherewith the great ones of the earth often think they must adorn themselves. If, thus stripped, he still find that that eternal life is with him to which the end of this Speech points, he will readily understand what I am aiming at in my presentation of the Christian faith. Furthermore, the parallel between the two ideas of God and immortality in respect of the different ways of conception here indicated, is not to be overlooked. The most anthropomorphic view of God usually presupposes a morally corrupt consciousness, and the same holds of such a conception of immortality as pictures the Elysian fields as just a more beautiful and wider earth. As there is a great difference between inability to think of God as in this way personal and the inability to think of a living God at all, so there is between one who does not hold such a sensuous conception of immortality and one who does not hope for any immortality. As we call everyone pious who believes in a living God, so without excluding any kind or manner we would hold the same of those who believe in an eternal life of the spirit.

absolute Spirit, God moves through a dialectic of self-consciousness that moves from immediacy or identity ("being in itself) to differentiation or cleavage ("being for another") and then a return to itself or reconciliation. In this movement, the infinite establishes a relationship with the finite by way of a twofold negation: it not only "negates" or differentiates itself from the finite spirit (by creating a reality different from it), but it also "negates" that negation or difference by reestablishing a relationship with it. As Spirit, God realizes God's determinate being or existence (*Dasein*)—and not merely God's abstract being as concept—by appearing in a concrete historical figure.

This concept of God is explicitly Trinitarian, and its *representational expression* is the incarnation. Within the divine life, absolute Spirit differentiates from itself—releasing the other (the Son) to exist as a free and independent being. From this release, the finite world is created and with it finite human spirits. But the very process of becoming what we are—conscious and morally responsible finite spirits—entails estrangement and separation from God, the universal and absolute. Evil arises out of this estrangement. To reconcile the estranged finite spirit with absolute Spirit, a concrete historical individual must appear, since the human spirit cannot achieve this reconciliation of its own accord. This individual must express the very history of God in a single consciousness that unites within itself divine and human nature.

Appearing in Jesus of Nazareth, the history of God is first embodied in his teachings. Directed to our *intuition*, our sensory consciousness, Jesus' teachings evoke images of the "kingdom of God"—"God's determinate being (*Dasein*)" or "spiritual actuality"—that revolutionize everything in our world, including its institutions, with its universal demands. Ultimately, God's history is embodied in Jesus' death, which is not simply the death of a martyr but the very death of God. God is "satisfied"—that is, the reconciliation between divine and human is accomplished not by human sacrifice but by God's own self. In this reconciliation, God is not merely the Father enclosed within "godself" but the Son, who becomes the other, or finite spirit. Expressed in the human Jesus, "God is at home with godself in humanity." His death is a moment in the divine nature and embodies divine love itself—"absolute love envisaged"—since in it God is not only reconciled with all of nature and history but also with God's own self, returning to godself as Spirit.

But further, the Son is raised to the right hand of God, where this history of God—the nature of God as Spirit—is "accomplished, interpreted and explicated for the community." In the community that emerges out of this event, our verification of this reconciliation takes place not through miracles but in the "immediate *witness of the Spirit to spirit*"—the "power over minds" by which the Spirit enables us to intuit its truth within our own self-consciousness. Here, the representation of Christ moves from external forms to the inner realm—to a Comforter, who comes when the immediacy of sensible history has passed away.

From *G. W. F. Hegel: Theologian of the Spirit*, ed. Peter Hodgson
(Minneapolis: Fortress Press, 1997), 212–45.

Our next step is to proceed to concrete representation, to the development and more specific determination of the idea.

We have defined the metaphysical concept as the concept that realizes itself, the one that is itself real; the whole of finitude subsists within it. God is the absolute idea, the fact that reality matches the concept. What we have called reality in the metaphysical concept is now reality as such, being, etc. But, more precisely, it is not *natural* being. In nature religion, "being" was naturalness in general—the sky, the sun, etc. The reality we are now speaking of constitutes the determinateness of God. It is not something natural. Similarly, God's determinateness is not constituted by a predicate or a plurality of predicates. "Predicates" (characteristics such as wisdom, justice, goodness) are not, to be sure, natural and immediate; but they are stabilized by reflection—(each predicate is) a content that has attained through reflection the form of universality, of relation to self. Thus each determinate content has become just as immovable, just as rigidly *for itself* as the natural content was to begin with. About the natural we say, "It is." These "predicates" are just as self-identical as (natural) immediacy. The predicates do not correspond to the reality of the concept; the reality of the concept is more precisely the first (natural) reality, namely, that the concept in itself is real, wholly free totality, free totality present to itself. The one side, spirit, the subjective side, the concept, is itself the idea, while the other side, reality, is likewise the whole or spirit, posited at the same time as distinct. Reality is thus the reality of the idea itself, in such a way that each side is the idea, the free idea, present to itself, so that spirit, this idea, knows itself, is present to itself. It is real, places itself vis-à-vis (itself) as another spirit, and is then the unity of the two. And this is what the idea is.

The next point is to explicate the idea (of God in its self-development) as follows. Universal spirit—the totality that it is—posits itself (*setzt sich*) in its three determinations, i.e., it develops itself, realizes itself; and it is complete only at the end, which is at the same time its presupposition (*Voraussetzung*). At first, it is in itself as the totality; [then] it sets itself forth (*setzt sich voraus*), and likewise it is only at the end.[9]

9. Hegel is here engaged in a wordplay based on the verb *setzen: sich setzt* ("posits itself"), *Voraussetzung* ("presupposition"), and *setzt sich voraus* ("sets itself forth [or forward]"). Spirit must not merely posit itself "in itself" *(an sich)*; it must also "set itself forth" or "appear" in the world in order to arrive at its end and thus *be* spirit in the full sense. For this reason the end is at the same time the "presupposition" *(Voraus-setzung)* of spirit. This wordplay is repeated several times below.

We thus have to consider spirit in the three forms, *the three elements*, into which it posits itself. These three forms are: (1) Eternal being, within and present to itself—the form of *universality*. (2) The form of *appearance*, that of *particularization*, of being for others. (3) The form of return from appearance into itself, the form of *absolute singularity*, of absolute presence-to-self.

It is in these three forms that the divine idea explicates itself. Spirit is the divine history, the process of self-differentiation, of diremption and return into self; it is the *divine* history and therefore is to be viewed in each of the three forms.

These three forms are also determined as follows in regard to *subjective consciousness*. The first form (is determined) as the element of *thought*, that God is in pure thought as God is in and for godself; God is manifest but not yet issued forth into appearance—God in God's eternal essence, present to godself, yet manifest. The second form is that God is (present) in the element of *representation*, in the element of particularization, that consciousness is entrapped in its relation to the other; this is appearance. The third element is that of *subjectivity* as such. Partly this subjectivity is immediate subjectivity, disposition, thought, representation, sensation, but also it is partly a subjectivity that is the concept, i.e., it is thinking reason, the thinking of free spirit, which is inwardly free only through the return (into itself). . . .

First Element: The Idea of God in and for Itself

. . . In the first place, God is spirit; in God's abstract character God is defined as universal spirit that particularizes itself. This is the absolute truth, and the religion that has this content is the true religion. In the Christian religion this is what is called the *Trinity*—it is "triune" insofar as number categories are applied. It is the God who differentiates godself but remains identical with godself in the process. The Trinity is called the *mystery* of God; its content is mystical, i.e., speculative. But what is for reason is not a secret. In the Christian religion one *knows*, and this is a secret only for the finite understanding, and for the thought that is based on sense experience. There the distinctions are immediate, and natural things are accepted as valid; this is the mode of externality. But as soon as God is defined as spirit, externality is sublated, and for sense this is a mystery; for sense everything is external to everything else—objects change, and the senses are aware of them in different ways. The changing is itself a sensible process, occurring in time. The sun exists: once it did not exist, some day it will not exist—all these states are external to one another in time. The being (of a thing) is now, and its nonbeing is separated from now; for time is what keeps the determinations apart from one another, external to one another. For the understanding too (nonbeing) is other (than being); thus the understanding, like the sensible (realm), is a holding fast to abstract characteristics in such a way that each exists on its own account. The negative is distinct from the positive; so for the understanding it is something else.

Certainly, when we say "Trinity" or "triune," the unfortunate formal pattern of a number series (1, 2, 3) comes into play. Reason can employ all the *relationships* of the understanding, but only insofar as it destroys the *forms* of the understanding. And so it is with the Trinity. Hence the very word "triune" is an extreme of misuse as far as the understanding is concerned—for it believes the mere fact of the formula being used establishes its rights; but to use it as one does here to say "three equals one" is to misuse it. Consequently it is an easy matter to point out contradictions in such ideas, distinctions that go to the point of being opposites. Everything concrete, everything living contains contradiction within itself; only the dead understanding is identical with itself. But the contradiction is also resolved in the idea, and the resolution is spiritual unity. The living thing is an example of what cannot be grasped by the understanding. "God is love" is an expression very much to the point: here God is present to sensation; as "love" God is a person, and the relationship is such that the consciousness of the One is to be had only in the consciousness of the other. God is conscious of godself, as Goethe says,[10] only in the other, in absolute externalization. This is spiritual unity in the form of feeling. In the relationship of friendship, of love, of the family, this identity of one with the other is also to be found. It is contrary to the understanding that I, who exist for myself and am therefore self-consciousness, should have my consciousness rather in another; but the reconciliation (of this conflict) is the abstract content—the substantial, universal *ethical* relationship as such.

The second remark is a reflection upon the foregoing. We can find traces of the Trinity in other religions. They occur, for example, in the Trimurti or in the triad of Plato, while Aristotle says: We believe we have invoked the gods completely only when we have invoked them three times.[11] But wherever else we turn, we encounter only imperfect definitions. In Plato,[12] the "one" and the "other" and the "mixture" are wholly abstract in character, while in the Trimurti the wildest mode (of fanciful imagination) has entered into play, and the third moment is not that of spiritual return, for, as Siva, it is merely alteration, not spirit.[13]

A further point is that in the Christian religion it is not merely asserted that God is triune but also that God subsists in *three persons*. This is being-for-self taken to the extreme, the extreme being not only *one* but *person*, personality. Being a person is the highest intensity of being-for-self. Here

10. This is an allusion to Goethe's *Die Braut von Corinth*, vv. 120–23.

11. Aristotle, *De caelo* 1.1 (268a10–15).

12. Plato, *Timaeus* 34c–35b.

13. On the Trimurti, see Hegel's discussion of Hinduism in part 2 of the 1824 lectures (*Lectures on the Philosophy of Religion*, 2:326–28).

the contradiction seems to be pushed so far that no resolution, no mingling of one person with another, is possible. But just this resolution is
expressed in the assertion that God is *only* one; the three persons are thus
posited merely as a transient moment or aspect. "Personality" expresses
the fact that the antithesis is to be taken as absolute, that it is not a mild
one, and it is only when it is pushed to this extreme that it sublates itself.
Of this too we have a representation. In love and friendship it is the *person*
that maintains itself and *through* its love achieves its subjectivity, which
is its personality. But in religion, if one holds fast to personality in the
abstract sense, then one has three gods, and subjectivity is likewise lost.
Infinite form, infinite power is then all there is to the moment of divinity.
Furthermore, if one holds fast to personality as an unresolved (moment),
one has *evil*. For the personality that does not sacrifice itself in the divine
idea is evil. It is precisely in the divine unity that personality, just as much
as it is posited, is posited as resolved; only in appearance does the negativity of personality appear distinct from that whereby it is sublated.

The Trinity has also been brought under the relationship of Father, Son,
and Spirit. This is a childlike relationship, a childlike form. The understanding has no other category, no other relationship that would be comparable with this in respect of its appropriateness. But we must be aware
that this is merely a figurative relationship; spirit does not enter into this
relationship. "Love" would be more suitable, for the spirit (of love) is assuredly what is truthful.

There is a third point that we must not overlook, because it has given
rise to many so-called heresies. As we have said,[14] the abstract God, the
Father, is the universal, what is all-encompassing, what is One. We are now
on the level of spirit; the universal here includes everything within itself.
The other, the Son, is infinite particularity, the (realm of) appearance; the
third, the Spirit, is singularity as such. But we must be aware that all three
are spirit. In the third, we say, God is the Spirit; but the Spirit is also "presupposing," the third is also the first. It is essential to hold on to this; it is
explained by the nature of the (logical) concept. We encounter it in every
goal and every kind of life process. Life maintains itself; self-maintenance
means entering into differentiation, into the struggle with particularity, (the organism) finding itself distinguished from an inorganic nature,
and its going outwards. Thus life is only a result because it has produced
itself and is a product; moreover if we are asked, "What is produced?" the
answer is that what is produced is the life process itself, i.e., life is its own
presupposition. This is just what the universal consists in: that it works
through its process and that the process gives rise to nothing new; what
is brought forth is already (there) from the beginning. It is the same with

14. In the preceding materials Hegel has not depicted the Father as universal in this explicit form,
but such a reference might not have been transmitted by the sources available for the 1824 lectures.

loving and being loved in return. Insofar as love is present, its utterance and all the activities to which it gives rise, whereby it is simultaneously brought forth and supported, merely confirm it. What is brought forth is already there: the confirmation of love is a confirmation whereby nothing comes forth save what is already there. Similarly, spirit sets itself forth, it is the initiating.

The differentiation that the divine life goes through is not an external (process) but must be defined solely as internal, so that the first, the Father, is to be grasped just like the last (the Spirit). Thus the process is nothing but a play of self-maintenance, a play of self-confirmation. . . .

The Second Element: Representation, Appearance
RECONCILIATION[15]

a. The Idea of Reconciliation and Its Appearance in a Single Individual . . . The harmony, the resolution of this contradiction, must be represented as something that is in and of itself, it must be a presupposition for the subject. Since the concept cognizes divine unity, it recognizes that God is in and of godself. The one-sidedness that appears as the activity and so forth of the subject is merely a moment [that] simply subsists; it is nothing on its own account but exists only by virtue of this presupposition. The truth must therefore appear to the subject as a presupposition, and the question is how and in what guise the truth can appear at the standpoint at which we now find ourselves, i.e., the standpoint of infinite flight and abstractness. This is the infinite anguish, the pure depth of soul, and it is for this anguish that the contradiction is to be resolved. To begin with, the resolution necessarily has the form of a presupposition because the subject is, as we have seen, a one-sided extreme. More precisely, the subject is now defined as this profound being-within-itself, this flight from reality, this complete withdrawal from immediate existence, from fulfillment. But at the same time this abstraction of the ego is defined, in its reality, as an immediate being. So this subjective [element], this ego, is itself something presupposed too. It does have the aspect of a reality as well, for the idea is the unity of concept and reality, and its reality is determined according to the definition of the concept; here it is subjective reality. The

15. Ed. note: This section on "reconciliation" is preceded by a section on "differentiation" that describes how the reality of the finite world is made possible because God posits within the divine life a distinction—a "representation" or "appearance"—that also takes place in time and place and leads to a creation and fall. In determining itself, the infinite divine idea releases an other, the finite creation, to exist as a free and independent being. Within this creation, finite spirits develop their own self-consciousness, but doing so leads to estrangement—and to the possibility of evil—because in developing self-consciousness, the human spirit separates itself from the infinite Spirit. Nonetheless, the very "disease" of this separation is also its "source of health" since healing begins with its recognizing that nothing finite can satisfy. This, then, sets the stage for Hegel's discussion of the "need" for "reconciliation" that will occur in the appearance of Christ.

subjective [element] is this profundity involved in the fact that the ego and its fulfillment [the world] is an other. But what is as idea is also actual, and hence it has the determinate character of reality. Empty, naked reality is, as sensible, defined in a strictly exclusive way. Thus there is consciousness, subjectivity and objectivity, objectivity being defined as abstractly as consciousness itself. Consciousness exists in the mode of sensible being; it is simple, abstract being-within-self and does not yet reflect, for reflecting is an inner relating, thinking; reflection is not abstract being-within-self— just as the thinking of Stoicism is not.

This infinite suffering that is wholly unfulfilled is without reflection. Hence for consciousness its sensible content is one that ought not to be, and it still lacks any extended world within itself; so in its infinite depth it relates to itself as sensible consciousness. Therefore, since the truth now has to be *for it*, there is on the one hand the *presupposition* of the unity of divine and human nature, and on the other hand, because it is *sensible* self-consciousness, this unity *appears*. God appears as the concrete God. For this reason the idea appears in sensible immediacy, in sensible presence too, for the form of being for others is the immediate and sensible form.

Consequently God appears in sensible presence; God has no other figure or shape [*Gestalt*] than that of the sensible mode of the spirit that is spirit in itself—the shape of the *singular human being*. This is the one and only sensible shape of spirit—it is *the appearance of God in the flesh*. This is the monstrous reality whose necessity we have seen. What it posits is that divine and human nature are not intrinsically different—God [is] in human shape. The truth is that there is only one reason, only one spirit; we have seen that spirit as finite does not have genuine existence.

The essential aspect of the shape of appearance is thus explicated. Because it is the appearance of God, it occurs essentially for the community; it must not and cannot be taken in isolation. Appearing is being for an other; this other is the *community*.

The verification of this appearance has two aspects. The first concerns the *content* of the appearance, which is the unity of the finite and the infinite, the fact that God is not an abstraction but what is utterly concrete. Inasmuch as God is *for consciousness*, the verification of this is from our present standpoint a purely inner verification, a witness of the Spirit. Philosophy has to make explicit that the witness is not merely this mute *inner* one; it has to bring it to light in the element of thinking. This is the one side, the imago-aspect of human nature; human beings are the image of God [Gen. 1:26–27].

The second aspect [of the verification] is the one that we have observed earlier, that God, considered in terms of God's eternal idea, *has* to generate the Son, has to distinguish godself from godself, in such a way that what is distinguished is wholly God godself; and their union is love and the Spirit. The suffering of the soul, this infinite anguish, is the witness of the Spirit, inasmuch as spirit is the negativity of finite and infinite, of subjectivity and objectivity being conjoined but still as conflicting elements; if there were no longer any conflict, there would be no anguish. Spirit is the absolute power to endure this anguish, i.e., to unite the two and to be in this way, in this oneness. Thus the anguish itself verifies the appearance of God.

As for the other mode of verification,[16] namely, that God appeared in *this* human being, at *this* time and in *this* place—this is quite a different matter, and can be recognized only from the point of view of world history. It is written: "When the time had come, God sent forth God's Son" (Gal. 4:4); and *that* the time had come can only be discerned from history.

b. *The Historical, Sensible Presence of Christ* The question is now more precisely this: "What content must present itself in this appearance?" The content can be nothing else than the history of spirit, the history of God (which is God godself), the divine history as that of a single self-consciousness which has united divine and human nature within itself—the divine nature in this [human] element.

The first [aspect] of this history is the *single, immediate human being* in all his contingency, in the whole range of temporal relationships and conditions. To this extent this is a divestment of the divine. What is to be seen here is that this aspect is for the community. There is in it the unity of the finite and the infinite, but there is at the same time in this sensible mode a divestment of the idea, and this has to be sublated.

The second point relates to the teaching. What must the *teaching* of this individual be? It cannot be what later became the doctrine of the church or community. The teaching of Christ is not Christian dogmatics, not the doctrine of the church; Christ did not expound what the church later produced as its doctrine. For his teaching evokes sensations through representation, and it has a content. It is this content, which at the highest level is an explication of the nature of God, that has to be initially directed specifically at the sentient consciousness, coming to it as an *intuition*. Hence it is not present as a doctrine, which begins with assertions.

The main content of this teaching can only be universal and abstract, it can only contain abstract and universal [images]. If something new, a new world, a new religion, a new concept of God is to be given to the world of representational awareness, then two aspects are involved. First there [is] the universal soil, and second there is what is particular, determinate, and concrete. The world of representational awareness, insofar as it thinks, can achieve only abstract thinking, it thinks only the universal. It is reserved

16. Hegel here actually introduces a *third* consideration, distinct from the second. These three paragraphs taken together summarize what might be described as a threefold argument for the *possibility, necessity,* and *actuality* of the appearance of God in a single human individual. The final point serves as a transition to the next section, since it requires attending to concrete historical matters.

solely for conceptualizing spirit to cognize the particular from the universal, to let the particular emerge from the concept by its own power. For the world of representational awareness, determinate [reality] and the soil of universal thought are mutually exclusive. So what can initially be produced here by teaching is the universal soil for the concept of God. This can be expressed briefly as the *kingdom of God*.[17] This has been taught: it is the real divinity, God in God's *determinate being [Dasein]* in God's *spiritual actuality*, the kingdom of heaven. This divine reality contains already within itself God and God's kingdom, the community—a concrete content. This is the main content.

This teaching, insofar as it cannot initially advance beyond the universal, has in this universal (as an abstract universal) the character of negation vis-à-vis everything in the present world. Insofar as it affirms the universal in this way, it is a *revolutionary* doctrine that partly leaves all standing institutions aside and partly destroys and overthrows them. All earthly, worldly things fall away as valueless, and they are expressly declared to be so. What is brought before the imagination is an elevation to an infinite energy in which the universal demands to be firmly maintained on its own account. This is how we interpret the following sayings. When Christ is among his disciples and his mother and brothers come to speak to him, he asks: "Who are my mother and my brothers? Behold my mother and my brothers! For whoever does the will of God is my brother, and sister, and mother" [Mark 3:31–35]. "To another he said, 'Follow me.' But he said, 'Lord, let me first go and bury my father.' But Jesus said to him, 'Leave the dead to bury their own dead; but as for you, go and proclaim the kingdom of God.' Another said, 'I will follow you, Lord; but let me first say farewell to those at my home.' Jesus said to him, 'No one who puts his hand to the plow and looks back is fit for the kingdom of God'" [Luke 9:59–62]. All of the relationships that refer to property disappear, but at the same time they inwardly sublate themselves—for if everything is given to the poor, there are no poor any more. Christ says: "Do not be anxious about another day, for each day is anxious for itself."[18] Such concerns, however, are proper for human beings. Family relationships, property, etc., recede in the face of something higher, namely, following Christ. This perfect independence is the abstract, primal soil of spirituality. On the one hand, morality as such has its place at a subordinate level here, and it is nothing peculiar; for the commands of Christ are for the most part already to be found in the Old Testament. On the other hand, *love* is made the principal commandment—not an impotent love of humanity in general but the mutual love

17. See Mark 1:15 and parallels.
18. Cf. Matt. 6:34: "Do not be anxious about tomorrow, for tomorrow will be anxious for itself. Let the day's own trouble be sufficient for the day."

of the community,[19] such that no one has any particular purpose (of his or her own); for this community the universal can consist in the spiritual tie that binds them together. . . .

And the particular *is* the determinate aspect that comes into play here in equally distinctive fashion. Although to be sure the soil for it is the universalism of (Christ's) teaching, and some individual traits point to that, still the main point is that this (particular) content does not impinge on our representation through teaching but through sense-intuition. This content is *nothing* other than the life,[20] passion, *and* death of Christ.

c. The Death of Christ and the Transition to Spiritual Presence For it is *this* suffering and death, this sacrificial death of the individual for all, that is the nature of God, the divine history, the being that is utterly universal and affirmative. This is, however, at the same time to posit God's negation; in death the moment of negation is envisaged. This is an essential moment in the nature of spirit, and it is this death itself that must come into view in this individual. It must not then be represented merely as the death of *this individual*, the death of this empirically existing individual. Heretics have interpreted it like that,[21] but what it means is rather that *God* has died, that *God godself is dead.*[22] God has died: this is negation, which is accordingly a moment of the divine nature, of God godself.

In this death, therefore, God is satisfied. God cannot be satisfied by something else, only by godself. The satisfaction consists in the fact that the first moment, that of immediacy, is negated; only then does God come to be at peace with godself, only then is spirituality posited. God is the true God, spirit, because God is not merely Father, and hence closed up within godself, but because God is Son, because God becomes the other and sublates this other. This negation is intuited as a moment of the divine nature in which all are reconciled. Set against God there are finite human beings; humanity, the finite, is posited in death itself as a moment of God, and death is what reconciles. Death is love itself; in it absolute love is envisaged. The identity of the divine and the human means that God is at home with godself in humanity, in the finite, and in [its] death this finitude is itself a determination of God. Through death God has reconciled the world and reconciles godself eternally with godself. This coming back again is God's return to godself, and through it God is spirit. So this third moment is that

19. Hegel seems to refer here not to the love of God but only to the love of neighbor (cf. Matt. 22:36–39).

20. Although Hegel mentions the "life" of Christ, he does not in fact discuss it further in the 1824 lectures, as he did in the 1821 manuscript, where he showed the "conformity" between the life of Christ and his teaching. In 1824 the discussion of the "life" has focused entirely on the teaching.

21. Hegel is apparently thinking especially of Gnostic teachings.

22. A phrase from the second stanza of the passion hymn "O Traurigkeit, O Herzeleid" by Johannes Rist (1641).

Christ has risen. Negation is thereby overcome, and the negation of negation is thus a moment of the divine nature.

The Son is raised up to the right hand of God. Thus in this history the nature of God, namely, spirit, is accomplished, interpreted, explicated for the community. This is the crucial point, and the meaning of the story is that it is the story of God. God is the absolute, self-contained movement that spirit is, and this movement is here represented in the individual. There are quite a number of ways in which the matter can be represented, which refer to finite, external relationships. In particular a number of false relationships have been introduced: for example, the sacrificial death offers occasion for representing God as a tyrant who demands sacrifice; this is untrue. On the contrary, the nature of God is spirit, and that being so, negation is an essential moment.

As for the *verification* of this individual, this involves essentially the witness of the Spirit, of the indwelling idea, of spirit in itself. Spirit is here brought to intuition; what is given is an immediate *witness of the Spirit to spirit*, which only conceptualizing spirit recognizes in its true necessity. Outward attestations are of a subordinate character and do not belong here.

Essentially the Son is recognized by the community as the one who has been raised to the right hand of God (i.e., that he is essentially a determination for the nature of God itself), not as he who was here in sense experience. So all sensory verification falls away, including miracles in the way in which they fall within the empirically external consciousness of faith. This is another field, another soil, but we readily imagine that the individual [Jesus] must have attested himself through the marvelous phenomenon of miracles and through absolute power over nature, since we humans ordinarily picture God as the power in nature. We have already discussed that. But it may be recalled that Christ himself renounces miracles, He says, "You wish to see signs and wonders."[23] It is not a matter of signs and wonders; Christ renounced them. In any event, this is by its very nature an external, spiritless mode of attestation. We are rightly aware that God and God's power are present in nature in and according to eternal laws; the true miracle is spirit itself. Even the animal is already a miracle vis-à-vis plant life, and still more spirit vis-à-vis life, vis-à-vis merely sentient nature. However, the genuine mode of verification is quite different— it is through power over minds. We must insist that this is the genuine (proof). But even this power over minds is not an external power like that of the church against heretics; rather it is power of a spiritual type, which leaves spirit's freedom completely intact. This power has subsequently

---

23. Cf. John 4:48: "Unless you see signs and wonders you will not believe." The renunciation of "signs and wonders" is found at various places in the Synoptic tradition.

been manifested through the great community of the Christian church. One can say that this again is only an effect and [thus] an external mode [of verification]. But to say this is to fall into self-contradiction, for what is demanded is proof of the *power*; and this consists merely in its effect; the proof of the *concept* requires no verification.

This, then, is what this history is. The first moment is the concept of this standpoint for consciousness; the second is what is given to this stand-point, what actually exists for the community; the third is the transition to the community.

This appearance of God in the flesh occurs in a specific time and in this single individual. Since it is an appearance of this kind, of itself it passes by and becomes past history. This sensible mode must disappear and rise again in the sphere of representation. The formation of the community has just this content—that the sensible form passes over into a spiritual element. The manner of this purification of immediate being preserves the sensible element precisely by letting it pass away; this is negation in the way that it is posited and appears in the sensible individual as such. Only in regard to that single individual is this intuition given; it is not capable of being inherited or renewed. This cannot happen because as "this" event, a sensible appearance is by its very nature momentary, and its destiny is to be spiritualized. It is therefore essentially something that *has been* and it will be raised up into the sphere of representation in general.

For the spirit that has need of it, sensible presence can be brought forth again in various ways, in pictures, relics, holy images. There is no lack of such mediations when they are needed. But for the spiritual community, immediate presence [the now] has passed away. At first, then, sensible rep-resentation reintegrates the past, which is a one-sided moment for repre-sentation; the present includes the past and the future as moments within itself. Hence sensible representation includes the coming again of Christ, which is essentially an absolute return, but then takes [the shape of] a turning from externality to the inner realm—a Comforter, who can come only when sensible history in its immediacy has passed by.[24]

This then is the point relating to the formation of the community, in other words the third point—namely, the Spirit.[25]

---

24. Cf. John 16:7.

25. Ed. note: This section is followed by a section on the "third element" in the development of the idea of God: the "community," which occurs after the historical Christ has passed away and the reconciliation he enacted in the past is realized in the present through the love objectively realized by the "outpouring of the Spirit" within the community.

SELECTION 7

Søren Kierkegaard

"The Sin of Despairing of the Forgiveness of Sins (Offense)"

A Danish Lutheran, Søren Kierke-
gaard (1813–1855) was highly critical of Hegelianism and "Christendom."
Neither, in his view, addressed the rigorous but practical task of becoming
a self "before God."

Written under a pseudonym, *The Sickness unto Death* analyzes despair,
the "sickness unto death" (John 11:4) that paradoxically can only be cured
by "dying to the world." First emerging as ignorance—not being conscious
of having a self who makes choices of eternal import—its next two stages
manifest an increasing consciousness of having an "eternal self": (1) despair
as weakness ("not willing to be oneself") and (2) despair in defiance ("willing to be oneself"). Despair becomes *sin* as it is intensified infinitely "before
God": one has "more self" the more God is one's criterion and goal. Its only
cure is *faith*: "The self in being itself and in willing to be itself rests transparently in God."

Directly before Christ, the self is further intensified by the "inordinate
concession from God": God became human, suffered, and died for the sake
of this individual, offering forgiveness of sin. In Christ, God is the goal and
criterion; thus, the greater one's concept of Christ, the more self one has. But
the more self, the more sin—although here the forms of despair intensify in
opposite directions: despair as "weakness" becomes "defiance" (not willing
to be what one is: a sinner) and despair as "defiance" becomes "weakness"
(willing to be oneself—a sinner—in such a way that there is no forgiveness).

The antithesis of sin and faith "before God" is what gives Christianity its
criterion, a criterion that rests on a claim—that God forgives sin and that
sin can be forgiven—which is not only absurd and paradoxical but also has
the possibility of "offense." We cannot comprehend something so great and
extraordinary. As "envy" is self-assertion in the face of those we admire, so
"offense" is self-assertion in the face of what we ought to adore. Since forgiveness is impossible to understand, Christianity can never be "defended."
Yet the command remains: "Thou shall believe in the forgiveness of sins."

The possibility of offense cannot be removed: it protects the infinite
qualitative abyss between God and humans, a gulf that is only intensified
when God forgives sins, holding the opposites—individual sinners and
God—in such a way that their contrasts appear more sharply by juxtaposition. The only way in all eternity that human beings can never be like

God is in forgiving sins. And there is only one predication about a human being that can never be stated of God, either *via negationis* (by denial) or *via eminentiae* (by idealization)): that God is a sinner. To say that God is not a sinner (in the same way one says God is not finite, and consequently, *via negationis*, that God is infinite) is blasphemy. Without the possibility of this offense, teaching about the God-man becomes "brazen." A suffering and forgiving God appears weak, and forgiveness only promises "peace of mind," not awareness of sin. Sin and humanity become mere abstract concepts. "Earnestness" about sin—that you and I are sinners—is lost. Before God, however, there are only individual sinners, whose consciences from eternity are accountable for what they commit and omit. Nonetheless, God encompasses the whole—even caring for sparrows. God is everywhere present at every moment, in every person at every point. But God's "concept" is unlike human concepts, which cannot be merged with single individuals (cf. Hegel). God's concept embraces everything, yet in another sense God has no concept: God comprehends actuality itself, in all its particulars.

From *The Sickness Unto Death: A Christian Psychological Exposition for Upbuilding and Awakening*, trans. and ed. Howard V. Hong and Edna H. Hong (Princeton, NJ: Princeton University Press, 1980), 113–24.

At this point the intensification of the consciousness of the self is the knowledge of Christ, a self directly before Christ. First came [in part 1] ignorance of having an eternal self, then knowledge of having a self in which there is something eternal. Then [in the transition to part 2] it was pointed out that this distinction is included under the self that has a human conception of itself or that has man as the criterion. The counterpart to this was a self directly before God, and this constituted the basis for the definition of sin.

Now a self comes directly before Christ, a self that in despair still does not will to be itself or in despair wills to be itself. Despair of the forgiveness of sins must be traceable to the one or to the other formula for despair, despair in weakness or the despair of defiance: despair in weakness, which is offended and does not dare to believe; the despair of defiance, which is offended and will not believe. But here weakness and defiance are the opposite of what they usually are (since here the point is not just about being oneself but about being oneself in the category of being a sinner, thus in the category of one's imperfection). Ordinarily weakness is: in despair not to will to be oneself. Here this is defiance, for here it is indeed the defiance of not willing to be oneself, what one is—a sinner—and for that reason wanting to dispense with the forgiveness of sins. Ordinarily defiance is: in despair to will to be oneself. Here this is weakness, in despair to will to be oneself—a sinner—in such a way that there is no forgiveness.

A self directly before Christ is a self intensified by the inordinate concession from God, intensified by the inordinate accent that falls upon it because God allowed himself to be born, become man, suffer, and die also for the sake of this self. As stated previously, the greater the conception of God, the more self; so it holds true here: the greater the conception of Christ, the more self. Qualitatively a self is what its criterion is. That Christ is the criterion is the expression, attested by God, for the staggering reality that a self has, for only in Christ is it true that God is man's goal and criterion, or the criterion and goal. —But the more self there is, the more intense is sin.

The intensification of sin can also be shown from another side. Sin was despair, the intensification was despair over sin. But now God offers reconciliation in the forgiveness of sin. Nevertheless, the sinner still despairs, and despair acquires a still deeper manifestation: it now relates to God in a way, and yet precisely because it is even further away it is even more intensively absorbed in sin. When the sinner despairs of the forgiveness of sins, it is almost as if he walked right up to God and said, "No, there is no forgiveness of sins, it is impossible," and it looks like close combat. Yet to be able to say this and for it to be heard, a person must become *qualitatively* distanced from God, and in order to fight *cominus* (in close combat) he must be *eminus* (at a distance)—so wondrously is the life of the spirit acoustically constructed, so wondrously are the ratios of distance established. In order that the "No," which in a way wants to grapple with God, can be heard, a person must get as far away from God as possible. The most offensive forwardness toward God is at the greatest distance; in order to be forward toward God, a person must go far away; if he comes closer, he cannot be forward, and if he is forward, this *eo ipso* means that he is far away. What human powerlessness directly before God! If a person is forward toward a man of rank and importance, he may very well be punished by being thrust far away from him, but in order to be able to be forward toward God, one has to go far away from him.

In life, this sin (to despair of the forgiveness of sins) is conceived erroneously more often than not, especially since the time when the ethical was abolished, so that an authentic ethical word is seldom or never heard. Despairing of the forgiveness of sins is esthetically-metaphysically esteemed as a sign of a deep nature, which is about the same as accepting naughtiness in a child as a sign of a deep nature. On the whole, it is unbelievable what confusion has entered the sphere of religion since the time when "thou shalt" was abolished as the sole regulative aspect of man's relationship to God. This "thou shalt" must be present in any determination of the religious; in its place, the God-idea or the concept of God has been fancifully used as an ingredient in human importance, in becoming self-important directly before God. Just as one becomes self-important in politics by belonging to the opposition and eventually comes to prefer to have an administration just to have something to oppose, so also there is eventually a reluctance to do away with God just to become even more self-important by being the opposition. Everything that in the old days was regarded with horror as the expression of ungodly insubordination is now regarded as genius, the sign of a deep nature. "Thou shalt believe" is the old-fashioned phrase, short and good, as sober as possible—nowadays it is a sign of genius and a deep nature not to be able to do so. "Thou shalt believe in the forgiveness of sins" were the words, and the only commentary on that was "You will harm yourself if you cannot do it, for one can do what one is supposed to do"[26]—nowadays it is a sign of genius and of a deep nature not to be able to believe that. What an excellent outcome Christendom has brought about! If not one word about Christianity were heard, men would not be so conceited, something paganism has never been; but since the Christian conceptions float unchristianly in the air, they have been used for the most aggravated rudeness—if not misused in some other but equally shameless manner. Is it not epigrammatic enough that cursing was not customary in paganism, whereas it really is right at home in Christendom, that out of a kind of horror and fear of the mysterious paganism as a rule named the name of God with tremendous solemnity, whereas in Christendom God's name is the word that most frequently appears in daily speech and is clearly the word that is given the least thought and used most carelessly, because the poor, revealed God (who instead of keeping himself hidden, as the upper class usually does, was careless and injudicious enough to become revealed) has become a personage far too familiar to the whole population, a personage for whom they then do the exceedingly great service of going to church every once in a while, for which they are also commended by the pastor, who on behalf of God thanks them for the honor of the visit, favors them with the title of pious, but is a little sarcastic about those who never show God the honor of going to church.

The sin of despairing of the forgiveness of sins is *offense*. The Jews had a perfect right to be offended by Christ because he claimed to forgive sins.[27] It takes a singularly high degree of spiritlessness (that is, as ordinarily found in Christendom), if one is not a believer (and if one is a believer, one does believe that Christ was God), not to be offended at someone's claim to forgive sins. And in the next place, it takes an equally singular spiritlessness not to be offended at the very idea that sin can be forgiven. For the human understanding, this is most impossible—but I do not therefore laud as genius the inability to believe it, for it *shall* be believed.

In paganism, of course, this sin could not be found. If the pagan could have had the true conception of sin (which he could not even have, since

26. Kant's ethics implies universal applicability as the main criterion of a maxim of action and presupposes that "ought" implies "can."

27. See Matthew 9:2–3; Mark 2:7.

he lacked the conception of God), he could not have gone any further than to despair over his sin. Indeed, more than that (and herein is all the concession that can be made to human understanding and thought), the pagan must be eulogized who actually reached the point of despairing not over the world, not over himself in general, but over his sin.[28] Humanly speaking, it takes both depth and ethical qualifications for that. Further than this, no human being as such can come, and rarely does anyone come so far. But, Christianly, everything is changed, for you shall believe in the forgiveness of sins.

And what is the situation of Christendom with regard to the forgiveness of sins? Well, the state of Christendom is actually despair of the forgiveness of sins; but this must be understood in the sense that Christendom is so far behind that its state never becomes apparent as being that. Even the consciousness of sin is not reached, and the only kinds of sins recognized are those that paganism also recognized—and life goes on happily in pagan peace of mind. By living in Christendom, however, men go beyond paganism, they go ahead and imagine that this peace of mind is—well, it cannot be otherwise in Christendom—consciousness of the forgiveness of sins, a notion that the clergy encourage the congregation to believe.

Christendom's basic trouble is really Christianity, that the teaching about the God-man (please note that, Christianly understood, this is safeguarded by the paradox and the possibility of offense) is profaned by being preached day in and day out, that the qualitative difference between God and man is pantheistically abolished (first in a highbrow way through speculation, then in a lowbrow way in the highways and byways).[29] No teaching on earth has ever really brought God and man so close together as Christianity, nor can any do so, for only God himself can do that, and any human fabrication remains just a dream, a precarious delusion. But neither has any teaching ever protected itself so painstakingly against the most dreadful of all blasphemies, that after God has taken this step it should be taken in vain, as if it all merges into one—God and man—never has any teaching been protected in the same way as Christianity, which protects itself by means of the offense. Woe to the babblers, woe to the loose thinkers, and woe, woe to all the hangers-on who have learned from them and praised them!

28. Note that here despair over sin is dialectically understood as pointing toward faith. The existence of this dialectic must never be forgotten (even though this book deals only with despair as sickness); in fact, it is implied in despair's also being the first element in faith. But when the direction is away from faith, away from the God-relationship, then despair over sin is the new sin. In the life of the spirit, everything is dialectical. Indeed, offense as annulled possibility is an element in faith, but offense directed away from faith is sin. That a person never once is capable of being offended by Christianity can be held against him. To speak that way implies that being offended is something good. But it must be said that to be offended is sin, SK.

29. The first refers to Hegel's idealism and the second to the materialism of the inverted Hegelian, Ludwig A. Feuerbach, and the assertion that in ordinary religion God is man's projection of himself.

If order is to be maintained in existence—and God does want that, for he is not a God of confusion[30]—then the first thing to keep in mind is that every human being is an individual human being and is to become conscious of being an individual human being. If men are first permitted to run together in what Aristotle calls the animal category[31]—the crowd— then this abstraction, instead of being less than nothing, even less than the most insignificant individual human being, comes to be regarded as being something—then it does not take long before this abstraction becomes God.[32] And then, *philosophice* (philosophically viewed), the doctrine of the God-man is correct. Then, just as we have learned that in governments the masses intimidate the king and the newspapers intimidate the cabinet ministers, so we have finally discovered that the *summa summarum* (sum total) of all men intimidates God. This is then called the doctrine of the God-man, or that God and man are *idem per idem* (the same). Of course, some of the philosophers who were involved in spreading the teaching about the predominance of the generation over the individual turn away in disgust when their teaching has so degenerated that the mob is the God-man. But these philosophers forget that it is still their doctrine; they ignore that it was not more true when the upper class accepted it, when the elite of the upper class accepted it, when the elite of the upper class or a select circle of philosophers was the incarnation.

This means that the doctrine of the God-man has made Christendom brazen. It almost seems as if God were too weak. It seems as if the same thing happened to him as happens to the good-natured person who makes too great concessions and then is repaid with ingratitude. It is God who devised the teaching about the God-man, and now Christendom has brazenly turned it around and foists kinship on God, so that the concession that God has made means practically what it means these days when a king grants a more independent constitution—and we certainly know what that means: "he was forced to do it."[33] It seems as if God had gotten himself into hot water; it seems as if the sensible man would be right if he said to God: It is your own fault. Why did you get so involved with man? It would never have occurred to any man, it would never have arisen in any man's heart that there should be this likeness between God and man. It was you yourself who had it announced—now you are reaping the harvest.

But Christianity has protected itself from the beginning. It begins with the teaching about sin. The category of sin is the category of individuality.

---

30. See 1 Cor. 14:33.

31. See *Politics*, 3, 2, 1281 a, 40–43 and 1281 b, 15–20. If this is the portion to which Kierkegaard refers, he makes selective use of it, for Aristotle argues both sides of the mass/individual-expert issue.

32. Presumably a reference to David F. Strauss, who in his *Leben Jesu* (Berlin, 1836), 2, para. 147, 734ff., maintains that the God-man is mankind.

33. A reference to political events in Denmark in 1848.

Sin cannot be thought speculatively at all. The individual human being lies beneath the concept; an individual human being cannot be thought, but only the concept "man."—That is why speculation promptly embarks upon the teaching about the *predominance* of the generation over the individual, for it is too much to expect that speculation should acknowledge the *impotence* of the concept in relation to actuality.—But just as one individual person cannot be thought, neither can one individual sinner; sin can be thought (then it becomes negation), but not one individual sinner. That is precisely why there is no earnestness about sin if it is only to be thought, for earnestness is simply this: that you and I are sinners. Earnestness is not sin in general; rather, the accent of earnestness rests on the sinner, who is the single individual. With respect to "the single individual," speculation, if it is consistent, must make light of being a single individual or being that which cannot be thought. If it cares to do anything along this line, it must say to the individual: Is this anything to waste your time on? Forget it! To be an individual human being is to be nothing! Think—then you are all mankind: *cogito ergo sum* (I think therefore I am). But perhaps that is a lie; perhaps instead the single individual human being and to be a single human being are the highest. Just suppose it is. To be completely consistent, then, speculation must also say: To be an individual sinner is not to be something; it lies beneath the concept; do not waste any time on it etc. And what then? Instead of being an individual sinner, is one to think sin (just as one is asked to think the concept "man" instead of being an individual human being)? And what then? By thinking sin, does a person himself become "sin"—*cogito ergo sum*? A brilliant suggestion! But there is no need to fear that one will become sin—pure sin—in this way, for sin cannot be thought. Even speculation has to admit this, inasmuch as sin does indeed fall outside the concept "sin." But let us terminate this arguing *e concessis* (on the basis of concessions)—the main issue is something else. Speculation does not take into consideration that with respect to sin the ethical is involved, always pointing in the direction opposite to that of speculation and taking the very opposite steps, for the ethical does not abstract from actuality but immerses itself in actuality and operates mainly with the help of that speculatively disregarded and scorned category: individuality. Sin is a qualification of the single individual; it is irresponsibility and new sin to pretend as if it were nothing to be an individual sinner—when one himself is this individual sinner. Here Christianity steps in, makes the sign of the cross before speculation; it is just as impossible for speculation to get around this issue as for a sailing vessel to sail directly against a contrary wind: The earnestness of sin is its actuality in the single individual, be it you or I. Speculatively, we are supposed to look away from the single individual; therefore, speculatively, we can speak only superficially about sin. The dialectic of sin is diametrically contrary to that of speculation.

Christianity begins here—with the teaching about sin, and thereby with the single individual.[34] Surely it is Christianity that has taught us about the God-man, about the likeness between God and man, but it has a great abhorrence of flippant or brazen forwardness. By means of the teaching about sin and particular sins, God and Christ, quite unlike any kings, have protected themselves once and for all against the nation, the people, the crowd, the public, etc. and also against every demand for a more independent constitution. All those abstractions simply do not exist for God; for God in Christ there live only single individuals (sinners). Yet God can very well encompass the whole; he can take care of the sparrows to boot. God is indeed a friend of order, and to that end he is present in person at every point, is everywhere present at every moment (in the textbook this is listed as one of the attributes of God, something people think about a little once in a while but certainly never try to think about continuously). His concept is not like man's, beneath which the single individual lies as that which cannot be merged in the concept; his concept embraces everything, and in another sense he has no concept. God does not avail himself of an abridgment; he comprehends (*comprehendit*) actuality itself, all its particulars; for him the single individual does not lie beneath the concept.

The teaching about sin—that you and I are sinners—a teaching that unconditionally splits up "the crowd," confirms the qualitative difference between God and man more radically than ever before, for again only God can do this; sin is indeed: *before God*. In no way is a man so different from God as in this, that he, and that means every man, is a sinner, and is that "before God," whereby the opposites are kept together in a double sense: they are held together (*continentur*), they are not allowed to go away from each other, but by being held together in this way the differences show up all the more sharply, just as when two colors are held together, *opposita juxta se posita magis illucesunt* (the opposites appear more clearly by

34. The teaching about the sin of the race has often been misused, because it has not been realized that sin, however common it is to all, does not gather men together in a common idea, into an association, into a partnership ("no more than the multitude of the dead out in the cemetery form some kind of society"); instead it splits men into single individuals and holds each individual fast as a sinner, a splitting up that in another sense is both harmonized with and teleologically oriented to the perfection of existence. This has not been observed and thus the fallen race has been regarded as reconciled by Christ once and for all. And so once again God has been saddled with an abstraction that claims, as abstraction, to have a closer kinship with him. But this is a mask that merely makes men brazen. If "the single individual" is to feel in kinship with God (and this is what Christianity teaches), then he also senses the full weight of it in fear and trembling, and he must discover—as if it were not an ancient discovery—the possibility of offense. But if the single individual is to come to this glory by means of an abstraction, then the matter becomes too easy and is essentially prostituted. Then the individual does not sense the enormous weight of God, which through humiliation weighs one down as far as it lifts one up; by participating in that abstraction, the individual fancies that he has everything as a matter of course. Being a human being is not like being an animal, for which the specimen is always less than the species. Man is distinguished from other animal species not only by the superiorities that are generally mentioned but is also qualitatively distinguished by the fact that the individual, the single individual, is more than the species. This qualification is in turn dialectical and signifies that the single individual is a sinner, but then against that it is a perfection to be the single individual, SK.

juxtaposition). Sin is the one and only predication about a human being that in no way, either *via negationis* (by denial) or *via eminentiæ* (by idealization), can be stated of God. To say of God (in the same sense as saying that he is not finite and, consequently, *via negationis*, that he is infinite) that he is not a sinner is blasphemy.

As sinner, man is separated from God by the most chasmal qualitative abyss. In turn, of course, God is separated from man by the same chasmal qualitative abyss when he forgives sins. If by some kind of reverse adjustment the divine could be shifted over to the human, there is one way in which man could never in all eternity come to be like God: in forgiving sins.

At this point lies the most extreme concentration of offense, and this has been found necessary by the very doctrine that has taught the likeness between God and man.

However, offense is the most decisive qualification of subjectivity, of the single individual, that is possible. To think offense without thinking a person offended is perhaps not as impossible as thinking flute playing when there is no flute player, but even thought has to admit that offense, even more than falling in love, is an illusive concept that does not become actual until someone, a single individual, is offended.

Thus offense is related to the single individual. And with this, Christianity begins, that is, with making every man a single individual, an individual sinner; and here everything that heaven and earth can muster regarding the possibility of offense (God alone has control of that) is concentrated—and this is Christianity. Then Christianity says to each individual: You shall believe—that is, either you shall be offended or you shall believe. Not one word more; there is nothing more to add. "Now I have spoken," declares God in heaven; "we shall discuss it again in eternity. In the meantime, you can do what you want to, but judgment is at hand."

A judgment! Of course, we men have learned, and experience teaches us, that when there is a mutiny on a ship or in an army there are so many who are guilty that punishment has to be abandoned, and when it is the public, the esteemed, cultured public, or a people, then there is not only no crime, then, according to the newspapers (upon which we can depend as upon the gospel and revelation), then it is God's will. How can this be? It follows from the fact that the concept "judgment" corresponds to the single individual; judgment is not made *en masse*. People can be put to death *en masse*, can be sprayed *en masse*, can be flattered *en masse*—in short, in many ways they can be treated as cattle, but they cannot be judged as cattle, for cattle cannot come under judgment. No matter how many are judged, if the judging is to have any earnestness and truth, then each individual is judged.[35] Now when so many are guilty, it is humanly impossible

---

35. This is why God is "the judge," because for him there is no crowd, only single individuals, SK.

to do it—that is why the whole thing is abandoned. It is obvious that there can be no judgment: there are too many to be judged; it is impossible to get hold of them or manage to get hold of them as single individuals, and therefore *judging* has to be abandoned.

And now in our enlightened age, when all anthropomorphic and anthropopathic conceptions of God are inappropriate, it is still not inappropriate to think of God as a judge comparable to an ordinary district judge or judge advocate who cannot get through such a complicated and protracted case—and the conclusion is that it will be exactly like this in eternity. Therefore, let us just stick together and make sure that the clergy preach this way. And should there happen to be an individual who dares to speak otherwise, an individual foolish enough to make his own life concerned and accountable in fear and trembling, and then in addition makes himself a nuisance to others—then let us protect ourselves by regarding him as mad or, if necessary, by putting him to death. If many of us do it, then there is no wrong. It is nonsense, an antiquated notion, that the many can do wrong. What many do is God's will. Before this wisdom—this we know from experience, for we are not inexperienced striplings; we do not talk glibly, we speak as men of experience—before this wisdom to this day all men have bowed—kings, emperors, and excellencies—by means of this wisdom all our animals have been improved up to now—and so you can wager that God, too, is going to learn to bow. It is just a matter of continuing to be many, a good majority who stick together; if we do that, then we are protected against the judgment of eternity.

Well, presumably they would be protected if they were not supposed to become single individuals except in eternity. But before God they were and are continually single individuals; the person sitting in a showcase is not as embarrassed as every human being is in his transparency before God. This is the relationship of conscience. The arrangement is such that through the conscience the report promptly follows each guilt, and the guilty one himself must write it. But it is written with invisible ink and therefore first becomes clearly legible only when it is held up to the light in eternity while eternity is auditing the consciences. Essentially, everyone arrives in eternity bringing along with him and delivering his own absolutely accurate record of every least trifle he has committed or omitted. Thus a child could hold court in eternity; there is really nothing for a third party to do, everything down to the most insignificant word spoken is in order. The situation of the guilty person traveling through life to eternity is like that of the murderer who fled the scene of his act—and his crime—on the express train: alas, just beneath the coach in which he sat ran the telegraph wires carrying his description and orders for his arrest at the first station. When he arrived at the station and left the coach, he was arrested—in a way, he had personally brought his own denunciation along with him.

Therefore, despair of the forgiveness of sins is offense. And offense is the intensification of sin. Usually people give this scarcely a thought, usually never identify offense with sin, of which they do not speak; instead, they speak of sins, among which offense does not find a place. Even less do they perceive offense as the intensification of sin. That is because the opposites are construed not as being sin/faith but as sin/virtue.

SELECTION **8**

Alfred North Whitehead | **"God and the World"**

An English philosopher, Alfred North Whitehead (1861–1947) developed process philosophy in line with Heraclitus's ancient idea that "all things flow." Presupposing that creativity lies at the heart of the universe, he argued for a "metaphysics of flux" as an alternative to philosophies based on the idea of substance. In the last chapter of his most influential book, *Process and Reality* (his Gifford Lectures, 1927–28), Whitehead seeks to depict metaphysically the story (found in religious cosmologies) of how the world's finite multiplicity passes into everlasting unity and how God's infinite unifying vision completes itself by taking in the world's multiplicity. But for Whitehead, God's nature is not static, a "barren hypothesis" removed from the flux of life. Both God and the world are "co-creators," instruments for each other's creative advance into novelty. Nonetheless, there is a difference between God and the world. If in each moment of actuality, there is a *physical pole* (driving finite "enjoyment") and a *conceptual pole* (driving infinite "appetition" or vision), then in God the conceptual pole (which is permanent) is prior, and in the world the physical pole (which is in flux) is prior. In the creative process, God receives flux from the world, and the world receives permanence from God.

God's nature, then, is inherently dipolar. God's *primordial nature* is God's "conceptual" experience of absolute potentiality, which is infinite, free, and eternal. Presupposed by the creativity at the heart of the universe, it gives eternal value to each new occasion of actuality. God's primordial nature "lures" the creative process with an "eternal urge of desire" that "moves without being moved." But this side of God is deficient in terms of "actual" experience; it is also unconscious. It needs God's *consequent nature*, which completes it as God consciously "feels" (i.e., experiences) the world "physically," participating in each new creative advance. If God's primordial nature is eternal, then God's consequent nature is "everlasting," bringing each new creative advance into the immediate unity of its feelings and experiences, which are always moving onward, never perishing.

Weaving together individual sufferings and joys, God gathers the multiplicity of actualities that lack solidarity with one another into an immediate unity—an enlargement of understanding— that does not negate their particularity. The purely self-regarding "revolts of destructive evil" are dismissed as trivial, individual facts. There is "redemption through suffering" as God's "tender care that nothing be lost" both judges and saves the world—not by force (whether productive or destructive) but in the infinite patience of God's overpowering conceptual harmony. As "poet of the world," God leads with a vision of truth, beauty, and goodness, enabling us to understand the incredible fact "that what cannot be, yet is." In this way, God's nature itself passes into the temporal world and qualifies it. As God embodies the world, so the world embodies God. This is the "love of God for the world," the "particular providence for particular occasions," the kingdom of heaven in our midst. In Whitehead's famous phrase, "God is the great companion—the fellow-sufferer who understands."

From *Process and Reality*, ed. David Ray Griffin and Donald W. Sherburne
(New York: Free Press, 1979), 342–52.

Section 1

So long as the temporal world is conceived as a self-sufficient completion of the creative act, explicable by its derivation from an ultimate principle which is at once eminently real and the unmoved mover, from this conclusion there is no escape: the best that we can say of the turmoil is, "For so he giveth his beloved—sleep." This is the message of religions of the Buddhistic type, and in some sense it is true. In this final discussion we have to ask, whether metaphysical principles impose the belief that it is the whole truth. The complexity of the world must be reflected in the answer. It is childish to enter upon thought with the simple-minded question, What is the world made of? The task of reason is to fathom the deeper depths of the many-sidedness of things. We must not expect simple answers to far-reaching questions. However far our gaze penetrates, there are always heights beyond which block our vision.

The notion of God as the "unmoved mover" is derived from Aristotle, at least so far as Western thought is concerned. The notion of God as "eminently real" is a favorite doctrine of Christian theology. The combination of the two into the doctrine of an aboriginal, eminently real, transcendent creator, at whose fiat the world came into being, and whose imposed will it obeys, is the fallacy which has infused tragedy into the histories of Christianity and of Islam.

When the Western world accepted Christianity, Caesar conquered; and the received text of Western theology was edited by his lawyers. The code of Justinian and the theology of Justinian are two volumes expressing one movement of the human spirit. The brief Galilean vision of humility flickered throughout the ages, uncertainly. In the official formulation of the religion it has assumed the trivial form of the mere attribution to the Jews that they cherished a misconception about their Messiah. But the deeper idolatry, of the fashioning of God in the image of the Egyptian, Persian, and Roman imperial rulers, was retained. The Church gave unto God the attributes which belonged exclusively to Caesar.

In the great formative period of theistic philosophy, which ended with the rise of Mahometanism, after a continuance coeval with civilization, three strains of thought emerge which, amid many variations in detail, respectively fashion God in the image of an imperial ruler, God in the image of a personification of moral energy, God in the image of an ultimate philosophical principle. Hume's *Dialogues* criticize unanswerably these modes of explaining the system of the world.

The three schools of thought can be associated respectively with the divine Caesars, the Hebrew prophets, and Aristotle. But Aristotle was antedated by Indian, and Buddhist, thought; the Hebrew prophets can be paralleled in traces of earlier thought; Islam and the divine Caesars merely represent the most natural, obvious, idolatrous theistic symbolism, at all epochs and places.

The history of theistic philosophy exhibits various stages of combination of these three diverse ways of entertaining the problem. There is, however, in the Galilean origin of Christianity yet another suggestion which does not fit very well with any of the three main strands of thought. It does not emphasize the ruling Caesar, or the ruthless moralist, or the unmoved mover. It dwells upon the tender elements in the world, which slowly and in quietness operate by love; and it finds purpose in the present immediacy of a kingdom not of this world. Love neither rules, nor is it unmoved; also it is a little oblivious as to morals. It does not look to the future; for it finds its own reward in the immediate present.

Section 2

Apart from any reference to existing religions as they are, or as they ought to be, we must investigate dispassionately what the metaphysical principles, here developed, require on these points, as to the nature of God. There is nothing here in the nature of proof. There is merely the confrontation of the theoretic system with a certain rendering of the facts. But the unsystematized report upon the facts is itself highly controversial, and the system is confessedly inadequate. The deductions from it in this particular sphere of thought cannot be looked upon as more than suggestions as to how the problem is transformed in the light of that system. What follows is merely an attempt to add another speaker to that masterpiece, Hume's *Dialogues Concerning Natural Religion*. Any cogency of argument entirely depends upon elucidation of somewhat exceptional elements in our conscious experience—those elements which may roughly be classed together as religious and moral intuitions.

In the first place, God is not to be treated as an exception to all metaphysical principles, invoked to save their collapse. He is their chief exemplification.

Viewed as primordial, he is the unlimited conceptual realization of the absolute wealth of potentiality. In this aspect, he is not before all creation, but with all creation. But, as primordial, so far is he from "eminent reality," that in this abstraction he is "deficiently actual"—and this in two ways. His feelings are only conceptual and so lack the fullness of actuality. Secondly, conceptual feelings, apart from complex integration with physical feelings, are devoid of consciousness in their subjective forms.

Thus, when we make a distinction of reason, and consider God in the abstraction of a primordial actuality, we must ascribe to him neither fullness of feeling, nor consciousness. He is the unconditioned actuality of conceptual feeling at the base of things; so that, by reason of this primordial actuality, there is an order in the relevance of eternal objects to the process of creation. His unity of conceptual operations is a free creative act, untrammeled by reference to any particular course of things. It is deflected neither by love, nor by hatred, for what in fact comes to pass. The particularities of the actual world presuppose it; while it merely presupposes the general metaphysical character of creative advance, of which it is the primordial exemplification. The primordial nature of God is the acquirement by creativity of a primordial character.

His conceptual actuality at once exemplifies and establishes the categoreal conditions. The conceptual feelings, which compose his primordial nature, exemplify in their subjective forms their mutual sensitivity and their subjective unity of subjective aim. These subjective forms are valuations determining the relative relevance of eternal objects for each occasion of actuality.

He is the lure for feeling, the eternal urge of desire. His particular relevance to each creative act, as it arises from its own conditioned standpoint in the world, constitutes him the initial "object of desire" establishing the initial phase of each subjective aim. A quotation from Aristotle's *Metaphysics* expresses some analogies to, and some differences from, this line of thought:

> And since that which is moved and moves is intermediate, there is something which moves without being moved, being eternal, substance, and actuality. And the object of desire and the object of thought move in this way; they move without being moved. The primary objects of desire and of thought are the same. For the apparent good is the object of appetite, and the real good is the primary object of rational wish. But desire is consequent on opinion rather than opinion on desire; for the thinking is the starting-point. And thought is moved by the object of thought, and one of the two columns of opposites is in itself the object of thought. . . .[36]

36. *Metaphysics* 1072a 23–32.

Aristotle had not made the distinction between conceptual feelings and the intellectual feelings which alone involve consciousness. But if "conceptual feeling," with its subjective form of valuation, be substituted for "thought," "thinking," and "opinion," in the above quotation, the agreement is exact.

Section 3

There is another side to the nature of God which cannot be omitted. Throughout this exposition of the philosophy of organism we have been considering the primary action of God on the world. From this point of view, he is the principle of concretion—the principle whereby there is initiated a definite outcome from a situation otherwise riddled with ambiguity. Thus, so far, the primordial side of the nature of God has alone been relevant.

But God, as well as being primordial, is also consequent. He is the beginning and the end. He is not the beginning in the sense of being in the past of all members. He is the presupposed actuality of conceptual operation, in unison of becoming with every other creative act. Thus, by reason of the relativity of all things, there is a reaction of the world on God. The completion of God's nature into a fullness of physical feeling is derived from the objectification of the world in God. He shares with every new creation its actual world; and the concrescent creature is objectified in God as a novel element in God's objectification of that actual world. This prehension into God of each creature is directed with the subjective aim, and clothed with the subjective form, wholly derivative from his all-inclusive primordial valuation. God's conceptual nature is unchanged, by reason of its final completeness. But his derivative nature is consequent upon the creative advance of the world.

Thus, analogously to all actual entities, the nature of God is dipolar. He has a primordial nature and a consequent nature. The consequent nature of God is conscious; and it is the realization of the actual world in the unity of his nature, and through the transformation of his wisdom. The primordial nature is conceptual, the consequent nature is the weaving of God's physical feelings upon his primordial concepts.

One side of God's nature is constituted by his conceptual experience. This experience is the primordial fact in the world, limited by no actuality which it presupposes. It is therefore infinite, devoid of all negative prehensions. This side of his nature is free, complete, primordial, eternal, actually deficient, and unconscious. The other side originates with physical experience derived from the temporal world, and then acquires integration with the primordial side. It is determined, incomplete, consequent, "everlasting," fully actual, and conscious. His necessary goodness expresses the determination of his consequent nature.

Conceptual experience can be infinite, but it belongs to the nature of physical experience that it is finite. An actual entity in the temporal world is to be conceived as originated by physical experience with its process of completion motivated by consequent, conceptual experience initially derived from God. God is to be conceived as originated by conceptual experience with his process of completion motivated by consequent, physical experience, initially derived from the temporal world.

Section 4

The perfection of God's subjective aim, derived from the completeness of his primordial nature, issues into the character of his consequent nature. In it there is no loss, no obstruction. The world is felt in a unison of immediacy. The property of combining creative advance with the retention of mutual immediacy is what in the previous section is meant by the term "everlasting."

The wisdom of subjective aim prehends every actuality for what it can be in such a perfected system—its sufferings, its sorrows, its failures, its triumphs, its immediacies of joy—woven by rightness of feeling into the harmony of the universal feeling, which is always immediate, always many, always one, always with novel advance, moving onward and never perishing. The revolts of destructive evil, purely self-regarding, are dismissed into their triviality of merely individual facts; and yet the good they did achieve in individual joy, in individual sorrow, in the introduction of needed contrast, is yet saved by its relation to the completed whole. The image—and it is but an image—the image under which this operative growth of God's nature is best conceived, is that of a tender care that nothing be lost.

The consequent nature of God is his judgment on the world. He saves the world as it passes into the immediacy of his own life. It is the judgment of a tenderness which loses nothing that can be saved. It is also the judgment of a wisdom which uses what in the temporal world is mere wreckage.

Another image which is also required to understand his consequent nature is that of his infinite patience. The universe includes a threefold creative act composed of (i) the one infinite conceptual realization, (ii) the multiple solidarity of free physical realizations in the temporal world, (iii) the ultimate unity of the multiplicity of actual fact with the primordial conceptual fact. If we conceive the first term and the last term in their unity over against the intermediate multiple freedom of physical realizations in the temporal world, we conceive of the patience of God, tenderly saving the turmoil of the intermediate world by the completion of his own nature. The sheer force of things lies in the intermediate physical process: this is the energy of physical production. God's role is not the combat of productive force with productive force, of destructive force with destructive force; it lies in the patient operation of the overpowering rationality of his conceptual harmonization. He does not create the world, he saves it: or, more accurately, he is the poet of the world, with tender patience leading it by his vision of truth, beauty, and goodness.

Section 5

The vicious separation of the flux from the permanence leads to the concept of an entirely static God, with eminent reality, in relation to an entirely fluent world, with deficient reality. But if the opposites, static and fluent, have once been so explained as separately to characterize diverse actualities, the interplay between the thing which is static and the things which are fluent involves contradiction at every step in its explanation. Such philosophies must include the notion of "illusion" as a fundamental principle—the notion of "mere appearance." This is the final Platonic problem.

Undoubtedly, the intuitions of Greek, Hebrew, and Christian thought have alike embodied the notions of a static God condescending to the world, and of a world either thoroughly fluent, or accidentally static, but finally fluent—"heaven and earth shall pass away." In some schools of thought, the fluency of the world is mitigated by the assumption that selected components in the world are exempt from this final fluency, and achieve a static survival. Such components are not separated by any decisive line from analogous components for which the assumption is not made. Further, the survival is construed in terms of a final pair of opposites, happiness for some, torture for others.

Such systems have the common character of starting with a fundamental intuition which we do mean to express, and of entangling themselves in verbal expressions, which carry consequences at variance with the initial intuition of permanence in fluency and of fluency in permanence.

But civilized intuition has always, although obscurely, grasped the problem as double and not as single. There is not the mere problem of fluency and permanence. There is the double problem: actuality with permanence, requiring fluency as its completion; and actuality with fluency, requiring permanence as its completion. The first half of the problem concerns the completion of God's primordial nature by the derivation of his consequent nature from the temporal world. The second half of the problem concerns the completion of each fluent actual occasion by its function of objective immortality, devoid of "perpetual perishing," that is to say, "everlasting."

This double problem cannot be separated into two distinct problems. Either side can only be explained in terms of the other. The consequent nature of God is the fluent world become "everlasting" by its objective immortality in God. Also the objective immortality of actual occasions requires the primordial permanence of God, whereby the creative advance ever re-establishes itself endowed with initial subjective aim derived from the relevance of God to the evolving world.

But objective immortality within the temporal world does not solve the problem set by the penetration of the finer religious intuition.

"Everlastingness" has been lost; and "everlastingness" is the content of that vision upon which the finer religions are built—the "many" absorbed everlastingly in the final unity. The problems of the fluency of God and of the everlastingness of passing experience are solved by the same factor in the universe. This factor is the temporal world perfected by its reception and its re-formation, as a fulfillment of the primordial appetition which is the basis of all order. In this way God is completed by the individual, fluent satisfactions of finite fact, and the temporal occasions are completed by their everlasting union with their transformed selves, purged into conformation with the eternal order which is the final absolute "wisdom." The final summary can only be expressed in terms of a group of antitheses, whose apparent self-contradictions depend on neglect of the diverse categories of existence. In each antithesis there is a shift of meaning which converts the opposition into a contrast.

It is as true to say that God is permanent and the World fluent, as that the World is permanent and God is fluent.

It is as true to say that God is one and the World many, as that the World is one and God many.

It is as true to say that, in comparison with the World, God is actual eminently, as that, in comparison with God, the World is actual eminently. It is as true to say that the World is immanent in God, as that God is immanent in the World.

It is as true to say that God transcends the World, as that the World transcends God.

It is as true to say that God creates the World, as that the World creates God.

God and the World are the contrasted opposites in terms of which Creativity achieves its supreme task of transforming disjoined multiplicity, with its diversities in opposition, into concrescent unity, with its diversities in contrast. In each actuality there are two concrescent poles of realization—"enjoyment" and "appetition," that is, the "physical" and the "conceptual." For God the conceptual is prior to the physical, for the World the physical poles are prior to the conceptual poles.

A physical pole is in its own nature exclusive, bounded by contradiction: a conceptual pole is in its own nature all-embracing, unbounded by contradiction. The former derives its share of infinity from the infinity of appetition: the latter derives its share of limitation from the exclusiveness of enjoyment. Thus, by reason of his priority of appetition, there can be but one primordial nature for God; and, by reason of their priority of enjoyment, there must be one history of many actualities in the physical world.

God and the World stand over against each other, expressing the final metaphysical truth that appetitive vision and physical enjoyment have equal claim to priority in creation. But no two actualities can be torn apart: each is all in all. Thus each temporal occasion embodies God, and is embodied in God. In God's nature, permanence is primordial and flux is derivative from the World: in the World's nature, flux is primordial and permanence is derivative from God. Also the World's nature is a primordial datum for God; and God's nature is a primordial datum for the World. Creation achieves the reconciliation of permanence and flux when it has reached its final term which is everlastingness—the Apotheosis of the World.

Opposed elements stand to each other in mutual requirement. In their unity, they inhibit or contrast. God and the World stand to each other in this opposed requirement. God is the infinite ground of all mentality, the unity of vision seeking physical multiplicity. The World is the multiplicity of finites, actualities seeking a perfected unity. Neither God, nor the World, reaches static completion. Both are in the grip of the ultimate metaphysical ground, the creative advance into novelty. Either of them, God and the World, is the instrument of novelty for the other.

In every respect God and the World move conversely to each other in respect to their process. God is primordially one, namely, he is the primordial unity of relevance of the many potential forms; in the process he acquires a consequent multiplicity, which the primordial character absorbs into its own unity. The World is primordially many, namely, the many actual occasions with their physical finitude; in the process it acquires a consequent unity, which is a novel occasion and is absorbed into the multiplicity of the primordial character. Thus God is to be conceived as one and as many in the converse sense in which the World is to be conceived as many and as one. The theme of Cosmology, which is the basis of all religions, is the story of the dynamic effort of the World passing into everlasting unity, and of the static majesty of God's vision, accomplishing its purpose of completion by absorption of the World's multiplicity of effort.

Section 6

The consequent nature of God is the fulfillment of his experience by his reception of the multiple freedom of actuality into the harmony of his own actualization. It is God as really actual, completing the deficiency of his mere conceptual actuality.

Every categoreal type of existence in the world presupposes the other types in terms of which it is explained. Thus the many eternal objects conceived in their bare isolated multiplicity lack any existent character. They require the transition to the conception of them as efficaciously existent by reason of God's conceptual realization of them.

But God's conceptual realization is nonsense if thought of under the guise of a barren, eternal hypothesis. It is God's conceptual realization performing an efficacious role in multiple unifications of the universe, which are free creations of actualities arising out of decided situations. Again this discordant multiplicity of actual things, requiring each other and neglecting each other, utilizing and discarding, perishing and yet claiming life as obstinate matter of fact, requires an enlargement of the understanding to the comprehension of another phase in the nature of things. In this later phase, the many actualities are one actuality, and the one actuality is many actualities. Each actuality has its present life and its immediate passage into novelty; but its passage is not its death. This final phase of passage in God's nature is ever enlarging itself. In it the complete adjustment of the immediacy of joy and suffering reaches the final end of creation. This end is existence in the perfect unity of adjustment as means, and in the perfect multiplicity of the attainment of individual types of self-existence. The function of being a means is not disjoined from the function of being an end. The sense of worth beyond itself is immediately enjoyed as an overpowering element in the individual self-attainment. It is in this way that the immediacy of sorrow and pain is transformed into an element of triumph. This is the notion of redemption through suffering which haunts the world. It is the generalization of its very minor exemplification as the aesthetic value of discords in art.

Thus the universe is to be conceived as attaining the active self-expression of its own variety of opposites—of its own freedom and its own necessity, of its own multiplicity and its own unity, of its own imperfection and its own perfection. All the "opposites" are elements in the nature of things, and are incorrigibly there. The concept of "God" is the way in which we understand this incredible fact—that what cannot be, yet is.

Section 7

Thus the consequent nature of God is composed of a multiplicity of elements with individual self-realization. It is just as much a multiplicity as it is a unity; it is just as much one immediate fact as it is an unresting advance beyond itself. Thus the actuality of God must also be understood as a multiplicity of actual components in process of creation. This is God in his function of the kingdom of heaven.

Each actuality in the temporal world has its reception into God's nature. The corresponding element in God's nature is not temporal actuality, but is the transmutation of that temporal actuality into a living, ever-present fact. An enduring personality in the temporal world is a route of occasions in which the successors with some peculiar completeness sum up their predecessors. The correlate fact in God's nature is an even more complete unity of life in a chain of elements for which succession does not mean loss of immediate unison. This element in God's nature inherits from the temporal counterpart according to the same principle as in the temporal world the future inherits from the past. Thus in the sense in which the present occasion is the person now, and yet with his own past, so the counterpart in God is that person in God.

But the principle of universal relativity is not to be stopped at the consequent nature of God. This nature itself passes into the temporal world according to its gradation of relevance to the various concrescent occasions. There are thus four creative phases in which the universe accomplishes its actuality. There is first the phase of conceptual origination, deficient in actuality, but infinite in its adjustment of valuation. Secondly, there is the temporal phase of physical origination, with its multiplicity of actualities. In this phase full actuality is attained; but there is deficiency in the solidarity of individuals with each other. This phase derives its determinate conditions from the first phase. Thirdly, there is the phase of perfected actuality, in which the many are one everlastingly, without the qualification of any loss either of individual identity or of completeness of unity. In everlastingness, immediacy is reconciled with objective immortality. This phase derives the conditions of its being from the two antecedent phases. In the fourth phase, the creative action completes itself. For the perfected actuality passes back into the temporal world, and qualifies this world so that each temporal actuality includes it as an immediate fact of relevant experience. For the kingdom of heaven is with us today. The action of the fourth phase is the love of God for the world. It is the particular providence for particular occasions. What is done in the world is transformed into a reality in heaven, and the reality in heaven passes back into the world. By reason of this reciprocal relation, the love in the world passes into the love in heaven, and floods back again into the world. In this sense, God is the great companion—the fellow-sufferer who understands.

We find here the final application of the doctrine of objective immortality. Throughout the perishing occasions in the life of each temporal Creature, the inward source of distaste or of refreshment, the judge arising out of the very nature of things, redeemer or goddess of mischief, is the transformation of Itself, everlasting in the Being of God. In this way, the insistent craving is justified—the insistent craving that zest for existence be refreshed by the ever-present, unfading importance of our immediate actions, which perish and yet live for evermore.

CHAPTER 5

God in Twentieth-century Theology

Karl Barth

"The Being of God as the One Who Loves in Freedom"

A Swiss Reformed theologian, Karl Barth (1886–1968) is the most important Protestant theologian of the twentieth century. Rejecting the anthropocentrism of liberal Protestant theology, Barth stressed the primacy of God in his act of revelation in Jesus Christ.

The doctrine of God is a centerpiece of Barth's *Church Dogmatics*. Arguing that God is "the one who loves in freedom," Barth contends that we must not treat God's "essence" in abstraction from his revelation. Rather, the doctrine of God must be derived from Trinitarian doctrine, which Barth equates with God's being God in the act of self-revelation as Father, Son, and Holy Spirit: as its subject, predicate, and object; and as the revealer, the act of revelation, and the revealed.

Instead of speculating about God's essence, we must encounter God where God deals with us as Lord and Savior. There we find God's being as *act, event,* and *life*. God's being is God's act of revelation where he declares his reality—not only for us but as God's own proper reality. This act is an *event*, a happening, that must be understood in its full *contemporaneity* with the reality of Jesus Christ—a reality that pertains to the past (once and for all), the present (here and now), and the future (in front of us). All of this points to God's being as *life*—the "living God"—not only as *actus purus* ("pure act," cf. Aquinas), but as *et singularis*, the unique and singular one who reveals himself to us.

This God is one who *loves*. God seeks and creates fellowship between himself and us—not only for us but as who God is in God's eternal essence. God does this both by creating us—establishing and maintaining us as creatures distinct from him—and by reconciling us as sinners to himself in the incarnation, death, and resurrection of Jesus Christ. God therefore is not solitary but wills to be in relationship with us—embracing within himself not only the antithesis between creator and creatures but also God's separation from and judgment over sinners (and thus even death, hell, and eternal damnation).

Finally, God lives and loves *freely*. This is what affirms God's divinity and lordship over all reality. Not merely an absence of limits, restrictions, and conditions, this freedom has to do with God's being grounded in God's own being—self-determined and moved by no other. What this means is that God is free—without sacrificing his distinction or freedom—to give himself in communion to us as our creator, our reconciler, and our redeemer.

From Karl Barth, *Church Dogmatics*, vol. 2, pt. 1, *The Doctrine of God*,
ed. G. W. Bromiley (New York: Scribner's, 1957), 261–75, 320–21.

God is who He is in the act of His revelation. God seeks and creates fellowship between Himself and us, and therefore He loves us. But He is this loving God without us as Father, Son and Holy Spirit, in the freedom of the Lord, who has His life from Himself.

1. The Being of God in Act

What does it mean to say that "God is"? What or who "is" God? If we want to answer this question legitimately and thoughtfully, we cannot for a moment turn our thoughts anywhere else than to God's act in His revelation. We cannot for a moment start from anywhere else than from there.

> We stand here before the fundamental error which dominated the doctrine of God of the older theology and which influenced Protestant orthodoxy at almost every point. For the greater part this doctrine of God tended elsewhere than to God's act in His revelation, and for the greater part it also started elsewhere than from there. It is of a piece with this fact that with a surprisingly common thoughtlessness it was usual to begin by deducing the doctrine of the Trinity—theoretically maintained to be the basis of all theology—from the premises of formal logic. In the vacuum which this created, there was no place for anything but general reflections on what God at any rate could be—reflections arising from specific human standpoints and ideas as incontestable data, and then interwoven rather feebly with all kinds of biblical reminiscences. In this way there was created a doctrine of God which could have either no meaning or only a disastrous one for the remaining contents of dogmatics. And also in this way there was created, involuntarily, the basis on which an anti-Christian philosophy (and at the same time and later a heretical theology) could only too easily attack the dogma of the Trinity, and with it all the decisive articles of faith and its knowledge of the Word of God. It was certainly right to define the essence of God: *Essentia Dei est ipsa Deitas, qua Deus a se et per se absolute est et existit*[1] (Polanus, *Synt. Theol. chr.*, 1609, col. 865). But even in the definition of this *a se et per se* there ought never to have been an abstraction from the Trinity, and that means from the act of divine revelation. In all the considerations that are brought before us in this chapter we must keep vigorously aloof from this tradition, remembering that a Church dogmatics derives from a doctrine of the Trinity, and therefore that there is no possibility of reckoning with the being of any other God, or with any other being of God, than that of the Father, the Son and the Holy Spirit as it is in God's revelation and in eternity. So then, as dogmatics describes and explains God as the One who is, it cannot make any free speculations about the nature of His being. Whatever may be the standpoints and ideas that are adduced, in this context it has always to win and explain their particular sense in the light of this revelation—the revelation of the being of the triune God.

---

1. Eng. trans.: The essence of God is God himself, whereby God in himself and by himself is absolute being and becoming.

What God is as God, the divine individuality and characteristics, the *essentia* or "essence" of God, is something which we shall encounter either at the place where God deals with us as Lord and Savior, or not at all. The act of revelation as such carries with it the fact that God has not withheld Himself from men as true being, but that He has given no less than Himself to men as the overcoming of their need, and light in their darkness— Himself as the Father in His own Son by the Holy Spirit. The act of God's revelation also carries with it the fact that man, as a sinner who of himself can only take wrong roads, is called back from all his own attempts to answer the question of true being, and is bound to the answer to the question given by God Himself. And finally the act of God's revelation carries with it the fact that by the Word of God in the Holy Spirit, with no other confidence but this unconquerable confidence, man allows being to the One in whom true being itself seeks and finds, and who meets him here as the source of his life, as comfort and command, as the power over him and over all things.

Therefore our first and decisive transcription of the statement that God is, must be that God is who He is in the act of His revelation. Hence we have already repeated this sentence in our chapter heading with the concept of "The Reality of God," which holds together being and act, instead of tearing them apart like the idea of "essence." It will be noticed that even in this transcription and comprehension the statement speaks of the being of God and therefore answers the particular question of the subject of all the other articles of the creed. We are in fact interpreting the being of God when we describe it as God's reality, as "God's being in act," namely, in the act of His revelation, in which the being of God declares His reality: not only His reality for us—certainly that—but at the same time His own, inner, proper reality, behind which and above which there is no other.

If we follow the path indicated, our first declaration must be the affirmation that in God's revelation, which is the content of His Word, we have in fact to do with His act. And first, this means generally with an event, with a happening. But as such this is an event which is in no sense to be transcended. It is not, therefore, an event which has merely happened and is now a past fact of history. God's revelation is, of course, this as well. But it is also an event happening in the present, here and now. Again, it is not this in such a way that it exhausts itself in the momentary movement from the past to the present, that is, in our today. But it is also an event that took place once for all, and an accomplished fact. And it is also future—the event which lies completely and wholly in front of us, which has not yet happened, but which simply comes upon us. Again, this happens without detriment to its historical completeness and its full contemporaneity. On the contrary, it is in its historical completeness and its full contemporaneity that it is truly future. "Jesus Christ the same yesterday and today and for ever" (Heb. 13:8). This is something which cannot be transcended or surpassed or dispensed with. What is concerned is always the birth, death and resurrection of Jesus Christ, always His justification of faith, always His lordship in the Church, always His coming again, and therefore Himself as our hope. We can only abandon revelation, and with it God's Word, if we are to dispense with it. With it we stand, no, we move necessarily in the circle of its event or, in biblical terms, in the circle of the life of the people of Israel, And in this very event God is who He is. God is He who in this event is subject, predicate and object; the revealer, the act of revelation, the revealed; Father, Son and Holy Spirit. God is the Lord active in this event. We say "active" in this event, and therefore for our salvation and for His glory, but in any case active. Seeking and finding God in His revelation, we cannot escape the action of God for a God who is not active. This is not only because we ourselves cannot, but because there is no surpassing or bypassing at all of the divine action, because a transcendence of His action is nonsense. We are dealing with the being of God: but with regard to the being of God, the word "event" or "act" is *final*, and cannot be surpassed or compromised. To its very deepest depths God's Godhead consists in the fact that it is an event—not any event, not events in general, but the event of His action, in which we have a share in God's revelation.

The definition that we must use as a starting-point is that God's being is life. Only the Living is God. Only the voice of the Living is God's voice. Only the work of the Living is God's work; only the worship and fellowship of the Living is God's worship and fellowship. So, too, only the knowledge of the Living is knowledge of God.

> We recall in this connection the emphatic Old and New Testament description of God as "the living God." This is no metaphor. Nor is it a mere description of God's relation to the world and to ourselves. But while it is that, it also describes God Himself as the One He is. "As I live" or "As the Lord (or God, or the God of Israel) liveth" is not for nothing the significant formula for an oath in the Old Testament. God is "the living fountain" (Jer. 2:13, 17:13), "the fountain of life" (Ps. 36:9). The Father has life in Himself (John 5:26). Christ is "the author of life" (Acts 3:15), even "the life" (John 14:6, Phil. 1:21, Col. 3:4, 1 John 1:2), and "eternal life" (1 John 5:20), "alive for evermore" (Rev. 1:18). The Holy Spirit is life (John 6:63, Rom. 8:10). All this is clearly in contradistinction to the gods and idols who "have no life" (Jer. 10:14, Acts 14:15). . . .

But we must be more precise. When on the basis of His revelation we always understand God as event, as act and as life, we have not in any way identified Him with a sum or content of event, act, or life generally. We can never expect to know generally what event or act or life is, in order from that point to conclude and assert that God is He to whom this is all proper in an unimaginable and incomprehensible fullness and completeness. When we know God as event, act and life, we have to admit that generally and apart from Him we do not know what this is. So then, when we know God as event, act and life, He is definitely something different—to be distinguished from what we are accustomed to understand by these views and concepts. God's revelation is a particular event, not identical with the sum, nor identical with any of the content of other existing happenings either in nature or in human history. It is a definite happening within general happening: so definite that, while it takes part in this happening, it also contradicts it, and can only be seen and comprehended together with it in its contradiction, without the possibility of a synthesis, apart from the synthesis proclaimed and already fulfilled in itself. So, too, the action of God that takes place in revelation is a particular action, different from any other happening, even in contradiction to it. *Actus purus* (pure act) is not sufficient as a description of God. To it there must be added at least "*et singularis*" (and singularly). The fact that in God the source, reconciliation and goal of all other happenings are together real and discernible, is another matter, which as such is only true in the separation of this action from every other happening. God is also the One who is event, act and life in His own way, as distinct from everything that He is not Himself, even though at the same time He is its source, reconciliation and goal. God is not merely differentiated from all other actuality as actuality generally and as such, or as its essence and principle, so that, while He is differentiated from all other actuality, He is still connected to it—and the idea is both immanent in the phenomenon and transcendent to it. He is, of course, differentiated from it in this way too. His work in the creation and preservation of the world can also up to a point—but only up to a point—be described in this way. But the particularity of His working and therefore His being as God is not exhausted by this dialectical transcendence which, however strictly it may be understood, must always be understood with equal strictness as immanence. On the contrary, without prejudice to and yet without dependence upon His relationship to what is event, act and life outside Him, God is in Himself free event, free act and free life. . . .

But we must take a further step forward. What is the particularity, what is therefore the specific freedom, of the event, act and life of God in His revelation? We are obviously speaking with a double meaning when in describing God we speak of event, act and life. Event, act and life could refer to an event in nature, or a transcendent happening, to be investigated after the fashion of what we know as natural events. Now it is true that we cannot simply neglect to seek the being of God along this line if we consider ourselves bound to speak of the God of revelation. Therefore, in the attempt to speak here more unequivocally, we must exercise some care. The differentiation of the divine happening from the non-divine does not coincide in Holy Scripture with the distinction between nature and grace, soul and body, inner and outer, visible and invisible. On the contrary, the event of revelation as described for us in Scripture has everywhere a natural, bodily, outward and visible component—from the creation (not only of heaven but also of earth), by way of the concrete existence of the people of Israel in Palestine, the birth of Jesus Christ, His physical miracles, His suffering and death under Pontius Pilate, His physical resurrection, right down to His coming again and the resurrection of the body. We cannot give a new meaning to this component without explaining away the specific sense of this revelation, and therefore the revelation itself, without giving over the field to another reflection foreign to the basis and message of the Church. And this state of affairs cannot be a matter of indifference for the description of the being of God. Whoever describes this as absolute "spirit," and by this absoluteness understands an as it were chemical purity as against "nature," must ask himself whether at the very source of his consideration of the matter he has not fallen into a misunderstanding of the most fundamental character and with the gravest consequences, confusing the reality of God with the reality of the spiritual world—a reality to be distinguished no less from the reality of God than from that of the world of nature. . . .

2. The Being of God as the One Who Loves
It would be dangerous and ambiguous if we tried to prolong the definition of the divine essence as His being in act generally, and therefore, the establishment of the form of this essence—His actuality or His life. Once said, the fact that God's being is absolutely His act will not be restated, but taken seriously in the insight that this act of His, which is His being, is not actuality in general and as such, but that in His revelation and in eternity it is a specific act with a definite content. It is personal being in the originality and uniqueness that is applicable only to Him. It is the being of a person, distinguished not by its formal completeness, but by its peculiar, distinctive act as such. We must now enquire further what is this act of His, the divine act which is the divine being, so that we have to conclude from it what is divine, i.e., what it is to be God, what makes God God, what God's "essence" is. Following the considerations of the first section this much is established, that God is what He is absolutely by Himself, and not by anything else that would confer divinity upon Him. Therefore the act that becomes visible to us in God's revelation, in which He is who He is, and from which we must conclude what and how He is, can only make manifest in fact that He is who He is. If it does not make this manifest, it has definitely not made manifest what is divine, what is the essence of God. But the act that is visible in God's revelation is not so constituted that we can conclude from it no more than the tautology "God is God." This very tautology as such we find clarified and explained in God's revelation. For it is nothing less than God's self-revelation. It is the revelation of the name by which He wills to be known and addressed by us, the name which does not add a second and extrinsic truth to the first intrinsic truth of His intimate, hidden essence, but which is the name and the criterion and the truth (i.e., the disclosure and description of the particularity) of His innermost

hidden essence. This essence of God which is seen in His revealed name is His being and therefore His act as Father, Son and Holy Spirit. The fact that He makes Himself visible in this name is the solution of the tautology. From this name of His we have to conclude what and how He is in His act and therefore in His being: what is divine, what is the character of Him who is God, what makes God God, what therefore His "essence" is. The fact that we cannot go behind His livingness for a definition of His being means in fact that we cannot go behind this name of His, because in the very revelation of His name there occurs the act which is His being to all eternity. However (in order to define this revealed and eternal being) we can, we may and we must ask what this name has to say to us about the particular being of God in His act.

As it is revealed to us as the definition of that which confronts us in His revelation, this name definitely has this primary and decisive thing to say to us in all its constituents—that God is He who, without having to do so, seeks and creates fellowship between Himself and us. He does not have to do it, because in Himself without us, and therefore without this, He has that which He seeks and creates between Himself and us. It implies so to speak an overflow of His essence that He turns to us. We must certainly regard this overflow as itself matching His essence, belonging to His essence. But it is an overflow which is not demanded or presupposed by any necessity, constraint, or obligation, least of all from outside, from our side, or by any law by which God Himself is bound and obliged. On the contrary, in itself and as such it is again rooted in Himself alone. Yet important as it is, we will postpone this explanation and keep to the positive statement that God is He who in His revelation seeks and creates fellowship with us, and who (because His revelation is also His self-revelation) does this in Himself and in His eternal essence. Creation itself, i.e., the establishment and maintenance of a reality really distinct from Himself, of which man confronted by God, may find himself the spiritual-natural unity, is already a seeking and creating of fellowship. This seeking and creating is heightened in the work of revelation itself, which is not so much a continuation of creation as its supersession, and is identical with the reconciliation of sinful man in the incarnation, death and resurrection of the Son of God. This seeking and creating finds its crown and final confirmation in the future destiny of mankind as redeemed in Jesus Christ, in his destiny for eternal salvation and life. What God does in all this, He is: and He is no other than He who does all this. But what is it that He does in virtue of His triune name, and therefore in this whole act of God seen in His revelation? If it is right and necessary to bring together the purpose and meaning of this act in order to understand it, and therefore to understand God, we must now say that He wills to be ours, and He wills that we should be His. He wills to belong to us and He wills that we should belong to Him. He does not will to be without us, and He does not will that we should be without Him. He wills certainly to be God and He does not will that we should be God. But He does not will to be God for Himself nor as God to be alone with Himself. He wills as God to be for us and with us who are not God. Inasmuch as He is Himself and affirms Himself, in distinction and opposition to everything that He is not, He places Himself in this relation to us. He does not will to be Himself in any other way than He is in this relationship. His life, that is, His life in Himself, which is originally and properly the one and only life, leans towards this unity with our life. The blessings of His Godhead are so great that they overflow as blessings to us, who are not God. This is God's conduct towards us in virtue of His revelation. There is no lack of contrariety in this conduct. It establishes and embraces the antithesis between the Creator and His creatures. It establishes and embraces necessarily, too, God's anger and struggle against sin, God's separation from sinners, God's judgment hanging over them and consummated on them. There is death and hell and eternal damnation in the scope of this relationship of His. But His attitude and action is always that He seeks and creates fellowship between Himself and us. For large stretches it may be for us doubtful, dark, and incomprehensible. For large stretches it will seem to us like the very opposite of this relationship. It will reveal itself as such through judgment and grace, through dying and making alive, through veiling and unveiling. It will always be the light that shines out of darkness when it is revealed to us as such. We shall have to learn ever and again what it really means to say that God seeks and creates fellowship between Himself and us. In itself, first and last, it will always be this and no other relationship. God wills and does nothing different, but only one thing—this one thing. And this one thing that He wills and does is the blessing of God, that which distinguishes His act as divine, and therefore also His person as divine. This one thing is therefore the divine, the θειον, the essence of God in the revelation of His name, which is the subject of our enquiry. That is to say, we shall find in God Himself, in His eternal being, nothing other than this one thing. As and before God seeks and creates fellowship with us, He wills and completes this fellowship in Himself. In Himself He does not will to exist for Himself, to exist alone. On the contrary, He is Father, Son and Holy Spirit and therefore alive in His unique being with and for and in another. The unbroken unity of His being, knowledge and will is at the same time an act of deliberation, decision and intercourse. He does not exist in solitude but in fellowship. Therefore what He seeks and creates between Himself and us is in fact nothing else but what He wills and completes and therefore is in Himself. It therefore follows that as He receives us through His Son into His fellowship with Himself, this is the one necessity, salvation, and blessing for us, than which there is no greater blessing—no greater, because God has nothing higher than this to give, namely Himself; because in giving us Himself, He has given us every blessing. We recognize and appreciate this blessing when we describe God's being more specifically in the statement that He is the One who loves. That He is God—the Godhead of God—consists in the fact that He loves, and it is the expression of His loving that He seeks and creates fellowship with us. It is correct and important in this connection to say emphatically His *loving, i.e.,* His act as that of the One who loves. . . .

3. The Being of God in Freedom

God's being as He who lives and loves is being in freedom. In this way, freely, He lives and loves. And in this way, and in the fact that He lives and loves in freedom, He is God, and distinguishes Himself from everything else that lives and loves. In this way, as the free person, He is distinguished from other persons. He is the one, original and authentic person through whose creative power and will alone all other persons are and are sustained. With the idea of freedom we simply affirm what we would be affirming if we were to characterize God as the Lord. But His lordship is in all circumstances the lordship of His living and loving. Our present question is that of the mode of His lordship and therefore of His living and loving—of the divine characteristics by which, as He who lives and loves, He manifests His sovereignty. This mode is characterized by the fact that it is absolutely God's own, in no sense dictated to Him from outside and conditioned by no higher necessity than that of His own choosing and deciding, willing and doing. If we enquire how, according to His revelation in Jesus Christ, God's lordship differs in its divinity from other types of rule, then we must answer that it is lordship in freedom. It would be senseless to ascribe this characteristic to other kind of sovereignty, or to any other living and loving but that of God. There are other sovereignties, but freedom is the prerogative of divine sovereignty. Freedom is, of course, more than the absence of limits, restrictions, or conditions. This is only its negative and to that extent improper aspect— improper to the extent that from this point of view it requires another, at least in so far as its freedom lies in its independence of this other. But freedom in its positive and proper qualities means to be grounded in one's own being, to be determined and moved by oneself. This is the freedom of the divine life and love. In this positive freedom of His, God is also unlimited, unrestricted and unconditioned from without. He is the free Creator, the free Reconciler, the free Redeemer. But His divinity is not exhausted in the fact that in His revelation it consists throughout in this freedom from external compulsion: in free utterance and action, free beginning and ending, free judgment and blessing, free power and spirit. On the contrary, it is only manifest in all this. For He has it in Himself quite apart from His relation to another from whom He is free. He in Himself is power, truth and right. Within the sphere of His own being He can live and love in absolute plenitude and power, as we see Him live and love in His revelation.

The loftiness, the sovereignty, the majesty, the holiness, the glory—even what is termed the transcendence of God—what is it but this self-determination, this freedom, of the divine living and loving, the divine person? If later on we shall not be able to portray fully the attributes of divine love except with close attention to their divinity, i.e., their divine excellence, conversely we shall have to understand this divinity of God in all its aspects as the sum of His freedom.

Our emphasis in defining the concept must not in any circumstances fall upon this negative aspect. To be sure, this negative side is extremely significant not only for God's relation to the world, but also for His being in itself. We cannot possibly grasp and expound the idea of divine creation and providence, nor even the ideas of divine omnipotence, omnipresence and eternity, without constantly referring to this negative aspect of His freedom. But we shall be able to do so properly only when we do so against the background of our realization that God's freedom constitutes the essential positive quality, not only of His action towards what is outside Himself, but also of His own inner being. The biblical witness to God sees His transcendence of all that is distinct from Himself, not only in the distinction as such, which is supremely and decisively characterized as His freedom from all conditioning by that which is distinct from Himself, but furthermore and supremely in the fact that without sacrificing His distinction and freedom, but in the exercise of them, He enters into and faithfully maintains communion with this reality other than Himself in His activity as Creator, Reconciler and Redeemer. According to the biblical testimony, God has the prerogative to be free without being limited by His freedom from external conditioning, free also with regard to His freedom, free not to surrender Himself to it, but to use it to give Himself to this communion and to practice this faithfulness in it, in this way being really free, free in Himself. God must not only be unconditioned but, in the absoluteness in which He sets up this fellowship, He can and will also be conditioned. He who can and does do this is the God of Holy Scripture, the triune God known to us in His revelation. This ability, proved and manifested to us in His action, constitutes His freedom.

SELECTION **2**

Karl Rahner

"Brief Creedal Statements"

A German Jesuit, Karl Rahner (1904–1984) is one of the most influential twentieth-century Roman Catholic theologians—alongside Bernard Lonergan and Hans Urs von Balthasar.

Not only did his theology play an important role in the Second Vatican Council, articulating a modern understanding of Catholicism, but he, along with Karl Barth, is credited with initiating the modern revival of Trinitarian theology.

Written at the end of his life, his *Foundations of Christian Faith* presents a systematic exposition of his theology, most of which had previously been developed in essays. The following excerpt (from its epilogue) contains three brief creedal statements that provide a succinct summary of the central themes in his doctrine of God.

For Rahner, God's essence and his existence can be characterized as the term (the source and goal) of human transcendence. Rather than seeking to "prove" God's existence, Rahner simply seeks to indicate how we might become aware of God's presence in our everyday lives. Although incomprehensible to us, the experience of God is implicit in our human experience of transcendence, which is always present in our everyday acts of knowing things and acting freely. It is, therefore, inescapable and universal in all human experiences—even when we are unaware of it.

God, however, is not merely the eternally unreached or "asymptotic" term of human transcendence. Rather, God, in fact, gives himself in *self-communication* to us as our own fulfillment. And since we are sinners, this self-communication always takes the form of forgiving love. Drawing on Augustine, Rahner describes this self-communication in terms of God's two "missions" in the economy of salvation. First, the mission of the "Spirit" is experienced as the grace of justification that divinizes us in the innermost center of our existence. Second, the mission of the "Logos" or "Son" is experienced in the history of salvation and revelation as the irreversible, victorious, and definite acceptance of this offer to human freedom within one man, Jesus Christ, for all of humanity (what the church has called the dogma of the God-Man or hypostatic union, which encompasses Jesus' death and resurrection). Finally, since the God who comes to us as Spirit and as Logos is always the ineffable and holy mystery, we call this God "Father."

One of Rahner's main contributions to contemporary Trinitarian theology is the axiom that "the economic Trinity is the immanent Trinity, and the immanent Trinity is the economic Trinity." In other words, the way God communicates himself to humanity (the "economic Trinity") is who God is within himself (the "immanent Trinity") since if there were no immanent Trinity, the former would not really be God's self-communication.

The three creeds below develop these themes in relation to the three persons of the Trinity: (1) the "theological creed" centers on the "Father" (the incomprehensible term of human transcendence); (2) the "anthropological creed" centers on the incarnate God or the "Son" (the God who in Jesus Christ is the condition for radical interpersonal love); and (3) the "future-oriented creed" centers on the "Spirit" (the God who, as the absolute future of humanity, is the free and loving Lord over history).

From Karl Rahner, *Foundations of Christian Faith:*
An Introduction to the Idea of Christianity, trans. William V. Dych
(New York: Crossroad, 1987), 452–59.

Requirements for a Basic Creedal Statement

Among the fundamental questions which have to be asked about basic creedal statements belongs of course the question what really has to be expressed in this kind of a creed and what can be left out. It is perhaps clear that these basic creeds may not be brief summaries of systematic or dogmatic theology. It cannot express at the same time everything which makes up the church's consciousness of the faith. None of the earlier creeds before Trent expressed everything which belongs to Christian faith. The Second Vatican Council's teaching about the "hierarchy of truths" says that not everything which is true must for this reason be equally significant. A basic creed would only have to contain what is of fundamental importance and what provides a basic starting point for reaching the whole of the faith. If in addition to this we consider that we can legitimately distinguish between an objective hierarchy of truths and an existentiell and situational hierarchy of truths, and that a basic creed which is only intended to be one among many may place the emphasis on expressing an approach to and a point of departure for the whole content of faith which are correct and effective from an existentiell and situational point of view, then it becomes clear that these basic creeds can also vary a great deal in their content.[2] It also becomes clear that this content should consist primarily and especially in what constitutes for the listeners in question an initial and hopefully successful point of departure for reaching an understanding of the whole of Christian faith.

A further question would be what the scope of a basic creed should be in a purely quantitative sense. On this point very considerable differences are conceivable, beginning with a basic creed in a few phrases, as in the Apostles' Creed, and extending to a creed which runs for several pages. The three brief creedal statements to be offered in what follows will aim for extreme brevity. But presumably the various possible basic or brief creedal statements of Christian faith do not have to be equal in this respect.

We must mention one further question about these basic creeds in general. For this kind of a creed really to be a Christian profession of faith, it has to give expression to our faith in the historical Jesus as our Lord and as the absolute savior, and it has to be related to this historical facticity. There is indeed something like an anonymous Christianity in which grace, the

---

2. Ed. note: Rahner uses the word "existentiell" to refer to what we actually experience in our everyday activities of knowing and acting freely. In doing so, he draws on Martin Heidegger's distinction between an "ontic" (or "existentielle") understanding of facts about things in their actual existence in the world in contrast to an "ontological" (or "existential") understanding that, however vague, is the precondition for our ontic understanding of them. See Heidegger's *Being and Time* (New York: Harper Perennial Modern Classics, 2008; reprint ed.), esp. 312–48.

forgiveness of sin, justification and salvation take place without the person in question being related explicitly in his objectified consciousness to the historical event of Jesus of Nazareth. Moreover, a great deal can be said about the most central reality of Christian faith without this being seen in an immediate connection with Jesus Christ. This is true especially because not every explicit relationship to the historical Jesus is already a relationship of faith, and hence the specific theological nature of this relationship itself has to be explained. In certain circumstances it can be explained in the light of other fundamental faith statements which in the first instance and *quoad nos* can he made without being explicitly related to Jesus Christ. An example of this would be the first article of the Apostles' Creed. But it is to be taken for granted that even a merely basic creedal statement of explicit Christian faith has to express explicitly the relationship of the other elements expressed to Christ, or the relationship of Jesus to these other elements, and hence it has to have an explicit Christological structure in its profession. To this extent the second of the following three brief creedal statements has to be read very carefully lest this Christological implication be overlooked.

In order to make what has been said so far a bit more concrete and to give some examples of it, we shall present three brief theological creeds and explain one possible way of understanding them. It can perhaps be better clarified at the end why there are precisely three brief creedal statements, and so we shall leave this question open for the moment.

Because of their brevity these three creeds are formulated very "abstractly." They will try to express briefly the innermost essence of the collective or individual history of salvation which Christianity is and will always remain. The abstract formulation which this implies is certainly not appropriate for everyone. It is to be taken for granted, then, that these brief creedal statements do not of themselves make any claim to be binding for everyone, and that they were formulated from out of a western milieu and are directed to a European situation.

A Brief Theological Creed

The incomprehensible term of human transcendence, which takes place in man's existentiell and original being and not only in theoretical or merely conceptual reflection, is called God, and he communicates himself in forgiving love to man both existentielly and historically as man's own fulfillment. The eschatological climax of God's historical self-communication, in which this self-communication becomes manifest as irreversible and victorious, is called Jesus Christ.

Explanatory Remarks

We shall offer a few reflections by way of commentary on this first brief creed, which we are calling a "theological" creed. It contains three fundamental statements. The first has to do with what we mean by *God*. It tries to suggest an understanding of God both in his essence and in his existence by characterizing God as the *term* of human transcendence, and hence precisely as a mystery which remains incomprehensible.

This emphasizes that the experience of God which is implicit in the experience of transcendence is not found in the first instance and originally in theoretical reflection, but rather takes place basically and originally in our everyday acts of knowledge and freedom. On the one hand, therefore, this experience of God is inescapable, and on the other hand it can take place in a very anonymous and preconceptual way. A person should be challenged to discover this universally present experience of God reflexively and to objectify it conceptually. This first theological creed, then, must not only say *that* God exists, a God about whom it is clear *that* he is, as Thomas Aquinas thought. The creedal statement intends rather to indicate how we reach an understanding of *what* God really means.

The second statement in this theological creed explains that God as understood in this way is not merely man's eternally asymptotic goal, but rather—and this is the first decisively Christian statement—he gives himself in his own reality in *self-communication* to man as man's own fulfillment. Indeed he does this on the presupposition that man is a sinner, and hence in forgiving love. It says that this self-communication takes place both existentielly and historically at the same time. This expresses two elements in their relationship of mutual conditioning: it expresses what is called in the usual theological terminology the grace of justification at least as an offer and this is the existentiell self-communication of God in the "Holy Spirit"; and it also expresses what is called the history of salvation and revelation. The latter is nothing else but the historical self-mediation and the historical and historically ongoing objectification of God's self-communication in grace which has been permanently imbedded in the ground of history at least as an offer. This statement about God's twofold self-communication to the world, that is, about the two "missions" in the economy of salvation, the existentiell mission of the "Spirit" and the historical mission of the "Logos" or the "Son," this statement, along with the fact that the original, incomprehensible and abiding mystery of God as "Father" has already been mentioned, gives us first of all the Trinity in the economy of salvation. And it also gives us the immanent Trinity, because if there were no immanent Trinity the former would not really be God's self-communication.

The third basic statement says that this historical self-communication of God, which makes the existentiell self-communication in grace objective historically and is its self-mediation, has its eschatological and victorious climax in *Jesus of Nazareth*. For when God's historical self-communication reaches the climax in which it is not merely present as directed and offered to man's individual and collective freedom, but also has been accepted irreversibly, victoriously and definitively in the human race as a whole (without this marking the absolute end of the history of salvation), then we have precisely what is called in the church's dogma the God-Man or the hypostatic union, and this includes the death and the resurrection of the God-Man. Hence the third statement in this creed professes that the eschatological climax of God's historical self-communication to the world has already taken place in the concrete in the historical person of Jesus of Nazareth. Since this eschatological event cannot be understood without understanding along with it its historical continuation in the still ongoing history of salvation, this creed also contains an adequate starting point for a theology of the *church*. For in its deepest essence the church can only be understood as the abiding sacrament of God's salvific act in Christ for the world.

A Brief Anthropological Creed

A person really discovers his true self in a genuine act of self-realization only if he risks himself radically for another. If he does this, he grasps unthematically or explicitly what we mean by God as the horizon, the guarantor and the radical depths of this love, the God who in his existentiell and historical self-communication made himself the realm within which such love is possible. This love is meant in both an interpersonal and a social sense, and in the radical unity of both of these elements it is the ground and the essence of the church.

Explanatory Remarks

Perhaps we can distinguish three statements here too. The first says that in the existentiell self-transcendence which takes place in the act of *loving one's neighbor* a person has an *experience of God* at least implicitly. This first statement is only a further specification of the first part of the theological creed. It makes concrete what was said in the first statement of the first creed, namely, that the basic and original actualization of human transcendence does not take place in theoretical reflection, but rather in the concrete and practical knowledge and freedom of "everyday life," and this is what is meant by interpersonal relationships. The first statement of this second creed is also established theologically by the truth about the unity between love of God and love of neighbor. This presupposes that this truth is not reduced to the platitude that a person cannot please God if he disobeys his commandment to love his neighbor.

The second statement in this creed says that it is precisely through his self-communication that God creates the possibility for the interpersonal love which in the concrete is possible for us and is our task. In other words, then, this second statement says that when interpersonal love really reaches its own deepest essence, it is borne by the supernatural, infused and justifying grace of the Holy Spirit. If we understand God's self-communication in the more exact sense in which it was nuanced in the first creedal statement—that is, in the unity, the difference and the relationship of mutual conditioning between God's existentiell self-communication in grace and God's historical self-communication with its climax in the Incarnation of the divine Logos—then the statement that by his self-communication God made himself the realm within which such radical interpersonal love is possible also contains everything which was said in the first creed and its explanation about God's self-communication as the very essence of Christian faith. If a person reflects upon Matthew 25, he certainly does not have to deny a priori that the entire salvific relationship between man and God and between man and Christ is already found implicitly in a radical love for one's neighbor which has been realized in practice. If someone should miss in the second statement of this anthropological creed a more explicit expression of the relationship which a person and his love for neighbor has to Jesus Christ, then we could say explicitly: The self-communication of God to man by which man's love for neighbor is borne has its eschatological, victorious and historical climax in Jesus Christ, and therefore he is loved at least anonymously in every other person.

The third statement of this second creed says that this love in which God is loved in our neighbor and our neighbor is loved in God has itself two dimensions: an existentiell dimension of intimacy, and an historical and social dimension. These two dimensions correspond to the two aspects of God's self-communication. When this love reaches its high point, and indeed in the unity of both of these aspects, then we have in fact what we call church. For what characterizes the church as distinguished from other social groups consists precisely in the eschatologically inseparable unity (not identity) between Spirit, truth and love on the one hand, and on the other hand the historical and institutional manifestation of this communication of the Spirit as truth and as love.

A Brief Future-Oriented Creed

Christianity is the religion which keeps open the question about the absolute future which wills to give itself in its own reality by self-communication, and which has established this will as eschatologically irreversible in Jesus Christ, and this future is called God.

Explanatory Remarks

This shortest of the creedal statements transposes the statement about man's *transcendentality* in the first creed by interpreting this transcendentality as an *orientation towards the future*, as man's futurity. A transcendentality which is absolutely unlimited implies by this very fact the question about an absolute future as distinguished from an indefinite series of finite and partial futures. The creedal statement says of this future that it is not merely the asymptotic goal of history which keeps this history in motion but is never reached in its own reality. Rather, this future wills to give itself through its own self-communication. It says of this self-communication of the absolute future, which is still in the process of historical realization, what was already said of God's self-communication in the first creedal statement, namely, that this self-communication which is always "existen-tiell" also has a *historical aspect*, and that in this aspect it has reached an *eschatological irreversibility in Jesus Christ*.

We do not have to show again in detail that the basic starting point of a divine self-communication to the world which has become eschatologi-cally irreversible in Jesus Christ already contains implicitly what the doc-trine of the Trinity and Christology say more explicitly. Nor do we have to show again in detail that in the experience of our orientation towards an absolute future, a future which wills to give itself immediately in its own reality, God is experienced, and indeed the God of the supernatural order of grace. Hence he is experienced as mystery in an absolute sense.

Insofar as Christianity is the worship of the one true God as opposed to all the idols which absolutize finite powers and dimensions of man, it is the religion which keeps man open for the absolute future. And inso-far as this future is and remains an absolute mystery even when this self-communication reaches fulfillment, Christianity is the religion which keeps open the *question* about the absolute future.

Reflections on the Trinitarian Faith

These three brief creeds to be sure are intended first of all as possible creeds alongside which there can also be other such creeds, and this is still true even when such creedal statements are conceived on a quite defi-nite level of conceptual abstractness. Perhaps, nevertheless, it is not merely empty theological speculation to try to understand these three creeds in their juxtaposition and in their interrelationships as reflections and con-sequences of Christian belief in the Trinity, or to interpret them as the three approaches and ways which human experience has for reaching an understanding of the Trinity in the economy of salvation first of all, and then from this an understanding of the immanent Trinity.

The first creedal statement speaks of God as the incomprehensible term of human transcendence. When we consider that this signifies the *prin-cipium inprincipiatum* of all conceivable reality who is absolutely with-out origin, then this incomprehensible and unoriginated term of human transcendence really signifies the "Father" of the Christian doctrine of the Trinity. If in the second creedal statement the God who in the man Jesus Christ made himself the realm within which there can be radical interper-sonal love is the real point of this creed, then this signifies the incarnate God or the "Son." But the absolute future of man, who is God and who communicates himself in his free Lordship over history, is in a special way the "Spirit" of God because he can be characterized as love and as freedom and as ever new and surprising.

Of course this triad of brief creedal statements which we presented would have to be thought out more precisely and more clearly in relation to their trinitarian background, and this is not possible here. But in any case we can say that if, on the one hand, a brief creedal statement should express the basic substance of the reality of Christian faith in such a way that the most intelligible approach possible is opened to this reality from out of man's existentiell experience, and if, on the other hand, this basic substance can certainly be found in God's turning to the world as Trinity in the economy of salvation, then one cannot dismiss out of hand the idea that there would have to be three basic types of these brief creedal statements corresponding to the dogma of the Trinity. This does not exclude the fact that each of these basic types can be very variable both because of further differentiations and emphases in its content, and also because it takes into account the differences among those for whom the basic creedal statement is intended.

SELECTION **3**

Paul Tillich

"God as the Power of Being Resisting Nonbeing"

A German American, Paul Tillich (1886–1965) is considered one of the four most-influential Protestant theologians of the twentieth century (along with Karl Barth, Rudolf Bultmann, and Reinhold Niebuhr). For Tillich, the symbol "God" answers the question implied in human finitude. God must be our "ultimate concern," following Luther's interpretation of the First Commandment that whatever we trust completely becomes a god for us. Our finite concerns are "demonic" or idolatrous when we attribute ultimate meaning and power to them; they are merely "secular" (or "profane") when we deny God's presence in all things. Only what is "holy" can demand our ultimate concern.

And only God is "holy" because only God is "being-itself." Qualitatively different from all others, God is not *a being* alongside or above others: God can never be conditioned by the categories of finitude (e.g., time, space, substance, and causality). Rather, as the power that creates "out of nothing," God is the "power of being" resisting "nonbeing." There is no contradiction within God (as there is in all other beings) between essence and existence. Beyond or prior to all distinctions, God both transcends and is immanent in all things as their creative power. God's infinity, therefore, encompasses the finite (and with it the element of nonbeing inherent in all finitude). Indeed, human beings are only aware of their finitude because of the power that enables them to transcend it and look at it.

Yet the Bible speaks of God as a "living God" and not simply as a pure absolute. We can only, however, speak of God as "living" in symbolic terms, that is, using language drawn from the ontological elements that describe our experience of power and meaning in life. Although "Spirit" refers both to God's entire reality (God *is* Spirit) and to an aspect of God's life (God *has* the Spirit as God has the Logos), it is the most embracing, direct, and unrestricted symbol for God because it includes all the ontological elements of our experience without needing to be balanced by other symbols. On one side, "Spirit" depicts God as the inherent *power* in all reality (with a centered personality, self-transcending vitality, and freedom of self-determination). On the other side, it depicts God as the *meaning* of reality (participating in all reality as the source of its forms and structures and its limiting and directing destiny).

God's life as Spirit embodies Trinitarian principles: (1) God is the abyss or depth of the divine, the inexhaustible power of being infinitely resisting nonbeing, giving the power of being to everything that is (the element of power); (2) God is the Logos, the meaning and structure of reality, the mirror of the divine depth and self-objectification by which God speaks his Word both in himself and beyond himself (the element of meaning); and (3) God is Spirit, uniting within himself both divine power and divine meaning. In the Spirit, God goes out of himself, giving actuality to what is potential in the divine abyss and outspoken in the divine Logos. In the Spirit, the finite is both posited as finite and reunited with the infinite. Thus, although divine life is infinite mystery, it is never infinite emptiness but rather the source of abundance in all reality.

From Paul Tillich, *Systematic Theology*, vol. 1 (Chicago: University of Chicago Press, 1951), 211, 214–18, 235–37, 241–44, 249–52.

A. The Meaning of "God"
1. A Phenomenological Description

a. God and Man's Ultimate Concern "God" is the answer to the question implied in man's finitude; he is the name for that which concerns man ultimately. This does not mean that first there is a being called God and then the demand that man should be ultimately concerned about him. It means that whatever concerns a man ultimately becomes god for him, and, conversely, it means that a man can be concerned ultimately only about that which is god for him. The phrase "being ultimately concerned" points to a tension in human experience. On the one hand, it is impossible to be concerned about something which cannot be encountered concretely, be it in the realm of reality or in the realm of imagination. Universals can become matters of ultimate concern only through their power of representing concrete experiences. The more concrete a thing is, the more the possible concern about it. The completely concrete being, the individual person, is the object of the most radical concern—the concern of love. On the other hand, ultimate concern must transcend every preliminary finite and concrete concern. It must transcend the whole realm of finitude in order to be the answer to the question implied in finitude. But in transcending the finite the religious concern loses the concreteness of a being-to-being relationship. It tends to become not only absolute but also abstract, provoking reactions from the concrete element. This is the inescapable inner tension in the idea of God. The conflict between the concreteness and the ultimacy of the religious concern is actual wherever God is experienced and this experience is expressed, from primitive prayer to the most elaborate theological system. It is the key to understanding the dynamics of the history of religion, and it is the basic problem of every doctrine of God, from the earliest priestly wisdom to the most refined discussions of the trinitarian dogma. . . .

If the word "existential" points to a participation which transcends both subjectivity and objectivity, then man's relation to the gods is rightly called "existential." Man cannot speak of the gods in detachment. The moment he tries to do so, he has lost the god and has established just one more object within the world of objects. Man can speak of the gods only on the basis of his relation to them. This relation oscillates between the concreteness of a give-and-take attitude, in which the divine beings easily become objects and tools for human purposes, and the absoluteness of a total surrender on the side of man. The absolute element of man's ultimate concern demands absolute intensity, infinite passion (Kierkegaard), in the religious relation. The concrete element drives men toward an unlimited amount of relative action and emotion in the cult in which the ultimate concern is embodied and actualized, and also outside it. The Catholic system of relativities represents the concrete element most fully, while Protestant radicalism predominantly emphasizes the absolute element. The tension in the nature of the gods, which is the tension in the structure of man's ultimate concern (and which, in the last analysis, is the tension in the human situation), determines the religions of mankind in all their major aspects.

b. God and the Idea of the Holy The sphere of the gods is the sphere of holiness. A sacred realm is established wherever the divine is manifest. Whatever is brought into the divine sphere is consecrated. The divine is the holy.

Holiness is an experienced phenomenon; it is open to phenomenological description. Therefore, it is a very important cognitive "doorway" to understanding the nature of religion, for it is the most adequate basis we have for understanding the divine. The holy and the divine must be interpreted correlatively. A doctrine of God which does not include the category of holiness is not only unholy but also untrue. Such a doctrine transforms the gods into secular objects whose existence is rightly denied by naturalism. On the other hand, a doctrine of the holy which does not interpret it as the sphere of the divine transforms the holy into something aesthetic-emotional, which is the danger of theologies like those of Schleiermacher and Rudolf Otto. Both mistakes can be avoided in a doctrine of God which analyzes the meaning of ultimate concern and which derives from it both the meaning of God and the meaning of the holy.

The holy is the quality of that which concerns man ultimately. Only that which is holy can give man ultimate concern, and only that which gives man ultimate concern has the quality of holiness.

The phenomenological description of the holy in Rudolf Otto's classical book *The Idea of the Holy* demonstrates the interdependence of the meaning of the holy and the meaning of the divine, and it demonstrates their common dependence on the nature of ultimate concern. When Otto calls the experience of the holy "numinous," he interprets the holy as the presence of the divine. When he points to the mysterious character of holiness, he indicates that the holy transcends the subject-object structure of reality. When he describes the mystery of the holy as *tremendum* and *fascinosum*, he expresses the experience of "the ultimate" in the double sense of that which is the abyss and that which is the ground of man's being. This is not directly asserted in Otto's merely phenomenological analysis, which, by the way, never should be called "psychological." However, it is implicit in his analysis, and it should be made explicit beyond Otto's own intention.

Such a concept of the holy opens large sections of the history of religion to theological understanding, by explaining the ambiguity of the concept of holiness at every religious level. Holiness cannot become actual except through holy "objects." But holy objects are not holy in and of themselves. They are holy only by negating themselves in pointing to the divine of which they are the mediums. If they establish themselves as holy, they become demonic. They still are "holy," but their holiness is anti-divine. A nation which looks upon itself as holy is correct in so far as everything can become a vehicle of man's ultimate concern, but the nation is incorrect in so far as it considers itself to be inherently holy. Innumerable things, all things in a way, have the power of becoming holy in a mediate sense. They can point to something beyond themselves. But, if their holiness comes to be considered inherent, it becomes demonic. This happens continually in the actual life of most religions. The representations of man's ultimate concern—holy objects—tend to become his ultimate concern. They are transformed into idols. Holiness provokes idolatry.

Justice is the criterion which judges idolatrous holiness. The prophets attack demonic forms of holiness in the name of justice. The Greek philosophers criticize a demonically distorted cult in the name of *Dike*. In the name of the justice which God gives, the Reformers destroy a system of sacred things and acts which has claimed holiness for itself. In the name of social justice, modern revolutionary movements challenge sacred institutions which protect social injustice. In all these cases it is demonic holiness, not holiness as such, which comes under attack.

However, it must be said with regard to each of these cases that to the degree to which the antidemonic struggle was successful historically, the meaning of holiness was transformed. The holy became the righteous, the morally good, usually with ascetic connotations. The divine command to be holy as God is holy was interpreted as a requirement of moral perfection. And since moral perfection is an ideal and not a reality, the notion of actual holiness disappeared, both inside and outside the religious sphere. The fact that there are no "saints" in the classical sense on Protestant soil supported this development in the modern world. One of the characteristics of our present situation is that the meaning of holiness has been rediscovered in liturgical practice as well as in theological theory, although in popular language holiness still is identified with moral perfection.

The concept of the holy stands in contrast with two other concepts, the unclean and the secular. In the classical sixth chapter of Isaiah the prophet must be purified by means of a burning coal before he can endure the manifestation of the holy. The holy and the unclean seem to exclude each other. However, the contrast is not unambiguous. Before it received the meaning of the immoral, the unclean designated something demonic, something which produced taboos and numinous awe. Divine and demonic holiness were not distinguished until the contrast became exclusive under the impact of the prophetic criticism. But if the holy is completely identified with the clean, and if the demonic element is completely rejected, then the holy approximates the secular. Moral law replaces the *tremendum* and *fascinosum* of holiness. The holy loses its depth, its mystery, its numinous character.

This is not true of Luther and many of his followers. The demonic elements in Luther's doctrine of God, his occasional identification of the wrath of God with Satan, the half-divine–half-demonic picture he gives of God's acting in nature and history—all this constitutes the greatness and the danger of Luther's understanding of the holy. The experience he describes certainly is numinous, tremendous, and fascinating, but it is not safeguarded against demonic distortion and against the resurgence of the unclean within the holy.

In Calvin and his followers the opposite trend prevails. Fear of the demonic permeates Calvin's doctrine of the divine holiness. An almost neurotic anxiety about the unclean develops in later Calvinism. The word "Puritan" is most indicative of this trend. The holy is the clean; cleanliness becomes holiness. This means the end of the numinous character of the holy. The *tremendum* becomes fear of the law and of judgment; the *fascinosum* becomes pride of self-control and repression. Many theological problems and many psychotherapeutic phenomena are rooted in the ambiguity of the contrast between the holy and the unclean.

The second contrast to the holy is the secular. The word "secular" is less expressive than the word "profane," which means "in front of the doors"—of the holy. But profane has received connotations of "unclean," while the term "secular" has remained neutral. Standing outside the doors of the sanctuary does not in itself imply the state of uncleanness. The profane *might* be invaded by unclean spirits but not necessarily. The German word *profan* preserves this idea of neutrality. The secular is the realm of preliminary concerns. It lacks ultimate concern; it lacks holiness. All finite relations are in themselves secular. None of them is holy. The holy and the secular seem to exclude each other. But again the contrast is ambiguous. The holy embraces itself and the secular, precisely as the divine embraces itself and the demonic. Everything secular is implicitly related to the holy. It can become the bearer of the holy. The divine can become manifest in it. Nothing is essentially and inescapably secular. Everything has the dimension of depth, and in the moment in which the third dimension is actualized, holiness appears. Everything secular is potentially sacred, open to consecration.

Furthermore, the holy needs to be expressed and can be expressed only through the secular, for it is through the finite alone that the infinite can express itself. It is through holy "objects" that holiness must become actual. The holy cannot appear except through that which in another respect is secular. In its essential nature the holy does not constitute a special realm in addition to the secular. The fact that under the conditions of existence it establishes itself as a special realm is the most striking expression of existential disruption. The very heart of what classical Christianity has called "sin" is the unreconciled duality of ultimate and preliminary concerns, of the finite and that which transcends finitude, of the secular and the holy. Sin is a state of things in which the holy and the secular are separated, struggling with each other and trying to conquer each other. It is the state in which God is not "all in all," the state in which God is "in addition to" all other things. The history of religion and culture is a continuous confirmation of this analysis of the meaning of holiness and of its relation to the unclean and to the secular. . . .

B. The Actuality of God
3. God as Being

a. God as Being and Finite Being The being of God is being-itself. The being of God cannot be understood as the existence of a being alongside others or above others. If God is a being, he is subject to the categories of finitude, especially to space and substance. Even if he is called the "highest being" in the sense of the "most perfect" and the "most powerful" being, this situation is not changed. When applied to God, superlatives become diminutives. They place him on the level of other beings while elevating him above all of them. Many theologians who have used the term "highest being" have known better. Actually they have described the highest as the absolute, as that which is on a level qualitatively different from the level of any being—even the highest being. Whenever infinite or unconditional power and meaning are attributed to the highest being, it has ceased to be a being and has become being-itself. Many confusions in the doctrine of God and many apologetic weaknesses could be avoided if God were understood first of all as being-itself or as the ground of being. The power of being is another way of expressing the same thing in a circumscribing phrase. Ever since the time of Plato it has been known—although it often has been disregarded, especially by the nominalists and their modern followers—that the concept of being as being, or being-itself, points to the power inherent in everything, the power of resisting nonbeing. Therefore, instead of saying that God is first of all being-itself, it is possible to say that he is the power of being in everything and above everything, the infinite power of being. A theology which does not dare to identify God and the power of being as the first step toward a doctrine of God relapses into monarchic monotheism, for if God is not being-itself, he is subordinate to it, just as Zeus is subordinate to fate in Greek religion. The structure of being-itself is his fate, as it is the fate of all other beings. But God is his own fate; he is "by himself"; he possesses "aseity." This can be said of him only if he is the power of being, if he is being-itself.

As being-itself God is beyond the contrast of essential and existential being. We have spoken of the transition of being into existence, which involves the possibility that being will contradict and lose itself. This transition is excluded from being-itself (except in terms of the christological paradox), for being-itself does not participate in nonbeing. In this it stands in contrast to every being. As classical theology has emphasized, God is beyond essence and existence. Logically, being-itself is "before," "prior to," the split which characterizes finite being.

For this reason it is as wrong to speak of God as the universal essence as it is to speak of him as existing. If God is understood as universal essence, as the form of all forms, he is identified with the unity and totality of finite potentialities; but he has ceased to be the power of the ground in all of them, and therefore he has ceased to transcend them. He has poured all his creative power into a system of forms, and he is bound to these forms. This is what pantheism means.

On the other hand, grave difficulties attend the attempt to speak of God as existing. In order to maintain the truth that God is beyond essence and existence while simultaneously arguing for the existence of God, Thomas Aquinas is forced to distinguish between two kinds of divine existence: that which is identical with essence and that which is not. But an existence of God which is not united with its essence is a contradiction in terms. It makes God a being whose existence does not fulfill his essential potentialities; being and not-yet-being are "mixed" in him, as they are in everything finite. God ceases to be God, the ground of being and meaning. What really has happened is that Thomas has had to unite two different traditions: the Augustinian, in which the divine existence is included in his essence, and the Aristotelian, which derives the existence of God from the existence of the world and which then asserts, in a second step, that his existence is identical with his essence. Thus the question of the existence of God can be neither asked nor answered. If asked, it is a question about that which by its very nature is above existence, and therefore the answer— whether negative or affirmative—implicitly denies the nature of God. It is as atheistic to affirm the existence of God as it is to deny it. God is being- itself, not a being. On this basis a first step can be taken toward the solu- tion of the problem which usually is discussed as the immanence and the transcendence of God. As the power of being, God transcends every being and also the totality of beings—the world. Being-itself is beyond finitude and infinity; otherwise it would be conditioned by something other than itself, and the real power of being would lie beyond both it and that which conditioned it. Being-itself infinitely transcends every finite being. There is no proportion or gradation between the finite and the infinite. There is an absolute break, an infinite "jump." On the other hand, everything finite participates in being-itself and in its infinity. Otherwise it would not have the power of being. It would be swallowed by nonbeing, or it never would have emerged out of nonbeing. This double relation of all beings to being- itself gives being-itself a double characteristic. In calling it creative, we point to the fact that everything participates in the infinite power of being. In calling it abysmal, we point to the fact that everything participates in the power of being in a finite way, that all beings are infinitely transcended by their creative ground. . . .

4. God as Living

a. God as Being and God as Living Life is the process in which poten- tial being becomes actual being. It is the actualization of the structural elements of being in their unity and in their tension. These elements move divergently and convergently in every life-process; they separate and reunite simultaneously. Life ceases in the moment of separation without union or of union without separation. Both complete identity and com- plete separation negate life. If we call God the "living God," we deny that he is a pure identity of being as being; and we also deny that there is a definite separation of being from being in him. We assert that he is the eternal process in which separation is posited and is overcome by reunion. In this sense, God lives. Few things about God are more emphasized in the Bible, especially in the Old Testament, than the truth that God is a living God. Most of the so-called anthropomorphisms of the biblical picture of God are expressions of his character as living. His actions, his passions, his remembrances and anticipations, his suffering and joy, his personal relations and his plans—all these make him a living God and distinguish him from the pure absolute, from being-itself.

Life is the actuality of being, or, more exactly, it is the process in which potential being becomes actual being. But in God as God there is no distinction between potentiality and actuality. Therefore, we cannot speak of God as living in the proper or non-symbolic sense of the word "life." We must speak of God as living in symbolic terms. Yet every true symbol participates in the reality which it symbolizes. God lives in so far as he is the ground of life.[3] Anthropomorphic symbols are adequate for speaking of God religiously. Only in this way can he be the living God for man. But even in the most primitive intuition of the divine a feeling should be, and usually is, present that there is a mystery about divine names which makes them improper, self-transcending, symbolic. Religious instruction should deepen this feeling without depriving the divine names of their reality and power. One of the most surprising qualities of the prophetic utterances in the Old Testament is that, on the one hand, they always appear concrete and anthropomorphic and that, on the other hand, they preserve the mystery of the divine ground. They never deal with being as being or with the absolute as the absolute; nevertheless, they never make God a being alongside others, into something conditioned by something else which also is conditioned. Nothing is more inadequate and disgusting than the attempt to translate the concrete symbols of the Bible into less concrete and less powerful symbols. Theology should not weaken the concrete symbols, but it must analyze them and interpret them in abstract ontological terms. Nothing is more inadequate and confusing than the attempt to restrict theological work to half-abstract, half-concrete terms which do justice neither to existential intuition nor to cognitive analysis.

The ontological structure of being supplies the material for the symbols which point to the divine life. However, this does not mean that a doctrine of God can be derived from an ontological system. The character of the divine life is made manifest in revelation. Theology can only explain and systematize the existential knowledge of revelation in theoretical terms, interpreting the symbolic significance of the ontological elements and categories.

---

3. "He that formed the eye, shall he not see?" (Ps. 94:9).

While the symbolic power of the categories appears in the relation of God to the creature, the elements give symbolic expression to the nature of the divine life itself. The polar character of the ontological elements is rooted in the divine life, but the divine life is not subject to this polarity. Within the divine life, every ontological element includes its polar element completely, without tension and without the threat of dissolution, for God is being-itself. However, there is a difference between the first and the second elements in each polarity with regard to their power of symbolizing the divine life. The elements of individualization, dynamics, and freedom represent the self or subject side of the basic ontological structure within the polarity to which they belong. The elements of participation, form, and destiny represent the world or object side of the basic ontological structure within the polarity to which they belong. Both sides are rooted in the divine life. But the first side determines the existential relationship between God and man, which is the source of all symbolization. Man is a self who has a world. As a self he is an individual person who participates universally, he is a dynamic self-transcending agent within a special and a general form, and he is freedom which has a special destiny and which participates in a general destiny. Therefore, man symbolizes that which is his ultimate concern in terms taken from his own being. From the subjective side of the polarities he takes—or more exactly, receives—the material with which he symbolizes the divine life. He sees the divine life as personal, dynamic, and free. He cannot see it in any other way, for God is man's ultimate concern, and therefore he stands in analogy to that which man himself is. But the religious mind—theologically speaking, man in the correlation of revelation—always realizes implicitly, if not explicitly, that the other side of the polarities also is completely present in the side he uses as symbolic material. God is called a person, but he is a person not in finite separation but in an absolute and unconditional participation in everything. God is called dynamic, but he is dynamic not in tension with form but in an absolute and unconditional unity with form, so that his self-transcendence never is in tension with his self-preservation, so that he always remains God. God is called "free," but he is free not in arbitrariness but in an absolute and unconditional identity with his destiny, so that he himself is his destiny, so that the essential structures of being are not strange to his freedom but are the actuality of his freedom. In this way, although the symbols used for the divine life are taken from the concrete situation of man's relationship to God, they imply God's ultimacy, the ultimacy in which the polarities of being disappear in the ground of being, in being-itself . . . .

c. God as Spirit and the Trinitarian Principles Spirit is the unity of the ontological elements and the *telos* of life. Actualized as life, being-itself is fulfilled as spirit. The word *telos* expresses the relation of life and spirit more precisely than the words "aim" or "goal." It expresses the inner directedness of life toward spirit, the urge of life to become spirit, to fulfill itself as spirit. *Telos* stands for an inner, essential, necessary aim, for that in *which* a being fulfils its own nature. God as living is God fulfilled in himself and therefore spirit. God *is* spirit. This is the most embracing, direct, and unrestricted *symbol* for the divine life. It does not need to be balanced with another symbol, because it includes all the ontological elements. . . .

The meaning of spirit is built up through the meaning of the ontological elements and their union. In terms of both sides of the three polarities one can say that spirit is the unity of power and meaning. On the side of power it includes centered personality, self-transcending vitality, and freedom of self-determination. On the side of meaning it includes universal participation, forms and structures of reality, and limiting and directing destiny. Life fulfilled as spirit embraces passion as much as truth, libido as much as surrender, will to power as much as justice. If one of these sides is absorbed by its correlate, either abstract law or chaotic movement remains. Spirit does not stand in contrast to body. Life as spirit transcends the duality of body and mind. It also transcends the triplicity of body, soul, and mind, in which soul is actual life-power and mind and body are its functions. Life as spirit is the life of the soul, which includes mind and body, but not as realities alongside the soul. Spirit is not a "part," nor is it a special function. It is the all-embracing function in which all elements of the structure of being participate. Life as spirit can be found by man only in man, for only in him is the structure of being completely realized.

The statement that God is Spirit means that life as spirit is the inclusive symbol for the divine life. It contains all the ontological elements. God is not nearer to one "part" of being or to a special function of being than he is to another. As Spirit he is as near to the creative darkness of the unconscious as he is to the critical light of cognitive reason. Spirit is the power through which meaning lives, and it is the meaning which gives direction to power. God as Spirit is the ultimate unity of both power and meaning. In contrast to Nietzsche, who identified the two assertions that God is Spirit and that God is dead, we must say that God is the living God because he is Spirit.

Any discussion of the *Christian* doctrine of the Trinity must begin with the christological assertion that Jesus is the Christ. The Christian doctrine of the Trinity is a corroboration of the christological dogma. The situation is different if we do not ask the question of the Christian doctrines but rather the question of the *presuppositions* of these doctrines in an idea of God. Then we must speak about the trinitarian principles, and we must begin with the Spirit rather than with the Logos. God is Spirit, and any trinitarian statement must be derived from this basic assertion.

God's life is life as spirit, and the trinitarian principles are moments within the process of the divine life. Human intuition of the divine always has distinguished between the abyss of the divine (the element of power) and the fullness of its content (the element of meaning), between the divine depth and the divine *logos*. The first principle is the basis of Godhead, that which makes God God. It is the root of his majesty, the unapproachable intensity of his being, the inexhaustible ground of being in which everything has its origin. It is the power of being infinitely resisting nonbeing, giving the power of being to everything that is. During the past centuries theological and philosophical rationalism have deprived the idea of God of this first principle, and by doing so they have robbed God of his divinity. He has become a hypostasized moral ideal or another name for the structural unity of reality. The power of the Godhead has disappeared.

The classical term *logos* is most adequate for the second principle, that of meaning and structure. It unites meaningful structure with creativity. Long before the Christian Era—in a way already in Heraclitus—*logos* received connotations of ultimacy as well as the meaning of being as being. According to Parmenides, being and the *logos* of being cannot be separated. The *logos* opens the divine ground, its infinity and its darkness, and it makes its fulness distinguishable, definite, finite. The *logos* has been called the mirror of the divine depth, the principle of God's self-objectification. In *the logos* God speaks his "word," both in himself and beyond himself. Without the second principle the first principle would be chaos, burning fire, but it would not be the creative ground. Without the second principle God is demonic, is characterized by absolute seclusion, is the "naked absolute" (Luther).

As the actualization of the other two principles, the Spirit is the third principle. Both power and meaning are contained in it and united in it. It makes them creative. The third principle is in a way the whole (God *is* Spirit), and in a way it is a special principle (God *has* the Spirit as he has the *logos*). It is the Spirit in whom God "goes out from" himself, the Spirit proceeds from the divine ground. He gives actuality to that which is potential in the divine ground and "outspoken" in the divine *logos*. Through the Spirit the divine fulness is posited in the divine life as something definite, and at the same time it is reunited in the divine ground. The finite is posited as finite within the process of the divine life, but it is reunited with the infinite within the same process. It is distinguished from the infinite, but it is not separated from it. The divine life is infinite mystery, but it is not infinite emptiness. It is the ground of all abundance, and it is abundant itself. . . .

The divine life is infinite, but in such a way that the finite is posited in it in a manner which transcends potentiality and actuality. Therefore, it is not precise to identify God with the infinite. This can be done on some levels of analysis. If man and his world are described as finite, God is infinite in contrast to them. But the analysis must go beyond this level in both directions. Man is aware of his finitude because he has the power of transcending it and of looking at it. Without this awareness he could not call himself mortal. On the other hand, that which is infinite would not be infinite if it were limited by the finite. God is infinite because he has the finite (and with it that element of nonbeing which belongs to finitude) within himself united with his infinity. One of the functions of the symbol "divine life" is to point to this situation.

SELECTION **4**

Wolfhart Pannenberg

"The Unity and Attributes of the Divine Essence"

Wolfhart Pannenberg (1928–) is widely regarded as an influential Protestant theologian. In the first volume of his *Systematic Theology,* he deals with questions about the truth of God in history. How is our indefinite awareness of a reality that infinitely transcends and embraces all that is finite related to the concrete revelation of God found in Scripture? How is the unity of God's eternal "essence" related to the specific manifestations of God's "existence" in salvation history— especially as these are revealed in the Trinity (Father, Son, and Spirit) and the multiplicity of the attributes identified with the biblical God? And how are the immanent and economic Trinity related?

Pannenberg answers these questions by relating two biblical statements: "God is love" (1 John 4:8, 16) and "I AM WHO I AM" (Exod. 3:14). Together, they tell us that God's self-identity is revealed in his actions. God's unity is not a numerical unity but the self-identity demonstrated in the Father's reconciling love through the Son and the Spirit.

In Scripture, the "essence" of this self-identity is the "holiness" that both opposes the profane world and brings it into fellowship with the holy God. Pannenberg relates this understanding of holiness to a concept of infinity defined not merely as the antithesis of the finite but as the "true Infinite" transcending and embracing its own antithesis to the finite. Thinking of God's essence as infinity is superior to thinking of it as a cause or substance unrelated to the world for two reasons. First, it enables us to take into account a modern scientific view of the world (which since Kant presupposes that the category of "relation" is more primary than that of "substance"). Second, it enables us to understand something not only about the reciprocal relationships among Trinitarian persons but also about God's relationship to the world.

Nonetheless, the infinite and finite cannot be synthesized in a single thought (as Hegel attempted). Rather, their unity can only be found in the concrete dynamic of God's Spirit—the biblical *ruah*, which is more like a "field of force," drawing on modern physics, than mind (*nous*), as Origen had affirmed. Embracing the tension between the infinite and the finite without setting their distinction aside, God's love is the concrete content of this dynamic. God's "essence" is manifest in the sum total of the moments of God's "existence" as love. The biblical attributes for God (goodness, grace, mercy, righteousness, faithfulness, patience, and wisdom) are all aspects of God's love. Even those most explicitly identified with God's infinity in its relation to time, space, and power (eternity, omnipresence, and omnipotence) have their true meaning in the divine love that eternally affirms the distinctiveness of creatures even as it seeks to reconcile their separation from God. Finally, the immanent Trinity and the economic Trinity are related in the unfolding of divine love in the world, a love that can only be grounded in and enacted by the true Infinite, the Trinitarian God manifest in the Father, Son, and Spirit.

Wolfhart Pannenberg, *Systematic Theology*, vol. 1, trans. Geoffrey W. Bromley (Grand Rapids: Wm. B. Eerdmans Publishing Co., 1988), 382–84, 440–48.

The Love of God

Already in ancient Israel wisdom has to do not only with the order of the cosmos but also with the determination of the times in the course of history.[4] The unsearchability of the future for us, and especially the divine transcendence over the inner logic of the nexus of actions and events in the course of history, necessarily strengthened the impression that the divine wisdom is hidden in the march of world occurrence. Only at the end of history will the divine counsel that underlies what takes place be knowable. But expectation of its disclosure combined with expectation of the definitive revelation of God's lordship over the course of history, and therefore of his deity, in the events of the end-time.[5] For primitive Christianity, then, the dawning of these events in the person of Jesus not only initiated the definitive revelation of God but a closely related manner showed what is the goal of the divine counsel (Eph. 1:9–10). It could thus regard Jesus Christ himself as the embodiment of the divine wisdom (1 Cor. 1:24) or the divine Logos.[6] In him the merciful love of God reaches its goal, the goal of the reconciliation of the world. In the fine saying of Barth, then, Jesus Christ is the "meaning of God's patience" (cf. CD, II/1, 432). In the rule of God's wisdom there may be seen the power of love over the march of history.

But is this really so? Even two thousand years after the birth of Christ does not humanity offer the picture of an unreconciled world? Have

4. Cf. von Rad, *Wisdom in Israel* (Nashville: Abingdon, 1972), pp. 263–83.
5. See above, pp. 207ff.
6. See above, pp. 213, 215–16.

Christians made much change? Has not the church itself been drawn into worldly conflicts? Has it not even multiplied and sharpened these conflicts by its impatience and divisions? Has not the Christian God of love proved to be powerless against the march of events in the world, powerless even in the lives of Christians and the fellowship of the church which by its unity ought to bear witness to Christ in the world? In fact, all this brings the truth of the biblical revelation into question.

The discussion in this section deals with the attributes that may be ascribed to God on the basis of the biblical witness to revelation. It shows that these attributes—goodness, grace, mercy, righteousness, faithfulness, patience, and wisdom—are all to be seen as aspects of the comprehensive statement that God is love. But this does not prove that God is in fact the eternal, omnipresent, and omnipotent author and finisher of the world, the Infinite who governs and embraces all things. Not without reason the exposition in this final section has hardly gone beyond the biblical testimonies, whereas § 6 above tried to show that the biblical statements about the holiness, eternity, omnipresence, and omnipotence of God give concrete form to the true Infinite which philosophical reflection advances as the sphere to which religious statements about divine powers refer.

But can the doctrine of God be expected to prove that the God of the biblical revelation, the God of love, is really the omnipresent, eternal, and omnipotent One who permeates and embraces all things, that he, then, and he alone is truly God? According to the biblical testimonies only God's own acts in history and not doctrinal arguments can prove this. The primitive Christian message certainly claimed that his self-demonstration has already been given in the history of Jesus, in the resurrection of the Crucified. But according to this message we have here only an anticipation of the end-time event whose consummation is awaited in the final accomplishment of the kingdom of God with the return of Christ, the resurrection of the dead, and the judgment of this world. Only the future consummation of God's kingdom can finally demonstrate that the deity of God is definitively revealed already in the history of Jesus and that the God of love is truly God. On the way to this ultimate future the truth claim of the Christian message concerning God remains unavoidably debatable. Theology can do nothing to alter this. Theology cannot replace faith. But it can try to show how far faith, in keeping with the truth claim of Christian proclamation, is aware of being in alliance with true reason.

The Unity of God

Is the eternal and omnipotent God, if there is such, really merciful and gracious, patient, and of great kindness? Is the God of love really almighty, all-embracing, omnipresent, and eternal, truly God?

This question might imply that we are to seek evidence of the deity of the God of love in the reality of the world. More comprehensively, it relates to the experience of worldly reality itself in the process of its history. In a more limited sense, with reference to reflection on the relation between worldly reality and the religious proclamation of God, the issue is whether the reality of the world as it is may even be thought of as the creation of the God of the Bible. The next chapters of this systematic theology, first the doctrine of creation and anthropology, but also christology, ecclesiology, and eschatology, will have to take up this question, for they will show that the world and humanity as they are do not fully correspond to the loving will of the Creator but stand in need of reconciliation and consummation.

The initial question, however, can be taken in a narrower sense. It is the question whether we can think of statements about God's love in conjunction with his infinity, holiness, eternity, omnipresence, and omnipotence. Stated thus, it is the question of the unity of God in the multiplicity of his attributes, and especially of the relation of the divine love to the attributes which in § 6 we saw to be concrete forms of the concept of the Infinite. In other words, what we have to show is that the Infinite is truly infinite. The place of this question is in the doctrine of God in the narrower sense.

We first have to clarify the status of the thought of God's unity. Is this another attribute that we have not yet discussed? This is suggested by the usual treatment of it within the doctrine of the divine attributes. Against this arrangement Schleiermacher rightly objected that unity cannot be viewed as an attribute at all. Strictly speaking it can never be an attribute of a thing that it exists only in a specific number.[7] Unity and plurality are not attributes. They come under the category of quantity. But we cannot say that God is numerically one if we cannot say that he is one among many. For this reason the older Protestant dogmatics differentiated between numerical and transcendental unity and related only the latter to God.[8] God is one, and as such distinct from others. This idea can be applied only to God. The thought of the true Infinite means that the distinction between one thing and another cannot be applied unrestrictedly to God as the true Infinite. As the one who is not one among others, God must be absolute.[9] As one, the Absolute is also all.[10] Yet it is not all in one

---

7. *Christian Faith*, I, #56.2. Schleiermacher explains that it is not the quality of the hand to be double but of human beings to have two hands and apes four. Thus it might be a quality of the world to be ruled by one God but not of God to be only one. In fact, in the history of philosophy from antiquity that unity of the world has been the decisive argument for the unity of its divine origin; cf. the examples in n.211 above; cf. my *Basic Questions*, 2 (Philadelphia: Fortress, 1971), 119ff., 126–27. Aquinas used the same argument in *Summa Theologiae*, 1.11.3. Here it is the last of three arguments, the second of which deduces God's unity from his infinity because several infinites would limit one another and thus mutually negate their infinity. The weakest of the three arguments is the first, which infers unity from simplicity.

8. D. Hollaz, *Examen*, I, 337; and A. Calov, *Systema*, II, 287.

9. Seneca's description of the Absolute (*Ep.* 52.1) as the incomparably perfect was first applied to God by Tertullian (*Adv. Marc.* 2.5) . . . . The term first appears more commonly in this sense in Anselm's *Monologion*. On God's unity as absolute unity cf. Nicholas of Cusa's *On Learned Ignorance* 1.5.14.

10. Nicholas of Cusa arrived at this thesis by way of the concept of the greatest (*On Learned*

(pantheism) but transcends the difference of one and all.[11] It is thus the One that also embraces all. Formulas like this, of course, are only logical postulates which can be developed out of analysis of the concept of absolute unity but cannot be shown to be possible, i.e., self-consistent, because in their deduction the opposing ideas of the one and the many are also in play. What is evident, however, is that we cannot think of God's unity as a quality or a number. The thought of God as the absolute one means not only his singularity but also the uniqueness and incomparability that lie in the idea of his holiness. The problems in the concept of absolute unity lie in its relation to the many. Reflection on the unity as such cannot solve them.

On the biblical view God's unity is not merely the presupposition of his revelatory action but also its content. When Moses asks God for his name, the reply refers to God's self-identification by his historical working: "I will be who I will be" (Exod. 3:14).[12] The identity here is not the timeless identity of a concept of being, but the self-identity of the truth of God which his faithfulness in historical action demonstrates by its holiness, goodness, patience, righteousness, and wisdom. It is to this that Israel's confession of the unity of God relates: "Hear, O Israel, the Lord (Yahweh) is our God, the Lord (Yahweh) alone (the only one)" (Deut. 6:4, margin). From the outset the oneness of God was an expression, and in the religious history of Israel it is also a result, of his zeal that will not tolerate any other gods alongside him (Deut. 6:15; Exod. 20:5). There is thus a connection between the oneness of the God of Israel and his love, namely, through the claim to sole deity which is grounded in his love, and to recognition of this claim by those to whom he reveals himself (cf. Matt. 6:33; Luke 12:31; also Matt. 6:24; Luke 16:13).

The love of God reaches beyond Israel to all creation. The righteousness

---

Ignorance 1.2.1). But it may be inferred directly from the relation between the one, the many, and the all (cf. Kant's *Critique of Pure* Reason, B 111), if we think of a unity that is not an element of plurality. In that case the one and the all coincide. In modern theology Dorner is one of the few who have examined this matter in connection with the divine unity. His conclusion is that the absolute unity or oneness of God must be "in some way" the basis of the possibility of everything else *(System of Christian Doctrine,* pp. 230ff., § 19.1).

11. For Plotinus, then, the one is not part of the all; cf. W. Beierwaltes, *Denken des Einen* (Frankfurt: Klostermann, 1985), pp. 41–42. As such the absolute One is *apeiron,* not something. More precisely, as truly infinite, it is both something and not (merely) something. This is in line with the view of the Areopagite that the divine unity is united in distinction (p. 214). As Beierwaltes sees it, we already have here the coincidence of opposites of Nicholas of Cusa (p. 215). On the other hand the inferring of equality from unity in Thierry of Chartres (pp. 369f) seems to me to have the character of outward reflection on the One, i.e., on the relation of the One of being to the One of super-being as this was developed in the first of the two hypotheses of the Platonic Parmenides (pp. 194–95). This applies also to the *homoousion* of the doctrine of the Trinity, which cannot be developed out of the concept of the One, as attempted by the school of Chartres (pp. 382ff.), but only out of a description of the historical relation of Jesus as Son of the Father.

12. See above, ch. 4, #2, esp. n.22.

and self-identity of the electing God are shown by his faithfulness not merely to his election of Israel but to his whole creation, which is the target of his electing action by means of the election of this people. For the sake of the identity of his name (Isa. 48:9; cf. 43:25; Ezek. 36:22–23) God will not let his elect or his whole creation sink into nothingness. He overcomes the turning of his creatures away from himself by sending his Son to reconcile the world. By the unity of reconciliation by love, which embraces the world and bridges the gulf between God and the world, the unity of God himself is realized in relation to the world. This takes us beyond the initially abstract idea of God's unity as a separate reality which is in mere opposition to the plurality of other gods and the world. By the love which manifests itself in his revelatory action God's unity is constituted the unity of the true Infinite which transcends the antithesis to what is distinct from it.

If the unity of God thus finds nuanced and concrete form only in the work of divine love, then the other attributes of the divine being may be shown to be either manifestations of the love of God or to have true meaning only insofar as their concrete manifestation is taken up into the sway of divine love. The latter is true especially of the qualities of God's infinity.

In the discussion of God's omnipotence and omnipresence we saw that the problems raised by these concepts are solved only by their trinitarian interpretation and therefore by viewing them as an expression of the love of God. Only the doctrine of the Trinity permits us so to unite God's transcendence as Father and his immanence in and with his creatures through Son and Spirit that the permanent distinction between God and creature is upheld. The same holds good for an understanding of God's omnipotence. The power of God over his creation as the transcendent Father finds completion only through the work of the Son and Spirit because only thus is it freed from the one-sided antithesis of the one who determines and that which is determined, and God's identity in his will for creation is led to its goal.

The same holds good also for an understanding of God's eternity. The incarnation of the Son sets aside the antithesis of eternity and time as the present of the Father and his kingdom is present to us through the Son. This present not only contains all the past within it, as the idea of Christ's descent into Hades shows, but it also invades our present in such a way that this becomes the past and needs to be made present and glorified by the work of the Spirit. The removal of the antithesis of eternity and time in the economy of God's saving action according to the wisdom of his love is the reconciliation of the antithesis between Creator and creature.

The same holds good finally for an understanding of the basic statement of God's infinity. The thought of the true Infinite, which demands that we do not think of the infinite and the finite as a mere antithesis but also think of the unity that transcends the antithesis, poses first a mere challenge, an intellectual task which seems at a first glance to involve a paradox. In the

abstractly logical form of the question there appears to be no way of showing how we can combine the unity of the infinite and the finite in a single
thought without expunging the difference between them. We cannot solve
this problem, as Hegel thought, by the logic of concept and conclusion.
The perfect unity of concept and reality in the idea is itself no more than
a mere postulate of metaphysical logic. The dynamic that in the process
has to be ascribed to the idea leaps over the frontiers of logic. It may be
found only in a very different field, that of the dynamic of the Spirit, but
of the Spirit in the OT sense, not in that of its fusion with thought. More
concretely this dynamic may be filled with content, and thus show itself to
be formally consistent, only through the thought of the divine love.

Love, of course, is infinite only as divine love. As infinite love it is divine
love only in the trinitarian riches of its living fulfilment. Divine love in its
trinitarian concreteness, in the freedom not merely of the Father but of
the Son (in the self-distinction by which he is at one with the Father) and
of the Spirit (in the spontaneity of his glorification of the Father and the
Son), embraces the tension of the infinite and the finite without setting
aside their distinction. It is the unity of God with his creature which is
grounded in the fact that the divine love eternally affirms the creature in
its distinctiveness and thus sets aside its separation from God but not its
difference from him.[13]

As love gives concrete form to the divine unity in its relation to the
world, it also represents the taking up of the plurality of the divine attributes into the unity of the divine life. The differences do not simply disappear, but they have reality only as moments in the living plenitude of the
divine love. Similarly, the relativity of the concept of essence and the differences between essence and attributes, essence and manifestation, and
essence and existence, have their concrete truth in the trinitarian dynamic
of the divine love. Love is the essence that is what it is only in its manifestation, in the forms of its existence, namely, in the Father, Son, and Spirit,
presenting and manifesting itself wholly and utterly in the attributes of
its manifestation. Because God is love, having once created a world in his
freedom, he finally does not have his own existence without this world,
but over against it and in it in the process of its ongoing consummation.

The thought of love makes it possible conceptually to link the unity of
the divine essence with God's existence and qualities and hence to link the
immanent Trinity and the economic Trinity in the distinctiveness of their
structure and basis. This is because the thought of divine love shows itself
to be of trinitarian structure, so that we can think of the trinitarian life of
God as an unfolding of his love. It is also because the thought of love permits us to think of God's relation to the world as grounded in God.

13. Maximus Confessor *Opusc. theol. polem.* 8; PG, 91, 97A; cf. 91, 877A, 1113 BC and 1385 BC;
and on this L. Thunberg, *Microcosm and Mediator: The Theological Anthropology of Maximus the
Confessor* (Lund: C.W.K. Gleerup 1965), pp. 32ff.

What we have not yet shown, however, is how God's relation to the world is to be understood in the light of the trinitarian understanding of God. After the trinity of Father, Son, and Spirit that is based on the biblical revelation gave rise to the problem how to preserve God's unity theologically, and after the Johannine equation of God and love provided a solution to this problem, the question arose as to the functions of the divine persons in God's relation to the world and of the specific form that the unity of the divine life takes in the relation between the immanent and the economic Trinity. In dealing with this issue our dogmatics will have to traverse the various areas of the creation, reconciliation, and redemption of the world. Only with the consummation of the world in the kingdom of God does God's love reach its goal and the doctrine of God reach its conclusion. Only then do we fully know God as the true Infinite who is not merely opposed by the world of the finite, and thus himself finite. To this extent Christian dogmatics in every part is the doctrine of God. Even the question of God's reality, of his existence in view of his debatability in the world as atheistic criticism in particular articulates it, can find a final answer only in the event of eschatological world renewal if God is viewed as love and therefore as the true Infinite. On the way to this goal of world history, from creation to the eschatological consummation, the distinctive features of the trinitarian persons, of Father, Son, and Holy Spirit, will also emerge more clearly, so that the course of systematic theology up to its conclusion in the treatment of eschatology may be expected to offer us a more nuanced understanding of what it means that God is love.

SELECTION **5**

Jürgen Moltmann

"A Trinitarian Theology of the Cross"

Jürgen Moltmann (1926–) is one of the leading twentieth-century Protestant theologians. Although Reformed, his theology has been deeply influenced by Luther's theology of the cross. Among his many works, his book *The Crucified God* has played an important role in contemporary Trinitarian theology.

Following Rahner, Moltmann assumes the inextricable connection between the economic and immanent Trinity. But he argues further that the cross of Christ must be both the material principle of Trinitarian doctrine and our formal principle for understanding it. The shortest summary of Trinitarian theology is the divine act of the cross, where the Father allows the Son to sacrifice himself through the Spirit.

Jesus was abandoned by his Father and died with a cry of forsakenness (Mark 15); God "delivered up" his own Son to an accursed death for our sakes (Rom. 8:32; cf. 2 Cor. 5:21; Gal. 3:13). However, as Paul proclaims, in the eschatological context of Jesus' resurrection (rather than in the historical context of his life), the godforsakenness of Jesus is the saving righteousness of Christ. In this "delivering up" of the Son by the Father, the godless and the godforsaken are spared.

In this event, the Father suffers the infinite grief of love. We must understand this neither in patripassionist terms (that the Father also suffered and died) nor in theospaschite terms (that "God is dead"), but in Trinitarian terms: as the Son suffers death, the Father suffers the death of the Son. Moreover, the Son willingly and consciously gives himself up for our sakes. His will is in deep conformity with the Father's will—a community expressed precisely at the point of their deepest separation, in the godforsaken and accursed death of Jesus. What proceeds from this event between the Father and the Son is the Spirit who opens up the future and creates new life—justifying the godless, filling the forsaken with love, and bringing the dead to life. Johannine theology sums this up: "God is love." Thus, rather than seeing the divine nature as incapable of suffering, Moltmann maintains that "all disaster, forsakenness by God, absolute death, the infinite curse of damnation and sinking into nothing" are taken into the community of divine life where it is created anew by God's indestructible life—God's eternal salvation and infinite joy.

Trinitarian doctrine differs radically from both monotheism (which thinks of God as all-powerful, perfect, and infinite in contrast to humans, who are helpless, imperfect, and finite) and atheism (which rejects this idea of God as a human projection). Rather, Moltmann asserts, to speak of God in Christian terms is to tell the history of Jesus as a history between the Son and the Father out of which the Spirit opens up the future and creates new life for all. Rather than seeking to think "God in history" we must by faith think the "history in God" that leads beyond guilt and death into new creation and *theopoeisis* (being made divine)—the absolute future contained in God's eternal life.

From Jürgen Moltmann, *The Crucified God: The Cross of Christ
as the Foundation and Criticism of Christian Theology*, trans. R. A. Wilson and
John Bowden (Minneapolis: Fortress Press, 1993), 239–49.

Karl Rahner has pointed out that after the supplanting of the *Sentences* of Peter Lombard by the *Summa* of Thomas Aquinas, a momentous distinction was introduced into the doctrine of God. This was the distinction between the tractates *De Deo uno* and *De Deo triuno* and the order in which they are put, which is still felt to be a matter of course even today. The purpose behind this separation and arrangement was apologetic.

Following Thomas, one began with the question "Is there a God?" and demonstrated with the help of the natural light of human reason and the cosmological arguments for the existence of God that there was a God and that God was one. Then, with the same method, conclusions were drawn as to the metaphysical, non-human properties of the divine nature. This knowledge was assigned to natural theology. Only then was a move made to describe the inner being of God with the aid of the supernatural light of grace, a move towards *theologica christiana, theologia salvifica*, the saving knowledge of God.

In the first tractate there was a discussion of the metaphysical properties of God in himself, and in the second of his salvation-historical relationships to us. Even in Protestant orthodoxy, first a general doctrine of God "*De deo*" was outlined, after which there followed teaching on the "*mysterium de sancta trinitate.*" The great Greek theology of the Cappadocians certainly understood all theology as the doctrine of the Trinity. But it made a distinction between the "immanent Trinity" and the "Trinity in the economy of salvation," and thus distinguished in its own way between the inner being of God and salvation history, as between original and copy, idea and manifestation. Karl Barth, who differed from the Protestant tradition of the nineteenth century by making his *Church Dogmatics* begin not with apologetic prolegomena or with basic rules for hermeneutics but with the doctrine of the Trinity, which for him was the hermeneutic canon for understanding the Christian principle "Jesus Christ the Lord," followed the Cappadocians in distinguishing between the immanent Trinity and the economy of the Trinity. God is "beforehand in himself" everything that he reveals in Christ. God corresponds to himself.

Karl Rahner[14] has advanced the thesis that both distinctions are inappropriate and that we must say: (1) The Trinity is the nature of God and the nature of God is the Trinity. (2) The economic Trinity is the immanent Trinity, and the immanent Trinity is the economic Trinity.

> God's relationship to us is three-fold. And this three-fold (free and unmerited) relationship to us is not merely an image or analogy of the immanent Trinity; it is this Trinity itself, even though communicated as free grace.[15]

Thus the unity and the Trinity of God belong together in one tractate. One cannot first describe the unity of the nature of God and then distinguish between the three divine persons or hypostases, as in that case one is essentially dealing with four beings. The being of God then becomes the hypostasis of God, so that the three persons can be renounced and one can think in monotheistic terms.

---

14. K. Rahner, *Theological Investigations*, vol. 4 (New York: Helicon Press, 1966), 87ff.
15. Ibid., 96.

Before we consider this question further, we must also look at the particular context in which trinitarian thought is necessary at all. Otherwise these considerations could easily become a new version of traditional teaching under the changed conditions of modern times, just for the sake of a tradition which once existed. As Schleiermacher rightly said, any new version of the doctrine of the Trinity must be "a transformation which goes right back to its first beginnings." The place of the doctrine of the Trinity is not the "thinking of thought," but the cross of Jesus. "Concepts without perception are empty" (Kant). The perception of the trinitarian concept of God is the cross of Jesus. "Perceptions without concepts are blind" (Kant). The theological concept for the perception of the crucified Christ is the doctrine of the Trinity. The material principle of the doctrine of the Trinity is the cross of Christ. The formal principle of knowledge of the cross is the doctrine of the Trinity. Where do the first beginnings lie? As is well known, the New Testament does not contain any developed doctrine of the Trinity. That only arose in the controversies of the early church over the unity of Christ with God himself. I believe that B. Steffen, in his long-forgotten book *Das Dogma vom Kreuz: Beitrag zu einer staurozentrischen Theologie* (1920: The Dogma of the Cross: A Contribution to a Staurocentric Theology), saw something quite astonishing:

> The scriptural basis for Christian belief in the triune God is not the scanty trinitarian formulas of the New Testament, but the thoroughgoing, unitary testimony of the cross; and the shortest expression of the Trinity is the divine act of the cross, in which the Father allows the Son to sacrifice himself through the Spirit.[16]

We must test this argument, according to which the theology of the cross must be the doctrine of the Trinity and the doctrine of the Trinity must be the theology of the cross, because otherwise the human, crucified God cannot be fully perceived.[17]

What happened on the cross of Christ between Christ and the God whom he called his Father and proclaimed as "having come near" to abandoned men? According to Paul and Mark, Jesus himself was abandoned by this very God, his Father, and died with a cry of godforsakenness.

> That God delivers up his Son is one of the most unheard-of statements in the New Testament. We must understand "deliver up" in its full sense and not water it down to mean "send" or "give." What happened here is what Abra-

---

16. B. Steffen, *Das Dogma vom Kreuz. Beitrag zu einer staurozentrische Theologie* (Gütersloh: Bertelsmann, 1920), 152. On this see H. Mühlen, *Der Veränderlichkeit Gottes als Horizont einer zukunftigen Christologie. Auf dem Wege zu einer Kreuzestheologie in Auseinandersetzung mit der altkirchlichen Christologie* (Münster: Aschendorff, 1969), 33, who also follows B. Steffen.

17. H. Urs von Balthasar, "Mysterium Paschale," in *Mysterium Salutis. Grundis heilgeschichtlicher Dogmatic* 3.2 (Einsiedeln: Johannes Verlag, 1969), 223: "The scandal of the cross is tolerable for believers only as the action of the triune God, indeed it is the only thing in which the believer can boast."

ham did not need to do to Isaac (cf. Rom. 8:32): Christ was quite deliberately abandoned by the Father to the fate of death: God subjected him to the power of corruption, whether this be called man or death. To express the idea in its most acute form, one might say in the words of the dogma of the early church: the first person of the Trinity casts out and annihilates the second . . . A theology of the cross cannot be expressed more radically than it is here.[18]

Consequently we shall begin with a theological interpretation of those sayings which express the abandonment of Christ by God.

In the passion narratives, which present Jesus' death in the light of the life that he lived, the word for deliver up, *paradidónai*, has a clearly negative connotation. It means: hand over, give up, deliver, betray, cast out, kill. The word "deliver up" (Rom. 1:18ff.) also appears in Pauline theology as an expression of the wrath and judgment of God and thus of the lostness of man. God's wrath over the godlessness of man is manifest in that he "delivers them up" to their godlessness and inhumanity. According to Israelite understanding, guilt and punishment lie in one and the same event. So too here: men who abandon God are abandoned by God. Godlessness and godforsakenness are two sides of the same event. The heathen turn the glory of the invisible God into a picture like corruptible being—"and God surrenders them to the lusts of their heart" (Rom. 1:24; par. 1:26 and 1:28). Judgment lies in the fact that God delivers men up to the corruption which they themselves have chosen and abandons them in their forsakenness. It is not the case that Paul threatens sinners, whether Jews or Gentiles, with a distant judgment; rather, he sees the wrath of God as now being manifest in the inhuman idolatry of the Gentiles and the inhuman righteousness by works of the Jews. Guilt and punishment are not separated temporally and juristically. In the godforsakenness of the godless idolaters Paul now already sees the revelation of the wrath of God, the judgment that is being accomplished.[19] In this situation (Rom. 1:18) he proclaims the saving righteousness of God in the crucified Christ. But how can deliverance and liberation for godforsaken man lie in the figure of the godforsaken, crucified Christ?

Paul introduces a radical change in the sense of "deliver up" when he recognizes and proclaims the godforsakenness of Jesus in the eschatological context of his resurrection rather than in the historical context of his life. In Rom. 8:31f., we read: "If God is for us, who is against us? He who did not spare his own Son but gave him up for us all, will he not also give us all things with him?" According to this God gave up his own Son, abandoned him, cast him out and delivered him up to an accursed death. Paul

---

18. W. Popkes, *Christus Traditus. Eine Untersuchung zum Begriff der Dahingabe im Neuen Testament* (Zürich: Zwingli, 1967), 286f.

19. Cf. on this G. Bornkamm, "The Revelation of God's Wrath (Romans 1–3)," in *Early Christian Experience* (London: SCM Press, 1969), 47–70.

says in even stronger terms: "He made him sin for us" (2 Cor. 5:21) and "He became a curse for us" (Gal. 3:13). Thus in the total, inextricable abandonment of Jesus by his God and Father, Paul sees the delivering up of the Son by the Father for godless and godforsaken man. Because God "does not spare" his Son, all the godless are spared. Though they are godless, they are not godforsaken, precisely because God has abandoned his own Son and has delivered him up for them. Thus the delivering up of the Son to godforsakenness is the ground for the justification of the godless and the acceptance of enmity by God. It may therefore be said that the Father delivers up his Son on the cross in order to be the Father of those who are delivered up. The Son is delivered up to this death in order to become the Lord of both dead and living. And if Paul speaks emphatically of God's "own Son," the not-sparing and abandoning also involves the Father himself. In the forsakenness of the Son the Father also forsakes himself. In the surrender of the Son the Father also surrenders himself, though not in the same way. For Jesus suffers dying in forsakenness, but not death itself; for men can no longer "suffer" death, because suffering presupposes life. But the Father who abandons him and delivers him up suffers the death of the Son in the infinite grief of love. We cannot therefore say here in patripassian terms that the Father also suffered and died. The suffering and dying of the Son, forsaken by the Father, is a different kind of suffering from the suffering of the Father in the death of the Son. Nor can the death of Jesus be understood in theopaschite terms as the "death of God." To understand what happened between Jesus and his God and Father on the cross, it is necessary to talk in trinitarian terms. The Son suffers dying, the Father suffers the death of the Son. The grief of the Father here is just as important as the death of the Son. The Fatherlessness of the Son is matched by the Sonlessness of the Father, and if God has constituted himself as the Father of Jesus Christ, then he also suffers the death of his Fatherhood in the death of the Son. Unless this were so, the doctrine of the Trinity would still have a monotheistic background.

In Gal. 2:20 the "delivering up" formula also occurs with Christ as its subject: ". . . the Son of God, who loved me and gave himself for me." According to this it is not just the Father who delivers Jesus up to die godforsaken on the cross, but the Son who gives himself up. This corresponds to the synoptic account of the passion story according to which Jesus consciously and willingly walked the way of the cross and was not overtaken by death as by an evil, unfortunate fate. It is theologically important to note that the formula in Paul occurs with both Father and Son as subject, since it expresses a deep conformity between the will of the Father and the will of the Son in the event of the cross, as the Gethsemane narrative also records. This deep community of will between Jesus and his God and Father is now expressed precisely at the point of their deepest separation, in the godforsaken and accursed death of Jesus on the cross. If both historical godforsakenness and eschatological surrender can be seen in Christ's death on the cross, then this event contains community between Jesus and his Father in separation, and separation in community.

As Rom. 8:32 and Gal. 2:20 show, Paul already described the godforsakenness of Jesus as a surrender and his surrender as love. Johannine theology sums this up in the sentence: "God so loved the world that he gave his only-begotten Son that all who believe in him should not perish but have everlasting life" (3:16). And 1 John sees the very existence of God himself in this event of love on the cross of Christ: "God is love" (4:16). In other words, God does not just love as he is angry, chooses or rejects. He is love, that is, he exists in love. He constitutes his existence in the event of his love. He exists as love in the event of the cross. Thus in the concepts of earlier systematic theology it is possible to talk of a *homoousion*, in respect of an identity of substance, the community of will of the Father and the Son on the cross. However, the unity contains not only identity of substance but also the wholly and utterly different character and inequality of the event on the cross. In the cross, Father and Son are most deeply separated in forsakenness and at the same time are most inwardly one in their surrender.[20] What proceeds from this event between Father and Son is the Spirit which justifies the godless, fills the forsaken with love and even brings the dead alive, since even the fact that they are dead cannot exclude them from this event of the cross; the death in God also includes them.

In this way we have already used trinitarian phrases to understand what happened on the cross between Jesus and his God and Father. If one wanted to present the event within the framework of the doctrine of two natures, one could only use the simple concept of God (*esse simplex*). In that case one would have to say: what happened on the cross was an event between God and God. It was a deep division in God himself, in so far as God abandoned God and contradicted himself, and at the same time a unity in God, in so far as God was at one with God and corresponded to himself. In that case one would have to put the formula in a paradoxical way: God died the death of the godless on the cross and yet did not die. God is dead and yet is not dead. If one can only use the simple concept of God from the doctrine of two natures, as tradition shows, one will always be inclined to restrict it to the person of the Father who abandons and accepts Jesus, delivers him and raises him up, and in so doing will "evacuate" the cross of deity. But if one begins by leaving on one side any concept of God which is already presupposed and taken from metaphysics, one must speak of the one whom Jesus called "Father" and in respect of whom he understood himself as "the Son." In that case one will understand the deadly aspect of the event between the Father who forsakes and the Son who is forsaken, and conversely the living aspect of the event between the

---

20. H. Mühlen, op. cit., 32.

Father who loves and the Son who loves. The Son suffers in his love being forsaken by the Father as he dies. The Father suffers in his love the grief of the death of the Son. In that case, whatever proceeds from the event between the Father and the Son must be understood as the spirit of the surrender of the Father and the Son, as the spirit which creates love for forsaken men, as the spirit which brings the dead alive. It is the unconditioned and therefore boundless love which proceeds from the grief of the Father and the dying of the Son and reaches forsaken men in order to create in them the possibility and the force of new life. The doctrine of two natures must understand the event of the cross statically as a reciprocal relationship between two qualitatively different natures, the divine nature which is incapable of suffering and the human nature which is capable of suffering. Here we have interpreted the event of the cross in trinitarian terms as an event concerned with a relationship between persons in which these persons constitute themselves in their relationship with each other. In so doing we have not just seen one person of the Trinity suffer in the event of the cross, as though the Trinity were already present in itself, in the divine nature. And we have not interpreted the death of Jesus as a divine-human event, but as a trinitarian event between the Son and the Father. What is in question in the relationship of Christ to his Father is not his divinity and humanity and their relationship to each other but the total, personal aspect of the Sonship of Jesus. This starting point is not the same as that to be found in the tradition. It overcomes the dichotomy between immanent and economic Trinity, and that between the nature of God and his inner tri-unity. It makes trinitarian thought necessary for the complete perception of the cross of Christ.

Faith understands the historical event between the Father who forsakes and the Son who is forsaken on the cross in eschatological terms as an event between the Father who loves and the Son who is loved in the present spirit of the love that creates life.

If the cross of Jesus is understood as a divine event, i.e. as an event between Jesus and his God and Father, it is necessary to speak in trinitarian terms of the Son and the Father and the Spirit. In that case the doctrine of the Trinity is no longer an exorbitant and impractical speculation about God, but is nothing other than a shorter version of the passion narrative of Christ in its significance for the eschatological freedom of faith and the life of oppressed nature. It protects faith from both monotheism and atheism because it keeps believers at the cross. The content of the doctrine of the Trinity is the real cross of Christ himself. The form of the crucified Christ is the Trinity. In that case, what is salvation? Only if all disaster, forsakenness by God, absolute death, the infinite curse of damnation and sinking into nothingness is in God himself, is community with this God eternal salvation, infinite joy, indestructible election and divine life. The "bifurcation" in God must contain the whole uproar of history within itself. Men must be able to recognize rejection, the curse and final nothingness in it. The cross stands between the Father and the Son in all the harshness of its forsakenness. If one describes the life of God within the Trinity as the "history of God" (Hegel), this history of God contains within itself the whole abyss of godforsakenness, absolute death and the non-God. "*Nemo contra Deum nisi Deus ipse.*" Because this death took place in the history between Father and Son on the cross on Golgotha, there proceeds from it the spirit of life, love and election to salvation. The concrete "history of God" in the death of Jesus on the cross on Golgotha therefore contains within itself all the depths and abysses of human history and therefore can be understood as the history of history. All human history, however much it may be determined by guilt and death, is taken up into this "history of God," i.e. into the Trinity, and integrated into the future of the "history of God." There is no suffering which in this history of God is not God's suffering; no death which has not been God's death in the history on Golgotha. Therefore there is no life, no fortune and no joy which have not been integrated by his history into eternal life, the eternal joy of God. To think of "God in history" always leads to theism and to atheism. To think of "history in God" leads beyond that, into new creation and *theopoiesis*. To "think of history in God" however, first means to understand humanity in the suffering and dying of Christ, and that means all humanity, with its dilemmas and its despairs.

In that case, what sense does it make to talk of "God"? I think that the unity of the dialectical history of Father and Son and Spirit in the cross on Golgotha, full of tension as it is, can be described so to speak retrospectively as "God." In that case, a trinitarian theology of the cross no longer interprets the event of the cross in the framework or in the name of a metaphysical or moral concept of God which has already been presupposed— we have shown that this does not do justice to the cross, but evacuates it of meaning—but develops from this history what is to be understood by "God." Anyone who speaks of God in Christian terms must tell of the history of Jesus as a history between the Son and the Father. In that case, "God" is not another nature or a heavenly person or a moral authority, but in fact an "event."[21] However, it is not the event of co-humanity, but the event of Golgotha, the event of the love of the Son and the grief of the Father from which the Spirit who opens up the future and creates life in fact derives.

In that case, is there no "personal God"? If "God" is an event, can one pray to him? One cannot pray to an "event." In that case there is in fact no

---

21. I have taken over this expression from H. Braun. According to his Greek understanding of God, God (more accurately, the divine) "happens" where one man helps another. However, this can only be applied in a very loose way to the Christian understanding of the Holy Spirit and quickly succumbs to popular Ritschlianism.

"personal God" as a person projected in heaven. But there are persons in God: the Son, the Father and the Spirit. In that case one does not simply pray to God as a heavenly Thou, but prays in God. One does not pray to an event but in this event. One prays through the Son to the Father in the Spirit. In the brotherhood of Jesus, the person who prays has access to the Fatherhood of the Father and to the Spirit of hope. Only in this way does the character of Christian prayer become clear. The New Testament made a very neat distinction in Christian prayer between the Son and the Father. We ought to take that up, and ought not to speak of "God" in such an undifferentiated way, thus opening up the way to atheism.

"God is love," says 1 John 4:16. Thus in view of all that has been said, the doctrine of the Trinity can be understood as an interpretation of the ground, the event and the experience of that love in which the one who has been condemned to love finds new possibility for life because he has found in it the grace of the impossibility of the death of rejection. It is not the interpretation of love as an ideal, a heavenly power or as a command-ment, but of love as an event in a loveless, legalistic world: the event of an unconditioned and boundless love which comes to meet man, which takes hold of those who are unloved and forsaken, unrighteous or outside the law, and gives them a new identity, liberates them from the norms of social identifications and from the guardians of social norms and idola-trous images. What Jesus commanded in the Sermon on the Mount as love of one's enemy has taken place on the cross through Jesus' dying and the grief of the Father in the power of the spirit, for the godless and the loveless. Just as the unconditional love of Jesus for the rejected made the Pharisees his enemies and brought him to the cross, so unconditional love also means enmity and persecution in a world in which the life of man is made dependent on particular social norms, conditions and achieve-ments. A love which takes precedence and robs these conditions of their force is folly and scandal in this world. But if the believer experiences his freedom and the new possibility of his life in the fact that the love of God reaches him, the loveless and the unloved, in the cross of Christ, what must be the thoughts of a theology which corresponds to this love? In that case it is a love which creates its own conditions, since it cannot accept the conditions of lovelessness and the law. Further, it cannot command love and counterlove. As its purpose is freedom, it is directed towards freedom. So it cannot prohibit slavery and enmity, but must suffer this contradic-tion, and can only take upon itself grief at this contradiction and the grief of protest against it, and manifest this grief in protest. That is what hap-pened on the cross of Christ. God is unconditional love, because he takes on himself grief at the contradiction in men and does not angrily suppress this contradiction. God allows himself to be forced out. God suffers, God allows himself to be crucified and is crucified, and in this consummates his unconditional love that is so full of hope. But that means that in the cross he becomes himself the condition of this love. The loving Father has a parallel in the loving Son and in the Spirit creates similar patterns of love in man in revolt. The fact of this love can be contradicted. It can be crucified, but in crucifixion it finds its fulfillment and becomes love of the enemy. Thus its suffering proves to be stronger than hate. Its might is powerful in weakness and gains power over its enemies in grief, because it gives life even to its enemies and opens up the future to change. If in the freedom given through experience of it the believer understands the crucifixion as an event of the love of the Son and the grief of the Father, that is, as an event between God and God, as an event within the Trinity, he perceives the liberating word of love which creates new life. By the death of the Son he is taken up into the grief of the Father and experiences a liberation which is a new element in this de-divinized and legalistic world, which is itself even a new element over against the original creation of the word. He is in fact taken up into the inner life of God, if in the cross of Christ he experiences the love of God for the godless, the enemies, in so far as the history of Christ is the inner life of God himself. In that case, if he lives in this love, he lives in God and God in him. If he lives in this freedom, he lives in God and God in him. If one conceives of the Trinity as an event of love in the suffering and the death of Jesus—and that is something which faith must do—then the Trinity is no self-contained group in heaven, but an eschatological process open for men on earth, which stems from the cross of Christ. By the secular cross on Golgotha, understood as open vulnerability and as the love of God for loveless and unloved, dehumanized men, God's being and God's life is open to true man. There is no "outside the gate" with God (W. Borchert), if God himself is the one who died outside the gate on Golgotha for those who are outside.

SELECTION **6**

Hans Urs von Balthasar

"The Cross and the Trinity"

Hans Urs von Balthasar (1905–1988) was a Swiss theologian and priest who (along with Bernard Lonergan and Karl Rahner) is considered one of the most important Roman Catholic theologians of the twentieth century. Influenced by Karl Barth and by the early church fathers (especially Irenaeus, Origen, Gregory of Nyssa, Augustine, and Maximus the Confessor), von Balthasar provides a Trinitarian framework for a comprehensive doctrine of salvation. In doing so, he seeks to encompass five motifs: (1) the *Son's self-surrender*, by which he gives himself through God the Father for the world's salvation; (2) the *commercium* ("exchange") whereby Jesus, as the sinless one, "changes places" with sinners (2 Cor. 5:21; Gal. 3:13); (3) the *redemption, understood as liberation and ransom,* that occurs when we are set free by Jesus from sin, death, and demonic power; (4) our *initiation into Trinitarian life* through the gift of grace that brings about our adoption as children of God and divinization; and finally (5) how all of this results from the divine initiative of love in the *Father's Trinitarian, self-giving surrender.*

In depicting the five motifs, Von Balthasar radicalizes the early church idea of the "exchange"—that in the incarnation God becomes human so that we could be divinized—by following modern accounts of the atonement (since Luther and Hegel) that draw out its full implications: Christ not only took on human finitude and death but also literally was "made sin" for our sakes (2 Cor. 5:21; Gal. 3:13). Nonetheless, in doing so, he seeks to "walk on a knife edge" in depicting the relationship between the "economic" Trinity (God in salvation history) and the "immanent" Trinity (the inner triune life). On one side, von Balthasar excludes (in line with the negative theology of the early church) any notion that God *has to* be involved in the world process (thus he excludes any "tragic mythology" within the divine life). On the other, he affirms (in line with what is revealed in the economy of salvation) that, indeed, "something happens in God" that not only justifies all suffering but also entails Christ's vicariously taking on human sin (i.e., human "God-lessness").

Thus, the precondition and source of the world's salvation lies in the infinite *distance* between the Father and the Son as the Son is "forsaken" by the Father in taking on our sin—a distance that is sustained by their even more profound *unity* through the Holy Spirit. Reading back from the cross to the covenant (both to Israel and through Jesus) on to our creation, von Balthasar argues that God's omnipotence is enacted as God's powerlessness. Not only does the Father give the Son an equal divine freedom, but through the Son (in creation and covenant) God also gives human creatures, made in the image of God, a genuine freedom. In this way, human freedom and its sinful perversion are always only enacted within the Son's *eucharistia* (self-giving) on the cross—the true precondition for any possible and real world.

From *Theo-Drama: Theological Dramatic Theory,* vol. 4, trans.
Graham Harrison (San Francisco: Ignatius Press, 1994), 319–32.

a. The Immanent and the Economic Trinity

Scripture clearly says that the events of the Cross can only be interpreted against the background of the Trinity and through faith; this is the thrust of its first and fifth motifs, namely, that God (the Father) gave up his Son out of love for the world and that all the Son's suffering, up to and including his being forsaken by God, is to be attributed to this same love. All soteriology must therefore start from this point. Of course, we must not leave consideration of the Hypostatic Union aside, for how could the man Jesus have borne away the world's sin, except as God? But Jesus understands his "hour" as something given him by the Father; it is only on the basis of this "hour" that the Spirit will be set loose in and for the world.

It is only from the Cross and in the context of the Son's forsakenness that the latter's distance from the Father is fully revealed; when the unity between them is exposed, the uniting Spirit, their "We," actually appears in the form of mere distance. The surrendered Son, in bearing sin, that is, what is simply alien to God, appears to have lost the Father; so it seems as if this revelation of the "economic" Trinity brings out, for the first time, the whole seriousness of the "immanent" Trinity. This is why Hegel incorporates the world process into the internal "history of God":[22] the true life of the Spirit is not that which preserves itself from death and dissolution but that which looks negativity in the eye. Many theologians, in attempting to establish the relationship between immanent and economic Trinity, seem to lay such weight on the latter that the immanent Trinity, even if it is still distinguished from the other, becomes merely a kind of precondition for God's true, earnest self-revelation and self-giving.

In K. Rahner, this may be because he sees God primarily in terms of mystery; accordingly, he is concerned to preserve God's inner, triune nature as the mystery of mysteries. In his axiom, "The economic Trinity is the immanent Trinity, and vice versa,"[23] the accent clearly lies on the divine Trinity that is genuinely revealed (uttered) and given to the world in the economy of grace: the Son is the self-utterance of the Father, the Spirit is the Father's self-giving together with the Son. Why not leave it at this (as, at times, P. Schoonenberg has done)? Surely this self-communication on God's part adequately shows him to be love, free and perfect? Why is the Son always held to be not only the *logos prophorikós* but also the *logos endiáthetos* of the Father? Because in the Gospel, says Rahner, Jesus experiences and proclaims himself to be *the* Son, not only vis-à-vis the Father but also in regard to men. That is, he thus distinguishes himself from the latter.[24] Is this sufficient to distinguish Jesus from a mere "advocate of God on earth," particularly if the "late" descendence-Christology of the New Testament is regarded as an over-interpretation? We cannot deal with this question here. On the other hand, Rahner maintains that God utters himself *substantially* in the (incarnate) Logos and communicates himself equally *substantially in* the Holy Spirit. This shows, in contrast to H. Kung, that "the immanent (and necessary) Trinity is the necessary condition for God to be able freely to communicate himself."[25] And, with regard to this

22. *Phänomenologie des Geistes* (1832), 26.
23. *Theological Investigations* (London and Baltimore: Helicon, 1961–1979); *Mysterium Salutis*, 2 (Einsiedeln: Benziger, 1967), 327f.
24. *Myst. Sal.* 2, 359.
25. Ibid., 384, note 21.

"necessary condition," Rahner can only say: "In one and the same God there exist real distinctions between him who is necessarily without origin, mediating himself to himself (the Father), him who is truly uttered to himself (the Son), and him who, for himself, is conceived and accepted in love (the Spirit). It is *because of this* that God can freely communicate himself 'ad extra.'"[26] These concrete modes of being of the one God are not like self-consciousness (in the modern "personalist" sense), for God has only one self-consciousness. They cannot address each other as "Thou."[27] Hence it is only as man, not as the Son of God, that Jesus calls the Father "Thou." The process whereby "self-communication" takes place in God retains a strangely formal aspect,[28] which is hardly credible as the infinite prototype of God's "economic" self-squandering. In Rahner, it is only in the realm of the economic Trinity that the concept of "self-communication" has a convincing ring about it.

In Moltmann, we come across another form of identification, nearer to Hegel. For him, the Cross is not the privileged (and ultimately the solely valid) locus of the Trinity's self-revelation. Rather, it is the locus of the Trinity's authentic actualization. "The briefest expression of the Trinity is the divine act of the Cross, in which the Father causes the Son to sacrifice himself through the Spirit."[29] Moltmann bases himself on Rahner's formula but goes beyond the latter's position: "The 'bifurcation' in God must contain within it the whole turmoil of history."[30] Thus "the Trinity is not a closed circle in heaven but an open eschatological process for men on earth, with the Cross as its origin."[31] So Moltmann is sucked into the undertow of Whitehead's "process theology,"[32] which "overcomes the dichotomy between immanent and economic Trinity, as well as that between God's nature and his inner tri-unity."[33] It overcomes this latter dichotomy, according to Moltmann, since the attempt to approach God on the basis of a "one-nature" knowledge of God actually blocks the path to the genuine, Christian knowledge of God; God is known in the true dimensions of his love, not by analogy, but in the contradiction of the Cross, that is, *sub contrario*.[34] The Son's forsakenness on the Cross becomes a directly

26. Ibid., 384.

27. Ibid., 366, note 29.

28. It is related to Augustine's *imago Trinitatis* within the soul (the ground of the soul, reason, will/ love).

29. *The Crucified God* (London: SCM, 1974), 241.

30. Ibid., 246.

31. Ibid., 249.

32. Ibid., 256.

33. Ibid., 245.

34. Ibid., 69, 32: "God is only (!) revealed as 'God' in his opposite: godlessness and abandonment by God." By contrast, "Man seeks to know God in the works and ordinances of the cosmos . . . in order to become divine himself . . . in pursuit of his own interests" (69). However, Moltmann does not stop at the level of these contradictions; for him, "the basis and starting point of analogy is this dialectic" (28); "Christian theology is not the 'end of metaphysics'"; rather, "it is free to take up metaphysics as a task of theology" (218).

trinitarian event: the Father himself is forsaken,[35] death is located in God,[36] Jesus' death on the Cross is "God's death and God's suffering."[37] The most profound communion between Father and Son is "expressed at the very point where they are most profoundly separated, when Jesus dies on the Cross, forsaken by God and accursed."[38] "In the Christ-event," therefore, in the genuinely Hegelian manner, salvation is to be defined as a "negation (expiation) of the negation (sin)."[39]

Interpretations of this kind, like all talk of God's suffering, become inevitable wherever the internal divine process, "pro-cession," is lumped together with the process of salvation history. Thus God is entangled in the world process and becomes a tragic, mythological God. A way must be found to see the immanent Trinity as the ground of the world process (including the crucifixion) in such a way that it is neither a formal process of self-communication in God, as in Rahner, nor entangled in the world process, as in Moltmann.[40] The immanent Trinity must be understood to be that eternal, absolute self-surrender whereby God is seen to be, in himself, absolute love; this in turn explains his free self-giving to the world as love, without suggesting that God "needed" the world process and the Cross in order to become himself (to "mediate himself").

It is possible to say, with Bulgakov, that the Father's self-utterance in the generation of the Son is an initial "kenosis" within the Godhead that underpins all subsequent kenosis. For the Father strips himself, without remainder, of his Godhead and hands it over to the Son; he "imparts" to the Son all that is his. "All that is thine is mine" (John 17:10). The Father

---

35. Ibid., 192.

36. Ibid., 215f.

37. Ibid., 190, cf. 192.

38. Ibid., 243f.

39. Ibid., 261, cf. 230.

40. The innumerable critical appraisals of Moltmann's work often raise this objection (yet perhaps not often enough!). Cf. *Diskussion über Jürgen Moltmanns Buch "Der gekreuzigte Gott"* (Munich: Kaiser, 1979: Ricoeur [25], Lochmann [33], Denbowski [36], Bauckham [52], Klappert, including an important comparison with K. Barth [70ff.], Miskotte [93], W. Kasper [146f], Markus Barth [161]). Moltmann's reply, which retracts nothing of his identification of the "economic" with the "immanent" Trinity, is unsatisfying. How can we know about a radical distinction between the world and God if the creature (whether in communication with God or "forsaken" by God) does not have a fundamental awareness that it is *not* God? Moltmann may reject the "two-natures" theology in connection with the concrete phenomenon of Jesus, but it remains the inner presupposition of his trinitarian theology of the Cross. Kasper has pointed out that this primary distinction is indispensable (147) and that it frustrates any attempt to equate God-in-himself (understood as inner-divine "process") with God's intervention in the world process. Moltmann's speculations concerning God's freedom are inconsistent—he suggests that the idea that God enjoys freedom of choice is a Nominalist impossibility (170). Questions such as, "Can God content himself with being self-sufficient?"; "Could God be really satisfied to enjoy his own, untouched glory?" (170), show that, for him, considered apart from the world process, God is only an "abstract, self-contained Being" (155) and that he can only be "love" by "doing the good," in the free "overflowing of goodness" (172–73). Hence the really naïve question, "What right have we to say that the revealed Trinity must have, as its presupposition, an independent, 'essential' Trinity?" (179).

must not be thought to exist "prior" to this self-surrender (in an Arian sense): he is this movement of self-giving that holds nothing back. This divine act that brings forth the Son, that is, the second way of participating in (and of *being*) the identical Godhead, involves the positing of an absolute, infinite "distance" that can contain and embrace all the other distances that are possible within the world of finitude, including the distance of sin. Inherent in the Father's love is an absolute renunciation: he will not be God for himself alone. He lets go of his divinity and, in this sense, manifests a (divine) God-lessness (of love, of course). The latter must not be confused with the godlessness that is found within the world, although it undergirds it, renders it possible and goes beyond it. The Son's answer to the gift of Godhead (of equal substance with the Father) can only be eternal thanksgiving (*eucharistia*) to the Father, the Source—a thanksgiving as selfless and unreserved as the Father's original self-surrender. Proceeding from both, as their subsistent "We," there breathes the "Spirit" who is common to both: as the essence of love, he maintains the infinite difference between them, seals it and, since he is the one Spirit of them both, bridges it.

We cannot entertain any form of "process theology" that identifies the world process (including God's involvement in it, even to the extent of the Cross) with the eternal and timeless "pro-cession" of the Hypostases in God. Accordingly, there is only one way to approach the trinitarian life in God: on the basis of what is manifest in God's kenosis in the theology of the covenant —and thence in the theology of the Cross—we must feel our way back into the mystery of the absolute, employing a negative theology that excludes from God all intramundane experience and suffering, while at the same time presupposing that the possibility of such experience and suffering—up to and including its christological and trinitarian implications—is grounded in God. To think in such a way is to walk on a knife edge: it avoids all the fashionable talk of "the pain of God" and yet is bound to say that something happens in God that not only justifies the possibility and actual occurrence of all suffering in the world but also justifies God's sharing in the latter, in which he goes to the length of vicariously taking on man's God-lessness. The very thing that negative ("philosophical") theology prohibits seems to be demanded by the *oikonomia* in Christ: faith, which is beyond both yet feels its way forward from both, has an intuition of the mystery of all mysteries, which we must posit as the unfathomable precondition and source of the world's salvation history.

The action whereby the Father utters and bestows his whole Godhead, an action he both "does" and "is," generates the Son. This Son is infinitely Other, but he is also the infinitely Other *of the Father*. Thus he both grounds and surpasses all we mean by separation, pain and alienation in the world and all we can envisage in terms of loving self-giving, interpersonal relationship and blessedness. He is not the direct identity of the two but their presupposition, sovereignly surpassing them. Hence, too, he is not the mere foundation of a potential "history of God," a God who would achieve unity through the pain involved in "bifurcation" (within himself and/or in the world): he is the concrete, complete presupposition ("prepositing") of this bifurcation. God the Father can give his divinity away in such a manner that it is not merely "lent" to the Son: the Son's possession of it is "equally substantial." This implies such an incomprehensible and unique "separation" of God from himself that it *includes* and grounds every other separation be it never so dark and bitter. This is the case even though this same communication is an action of absolute love, whose blessedness consists in bestowing, not only something, but itself. However, though we may have a stereoscopic view of these two aspects, we have no right to regard the Trinity one-sidedly as the "play" of an absolute "blessedness" that abstracts from concrete pain and lacks the "seriousness" of separation and death. Such a view would lead necessarily to a Hegelian process theology. "Love is as strong as hell" (". . . as death" AV, RSV): no, it is stronger, for hell is only possible given the absolute and real separation of Father and Son.

If, with believing hearts, we are to come to a deeper grasp of the primal divine drama—which is not a matter of temporal process—we must remember this: the Father, in uttering and surrendering himself without reserve, does not lose himself. He does not extinguish himself by self-giving, just as he does not keep back anything of himself either. For, in this self-surrender, he is the whole divine essence. Here we see both God's infinite power and his powerlessness; he cannot be God in any other way but in this "kenosis" within the Godhead itself. (Yet what omnipotence is revealed here! He brings forth a God who is of equal substance and therefore uncreated, even if, in this self-surrender, he must go to the very extreme of self-lessness.) It follows that the Son, for his part, cannot be and possess the absolute nature of God except in the mode of receptivity: he receives this unity of omnipotence and powerlessness from the Father. This receptivity simultaneously includes the Son's self-givenness (which is the absolute presupposition for all the different ways in which he is delivered up to the world) and his filial thanksgiving (Eucharist) for the gift of consubstantial divinity. The world can only be created within the Son's "generation"; the world belongs to him and has him as its goal; only in the Son can the world be "re-capitulated." Accordingly, in whatever way the Son is sent into the world (*processio* here is seen to be *missio*, up to and including the Cross), it is an integral part of his "co-original" thanksgiving for the world. He is delivered up to the world, yet the world is already his, even if it does not accept him. His thanksgiving is the eternal Yes to the gift of consubstantial divinity (that is, a divinity that is equally absolute). It is a Yes to the primal kenosis of the Father in the unity of omnipotence and powerlessness: omnipotence, since he can give all; powerlessness, since nothing is as truly powerful as the gift. Here, spanning the gulf of the Divine Persons' total distinctness, we have a correspondence between the Father's self-giving, expressed in generation, and the Son's thanksgiving and readiness (a readiness that goes to the limit of forgiveness). It is a profound mystery of faith. Thus the absolute is manifest as "We" in the identity of the gift-as-given and the gift-as-received in thanksgiving, which can only be such by attesting, maintaining and fueling the infinite distinction between Father and Son. Thus, within the distinction, the gift is not only the presupposition of an unsurpassable love: it is also the realized union of this love.

It is pointless to call this primal drama, which is above all time, "static," "abstract," "self-enclosed." Those who do so imagine that the divine drama only acquires its dynamism and its many hues by going through a created, temporal world and only acquires its seriousness and depth by going through sin, the Cross and hell. This view betrays a hubris, an exaggerated self-importance, on the part of creaturely freedom; it has succumbed to the illusion that man's ability to say No to God actually limits the divine omnipotence. It imagines that, by saying No to God, it is man who has drawn God into a momentous drama and made him consider how he (God) may extract himself from a trap he himself has set. On the contrary, it is the drama of the "emptying" of the Father's heart, in the generation of the Son, that contains and surpasses all possible drama between God and a world. For any world only has its place within that distinction between Father and Son that is maintained and bridged by the Holy Spirit. The drama of the Trinity lasts forever: the Father was never without the Son, nor were Father and Son ever without the Spirit. Everything temporal takes place within the embrace of the eternal action and as its consequence (hence *opera trinitatis ad extra communia*). So it is unnecessary—in fact, it is nonsense to imagine a point of time within infinity when the triune God decides to create a world.[41]

We are not saying that the eternal separation in God is, in itself, "tragic" or that the Spirit's bridging of the distinction is the sublation of tragedy, that is, "comedy." Nor are we saying, in a Hegelian sense, that the trinitarian drama needs to pass through the contradictions of the world in order to go beyond the "play," to go beyond the "abstract," and become serious and concrete. Rather, we approach the mystery from two sides, that is, from that of negative theology, which excludes as "mythology" any notion that God has to be involved in the world process; and from the point of view of the world drama, the possibilities of which must be grounded in God. In pursuing these paths, we are led by the hand through the trinitarian

---

41. This renders questionable Moltmann's assertion: "By assuming that God makes a decision with regard to himself (that is, to create a world), one is projecting time into God's eternity, for every 'decision' is characterized by the before-and-after structure of time." "Antwort auf die Kritik an 'Der gekreuzigte Gott'" in *Diskussion* (see previous note), 171–72.

passages of Scripture, particularly John, whose writings are most transparent to the Trinity. It is irrelevant to suggest that the Father's generation of the Son involves no risk and is therefore "undramatic": a world that is full of risks can only be created within the Son's *processio* (prolonged as *missio*); this shows that every "risk" on God's part is undergirded by, and enabled by, the power-less power of the divine self-giving. We cannot say that the Father is involved in "risk" by allowing his Son to go to the Cross, as if only then could he be sure of the earnestness of the Son's indebtedness and gratitude. However, if we ask whether there is suffering in God, the answer is this: there is something in God that can develop into suffering. This suffering occurs when the recklessness with which the Father gives away himself (and all that is his) encounters a freedom that, instead of responding in kind to this magnanimity, changes it into a calculating, cautious self-preservation. This contrasts with the essentially divine recklessness of the Son, who allows himself to be squandered, and of the Spirit who accompanies him.

b. The Creation, the Covenant, and the Cross-Eucharist

In creation, God fashions a genuine creaturely freedom and sets it over against his own, thus in some sense binding himself. It is possible to call this creation, together with the covenant associated with it—in Noah, and more patently in Abraham and Moses—a new "kenosis" on God's part, since he is thereby restricted, implicitly by creaturely freedom and explicitly by the covenant with its stated terms. He is "bound" in two ways. First, he has endowed man with a freedom that, in responding to the divine freedom, depends on nothing but itself. Like the ultimate ground that cannot have some further rationale beyond it and is hence ground-less—that is, the Father's self-surrender to the Son and their relationship in the Spirit (which grounds everything)—human freedom participates in the divine autonomy, both when it says Yes and when it says No. This is analogous to the way in which the Son receives the autonomy of the divine nature in the mode of receptivity (not, like the creature, in being created): the Father "has granted the Son also to have life in himself" (John 5:26).

The creature can refuse to acknowledge that it owes its freedom to the Creator. This is because freedom has no other origin but itself; it is not "caused" by anything but itself; in refusing, it deliberately ignores the fact that it did not acquire this self-origin by its own efforts. Absurdly, it tries to arrogate divine nature to itself without sharing in the Person who is always endowing, receiving, pouring forth and giving thanks for that nature—and who embodies its self-giving. Man's refusal reveals that abyss in the creature whereby it contradicts its own character as analogy and image, a character that arises necessarily from its position within the trinitarian relations. As a result of the creation, the most positive Godlessness on God's part has produced a real, negative godlessness; the latter is impossible to God because he is always in a covenant relationship with his creation, and particularly because of his formal covenant with Noah and Israel. It is "unbearable" for the rebellious, sinful, self-sufficient creature to look divine love in the face; this means that God too finds it "unbearable"—precisely because he has to "bear" it and it causes him to suffer. Man's refusal was possible because of the trinitarian "recklessness" of divine love, which, in its self-giving, observed no limits and had no regard for itself. In this, it showed both its power and its powerlessness and fundamental vulnerability (the two are inseparable). So we must say both things at once: within God's own self—for where else is the creature to be found?—and in the defenselessness of absolute love, God endures the refusal of this love; and, on the other hand, in the omnipotence of the same love, he cannot and will not suffer it.

We must remember that the creature's No, its wanting to be autonomous without acknowledging its origin, must be located within the Son's all-embracing Yes to the Father, in the Spirit; it is the refusal to participate in the autonomy with which the Son is endowed. This negation, however, is restriction: it is the refusal to follow truth to the very end. It is the lie, which only exists by courtesy of the truth and has already been overtaken by it. For the Son, following truth to the end means making a fitting response to the Father's total gift of himself [42] by freely and thankfully allowing himself to be poured forth by the Father, a response that is made in absolute spontaneity and in absolute "obedience" to the Father (and "obedience" here means the readiness to respond and correspond to the Father). Both take place in a generous, eucharistic availability (*Gelöstheit*) that matches the limitless proportions of the divine nature. The creature's No is merely a twisted knot within the Son's pouring-forth; it is left behind by the current of love.

We can indeed say, as Greek "emanation" theology does, that the Father expresses his own fullness in the Son, so that the Son imitates God (his "world of ideas") in every possible way. At the same time, we must maintain that the Son, in responding to and accepting his Father's self-giving, is ready to pour *himself* forth in any way the Father may determine. Given

---

42. Some object that the "generation" of the Son, as his identification with the "Word" of God shows, is intellectual by nature, whereas the volitional (love) only appears at the procession of the Holy Spirit. This view is partly based on arguments from anthropology (Augustine, Thomas) or from the Old Testament (the "word" that Yahweh addresses to Israel is primarily an instruction). But the latter argument forgets that Yahweh's word to Israel presupposes his election of Israel in an unfathomable love, and the former fails to realize that the entire psychological process of self-consciousness is initiated by the prior address of a "thou": it cannot, therefore, be applied to God, who has no antecedent conditions. In the Wisdom literature, there is a definite link between man's love for the divine word (as Wisdom) and the word that God himself communicates to man out of love; love is not limited to the gift of *ruach* (spirit). In the New Covenant, God (primarily as Father) is utter love, particularly in the sending (the surrender) of the Son. The Son's sending refers back to his coming forth from the Father (cf. the context of John 1:13, according to the reading "*hos . . . egennēthē*").

the plan to bring about creatures endowed with freedom, the ultimate form of this pouring-forth will be that of the Eucharist, which, as we know it, is intimately connected with the Passion, *pro nobis*. This "readiness" (active, eager obedience) can and must also be understood as a spontaneous "offer," so that there can be no question of the Son being "forced" to do something by a will that is exclusively the Father's. Creation, if it is to be free, can only be envisaged and decided upon by the entire triune God; it follows that this decision must be regarded as standing from all eternity.

This being so, we are justified in thinking backward from the Eucharist—the Son's ultimate self-giving—to the covenant that it makes possible, and from there again to the creation that gains its meaning from the covenant. Covenant and creation are not only rendered possible by the Son's "eucharistic" response to the Father: they are "surpassed" by it, since both of them can only become reality within the embrace of the Son's response. This does not rob the creature of its inherent freedom, its freedom to act within the covenant with God; its own ground-lessness is not expropriated and stifled by the "omnipotence" of divine goodness (as in Islam, for instance). Within the Trinity, God's all-powerful love is also powerlessness, not only giving the Son an equal, divine freedom but also giving the creature itself—the image of God—a genuine power of freedom and taking it utterly seriously. What it *does* mean is that, because of the Son's all-embracing *eucharistia*, God cannot be entangled in some kind of tragic role; he is not torn in two, which would signify a persistent, unconquerable hell in God.

We spoke of a first "kenosis" of the Father, expropriating himself by "generating" the consubstantial Son. Almost automatically, this first kenosis expands to a kenosis involving the whole Trinity. For the Son could not be consubstantial with the Father except by self-expropriation; and their "We," that is, the Spirit, must also be God if he is to be the "personal" seal of that self-expropriation that is identical in Father and Son. For the Spirit does not want anything "for himself" but, as his revelation in the world shows, wants simply to be the pure manifestation and communication of the love between Father and Son (John 14:26; 16:13–18). This primal kenosis makes possible all other kenotic movements of God into the world; they are simply its consequences. The first "self-limitation" of the triune God arises through endowing his creatures with freedom. The second, deeper, "limitation" of the same triune God occurs as a result of the covenant, which, on God's side, is indissoluble, whatever may become of Israel. The third kenosis, which is not only christological but involves the whole Trinity, arises through the Incarnation of the Son alone: henceforth he manifests his eucharistic attitude (which was always his) in the *pro nobis* of the Cross and Resurrection for the sake of the world.

Man's freedom is left intact, even when perverted into sin. This has been a patristic *theologoumenon* since the time of Irenaeus: God does not overwhelm man; he leads him to his goals *peithei, suadelā*.[43] This indicates no inability on God's part; it is not that he is uncertain whether he can convince rebellious man. It arises from the power-lessness that, as we have seen, is identical with his omnipotence: he is above the necessity to dominate, let alone use violence. This identity of powerlessness and omnipotence sheds much light on what we have already said about God's "holiness" and on John's use of the term "glorification," where the powerlessness of the Cross and the omnipotence of the Resurrection are seen together.

The fact that human freedom and its perversion are always exercised within the Son's *eucharistia*—since, reading backward from the Cross to the covenant and from there to the creation, the latter is the precondition for every possible and real world—shows the confrontation between ground-less divine love and ground-less human sin: "It is to fulfill the word . . . 'They hated me without a cause.'" But "If I had not come and spoken to them, they would not have sin" (John 15:24, 22). Here, the "light" that has come into the world shines in the darkness from the beginning of creation (John 1:4–5) and "lightens every man" (9).

All this is preparatory to a doctrine of salvation that—by providing what we might call a trinitarian substructure—endeavors to avoid all the one-sidedness found in the historico-theological systems. Now that the patristic "exchange of places" no longer stands unsupported and unprepared, it is not in need of the Lutheran complement (which is in fact just as unsupported). The second motif, the *commercium*, is now firmly based on the first, that is, *the Son's self-surrender*, insofar as the latter is the "economic" representation of *the Father's trinitarian, loving self-surrender* (the fifth motif). In this context, the third scriptural topic, that is, *redemption, understood as liberation and ransom*, becomes accessible. It will be discussed in connection with the motif of the "exchange." Finally, the context also accommodates the fourth motif, namely, *initiation into the life of the Trinity*, which arises directly from the foregoing.

SELECTION 7

Vladimir Lossky

"The Divine Darkness"

An exile from Russia, Vladimir Lossky (1903–1958) is one the most influential Eastern Orthodox theologians of the twentieth century. His well-known book *The Mystical Theology of the Eastern Church* argues that the Eastern church preserved the

---

43. The motif appears in a different form in Augustine and his "*voluptate trahi*" (In *Joh.* tr. 26).

mysticism of the early church in ways that the church in the West did not (after the schism between the Roman Catholic and Orthodox churches in 1054). Synthesizing the theology of the Eastern church, he maintains that Christian mystical experience must not be separated from dogmatic theology: Christian theory must always be practical; it must ultimately lead to union with God—deification (*theōsis*).

Lossky draws primarily on Dionysius the Areopagite but also on Gregory Nazianzen, Gregory of Nyssa, Gregory Palamas, and others, in order to distinguish two ways of knowing God: the *apophatic* (which proceeds by negations) and the *cataphatic* (which proceeds by affirmations). "Apophatic" theology is the way of unknowing (*agnosis*), the rejection of all knowledge (*gnosis*) that attempts to comprehend God's essence. It differs not only from an agnosticism that refuses to know God (since apophatic theology's goal is union with God) but also from the intellectual purification of Neoplatonic mysticism, which seeks to cast off the "multiplicity" of being in order to arrive at "the One" (*hen*) that lies beyond being. The God of revelation, by contrast, transcends even the antinomy between the one and the many; because of the radical difference between God and creatures, God's "uncreated" essence will always remain incomprehensible to us. We can only know God through an ascent toward union that surpasses all understanding, even as it radically changes our hearts and our minds. In turn, "cataphatic" theology describes how God's "energies" descend to us in a ladder of "theophanies" or manifestations in creation. Revealed in the divine names of Scripture (e.g., wisdom, life, power, justice, love, being, etc.), these "energies" are not rational notions that give us a positive science of the divine nature but are instead images or ideas that lead us, according to our capacities, to the contemplation of God.

Throughout *The Mystical Theology*, Lossky maintains that the distinction between apophatic and cataphatic theology is rooted in the distinction between God's unspeakable essence and God's self-revealing energies, a distinction that is central to the Eastern Orthodox doctrine of God. If the eternal procession of persons within the Trinity is manifest in the world through the missions of the Son and the Holy Spirit (in the economy), then it is through the energies—which originate in the Father and are communicated through the Son in the Spirit (and therefore belong both to God's eternal essence and to the economy)—that God manifests himself to creatures. In other words, the energies are what make deification possible. By means of the energies common to the three Persons, the Holy Trinity indwells us, enabling us, who remain creatures by nature, to partake in what God is by nature (through grace). Thus, the apophatic way leads not to absence or utter emptiness but to participation in Trinitarian life. The basis and goal of all theology and spirituality—the "kingdom of heaven"— is not a vision of divine essence but participation in Trinitarian life as deified coheirs of the divine nature who possess by grace all that the Holy Trinity possesses by nature.

From Vladimir Lossky, *The Mystical Theology of the Eastern Church*
(London: James Clarke & Co., 1944), 36–43.

It would be possible to go on indefinitely finding examples of apophaticism in the theology of the eastern tradition. We will confine ourselves to quoting a passage from a great Byzantine theologian of the fourteenth century, St. Gregory Palamas: "The super-essential nature of God is not a subject for speech or thought or even contemplation, for it is far removed from all that exists and more than unknowable, being founded upon the uncircumscribed might of the celestial spirits—incomprehensible and ineffable to all forever. There is no name whereby it can be named, neither in this age nor in the age to come, nor word found in the soul and uttered by the tongue, nor contact whether sensible or intellectual, nor yet any image which may afford any knowledge of its subject, if this be not that perfect incomprehensibility which one acknowledges in denying all that can be named. None can properly name its essence or nature if he be truly seeking the truth that is above all truth."[44] "For if God be nature, then all else is not nature. If that which is not God be nature, God is not nature, and likewise He is not being if that which is not God is being."[45]

Face to face with this radical apophaticism, characteristic of the theological tradition of the East, we may ask whether or not it corresponds to an ecstatic approach: whether there is a quest of ecstasy whenever the knowledge of God is sought by the way of negations. Is this negative theology necessarily a theology of ecstasy, or is it susceptible of a more general interpretation? We have seen, in examining the *Mystical Theology* of Dionysius, that the apophatic way is not merely an intellectual quest, that it is something more than a spinning of abstractions. As in the ecstatic Platonists, as also in Plotinus, it is a question of a *kátharsis*: of an inward purification. There is, however, this difference: the Platonic purification was above all of an intellectual nature, intended to free the understanding from the multiplicity which is inseparable from being. For Dionysius, on the other hand, it is a refusal to accept being as such, in so far as it conceals the divine non-being: it is a renunciation of the realm of created things in order to gain access to that of the uncreated; a more existential liberation involving the whole being of him who would know God. In both cases it is a question of union. But union with the *hen* of Plotinus can in fact mean a perception of the primordial and ontological union of man with God: in Dionysius the mystical union is a new condition which implies a progress, a series of changes, a transition from the created to the uncreated, the acquiring of something which man did not hitherto

44. "Theophanes," PG 150, 937 A.
45. "*Capita 150 physica, theologica, moralia et practica*, cap. 78," PG 150, 1176 B.

possess by nature. Indeed, not only does he go forth from his own self (for this happens also in Plotinus), but he belongs wholly to the Unknowable, being deified in this union with the uncreated. Here union means deification. At the same time, while intimately united with God he knows Him only as Unknowable, in other words as infinitely set apart by His nature, remaining even in union, inaccessible in that which He is in His essential being. Though Dionysius speaks of ecstasy and of union, though his negative theology, far from being a purely intellectual exercise involves a mystical experience, an ascent towards God; he makes it none the less clear that even though we attain to the highest peaks accessible to created beings, the only rational notion which we can have of God will still be that of His incomprehensibility. Consequently, theology must be not so much a quest of positive notions about the divine being as an experience which surpasses all understanding. "It is a great thing to speak of God, but still better to purify oneself for God," says St. Gregory Nazianzen.[46] Apophaticism is not necessarily a theology of ecstasy. It is, above all, an attitude of mind which refuses to form concepts about God. Such an attitude utterly excludes all abstract and purely intellectual theology which would adapt the mysteries of the wisdom of God to human ways of thoughts. It is an existential attitude which involves the whole man: there is no theology apart from experience; it is necessary to change, to become a new man. To know God one must draw near to Him. No one who does not follow the path of union with God can be a theologian. The way of the knowledge of God is necessarily the way of deification. He who, in following this path, imagines at a given moment that he has known what God is has a depraved spirit, according to St. Gregory Nazianzen.[47] Apophaticism is, therefore, a criterion: the sure sign of an attitude of mind conformed to truth. In this sense all true theology is fundamentally apophatic.

It will naturally be asked what is the function of "cataphatic" or affirmative theology, the theology of the "divine names" which we find made manifest in the order of creation? Unlike the negative way, which is an ascent towards union, this is a way which comes down towards us: a ladder of "theophanies" or manifestations of God in creation. It may even be said to be one and the same way which can be followed in two different directions: God condescends towards us in the "energies" in which He is manifested; we mount towards Him in the "unions" in which He remains incomprehensible by nature. The "supreme theophany," the perfect manifestation of God in the world by the incarnation of the Word, retains for us its apophatic character. "In the humanity of Christ," says Dionysius, "the Super-essential was manifested in human substance without ceasing to be hidden after this manifestation, or, to express myself after a more

---

46. "Oratio 32.12," PG 36, 188 C.
47. "*Carmina moralia.* 10: *Perì aretēs*," PG 37, 748.

heavenly fashion, in this manifestation itself."[48] "The affirmations of which the sacred humanity of Jesus Christ are the object have all the force of the most pre-eminent negations."[49] So much the more the partial theophanies of inferior degree conceal God in that which He is, whilst manifesting Him in that which He is not by nature. The ladder of cataphatic theology which discloses the divine names drawn, above all, from Holy Scripture, is a series of steps up which the soul can mount to contemplation. These are not the rational notions which we formulate, the concepts with which our intellect constructs a positive science of the divine nature; they are rather images or ideas intended to guide us and to fit our faculties for the contemplation of that which transcends all understanding.[50] On the lower steps, especially, these images are fashioned from the material objects least calculated to lead spirits inexperienced in contemplation into error. It is, indeed, more difficult to identify God with stone or with fire than with intelligence, unity, being or goodness.[51] What seemed evident at the beginning of the ascent—"God is not stone, He is not fire"—is less and less so as we attain to the heights of contemplation, impelled by that same apophatic spirit which now causes us to say: "God is not being, He is not the good." At each step of this ascent as one comes upon loftier images or ideas, it is necessary to guard against making of them a concept, "an idol of God." Then one can contemplate the divine beauty itself: God, in so far as He manifests Himself in creation. Speculation gradually gives place to contemplation, knowledge to experience; for, in casting off the concepts which shackle the spirit, the apophatic disposition reveals boundless horizons of contemplation at each step of positive theology. Thus, there are different levels in theology, each appropriate to the differing capacities of the human understandings which reach up to the mysteries of God. In this connection St. Gregory Nazianzen takes up again the image of Moses on Mount Sinai: "God commands me to enter within the cloud and hold converse with Him; if any be an Aaron, let him go up with me, and let him stand near, being ready, if it must be so, to remain outside the cloud. But if any be a Nadad or an Abihu, or of the order of the elders, let him go up indeed, but let him stand afar off. . . . But if any be of the multitude, who are unworthy of this height of contemplation, if he be altogether impure let him not approach at all, for it would be dangerous to him; but if he be at least temporarily purified, let him remain below and listen to the voice alone, and the trumpet, the bare words of piety, and let him see the mount smoking and lightening. . . . But if any be an evil and savage beast, and altogether incapable of taking in the matter of contemplation and theology,

---

48. "Epist. 3," PG 3, 106g B.
49. "Epist. 4," ibid., 1072 B.
50. Gregory of Nyssa, "*Con. Eunom.*," PG 45, 939–41.
51. *De Coel. hier.*, 2.3-5, ibid., 140–5.

let him not hurtfully and malignantly lurk in his den amongst the woods, to catch hold of some dogma or saying by a sudden spring . . . but let him stand yet afar off and withdraw from the mount, or he shall be stoned."[52] This is not a more perfect or esoteric teaching hidden from the profane; nor is it a gnostic separation between those who are spiritual, psychic or carnal, but a school of contemplation wherein each receives his share in the experience of the Christian mystery lived by the Church. This contemplation of the hidden treasures of the divine Wisdom can be practiced in varying degrees, with greater or lesser intensity: whether it be a lifting up of the spirit towards God and away from creatures, which allows His splendor to become visible; whether it be a meditation on the Holy Scriptures in which God hides Himself, as it were behind a screen, beneath the words which express the revelation (so Gregory of Nyssa); whether it be through the dogmas of the Church or through her liturgical life; whether, finally, it be through ecstasy that we penetrate to the divine mystery, this experience of God will always be the fruit of that apophatic attitude which Dionysius commends to us in his *Mystical Theology.*

All that we have said about apophaticism may be summed up in a few words. Negative theology is not merely a theory of ecstasy. It is an expression of that fundamental attitude which transforms the whole of theology into a contemplation of the mysteries of revelation. It is not a branch of theology, a chapter, or an inevitable introduction on the incomprehensibility of God from which one passes unruffled to a doctrinal exposition in the usual terminology of human reason and philosophy in general. Apophaticism teaches us to see above all a negative meaning in the dogmas of the Church: it forbids us to follow natural ways of thought and to form concepts which would usurp the place of spiritual realities. For Christianity is not a philosophical school for speculating about abstract concepts, but is essentially a communion with the living God. That is why, despite all their philosophical learning and natural bent towards speculation, the Fathers of the eastern tradition in remaining faithful to the apophatic principle of theology, never allowed their thought to cross the threshold of the mystery, or to substitute idols of God for God Himself. That is also why there is no philosophy more or less Christian. Plato is not more Christian than Aristotle. The question of the relations between theology and philosophy has never arisen in the East. The apophatic attitude gave to the Fathers of the Church that freedom and liberality with which they employed philosophical terms without running the risk of being misunderstood or of falling into a "theology of concepts." Whenever theology is transformed into a religious philosophy (as in the case of Origen) it is always the result of forsaking the apophaticism which is truly characteristic of the whole tradition of the Eastern Church.

52. "Oratio 28.2," PG 36, 28 AC.

Unknowability does not mean agnosticism or refusal to know God. Nevertheless, this knowledge will only be attained in the way which leads not to knowledge but to union—to deification. Thus theology will never be abstract, working through concepts, but contemplative: raising the mind to those realities which pass all understanding. This is why the dogmas of the Church often present themselves to the human reason as antinomies, the more difficult to resolve the more sublime the mystery which they express. It is not a question of suppressing the antinomy by adapting dogma to our understanding, but of a change of heart and mind enabling us to attain to the contemplation of the reality which reveals itself to us as it raises us to God, and unites us, according to our several capacities, to Him.

The highest point of revelation, the dogma of the Holy Trinity, is preeminently an antimony. To attain to the contemplation of this primordial reality in all its fullness, it is necessary to reach the goal which it set before us, to attain to the state of deification; for, in the words of St. Gregory Nazianzen, "they will be welcomed by the ineffable light, and the vision of the holy and sovereign Trinity . . . uniting themselves wholly to the whole Spirit; wherein alone and beyond all else I take it that the Kingdom of Heaven consists."[53] The apophatic way does not lead to an absence, to an utter emptiness; for the unknowable God of the Christian is not the impersonal God of the philosophers. It is to the Holy Trinity, "super-essential, more than divine and more than good" (*Triàs huperoúsie, kaì hupérthee, kaì huperágathe*)[54] that the author of the *Mystical Theology* commends himself in entering upon the way which is to bring him to a presence and a fullness which are without measure.

SELECTION **8**

Dumitru Stăniloae

"The Relation of Being and Operation in God"

Along with Vladimir Lossky, the Romanian Eastern Orthodox priest and theologian Dumitru Stăniloae (1903–1993) is recognized as one of the greatest Orthodox theologians of the twentieth century. His primary influence is Maximus Confessor, although he also frequently cites Gregory of Nazianzus, Gregory of Nyssa, Cyril of Alexandria, Dionysius the Areopagite, and Gregory Palamas, among others.

---

53. "Oratio 16," PG 35, 945 C.
54. "Mystical Theology," 1.1, PG 3, 997.

His style of thinking is patristic, but he also appropriates a modern understanding of personhood and interpersonal relationships in his interpretation of the dogmatic tradition.

Central to his theological vision is Maximus Confessor's cosmology and distinction between the Logos and *logoi*, which he uses to depict how the transcendent and profoundly personal God brings all things into being and calls them to fulfillment. Stăniloae affirms the profound interconnection between natural and supernatural revelation: the latter strengthens, clarifies, and expands the former, bringing believers into communion with God. Drawing on Dionysius the Areopagite and patristic thinkers, he also discusses how purifying ourselves from passions develops into an "ignorance" or apophatic vision of the presence of God as person—an experience that transcends all that we know through our senses and our mind. Central as well to his doctrine of God is Gregory Palamas's distinction between the essence and the energies or operations of God. As discussed in the selection below, Stăniloae uses this distinction to distinguish between what can be experienced but not defined (i.e., the energies of God) and what cannot even be experienced (i.e., the essence of God). For Stăniloae, God is incomprehensible and infinitely beyond us yet also the deep meaning of all things and closer to us than we are to ourselves.

Stăniloae's profound understanding of God as a personal God means that his doctrine of the Trinity is inseparable from the rest of his discussion of who God is and how we know God. He describes the Holy Trinity as the "structure of supreme love." God is love and thus the "divine intersubjectivity," who alone ensures not only our existences as human persons but also the world's existence as a theophany, a sacrament of God's personal presence.

From Dumitru Stăniloae, *The Experience of God*, vol. 1, trans. and ed. loan Ionita and Robert Barringer; foreword by Bishop Kallistos Ware (Brookline, MA: Holy Cross Orthodox Press, 1994), 125–30.

The Eastern Fathers have made a distinction between the being and the operations of God.[55] Saint Gregory Palamas did nothing more than hold fast to this distinction between the being of God and the uncreated operations flowing from it. Nevertheless, while speaking of the variety of the divine works, we can sometimes forget to observe that, through each of these operations, it is God, who is one in being, who is at work. We must always keep in mind, however, the paradoxical fact that, although God

---

55. Translator's note: The Romanian word *lucrare* is translated here as "operation" to suggest its active, verbal quality, but "operation" should not be taken as pointing to a philosophical-theological context dependent on Western scholastic tradition. *Lucrare* as used by the author is much closer to "energy" in the Byzantine context of the essence-energies distinction, but because the explicit word for "energy" is also used in the text, it has seemed better to adopt a less technical approach to the translation of the many uses of *lucrare*.

effects something on each occasion through a particular operation, yet he is wholly within each operation. On the other hand, through each operation God produces or sustains a certain aspect of reality; consequently this aspect of reality has its cause in something corresponding to it, though in an incomprehensible way, within God himself. The operations which produce the attributes of the world are, therefore, bearers of certain attributes found in God in a simple and incomprehensible way. The operations, therefore, are nothing other than the attributes of God in motion—or God himself, the simply One, in a motion which is, on every occasion, specific, or again, in a number of different kinds of motion, specified and united among themselves. God himself is in each of these operations or energies, simultaneously whole, active, and beyond operation or movement. Thus his operations are what makes God's qualities visible in creatures, creating these with qualities analogous, but infinitely inferior, to God himself, and then imparting his uncreated operations or energies to them in higher and higher degrees.[56]

That is why Dionysius the Areopagite sees God as above any name and yet at the same time indicated wholly through many names: "This surely is the wonderful 'name which is above every name.' . . . These same wise writers, when praising the Cause of everything that is, use names drawn from all the things caused: good, beautiful, wise, beloved, God of Gods, Lord of Lords, Holy of Holies, eternal, existence, Cause of the ages. They call him source of life, wisdom, mind, word, knower, possessor beforehand of all the treasures of knowledge, power, powerful. . . ."[57] He sees God in his entirety in all the actions directed toward the world. But he also sees him as beyond all these operations.

All those names have reference to the "beneficent processions" from the source of divinization, not to these qualities.[58]

We only know the attributes of God in their dynamism and to the extent to which we participate in them. This does not mean, however, that God himself remains passive in his simplicity and in the diverse motion we project upon him. It is from God himself that the operations originate

---

56. Dionysius the Areopagite, *The Divine Names* 9.9; ET: *Pseudo Dionysius: The Complete Works*, ed. Karlfried Froehlich (New York: Paulist Press, 1987), 118: "And yet what do the theologians mean when they assert that the unstirring God moves and goes out into everything? This is surely something which has to be understood in a way befitting God, and out of our reverence for him, we must assume that this motion of his does not in any way signify a change of place, a variation, an alteration, a turning, a movement in space either straight or in a circular fashion or in a way compounded of both. Nor is this motion to be imagined as occurring in the mind, in the soul, or in respect of the nature of God. What is signified, rather, is that God brings everything into being, that he sustains them, that he exercises all manner of providence over them, that he is present to all of them, that he embraces all of them in a way which no mind can grasp, and that, from him, providing for everything, arise countless processions and activities."

57. *The Divine Names*, 1.6; ET, 54, 55.

58. Ibid., 1.4; ET, 51.

which are productive of new and various qualities in the world. But we only know them through the prism of the effect they produce in the world. God himself changes for our sake in his operations, remaining simple as the source of these operations and being wholly present in each one of them. "For the truth is that everything divine and even everything revealed to us is known only by way of whatever share of them is granted. Their actual nature, what they are ultimately in their own source and ground, is beyond all intellect and all being and all knowledge. When for instance, we give the name of 'God' to that transcendent hiddenness, when we call it 'life' or 'being' or 'light' or 'Word,' what our minds lay hold of is in fact nothing other than certain activities apparent to us, activities which deify, cause being, bear life, and give wisdom."[59]

We experience nothing from God, in content, other than his varied operations that have to do with the world, which is to say, in relation to us. Beyond this we know that at their basis is the personally subsistent essence, but how it is, we do not know, for it is an essence beyond all essence. All we know in God is his dynamism experienced in relation to the world or through the prism that we ourselves are, a dynamism not subject to any necessity at all, that is, not subject to passion and totally free.

In fact, the human person itself—as subsistence of a being, which, as such maintains the being as an inexhaustible source of acts—does not have a name by which it can be characterized in itself. The names we give to persons (John, Paul, etc.) are conventional. They do not tell what the person is. All other names by which we wish to characterize the person refer to its modes of manifestation. That is why the person himself uses a pronoun— something that takes place of a name—("I") in order to indicate himself. And in intimate relation with the other, it calls the other "Thou." How much less, then, is it possible for the supreme subject to have a name. The name does not indicate the content of the person, instead it limits and governs. But the person cannot be limited and governed by knowledge; in a general way and *par excellence* the person is apophatic. It transcends existence that can be perceived directly. It is perceived though its acts. It exists on another plane, one which transcends existence. How much more, then, is this true of supreme Person. Moreover, the attributes themselves cannot be contained in names. They have a dynamic character and, through different acts, they activate their effectiveness, or rather the inexhaustible simplicity itself of the divine essence is activated under the form of certain varied qualities through its acts.

The qualities of God, as we know them, disclose their richness gradually as we develop the capacity to participate in them. Yet, as a personally subsisting being, God remains always above them, although in a certain

---

59. Ibid., 2.7; ET, pp. 63–64.

manner he is their source. Therefore, we do not err if we consider them in their totality as existent in his being in a manner beyond all understanding and in an inexhaustible simplicity. Thus, as dynamic manifestations of God, they are "around his being," and are not identical with his being itself.

We know the God who is for us, but this knowledge does not show him to us as if this God were to be opposed to God understood in himself.

In his descent to us, God communicates to us in modes adapted to our condition something of what he is in fact, leading us to stages which correspond more and more to himself. In a rational manner, under the form of the attributes, we know, understand, and express him very schematically and generally. But in his operations we know God more concretely, more intensely. Yet, the expression always remains inadequate, and mostly makes use of symbols and images.

In the varied and gradual communication of his inexhaustible content, in the gradual and varied disclosure of the content of his attributes, the infinite richness itself of God's uncreated operations is revealed. Through a new operation or energy we receive an added element or a nuance of his content imparted to us. An attribute, in this sense, appears as the expression of various multiple operations that impart to us a divine good which is, to a certain extent, common to them and which we experience. If, in attributes, the divine being gives us the appearance of having come down to the level of our understanding under a certain number of aspects, the operations make these aspects or attributes even more specific and innumerable. Frequently they make God known to us through experience both in the general aspects under which God has descended to meet us and also in the innumerable, more specific ways in which they are imparted to us at every moment.

On the other hand, the same God in his entirety makes himself known to us and, frequently enough, causes us to experience him through each operation and, through them, the same God in his entirety makes himself known to us as bearer of a number of general attributes. God is good. But how many nuances does this goodness of his not have as we see it shown to us in innumerable operations that correspond to the need we have at each moment and to the needs of all? Through his attributes God makes something of his being evident to us, but this something is made specific within one vast and uninterrupted symphony of continually new acts that guide creation and each element of it separated toward the final goal of full union with him. Through all these God pursues the fulfillment of this plan.

Thus, the operation of God does not appear to us as grouped only according to the attributes which they actuate and impart to us, but also according to the various sections of the plan God follows in creation. Through some of these operations new periods are inaugurated which come about through more climactic acts anticipated and prolonged through operations connected with them. The creation of the world is an operation or a sum of operations followed by the operations culminating in the incarnation and resurrection of the Son of God. Salvation has its subsequent application through a succession of other operations that derive from these. The entire dynamism or movement of creation toward deification has its cause in the dynamism of the divine operations which aim at leading creation toward deification. The power for these acts which proceed from God, and through which creation is led to him, is to be found in God. These acts neither enrich nor change God himself, for he is above all his acts and above all the divine attributes which he manifests through them.

The words which have reference to divine operation can also serve as names of God's being, for it is the being that produces the operations. They can also be new, moreover, inasmuch as the operations are new; nevertheless, some fundamental words still remain at the basis of the new words because in the new operations it is the same divine attributes that are imparted to the world, though these display an ever greater profundity, richness and subtlety. But the mystery of the personal reality of God is experienced, properly speaking, through the renunciation of all the words that point to the attributes and operations of God directed towards us.

Dionysius the Areopagite holds that, inasmuch as we possess the various aspects of our existence through a participation in the participable qualities of God, these aspects can be thought of as being "of themselves." Yet they have a support which transcends any quality or attribute of God that is "of/in itself." Dionysius places "existence in itself" above all the other attributes of this kind, however, and seems to identify this existence with God's essence (*esse—essentia*). But inasmuch as the essence is only really given in a subject, or hypostasis, it could be said that what supports all the attributes of God, in which creatures participate, or the very support of existence itself, is the hypostatic reality or the threefold divine hypostatic reality. "Being in itself is more revered than the being of Life itself and Wisdom itself and Likeness to divinity itself. Whatever beings participate in these things must, before all else, participate in Being."[60] "[The Preexistent] is not a facet of being. Rather being is a facet of him. He does not possess being, but being possesses him."[61] "The God who is transcends everything by virtue of his power. He is the substantive Cause and maker of being, subsistence, of existence, of substance, and of nature. . . . He is being for whatever is . . . . For God is not some kind of being. No. But in a way that is simply and indefinable he gathers into himself and anticipates every existence."[62]

60. Ibid., 5.5; ET, 99.
61. Ibid., 5.8; ET, 101.
62. Ibid., 5.4; ET, 98.

As personal reality, God is the undetermined source of all the qualities which are determined in some way through their procession from him. The personal divine reality is undetermined in an eminent way because it is the hypostasizing of the superessence from which every created essence receives its existence. God can be said to be the tripersonal superessence, or the superessential tripersonality. What this superessence is, we do not know. But it exists of itself; like any essence, however, it is not real except by the fact that it subsists hypostatically, in persons.

As superessential hypostatic existence, however, God is not encompassed by the category of existence as this is known or imagined by us, but transcends it. For all the things that we know as existing have their existence from something else and, in their existence, they depend on a system of references. This points to a relativity or a weakness of existences. He who exists of himself, however, has an existence free of all relativity. He is not integrated within a system of references and he has no weakness at all. He is existence not only in the highest sense, but he is also super-existent existence. As such, he does not sustain existence passively, nor is he subject to any passion or suffering. This is the meaning of the Greek word *apathēs* applied to God; it does not have the meaning "indifferent."[63] The entire life of God is act or power. All his attributes he has of himself, hence not through participation in some other sources. That is why he possesses them all in a mode incomparably superior to that of creatures, for all these possess their attributes through participation in the attributes of God, through his operations.

Very life itself, every existence itself, very wisdom itself cannot exist as general attributes belong to a multitude of entities which themselves depend on one another. In such a case these attributes would not be experienced concretely by any of the entities as *per se* attributes. Their very existence would be an abstraction. Since, in reality, the world exists as a sum of dependent entities, it cannot be—taken as a whole—an independent reality.

These attributes can only have existence as attributes of a unique personal reality. In fact only supreme person—in his own right and in all that belongs to him—can be *per se* "of himself."

---

63. This is what Dionysius the Areopagite and Saint Maximus Confessor call *aschetos*: *The Divine Names*, 5.8; *The Ambigua*. The same thing is expressed by the Fathers through the term *exērēménos* (detached from everything): *The Divine Names*, 2.8, 9.10.

CHAPTER 6

Recent Developments

Nicholas Wolterstorff

**"Can Belief in God
Be Rational?"**

Along with Alvin Plantinga, Nicholas
Wolterstorff (1932–) launched the position called "Reformed epistemology." Drawing on John Calvin's theology and the Scottish common sense
philosophy of Thomas Reid, Reformed epistemology maintains that believers are entitled to their beliefs in God even if their arguments for that belief
are unsuccessful. Seeking to counter the "evidentialist" claim that belief in
God is only justified if there is sufficient *evidence* for God's existence (based
on inferences from other beliefs one holds to be true), it rejects the "foundationalist" assumption (identified with Descartes) that beliefs are either
properly basic or justified by *inference* from properly basic beliefs and that it
is thus possible to specify in advance (based on one's properly basic beliefs)
what would qualify as evidence for belief in God. Instead, Reformed epistemology maintains that believers are reasonable in presuming that their
spontaneous beliefs about God are properly basic and therefore justified
even without evidence based on other beliefs.

In the essay "Can Belief in God Be Rational?" Wolterstorff asks whether
someone who has an immediate belief in God can rationally justify this
belief. Countering the "evidentialist" challenge, he proposes a "criterion"
that enables us to consider whether a person can be rational if he or she holds
that God exists as one of his or her *immediate* beliefs and at the same time
has no reason to surrender that belief. Can such a person still be intellectually responsible? This question, Wolterstorff maintains, cannot be answered
in the abstract. It can only be answered by examining individual cases. People come to believe in God in a variety of ways (from parents, in situations of
guilt or despair, through mystical experience, etc.) and the reasons they give
for their beliefs are situation specific. The situation may arise, for instance,
that a person might be persuaded by arguments that deny God's existence.
But even if one's theistic convictions are proved nonrational, it does not follow that one ought to give up belief in God. Drawing on the biblical category
of *trial,* Wolterstorff asks whether the nonrationality of one's belief in God
(in the face of other conflicting beliefs) may not, at times, be a trial to be
endured—and even suffered.

From *Reason and Belief in God*, ed. Alvin Plantinga and Nicholas Wolterstorff
(Notre Dame, IN: University of Notre Dame Press, 1983), 175–77.

And now at last we can return to our beginning. Can belief in God be rational if it has no foundations? Could a person be justified in believing that God exists (or some other affirmative theistic proposition) without the justifying circumstance consisting in the fact that he believes it on the basis of other beliefs of his which he judges to be good evidence for it? Could a person whose belief that God exists is one of his immediate beliefs nonetheless be rationally justified in that belief? Or is it the case that if our theistic convictions are to be rational, they must be formed or reinforced in us exclusively by the "mechanism" of inference?

People come to the conviction that God exists in the most astonishing diversity of ways. Some pick up their theistic convictions from their parents; presumably it is the credulity disposition which is at work in such cases. Some find themselves overcome with a sense of guilt so vast and cosmic that no human being is adequate as its object. Some fall into a mystic trance and find themselves overcome with the conviction that they have met God. Some in suicidal desperation find themselves saying, "Yes, I do believe," whereupon they have a sense of overwhelming peace. The evidentialist proposes slicing through all this diversity. One's belief that God exists is rational only if it is formed or sustained by good inference— by inferring it from others of one's beliefs which in fact provide adequate evidence for it. In the light of the criterion proposed, what is to be said about this claim?

What our criterion instructs us to consider is whether it is possible that there be a person who believes *immediately* that God exists, and at the same time has no adequate reason to surrender that belief. Or more precisely, whether there is a person who at the same time neither has nor ought to believe that he has any adequate reason to surrender that belief. Might a person's being in the situation of believing immediately that God exists represent no failure on his part to govern his beliefs as well as can rightly be demanded of him with respect to the goal of getting more amply in touch with reality?

I see no reason whatsoever to suppose that by the criterion offered the evidentialist challenge is tenable. I see no reason to suppose that people who hold as one of their immediate beliefs that God exists always have adequate reason to surrender that belief—or ought to believe that they do. I see no reason to suppose that holding the belief that God exists as one of one's immediate beliefs always represents some failure on one's part to govern one's assent as well as one ought.

However, those abstract and highly general theses of evidentialism no longer look very interesting, once we regard them in the light of the criterion offered. One of the burdens of this paper has been that issues of rationality are always situation specific. Once the impact of that sinks in, then no longer is it of much interest to spend time pondering whether evidentialism is false. It seems highly likely that it is. But the interesting and important question has become whether some specific person—I, or you, or whoever—who believes immediately that God exists is rational in that belief. Whether a given person is in fact rational in such belief cannot be answered in general and in the abstract, however. It can only be answered by scrutinizing the belief system of the individual believer, and the ways in which that believer has used his noetic capacities.

Perhaps a theistic believer who is not of any great philosophical sophistication has heard a lecture of Anthony Flew attacking religious belief, and perhaps he finds himself unable to uncover any flaws in the argument. Or perhaps he has heard a powerful lecture by some disciple of Freud arguing that religious belief represents nothing more than a surrogate satisfaction of one's need to feel secure, and perhaps, once again, he can find no flaw in the argument. It would appear that if this believer has puzzled over these arguments for a reasonable length of time, has talked to people who seem to him insightful, and so on, and still sees no flaws in the argument, then he is no longer rationally justified in his belief—provided, of course, he does not have evidence in favor of God's existence which counterbalance these. And it makes no difference now by what "mechanism" his theistic convictions were formed in him! By contrast, the person who has never heard of these arguments, and the person who justifiably believes them not sound, is in a relevantly different situation.

It is important to keep in mind here our main earlier conclusion, however. From the fact that it is not rational for some person to believe that God exists it does not follow that he ought to give up that belief. Rationality is only *prima facie* justification; lack of rationality, only *prima facie* impermissibility. Perhaps, in spite of its irrationality for him, the person ought to continue believing that God exists. Perhaps it is our duty to believe more firmly that God exists than any proposition which conflicts with this, and/or more firmly than we believe that a certain proposition *does* conflict with it. Of course, for a believer who is a member of the modern Western intelligentsia to have his theistic convictions prove nonrational is to be put into a deeply troubling situation. There is a biblical category which applies to such a situation. It is a *trial*, which the believer is called to endure. Sometimes suffering is a trial. May it not also be that sometimes the nonrationality of one's conviction that God exists is a trial, to be endured?

Gordon D. Kaufman

"Christian Theocentrism"

At the heart of Gordon Kaufman's theology is the attempt to understand what faith in God means once we recognize that all our images and ideas of God (both ancient and modern) are imaginative constructs. Moving away from Scripture's personal and political metaphors, he understands the symbol "God" to signify the ultimate mystery that unifies and holds together the cosmic evolutionary and historical processes undergirding human life, drawing us on toward more profound "humanization."

Given this understanding of God, he presents five steps toward the development of faith. The first four are (1) moving from bare "facts" (science, history, and common sense) to metaphysical reflection; (2) thinking of the world as cosmic evolution; (3) discerning serendipitous creativity in that evolution; and (4) moving in a trajectory toward the human and humane. In the excerpt that follows, he discusses a fifth and final step of faith centered on the Christian affirmation that Christ is key for understanding not only human life (and how it is to be lived) but also God (the ultimate reality of human beings). Christ is a fourth category that modifies—and complicates—the three principle categories of monotheistic faith, perspectives he has discussed earlier in the book: God (the ultimate point of reference); humanity (free and responsible beings needing orientation in life); and the world (the context of human life).

Trinitarian doctrine provides a way of integrating christocentrism into a theocentric framework. The ultimate mystery of all reality (the first person of the Trinity) is construed in terms of images and stories of Christ that sharpen what it means to sustain our biohistorical existence in ways that are truly humane (the second person of the Trinity) within the ecology of a universe sustained by serendipitous creative activity (the third person of the Trinity). Not merely a speculative concept, the Trinity is a practical notion that has to do with how life is to be lived. Thus, the move into christocentrism and a Trinitarian interpretation of it entail a life commitment. The classic Christian virtues summarize what this commitment means in the face of ultimate mystery. *Faith* gives our biohistorical existence a center of meaning and value. *Hope* gives us an attitude of positive expectation and the prospect of creativity. *Love* sustains us in interdependent relationships of mutual support. Throughout, this vision of Trinitarian faith emphasizes the interconnectedness of all that is, and in doing so, expresses a *radical naturalism* that affirms that in God meaning and value are inherent to our biohistorical existence.

From *In Face of Mystery: A Constructive Theology*
(Cambridge, MA: Harvard University Press, 1993), 456–58.

In Christian faith . . . the conceptions of God and of humanity are not developed simply in terms of relatively vague notions of humaneness, freedom, justice, well-being, ecological responsibility, and the like, nor in terms of such widely admired human images as Socrates, the Buddha, Faust, the Nietzschean *Uebermensch*, the "common man"; it is, rather, Christ—the historical events "surrounding, including, and following upon" the ministry of Jesus of Nazareth (as I put it)—that is regarded as having paradigmatic, and thus normative, standing in the construction of these notions. What it is to be truly human and truly humane is depicted sharply and clearly and dramatically in the Christ-imagery and stories of the New Testament; these, thus, supply criteria for constructing both a Christian conception of what human life is and how it is to be lived, and a Christian understanding of God—the ultimate reality with which we humans have to do. Christians have developed their views of the normative conception of Christ in many different ways in the course of the past two thousand years, and they continue to do so today. (In our theological construction here "Christ" is understood in "the wider sense" that includes the life of the early Christian communities.) . . . I want to emphasize again that it has always been the centrality which Christian faith has given to *Christ*, in its understanding of both humanity and God (Chalcedon), that has given Christian faith its distinctive marks; working out the meaning of that centrality for the theocentric framework developed in this book constituted the fifth (and final) major step of faith undertaken here.

This christocentrism introduces into the Christian frame of orientation a fourth category, thus substantially modifying—and complicating—the triadic structure generally characteristic of monotheistic faith-perspectives: without in any way giving up its theocentrism, Christian faith seeks to be christocentric as well. But is this really possible? Does not a move of this sort weaken the theocentric framework to the point where it may self-destruct? It was above all through their development of the concept of the trinity that Christian theologians attempted to address this problem, by drawing together the several strands that constituted their understanding of God in a way that insured both its christocentrism and its basic monotheistic intent . . . What is affirmed in the trinitarian conception (as I have interpreted it here) is that (a) the ultimate mystery of things, the ultimate reality behind and working in and through all that exists, is to be construed (when it is the question of how we are to orient our biohistorical existence that is at stake) (b) in terms suggested by the images and stories of Christ (taken in the "wider sense"); these images and stories focus in the sharpest and most dramatic way what is required of us humans if our existence is to become truly humane, and they help women and men discern what it means to be living in a universe in which evolutionary and historical processes have produced and continue to sustain our biohistorical mode of existence, and which, it can be hoped (in the light of Christ), will continue to draw us toward a truly humane ordering of human life within our ecological niche on planet Earth; for (c) this is a universe in which serendipitously creative activity is everywhere at work. Stated in this way, the trinitarian doctrine sums up the central Christian claims about human life, the world, and God; and it does this in a manner that shows the trinity to be a *practical* notion having to do with the way in which life is to be lived (not a speculative concept pretending to set forth the inner structure of the divine being—something about which we can have no knowledge). The move into christocentrism, and into a trinitarian interpretation of this christocentrism, it should be clear, involves a fifth major step of faith—of life commitment—with implications significantly different from those of other monotheisms.

The form of life in which the trinitarian faith articulated here issues can be characterized conveniently in terms of the threefold pattern of the "Christian virtues": faith, hope, and love.[1] These three virtues taken together provide a nice summary framework for sketching the human situation in face of the ultimate mystery of things. As biohistorical beings we must, in the first place, live in *faith*—*faith* in some frame of orientation or other, faith in some center of meaning and value. To the extent that our faith is placed in God—to the extent that we construe the ultimate mystery as God—it is possible to live with a deep confidence in the basic order and goodness and meaning of the world, and of human existence within the world. Faith in God, that is to say, can overcome the terror of historicity, enabling women and men to face both the problems of the present and the unknownness of the future with confidence and strength. Faith does this (in part) through giving rise to *hope* (Rom 5:1–5), an attitude of positive expectation regarding the possibilities for human life that will emerge in the future: the relentless movement of time becomes the gift of openness and the prospect of creativity rather than the threat of dissolution and destruction. This hope, it must be noted, is not some mere abstract hope-in-general: it is the very specific expectation of a new human existence to be lived out in love, in relationships of interdependence and mutual support with our fellow humans and the rest of reality. Thus, the hope born of

---

1. Another formula that is often used to characterize Christian existence is derived from Jesus' double commandment to love God and love one's neighbor as oneself (Mark 12:30–31). Here, however, attention is focused on only two primary objects for love—God and human beings. This formula, therefore, tends to reinforce a long-standing weakness of Christian faith, its tendency to see everything of importance in terms of human relations to God and to other humans, thus not giving proper attention to our embeddedness in, and responsibility for, the natural order within which human existence falls. When this emphasis is combined with the traditional tendencies to reify God into a position of utterly dominative importance, it becomes a poor guide in today's ecologically threatened world.

faith looks forward to a new order in which human life will be in full harmony with the entire ecological web of which it is part; in light of that hope it becomes possible, even now, to begin to take up a stance of love for all that is, what Jonathan Edwards called "benevolence to being in general."[2]

Nothing of the ultimate mystery of things is sacrificed in this version of Christian faith; on the contrary, the mystery is presupposed, and what is proposed here is a way of living in face of it. Nor is an openness to all of reality as it is—our own human reality and the reality of the world—in any respect restricted here; on the contrary, all of reality is to be affirmed, indeed loved. This faith, in its trinitarian emphasis on the interconnectedness of all that is, expresses, one could say, a kind of radical naturalism: not a reductive naturalism, of course, but one that affirms the deep value and meaning of our human historicity as well as of the wider world in which it emerges. In this vision of things meaning and value are no longer something extraneous to the natural order, something that must be super-added to it. Rather, they belong to it "naturally": in human beings this interconnectedness of value and being becomes visible as an empirical fact within the world; in God this interconnectedness takes on ultimate metaphysical meaning.[3] This is a faith, therefore, well suited to bio-historical beings like us. The word "bio-historical," which we have been using throughout to characterize the human, itself suggests precisely the inseparability of being and value in our own human existence; faith in God, as we have seen, is essentially a trust in and affirmation of the religious and metaphysical implications to be drawn from this bio-historical existence which we daily live out.

SELECTION **3**

Clark Pinnock

"The Openness of God"

Along with some other evangelical theologians, Clark Pinnock (1937–2010) advocated "open theism." Affirming that the God we know through Christ desires a "responsive" relationship with creatures, open theism seeks to reconceptualize classical theism (especially its doctrines of divine immutability, impassibility, and foreknowledge) even as its proponents also distance themselves from process theology.

---

2. Jonathan Edwards, *The Nature of True Virtue* (Ann Arbor: University of Michigan Press, 1960), chap. 1.

3. Cf. H. R. Niebuhr on God as the unity of value and being; see esp. *Radical Monotheism and Western Culture* (New York: Harper and Bros., 1960), chaps. 1–2, supplementary essays 2–3.

The following excerpt contrasts a model of God as an aloof monarch—unaffected by the world, unchangeable, and all-determining—with one that views God as a loving parent—responsive, generous, sensitive, open, and vulnerable. The God of the Bible voluntarily creates a world with free personal agents who can accept or reject God's plans for them. Upholding created structures, God gives liberty to creatures and lets what we do affect God. Thus, God gladly accepts a future that is "open" and relates to us in a way that is dynamic, not static.

Trinitarian doctrine reinforces this model of God. As a community of persons, God embodies a relational fullness and richness of being. Not a solitary domineering individual, the Trinitarian God is the essence of a loving community that is open and dynamic. Further, in contrast to substantialist conceptions of God as a "thing," Trinitarian theology depicts God as a dynamic event—relational, ecstatic, and alive. Thus, it enables us to say that God is both self-sufficient in fullness and yet open to the world in overflowing love. In addition to criticizing classical theism, Pinnock also distances himself from process theology because it limits God's freedom by viewing the world as necessary to God. By contrast, Pinnock maintains that God does not need the world but creates it out of the abundance of God's rich inner life. As event of relationship, the Trinity is open to the world by choice and works toward a mutuality in history already present in God's being.

From *The Openness of God: A Biblical Challenge to the Traditional Understanding of God*, ed. Clark Pinnock, Richard Rice, John Sanders, William Hasker, and David Basinger (Downers Grove, IL: InterVarsity Press, 1994), 103–4, 107–9.

Basic Models

Interpretation is a human activity in which we distinguish between the primary biblical data and any presuppositions and interests we bring to the task. In theology, as in science, we also make use of models. Models help us to deal with complex subjects like Christology, ecclesiology, salvation and so forth. We face a great variety of data needing interpretation and are compelled to choose an angle of approach to them. In the case of the doctrine of God, we all have a basic portrait of God's identity in our minds when we search the Scriptures, and this model influences our exposition. What a great difference it makes, for example, whether we think of God as a stern judge, a loving parent or an indulgent grandfather. In theology we experiment with plausible angles of vision and try them out.[4]

Two models of God in particular are the most influential that people commonly carry around in their minds. We may think of God primarily

---

4. On the use of models in theology see Richard Rice and John Sanders in *The Grace of God, the Will of Man: A Case for Arminianism*, ed. Clark Pinnock (Grand Rapids: Zondervan, 1989), 130–37, 167–78.

as an aloof monarch, removed from the contingencies of the world, unchangeable in every aspect of being, as an all-determining and irresistible power, aware of everything that will ever happen and never taking risks. Or we may understand God as a caring parent with qualities of love and responsiveness, generosity and sensitivity, openness and vulnerability, a person (rather than a metaphysical principle) who experiences the world, responds to what happens, relates to us and interacts dynamically with humans. These correspond to the differences Sanders has noted between the God of Greek philosophy and the God of the Bible. God is sovereign in both models, but the mode of his sovereignty differs.

In this book we are advancing the second, or the open, view of God. Our understanding of the Scriptures leads us to depict God, the sovereign Creator, as voluntarily bringing into existence a world with significantly free personal agents in it, agents who can respond positively to God or reject his plans for them. In line with the decision to make this kind of world, God rules in such a way as to uphold the created structures and, because he gives liberty to his creatures, is happy to accept the future as open, not closed, and a relationship with the world that is dynamic, not static. We believe that the Bible presents an open view of God as living and active, involved in history, relating to us and changing in relation to us. We see the universe as a context in which there are real choices, alternatives and surprises. God's openness means that God is open to the changing realities of history, that God cares about us and lets what we do impact him. Our lives make a difference to God—they are truly significant. God is delighted when we trust him and saddened when we rebel against him. God made us significant creatures and treats us as such. We are significant to God and the apple of his eye (Ps 17:8).[5]

We hope to persuade people both inside and outside the church to regard God in this fashion, because we believe it is more biblical and meaningful to do so. Some critics may speak of "a battle of the gods," as if we were advocating a God other than the God of historic Christianity.[6] What we are really doing is conducting a competition between models of God. We are trying to understand the God of Christian revelation better. I realize that reconsidering one's model of God may be a delicate issue for some readers. It may feel as if, when a familiar way of thinking about God is questioned, God himself is lost or has become distant. But the experience of reconceptualizing can be positive. After the initial anxiety of rethinking, one will find God again in a fresh way around the next bend

---

5. The open view of God is also sketched out in Keith Ward, *Holding Fast to God: A Reply to Don Cupitt* (London: SPCK, 1982), chap. 3.

6. See Robert A. Morey, *Battle of the Gods: The Gathering Storm in Modern Evangelicalism* (Southbridge, MA: Crown, 1989). Morey equates the open view of God with what he calls finite godism. What troubles me about this view is not the charge of heresy so much as the distance I feel between his vision of God and the loving heart of the Father.

in the reflective road. Rather than worry about our discomfort, perhaps we should be concerned about God's reputation. Does it not concern us that God's name is often dishonored because of poor theologies of God? How can we expect Christians to delight in God or outsiders to seek God if we portray God in biblically flawed, rationally suspect and existentially repugnant ways? . . .

The Trinity

The doctrine of the Trinity is the centerpiece of Christian theism. The church has always confessed that the God who created all things is one and many (not an undifferentiated simple unity) and embodies a relational fullness and richness of being in himself. Given the fact that Father and Son are persons and that the Spirit is spoken of in personal terms in the Scriptures, it is appropriate to speak of God as a community of persons rather than as modes of being.[7]

This doctrine is relevant to the openness of God because the social trinity is an open and dynamic structure. It does not portray God as a solitary, domineering individual but as the essence of loving community. When presented as a solitary potentate, God appears as the enemy of human freedom and atheism flourishes, but when seen as social trinity, God is the ultimate in community, mutuality and sharing. The doctrine enables us to break with substantialist assumptions about God being a "thing" and puts the idea of three relationally interconnected persons in its place. The Trinity points to a relational ontology in which God is more like a dynamic event than a simple substance and is essentially relational, ecstatic and alive. God exists as diverse persons united in a communion of love and freedom. God is the perfection of love and communion, the very antithesis of self-sufficiency.[8]

The Trinity lets us say simultaneously two very important things about God—that God is (on the one hand) self-sufficient in fullness and (on the other hand) open to the world in overflowing love. It sheds light on God's genuine delight in creatures as social beings themselves and on why he would invite them to share the richness of the divine fellowship as his friends. His love for us is not the benevolence of a distant king but like the tender love of a nursing mother (Isa 49:15).[9]

---

7. The social analogy of the Trinity is gaining ground; see Ted Peters, *God as Trinity: Relationality and Temporality in Divine Life* (Louisville: Westminster/John Knox, 1993); Colin E. Gunton, *The Promise of Trinitarian Life* (Edinburgh: T & T Clark, 1991), chap. 5; Wolfhart Pannenberg, *Systematic Theology*, vol. 1, trans. Geoffrey W. Bromley (Grand Rapids: Eerdmans, 1991), chap. 5; and Jürgen Moltmann, *The Trinity and the Kingdom: The Doctrine of God* (San Francisco: Harper & Row, 1981).

8. On God as three persons in communion, see Catherine M. LaCugna, *God for Us: The Trinity and the Christian Life* (San Francisco: HarperSanFrancisco, 1991), especially chap. 8, and Cornelius Plantinga Jr., "The Hodgson-Welch Debate on the Social Analogy of the Trinity," Ph.D. diss., Princeton University, 1982.

9. Moltmann accents this in *Trinity and the Kingdom*, chap. 6. Like LaCugna, he is sensitive to a relational ontology.

The trinitarian model seems superior to process theism in this matter of the divine openness. It lets us criticize classical theism without moving in that direction. Process thinking does not have a patent on the dynamic, relational and temporal nature of God. The triune God (unlike God in process theism) does not need the world to make up for a love and mutuality lacking in his nature. The Trinity allows the church to confess that God is both self-sufficient and loving at the same time. The problem in process theology seems to be the fact that it requires us to view the world as necessary to God, with the implication that God is not free in creation but necessarily tied to a world. The Trinity, being an event of relationship, can be open to the world by choice and can work toward the mutuality in history already present in God's being.

The Trinity depicts a relational God who is ontologically other and a dynamic world that has real value. As internally social and self-sufficient, God does not need the world but creates it out of the abundance of his rich inner life. This makes God free to create and respond to the world, free to be gracious and take the initiative where necessary. Gregory Boyd writes:

> Only if God is antecedently actual, relational, and self-sufficient in relation to the world can God be free enough to do what scripture proclaims that God did in fact do in Jesus Christ. Only a God who is internally social within Godself can perform the more than necessary feat of opening up this sociality to what is fundamentally other than Godself. Only a God who is socially and self-sufficiently triune as lover, beloved, and loving can take the radical and completely unprovoked initiative to take on within this One's self the full nature of a non-divine self in order to effect wholeness in the whole of the non-divine creation.[10]

SELECTION **4**

Kathryn Tanner

"God, the Giver of All Good Gifts"

Kathryn Tanner (1957–) presents a vision of God as the already-abundant fullness who freely desires to replenish the fullness of life in what is not God. Two principles undergird this vision. The first is a noncompetitive relationship between God and the world. God's glorification does not compete with creaturely experience; the dependence of creatures on God does not take away from their inherent dignity. Creaturely life is perfected in its *difference* from God, a difference

---

10. This is the basic point of Gregory A. Boyd's entire thesis: see *Trinity and Process: A Critical Evaluation and Reconstruction of Hartshorne's Di-polar Theism Towards a Trinitarian Metaphysics* (New York: Peter Lang, 1992), 332–33.

that increases in proportion to the perfection of its *relationship* with God, the closer the better. The second principle, a radical interpretation of God's transcendence, is the precondition for the first. A noncompetitive relationship between God and creatures is only possible because God is the fecund provider of all that creatures are in themselves. Creatures do not compete with God because God and creatures are on different levels of being and different planes of causality—something that God's transcendence implies.

From *Jesus, Humanity and the Trinity: A Brief Systematic Theology*
(Minneapolis: Fortress Press, 2001), 1–4.

At the heart of this systematic theology is the sense of God as the giver of all good gifts, their fount, luminous source, fecund treasury and store house. Like an "overflowing radiance," God "sends forth upon all things . . . the rays of Its undivided Goodness"; "the divine Goodness . . . maintains . . . and protects [all creation] and feasts them with its good things."[11] In establishing the world in relationship to Godself, God's intent is to communicate such gifts to us. The history of the world is God's working for the fuller bestowal of such gifts, each stage of this history—creation, covenant, salvation in Christ—representing a greater communication of goodness to the creature and the overcoming of any sinful opposition to these gifts' distribution.

Corresponding to such stages of increase in gifts bestowed are changed relations with God. The world is perfected by being brought into closer relations with the God who perfects it. In union with God, in being brought near to God, all the trials and sorrows of life—suffering, loss, moral failing, the oppressive stunting of opportunities and vitality, grief, worry, tribulation and strife — are purified, remedied, and reworked through the gifts of God's grace.

In short, God, who is already abundant fullness, freely wishes to replicate to every degree possible this fullness of life, light, and love outward in what is not God; this is possible in its fullness only to the extent the world is united by God to Godself over the course of the world's time. Met by human refusal to receive from God's hands in God's own time, by the creature's efforts to separate itself and others from the life-giving fount of divine beneficence, met by the human refusal to minister God's gift-giving to others, this history or process of God's giving to creatures becomes a struggle, a fight to bring the graced kingdom of God into an arena marked by sin and death.[12] The struggle is won by the same means necessary for increase in gifts of grace: growth in unity with God.

---

11. Dionysius the Areopagite, "The Divine Names," trans. C. E. Rolt, in *The Divine Names and Mystical Theology* (London: SPCK, 1940), 94, 87; see the whole of the influential imagery in chapter 4.

12. This sense of sin (as a refusal to receive from God for the good of creation) and of struggle follow those of Irenaeus in his *Against Heresies*.

The most general or abstract principles underlying this systematic vision are the following: firstly, a non-competitive relation between creatures and God, and secondly, a radical interpretation of divine transcendence.[13] The second principle, as we shall see, is the pre-condition of the first.

A non-competitive relation between creatures and God means that the creature does not decrease so that God may increase. The glorification of God does not come at the expense of creatures. The more full the creature is with gifts the more the creature should look in gratitude to the fullness of the gift-giver. The fuller the giver the greater the bounty to others.[14]

Similarly, connection with God does not take away from the creature's own dignity as the being it is. The greater one's dependence upon God, the more one receives for one's own good. As Karl Rahner makes the point: "genuine reality and radical dependence [on God] are simply . . . two sides of one and the same reality, and therefore vary in direct and not in inverse proportion. We and the existents of our world really and truly are and are different from God not in spite of, but because we are established in being by God."[15] The distinctness of the creature is thus the consequence of relationship with God as its creator; here difference is the product of unity, of what brings together, of relationship. The perfection of created life, the perfection of the creature in its difference from God, increases with the perfection of relationship with God: the closer the better.

This non-competitive relation between creatures and God is possible, it seems, only if God is the fecund provider of all that the creature is in itself; the creature in its giftedness, in its goodness, does not compete with God's gift-fullness and goodness because God is the giver of all that the creature is for the good. This relationship of total giver to total gift is possible, in turn, only if God and creatures are, so to speak, on different levels of being, and different planes of causality—something that God's transcendence implies.

God does not give on the same plane of being and activity as creatures, as one among other givers and therefore God is not in potential competition (or co-operation) with them. Non-competitiveness among creatures—their co-operation on the same plane of causality—always brings

---

13. For a more technically precise exposition of these principles than I can offer here, see my *God and Creation in Christian Theology: Tyranny or Empowerment?* (Oxford: Basil Blackwell, 1988), chaps. 2 and 3.

14. This kind of non-competitiveness as an affirmation of both God's gift-fullness and our bounty as recipients of God's giving is perhaps given clearest expression in the theology of Thomas Aquinas. John Calvin's theology is also notable for this sense that all we have is from God, so that the more we have the more we should be grateful to God as giver. In Reformation theology, however, this principle takes on a negative cast: worry that creatures will not thank God for all that they are deflates reveling in the gifts themselves. So, for example, Calvin, *Institutes of the Christian Religion*, ed. J. McNeil, trans. F. Battles, vol. 1 (Philadelphia: Westminster Press, 1960), Book 3, chap. 15, section 5, 793: "because all his things are ours and we have all things in him, in us there is nothing." See Tanner, *God and Creation*, 105–19.

15. *Foundations of Christian Faith*, trans. W. Dych (New York: Crossroad, 1978), 79.

with it the potential for competition: Since I perform part of what needs to be done and you perform the rest, to the extent I act, you need not; and the more I act, the less you need to. Even when we co-operate, therefore, our actions involve a kind of competitive either/or of scope and extent. Unlike this co-operation among creatures, relations with God are utterly non-competitive because God, from beyond this plane of created reality, brings about the whole plane of creaturely being and activity in its goodness. The creature's receiving from God does not then require its passivity in the world: God's activity as the giver of ourselves need not come at the expense of our own activity. Instead, the creature receives from God its very activity as a good.

SELECTION   **5**

Kosuke Koyama

"Heating the Cool Ideals of *Dukkha*, *Anicca*, and *Anatta*"

The memos and short reflections that were gathered together in *Water Buffalo Theology* emerged out of Kosuke Koyama's experience as a missionary teacher sent by the United Church of Christ in Japan to Thailand in the early 1960s. In the following excerpt, Koyama (1929–2009) sets Theravada Buddhism in conversation with biblical faith.

In Buddhism, the "*arhat*-ideal" is a person detached from all involvements. *Arhat* literally means "worthy one" and refers to a person freed from passions (e.g., anger, pride, fear, fettering ideas, and worry). The *arhat*-ideal seeks to address the three marks of humanity illuminated by the Buddha: *dukkha* ("unsatisfactoriness"), *anicca* ("transitoriness" and "impermanence"), and *anatta* ("self-destruction," which inspires one to eliminate "I," the source of all personal troubles). These three marks, Koyama observes, receive new meaning when placed within the context of the story of the people of Israel. In this story, God is involved in history. God liberates Israelite slaves from oppression in Egypt. Far from being "worthy ones" in the *sotas* ("streams") of salvation, the people of Israel lack *arhatic* concentration and dedication. From the perspective of God's experience of history, humankind is marked by *dukkha* (which characterizes not life itself but humanity's relationship to God), *anicca* (the impermanence of creatureliness), and *anatta* (the destruction that occurs when humans reject God's covenantal faithfulness).

All three marks are *historicized* when seen as marks of humanity in covenantal relationship with God, who is none of the three. Historicization points to the reality of a broken covenantal relationship, whose wound becomes useful in human salvation. Both Buddhist and biblical forms of spirituality address the distance between thought and existence. Yet biblical spirituality seeks to erase that distance not by a spirituality seeking nirvana but by a spirit of engagement in covenantal history—a spirit that emphasizes "attachment" to history (an urgency involved in history), not detachment from history (an urgency freed from history).

From Kosuke Koyama, *Water Buffalo Theology*
(Maryknoll, NY: Orbis Books, 1974), 113–16.

The *arhat*-ideal is radically different from the spirituality expressed in the lives of the people of Israel (the Old Testament) and of the church (the New Testament). God rules history. God's direction is not away from history (detachment—"eyes lowered"), but toward history (attachment—"I have seen the affliction of my people who are in Egypt"). Perhaps this is the basic contrast between Theravada Buddhism and the Judeo-Christian faith: the two histories, the two eyes.

In order to study the theological significance of this encounter, we may be helped by the covenant read to Israel at the time of Josiah's reformation.

> For you are a people holy to the LORD your God; the LORD your God has chosen you to be a people for his own possession, out of all the peoples that are on the face of the earth. It was not because you were more in number than any other people that the LORD set his love upon you and chose you, for you were the fewest of all peoples; but it is because the LORD loves you, and is keeping the oath which he swore to your fathers, that the LORD has brought you out with a mighty hand, and redeemed you from the house of bondage, from the hand of Pharaoh king of Egypt (Deut. 7:6–8).

God saved the nation, "the fewest of all peoples," from the oppression of Egypt. This is the foundation of the faith of Israel. Israel experienced this. Her God experienced this. Israel experienced it as the one who is saved and God experienced it as the One who saved "with a mighty hand." Israel, "the fewest of all peoples," is a stubborn people (Exod. 32:7–9).

They are, as it were, not "worthy ones." They are not really in the *sotas* of salvation and they lack the *arhatic* concentration and dedication.

> Remember and do not forget how you provoked the LORD your God to wrath in the wilderness; from the day you came out of the land of Egypt, until you came to this place, you have been rebellious against the LORD (Deut. 9:7).

Israel is "unsatisfactory" (*dukkha*) to God. This is God's experience of them. Israel's devotion to God is "transitory" and "impermanent" (*anicca*):

> What shall I do with you, O Ephraim? What shall I do with you, O Judah? Your love is like a morning cloud, like the dew that goes early away (Hos. 6:4).

They destroyed themselves (*anatta*) by rebelling against their God:

I sent among you a pestilence after the manner of Egypt; I slew your young
men with the sword; I carried away your horses; and I made the stench of your
camp go up into your nostrils; yet you did not return to me, says the LORD
(Amos 4:10).

In spite of Israel's "unsatisfactoriness," "transitoriness," and "self-
destruction," God remains in a saving covenant with her.

I will not execute my fierce anger, I will not again destroy Ephraim; for I am
God and not man, the Holy One in your midst, and I will not come to destroy
(Hos. 11:9).

This is what is meant when it is said that God does not go away from
history, but engages in history. God's faithfulness is faithfulness directed
into history, even though that history is full of "unsatisfactoriness," "transitoriness," and "self-devastation" as represented by the covenant people,
Israel. God "will not come to destroy" the "unworthy ones." Viewed from
the side of God's experience of history, humankind is marked by *dukkha*,
anicca, and *anatta*. It is to God *dukkha*, *anicca*, and *anatta*. This theological context changes the meaning of these three marks of humankind
radically. *Dukkha* does not simply mean "unsatisfactoriness" of life. It signifies specifically humankind's unsatisfactory commitment and devotion
to God. *Anicca*, in the same way, does not mean humankind's realization
of its existence as impermanent and transitory. It means that humankind
breaks its covenant relationship with God through its changeable and
transitory devotion to God. The doctrine of *anatta*, which inspires a person to eliminate "I," the source of all personal troubles, becomes a useful indicator that when the person rejects God's covenantal faithfulness,
he or she moves toward destruction and the elimination of oneself. The
three basic marks of humankind illuminated by the Enlightened One thus
receive new meaning when they are placed in the context of the life of the
"fewest of all peoples" God has chosen, this strange nation called Israel.
The depth-psychological analysis of humankind given by the Buddha is
now historicized. The agent of this historicization is God who is neither
dukkha, nor *anicca*, nor *anatta*.

Turn to me and be saved, all the ends of the earth! For I am God, and there is
no other. By myself I have sworn, from my mouth has gone forth in righteousness a word that shall not return (Isa. 45:22–23).

When *dukkha*, *anicca*, and *anatta* are placed as marks of humankind in
the covenant relationship with God, they are historicized. In this theological perspective of God's experience of history—in the context of "turn to
me and be saved, all the ends of the earth"—the insight of the Buddha and
the message of Israel encounter one another. This point is the point of historicization. "Man is shot by a poisonous arrow" must now be understood
in the concept of the broken covenant relationship. When it is so taken up,

the incident of wounding by a poisonous arrow will become "useful" for human salvation. That strange "distance" between thought and existence is not, indeed, a useful distance. But that distance must be erased not by the spiritual energy seeking nirvana, but by the spirit of engagement in history. The distance must be removed by the principle of "attachment" to history, not by the principle of "detachment" from history. The poison is circulating! The situation is urgent. Urgency to be free from history and urgency to be involved in history are two different kinds of urgencies. The message of Israel is that "urgency" is a history-concept. Urgency can be truly what it is when it is considered within the live relationship of "covenant." Historicization here, then, means to bring the profound insights of the Enlightened One to Israel's experience of history.

This special "bringing," the Hebraization of the Buddha's teaching, is significant in that it will help us to see the radical difference between "detachment" from history and "attachment" to history. And while it engages in this theological operation, it will clarify also the centrality of "God in history," who is the Lord over all doctrines, *dukkha*, *anicca*, and *anatta*, by the power of God's presence and work in history. The strongly historical God can make use of all weakly historical as well as ahistorical thoughts, convictions, and enlightenments. But the reverse is hardly a possibility.

Then God is the One who gives meaning to all people who live in history. God does not reject *dukkha*, *anicca*, and *anatta* but historicizes them by God's historical covenant-relationship. The new meaning to *dukkha*, *anicca*, and *anatta* is to interpret these essential marks of human life as the factors contributing to the elucidation of God who is involved in history. Beyond-history and ahistorical concepts are now placed in the this-history context of God's covenant-relationship. This must be the starting point for our theological response to the *arhat*-orientation. And this placing does not produce syncretism. It must be, rather, understood as participation of the insights of the Buddha in the Christian understanding of history, namely, that "history is experienced and ruled by the covenant God."

The bringing of *dukkha*, *anicca*, and *anatta* to the spirituality of Israel is called here Hebraization. Before we proceed further, I must make two brief comments on Hebraization.

(1) Hebraization in this context consists of injecting the covenant concept into the Thai indigenous spiritual and religious concepts. In short, Hebraization is "covenantization." There are all kinds of covenants. But here we are speaking of the specific kind of covenant experienced by the people of Israel. Israel's covenant-life is unique in history. It is a theological experience of faith and unfaith, gathering and scattering, salvation and destruction, yet all under guidance of God who rules her history and the world's. Our primary target is to bring the historical experience of the covenant-life of this "fewest of all peoples" to the *dukkha*, *anicca*,

and *anatta* concepts, since this is the greatest message of Israel to the Thai people today. And within this context of the appreciation of Israel's experience of history, we are invited to evolve further theological response to the *arhat*-orientation. Our theological response cannot be based on Japanization or Indianization or Filipinization of *dukkha*, *anicca*, and *anatta*. Theological response begins when we bring *dukkha*, *anicca*, and *anatta* to Israel's experience of covenant life.

(2) Japanization of *dukkha*, *anicca*, and *anatta* would invite fewer frictions than Hebraization of them. The bringing of *dukkha*, *anicca*, and *anatta* to Japanese spirituality would not occasion radical reversal of the original intentions and message of these three doctrines. It is because the spiritual and cultural context in which the two live are basically the same. It is like, to use an image, the movement of a fish from salt water to salt water. The fish may notice some unfamiliar scenes and perhaps difference in water temperature, but basically the environment is the same. It is salt water. Without special difficulty fish can live in the new water. But when a fish moves from salt water to fresh water, it immediately realizes the basic (vital) difference in its surroundings. The change is immense. This is what happens when *dukkha*, *anicca*, and *anatta* concepts are brought to the history of Israel's covenant life. The context is basically unfamiliar and even threatening. It is not a smooth transition.

The fish which lived in the salt water (the thought-world of "detachment") is now loved in the fresh water (the thought-world of "attachment"). When the principle of detachment is embraced by the principle of attachment, the former will inevitably be "altered." But this special "alteration" is a theologically valuable "alteration." *Dukkha*, *anicca*, and *anatta*, by themselves, contain high spiritual values. The "altered" *dukkha*, *anicca*, and *anatta* yield tremendous theological value for the people of Thailand. Insights of the Enlightened One and the theology of the covenant God are mutually related in a paradoxical way. The former contradicts the latter, but simultaneously, the former participates in the latter by supplying the valuable raw material without which theological values cannot be established for the people of the thought-world of detachment. In a similar way, theological covenant-awareness rejects the Buddhist doctrines, but at the same time, it theologizes them and thus accepts them.

Dear Elder Malunkyaputta,
I am afraid that I have involved you in a discussion very unfamiliar to you! Pardon me. It has been more a discussion with myself, a monologue. I do not hesitate at all in showing my sincere respect to the Buddha. He was one of the greatest sages that humankind ever produced. I listen to him. I want, then, to see how I can theologically historicize him. Yes. You are right. This business of what I call "theological historicization" (what a monstrous expression!) is my concern and not yours. For me, what the Buddha said

will be tremendously significant if I place it, yes, all of it, in the context of the life of that strange (and insignificant) people called Israel. I am not speaking of the Israel of today. The biblical Israel is the Israel that attracts so much of my attention. I do not want to ignore the words of wisdom of your Master. I try, instead, to place it in my theological existential context of thinking—the covenant-relationship between God and Israel (and the church).

My sincere thanks to you for opening up my discussion by that wonderful parable. My God is (to say this is pretty hot already! isn't it!?) a "hot" God! This hot God cannot be approached by way of "whethers . . ." God will burn all the "whethers . . ." God burns them, not by the principle of detachment, but by that of attachment! It is a creative and life-giving attachment! (How strange this must sound to you!) I have an interesting and special story to tell you on this point. That is the story of someone who came, chronologically speaking, after you—Jesus of Nazareth. But that has to wait for the moment.

"Let the poison be pulled out immediately. The situation is that of emergency! Speculations must go out the window!" This great spirit of the parable must be deeply appreciated by all of us. In my case this sense of urgency has a special message since I historicize this spirit of urgency and the contents of urgency by placing them in the context of specific historical urgency. The basis which enables me to do this placing is that God "warms" the cool person not by rejecting, but by accepting human *dukkha*, *anicca*, and *anatta*.

Sincerely yours,

SELECTION **6**

Raimon Panikkar

"A Non-dualist Vision of the Trinitarian God"

Raimon Panikkar (1918–2010) was been a proponent of interreligious dialogue throughout his life. A Roman Catholic priest, he was born in Barcelona, Spain (the son of a Hindu Indian and a Catholic Catalan) and received training in Western philosophy and Christian theology in Europe and Hindu philosophy and religion in India.

In the following excerpt, Panikkar speaks of "a possible Christian experience of God" in relation to three visions of understanding God's relation to creatures: a dualist vision (which stresses the infinite distance between God and creatures), the monist vision (which stresses that everything is God), and a nondual vision (which stresses the way God is neither separate from the rest of reality nor totally identical to it). If the wisdom of the East offers the West a nondualist vision of reality, then Panikkar maintains that such a vision offers a more complete image of the Trinity. Such a vision enables us to understand more clearly the reasons Christians worship the one God in three persons and the reason they affirm that Christ, as Messiah, was not merely "a king in the manner of David" but the "veritable icon of Divinity, the perfect image of Yahweh, generated directly by God."

From *The Experience of God: Icons of the Mystery*
(Minneapolis: Fortress Press, 2006), 61–68.

Three Visions of God and World

To approach a possible Christian experience of God, it is appropriate first to locate the place of *God* in human consciousness. Let us emphasize here that we are not speaking of conceptions of divinity but of the more concrete problem of the relation of God to the world, for it is in the world that the Christian event will make its appearance. What is this world that God has loved so much (John 3:16) and that we are then ordered not to love (John 16:33; 1 John 2:15–16; 4:4)? Although these texts refer to two different worlds, when all is said and done, it is the world that the Christian ought to confront. The history of humanity bears witness that human consciousness has approached the relation of God to creatures within three principal frameworks:

— *The dualist vision,* in which God is the "absolutely Other." There is an infinite distance between Creator and creature; there is no way of understanding, as in Vedanta or Thomism, the relation of God with creatures as a "relationship of reason": the unique target of human understanding. Such a God does not deal with human beings, because God is immutable, infinite. We experience God as wholly "Other" precisely because we start with the I as subject of the experience.

— *The monist vision,* which in theological terms would be pantheism. Everything is God, and we all experience God insofar as we all experience things. *Deus sive natura,* Spinoza says: God or Nature. There is no other God than this *natura,* in which the relation between Creator and creature is also that "of reason," but in an inverse perspective. In this context, creatureliness does not imply a distinction from the Creator.

— *The non-dualist vision (advaita),* in which divinity is neither individually separate from the rest of reality nor totally identical with it. The *Upanishads,* for example, present a religious attitude that is based neither on dialogue nor monologue, but on the super-rational experience of a "reality" that in a certain sense "inhales" to the interior of itself.

In the simplest terms, a great part of the wisdom the East offers to the West is the non-dualist vision of reality. Yet this vision also suggests a more complete image of the Trinity.

God is neither the Same (monism) nor the Other (dualism). God is one pole of reality, a constitutive pole. Although silent and hence ineffable in itself, it nevertheless speaks to us. It is transcendent but immanent in the world, infinite but delimited in things. This pole is nothing in itself. It exists only in its polarity, in its relationship. God is relationship, intimate internal relationship with all.

Once this is said, though we still can argue, we cannot avoid a definitive choice either for or against one of these three millennial options in human history. None of them can be refuted, although we may find them more or less convincing. It is quite obvious that reason cannot have the last word in a matter where, as part of reality, its own position is itself under question. Otherwise, reason would divinize itself. Even so, we cannot make an abstraction of the limited human being who interprets reason. Nevertheless, the three visions do seek, each in itself, an interior coherence. Here we have a reasonable argument in favor of pluralism. Certain ultimate options cannot be settled by either the intellect or logic. "God has abandoned the world to the disputes of men," says a text from the Latin Bible (Eccl 31:11).

Conceiving the Divine

In itself, the Christian event constitutes a challenge to both monism and dualism. The principal dogmas of Christianity are non-dualist: Christ is neither uniquely God nor uniquely human; at the same time he is not half-God and half-human. Neither an absolutely "Other" God, any more than a God who is All, fits into the conception of Christ's divinity. Neither monotheism nor dualism is compatible with the orthodox and traditional conception of the *Incarnation*.

The Trinity is as much a challenge to monism as to dualism. If there is one and only one God, the Trinity is either superfluous or no more than a simple modality. If there are three gods, the Trinity is an aberration. And if God is neither "one" nor "three," what does the Trinity mean? Precisely that: God is neither one nor three. God does not allow himself to be enclosed in any number. *Qui incipit numerare incipit errare* (Who begins to count begins with a mistake), says Saint Augustine. Hence it is inaccurate to say that God is three persons. The concept of person applied to the Trinity, to Father, Son, and Spirit, is not univocal (three absolutely equal persons would be three Gods), nor is it analogical. As Saint Thomas says, speaking of three persons is a concession to current language and nothing can be called "three" in the Trinity. If I utilize the word *person*, applied to three persons, and the three persons are not equal (that would be a tritheism), they would then be analogues. But if they were analogues, there would have to be a *primum analogatum* (a primary reference in the analogy), superior and prior to the three persons, which founds their analogy and permits us to apply it analogically to *A*, *B*, and *C*. But if there is a *primum analogatum* distinct from the three analogues *A*, *B*, and *C*, it would be a matter of something superior to the three persons, above divinity, which would permit us to say that the Father is divine, the Son is divine, and the Spirit is divine. The divinity of the persons would be simple participation. But that would be the famous *quaternitas* that the church condemned, or Gilbert de la Porrée's *divinitas*. This was also Meister Eckhart's misunderstanding. His *Gottheit* was precisely the "Father." Both Gilbert and Eckhart were too entangled with the metaphysics of the One.

But we have known for a long time and under almost all latitudes that One is not a number; it is rather the symbol of intelligibility. That is the challenge of the Trinity and of non-dualism. The concept of person in the Trinity, therefore, is equivocal. The difference between the "persons" is infinite. There is no divine nature apart from the persons. It is not without reason that the Greeks in the early church controversies preferred the concept of *hypostasis*. The One is neither three nor persons. We just as well could say *sun*, *person*, and *wind*. But I will not explain now my conviction that the unique divine "person" is Christ. We already have suggested that the Trinity is not a simple, accidental modification of monotheism.

Although the One is certainly not a numerical value, it surely implies the negation of all multiplicity; it is the expression of unity, and is in that way the seat of intelligibility. To say that God is not One means that the rationalizing human mind cannot reduce reality *ad unum*, and at the same time cannot make unity an abstraction. If, in the monotheistic perspective, there is one absolutely omniscient being who embraces and understands all of reality, that is not the case for the Trinity. Nevertheless, there are not three Gods: this is non-dualism. God is not one, but neither is God two, nor any multiplicity. It is only through the constant negation of duality, by the refusal to close the process, in the conscious renunciation of trying to understand everything, in the *neti neti* of apophatic mysticism, that we can approach the trinitarian mystery.

One challenge for the theology of the third millennium will be taking far more seriously than before the mystery of the Trinity. Indeed, what has the Trinity meant until now in the spiritual life of the majority of Christians? They scarcely know what it means, and as a result it has little impact on their personal lives. Nevertheless, the trinitarian vision of reality is nothing less than a human invariant that is found, implicitly or explicitly, in practically all the traditions of humanity. A certain elitist and self-sufficient idea of the Christian Trinity has propagated the idea of a

Christian monopoly in regard to the Trinity, thereby reducing it to a clever intellectual game.

God, the Human, and the World are not one, nor two, nor three. They are not three things, neither are they one. There is a radical relativity, an irreducible connection between the Source of what is, that which Is, and its very Dynamism; Father, Son, and Spirit; *Sat, Cit,* and *Ananda*; the Divine, the Human, and the Cosmic; Liberty, Consciousness, and Matter; or however we might name this triad that constitutes the real. Reality is trinitarian, not dualist, neither one nor two. Only by denying duality (*advaita*), without reducing everything to unity, are we able consciously to approach it.

The discovery of the Christian trinitarian God, which is not conceived identically to the God of Jewish monotheism, even if Jews are able to bring precise nuances to this terminology, is the great theological challenge for Christianity in the third millennium.

Certainly the reasons for condemning Jesus were not insignificant. It was not a question of petty quarrels or envies. In my reading, the Jews did everything possible to save Jesus, but he himself renounced the fundamental basis of the Torah. It was a problem of conscience for Israel and not a plot of scoundrels. Jesus was not condemned for calling himself divine, for the idea of human divinization was neither new nor scandalous. He was condemned for proclaiming himself the Son of God in the trinitarian sense of the expression, as it will be interpreted later: the only Son of God—equal to God, proceeding from God. In other words, he was condemned for having defied the people of Israel by presenting himself as the divine icon without having denied his human condition. In the eyes of the Jews, the crime of Jesus was to have dared to supplant Yahweh, the icon of Israel, by putting himself in Yahweh's place, and it was in this way that the Christians of the first generations understood it. If "the people of God" had refused to adore other gods, how much more strongly should they get rid of someone who dared to affirm that the Messiah was not a king in the manner of David but the veritable icon of Divinity, the perfect image of Yahweh, generated directly by God. The rupture with Israel was consummated by what has come to be called the (first) Council of Jerusalem (Acts 15:1ff.), in the course of which the apostles had the audacity to abolish circumcision, the fundamental sign of Judaism (Gen 17).

But the trinitarian scandal that, according to the theology of the first centuries, cost Jesus his life ended in time by becoming blurred. Some Christian consciences, in an almost imperceptible manner, slipped again, little by little, toward the legalism that Paul denounced with such vigor. This is an important and neglected theme of political theology. The Trinity did not fit in with the Christian empire. Theocracy is more in accord with monotheism. From the doctrinal point of view, the mystico-speculative progress in the approach of the trinitarian mystery was not supported sufficiently by practice and had relatively little influence on Christian life.

The monotheism of orthodox Judaism emerged again in the way Christianity was lived. The God of the Hebrew Bible was identified with the Christian God, and the people of Israel corresponded to "the people of God." For many, Jesus became simply the God of Christians; that is the impression, for example, that Hindus have if they happen to hear the preaching of the gospel. For them, Christians are a people who adore God under the name and form of Jesus.

Our presentation of the Christian vision does not, of course, invalidate other visions; still less does it condemn other religions. Although we are prepared to defend our opinion in the public arena, that would be to reduce the mystery of what we have agreed to call God, if it were indeed possible for us to have the slightest notion of God.

SELECTION **7**

James Kombo

"The Doctrine of God in African Thought"

In *The Doctrine of God in African Christian Thought*, the Kenyan theologian James Kombo uses an African conceptual framework to articulate the Christian doctrine of God. In the same way that Christians used Neoplatonic metaphysics and later German idealism to conceptualize the doctrine of God in the history of Western thought, so Kombo argues for the use of an African metaphysics to interpret biblical themes and Trinitarian doctrine within an African setting. His goal is "inculturation," the dynamic process whereby the Christian message is incarnated in its cultural milieu and that milieu, in turn, is transformed by the gospel.

In addition to appropriating African names and concepts for God (e.g., *Nyame, Leza, Nyambe, Modimo*), Kombo also employs categories from the *Ntu* metaphysics of Bantu reflection. *Ntu* refers to "Being itself," the universal life force that is inseparably intertwined with its manifestations within the four major aspects of existence: *Umuntu* (life forces with intelligence, e.g., God, spirits, humans, the living dead); *Ikintu* (beings without intelligence, e.g., things, animals, plants, minerals); *Ahantu* (the power of time and place); and *Ukuntu* (modalities in which power is enacted, e.g., quality, quantity, relation, action, passion, position, and possession). For Africans, God is the great *Muntu*, who, though constantly experienced, is in a radically different category than any other aspect of *Ntu* metaphysics. A personal life force, the great *Muntu* is the fathomless Spirit, the source of life flowing into indeterminate future.

The African category of *Umuntu*, a personal life force, identifies being a "person" not merely with humans but also with God, spirits, and the living dead. To be a "person" in the African context is to "reveal God"—to exist in the way God exists—and to do so within community, linked with others in space and time (backward to ancestors and forward to generations yet unborn). As the following excerpt suggests, the category of *Umuntu* offers fresh insight not only into what it means to be human but into classical Christian understandings of the Trinitarian persons—Father, Son, and Spirit—and how they exist together as one God. Nonetheless, as Kombo also points out, the God of Christian faith is not merely the supreme vital force, the power par excellence that accounts for all other forms of power. As the great *Muntu*, the God of Christian faith is also the "powerless power," whose power is stronger than human strength (Phil. 2:5-11).

From *The Doctrine of God in African Christian Thought: The Holy Trinity, Theological Hermeneutics and the African Intellectual Culture* (Leiden: Brill, 2007), 238–44.

Inculturation of the Christian View of God

Whereas "Christianization" is significant, the real goal of African theology should be "inculturation."[16] Inculturation as a theological process is a dynamic interaction between the Christian message and the culture of reception. In the process of the interaction the Christian message is incarnated in the cultural milieu of the recipients, and the culture is also impacted and changed by the gospel. The concept of inculturation is the equivalent of the Hellenization of the Christian faith from the second to the fourth centuries of the church. Under Hellenization the church utilized the Greek metaphysics to explain the Christian concepts to the indigenous Greek culture. In the process, the gospel was incarnated in the Greek culture, but the Greek culture was also changed by the gospel. A similar principle is clearly noticeable in Augustine, Boethius, and Aquinas, who were attempting to use the Latin metaphysics to convey the Christian view of *divinitas* to the Latin West. Inculturation as a theological strategy for the

16. T. S. Maluleke argues that positing Africanization as the new task of African inculturation theology, as [Kwame] Bediako does, may not be as ground-breaking as it may seem. He reasons that the proposal is based on juxtaposing Christianization and Africanization (T. S. Maluleke, "Half Century of African Christian Theology" in *Journal of Theology for Southern Africa* 99 [1997]: 4–23). But the concern of Bediako is clearly not to place a wall between that which is Christian and that which is African. The point of Bediako is that the Christian thought in the African context has done well to show the areas of continuity between the African culture and the Christian faith. And without taking away this credit, Bediako now urges African theology to engage in a kind of scholarship which utilizes the African conceptual framework to explain the Christian concepts. This, in my opinion, is why Bediako took such pains to explore the significance of the developments of the Christian faith in the second century to modern Africa. See Bediako, *Theology and Identity* (London: SPCK, 1992).

African context is an effort to use the African metaphysics to explain "the new content," viz. the Christian interpretation of *Nyame, Leza, Nyambe,* and *Modimo* to the African audience. This is groundbreaking, and it is yet to be done.

In order to inculturate the Christian view of God into the African conceptual framework, it is important that we first consider the issue of the referentiality of the God language. According to Christian faith, God is the One who has revealed himself in the Son and in the Holy Spirit. This concept is encapsulated in the traditional theological language or formula, "One God Three Persons." Having understood the referent designated by the theological language, we then seek to have a thorough understanding of the African conceptual framework. Mugambi warns that if this basic requirement is not met, we are likely to have a "mutual misunderstanding which would be difficult to reconcile."[17]

For the Africans, being *Ntu* is not just defined substantially. There are categories of existence such as *Ikintu* or the time aspect of *Ahantu* that cannot be defined substantially. The underlying principle here is that force and its manifestation are inseparably intertwined. God exists in a non-substantial category. Moreover, He is known to be a category of existence that is outside *Umuntu, Ikintu, Ahantu,* and *Ukuntu.* In a way, God is unknown. He is not even as tangible as the wind, yet he is experienced constantly. He is experienced in ways other than "the world of senses."[18] For this reason, some African peoples simply call God "the Great Spirit, the Fathomless Spirit, the ever-present Spirit or the God of wind and breath."[19] Although the African people admit that they know nothing of the substantial nature of God,[20] they insist that this "Great *Muntu*" is "the source, originating in unrecorded time, of stream of life which flows into indeterminate future."[21] Therefore the African peoples do not describe God in substantial terms. In view of this consideration, the term that can best capture the unity factor in the context of the Trinity is the "Great *Muntu.*"

Person (*Umuntu*) in the African metaphysics is life force.[22] This is what remains when a man dies. Tempels calls it "genuine *Muntu* (person)." Tempels says that he "always heard the old men say that man himself goes on existing, he-himself, the little man who sits in hiding behind the outwardly

---

17. J. N. K. Mugambi, *The African Heritage and Contemporary Christianity* (Nairobi: Longman, 1989), 58.

18. [Gabriel] Setiloane, "MODIMO: GOD Among the Sotho-Tswana," 13; cf. Setiloane, *The Image of God among the Sotho-Tswana* (Rotterdam: A. A. Balkema, 1976), 80.

19. [John] Mbiti, *Introduction to African Religion* (Nairobi: East African Educational Publishers, 1975), 53.

20. Mbiti, *African Religions and Philosophy* (Johannesburg: Heinemann, 1969), 35; cf. Mbiti, *Introduction to African Religion,* 53.

21. Setiloane, *The Image of God among the Sotho-Tswana,* 80.

22. [Jenheinz] Jahn, *Muntu: An Outline of the New African Culture* (New York: Grove Press, 1961), 107.

visible form, the *muntu* that went away from the living ones."[23] Personality in human beings is said to be "a tributary of the Supreme Vital Force.[24] To be person is not just to be divine, sacred, weird, and holy, but to be person is also to reveal God.[25] Moreover, to be person is to be in a community.[26] Archbishop Desmond Tutu puts this point well:

> The African would understand perfectly well what the Old Testament meant when it said, "man belongs to the bundle of life", that he is not a solitary individual. He is linked backwards to the ancestors whom he reveres and forward with all generations yet to be born. . . . Even today when you ask an African how he is, you usually in fact speak in the plural "How are you?" and he will usually answer, "We are well, we are here", or the opposite; he will not be well because his grandmother is unwell, his vitality will be diminished in so far as one member has reduced life force.[27]

This understanding of "person" is crucial for theology's formulation of the doctrine of the Trinity. It means that theology relevant for the African context must view person not just as coinciding with "human being." Personality in the African context, as we have already indicated elsewhere, can also be applied to God, spirits, and the living dead. Moreover, we cannot just describe person as "individuals with rationality" (see "God as subject") or as "pure relations" (see "God as essence"). While a person has these qualities, what is determinative is that he is in an existence that is consistent with the way God himself exists.[28]

From the African metaphysics of *Ntu*, the fatherhood of God in the context of the Trinity has several implications. First, it means that we are to continue to view God as "the 'Great *Muntu*,' First Creator and First Begetter in one."[29] The significant metaphysical characteristics of this Great *Muntu* as noted by Kagame include:

> (i) God as an external existent: God does not form part of the four metaphysical categories and, therefore, is on the outside of created or qualified beings—*Ntu*; He is external.
>
> (ii) God as the Creator: God is considered as the existent which puts the existence [Fr. *l'exister*] of beings—*Ntu*—there, and confers to them the property of reproduction and activity.
>
> (iii) God as the conserver [*Consevateur*]: the actual existence of beings is thought to be regulated [begin and end] by his decision.[30]

23. [Placide] Tempels, *Bantu Philosophy* (Paris: Editions Présence Africaine), 28.

24. Setiloane, *African Theology: An Introduction* (Johannesburg: Skotaville Publishers, 198), 42.

25. [Bolaji] Idowu, *Towards an Indigenous Church* (London: Oxford University Press, 1965), 19.

26. Mbiti, *African Religions and Philosophy,* 108f.

27. D. Tutu, "Some African insights and the Old Testament" in *Journal of Theology for Southern Africa,* no. 1 (Dec. 1972), 20.

28. Idowu, *Towards an Indigenous Church,* 19; cf. "God as community in unity."

29. Jahn, *Muntu: An Outline of the New African Culture,* 105.

30. [D. A.] Masolo, *African Philosophy in Search of Identity* (Bloomington: Indiana University Press, 1994), 92.

Second, the fatherhood of God in the context of the Trinity means two things to an African reader. First, it means that the Father is to be understood as the Divine *principium*. The Father is the *principium* of the persons of the Son and of the Holy Spirit.[31] If the Father is the *principium*, then it logically follows that the Fatherhood of God also means that the Father, the Son, and the Holy Spirit share a common category of existence that is different from all other beings. It is not only the Father who does not belong to the series of objects for which the African cosmology developed categories; the Son and the Holy Spirit are also not part of the four metaphysical categories which qualify created beings.

In other words, the Father, the Son, and the Holy Spirit belong to the divine category and in this category there is only one existence, the Great *Muntu*. The Sotho-Tswana, for example, refer to this Great *Muntu* (*Modimo*) as "hla'a-Macholo" (ancient of days); "MODIMO wa borare" (of my forefathers—thus the forefathers know *Modimo* better); "Na Choeng Tsa Dithaba" (whose abode is on the highest peak of the mountains); "Monga Tschle" (owner or master of all, Lord). The point of these attributes and names is that *Modimo's* existence is consistent at all points with the nature of *Modimo*, and that there is only one such nature.[32]

Christian theology teaches that the existence of the Son and the existence of the Holy Spirit are consistent at all points with the nature of *Modimo*. But since there is only one such nature, one who shares in that one nature must of necessity be *Modimo* since it is impossible to talk of more than one *Modimo*. Thus we can speak of *Modimo* as having manifested or revealed himself in the Son and in the Holy Spirit. This phenomenon can be diagrammed as follows:

Category I
Modimo revealed in the Son and the Holy Spirit. The three
as the ultimate explanation of the origin and sustenance of *Ntu*

Third, the concept of *Ntu* helps us to grasp the theological ideas of *homoousios*, eternal generation, and procession. To say, for example, that *Modimo* is consubstantial with the Son and the Holy Spirit is to say that the three share *Ntu*. Since there is only one *Ntu* of God, and only an existence within the context of that *Ntu* can be consistent with the existence of God, we can say with Hilary that the Son is a perfect offspring of the

---

31. Calvin, *Institutes*, 1.13.2, 711, 23.
32. Setiloane, "MODIMO: GOD Among the Sotho-Tswana," 9, 10; cf. Setiloane, *The Image of God among the Sotho-Tswana*, 80. To say that there is only "one such nature" of *Modimo*, for instance, is to say that God, according to the conceptual framework of the African peoples, is not a count noun. Because of this we cannot, for example, speak about *Modimo* in the plural. We also cannot say "this is the same God as Modimo or a different God from Modimo."

Father, and that he is endowed with the properties that are in the Father.[33] Elsewhere Hilary argues that the Son is derived wholly from the whole of His Father's nature (*Ntu*). He has the whole of his Father's nature (*Ntu*), and thus he abides in the Father because he is God. The Bible identifies the Holy Spirit as the Spirit of God and the Spirit of Christ. The Holy Spirit is divine because he only has the nature (*Ntu*) of God shared by both the Father and the Son. Moreover, the individual existence of the Son and of the Holy Spirit is consistent at all points with the only Being (*Ntu*) of the Father, viz. the Great *Muntu*. And so the Father is God; the Son is God; and the Holy Spirit is God.

Fourth, whereas the *Ntu* concept may be important in the interpretation of the doctrine of the Trinity by the African audiences, it is worthwhile to note that we cannot apply the concept to the doctrine of the Trinity in an absolute sense. If we applied the concept of *Ntu* in its absolute sense to God, we will understand him as ". . . the Supreme Vital Force"[34] or simply power *par excellence*. The Great *Muntu* will then be all powerful and exist as the explanation of all powers. This way of understanding God would suffice if we accepted a one-sided transcendental view of God. But the Christian faith does not understand God simply as "power *par excellence*." God, worshipped in the Christian faith, brings power and powerlessness together in a profound way.[35] According to Berkhof, God who is present as almighty is also experienced as:

> . . . the one who is hidden or angry or provoked or unrecognized . . . . that is how we see him present in Israel . . . . God's history with Israel is to a large degree the history of a God who sees his plans fail and who repeatedly must react to the hostile or at least disobedient initiative of his partner, without apparently having (or wanting to have) the power to force that partner to his will.[36]

In the New Testament's parables, the almighty God is depicted as a man who has gone on a journey and is absent.[37] The Son, who is the revelation of the Father, refuses to establish his kingdom by force,[38] and instead renounces power and becomes powerless in order to bring succor to humankind and to the entire creation. According to Paul's letter to the Philippians: "Though he was divine by nature, he did not set store upon equality with God, but emptied himself by taking the nature of a servant; born in human guise and appearing in human form, he humbly stooped in

---

33. Hilary of Poitiers, *On the Trinity*, 3.1; 2, 4.
34. Setiloane, *African Theology: An Introduction*, 42.
35. [Hendrikus] Berkhof, *Christian Faith: An Introduction to the Study of Faith*, trans. S. Woudstra (Grand Rapids: Eerdmans, 1979), 133–40.
36. Berkhof, *Christian Faith*, 135.
37. Matt 24:50; 25:14; and Mark 12:1.
38. Matt 26:51f.; Luke 22:38; John 6:15;18:36.

his obedience even to die, and to die upon the cross."[39] On the cross we see the climax of the divine defenselessness. Here God is unable to save himself; the Father is depicted as in complete silence and as having deserted him who is his manifestation, and man triumphs over God by nailing the Son to the cross.[40] The scripture also depicts the Holy Spirit as the source of the power which the Christian has, yet the Holy Spirit is also depicted as defenseless. He must persuade men to accept the salvation of God, and, in most cases, he is resisted[41] and even quenched.[42]

The defenselessness of God—or as we have said here, his weakness—implies a paradigm shift that is important in how we in the African context are to understand the Great *Muntu*. As Great *Muntu* he is all powerful. He is in a different category of existence, and he exists as the explanation for all powers. Yet in the context of the Christian faith we must understand the Great *Muntu* as a "powerless power." This is because the powerlessness of God is the expression of his superiority. The scripture is clear that in the weakness of God there is power *par excellence*, viz. power that is stronger than man's strength.[43] This is a different way of understanding the power of the Great *Muntu*. He is powerful, but in a different way, in a hidden yet active sense.

We can organize the first category of the African cosmology in the light of the Christian information and have it look like this

Category I

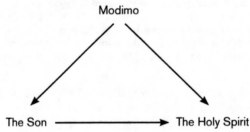

39. Phil 2:6–8.
40. Mark 15:31, 34.
41. Acts 7:51; cf. Isa 63:10.
42. 1 Thess 5:19.
43. I Cor 1:25.

SELECTION **8**

Leonardo Boff

"Amen: The Whole Mystery in a Nutshell"

Leonardo Boff (1938–) is a former Franciscan priest who, along with Gustavo Gutíerrez, was one of the early leading liberation theologians whose work led to the development of "ecclesial base communities" (*Communidades Eclesaises de Base*) among poor Catholics in Brazil and throughout Latin America.

The following excerpt summarizes the main points of *Trinity and Society*, where Boff provides an interpretation of the history and theology of Trinitarian doctrine that underscores its critical and constructive import for understanding the universe and human society. Its central thesis is that the Trinitarian Persons live in eternal *perichoresis* (defined as "being one in the others, through the others, with the others and for the others"), which is a source and model for understanding how we are to exist as a communion of creatures (interpenetrating one another). The *perichoresis* of the three divine Persons calls human individuals to rise above egoism and live out a vocation of communion. It calls societies to reject inequality in favor of sharing and communion, a call that implies justice and equality for all. It calls the church as a sacrament of Trinitarian communion to reduce inequalities among various ministries and to nourish the unity and diversity of gifts within the body of Christ. And it calls the poor to reject their poverty as sin and work for a society based on mutual and egalitarian collaboration and respect for individual differences. In sum, Boff argues, the entire universe exists to manifest the abundance of Trinitarian communion until that time when, in eschatological fullness, all of creation will be inserted (in the mode proper to each creature) into the communion of the three Persons—when the Trinity will be all in all (1 Cor. 15).

From *Trinity and Society*, trans. Paul Burns
(New York: Orbis Books, 1988), 232–37.

At the end of this journey in faith and thought, all that is left for us to say is a biblical *Amen. Amen* is a Hebrew expression of assent (cf. Deut. 27:14ff; 1 Cor. 14:16) deriving from *amin*, which means believing in, accepting and handing oneself over to God and God's plan. *Amen* is humankind's response to the revelation of the triune God: So be it! How good that it should be so! Come, most holy Trinity, come! It is pronounced in an atmosphere of worship and reverence for the unspeakable mystery. But before finally praying *Amen* and falling respectfully silent in the face of the august Trinity, let us give reason one last turn, in an attempt to sum up in a number of propositions the basis of the trinitarian doctrine developed above:

1. By "God" in the Christian faith we should understand the Father, the Son and the Holy Spirit in communion with each other, in such a way that they form a one and only God.

2. In relation to the Trinity, doxology precedes theology. First we profess faith in Father, Son and Holy Spirit in prayer and praise (doxology). Then we reflect on how the divine Three are one single God in perichoretic communion between themselves (theology).

3. In theological reflection, the economic Trinity precedes the immanent Trinity. By "economic Trinity" we mean the manifestation (the self-communication in the case of the Son and Holy Spirit) of the divine Three in human history, whether together or separately, for the purposes of our salvation. By "immanent Trinity" we mean Father, Son and Holy Spirit in their inner, eternal life, considered in itself. Starting with the economic Trinity, we can glimpse something of the immanent Trinity. Only by referring to the incarnation of the Son and the sending of the Holy Spirit can we say that the economic Trinity is the immanent Trinity and vice-versa. Outside these historic, salvific events, the immanent Trinity remains an apophatic mystery.

(i) The Trinity is revealed in the life of Jesus of Nazareth and the manifestations of the Holy Spirit as these were witnessed by the communities of disciples and recorded by them in the New Testament. The triadic expressions found in the Old Testament have trinitarian meaning only on the basis of a Christian reading of them in the light of the New Testament.

(ii) As they appear in the New Testament, Father, Son and Holy Spirit are always mutually related and reciprocally implied. The Father sends the Son into the world; the Son feels himself of one being with the Father; the Holy Spirit is also sent into the world by the Father, at the Son's request. The Holy Spirit takes what is of the Son and enables us to know the Son; it teaches us to cry "Abba, Father."

(iii) The triadic formulas of the New Testament, especially that in Matthew 28:19, show a way of thinking that always associates the divine Three in the work of salvation. This and similar formulas helped in the later elaboration of trinitarian doctrine.

4. The central problem of trinitarian doctrine is this: how to express the fact that the divine Three are one God. Faith says: Father, Son and Holy Spirit are really three and distinct; but they are always related; they are one God. How to equate trinity in unity and unity in trinity?

5. Three solutions put forward are unacceptable to Christian faith because they fail either to preserve trinity, or to maintain unity, or to keep the equality between the Three.

(i) *Tritheism*: affirms the existence of three gods, separate and distinct, each eternal and infinite. This interpretation preserves trinity; however, besides containing serious philosophical errors, it destroys unity.

(ii) *Modalism*: Father, Son and Holy Spirit are three pseudonyms of the same, single God, or three modes of presentation (masks) of the same divine substance. God would be three only for us, not in God's self. This interpretation (Sabellianism) preserves unity, but abandons trinity.

(iii) *Subordinationism*: Strictly speaking, there is only one God—the Father. The Son and Holy Spirit receive their divine substance from the Father in subordinate form, so that they are not consubstantial with the Father but rather creatures adopted (*adoptionism*) to share in his life. This interpretation (Arianism) denies the equality of the Three, since the Son and the Holy Spirit are not fully divine.

6. The orthodox Christian reply is expressed in basically philosophical terms drawn from the prevailing culture and says: God is one nature in three Persons, or, God is one substance in three hypostases. The concepts *nature* and *substance* (or essence) denote unity in the Trinity; the concepts *person* and *hypostasis* safeguard trinity in unity.

7. There are three classic currents of thought that seek to deepen this expression of faith by elaborating a doctrine of the Trinity: Greek, Latin and modern.

(i) *Greek*: This starts from the Father, seen as source and origin of all divinity. There are two ways out from the Father: the Son by begetting and the Spirit by proceeding. The Father communicates his whole substance to the Son and the Holy Spirit, so both are consubstantial with the Father and equally God. The Father also forms the Persons of the Son and of the Holy Spirit in an eternal process. This current runs the risk of being understood as subordinationism.

(ii) *Latin*: This starts from the divine nature, which is equal in all three Persons. This divine nature is spiritual; this gives it an inner dynamic: absolute spirit is the Father, understanding is the Son and will is the Holy Spirit. The Three appropriate the same nature in distinct modes: the Father without beginning, the Son begotten by the Father, and the Spirit breathed out by the Father and the Son. The three are in the same nature, consubstantial, and therefore one God. This current runs the risk of being interpreted as modalism.

(iii) *Modern*: This starts from the Trinity of Persons—Father, Son and Holy Spirit. But the Three live in eternal perichoresis, being one in the others, through the others, with the others and for the others. The unity of the Trinity means the union of the three Persons by virtue of their perichoresis and eternal communion. Since this union is eternal and infinite, we can speak of one God. This interpretation runs the risk of being seen as tritheism. We follow this current: first, because it starts from the *datum* of faith—the existence of Father, Son and Holy Spirit as distinct and in communion; and second, because it allows a better understanding of the universe and human society as a process of communication, communion and union through the interpenetration of creatures with one another (perichoresis). This interpretation strengthens the cause of the oppressed struggling to liberate themselves so that there can be greater sharing and communion.

8. Trinitarian language is highly figurative and approximative, the more so in that the mystery of the Trinity is the deepest and most absolute mystery of the Christian faith. Expressions such as "cause" referring to the Father, "begetting" referring to the Son, and "breathing-out" applied to the Holy Spirit, like "processions," "mission," "nature" and "persons" are analogical or descriptive and do not claim to be causal explanations in the philosophical sense. The inner meaning of such expressions shows the diversity that exists in the divine reality on one hand, and the communion on the other. We use terminology hallowed by tradition and also biblical terminology because they are less ambiguous and because they are used by some modern theologians. Some of those terms are: revelation, acceptance, communion.

9. The conceptual language of devout reason is not the only means of access to the mystery of the Trinity. The church has also developed the symbolic language of imagery. This emphasizes the significance the Trinity has for human existence, particularly in its longing for wholeness. This wholeness is the mystery of the Trinity. It is best expressed through symbols which spring from the depths of the individual and collective unconscious, or from humanity's common religious stock. Symbolic language does not replace conceptual language, but is basic to the formation of religious attitudes.

10. Humanity, male and female, was created in the image and likeness of the triune God. Male and female find their ultimate raison d'être in the mystery of trinitarian communion. Though the Trinity is transsexual, we can use male and female forms in speaking of the divine Persons. So we can say "maternal God-Father" and "paternal God-Mother."

11. The *Filioque* question (the Holy Spirit breathed out by the Father and the Son, or through the Son) is bound up with the theological sensitivity of the Eastern church vis-à-vis the Western, as is a certain type of terminology adopted by one or the other (the Father as source or principle of all divinity—Eastern; or the Son as sourced source—Western). Another theological strand starting from the perichoresis of the divine Persons would have not only *Filioque*, but *Spirituque* and *Patreque* as well, since in the Trinity everything is triadic.

12. By virtue of perichoresis, everything in the Trinity is trinitarian—shared by each of the divine Persons. This does not preclude there being

actions proper to each of the Persons, through which the property of each person is shown.

(i) The proper action of the Father is creation. In revealing himself to the Son in the Spirit, the Father projects all creatable beings as expressions of himself, of the Son and of the Holy Spirit. Once created, all beings express the mystery of the Father, have a filial nature (since they come from the Father), a brotherly and sisterly nature (since they are created in the Son) and a "spiritual" nature (meaning full of meaning, of dynamism, since they were created by the power of the Holy Spirit).

(ii) The action proper to the Son is the incarnation in Jesus of Nazareth, through which he divinizes all creation and redeems it from sin. Through the Son, maleness shares in divinity.

(iii) The action proper to the Holy Spirit is the "pneumatization" through which created life is inserted into the mystery of the life of the Trinity, and redeemed from all threat of death. Through the Holy Spirit, femaleness is introduced into the divine mystery.

13. From the perichoresis-communion of the three divine Persons derive impulses to liberation: of each and every human person, of society, of the church and of the poor, in the double —critical and constructive— sense. *Human beings* are called to rise above all mechanisms of egoism and live their vocation of communion. *Society* offends the Trinity by organizing itself on a basis of inequality and honors it the more it favors sharing and communion for all, thereby bringing about justice and equality for all. The *church* is more the sacrament of trinitarian communion the more it reduces inequalities between Christians and between the various ministries in it, and the more it understands and practices unity as co-existence in diversity. The *poor* reject their impoverishment as sin against trinitarian communion and see the inter-relatedness of the divine "Differents" as the model for a human society based on mutual collaboration—all on an equal footing—and based on individual differences; that society's structures would be humane, open, just and egalitarian.

14. The universe exists in order to manifest the abundance of divine communion. The final meaning of all that is created is to allow the divine Persons to communicate themselves. So in the eschatological fullness, the universe—in the mode proper to each creature, culminating in man and woman in the likeness of Jesus of Nazareth and Mary—will be inserted into the very communion of Father, Son and Holy Spirit. Then the Trinity will be all in all.

The Holy Trinity is a sacramental mystery. As *sacramental*, it can be understood progressively, as the Trinity communicates itself and the understanding heart assimilates it. As mystery it will always remain the Unknown in all understanding, since the mystery is the Father himself, the Son himself and the Spirit itself. And the mystery will last for all eternity.

SELECTION **9**

Elizabeth Johnson

"She Who Is"

A Roman Catholic nun, Elizabeth Johnson (1941–) wrote *She Who Is,* widely recognized as a classic in feminist theology. In the following excerpt, she suggests that we can call God "SHE WHO IS" by translating with a female pronoun the original Latin "*qui est*" ("the one who is") in Aquinas's classic statement that "being" is the most appropriate name for God (cf. Exod. 3:14). Not only is God neither male nor female, but like men, women are also created in God's image (Gen. 1:27); indeed, they only exist in all their uniqueness and difference as women by participating in God's being. Because the name "SHE WHO IS" discloses that women's human nature is also created in God's image, it enables us to affirm women in their own dignity, power, and value (as women) and to reject the idolatry of all that would promote the ontological superiority of men on theological grounds (and thus reinforce the inferior status of women).

As a name for God, "SHE WHO IS" has both ontological and historical connotations. It brings with it all the ontological force carried by a symbol of absolute aliveness—the absolutely overflowing wellspring of divine energy—and of the profoundly relational source of being that causes us "to be" in the midst of situations marked by sin and suffering, death and destruction. Moreover, because the one who speaks in the burning bush— the fire that does not destroy—is a personal mystery who promises deliverance and empowers a human sense of mission and responsibility, the idea of God in Christian orthodoxy is a practical idea. Words and deeds of liberation and covenant belong to the name of God. Speaking rightly about God from a feminist perspective, then, simply entails incorporating the stories of women and women's ways of being into the stories of liberation and covenant that Jews and Christians tell. It entails appropriating for women stories about God's giving life to the dead and calling into existence things that do not exist (Rom. 4:17)—wherever there is systemic oppression (whether because of the sins of others or one's own folly and wrongdoing, or any combination thereof). In turn, it entails appropriating for women stories about God's calling forth responsibility for the good of the world: women too can share in her power of love to create, struggle, and hope on behalf of the new creation in the face of suffering and evil.

From *She Who Is: The Mystery of God in Feminist*
Theological Discourse (New York: Crossroad, 1993), 241–45.

Speaking about the Living God: SHE WHO IS

Near the start of the biblical story of deliverance and covenant stands an
enigmatic encounter. A bush is burning in the wilderness without being
consumed. In respect for the presence of the holy, Moses removes his
shoes. From the bush he hears words of divine compassion for people who
are enslaved, and feels challenged to partner this God of the Hebrews in
winning their release. In this context the exiled shepherd asks the ancestral
God for a self-identifying name. It is graciously given: "I AM WHO I AM"
(Ex 3:14), *'ehyeh 'asher 'ehyeh*, safeguarded in the sacred tetragrammaton
YHWH.

The exegetical difficulties of this passage are numerous, and have given
rise to a variety of interpretations of the personal name of the liberating
God.[44]

Given the virtually untranslatable nature of the name, some scholars
see here an affirmation of the mystery of God. YHWH is a limit expression, not a defining name but an unnameable one. There is no name that
we can comprehend that would satisfactorily designate the Holy One. We
are left in salutary darkness.

Others argue that the name should be interpreted in a causative sense
to signify that God brings about whatever exists and whatever occurs in
history. Thus the name YHWH means "I bring to pass" or "I cause to be"
or "I make to be whatever comes to be." This explanation builds on an
affinity between the letters of the name and a Hebrew verb denoting to be
to evoke the idea that God is the Creator of all things who lets creatures be
in life-giving fashion.

Still another position holds that the name carries the promise of divine
accompaniment to people struggling under bitter oppression. In uttering
the divine name God is saying, "I shall be there, as who I am, shall I be
there with you." In this reading the transcendent mystery of God ("as who
I am") is made known in and through the promise to bring about deliverance from bondage and to initiate the covenant relationship. Here the
sense of the verb to be is interpreted relationally and historically. To be
means to be with and for others, actively and concretely engaged on their
behalf.[45]

---

44. *TDOT* 5:500–521; *TDNT* 3:1058-81; B. W. Anderson, "God, Names of," *The Interpreter's Dic-
tionary of the Bible*, ed. G. A. Buttrick et al. (Nashville: Abingdon, 1962), 2:407–17; 407–17; and S.
Goitein, "YHWH the Passionate: The Monotheistic Meaning and Origin of the Name YHWH," *Vetus
Testamentum* 6 (1956), 1–9.

45. John Courtney Murray mounts a persuasive argument for this reading in *The Problem of God*
(New Haven: Yale University Press, 1964), 5–25; so too does Martin Buber, *Eclipse of God* (New York:
Harper & Row, 1952), 62.

Of all the interpretations of the name given at the burning bush, however, the one with the strongest impact on subsequent theological tradition links the name with the metaphysical notion of being. YHWH means "I am who I am" or simply "I am" in a sense that identifies divine mystery with being itself. Biblical exegetes are unanimous in criticizing the anachronistic tendency to read this philosophical meaning back into the original text, let alone to the events that gave rise to it, for the Hebrew mind did not resonate with such metaphysical nuances until it came into contact with Hellenistic culture. Nevertheless, from the Septuagint translation onward the idea that the name YHWH discloses the ontological nature of God gained precedence in Jewish circles and was widely used in early Christian theology.[46]

It is thus to a long and venerable tradition that Aquinas appeals when he calls on the metaphysical interpretation to support his demonstration that the divine essence is identical with divine existence, or that God's very nature is to be. He finds the term "being" particularly apt because it refers to no partial aspect of God but rather to the whole in an indeterminate way, as to an infinite ocean. Its excellence is further seen in that it highlights the uniqueness of God, for of no one else can it be said that their essence is to exist. At the climax of this argument he proposes that being can serve even to name God in a particularly apt way. He asks, "Is HE WHO IS the most appropriate name for God?" Referring to the burning bush scene interpreted metaphysically, he answers in the affirmative: "Therefore this name HE WHO IS is the most appropriate name for God." Aquinas fills this name with all the transcendent significance that accrues to pure, absolute being in his system. God whose proper name is HE WHO IS is sheer, unimaginable livingness in whose being the whole created universe participates.

The androcentric character of the standard English translation of God's name as HE WHO IS is piercingly evident. That character is not accidental but coheres with the androcentric nature of Aquinas's thought as a whole, expressed most infamously in his assessment of women as deficient males. The original Latin, however, could be rendered differently. It reads, *Ergo hoc nomen, "qui est," est maxime proprium nomen Dei. Qui est* is a construction composed of a singular pronoun and singular verb. The grammatical gender of the pronoun *qui* is masculine to agree with its intended referent *Deus*, the word for God which is also of grammatically masculine gender. The name could be translated quite literally "who is" or "the one who is," with the understanding that the antecedent is grammatically masculine.

Naming toward God from the perspective of women's dignity, I suggest a feminist gloss on this highly influential text. In English the "who"

---

46. For the history of how the name of historical promise became a metaphysical definition, see Walter Kasper, *God of Jesus Christ*, trans. Matthew O'Connell (New York: Crossroad, 1984), 147–52.

of *qui est* is open to inclusive interpretation, and this indicates a way to proceed. If God is not intrinsically male, if women are truly created in the image of God, if being female is an excellence, if what makes women exist as women in all difference is participation in divine being, then there is cogent reason to name toward Sophia-God, "the one who is," with implicit reference to an antecedent of the grammatically and symbolically feminine gender. SHE WHO IS can be spoken as a robust, appropriate name for God. With this name we bring to bear in a female metaphor all the power carried in the ontological symbol of absolute, relational liveliness that energizes the world.

But not only that. The light of the biblical burning bush narrative adds a further precision. The one who speaks there is mystery in a personal key, pouring out compassion, promising deliverance, galvanizing a human sense of mission toward that end. Symbolized by fire that does not destroy, this one will be known by the words and deeds of liberation and covenant that follow. SHE WHO IS, the one whose very nature is sheer aliveness, is the profoundly relational source of the being of the whole universe, still under historical threat. She is the freely overflowing wellspring of the energy of all creatures who flourish, and of the energy of all those who resist the absence of flourishing, both made possible by participating in her dynamic act. In the power of her being she causes to be. In the strength of her love she gives her name as the faithful promise always to be there amidst oppression to resist and bring forth.

SHE WHO IS: linguistically this is possible; theologically it is legitimate; existentially and religiously it is necessary if speech about God is to shake off the shackles of idolatry and be a blessing for women. In the present sexist situation where structures and language, praxis and personal attitudes convey an ontology of inferiority to women, naming toward God in this way is a gleam of light on the road to genuine community.

Spiritually, SHE WHO IS, spoken as the symbol of ultimate reality, of the highest beauty and truth and goodness, of the mystery of life in the midst of death, affirms women in their struggle toward dignity, power, and value. It discloses women's human nature as *imago Dei*, and reveals divine nature to be the relational mystery of life who desires the liberated human existence of all women made in her image. In promoting the flourishing of women SHE WHO IS attends to an essential element for the well-being of all creation, human beings and the earth inclusively.

Politically, this symbol challenges every structure and attitude that assigns superiority to ruling men on the basis of their supposed greater godlikeness. If the mystery of God is no longer spoken about exclusively or even primarily in terms of the dominating male, a forceful linchpin holding up structures of patriarchal rule is removed.

In a word, SHE WHO IS discloses in an elusive female metaphor the mystery of Sophia-God as sheer, exuberant, relational aliveness in the midst of the history of suffering, inexhaustible source of new being in situations of death and destruction, ground of hope for the whole created universe, to practical and critical effect.

To Practical and Critical Effect

When done with eyes open to the magnitude of evil plaguing the world, speaking about God in the language of being moves from the ontological to the historical in short order. This is due to the belief that God's passion is for the world, which is under duress. Any words that are true must take this care into account. J. B. Metz sums this up in an illuminating way:

> The idea of God to which Christian orthodoxy binds us is itself a practical idea. The stories of exodus, of conversion, of resistance and suffering belong to its doctrinal expression. The pure idea of God is, in reality, an abbreviation, a shorthand for stories without which there is no Christian truth in this idea of God.[47]

Speaking rightly about God from a feminist perspective means weaving the stories of women and women's ways of being into the stories of God that the Jewish and Christian traditions habitually tell. This in turn bubbles up to color even the "pure idea of God," in the direction of the praxis of freedom. And so we say:

The mystery of God, Holy Wisdom, SHE WHO IS, is the dark radiance of love in solidarity with the struggle of denigrated persons, including long generations of women, to shuck off their mean estate and lay hold of their genuine human dignity and value. Wherever the human project comes crashing down through systemic oppression, through the sin of others that delights in hurting or remaining indifferent, through personal folly and wrongdoing, through any contingent combination of factors, or wherever the earth and its life-systems are being damaged or destroyed, there the pain and suffering and degradation do not necessarily have the last word. They are bounded by the livingness of Sophia-God who gives life to the dead and calls into being the things that do not exist (Rom 4:17). She accompanies the lost and defeated, even violated women, on the journey to new, unimaginable life.

Conversely, mutuality in relation with God calls forth human responsibility for the good of the world. Alive in the *koinonia* of SHE WHO IS, women and men are called to be friends of God and prophets, that is, appreciators of her wonders, sympathizers with her resistance to whatever degrades beloved creation, companions to her passion for the world's flourishing, starting with the nearest neighbor in need and extending to the farthest flung system by which we order, or disorder, our common life. The nearest woman in need with her dependent children and systemic sexism are prime candidates for transforming attention.

47. Johannes Baptist Metz, "Theology Today: New Crises and New Visions," *Catholic Theological Society of America Prodeedings* 40 (1985): 7.

This way of speaking crafts a partnership amid the ambiguity of history: SHE WHO IS, Holy Wisdom herself, lives as the transcendent matrix who underlies and supports all existence and potential for new being, all resistance to oppression and the powers that destroy, while women and men, through all the ambivalence of their own fidelity, share in her power of love to create, struggle, and hope on behalf of the new creation in the face of suffering and evil.

SELECTION 10

Catherine Mowry LaCugna

"The Practicality of the Doctrine of the Trinity"

Catherine Mowry LaCugna (1952–1997) was a feminist Catholic theologian whose book, *God For Us: The Trinity and Christian Life*, made an important contribution to the revival of Trinitarian doctrine as a practical doctrine with profound relevance for the everyday lives of Christians. Drawing on Karl Rahner's axiom that the "immanent Trinity" (God in Godself) is intrinsically connected to the "economic Trinity" (God's activity in the world), she argued that there is, indeed, an essential unity between *theologia* ("theology," the contemplation of God) and *oikonomia* ("economy," God's activity in creating, redeeming, and sanctifying us). It is only in the economy of creation and salvation, experienced in our own personal histories, that we come to know, love, and worship the true living God. It is there that God's face and name are proclaimed to us—not only in creation but most profoundly in the life, the death, and resurrection of Jesus Christ and the new community gathered in Holy Spirit. Trinitarian doctrine is inextricably linked with the practice of Christian faith, the form of life appropriate to God's economy.

From God for Us: The Trinity and Christian Life
(San Francisco: HarperSanFrancisco, 1973), 377–81.

The doctrine of the Trinity is ultimately a practical doctrine with radical consequences for Christian life. Because of the essential unity of *theologia* and *oikonomia*, the subject matter of the doctrine of the Trinity is the shared life between God and creature. . . . Through the economy of creation, redemption, deification, and consummation, experienced in the context of our own personal histories, we are enabled to know, love, and worship the true living God. God's face and name are proclaimed before us in creation, in God's words and deeds on our behalf, in the life and death of

Jesus Christ, in the new community gathered by the Holy Spirit. The form of God's life in the economy dictates both the shape of our experience of that life and our reflection on that experience. Led by the Spirit more deeply into the life of Christ, we see the unveiled face of the living God. God's glory is beheld in Jesus Christ who is the instrument of our election, our adoption as daughters and sons of God, our redemption through his blood, the forgiveness of our sins, and the cause of our everlasting inheritance of glory (Ephesians). In order to formulate an ethics that is authentically Christian, an ecclesiology and sacramental theology that are christological and pneumatological, a spirituality that is not generic but is shaped by the Spirit of God, Spirit of Christ, we must adhere to the form of God's self-revelation, God's concrete existence as Christ and Spirit. The purpose of the discipline of theology is to contemplate and serve that economy, to throw light on it if possible, so that we may behold the glory of God, *doxa theou*, ever more acutely.

According to the doctrine of the Trinity, God lives as the mystery of love among persons. If we are created in the image of this God, and if our destiny is to live forever with this God and with God's beloved creatures, then what forms of life best enable us to live as Christ lived, to show forth the Spirit of God, and ultimately to be deified? These questions are best answered in light of what is revealed of God's life in Jesus Christ. Jesus preached the reign of God (*basileia*), he revealed the order of a new household (*oikos*), a new dwelling place where the Samaritan woman, the tax collector, and the leper are equally at home.[48] The economy where the great drama of salvation takes place is the dwelling place both of God and of God's beloved. This common life of God and creature, lived out within a common dwelling place, is the subject matter of theology. Inasmuch as the doctrine of the Trinity is bound up with every dimension of the economy where God and creature live together as one, it is inherently practical. As such it is an underutilized source for articulating what we understand to be the demands of the gospel, what constitutes right relationship, what serves the glory of God, what it means to confess faith in and be baptized into the name and life of the God of Jesus Christ. Both theology and praxis would be quite different if the doctrine of the Trinity were allowed to serve at the center of Christian faith.

The practical nature of the doctrine of the Trinity does not mean it is a pragmatic principle that furnishes an easy solution to war and violence, or yields the blueprint for a catechetical program, or settles vexing

---

48. The metaphors of household and economy are used effectively by M. D. Meeks, *God the Economist: The Doctrine of God and Political Economy* (Minneapolis: Fortress, 1989), and by feminist theologian L. Russell in *The Future of Partnership* (Philadelphia: Westminster, 1979) and *Household of Freedom, Authority in Feminist Theology* (Philadelphia: Westminster, 1987). The metaphor of being homeless (*paroikos*) is the basis of J. H. Elliott's *A Home for the Homeless: A Sociological Exegesis of 1 Peter, Its Situation and Strategy* (Philadelphia: Fortress, 1981).

disagreements over the church's public prayer. Rather, the theoretical framework of trinitarian theology yields a wisdom, a discernment, a guide for seeing the "two hands of God" (Irenaeus) at work in our salvation . . . . The doctrine of the Trinity is a way of contemplating the mystery of God and of ourselves, a heuristic framework for thinking correctly about God and about ourselves in relation to God. When we try to apply it to concrete situations, the sands start to shift.

In the desire to remedy some of the great problems of the day, the temptation is to use the doctrine of the Trinity as "an autonomous datum and even premise for theology"[49] that is applied to a particular problem, for example, unequal distribution of resources. It is as if the goal is to figure out God "in se"—the number of persons, relations and processions and how they are configured—and then project this "intra-divine" structure onto human community, or vice versa. But as we have seen, this strategy, whether it supports a hierarchical or egalitarian vision, inevitably appears to be a transcendental projection of human preferences onto God. Moreover, an appeal to the structure of "intra-divine" life to support a vision of human persons or community, or the place of all creatures within God's providential plan, is not the purpose of the doctrine of the Trinity and in the end defeats it. Rather, the purpose of the doctrine of the Trinity is to affirm that God who comes to us and saves us in Christ and remains with us as Spirit is the true living God. Its purpose is to clarify the relationship between God's self-revelation in the economy, and God's being as such. From this perspective the doctrine of the Trinity serves a critical theological function, to critique the tendency of praxiological theologies to promote a particular construal of reality as the only legitimate one, or as the one that perfectly mirrors intradivine life. Similarly the doctrine of the Trinity exposes the degree to which (classical) theologies are blind to their own ideological construction of reality, likewise supposedly rooted in the nature of God's inner life.[50] By carefully qualifying the concept of God's "inner life," and by making all metaphysical claims function directly with respect to the economy of salvation, a revitalized doctrine of the Trinity calls to account all theologies of God, it forces us to admit their partiality and inadequacy, and it requires that every interpretation of who God is be measured against what is revealed of God in the economy. The doctrine of the Trinity is in this sense not a teaching about God but the doctrine that specifies the conditions and criteria under which we may speak of God.

---

49. R. Haight, "The Point of Trinitarian Theology," *Toronto Journal of Theology* 4 (1988): 192.

50. An example would be W. Moll, *The Christian Image of Woman* (Notre Dame: Fides Publishers, 1967). Moll argues on the basis of his understanding of the doctrine of the Trinity that "representing and incorporating God's anonymity on earth is woman" (24); the specific dignity of woman is to be Thou, never I, always response, never the word spoken (25); the Holy Spirit and woman are alike in that both are passive receivers (37–38); just as the Spirit is the conjoining principle between Father and Son, woman is conjoining principle within "man"; woman is "merely the 'or' of humanity" (110); the hierarchy between male and female belongs to the natural order (111–12).

Even so, the doctrine of the Trinity has more than a purely grammatical function. The doctrine of the Trinity does more than set out criteria for orthodoxy. It is also the framework for reflecting on the nature of the human person, on the relationship between humankind and all other creatures of the earth, on the relationship between ourselves and God. In short, all theological reflection, whether conducted under the rubric of ethics, sacramental-theology, ecclesiology, or spirituality, is potentially a mode of trinitarian theology.

Despite its practical character, the doctrine of the Trinity remains derivative, derived from the economy.[51] It is the summary of Christian faith, not its premise. The life of God with us is the premise, context, horizon of faith; doctrine articulates the nature or meaning of that faith. It is quite plain that there always have been and always will be many readings of the economy, many disagreements about what God's providential will is. The doctrine of the Trinity does not settle but concedes a variety of views because the path through the economy is both an unknowing as well as a knowing. Since the economy is the ongoing life of God with us, theological reflection on the economy necessarily will be open-ended.[52] Theologians inevitably will make mistakes, since no one theologian or school of theology can presume to have unraveled the mystery of the divine-human relationship. Each theology is one reading of the economy, one interpretation of God's self-revelation in Jesus Christ. There will always be many theologies and doctrines, and no meta-theological standpoint, neither ecclesiastical nor biblical, from which to adjudicate among differences. While the theologian strives within the context of a whole tradition of interpretation to achieve orthodoxy, or right opinion about the economy, right perception of the glory of God, the criterion for theological truth remains the Spirit of God who transforms our inarticulate words into praise. The Spirit of God accomplishes the work of salvation: The Spirit enables us to see the glory of God passing before us, to confess Jesus Christ as Lord, to know, love, and worship the true living God, to "become God" (2 Pet. 1:4). The very same Spirit conforms theological statements to this ever-greater mystery. This is where the idea of God's incomprehensibility becomes much more than a mere formality: The economy is ineffable because the economy is God's life with us. This renders theology inherently practical but at the same time calls for a genuine modesty and humility on the part of theologians who would place their words at the service of God's Holy Spirit.

The doctrine of the Trinity, then, is unavoidably bound up with the praxis of Christian faith, with the form of life appropriate to God's economy. The details must be worked out amidst all the ambiguities of the

---

51. Haight, "The Point of Trinitarian Theology," 192.
52. This is the basis for the possibility of genuinely indigenous theologies, different Christian readings of the economy, different symbols, doctrines, and rites.

economy, all the competing notions of what God's will is, all the disagreements about whose experience should be normative. Anything less would simply be a massive projection.

SELECTION **1 1**

Rowan Williams

"Trinity and Revelation"

A theologian and poet, Rowan Williams (1950–) has been the archbishop of Canterbury since 2003. The following excerpt from his essay "Trinity and Revelation" describes how the internal logic of Trinitarian theology ascribes divinity to Jesus and the Holy Spirit. In the memory and presence of Jesus, Christians have experienced radical generative power or absolute creativity. Jesus reconstitutes their lives—liberating them from sinful and destructive patterns, healing their diseases, and restoring them to wholeness and integrity (what traditional theology calls "grace," "forgiveness of sins," or "justification"). Yet Jesus is also part of our human, contingent world. Unlike the Father, the "generative" source of creative power, he is "generated," derived from something else. Fourth-century Trinitarian theologians distinguished between being "generated" and being "created": the Godhead of Jesus shares in God's creativity—not as a second God but as one "generated" as a response to or a reflection of that prior absolute creativity (thus, the metaphors of Word, Wisdom, Image, and Son). Like that ascribed to Jesus, the Spirit's creative power is also derived and responsive. But it is not reducible to what happened in Jesus. We find it rather in the way the Spirit forms Christ in our corporate and individual lives as believers. The same creative space enacted in Jesus is now enacted as creative grace between human beings in the church, in the fellowship of the Spirit. In sum, a Trinitarian account of God brings to the fore the fact that absolute creativity is not simply initiatory but also responsive. This creativity and radical newness appears in the world as grace—love, mercy, and gift.

From *Modern Theology* 2:3 (1986): 200–205.

Thus the claim that Jesus of Nazareth "reveals" God (more specifically, the God of Israel) is a statement affirming that what is thought to be characteristic of God alone—radical "generative power," global creativity, the capacity to constitute the limits of human existence, and so forth—has been experienced in connection with the life and death of a human being; that direct and immediate knowledge of God is to be had definitively in the leading of a life governed by the memory and the presence of Jesus. The drastic liberty or creativity which we call "God's" because it cannot be contained in language descriptive of the "contents of the world" is reflected, echoed, embodied—incarnated—in what Jesus is experienced as affecting. Jesus' reconstruction of humanity, liberating men and women from the dominance of past patterns, is Godlike. Using the traditional dogmatic language, we could say that "grace," or "the forgiveness of sins," or "justification" is seen as a comprehensive enough transaction to be called creative and divine: if creation is to be saved from its diseases and restored to wholeness and integrity, the restoring agency must be level with, comparable to, the creative itself.

This at once poses a problem: we have said that we call radical creativity God's because it cannot be contained in "worldly" language; yet Jesus as a human being is containable in worldly language, he belongs in the same network of historical contingencies as we ourselves do. And even more obviously, the mediation of his grace in the believing community operates within that finite network. The notion of radical divine initiative is a regulative idea, "holding the ring" for our variegated apprehensions of generative power: must it not, therefore, be a concept of a different order from anything we can use in respect of any human event? All events in the world are generated, even if in important respect they are also generative; while God is not generated, but purely generative. It is precisely this problem that produced the long-drawn out dogmatic crisis of the fourth century[53] in the Christian Church (though the issue was less about the "generatedness" of the human Jesus than about the derivative status of the heavenly Logos). And in response to this crisis, the anti-Arian wing of the Church gradually developed its insistence that a distinction could properly be drawn between being "derived" or dependent and being created (i.e., being contingent and mutable): the Godhead of Jesus is unquestionably the former; but this does not simply reduce what is at work in his history to a level inferior to that of the creator.

Does this help? It allows us to say that radical liberty and creativity is not such a simple, univocally applicable concept as might be supposed: there is a proper liberty generated out of dependence, a proper creativity which is responsive rather than simply initiatory. Absolute creativity is not a part of the world; but it is possible to imagine a creativity of comparable generality in its effect which nevertheless arises as response to, or reflection of, that prior "absolute" creativity. What needs to be said of Jesus is that his power to remold the image of human being, his liberty

---

53. As to whether the Son, being *begotten* (*gennētos*), can be rightly said to share the same absolute and self-sufficient (*agenētos*) nature as the Father, who is both unbegotten (*agennētos*, from *gennaō*) and self-sufficient (*agenētos*, from *ginomai*). The answer of developed orthodoxy is that the *life* of the Father and Son is equally *agenētos*, but it is a life they share precisely in their mutual relation—i.e. neither is *agenētos* qua person, but only by nature.

in reconstituting the boundaries of human vocation and identity, is not limited by the history of which he is the inheritor or the society of which he is a member. Without ceasing to be an inheritor of that history and a member of that society, he acknowledges as his "limit" only the will of the God he calls Father: his liberty is itself a function of his obedience. So Jesus shares the creativity of God, yet not as a "second God," a separate individual:[54] he is God as dependent—for whom the metaphors of Word, Image, Son are appropriate.

What I am suggesting is a tentative sketch of what might be meant by ascribing "divinity" to Jesus without simply walking into the logical absurdity of saying that Jesus "is" the creator of the world, *tout court*. It may be worth noting that the tradition of classical trinitarian theology has been far from indifferent to these issues: Aquinas makes it plain that the second person of the Trinity is "apt" to be incarnate (as the Father is not) because he is both image of the Father and exemplar of the creation; and also because, as Son, he is eternally what we are called to be. Our salvation is in becoming adoptive children of God, and it is proper that this should be realized through the mediation of the God who is already and forever "Son," God as eternal issue or response.[55]

If we then go on to ask about the divinity of the agency which perpetually renews the experience of grace and re-creation in the believing community, yet which is not straightforwardly identical either with the absolute creativity which is the source and context of all things, or with the historical event generating the reconstruction of the human world, similar points emerge. Radical generative power is ascribed to the life of Jesus, but it is also ascribable to those events in which, through the ages, the community learns and re-learns to interpret itself by means of Jesus (and nothing else and nothing less). Once again, we have to do with a derived or responsive creativity: it is the same radical renewing energy as is encountered in the event of Jesus, which is in turn continuous with the absolute generative power which founds the world. It is not reducible to a human recollecting of Jesus; it is rather the process of continuing participation in the foundational event—the forming of Christ in the corporate and individual life of believers. It is on this basis that we speak of the rite of initiation into the believing community both as an "immersion" in the death and resurrection of Jesus—a being engulfed in that paradigm—and as a receiving of God as "Spirit"—a perilously vague term, as theologians have long recognized,[56] but a useful cipher for that mode of creative presence and action which cannot simply be identified with "the Father" and "the

---

54. This answers the Arian criticism that Alexandrian episcopal orthodoxy involved belief in two rival first principles. See, e.g. the letter of Eusebius of Nicomedia to Paulinus of Tyre, in Theodoret, *Historica ecclesiastica* 1.6 (ed. Parmentier; Leipzig, 1911), 27–8.

55. See, e.g., *Summa Theologiae* 3.3.8.

56. See, e.g., Augustine, *De trinitate* 5.11.12: *potest appellari trinitas et spiritus et sanctus.*

Son." So, as with the Son, we do not say that the process of re-presentation and re-apprehension of Jesus in the Church is straightforwardly the ultimate initiating source of divine life; but the creative grace which is enacted in Jesus is the same creative grace enacted between human beings in the Church, in the "fellowship of the Holy Spirit." The Spirit is Jesus' Spirit and therefore God's Spirit: it is what God gives in Jesus, and that gift is always and invariably the breaking of bondage and the dawn of hope.

In the events of Jesus and the Spirit-in-the-Church,[57] incarnation and Pentecost, creative and generative power is shown in the form of grace. That is, creativity is seen to be exercised in terms of compassionate acceptance, the refusal of condemnation, the assurance of an abiding relationship of healing love. God is glorified as Lord of creation by the act which brings unpredicted and unprecedented fulfillment to his creatures. And so it is through what we learn to say of Son and Spirit that we can interpret the abstract notion of "absolute creativity" as the absolute gratuity of love, rather than the exercise of simple untrammeled power for its own sake. If creativity, radical newness, appears decisively in the human world as grace, the final ground of creativity is, at the very least, not alien to love, to mercy and gift. "The Father" loves and does not negate, frustrate or destroy. "The Father himself loves you, because you have loved me and have believed that I came from the Father."[58] Initially, the notion of radical creativity renders problematic any account of truly generative occurrence within the world; but a fuller understanding of what this generative power in the world actually consists in, as grace and absolution or renewal, does at least render the idea of creativity, and thus the idea of "God" itself, more than a content-less postulate. None of this finally resolves the basic difficulty of spelling out the nature of the continuity between absolute and derivative; but for a Christian committed to some kind of talk about God as a "gracious" or "loving" or even "personal" God, only a trinitarian account of God seems able to safeguard theology against agnosticism and formalism.

---

57. Cf. Rahner's account of the "modalities of self-communication" in *The Trinity* (London: Herder and Herder, 1970), especially 82–99. But I am extremely uneasy with the distinction drawn between communication as "history" and communication as "spirit," as this threatens to confine the spirit to a rather abstractly conceived future rather than identifying Spirit in the concrete life, work, prayer, and conflict of the community.

58. Jn 16:27.

SELECTION **12**

Jean-Luc Marion

God Without Being

Jean-Luc Marion (1946–) is a leading French philosopher who seeks to address the contemporary spiritual and intellectual crisis of nihilism (especially in France since 1968) in light of Christian revelation. Located within the "postmodern" horizon established by Nietzsche, Heidegger, and Wittgenstein, his work has also been influenced by the philosophers Jacques Derrida and Emmanuel Levinas and the theologian Hans Urs von Balthasar.

Like other postmodern thinkers, Marion rejects the "modern" attempt (since Descartes) to think "God" on the basis of "onto-theo-logy"—that is, the metaphysical concept of a supreme being (the "Being of beings") that grounds all other derived beings. For Marion, Nietzsche's nihilistic declaration of the "death of God" brought to light not only the failure but also the idolatry of this metaphysical concept of God. In addition, Marion rejects Heidegger's attempt to think of God according to the "question of Being" (*Seinsfrage*).

In his critique of God as "Being," Marion makes clear that Thomas's concept of *esse* is not the "Being" of onto-theo-logy: he acknowledges that for Thomas God's *esse* far surpasses the *ens commune* (common being or being in general) of creatures. Yet Thomas diverged from tradition (e.g., Dionysius and Bonaventure) by substituting *esse* for the good *(bonum, summum bonum)* as the first divine name. Marion takes a path Thomas does not take by thinking of God not within the horizon of Being but within the horizon of gift—*agape*. As humans we have to "be" in order to "live," to "move" (Acts 17:28), and eventually to love, but with God this order is reversed: God loves before being. If we seek to think of God as God gives himself to be known—insofar as God gives himself in Christ—then we must think of the name revealed in 1 John 4:8—"God is love"—as prior to the name revealed in Exod. 3:14—"I AM WHO I AM."

In his important book *God Without Being*, Marion seeks both to deconstruct the history of Western metaphysics by way of a phenomenology that brings to light the "vanity" of all beings and Being and to depict two figures of gift that Christian theology offers (without being able to or having to justify): the Eucharist and the confession of faith. Irreducible to Being and its beings, these two "facts" are only intelligible in terms of gift—*agape* as a pure given.

From the "Preface to the English Edition," in *God Without Being*,
trans. Thomas A. Carlson (Chicago: University of Chicago Press, 1991), xix–xxv.

Written at the border between philosophy and theology, this essay remains deeply marked by the spiritual and cultural crisis in which it was thought and written. That crisis, shared by an entire generation (at least), had a time and a stake. A time: the test of nihilism which, in France, marked the years dominated by 1968. A stake: the obscuring of God in the indistinct haze of the "human sciences," which at the time were elevated by "structuralism" to the rank of dominant doctrine. Later I shall have to say what this field of passions, discoveries, strife, and work actually was—this field in which I struggled like many others, having as close teachers Beaufret, Derrida, but also Althusser; as masters, Alquié and Levinas, but also Gilson, Daniélou, and H. U von Balthasar; and, as horizon, Nietzsche, Wittgenstein, and Heidegger. For the moment, it is sufficient to understand that, in a confused and sometimes unpolished form, the issue was a confrontation between the philosophical prohibitions of nihilism and the demanding openings of Christian revelation in a debate so close that it sometimes brought the antagonists together on a common course.

At the time of its first publication, *God Without Being* provoked some fairly animated debates, in France and elsewhere. Curiously, its theses were better received by the philosophers and academics than by the theologians and believers. The whole book suffered from the inevitable and assumed equivocation of its title: was it insinuating that the God "without being" is not, or does not exist? Let me repeat now the answer I gave then: no, definitely not. God is, exists, and that is the least of things. At issue here is not the possibility of God's attaining Being, but, quite the opposite, the possibility of Being's attaining to God. With respect to God, is it self-evident that the first question comes down to asking, before anything else, whether he is? Does Being define the first and the highest of the divine names? When God offers himself to be contemplated and gives himself to be prayed to, is he concerned primarily with Being? When he appears as and in Jesus Christ, who dies and rises from the dead, is he concerned primarily with Being? No doubt, God can and must in the end also be; but does his relation to Being determine him as radically as the relation to his Being defines all other beings? To be or not to be—that is indeed the first and indispensable question for everything and everyone, and for man in particular. But with respect to Being, does God have to behave like Hamlet? Under the title *God Without Being*, I am attempting to bring out the absolute freedom of God with regard to all determinations, including, first of all, the basic condition that renders all other conditions possible and even necessary—for us, humans—the fact of Being. Because, *for us*, as for all the beings of the world, it is first necessary "to be" in order, indissolubly, "to live and to move" (Acts, 17:28), and thus eventually also to love. But *for*

God, if at least we resist the temptation to reduce him immediately to our own measure, does the same still apply? Or, on the contrary, are not all the determinations that are necessary for the finite reversed for Him, and for Him alone? If, to begin with, "God is love," then God loves before being, He only is as He embodies himself—in order to love more closely that which and those who, themselves, have first to be. This radical reversal of the relations between Being and loving, between the name revealed by the Old Testament (Exodus, 3:14) and the name revealed, more profoundly though not inconsistently, by the New (First Letter of John, 4:8), presupposes taking a stand that is at once theological and philosophical.

The philosophical decision takes place within the framework, perhaps, of what is conventionally called "postmodernity." If we understand by modernity the completed and therefore terminal figure of metaphysics, such as it develops from Descartes to Nietzsche, then "postmodernity" begins when, among other things, the metaphysical determination of God is called into question. Following the thematic elaborated by Heidegger, I admit that metaphysics imposes on what it still designates under the disputable title of "God" a function in the onto-theo-logy constitution of metaphysics: as supreme being, "God" assures the ground (itself grounded according to the Being of beings in general) of all other derived beings. In two studies on Descartes,[59] I have examined in more detail the construction of the system of the metaphysical names imposed on "God." Inevitably, though it did not become apparent for three centuries, these names reflect purely metaphysical functions of "God" and hide that much more the mystery of God as such. Nietzsche not only proclaimed the "death of God," he brought the grounds for it to light: under the conceptual names of "God" only metaphysical "idols" emerge, imposed on a God who is still to be encountered. A few years before *God Without Being*,[60] I had noted this paradox in the framework of the short-lived "new philosophers" movement: the "death of God" exclusively concerns the failure of the metaphysical concepts of "God"; in taking its distance from all metaphysics, it therefore allows the emergence of a God who is free from onto-theo-logy; in short, the "death of God" immediately implies the death of the "death

59. *Sur la théologie blanche de Descartes: Analogie, création des vérités eternelles et fondement* (Paris: Presses Universitaires de France, 1981; 2d ed., 1991), and *Sur le prisme métaphysique de Descartes* (Paris: Presses Universitaires de France, 1986). See the discussions of E. Jennifer Ashworth, *Studia Cartesian,* 2 (Amsterdam, 1981), 219–24; Charles Larmore, *Journal of Philosophy* 81:3 (1984): 156–62; John G. Cottingham, *Times Higher Education Supplement,* 29 November 1985; Richard A. Watson, *Independent Journal of Philosophy* 5:6 (1988): 147–49, etc. See also my essays, "The Essential Incoherence of Descartes' Definition of Divinity," in Amélie O. Rorty (ed.), *Essays on Descartes' Meditations* (Berkeley and Los Angeles: University of California Press, 1986), 297–337; "On Descartes' Constitution of Metaphysics," *Graduate Faculty Philosophy Journal,* New School for Social Research, 11:1, 21–34; and "The Idea of God," in M. Ayers and D. Garber (eds.), *Cambridge History of Seventeenth Century Philosophy* (Cambridge: Cambridge University Press, forthcoming).

60. In *L' idole et la distance* (Paris: Grasset, 1977; 2nd ed., 1989; 3rd ed., Paris: Hachette, "Poche-biblio," 1991).

of God." But, according to the logic of "post-modernity," the critique thus initiated had to be made deeper: to release God from the constraints of onto-theo-logy can still signify that Being, thought as such, without its metaphysical figure, in the way that Heidegger attempted, is still imposed on him. This second idolatry—"God according to Being"—only appears once one has unmasked the first—"God" according to onto-theo-logy. In *God Without Being*, therefore, I no longer play Heidegger and Nietzsche against metaphysics, but rather, playing against Heidegger and the primacy of the *Seinsfrage*, I shoot for God according to his most theological name—charity. My enterprise remains "postmodern" in this sense, and, in this precise sense, I remain close to Derrida.[61]

My enterprise does not remain "postmodern" all the way through, however, since it claims in the end to be able to refer to charity, the *agape* properly revealed in and as the Christ, according to an essential anachronism: charity belongs neither to pre-, nor to post-, nor to modernity, but rather, at once abandoned to and removed from historical destiny, it dominates any situation of thought. The thematic of destitution, which strikes all beings and all Being with vanity (chap. 4), develops an a-historical "deconstruction" of the history of metaphysics. At least it claims to outline this "deconstruction" within the framework of a phenomenology that is pushed to its utmost possibilities.[62]

A theological decision supports the philosophical decision. In rejecting the denomination of God by Being, am I not colliding with one of Thomas Aquinas's major theses? Am I not distancing myself from one of the most explicit benchmarks of properly Catholic theology (since *Aeterni Patris* in 1879, but even at Vatican II in 1965)? This of course is exactly what I was reproached for by a number of theologians, "Thomist" or not.[63] There is certainly a serious question here that no quick answer can satisfy. Without prejudicing other research, I will limit myself to sketching a few arguments.

First argument: the Being from which God is liberated in *God Without Being* is defined in terms of two different domains. On the one hand, we

61. Derrida takes up my theses in "Comment ne pas parley" in *Psyche* (Paris, 1987), 535 ff. [trans. Frieden].

62. See *Réduction et donation: Recherches sur Husserl, Heidegger et la phénoménologie* (Paris: Presses Universitaires de France, 1989); and "L'interloqué," in "Topos: Who Comes After the Subject?" *Topoi: An International Review of Philosophy* 7:2 (September 1988): 175 ff.

63. See, for example, in France, reviews by J.-H. Nicolas, "La suprême logique de l'amour et la théologie," *Revue Thomiste*, October-December 1983, 639–49; and J. D. Robert, "Dieu sans l'être: A propos d'un livre récent," *Nouvelle Revue Théologique*, 1983, 406 ff. See also the discussions by R. Virgoulay, "Dieu ou l'être? Relecture de Heidegger en marge de J.-L. Marion, *Dieu sans l'être*," *Recherches de Science Religieuses* 72:2 (1984): 163–98; and J.-Y. Lacoste, "Penser Dieu en l'aimant: Philosophie et théologie de Jean-Luc Marion," *Archives de Philosophie* 50:2 (1987). This debate led to D. Dubarle's collection of studies, *Dieu avec l'être: De Parménide à Saint Thomas. Essai d'ontologie théologale*, introduced by J. Greisch (Paris: Beauchesne, 1986), and to the collective work, *L'être et Dieu*. Travaux du C.E.R.I.T. (Paris: Cerf, 1986) (D. Bourg, S. Breton, A. Delzant, C. Geffré, J. Grosjean, G. Lafon, J.-L. Marion, G. Vahanian, H.-B. Vergotte, etc.).

have the metaphysical tradition of the *ens commune*, then of the objective concept of being, of its abstract univocity, such as it collapses under the critiques of Hegel and Nietzsche; but then, according to so incontestable a Thomist as E. Gilson, this "Being" no longer has anything to do with the *esse* that Saint Thomas assigns to the Christian God. So my thesis does not oppose but, rather, confirms the antagonism between the Thomistic *esse* and the "Being" of nihilism by disqualifying the claim of the latter to think God.[64] On the other hand, we have Being such as Heidegger understands it, as a phenomenological horizon, and then as *Ereignis*;[65] in both cases, the enthusiastic naïveté of the beginnings has largely given way, among the theologians, to great caution: Heidegger could indeed run the risk of a gnostic drift, even of an "ontologist" idolatry, whose famous "God alone who can save us" bears all the ambiguities. Within this perspective, *God Without Being* would offer a warning against a danger that is still to come, but already threatening for Christian faith.

Hence the second argument. In supposing (as certain passages in this book indisputably suggest) that it is necessary to liberate God from *esse* in the very sense that Saint Thomas understood it, this conflict would still have to be resituated within the wider theological debate of the divine names. Historically, in the tradition of Denys's treatise *On Divine Names* and its commentaries, Saint Thomas certainly marks a rupture: contrary to most of his predecessors (including Saint Bonaventure), as well as to several of his successors (including Duns Scotus), he substitutes *esse* for the good (*bonum, summum bonum*) as the first divine name. This initiative is not self-evident. In order to confirm it, we must first locate and meditate on it, which is what I attempted by sketching the path that Saint Thomas did *not* take and by stressing that that path also offers a solution. One last argument follows from this: even when he thinks God as *esse*, Saint Thomas nevertheless does not chain God either to Being or to metaphysics.

He does not chain God to Being because the divine *esse* immeasurably surpasses (and hardly maintains an *analogia* with) the *ens commune* of creatures, which are characterized by the real distinction between *esse* and their essence, whereas God, and He alone, absolutely merges essence with *esse*: God is expressed as esse, but this esse is expressed only of God, not of the beings of metaphysics. In this sense, Being does not erect an idol before God, but saves his distance.

Saint Thomas doesn't chain God to metaphysics either, since he explicitly stresses that "*res divinae non tractantur a philosophis, nisi prout sunt*

64. See E. Gilson, *L'être et l'essence* (Paris: J. Vrin, 1948, esp. 2d ed., 1962), as well as *Being and Some Philosophers* (Toronto: Pontifical Institute of Mediaeval Studies, 1952). The record of the interpretation of the *Seinsfrage* by Gilson can be found in large part in M. Couratier (ed.), *Etienne Gilson et Nous: La philosophie et son histoire* (third section, P. Aubenque, J. Beaufret, J.-F. Courtine and P. Hadot) (Paris: J. Vrin, 1980).

65. Ed. note: *Ereignis* means "event" or "coming into view."

rerum omnium principia": divine things do not belong to metaphysics as one of its objects; rather, they only intervene in metaphysics indirectly in the capacity of principles for its objects, "*non tanquam subjectum scientiae, sed tanquam principia subjecti*."[66] Between metaphysics (with its domain, common Being) and God, the relation, even and especially for Saint Thomas, has to do not with inclusion but with subordination: God, as principle, subjugates the subjects of philosophy to himself. Consequently, since the subjects of philosophy belong to Being, we must go so far as to conclude that their cause, God, also causes Being itself: "*Deus est causa universalis totius esse*."[67] But if God causes Being, wouldn't we have to admit that, for Saint Thomas himself, God can be expressed without Being? At the very least, we should have to grant that Thomism does not amount to the identification of the *esse commune* with God, and that, if *esse* characterizes God in Thomism, *esse* itself must be understood divinely, thus having no common measure with what Being can signify in metaphysics—and especially in the onto-theo-logy of modern metaphysics.

These debates, animated as they may have been, nevertheless do not get at the heart of the question, where something entirely different is at stake: can the conceptual thought of God (conceptual, or rational, and not intuitive or "mystical" in the vulgar sense) be developed outside of the doctrine of Being (in the metaphysical sense, or even in the nonmetaphysical sense)? Does God give himself to be known according to the horizon of Being or according to a more radical horizon? *God Without Being* barely sketches an answer, but does sketch it: God gives Himself to be known insofar as He gives Himself—according to the horizon of the gift itself. The gift constitutes at once the mode and the body of his revelation. In the end the gift gives only itself, but in this way it gives absolutely everything. The approach and reception of the gift are only described here with difficulty. First in a negative way: the experience of vanity indicates that even that which is finds itself disqualified as if it were not, so long as it does not have added to its status as a being the dignity of that which finds itself loved. Next in a dogmatic way: I attempt a pure and simple description of two emblematic figures of the gift, which Christian theology offers without being able or having to justify them—the Eucharist and the confession of faith. We describe these as two facts that are absolutely irreducible to Being and to its logic, facts that are only intelligible in terms of the gift. In conclusion, *agape* appears only as a pure given, with neither deduction nor legitimation. But in this way the given appears all the more as a given.

To give pure giving to be thought—that, in retrospect it seems to me, is what is at stake in *God Without Being*. It is also the task of my future work and, I expect, of the work of many others.

---

66. Saint Thomas Aquinas, *In Boethii De Trinitate*, q.5, a.4, *resp.*
67. Saint Thomas Aquinas, *Summa Theologica*, Ia, q.45, a.2.

Permissions

Suggestions for Further Reading

The list below includes recent translations of Christian classics (in addition to those used in this volume). It also contains biblical studies, histories of ancient and modern Christian thought, major twentieth-century works, and significant books published over the last century (including some from which selections in this volume have been taken). Although the list takes account of a broad range of perspectives, it is not exhaustive.

Christian Classics on God and the Trinity

Anselm. "Proslogion." In *Anselm*. Translated by Sidney Norton Deane, 3–35. Chicago: Open Court, 1903. See also *Anselm of Canterbury: The Major Works*. Edited by Brian Davis and G. R. Evans. New York: Oxford University Press, 2008.

Aquinas, Thomas. *The Summa Theologica of St. Thomas Aquinas*. Pt. 1. Translated by the Fathers of the English Dominican Province. New York: Benziger Bros., 1981.

Augustine, Saint. *Augustine: Later Works*. LCC, vol. 8. Translated and edited by John Burnaby, 128–42. See also *Trinity*. Translated by Edmund Hill with introduction. New York: New City Press, 1991.

Bonaventure. "The Journey of the Mind into God." In the *Opera Omnia S. Bonaventurae*. Vol. 5, 295–316. Quaracchi: Collegii S. Bonaventurae, 1890. See also *The Soul's Journey into God, the Tree of Life, the Life of St. Francis*. Translated and edited by Ewert Cousins. New York: Paulist Press, 1978.

Calvin, John. *Institutes of the Christian Religion*. Vol. 1. Edited by John T. McNeill. Translated by Ford Lewis Battles. Library of Christian Classics. Philadelphia: Westminster Press, 1960.

Descartes, René. *The Method, Meditations and Philosophy of Descartes*. Translated by John Veitch. Washington, D.C.: M. Walter Dunne, 1901. See also *Meditations and Other Metaphysical Writings*. Translated and edited by Desmond M. Clarke. London: Penguin Classics, 1999.

Dionysius the Areopagite. "The Divine Names" and "Mystical Theology." In *On the Divine Names and On the Mystical Theology*. Translated by C. E. Rolt, 51–81, 191–201. London: SPCK, 1920. See also *Pseudo Dionysius: The Complete Works*. Edited by Karlfried Froehlich. New York: Paulist Press, 1987.

Eckhart, Meister. *Meister Eckhart: The Essential Sermons, Commentaries, Treatises and Defense*. Edited by Edmund Colledge, Bernard McGinn, and Houston Smith. New York: Paulist Press, 1981.

Edwards, Jonathan. "The End for Which God Created the World." In *Works of Jonathan Edwards*. Vol. 8, *Ethical Writings*. Edited by Paul Ramsey, 526–36. New Haven, CT: Yale University Press, 1989.

———. *The Works of Jonathan Edwards*. Vol. 21, *Writings on the Trinity, Grace, and Faith*. Edited by Sang Hyun Lee. New Haven, CT: Yale University Press, 2002.

Gregory of Nazianzus. *The Fathers of the Church, St. Gregory of Nazianzus, Select Orations*. Translated by Martha Vinson. Washington, D.C.: Catholic University Press of America.

———. *On God and Christ: The Five Theological Orations and Two Letters to Cledonius*. Translated and edited by Frederick Williams et al. Yonkers, NY: St. Vladimir's Seminary Press, 2002.

Gregory of Nyssa. *The Catechetical Oration of St. Gregory of Nyssa*. Translated by J. H. Strawley. Cambridge: Cambridge University Press, 1903.

———. *Gregory of Nyssa: Dogmatic Treatises, Etc.*. Vol. 5, pt. 2, *NPNF* 2.5.131–37.

———. *The Life of Moses*. Trans. and intro. Abraham J. Malherbe and Everett Ferguson. New York: Paulist Press, 1978.

Hegel, Georg Wilhelm Friedrich. *Theologian of the Spirit*. Translated and edited by Peter Hodgson. Minneapolis: Augsburg Fortress, 1997.

Irenaeus of Lyons. *Against the Heresies*, in *Apostolic Fathers, Justin Martyr, Irenaeus*. Vol. 1, *ANF*, 487–93.

Julian of Norwich. *Revelations of Divine Love*. Translated by Grace Warrack, 140–57. London: Musuen & Co. Ltd., 1901. See also *Showings*. Translated by Edmund Colledge and James Walsh. New York: Paulist Press, 1977.

Kierkegaard, Soren. *The Sickness Unto Death: A Christian Psychological Exposition For Upbuilding And Awakening*. Translated and edited by Howard Hong and Edna Hong. Princeton, NJ: Princeton University Press, 1983.

Luther, Martin. *Martin Luther: Selections from His Writings*. Translated and edited by John Dillenberger. New York: Anchor, 1958.

Maximus the Confessor. *Maximus Confessor: Selected Writings*. Translated with notes by George Berthold. Introduction by Jaroslav Pelikan. New York: Paulist Press, 1985.

Nicholas of Cusa. "Vision of God." In *Nicholas of Cusa: Selected Spiritual Writings*. Edited by H. Lawrence Bond, 252–54. New York: Paulist Press, 1997.

Origen. "On First Principles." In *Fathers of the Third Century*. Vol. 4, *ANF*, 242–57. See also *On First Principles*. Translated by Henry Butterworth. Gloucester: Peter Smith, 1973.

Pascal, Blaise. *The Thoughts of Pascal*. Translated by W. F. Trotter. London: Gollancz, 1904. See also *Pensées and Other Writings*.

Edited by Anthony Levi. Translated by Honor Levi. Oxford: Oxford University Press, 2008.

Schleiermacher, Friedrich. *The Christian Faith*. Edited by H. R. MacKintosh and J. S. Stewart. Edinburgh: T. & T. Clark, 1999.

———. *On Religion: Speeches to Its Cultured Despisers*. Translated by John Oman. London: K. Paul, Trench, Trubner & Co., 1893. See also *On Religion: Speeches to its Cultured Despisers*. Edited by Richard Crouter. Cambridge: Cambridge University Press, 1996.

Tertullian. "Against Praxeas." In *Latin Christianity: Its Founder, Tertullian*. Vol. 3, *ANF*, 597–628. See also *Tertullian's Treatise Against Praxeas*. Translated by Henry Butterworth. London: SPCK, 1948.

Whitehead, Alfred North. *Process and Reality*. New York: Free Press, 1979.

Books on God in the Bible and in the History of Christian Thought

Armstrong, Karen. *The Case for God*. New York: Anchor, 2010.

Ayres, Lewis. *Nicaea and Its Legacy: An Approach to Fourth-Century Trinitarian Theology*. Oxford: Oxford University Press, 2006.

Bauckham, Richard. *Jesus and the God of Israel: God Crucified and Other Studies on the New Testament's Christology of Divine Identity*. Grand Rapids: Wm. B. Eerdmans Publishing Co., 2008.

Buckley, Michael, SJ. *At the Origins of Modern Atheism*. New Haven, CT: Yale University Press, 1990.

Clayton, Philip. *The Problem of God in Modern Thought*. Grand Rapids: Wm. B. Eerdmans Publishing Co., 2000.

Davis, Leo Donald. *The First Seven Ecumenical Councils (325–787): Their History and Theology*. Collegeville, MN: Liturgical Press, 1990.

Dunn, James D. G. *Christology in the Making: A New Testament Inquiry into the Origins of the Doctrine of the Incarnation*. 2d ed. Grand Rapids: Wm. B. Eerdmans Publishing Co., 1996.

———. *Jesus and the Spirit: A Study of the Religious and Charismatic Experience of Jesus and the First Christians as Reflected in the New Testament*. Grand Rapids: Wm. B. Eerdmans Publishing Co., 1997.

Fortman, Edmund J. *The Triune God: A Historical Study of the Doctrine of the Trinity*. Philadelphia: Westminster Press, 1972.

Frethheim, Terence E. *The Suffering of God: An Old Testament Perspective*. Minneapolis: Fortress Press, 1984.

Gillespie, Michael Allen. *The Theological Origins of Modernity*. Chicago: University of Chicago Press, 2009.

Grant, Robert. *Early Christian Doctrine of God*. Charlottesville: University Press of Virginia, 1966.

Hanson, R. P. C. *The Search for the Christian Doctrine of God: The Arian Controversy 318–281*. Edinburgh: T. & T. Clark, 1988.

Kelly, J. N. D. *Early Christian Creeds*. New York: Continuum, 2006.

Levenson, Jon D. *Creation and the Persistence of Evil: The Jewish Drama of Divine Omnipotence*. Princeton, NJ: Princeton University Press, 1994.

Livingston, James C. *Modern Christian Thought: The Enlightenment and the Nineteenth Century*. Minneapolis: Fortress Press, 2006.

Livingston, James C., Francis Schüssler Fiorenza, Sarah Coakley, and James H. Evans Jr., eds. *Modern Christian Thought: The Twentieth Century*. Minneapolis: Fortress Press, 2006.

Louth, Andrew. *Discerning the Mystery: An Essay on the Nature of Theology*. Oxford: Clarendon Press, 1983.

———. *The Origins of the Christian Mystical Tradition: From Plato to Denys*. Oxford: Oxford University Press, 2007.

Macquarrie, John. *In Search of Deity: An Essay in Dialectical Theism*. New York: Crossroad, 1985.

McGinn, Bernard. *The Foundations of Mysticism*. Vol. 1, *Presence of God: A History of Western Christian Mysticism*. New York: Crossroad, 2004.

McGuckin, John Anthony. *Westminster Handbook to Patristic Theology*. Louisville, KY: Westminster John Knox Press, 2004.

Norris, Richard A. *God and the World in Early Christian Theology: A Study in Justin Martyr, Irenaeus, Tertullian, and Origen*. New York: Seabury, 1965.

Otto, R. *The Idea of the Holy*. Oxford: Oxford University Press, 1958.

Pelikan, Jaroslav. *The Christian Tradition: A History of the Development of Doctrine*. Vol. 1, *The Emergence of the Catholic Tradition*. Chicago: University of Chicago Press, 1975.

Powell, Samuel. *The Trinity in German Thought*. Cambridge: Cambridge University Press, 2000.

Prestige, George L. *God in Patristic Thought*. London: W. Heinemann, 1936.

Taylor, Charles. *A Secular Age*. Cambridge, MA: Harvard University Press, 2007.

Tillich, Paul. *A History of Christian Thought*. New York: Touchstone, 1972.

Turner, Denys. *The Darkness of God: Negativity in Christian Mysticism*. Cambridge: Cambridge University Press, 1995.

Wainright, Arthur W. *The Trinity in the New Testament*. London: SPCK, 1962.

Significant Books on God and the Trinity in the Twentieth Century

Balthasar, Hans Urs von. *Theo-Drama: Theological Dramatic Theory*. Vols. 1–5. Translated by Graham Harrison. San Francisco: Ignatius Press, 1988–1998.

Barth, Karl. *Church Dogmatics.* Vols. 1–4. Edited by Geoffrey Bromiley and T. F. Torrance. Edinburgh: T. & T. Clark, 1936–1969.

Brunner, Emil. *The Christian Doctrine of God.* Translated by Olive Wyon. Philadelphia: Westminster, 1949.

Cone, James H. *God of the Oppressed.* Maryknoll, NY: Orbis Books, 1975.

Gilkey, Langdon. *Naming the Whirlwind: The Renewal of God-language.* Indianapolis: Bobbs-Merrill, 1969.

Hartshorne, Charles. *The Divine Relativity: A Social Conception of God.* New Haven, CT: Yale University Press, 1982.

Hick, John H., and Arthur C. McGill, eds. *The Many-faced Argument.* New York: Macmillan and Company, 1967.

Jenson, Robert W. *Systematic Theology.* Vol. 1, *The Triune God.* Oxford: Oxford University Press, 1997.

Johnson, Elizabeth A. *She Who Is: The Mystery of God in Feminist Theological Discourse.* New York: Crossroad, 1992.

Jüngel, Eberhard. *God as the Mystery of the World: On the Foundation of the Theology of the Crucified One in the Dispute between Theism and Atheism.* Translated by Darrell L. Guder. Grand Rapids: Wm. B. Eerdmans Publishing Co., 1983.

Kasper, Walter. *The God of Jesus Christ.* New York: Herder & Herder, 1986.

Küng, Hans. *Does God Exist? An Answer for Today.* Translated by Edward Quinn. New York: Doubleday, 1980.

Lossky, Vladimir. *The Mystical Theology of the Eastern Church.* London: James Clarke & Co., 1944.

Moltmann, Jürgen. *The Crucified God: The Cross of Christ as the Foundation and Criticism of Christian Theology.* London: SCM Press, 1974.

———. *The Trinity and the Kingdom: The Doctrine of God.* Minneapolis: Fortress Press, 1993.

Ogden, Schubert M. *The Reality of God and Other Essays.* Dallas: Southern Methodist University Press, 1992.

Owen, H. P. *Concepts of Deity.* New York: Herder & Herder, 1971.

Pannenberg, Wolfhart. *Systematic Theology.* Vol. 1. Translated by Geoffrey W. Bromiley. Grand Rapids: Wm. B. Eerdmans Publishing Co., 2010.

Rahner, Karl. *Foundations of Christian Faith: An Introduction to the Idea of Christianity.* New York: Crossroad, 1982.

———. *The Trinity.* New York: Herder & Herder, 2007.

Stăniloae, Dumitru. *The Experience of God.* Vol. 1. Translated and edited by Ioan Ionita and Robert Barringer. Foreword by Bishop Kallistos Ware. Brookline, MA: Holy Cross Orthodox Press, 1994.

Tillich, Paul. *Systematic Theology.* Vol. 1. Chicago: University of Chicago Press, 1973.

Torrance, Thomas F. *Christian Doctrine of God, One Being, Three Persons.* Edinburgh: T. & T. Clark, 2001.

Tracy, David. *Blessed Rage for Order: The New Pluralism in Theology.* Chicago: University of Chicago Press, 1996.

Welch, Claude. *In This Name: The Doctrine of the Trinity in Contemporary Theology.* New York: Charles Scribner's Sons, 1952.

Zizioulas, John D. *Being as Communion: Studies in Personhood and the Church.* Yonkers, NY: St. Vladimir's Seminary Press, 1997.

Recent Philosophical Books on God

Allen, Diogenes. *Philosophy for Understanding Theology.* Louisville, KY: Westminster John Knox Press, 2007.

Alston, William P. *Perceiving God: The Epistemology of Religious Experience.* Ithaca, NY: Cornell University Press, 1993.

Burrell, David B. *Knowing the Unknowable God: Theology.* Notre Dame, IN: University of Notre Dame Press, 1992.

Daly, Mary. *Beyond God the Father: Toward a Philosophy of Women's Liberation.* Boston: Beacon Press, 1973.

Gilson, Etienne. *God and Philosophy.* New Haven, CT: Yale University Press, 2002.

Kenny, Anthony. *The God of the Philosophers.* Oxford: Oxford University Press, 1987.

Mascall, E. L. *The Openness of Being: Natural Theology Today.* Philadelphia: Westminster Press, 1972.

Morris, Thomas V. *God and the Philosophers: The Reconciliation of Faith and Reason.* Oxford: Oxford University Press, 1996.

Pannenberg, Wolfhart. *Metaphysics and the Idea of God.* Grand Rapids: Wm. B. Eerdmans Publishing Co., 2001.

Plantinga, Alvin. *God and Other Minds: A Study of the Rational Justification of Belief in God.* Ithaca, NY: Cornell University Press, 1990.

Swinburne, Richard. *The Christian God.* Oxford: Clarendon Press, 1994.

———. *The Existence of God.* Oxford: Oxford University Press, 2004.

Turner, Denys. *Faith, Reason, and the Existence of God.* Cambridge: Cambridge University Press, 2004.

Recent Theological Books on God and the Trinity

Boff, Leonardo. *Trinity and Society.* Maryknoll, NY: Orbis Books, 1998.

Bracken, Joseph A. *God: Three Who Are One.* Collegeville, MN: Liturgical Press, 2008.

Caputo, John D. *The Weakness of God: A Theology of the Event.* Bloomington: Indiana University Press, 2006.

Cunningham, David. *These Three Are One: The Practice of Trinitarian Theology.* Cambridge, MA: Blackwell, 1998.

D'Costa, Gavin. *The Meeting of Religions and the Trinity*. Maryknoll, NY: Orbis Books, 2000.

Davis, Stephen T., Daniel Kendall, and Gerald O'Collins, eds. *An Interdisciplinary Symposium on the Trinity*. Oxford: Oxford University Press, 1999.

Erickson, Millard J. *God in Three Persons: A Contemporary Interpretation of the Trinity*. Grand Rapids: Baker Books, 1995.

Fiddes, Paul S. *Participating in a Pastoral Doctrine of the Trinity*. Louisville, KY: Westminster John Knox Press, 2001.

Grenz, Stanley J. *The Named God and the Question of Being: A Trinitarian Theo-Ontology*. Louisville, KY: Westminster John Knox Press, 2005.

Gunton, Colin. *The One, the Three and the Many: God, Creation, and the Culture of Modernity*. Cambridge: Cambridge University Press, 1993.

Gutiérrez, Gustavo. *The God of Life*. Maryknoll, NY: Orbis Books, 1991.

Hart, David Bentley. *The Beauty of the Infinite: The Aesthetics of Christian Truth*. Grand Rapids: Wm. B. Eerdmans Publishing Co., 2004.

Heim, S. Mark. *The Depths of Riches: A Trinitarian Theology of Religious Ends*. Grand Rapids: Wm. B. Eerdmans Publishing Co., 2001.

Jeanrond, Werner G., and Aasulv Lande, eds. *The Concept of God in Global Dialogue*. Faith Meets Faith Series. Maryknoll, NY: Orbis Books, 2005.

Kaufman, Gordon. *In the Face of Mystery: A Constructive Theology*. Cambridge, MA: Harvard University Press, 2006.

Keller, Catherine. *On the Mystery: Discerning Divinity in Process*. Minneapolis: Fortress Press, 2008.

LaCugna, Catherine M. *God for Us: The Trinity and Christian Life*. New York: HarperOne, 1993.

Marion, Jean-Luc. *God without Being: Hors-Texte*. Chicago: University of Chicago Press, 1995.

McFague, Sallie. *Models of God: Theology for an Ecological, Nuclear Age*. Philadelphia: Fortress Press, 1987.

McIntosh, Mark A. *Mystical Theology: The Integrity of Spirituality and Theology*. London: Wiley-Blackwell, 1998.

O'Collins, Gerald. *The Tripersonal God: Understanding and Interpreting the Trinity*. Mahwah, NJ: Paulist Press, 1999.

Panikkar, Raimon. *The Experience of God: Icons of the Mystery*. Minneapolis: Fortress Press, 2006.

Peters, Ted. *God—The World's Future: Systematic Theology for a Postmodern Era*. Minneapolis: Fortress Press, 1992.

Pinnock, Clark, Richard Rice, John Sanders, William Hasker, and David Basinger, eds. *The Openness of God: A Biblical Challenge to the Traditional Understanding of God*. Downers Grove, IL: InterVarsity Press, 1994.

Shults, F. LeRon. *Reforming the Doctrine of God*. Grand Rapids: Wm. B. Eerdmans Publishing Co., 2005.

Smart, Ninian, and Steve Konstantine. *Christian Systematic Theology in World Context*. Minneapolis: Fortress Press, 1991.

Spencer, Aida Besancon, and William David Spencer, eds. *The Global God: Multicultural Evangelical Views of God*. Grand Rapids: Wm. B. Eerdmans Publishing Co., 1998.

Tanner, Kathryn. *God and Creation in Christian Theology: Tyranny and Empowerment*. Minneapolis: Fortress Press, 2006.

Tracy, David. *Dialogue with the Other: The Inter-Religious Dialogue*. Grand Rapids: Wm. B. Eerdmans Publishing Co., 1991.

Volf, Miroslav. *After Our Likeness: The Church as the Image of the Trinity*. Grand Rapids: Wm. B. Eerdmans Publishing Co., 1997.

Index

CPSIA information can be obtained at www.ICGtesting.com
Printed in the USA
LVOW051624210213

321164LV00005B/605/P